A Practical Guide to FDA's Food and Drug Law and Regulation

Sixth Edition

Edited by Kenneth R. Piña and Wayne L. Pines

FDLI
Food and Drug Law Institute

ISBN 978-1-935065-84-5

Food and Drug Law Institute

1155 15th Street NW
Ste. 910
Washington, D.C. 20005
p: 202-371-1420
info@fdli.org
www.fdli.org

Contents

Introduction

It is with gratitude that we provide you with this sixth edition of *A Practical Guide to FDA's Food and Drug Law and Regulation*. Neither of us would have predicted that our text would play such a prominent role as a teaching tool and as an essential reference when we prepared the first edition back in the 1990s!

The sixth edition has been updated to reflect important regulatory changes and to maintain the usefulness of *A Practical Guide to FDA's Food and Drug Law and Regulation* as an up-to-date primer that explains these laws and regulations in simple, non-technical terms.

We are gratified that so many people have found the text to be useful. The idea for this book originated when Ken was teaching the food and drug law course for the Temple University School of Pharmacy's Graduate Studies Program for Quality Assurance and Regulatory Affairs. He noted that existing books on food and drug law were written in the "case law" format commonly used to teach law students, or were written for audiences with pre-existing knowledge of Food and Drug Administration (FDA) law. What was needed was a practical legal/regulatory primer that was substantive but that could also be readily understood by a wide range of persons with an interest in FDA-related laws and regulations.

The Food and Drug Law Institute (FDLI) welcomed the idea for such a text and suggested that Ken work with Wayne to develop the book. Wayne, a non-lawyer with extensive FDA regulatory experience, had edited earlier books for FDLI. He embraced the idea and joined Ken as co-editor. We were on our way!

This book has become a popular, basic resource both academically and within regulated industries. It is used as a standard textbook in a number of law school food and drug law courses, is used frequently to teach graduate-level regulatory courses, is a common reference text in many life science companies, and has been cited as a reference in judicial opinions (including a U.S. Supreme Court opinion). For many entering the FDA regulatory world, it is their first primer on the laws and regulations that govern the development, marketing, and sale of food, medical products, cosmetics, and tobacco products.

The intended readers of this book include students in law schools and in other professional academic programs, plus professionals who work for regulated companies and in related fields. Their commonality is that they want and need to understand how the laws and regulations that guide FDA's activities work, and they need the information to be provided in practical, real-world terms.

Like past editions, this edition stays true to our original goal. The format of *A Practical Guide to FDA's Food and Drug Law and Regulation* remains structured so as to provide a natural progression from subject to subject, so that each chapter is useful not only as a resource but also as a teaching tool. Every chapter has been updated so as to reflect the most current status of relevant laws and regulations.

We hope that you find this text useful. Should you have any questions or feedback, please feel free to contact us via FDLI or at our below email addresses.

In closing, we would like to thank our families, as well as FDLI staff members Judy Rein and Nina Seebeck, for their support of us and this project. We also would be remiss if we did not extend our deep gratitude to the chapter authors. Each of them is a recognized leader in their field, with extremely hectic schedules, yet they have kindly dedicated substantial time and energy not just to their original authorship, but also to updating their chapters. They continue to provide not just their practical knowledge but their valuable insights as well.

On a final note, after six editions, Ken has decided to "pass the baton." Beginning with the seventh edition of the text, Steve Kanovsky, General Counsel, Global Innovations at GE Healthcare, will take over Ken's role. Ken wishes Steve and Wayne well and thanks everyone who has been involved with this text for their support, encouragement, and assistance.

Kenneth R. Piña
pinakr@aol.com

Wayne L. Pines
wpines@apcoworldwide.com

About the Editors

Kenneth R. Piña, J.D., R.Ph.

Kenneth R. Piña is the Senior Vice President, Chief Legal and Compliance Officer & Corporate Secretary of Pernix Therapeutics.

Most recently, Mr. Piña was a Founder and the Managing Principal of Core Risks Ltd. (CRL), a global compliance and risk management consultancy firm that was acquired by Jardine Lloyd Thompson. He formerly served as the Senior Vice President, Chief Legal Officer and Secretary for Henkel Corporation. Before joining Henkel, Mr. Piña served as Vice President, General Counsel and Secretary of Rhone-Poulenc Rorer Pharmaceuticals Inc.

Mr. Piña received his Juris Doctorate from the Dickinson School of Law, Pennsylvania State University, and earned his B.S. degree from the Rutgers University College of Pharmacy. He has served as an adjunct professor of food and drug law at Temple University and as a lecturer in law at the Villanova School of Law.

Wayne L. Pines

Wayne L. Pines is President of Health Care and Regulatory Services at APCO Worldwide in Washington, D.C. He is an international consultant on FDA-related issues, specializing in crisis management, drug/device approvals, advertising and promotion issues, advisory committee preparation, and media outreach.

A graduate of Rutgers University, Mr. Pines served 10 years at the Food and Drug Administration as Director of Consumer Education, Chief of Press Relations, and as Associate Commissioner for Public Affairs. He has written or edited a dozen books, including *How to Work with the FDA* and *FDA: A Century of Consumer Protection*; two books on risk management; three books on crisis management; and the *FDA Advertising and Promotion Manual*. He has chaired since their inception in the late 1980s the annual promotion/advertising education conferences for both the Food and Drug Law Institute and the Drug Information Association, and is a frequent speaker at other conferences.

Mr. Pines was the founding president and is a current director of the Alliance for a Stronger FDA, which supports increased funding for FDA; is a founding director of the FDA Alumni Association and the current chair of its communications committee; is former chairman and a current director of the MedStar Health Research Institute which oversees medical research at 10 hospitals; and is a member of the executive committee of the regional board of the Anti-Defamation League.

About the Authors

Edward John Allera, Buchanan Ingersoll & Rooney PC

Edward John Allera focuses his practice on the development of new products and business opportunities in the areas of pharmaceuticals and technology, especially regarding the regulation and promotion of drugs, biologics, and devices. Mr. Allera is chairman of the firm's FDA/Biotechnology Section. He began his career at FDA, where he served as associate chief counsel. As a pharmacist, one of Mr. Allera's strengths is the ability to integrate science into the law.

Sarah Baumann, Navigant Consulting, Inc.

Sarah Baumann, MS, RAC, is a Managing Consultant at Navigant Consulting, Inc., where she provides regulatory support to clients across the product lifecycle. She has more than a decade of experience providing regulatory support to U.S. and global medical device companies, with specialization in the *in vitro* diagnostics (IVD) space. She has extensive experience in regulatory strategy and the submission and maintenance of complex 510(k) Premarket Notifications, Premarket Approval Applications (PMAs), and CLIA Categorization Requests to FDA for a variety of IVDs. Ms. Baumann holds a Master of Science degree in molecular biology from Purdue University.

Ann M. Begley, Morgan Lewis

Ann M. Begley, a partner in Morgan Lewis' FDA Practice, focuses her practice on regulatory issues concerning food, drug, cosmetic, and medical device products. With an emphasis on legal/regulatory issues involving clinical research practice, she advises clients on compliance and strategic issues, procedure development, and clinical trial-related agreements and transactions, and provides due diligence services. Ms. Begley's practice results in regular interaction with regulatory bodies, including FDA, OHRP, and the independent accrediting body, AAHRPP.

David L. Chesney, DL Chesney Consulting, LLC

David L. Chesney is the Principal and General Manager of DL Chesney Consulting, LLC. His career includes 23 years with FDA and 22 years in GMP and GCP consulting worldwide. In his consulting practice, Mr. Chesney helps clients prevent quality and compliance problems through proactive assessment and planning, and when necessary, with remediation planning and health regulatory authority communications. He has a bachelor's degree and postgraduate credits in biology from California State University, Northridge and San Diego, and received a Certificate in Health Care Compliance from Seton Hall University School of Law. He is presently studying for an M.S. in jurisprudence from Seton Hall with a concentration in pharmaceutical and medical device law. He serves as an instructor for the PDA Training and Research Institute, and with the Food and Drug Law Institute where he helps teach the Introduction to Drug Law program of legal continuing education.

Richard M. Cooper, Williams & Connolly LLP
Richard M. Cooper is of counsel (formerly, a partner) at Williams & Connolly LLP. He was FDA Chief Counsel 1977-1979, and has taught food and drug law at Georgetown University Law Center. He was a law clerk to U.S. Supreme Court Justice William J. Brennan, Jr. Education: Haverford College, B.A. *summa cum laude*; Rhodes Scholar; Oxford University, B.A., First Class with Congratulations; Harvard Law School, J.D., *summa cum laude*; President, *Harvard Law Review*.

Joseph W. Cormier, Hyman, Phelps & McNamara, PC
Joseph "Jay" Cormier is an attorney who focuses on regulatory strategy, policy, and compliance for various clients regulated by FDA. He has served in FDA's Center for Veterinary Medicine, where he developed policies regarding genetically engineered animals. He is a recipient of the FDA Scientific Achievement Award, the CBER Scientific Achievement Award, and the Commissioner's Special Citation. Mr. Cormier earned his A.B. from Dartmouth College, his Ph.D. from Columbia University, and his J.D. from Georgetown.

Fred H. Degnan, King & Spalding, LLP
Fred H. Degnan is a partner in King & Spalding's FDA practice. From 1977 to 1988 he served in FDA's Office of General Counsel where he had substantial FDA litigation and enforcement experience. For 21 years, he also taught food and drug law at the Catholic University/Columbus School of Law. He has published and lectured extensively on FDA-related issues. While at FDA he received the agency's highest awards and in 2002 he received the FDLI Distinguished Leadership Award. From 2009 to 2010 he served as Chair of the FDLI Board. He has consistently been recognized in independently conducted surveys as one of the nation's top food and drug lawyers.

Alexandre Gapihan, Buchanan Ingersoll & Rooney PC
Alexandre (Alex) Gapihan's practice focuses on matters relating to the Food and Drug Administration, the pharmaceutical industry, regulatory/compliance matters, and commercial litigation. His work extends to both federal and state courts, as well as mediation and arbitration. Mr. Gapihan is a graduate of the University of Pennsylvania Law School, where he served as Senior Editor for the school's *East Asia Law Review*.

Paula Gray, Navigant Consulting, Inc.
Paula Gray is a Senior Consultant at Navigant Consulting where she specializes in regulatory compliance, quality systems, and auditing for companies operating in the device, diagnostics, and combination product spaces. She has particular expertise in design and development activities for combination product manufacturers wishing to comply with U.S. and international standards and regulatory requirements for medical devices. As a quality expert, Ms. Gray has developed, implemented,

and maintained processes within quality management systems. In the regulatory arena, she has experience with reviewing records and preparing regulatory submissions for both stand-alone medical devices and combination products.

Benjamin M. Greenblum, Williams & Connolly LLP

Benjamin M. Greenblum is a partner at Williams & Connolly LLP. He represents several companies in litigations involving food and drug law. He was a law clerk to then-Chief Judge Dennis Jacobs of the U.S. Court of Appeals for the Second Circuit. Education: University of Pennsylvania, B.A./B.S., *summa cum laude*; Columbia Law School, J.D., Kent Scholar (2004-2006).

Sam Halabi, University of Missouri School of Law

Sam Halabi is an Associate Professor at the University of Missouri School of Law, the 2017-18 Fulbright Canada Research Chair in Health Law, Policy, and Ethics at the University of Ottawa, and a Scholar at the O'Neill Institute for National and Global Health Law at Georgetown University. He is the editor (with Larry Gostin and Jeff Crowley) of *Global Management of Infectious Disease after Ebola* (OUP 2017) and *Food and Drug Regulation in an Era of Globalized Markets* (Elsevier 2015). He is a regular contributor to the *Yale Journal on Regulation's* Notice and Comment Blog. Before earning his J.D. from Harvard Law School, Professor Halabi was awarded a British Marshall scholarship to study in the United Kingdom where he earned an M.Phil in international relations from the University of Oxford.

Dorothy Henckel, Navigant Consulting, Inc.

Dorothy Henckel is a Senior Consultant at Navigant Consulting, where clients regularly leverage her expertise on projects related to medical devices, IVDs, and combination products regulated by the U.S. FDA. She started her career at a leading multinational diagnostics company where she gained hands-on experience in nearly every aspect of a quality management system by working in R&D, operations, and quality departments. She has extensive experience working with quality systems, GMPs, design controls, validation, design transfer, CAPA, risk assessment, root cause analysis, and medical device reporting. She is a Certified Lead Auditor. Ms. Henckel holds a B.S. in chemistry from Indiana University – Bloomington.

Michael S. Heyl, Hogan Lovells US LLP

Michael S. Heyl's practice focuses on medical device regulation with an emphasis on postmarket enforcement matters. He focuses extensively on postmarket compliance issues, including the FDA's Quality System Regulation (QSR), adverse event reporting, and field action requirements. His experience includes assisting in the defense of criminal investigations, responding to Warning Letters and 483s, conducting internal investigations of alleged regulatory violations, assisting with import and export issues, and conducting regulatory due diligence and negotiation of corporate transactions.

Tina Hu-Rodgers, Buchanan Ingersoll & Rooney PC

Tina Hu-Rodgers focuses her practice on matters relating to FDA and the pharmaceutical industry, including the approval, regulation, promotion, and sale of drugs, medical devices, and dietary supplements. Ms. Hu-Rodgers assists clients in their interactions with various federal agencies, including FDA and the Drug Enforcement Administration (DEA), and advises clients on numerous issues related to these agencies.

Paul Hyman, Hyman, Phelps & McNamara, PC

Paul M. Hyman is a founding member of Hyman, Phelps & McNamara, PC, the largest FDA law practice in the United States. Mr. Hyman covers all aspects of FDA regulation, including product approvals and notifications, regulatory compliance, recalls, inspections, and labeling and advertising review. He also has broad experience in related government regulatory matters, particularly including FTC regulation of advertising. He brings more than five decades of perspective on FDA priorities, providing insight on their corresponding cycles of enforcement activity.

Miles Johnson, Navigant Consulting, Inc.

Miles Johnson is a consultant at Navigant Consulting, Inc., specializing in user experience research and software used in medical devices. He assists clients with a variety of FDA regulatory matters, including pre- and postmarket compliance, quality system remediation, adverse event reporting, and regulatory due diligence assessments in connection with corporate transactions. He earned a B.S. in biology and minor in anthropology from Indiana University and his M.S. from Purdue University in biotechnology.

Steve Kanovsky, GE Healthcare

Steve Kanovsky is General Counsel for the GE Healthcare Global Innovation legal group, covering most GE Healthcare products, research, regulatory, quality, intellectual property, and U.S. commercial. He joined GE after various in-house general counsel and compliance officer roles in the pharmaceutical industry (Sanofi, Abraxis BioSciences, and Archimedes Pharma). Prior to his in-house roles, he had a litigation practice at Drinker Biddle LLP and worked at Merck in basic research, regulatory affairs, and project management. Mr. Kanovsky received a B.A. (chemistry and biophysics) from the University of Pennsylvania, an M.S. (pharmacology) and a J.D. from Temple University, and an MBA (Pharmaceutical Marketing) from St. Joseph's University. He was an Adjunct Professor at the St. Joseph's Haub Graduate School of Business from 2005-2014.

Richard Kingham, Covington & Burling LLP

Richard Kingham is a partner in Covington & Burling LLP. He has advised most of the major pharmaceutical manufacturers in the United States and Europe as well as trade associations of the pharmaceutical and biotechnology industries, served on committees of the Institute of Medicine of the National Academy of Sciences, the National Institutes of Health, and the World Health Organization, and taught at universities in the U.S. and U.K.

Daniel A. Kracov, Arnold & Porter Kaye Scholer LLP
Daniel A. Kracov is a partner in the law firm of Arnold & Porter Kaye Scholer LLP in Washington, D.C. where he chairs the FDA and Healthcare Practice. He assists clients, including start-up companies, trade associations, and large manufacturing companies, in negotiating the challenges relating to the development, approval, and marketing of drugs, biologics, and medical devices. Mr. Kracov received his undergraduate degree, *magna cum laude*, from the University of Maryland and his J.D. from the University of Virginia.

Geoffrey M. Levitt, Pfizer Inc
Geoffrey M. Levitt is Senior Vice President and Associate General Counsel for Regulatory, Environmental, and Global Supply at Pfizer Inc, where he is responsible for managing global legal support for regulatory, medical, safety, clinical research, manufacturing, and environmental operations. Mr. Levitt has published and lectured extensively on regulatory law. He is a past member of the editorial board of the *Food and Drug Law Journal* and a current member of the editorial board of the *FDA Advertising and Promotion Manual*. Mr. Levitt is past Chairman of the Board of the Food and Drug Law Institute and received the Institute's 2009 Distinguished Service and Leadership Award and the 2017 inaugural Service to FDLI Award. He has also served as Chair of the PhRMA Law Section Executive Committee and is a current member of the Board of the Friedreich's Ataxia Research Alliance. He earned his J.D. from Harvard Law School and his B.A. from Columbia University.

Cynthia L. Meyer, Kleinfeld, Kaplan and Becker, LLP
Cynthia L. Meyer is an associate who joined the firm in 2011. Her practice focuses primarily on counseling and advocating on behalf of companies and individuals in the pharmaceutical, medical device, food, cosmetic, dietary supplement, and alcoholic beverage industries on legal and regulatory matters involving the FDA, USDA, FTC, TTB, and other related federal and state agencies. Prior to joining the firm, Ms. Meyer worked as a biologist at the National Cancer Institute at NIH. She received her B.S. from Duke University and her J.D. from Georgetown University Law Center.

Anisa Mohanty, McDermott Will & Emery
Anisa Mohanty is a member of McDermott Will & Emery's FDA practice. She advises life sciences companies on regulatory, compliance, enforcement, policy, and legislative matters and counsels companies on premarket pathways, advertising and promotion, and current Good Manufacturing Practice and Quality System requirements. She also assists clients with FDA engagement strategies and responding to FDA administrative and enforcement actions. Prior to joining McDermott, she served

as a Regulatory Counsel in the Office of Compliance and Enforcement in FDA's Center for Tobacco Products. In addition to advising agency policymakers and regulatory personnel, she conducted routine and directed inspections of manufacturing establishments and investigations of distribution and marketing activities and coordinated enforcement actions, on behalf of the agency. Ms. Mohanty received her B.A. in biology and political science from University of North Carolina at Chapel Hill and her J.D. from University of Richmond School of Law.

Thomas F. Myers, Personal Care Products Council

Thomas F. Myers is the Executive Vice President-Legal & General Counsel for the Personal Care Products Council, the leading national trade association for the cosmetics industry. His responsibilities include all legal and regulatory issues facing the cosmetics industry. Mr. Myers previously worked at the U.S. Chamber of Commerce and as an attorney with the international law firms of Jones Day and Greenberg Traurig. He is a member of the state bars of Michigan and the District of Columbia.

Suzanne O'Shea, Navigant Consulting, Inc.

Suzanne O'Shea is a Director in the regulatory practice at Navigant Consulting. She helps sponsors of drugs, devices, biological products, human tissue, and combination products navigate through FDA. Before joining Navigant, she worked in the FDA Regulatory Practice at Faegre Baker Daniels. She served as Regulatory Counsel at FDA headquarters for 21 years, including several years in the Office of Combination Products. Ms. O'Shea works with an outstanding team of professionals at Navigant, many of whom assisted with the chapter on Combination Products.

Joseph A. Page, Georgetown University Law Center

Joseph A. Page is a law professor emeritus at the Georgetown University Law Center and is the faculty advisor to the Georgetown law student editors of the *Food and Drug Law Journal*. He has contributed a chapter on the regulation of tobacco products for the third edition of *Food and Drug Law and Regulation*. Professor Page also writes about Latin America and has published books entitled *Perón: A Biography* and *The Brazilians*.

Raqiyyah R. Pippins, Arnold & Porter Kaye Scholer LLP

Raqiyyah Pippins focuses her practice in the areas of FDA's regulation of food, dietary supplement, cosmetic, drug, and medical device products sold directly to consumers as well as FTC and state regulation of the marketing and sale of consumer products. Ms. Pippins represents companies that are engaged in the development, marketing, import, and export of consumer products, including conventional food, dietary supplements, drugs, cosmetics, medical devices, apparel, and appliances. She also represents consumer product companies in advertising challenges (including numerous challenges before the National Advertising Division (NAD) of the Advertising Self-Regulatory Council), and defends companies in investigations conducted by FDA, the FTC, and state agencies regarding product marketing practices.

Vernessa T. Pollard, McDermott Will & Emery, LLP
Vernessa T. Pollard is co-leader of McDermott Will & Emery's FDA practice. She provides strategic business and regulatory advice to FDA-regulated companies on complex issues related to the development, manufacture, marketing, postmarket safety, and compliance for FDA-regulated products, including drugs, medical devices, and digital health technology. Ms. Pollard counsels companies on product development and premarket strategy, good manufacturing practice and quality system requirements, advertising and promotion, adverse event reporting, FDA Warning Letters, FDA inspections, recalls, import detentions, corporate compliance programs, and regulatory due diligence in mergers and acquisitions. She is a former Associate Chief Counsel for Enforcement in FDA's Office of Chief Counsel. She has been recognized in numerous Law and Life Sciences publications, including *Chambers USA* 2014 to 2016, Healthcare: Pharmaceutical/Medical Products Regulatory (District of Columbia). She received her B.A. in communications from Howard University and her J.D. from Temple University School of Law.

Edward P. Richards, III, J.D., M.P.H., Louisiana State University Law Center
Edward P. Richards is Director of the Program in Law, Science, and Public Health at Louisiana State University Law Center. He received his undergraduate degree in biology and behavioral science from Rice University, studied human physiology and biochemistry as a graduate student at Baylor College of Medicine and then the University of Michigan, before receiving his J.D. from the University of Houston and his M.P.H. in disease control from the University of Texas School of Public Health. He is the Clarence W. Edwards Professor of Law at the Louisiana State University Law Center.

Genevieve M. Spires, Buchanan Ingersoll & Rooney PC
Genevieve M. Spires is counsel in the firm's Food & Drug Administration and Pharmaceuticals Section. Ms. Spires counsels life sciences companies on the laws and industry standards applicable to the sale and marketing of FDA-regulated products. Her experience includes reviewing promotional materials and drafting sponsorship, consulting, and other agreements. She is an active member of the American Bar Association. Ms. Spires currently serves as the Director of Communications and Technology for the ABA Young Lawyers Division.

Smitha Stansbury, King & Spalding, LLP
Smitha G. Stansbury is a partner in King & Spalding's FDA & Life Sciences practice group in Washington, D.C. She assists clients with regulatory matters before FDA, the USDA, the FTC, and other health and safety regulatory agencies at the federal and state levels. Ms. Stansbury has particular expertise in

food law, and has worked extensively with various food and beverage manufacturers and distributors, food industry trade associations, equipment suppliers, retailers, and restaurants on issues related to food safety, ingredients and product formulation, and food labeling and advertising. She is a frequent speaker and author on food-related issues and a member of the editorial advisory boards of *Food Logistics* magazine and King & Spalding's *International Food Law Gazette*. Ms. Stansbury received her J.D. from the University of Virginia School of Law and her B.A. from the University of Virginia.

Ronald F. Tetzlaff, Ph.D., PAREXEL Consulting

Ronald F. Tetzlaff is currently Corporate Vice President with PAREXEL International providing worldwide GMP compliance consulting and quality systems services to the food and drug legal community and clients in the pharmaceutical, biotechnology, and medical device industries. He has more than 48 years' experience performing inspections and conducting audits of pharmaceutical manufacturing facilities on a worldwide basis including a 27-year career with the Food and Drug Administration where he held the position of the FDA's National Expert.

William Vodra, Arnold & Porter Kaye Scholer LLP

William Vodra served at DEA and FDA from 1971 into 1979, where he drafted many major regulations (e.g., GLPs, GCPs, drug GMPs, bioequivalency and *Orange Book* standards) and handled FDA's only imminent hazard proceeding. In 1979, he joined Arnold & Porter LLP, specializing in crisis management and regulatory issues involving the safety, effectiveness, quality, and marketing of medical products. Mr. Vodra retired from active practice in 2010. Education: B.A., College of Wooster; J.D., Columbia University.

Edward C. Wilson, Jr., Hogan Lovells US LLP

Edward Wilson's medical device practice focuses on enforcement and premarket submission matters. His experience includes assisting companies in complying with the Quality System Regulation; reviewing and drafting product submissions; and providing general advice on a variety of regulatory issues. He graduated *cum laude* from Davidson College where he was elected to Phi Beta Kappa. He received his J.D. from the University of Virginia School of Law, where he was awarded the Charles J. Frankel Award in Health Law.

James William Woodlee, Kleinfeld, Kaplan and Becker, LLP

Will Woodlee is a partner in the law firm of Kleinfeld, Kaplan and Becker, LLP, in Washington, D.C. His practice focuses primarily on counseling and advocating on behalf of food, dietary supplement, cosmetic, pharmaceutical, medical device, tobacco product, and consumer product companies on regulatory and advertising law matters. Mr. Woodlee currently serves on the Editorial Advisory Board of the *Food and Drug Law Journal* and has previously served on the Food and Drug Law Institute's (FDLI's)

Food, Dietary Supplements, and Cosmetics Committee and on the Editorial Advisory Board of FDLI's *Update* magazine. He earned his B.A. from Wake Forest University, graduating *magna cum laude*, with Honors in English, and as a member of Phi Beta Kappa. He earned his J.D. from Wake Forest University School of Law, where he served as an Executive Editor for the *Wake Forest Law Review*.

Gary L. Yingling, Morgan Lewis

Gary Yingling of Morgan Lewis focuses on issues involving the Food and Drug Administration, guiding clients through matters involving IND, NDA submissions, ANDA applications, paragraph IV filings, REMS, labeling, importation, regulatory marketing strategy, etc., and counsels on FDA pre-approval manufacturing and clinical site inspections and more. Mr. Yingling earned his J.D. from Emory University; M.S. from Purdue University; B.S. from University of North Carolina. He is a registered pharmacist in Maryland and the District of Columbia.

Anthony L. Young, Kleinfeld, Kaplan & Becker, LLP

Anthony L. Young is a partner with the law firm Kleinfeld, Kaplan and Becker, LLP, Washington, D.C., a firm that has counseled clients in the food, drug, and allied industries for more than 50 years. Mr. Young has practiced food, drug, and environmental law since 1974. A member of the District of Columbia and California bars, Mr. Young received his B.A. from the University of Southern California and his J.D. from Georgetown University Law Center.

Chapter 1

Overview of the U.S. Legal System

Edward P. Richards, III, J.D., M.P.H., Director, Program in Law, Science, and Public Health, and Clarence W. Edwards Professor of Law, Louisiana State University Law Center, Baton Rouge, LA

Key Points

- The Constitution is the fundamental source of U.S. law.
- The Constitution divides legal powers between the states and the federal government.
- The federal government is divided into three parts to create checks and balances on its power.
- The Supreme Court ensures that other branches of the government do not violate the Constitution.
- Agencies are created by Congress and overseen by the President.
- Enforcement agencies such as the Food and Drug Administration (FDA) are in the executive branch of the federal government.
- FDA may only regulate products that affect interstate commerce.
- The courts defer to agency decisions.
- Agencies may take emergency actions to protect the public health and safety.
- Formal agency regulations are subject to public notice and comment.

INTRODUCTION

The food, drug, and medical devices industries are unique in their breadth and complexity, and their intimate impact on individual lives. They are heavily regulated by state and federal government agencies to ensure that the public is protected from unsafe goods and from intentional contamination. This chapter introduces the basic structure and process of the legal system as it affects food, drug, and medical device regulation.

FEDERALISM

The American legal system is a federal system, with powers divided between the states and the central government. The sharing of power between state and federal governments, and the primacy of the federal government's powers, are key characteristics of the American legal system. This system was shaped by the Revolutionary War. Each of the 13 original colonies had an independent government that was overseen by England. Communications were slow, and England's concerns generally were limited to taxes and keeping the exports and imports flowing. The colonies had some freedom to govern themselves in domestic matters. With the Declaration of Independence, they became separate nations with complete control over their legal affairs. When they joined together under the Articles of Confederation to fight the Revolutionary War, none was willing to give up control of its government to a central authority. The result was a weak federation that almost lost the war because it could not muster troops and supplies.

The drafters of the Constitution wanted to assure that the United States would present a unified face to the world and would be able to defend itself in future conflicts. The federal government was given the sole power to deal with foreign governments. This includes the power of Congress to declare war, and the President's broad national security powers to counter both foreign and domestic threats to the nation. Trade fights between the states under the Articles of Confederation led the drafters to give the federal government primary authority over interstate commerce. The states retained the powers that were not given to the federal government. These included the police power: the power to protect the public health and safety. The Supremacy Clause of the Constitution allows Congress to preempt state regulation in areas where the states and the federal government share legal authority.

The Supremacy Clause of the Constitution allows Congress to preempt state regulation in areas where the states and the federal government share legal authority.

The powers of the federal government are constrained by the Bill of Rights, a series of 10 amendments to the Constitution that protect individual liberty. Constitutional amendments adopted after the Civil War ban slavery and give the federal government additional power to protect individual rights from state abuses. These amendments provided the legal authority to extend the Bill of Rights protections to actions by state governments, which was done by the Supreme Court over the next 100 years.

Federal Commerce Powers

The import and export of foods, drugs, and medical devices is regulated through treaties with other countries and statutes passed by Congress. Unless specifically authorized by Congress, states have no role in the regulation of foreign trade. At the federal level, domestic food and drug law is authorized through the Commerce Clause of the Constitution. States may not pass laws that attempt to limit interstate commerce by favoring in-state businesses. Thus, state laws that banned milk from out-of-state dairies were held unconstitutional because they interfered with interstate commerce in their attempts to protect local businesses. State consumer protection laws, such as those requiring the inspection of imported milk and banning the import of contaminated milk, are constitutional, provided they also apply to milk produced within the state. The breadth of federal power to regulate interstate commerce is defined by Congress, subject to limits imposed by the Supreme Court. Generally speaking, anything that moves between the states, any business that uses raw materials that come from out of state, or any business that affects interstate commerce is subject to regulation under the Commerce Clause. The Civil Rights Acts use this broad definition of interstate commerce, and a court found that a barbecue restaurant whose only customers were local in-state residents was involved in interstate commerce because it bought condiments that originated outside the state.

While the courts have found that medical practice is an interstate business, Congress has traditionally limited the Food and Drug Administration's (FDA's) regulatory authority to products that in whole or part actually travel in interstate commerce. Thus, a pharmaceutical firm that wants to market a new drug must have FDA approval before it can advertise or ship the drug in interstate commerce. While some states require FDA approval for drugs sold within the state, there are states that permit the sale and use of non-FDA approved drugs. As long as these drugs are made wholly within the state and used only by physicians in the same state, FDA has no authority to ban the use of the drug. This is a congressional, rather than a constitutional, limit. Congress could allow FDA to use the broad definition of interstate commerce and regulate all drug sales and the practice of medicine. The Drug Enforcement Administration has broader authority and can prosecute the sale and use of drugs used only intrastate, even if, as in the case of medical marijuana, the state has approved the sale of the drug.

The Police and National Security Powers

Police power is the state power to protect against threats to the public health and safety. The police power predates police forces and was historically more about public health threats such as smallpox. These threatened the survival of the state itself, not just individuals. Thus the police power is the state equivalent of the federal national security power. The police power was left to the states in the Constitution, although the federal government can wield what looks like the same power for domestic threats through the Commerce Clause. If the threat has national security implications, such as bioterrorism, the President can exercise broad authority through his national security powers.

Police power is the state power to protect against threats to the public health and safety.

Most public health and safety regulation, such as assuring clean drinking water, food sanitation, and communicable disease control, is still done by the states. The federal government also protects public health and safety through its Commerce Clause authority, such as food, drug, and medical device regulation.

In many areas the federal government sets basic standards and shares enforcement with the states. Thus in environmental law, the states are free to be stricter than the federal government, but cannot have lower pollution standards than those set by the Environmental Protection Agency (EPA).

The courts allow broad governmental powers during natural disasters, such as Hurricanes Katrina and Sandy, and to prevent threats to national security, such as the terrorist attacks on September 11, 2001. After the terrorist attacks, Congress passed laws dealing with the prevention and mitigation of bioterrorism acts, which also include powers to respond to threats such as pandemic influenza. These powers overlap and in some cases preempt traditional state police powers. They allow the use of drugs and vaccines during public health emergencies that are not FDA approved and provide comprehensive immunity from damage claims for manufacturers of drugs and biological agents used under a presidential emergency or national security directive.

Federal Preemption of State Law

The Constitution provides that federal law preempts conflicting state regulation.

Since food and drug law implicates both interstate commerce and local public health and safety, the states and the federal government share regulatory power in many areas. Areas of shared power require national businesses to deal with 50 state governments and with the federal government. As long as the laws do not conflict, each can be enforced by the appropriate level of government. If they do conflict, the Constitution provides that federal law preempts the conflicting state regulation. This conflict can arise because the federal law *explicitly* states that it is taking away the states' power to regulate. For example, federal law specifies the necessary labeling for hearing aids and limits what additional requirements a state may impose without FDA permission. When Massachusetts passed a law requiring more information on hearing aid labels, a federal court barred enforcement of the law.

Federal law can *implicitly* preempt a state's right to regulate if the federal government so completely controls the area there is no room for state regulation. The federal government regulates use of the electromagnetic spectrum for communications such as broadcast television, radio, and cell phones. These are intrinsically interstate activities because electronic signals do not respect state lines. These regulations cover all aspects of airwave broadcast communication, leaving no room for state regulation.

In some cases, federal law also preempts private lawsuits brought under state law. The Cigarette Labeling and Advertising Act (Cigarette Labeling Act) provided that states cannot require more or different health warnings on a cigarette package than those required by federal law. The Supreme Court found that this preempted state court lawsuits by smokers who claimed that the cigarettes were defective because the packages did not carry adequate warnings. Federal law also preempts certain lawsuits alleging vaccine-related injuries, substituting an administrative compensation fund for possible state tort recoveries. FDA regulation of drugs does not provide any preemption of state tort law claims, but the Medical Device Amendments of 1976 do preempt claims against medical device manufacturers for aspects of devices that have been comprehensively regulated by FDA. Compensation for persons injured by defective prescription drugs is determined by state law, which differs substantially among the states. While Congress could preempt state tort claims for drugs under the same logic as for medical devices, it has not done so.

Limits to Federal Power

While federal power under the Commerce Clause is very broad, there are limits to Congress commandeering state governments to enforce federal laws. The states have to obey federal law themselves, but the Supreme Court has limited the extent to which Congress can force states to use their own resources to enforce federal law. Despite this ruling, legislation passed after the terrorist attacks on September 11, 2001, and the Hurricane Katrina disaster gives the President broad emergency authority and the National Response Plan anticipates that state and local authorities will follow orders from the President.

While federal power under the Commerce Clause is very broad, there are limits to Congress commandeering state governments to enforce federal laws.

If Congress wants the states to follow federal guidance or enforce federal laws, it can avoid questions of constitutional limits by giving states financial incentives to do its bidding. (These funding restrictions cannot be used to require otherwise unconstitutional actions by the states.) When Congress wanted the states to pass laws requiring people in cars to wear seatbelts, it told the states to pass seatbelt laws or lose some of their federal highway construction money. The Centers for Disease Control and Prevention uses grant funding to impose some uniformity on state public health programs such as childhood vaccination requirements and communicable disease reporting. The federal government has historically used the power of the purse much more than legal coercion to impose uniform standards on the states. In rare cases, such as the requirement that states expand their Medicaid programs to continue to receive any Medicaid funding, the Supreme Court can find that the funding restrictions overly restrict state authority and strike them down.

Separation of Powers

The Constitution divides the federal government into three branches: the legislative (Congress), the executive (President), and the judicial (federal courts). The founders believed that each branch would try to preserve its own power, and

The Constitution divides the federal government into three branches: the legislative (Congress), the executive (President), and the judicial (federal courts).

thus act as a check on the power of the other branches. The states have basically the same organizational structure, although some states make one branch of the government much stronger than the others. This chapter focuses on the federal system, which is most important to FDA law.

The Legislative Branch

Congress has two houses: the Senate and the House of Representatives. These houses have different procedural rules and their members serve terms of different lengths. Congress is the only branch of government that can authorize the spending of government funds and the imposition of taxes.

Each proposed law (bill) must be passed by both houses of Congress and signed by the President. The President can veto legislation, and Congress can override a presidential veto by a two-thirds majority vote. The President can propose legislation, and does so each year when presenting the proposed budget. Ultimately, however, it is Congress that passes laws. To keep Congress from becoming too powerful, the Constitution gave the power to enforce the laws to the President.

The Executive Branch

The President is head of the executive branch and is charged with enforcing the laws passed by Congress. The President has two areas of power: domestic and international. In domestic affairs, most of the President's power comes from laws passed by Congress, such as the Federal Food, Drug, and Cosmetic Act (FDCA). These laws constrain domestic action to areas specifically approved by Congress, although the President does have some flexibility to respond to emergencies. Enforcement is carried out through various agencies, including FDA. The Constitution grants the President broad powers over international affairs, including international trade, foreign policy, and national security. These powers are subject to only limited review by Congress and the courts.

The Judicial Branch

The judicial branch consists of the Supreme Court, the courts of appeal (circuit courts), and the district (local) federal courts. The district courts hold trials for federal criminal cases, decide disputes arising under federal law or the Constitution, and hear cases involving citizens of different states under "diversity jurisdiction." The courts of appeal do not conduct trials but review the trial records from the district courts. Since many agency actions generate a record like a trial, Congress often provides that these agency actions be reviewed directly by the court of appeals. When a case is heard on appeal, the court does not collect new evidence or hear the testimony of the witnesses; it only considers the record generated at the district court or administrative level.

The Constitution gives the Supreme Court original jurisdiction over cases affecting ambassadors, other public ministers and consuls, and those in which a state is a party. Congress gave the Court the power to hear cases that arise from courts of appeal rulings and cases reviewing state court decisions involving questions of federal law or rights under the Constitution. The Supreme Court ensures that federal laws are given the same meaning by all courts of appeal, it resolves conflicts between state and federal laws, and it determines if state or federal laws impermissibly infringe on rights guaranteed by the Constitution. If the Supreme Court determines that a state law, federal law, or administrative regulation, such as an FDA rule, conflicts with the Constitution, it will strike the law down so that it may no longer be enforced.

How the Courts Work

When people think of law, they think of the courtroom. While most law and law practice does not happen in the courtroom, it is important to understand how the courts work because the courtroom is where disputes, both private and governmental, end up if they cannot be resolved in any other way. The U.S. litigation system has three key characteristics: 1) it is a common law system, meaning that it evolved through the opinions of judges; 2) it is an adversarial system (i.e., it is driven by the litigants rather than the judges); and 3) it is divided into civil and criminal law, with the greatest legal protections reserved for persons accused of a crime and at risk of imprisonment or execution.

Characteristics of the U.S. litigation system:
- *a common law system*
- *an adversarial system*
- *divided into civil and criminal law*

Understanding the Common Law

England is a common law country, which brought this system to the British colonies in America. Common law means that the law evolves through judges applying the law to specific cases and writing opinions about how the law applies in those cases. The laws they apply may be from earlier court decisions enforcing even earlier traditions, or they may apply statutes passed by legislatures. Cases still arise that involve rules laid down in cases decided more than 200 years ago. Each case decided by a common law court becomes a precedent, or guideline, for subsequent decisions involving similar disputes. The Constitution accepted most of the English common law that was in force when it was written.

The evolution of the law on the preemption of state tort claims against medical device manufacturers is a good example of how the common law system functions. The Medical Device Amendments of 1976 (MDA) gave FDA the authority to regulate medical devices. Congress wanted to assure uniform standards for medical devices so the MDA says that states cannot impose standards in addition to the FDA standards on medical devices. In an early case under the MDA, the court ruled that state regulation of hearing aids was preempted by the MDA because it conflicted with federal regulations. This was a simple application of the law to a direct regulatory conflict.

In 1992, the United States Supreme Court ruled that the Cigarette Labeling Act preempted state tort claims against tobacco companies, holding that tort claims were a form of state regulation. Since the language in the Cigarette Labeling Act was similar to the MDA, defendants in tort cases involving medical devices began to argue that the MDA preempted these tort claims. Some federal courts accepted this argument, and some rejected it. In 1996, the United States Supreme Court reviewed the law to resolve these conflicting opinions. The court found that there could be preemption, but only if FDA really regulated the device, rather than just letting it be sold because it was like a device already on the market. This led to a second wave of cases with conflicting decisions over how much oversight FDA had to have over the device before preemption was triggered. The United States Supreme Court further clarified the extent of preemption in a case decided in 2008.

The value of a common law system is that the law can be adapted to situations that were not contemplated by the legislature.

The value of a common law system is that the law can be adapted to situations that were not contemplated by the legislature. There are two disadvantages. First, the law will often be unclear for years, with the outcome of cases depending on which court decides them. Second, the court will only resolve the issues before it, so even the 2008 case on the MDA, decided more than 30 years after the passage of the MDA, still leaves some preemption issues unresolved.

The Adversarial System

The U.S. judicial system uses an adversarial model in which the judge acts as an impartial referee to ensure that the case is presented properly to jurors but does not assist the parties in developing their cases (although, in some instances, cases can be decided by the judge without a jury).

The U.S. judicial system uses an adversarial model in which the judge acts as an impartial referee to ensure that the case is presented properly to jurors but does not assist the parties in developing their cases (although, in some instances, cases can be decided by the judge without a jury). In private litigation, the plaintiff—the person who brings the litigation—hires a lawyer to file a complaint against the defendant. The defendant then hires a lawyer to oppose the plaintiff's charges and to bring any possible counterclaims against the plaintiff. In criminal cases and in agency enforcement actions, it is the government that brings the proceedings against the defendant. There are some federal statutes, such as the False Claims Act, that allow a private person to bring a civil action on behalf of the government and share in any recovery as an incentive to vindicate the government's interest. A few states allow private citizens to bring criminal actions in limited circumstances.

The courts protect against bias by excluding judges or jurors who have a relationship with the plaintiff or the defendant or are familiar with the factual issues in the case. Each side presents its case to the court or the jury, and the opposing side tries to discredit it. Lawyers must be truthful in what they say, but have no duty to volunteer information, even if not doing so misleads the judge or jury. If the case involves scientific or medical matters, each side will present experts who testify to why the facts support their client's case. Because neither the jurors nor the judge are knowledgeable about the specific facts being litigated, they have to decide which expert to trust based on credentials and demeanor. The great strength of the jury system is that it allows citizens to control the power of the government in criminal cases and to resolve difficult policy problems when these involve only the parties to the case. The great weakness of the jury system is that it cannot deal with complex scientific issues and it cannot balance the rights of persons not involved in the case. For example, in product liability cases involving persons claiming to have been injured by pharmaceuticals, the jury has no way to balance the interests of the injured person against those who may be denied access to a beneficial drug if the litigation is successful.

Criminal Law

The United States has two types of law: civil law and criminal law. The key distinction between civil and criminal law is that criminal laws punish for past conduct and can use imprisonment or execution. A law that imposes a five-year prison sentence for selling adulterated drugs would be a criminal law. (There are also criminal laws that punish with a fine.) Mental health commitment laws and communicable disease isolation and quarantine laws are not criminal laws, even if they require the person to be locked up. Their purpose is to protect the person or the public from future injury, not to punish for past conduct.

The key distinction between civil and criminal law is that criminal laws punish for past conduct and can use imprisonment or execution.

Criminal laws are enforced by the government in its own name. In the federal system, only the Department of Justice (DOJ) can bring criminal cases; for example, *United States v. Leichter*, in which Leichter was prosecuted for defrauding FDA. Because the federal and state governments are so powerful, the Constitution provides special protections for criminal defendants; criminal defendants have a right to: 1) free legal counsel if they are indigent, 2) a jury trial, 3) not be forced to testify against themselves, 4) refuse to talk to the police, 5) be free from unreasonable searches and seizures, and 6) force the government to prove its case beyond a reasonable doubt.

The Constitution bars laws that criminalize actions that happened before the law was passed (ex post facto laws) and laws that declare a person to be a criminal without a trial (a bill of attainder). If the jury finds the defendant not guilty, the same government cannot try the defendant again for the same crime (no double jeopardy). This does not bar another level of government from prosecuting the defendant. Thus, the federal government may retry a defendant who has been acquitted by a jury in state court. The second prosecution must be a federal crime, such as the federal law prohibiting violations of civil rights.

Criminal prosecutions can be devastating to a legitimate business, even if the business is ultimately found not guilty. The publicity can hurt the value of the stock, the company records may be seized as evidence, and individual employees may have to hire lawyers because their interests are different from the company's. Criminal defense is very expensive, and is not covered by most insurance policies. A regulated industry may be forced to give up its operating license if indicted. The Draconian consequences allow the government to use the threat of criminal prosecution to persuade a company to settle, rather than fight, civil regulatory charges.

Civil Law

Civil lawsuits can be brought by the government or by private citizens.

Civil lawsuits can be brought by the government or by private citizens. Government agencies use civil litigation to enforce regulatory rulings and statutes. Private civil litigation includes business disputes over private law matters, such as compliance with contracts, ownership of property, and tort claims for compensation for personal injuries. Private plaintiffs can sue FDA to enjoin it from enforcing questionable statutes or regulations.

In most civil cases, there is no right to government-supplied counsel and the defendant can be penalized for refusing to testify. The case need only be proved by a preponderance (>50 percent) of the evidence, which is much lower than the "beyond a reasonable doubt" standard used in criminal cases. The more the case resembles a criminal law case, however, the more protections to which the defendant is entitled. Thus, while a case to institutionalize a person who is dangerous because of mental illness is a civil case, the defendant may be entitled to a lawyer and a higher standard of proof than in a proceeding to collect money.

Civil lawsuits called injunctions ask the court to order the defendant to stop doing something illegal, such as selling unpasteurized milk. If the defendant disobeys the injunction, the court may hold the defendant in contempt of court and impose a fine or imprisonment. FDA can also bring a civil seizure or embargo action to take possession or forbid the sale of goods. These are very powerful measures in the food and drug industry, where seized or embargoed inventory can go out of date faster than the defendant can get a trial to contest the court's order. The agency has great leverage to negotiate a settlement if the defendant has 1,000 tons of fresh fruit that cannot be moved off a ship.

Tort Damage Claims

Simple tort lawsuits generally are based on negligence, which means proving that the defendant did not act as a reasonable person and thus exposed the plaintiff to unnecessary risk. An example would be a diagnostic laboratory that improperly reads a lab test and thus delays a patient's diagnosis of cancer. To win a negligence case, the plaintiff must show what a reasonable laboratory would have done, how the defendant laboratory failed to meet this standard, and that this failure caused plaintiff's harm. This generally requires a lot of information from the defendant, which is obtained by court orders in a process called "discovery."

The most expensive tort lawsuits are brought against product manufacturers under the theory of strict liability. All states have adopted some form of strict liability. To recover damages, an injured person must show that the product was defective and unreasonably dangerous, and that the defect was the cause of his or her injury. Unlike a negligence lawsuit, the plaintiff does not need to prove that the defendant acted "unreasonably." Thus, even if the defendant was more careful than other manufacturers and the plaintiff cannot show that the defendant could have prevented the injury, the plaintiff still can recover. For example, assume that after a drug has been on the market for three years, some patients begin to show serious liver damage. The evidence shows that this could not have been detected during clinical testing because it was either too rare or required a cofactor that could not have been anticipated during the clinical trial. Under the theory of strict (products) liability, the manufacturer could be held liable to the patients for their injuries.

The most expensive tort lawsuits are brought against product manufacturers under the theory of strict liability.

FDA can be sued for negligence causing personal injury under the Federal Tort Claims Act (FTCA). The FTCA allows ordinary negligence actions, such as suing FDA for failing to test and detect a dangerous batch of polio vaccine when its regulations required testing every batch of vaccine. Unlike private tort actions, however, if the plaintiff is injured because of an intentional policy choice, the agency is not liable. For example, the government tested atomic weapons in the western desert, knowing that this would put local residents at risk. When these residents sued, the case was eventually dismissed because the injuries were the result of a policy decision, rather than negligence. Agencies cannot be sued when regulatory decisions reduce or destroy the value of regulated products, such as when FDA pulls a drug from the market because it endangers the public.

Discovery

Discovery is the process for obtaining information in legal proceedings. Discovery is used in civil and criminal litigation, and in administrative proceedings. There are three types of discovery: 1) depositions, where the witness answers questions in person and the answers are recorded by a court reporter or electronically; 2) interrogatories, which are written questions to a party to a lawsuit and which are filled out with the help of the party's lawyer; and 3) subpoenas, which are legal orders to produce documents or other physical evidence, such as a batch of allegedly contaminated drugs. As companies have moved to electronic communications and document storage, the courts have extended discovery rules to electronic records and email. Discovery of electronic records ("e-discovery") poses new legal and practical issues. It is easier for parties to convince the court to grant very broad discovery orders when the data can be delivered on a small portable hard drive, rather than as truckloads of paper records.

Discovery is the process for obtaining information in legal proceedings.

Discovery is the most time-consuming and expensive part of litigation. For example, in a product liability lawsuit over the side effects of a new drug, a plaintiff will want copies of all the documents that contain any information about the drug, including the thousands of pages contained within the New Drug Application submitted to FDA. These will be reviewed and searched by computer for comments by researchers or others that indicate that the company knew of the problem or structured the research in ways that would minimize discovery of side effects. The plaintiff also would want to depose the senior executives of the company.

Privileged Information

U.S. law recognizes several circumstances where information is privileged from discovery, particularly in criminal trials. Traditional common law privileges protect information that a priest hears in confession, communications between spouses, and communications to a person's attorney. There are also statutory privileges, such as the physician-patient privilege, and restrictions on the discovery of drug and alcohol abuse treatment records. Statutory privileges usually contain exceptions, and even the attorney-client privilege does not protect information about future crimes or conspiracies with the attorney to commit crimes.

U.S. law recognizes several circumstances where information is privileged from discovery.

The attorney-client privilege protects information a client tells his or her attorney. It does not protect documents or other materials that the client gives the attorney, unless these were protected already under a different privilege. If the client tells the same information to a non-attorney, such as a co-worker, then the information can be obtained by deposing the co-worker. If the attorney is the corporation's employee, the attorney-client privilege runs to the corporation, not to employees or corporate officers who may talk to the attorney. If there is a conflict between the corporation's interests and employee's interests, the attorney must choose to protect the corporation. Thus, in criminal cases, employees being investigated need to retain their own attorneys.

The work that the attorney does for the client is also protected through the attorney work product doctrine. It applies to work done for the client in anticipation of litigation, meaning that it is not available if the attorney is acting as a business advisor rather than as legal counsel. This doctrine protects information, such as accident investigation reports, if they are done under the supervision of the attorney. It also protects the legal research done by the attorney. The protection is not absolute, however. A court can order the discovery of attorney work product if necessary to ensure fairness in the case. For example, assume that the attorney has an engineer test a medical device that was involved in an accident. The test destroys the device, making the engineer's report the only evidence of performance of the device. Even though the report was prepared at the instruction and under the supervision of an attorney, the court could order discovery of the report.

The Administrative Law System

Most food, drug, and medical device law is administrative law enforced by executive branch agencies, primarily FDA. In the United States, administrative law dates back to sanitary commissions and other citizens' boards in the colonial period. The growth of federal agencies reflects the growth of federal government after World War II. Administrative law is civil law, although agencies can refer cases to the DOJ or state prosecutors if they find criminal activity. Administrative agencies are diverse, ranging in size and power from the Department of Health and Human Services, which has a budget exceeding many small states, to specialized state agencies that have very small budgets and no full-time staff.

Creating Agencies

Congress creates agencies and gives them power through laws called "enabling legislation," which specifies what the agency is to do, how the agency is structured, and its budget. Once an agency is established, Congress can modify or expand its duties with subsequent legislation; for example, FDA was given authority to regulate medical devices by amendments that were made in 1976 to its enabling legislation. Congress also controls agency action through setting

Congress creates agencies and gives them power through laws called "enabling legislation," which specifies what the agency is to do, how the agency is structured, and its budget.

the agency's budget, which can include specific limits on money for each agency activity. While Congress may not directly interfere with agency management, it may require agency personnel to testify before Congress and justify their actions.

The heads of most agencies and their top administrators, such as FDA's Commissioner of Food and Drugs, are officers of the United States. The Constitution requires that these officials be appointed by the President and confirmed by the Senate. The President is free to replace them with new appointees at will. This allows the President to set agency policy through his political appointments, subject to review and delay by the Senate confirmation process.

Some agencies, such as the Securities and Exchange Commission (SEC) and the Federal Trade Commission (FTC), are governed by appointed boards whose members have staggered terms. The President can replace board members only when their terms expire. While these are called independent agencies, they are still in the executive branch. A newly elected President will only be able to change the governance of an independent agency by replacing the board members as their terms expire. This gives the agency greater political independence. Congress creates independent agencies when it wants to insulate an agency that is charged with politically sensitive enforcement.

Deference to Agency Expertise

Deference to Agency Expertise
Agencies occupy a privileged legal position because courts generally defer to agency decisions, as long as the agency is acting within the legal authority it was given by Congress in its enabling legislation.

Agencies occupy a privileged legal position because courts generally defer to agency decisions, as long as the agency is acting within the legal authority it was given by Congress in its enabling legislation. The courts recognize that there are many regulatory matters that can be resolved only through expert decision-making because they turn on highly technical issues, they demand quick action, or some combination of both. For example, when FDA orders a food recall, such as the 2012 recall of cantaloupes potentially tainted with *Salmonella*, the courts are very reluctant to second-guess the agency's expert determination that the recall is scientifically justified. Despite the financial injury to the cantaloupe producer, it would imperil the public's health to allow the regulated party to stop the recall while it was being litigated in court.

This deference to agency decision-making gives agencies flexibility in responding to problems. If a foodborne illness such as listeriosis breaks out because of problems with cheese made from unpasteurized milk, health agencies can institute control measures much faster than Congress or the state legislatures could pass specific laws on the subject. The agency also has the freedom to modify its strategies as it learns more about a problem.

ADMINISTRATIVE PROCEDURE

While agencies may act quickly and with little oversight during emergencies, they are more limited in their actions that deal with routine matters. Federal agencies are governed by the Administrative Procedure Act (APA), and each state has a comparable set of rules for its agencies. The APA establishes the basic framework for making regulations (rules), conducting adjudications (hearings and trials), and for challenging agency actions in court. Congress may supersede the APA and specify different procedures in the agency's enabling act.

Rulemaking

A federal agency can do only what Congress gives it the power to do in its enabling legislation. In many cases, however, that enabling legislation is broad and general. This gives the agency flexibility, but makes it difficult to know how to comply with the law. Agencies can write regulations to provide industries and individuals with more detailed legal standards than are in the general enabling legislation. The APA and an agency's enabling legislation specify the process for promulgating regulations. Properly promulgated regulations have the same force as a law passed by Congress. Like statutes, regulations control future conduct and bind the public and the agency.

For example, a rule might define how many insect parts are allowed in a pound of butter. FDA would publish its proposed regulation in the *Federal Register*, which is a compilation of federal notices—including proposed and final rules—issued by agencies. The proposed regulation must include the scientific and economic basis for the proposed rule, as well as the rule itself. All interested persons, which might include butter and cookie makers as well as cookie eaters, are given a period (often 90 days) to comment on the rule by mail or electronically. If the proposed rule allows three insect parts per pound, the butter industry might complain that the agency does not have scientific evidence that having more that three insect parts per pound poses a health risk. A public interest group might comment that there should be no insect parts in butter and, if there are, they should appear on the label so consumers know what they are buying.

Rulemaking:
FDA must follow a defined process before it can make a rule. It must publish the proposed rule in the Federal Register *and take comments from the public.*

FDA must review the comments, and in some cases it may be required to hold public hearings. It then decides whether it wants to change the regulation in response to the comments. In this case, assume it decides to raise the level to five parts per pound. It then publishes a final rule with this standard in the *Federal Register*. The final rule will include a summary of the comments FDA received and explanations of why it did or did not follow them. In this case, the agency would say that it was persuaded that three would be too expensive, but that 20 was too many and indicated filthy conditions. It also would say that it is too expensive to ban insect parts, and because they do not carry disease, putting insect parts on the label would give consumers the wrong impression that the butter was unsafe. Industry or the consumer group can only challenge the rule in court if it can show that the agency lacked the legal authority for the rule or that the agency withheld necessary information when it published the proposed rule.

When the final rule goes into effect, it is published as part of a series of books called the *Code of Federal Regulations* (C.F.R.). A food manufacturer who wants to start producing butter could look in Title 21 of the C.F.R., where the FDA regulations are codified. Agencies also publish informal guides for the industries they regulate. While these do not have the same legal standing as regulations that were subject to notice and comment in the *Federal Register*, they are very useful guides to agency practice. FDA publishes both notice-and-comment regulations and informational guidelines to help industry comply with its requirements.

Administrative Searches

The Right to Inspect: FDA inspectors may enter regulated facilities to check for violations without a search warrant.

When a party to a lawsuit wants discovery, it must file its request with the court. The opposing party can contest the request and the court will have a hearing to determine if the request must be complied with or if it will be quashed (denied). When the government wants to enter the premises of a business to collect evidence for a criminal case, it must get a search warrant from a judge. The warrant must show that there is probable cause to believe that specific evidence of a known crime will be found on the premises to be searched. In contrast, an administrative search warrant, say to look for fire code violations, need only show the legal authority to do a search and the general area to be searched. It need not be based on any specific information about the premises to be searched or be based on probable cause that a crime has been committed.

Regulated industries must consent to allow warrantless searches and to comply with reporting requirements as a condition of licensure or permitting. Thus, a drug company has to allow an FDA inspector onto its manufacturing site to check for current Good Manufacturing Practices (cGMPs) because the permit to produce drugs includes the right to inspect. If the company refuses and demands that the agency get a search warrant, the agency can revoke its permit to make drugs at the facility while it seeks the warrant.

Information collected during administrative searches can be used for regulatory actions, but there are limits on how it can be used in criminal prosecutions. If FDA believes that a criminal prosecution is possible, it will refer the case to the DOJ so the prosecutors can determine if a probable cause criminal warrant should be used, rather than an administrative warrant, or a warrantless search.

Adjudications

Statutes and regulations set the standard. Adjudications are used to determine facts about specific businesses or individuals. Adjudications take many forms. Some look like trials. The New Drug Application process is a form of adjudication. An inspection of a manufacturing facility for GMP violations is also a form of adjudication—it determines whether the facility is meeting the standards through a physical inspection. No matter the form, the primary difference between an adjudication and a civil trial is that adjudications are inquisitorial, not adversary proceedings.

Unlike the previously discussed adversarial system, where the judge is just a referee without knowledge of the subject matter, the inquisitorial judge is knowledgeable and is often an expert. The judges who conduct adjudications that look like hearings or trials are called administrative law judges (ALJs). Agency hearings do not have juries. The ALJ will question witnesses and the parties before the agency to fully develop the facts. Often the ALJ is the representative of the agency, so the ALJ is acting as both judge and prosecutor. At the end of the adjudication, the ALJ will issue a recommended opinion. The agency may adopt this as the final decision or modify it.

Most agency proceedings are less formal than civil trials. The regulated parties talk directly to relevant agency staff, who are usually encouraged to help the regulated party prepare their case or comply with the regulation. While live witness testimony is permitted, agencies generally prefer written reports from experts because they are easier to evaluate than live testimony. In agency practice, lawyers and their clients will deal with the same agency personnel on many different matters. The agency will know whether they are credible and will act accordingly. Parties that have a reputation for cutting corners will be regulated more closely.

Judicial Review of Agency Actions

In situations where an agency believes a public health and safety risk is imminent, it can act without first going to court. In a classic case from 1908, a public health agency seized chicken from a freezer plant that had experienced a power failure. The agency did not have a court order and was sued for unconstitutionally seizing the property. The court ruled that the seizure was proper, given the imminent threat to the public health and that the defendant's due process rights were satisfied by a post-seizure hearing. If an agency is found to have acted without proper authority or justification, it can be ordered to pay damages. The U.S. Supreme Court has ruled that in reviewing the order of a public health agency, the courts should not second-guess the underlying scientific basis of the agency's decision: "It is not for the courts to determine which scientific view is correct in ruling upon whether the police power has been properly exercised.

In situations where an agency believes a public health and safety risk is imminent, it can act without first going to court.

The judicial function is exhausted with the discovery that the relation between means and end is not wholly vain and fanciful, an illusory pretense." To successfully attack an agency's expert decision making, it must be shown that the agency acted "arbitrarily or capriciously," which means that the agency acted without a rational basis for its decision. To defeat such a challenge, the agency must present a proper record explaining the factual and legal basis for its actions.

The courts do not defer to agencies' interpretation of laws because that is the area of the courts' expertise. However, if the law is subject to more than one interpretation—very frequently the case—the courts will defer to the agency's choice of interpretation, as long as it is reasonable. In *Chevron U.S.A., Inc. v. Natural Resources Defense Council, Inc.,* 467 U.S. 837 (1984), an early case under the Clean Air Act, the court found that the Clean Air Act allowed the EPA more than one option for controlling air pollution at the Chevron facility. The agency was free to choose any method that was reasonable under the statute. It was the agency's decision, not the court's, in how to implement the law. The court held that substituting its decision for that of the agency would undermine separation of powers because agency policy is an executive branch function. In contrast, when FDA tried to regulate tobacco, the Supreme Court found that while the FDCA could be interpreted to allow tobacco regulation, it was clear from the history of FDA that Congress did not intend FDA to regulate tobacco. Congress had to pass new legislation to allow tobacco regulation by FDA.

In rare cases, courts will review an agency's failure to act.

In rare cases, the courts will also review an agency's failure to act. In one case, the Secretary of the Department of Health and Human Services refused to promulgate a rule banning the interstate shipment of unpasteurized milk. A public interest group sued the agency, arguing that such a rule was necessary to protect the public's health. The agency record showed that FDA scientists had built an overwhelming record that unpasteurized milk posed a threat to the public health. The court found that the Secretary was acting arbitrarily and capriciously in refusing to promulgate the rule, and ordered her do so.

SUMMARY

Food, drug, and medical device regulation can be understood only in the larger context of the U.S. legal system.

Food, drug, and medical device regulation can be understood only in the larger context of the U.S. legal system. FDA regulation is administrative law, governed by the APA and statutes passed by Congress. FDA is under executive branch control through the presidential appointment of the Commissioner and ongoing White House oversight. FDA can bring civil enforcement actions and can refer cases to the DOJ for criminal prosecution. Any industry regulated by FDA must be familiar with the statutes and the specific regulations promulgated by FDA governing their industry. Failure to follow these regulations can result in seizures, closing of facilities, and civil and criminal penalties.

Chapter 2

U.S. Food and Drug Law and FDA— A Historical Background

Paul Hyman, Hyman, Phelps & McNamara, PC, Washington, D.C.*

Key Points

- Food and drug law dates back to the beginning of commerce, arising with laws to protect consumers of food from false weights and measures.
- U.S. food and drug law derives primarily from British food laws adopted by the colonies and the states after the Revolutionary War.
- Until the mid-19th century, almost all food and drug regulation occurred at the local level, reflecting the prevailing pattern of commerce.
- With regional and national expansion of food distribution, the states became more involved; the few federal laws focused primarily on imports, taxes, and duties rather than consumer protection.
- The Vaccine Act of 1902 marked the federal government's venture into domestic drug regulation, and included premarket approval.
- The Food and Drugs Act of 1906, the first comprehensive federal law regulating foods and drugs, was strictly an enforcement statute, designed to punish violations.
- A tragedy involving a new dosage form of a sulfa drug, Elixir Sulfanilamide, which contained an unlabeled solvent and killed almost 100 people, helped induce Congress to enact the Federal Food, Drug, and Cosmetic Act of 1938 (FDCA), the basic law today.
- In addition to strengthening enforcement and federal jurisdiction, the 1938 act included government premarket clearance of drugs for safety.
- The FDCA has been amended numerous times, strengthening the regulation of drugs, food, and color additives, and medical devices; adding user fees; and, more recently, promoting the availability of generic drugs, new therapeutic agents, nutrition information for foods and dietary supplements, regulating tobacco products, and enhancing food safety.
- The Food and Drug Administration (FDA), which enforces the FDCA, is the oldest federal regulatory agency, beginning in 1848 as the Agricultural Division of the Patent Office, subsequently becoming part of the U.S. Department of Agriculture; the Federal Security Agency; the Department of Health, Education and Welfare; and now the Department of Health and Human Services, but lacking a statutory existence until 1988.

*The author gratefully acknowledges the invaluable assistance of Joseph W. Cormier and Andrew J. Hull in the update of this chapter.

INTRODUCTION

The basic statute under which the federal government regulates food, drugs, medical devices, cosmetics, and, most recently, tobacco products is the Federal Food, Drug, and Cosmetic Act of 1938 (FDCA). The history of food and drug regulation, however, goes back virtually to the beginning of recorded history, or at least since such products were offered for sale to consumers. Moreover, that history did not stop with the 1938 act. There have been numerous amendments to the statute, both expanding and contracting its reach, as well as court decisions that have changed the interpretation of the statutory language in ways that frequently have surprised the law's congressional proponents, government regulators, regulated industry, and consumers.

ROOTS OF FOOD AND DRUG LAW AND REGULATION

The development of food and drug law can be said to have paralleled the development of civilization.

The development of food and drug law can be said to have paralleled the development of civilization. Laws to protect consumers from adulterated food products and from false weights and measures date back at least to biblical times and can be found in all civilizations. Until relatively recent times, and the development of analytical chemistry and the beginnings of modern medicine, the regulation of food encompassed drugs as well. With the development of "consumer" products, early civilizations had to take steps to protect consumers who, like today's consumers, could not readily protect themselves from fraudulent practices. Early regulations can be found in the Code of Hammurabi in the 18th century B.C., and in early Chinese and Indian laws.

The Greeks and Romans enacted increasingly complicated food laws, addressing adulteration of staples such as wine, wheat, flour, and bread. In Rome, the sale of watered, flavored, and colored wines; the use of false weights and measures; and other fraudulent practices could give rise to a private right of action or to a civil crime punishable by condemnation to the mines or temporary exile. Thus, the Romans did not rely entirely on the doctrine of *caveat emptor* ("buyer beware") to regulate foods.

In the Middle Ages, following the Crusades, certain regulatory functions, particularly with respect to short weights and measures, were the responsibility of mercantile guilds. For instance, King Henry III of England appointed the Pepperers Guild custodian of official weight standards in the 13th century and its members became the first public food inspectors in England.

Concern over inadequate policing by these private, commercial interests eventually led to the enactment of local ordinances or state laws to regulate sales of particular commodities. Laws in England and the Continent regulated the quality of bread, wine, beer, ale, meat, fish, honey, spices, butter, milk, and water. Punishment for violations of these laws could range from public humiliation to fines to corporal or even capital punishment.

During the 16th and 17th centuries, colonial expansion brought more exotic goods—such as chocolate, tea, coffee, and sugar—to Europe. The substitution of cheaper ingredients and other fraudulent practices became more sophisticated and more widespread. The ability of regulatory officials to detect these adulterated foods was limited, although many ordinances and laws were enacted to try to prevent these practices. It was only with the development of the science of chemistry, however, that modern food and drug regulation could begin to develop. By the middle of the 19th century, the advance of analytical chemistry and the use of the microscope to analyze foods led at last to broad food and drug laws in Europe and the United States.

The American colonies followed English legal precedents for food regulation, but the early laws and ordinances primarily were intended to protect trade in the colonies. Independence did not change this legal tradition. Most states, like Virginia, formally adopted all of the English common law. Massachusetts enacted its own food adulteration law as early as 1785, again modeled on British regulations. Throughout the 19th century and into the 20th century, the United States was influenced most strongly by British law and regulation.

In the 1800s, Great Britain and other European countries began to update their laws to protect the public from unsafe and fraudulently presented foods and drugs. Their laws shifted from protection of revenue to protection of consumers as more fraud and adulteration were recognized and the public demanded better protection.

In 1820, a German chemist working in London, Frederick Accum, published *A Treatise on Adulteration of Food and Culinary Poisons*, which described the fraudulent adulteration of bread, beer, wine, liquor, tea, coffee, cream, confectionery, vinegar, mustard, pepper, cheese, olive oil, and pickles. Accum bravely identified merchants who were selling adulterated foods and drugs. His book also discussed various methods available to detect these frauds.

1820
Frederick Accum, a German chemist working in London, publishes A Treatise on Adulteration of Food and Culinary Poisons.

As exposed by Accum and others, adulteration of food and drugs was widespread. Candy was colored with highly toxic mineral pigments such as compounds of lead, arsenic, copper, mercury, and chromium. "Rock-and-rye" candy, popular among children, was made of glucose, flour, and fusel oil. Coffee was regularly adulterated with chicory, as well as roasted ox or horse liver. Tea was adulterated with copper arsenite, lead chromate, and indigo.

Dr. A.H. Hassall, an English physician, performed microscopic analyses on common food adulterations that were published in the medical journal *The Lancet*, and then republished in a book in 1855. Like Accum, Dr. Hassall's articles identified merchants responsible for the adulterations, and they received much public attention. In analyses of many samples of foods such as coffee, bread, flour, milk, and tea, Dr. Hassall found most to be adulterated with cheaper food ingredients and such extraneous materials as metals, colors, shells, husks, sand, and grit.

In response to public pressure, in 1860 the English Parliament enacted the first general food law in England, the Adulteration of Food and Drink Act. This legislation was extended to medicines in 1868 and 1872. In 1875, these acts were replaced by the Sale of Food and Drugs Act.

In the United States, until the middle of the 19th century, most food and drug regulation was carried out on a local level, reflecting the type of commerce prevalent at that time. As with other commerce, however, food distribution expanded regionally and nationally, and the states became more involved. By 1900, almost every state had some type of food and drug law in place.

Federal legislation through the 19th century focused on foreign commerce. Thus, in 1848, Congress passed the Drug Importation Act that ordered U.S. Customs to prevent entry of foreign adulterated drugs. The law's primary purpose was to levy taxes and duties on imported articles, and to protect U.S. industry. Protecting consumers was of secondary importance. Other laws enacted during the latter half of the 19th century included the Tea Acts of 1883 and 1897, the Oleomargarine Act of 1886, and the Filled Cheese Act of 1896. All were enforced by the Treasury Department and had similar commercial purposes.

1850

Lemuel Shattuck attributes a decrease in average life expectancy to adulterated food and drugs, and he recommends establishing boards of health to counter the problems.

Accum's treatise had raised public concern in the United States, as well as in Europe, about food adulteration. Several similar investigations in the United States added to this concern. Among these was a report by Lemuel Shattuck in 1850 that showed that average life expectancy had decreased in Boston from 27.85 years to 21.43 years and in New York from 26.15 years to 19.69 years between the years 1810 to 1820, and 1840 to 1845. He attributed this in part to adulterated food and drugs and recommended establishing boards of health to counter the problems.

Findings of this type helped put pressure on Congress to pass federal legislation. Many scientists, journalists, and social reformers joined the effort. Dr. Harvey W. Wiley, who became the Chief Chemist of the U.S. Department of Agriculture (USDA) (the forerunner of Commissioner of Food and Drugs) in 1883, took an aggressive public role in exposing food adulteration and demanding a federal response. Some industry leaders also spoke out on the need for federal regulation, based both on their concerns over lax enforcement and on the difficulties of complying with the patchwork of state and local laws. More than 100 food and drug bills were introduced in Congress, unsuccessfully save one, from the 1880s to 1906.

The one federal law enacted in that period was the Virus Act of 1902 (subsequently known as the Biologics Control Act), which was intended to ensure purity and safety of therapeutic serums, vaccines, toxins, anti-toxins, and similar products used to prevent, treat, or cure diseases in humans. Vaccines had long been widely accepted in the United States, but regulation of their safety and purity was left to the states. The direct impetus for the 1902 federal law arose from two tragedies that occurred in 1901: one involving contaminated smallpox vaccine that caused an outbreak of tetanus in Camden, New Jersey; the other involving diphtheria antitoxin contaminated with tetanus in St. Louis, Missouri. These incidents convinced Congress that federal action was necessary to protect the public from contaminated products. Ironically, vaccines originally were regulated by the Vaccines Act of 1813, apparently the first federal regulatory law, but that law was repealed in 1822 after similar incidents of contaminated batches occurred.

The 1902 act for the first time required government premarket approval of a product. Biologics manufacturers were required to obtain both product and establishment licenses. The act also, for the first time, authorized federal agents (from the Treasury Department) to inspect biologics establishments. Enforcement of the human biologics law subsequently was transferred to the National Institutes of Health and became the Food and Drug Administration's (FDA's) responsibility in 1972. Animal biologics are still regulated by USDA.

THE FOOD AND DRUGS ACT OF 1906

The pressure on Congress to enact federal legislation from Dr. Wiley and others was heightened around the turn of the century by public opinion whipped up by "muckrakers," "investigative reporters" who exposed food and drug adulteration, consumer fraud, and other social issues. Probably the most influential was Upton Sinclair, whose 1906 novel *The Jungle* dramatically portrayed food

1906

The original Food and Drugs Act is passed by Congress and signed by President Theodore Roosevelt. It prohibits interstate commerce in misbranded and adulterated foods, drinks, and drugs.

adulteration in the meat industry as part of his description of the exploitation of workers and the poor in Chicago. In response, President Theodore Roosevelt sent his own representatives to Chicago who confirmed the abominable conditions. President Roosevelt then added his support for federal legislation. On June 30, 1906, both the Food and Drugs Act (often called the "Pure Food and Drugs Act") and the Meat Inspection Act were signed into law. The former was enforced by the predecessor to today's FDA. The latter was, and remains, the jurisdiction of the USDA, continuing the historic split in regulatory authority between the two agencies and the corresponding segments of the food industry.

The 1906 act commanded the federal government to ferret out adulterated and misbranded foods and drugs in interstate commerce but it did not authorize the government to establish industry-wide standards or broad rules to protect the public health.

The 1906 act was the first comprehensive U.S. legislation relating to foods and drugs. It was designed as an "enforcement" statute intended to punish violations by criminal prosecution or by seizure of the offending goods. In concise and simple terms, the 1906 act commanded the federal government to ferret out adulterated and misbranded foods and drugs in interstate commerce. The government was not authorized to establish industry-wide standards or broad rules to protect the public health or to approve any products before they could be marketed.

Section 2 of the 1906 act prohibited the interstate shipment, including import from and export to a foreign country, of any adulterated or misbranded food or drug. The person who delivered a violative product *and* the person who subsequently delivered such an article "in original unbroken packages" were guilty of a misdemeanor and subject to a fine of up to $200. A subsequent offense was punishable by either or both a $300 fine and one year in prison. A dealer who could show a "guaranty" from a U.S. supplier to the effect that the article was not adulterated or misbranded would be exempt from prosecution (section 9 of the 1906 act).

Section 6 of the 1906 act defined "drug" to include "all medicines and preparations recognized in the United States Pharmacopoeia [USP] or National Formulary [NF] for internal or external use, and any substance or mixture of substances intended to be used for the cure, mitigation, or prevention of disease of either man or animals." The act provided that a drug was "adulterated" if: 1) the drug failed to meet the standards of "strength, quality, or purity" as prescribed by the USP or the NF, unless the drug's container "plainly stated" a different standard of purity; or 2) the drug failed to meet its own labeled strength or purity (section 7 of the 1906 act).

Section 6 of the 1906 act also defined "food" to include "all articles used for food, drink, confectionary, or condiment by man or other animals, whether simple, mixed, or compound." A food was adulterated:

First. If any substance has been mixed and packed with it so as to reduce or lower or injuriously affect its quality or strength.

Second. If any substance has been substituted wholly or in part for the article.

Third. If any valuable constituent of the article has been wholly or in part abstracted.

Fourth. If it be mixed, colored, powdered, coated, or stained in a manner whereby damage or inferiority is concealed.

Fifth. If it contain any added poisonous or other added deleterious ingredient which may render such article injurious to health. . . .

Sixth. If it consists in whole or in part of a filthy, decomposed, or putrid animal or vegetable substance, or any portion of an animal unfit for food, whether manufactured or not, or if it is the product of a diseased animal, or one that has died otherwise than by slaughter.

The statute further declared confectionary to be adulterated if it contained certain minerals, poisonous color, or flavor, other ingredients harmful to health, "spirituous liquor," or narcotic drugs (section 7 of the 1906 act).

The 1906 act also listed several acts that would constitute "misbranding" as to both food and drugs. In particular, any drug, food, or food ingredient "the package or label of which shall bear any statement, design, or device regarding such article [or its components] which shall be false or misleading in any particular" would be misbranded (section 8 of the 1906 act). A drug could also be misbranded if: 1) it was an imitation of or was offered for sale under the name of another drug; 2) the original contents were replaced by other materials; or 3) the package label failed to state "the quantity or proportion of any alcohol, morphine, opium, cocaine, heroine, alpha or beta eucaine, chloroform, cannabis indica, chloral hydrate, or acetanilide" or any derivatives of those substances. A food could be misbranded for the same conditions and also if the package contained: 1) an inaccurate quantity of contents statement or 2) a false statement about the food's ingredients.

"Misbranded" as defined in the 1906 act:
In particular, any drug, food, or food ingredient "the package or label of which shall bear any statement, design, or device regarding such article [or its components] which shall be false or misleading in any particular" would be misbranded.

An adulterated or misbranded article in interstate commerce, or still "unloaded, unsold, or in original unbroken packages," could be seized and condemned by a U.S. district court (section 10 of the 1906 act). The procedures were to conform to admiralty proceedings except that either the claimant of the article or the government could demand a jury trial.

The act was administered jointly under "uniform rules and regulations" established by the Secretaries of Agriculture, Commerce, and Treasury, including "collection and examination of specimens of foods and drugs" (section 3 of the 1906 act). The Secretaries established a committee to draw up rules and regulations for enforcement of the law. The committee included Dr. Wiley, Chief of the USDA Bureau of Chemistry, which was primarily responsible for the enforcement of the act. The bureau, in particular, examined samples and, if they appeared to be violative, notified and provided the party from which the samples were obtained an opportunity to be heard. "[I]f it appears that any of the provisions of [the 1906] Act have been violated," the Secretary of Agriculture certified the matter to the appropriate U.S. District Attorney for formal action in the federal district court (sections 4 and 5 of the 1906 act).

A controversy soon arose over whether a drug label was "false or misleading in any particular" if it contained unproved therapeutic claims.

A controversy soon arose over whether a drug label was "false or misleading in any particular" if it contained unproved therapeutic claims. The Supreme Court, in *United States v. Johnson*, 211 U.S. 488 (1911), held that "Cancerine tablets," offered as part of "Dr. Johnson's Mild Combination Treatment for Cancer, Tumor and Other Chronic Diseases," were not misbranded because the statute prohibited only misleading statements about the ingredients of a drug, not about the drug's effectiveness.

Congress reacted in 1912 with the Sherley Amendment, which expanded the definition of misbranding for drugs to include "any statement, design, or device regarding the curative or therapeutic effect of such article or [its components], which is false and fraudulent." Significantly, the government still had the burden of proving fraudulent intent.

Five amendments to the 1906 act:
- *The Net Weight Amendment*
- *The Kenyon Amendment*
- *Butter Amendment*
- *McNary-Napes Amendment*
- *Shrimp Inspection Amendment*

There were only five other amendments to the 1906 act before it was replaced by the FDCA in 1938:

◆ The Net Weight Amendment of 1913 required the quantity of a packaged food's contents to be plainly and conspicuously marked on the outer package in terms of weight, measure, or numerical count.

◆ The Kenyon Amendment of 1919 overturned an adverse administrative decision by defining the word "package," as used in the act, to include "wrapped meats inclosed [sic] in papers."

◆ In 1923 Congress responded to requests from the dairy industry to provide the first standard definition of a food product in "An Act to Define Butter and to Provide a Standard Therefore."

◆ At the urging of the canned foods industry, Congress passed the McNary-Napes Amendment in 1930, authorizing the Secretary of Agriculture to establish standards of quality, condition, and fill of container for each class of canned foods.

◆ In 1934 Congress implemented the Shrimp Inspection Amendment, which authorized the Secretary of Agriculture to create a voluntary seafood inspection program that would allow a participant to market its shrimp as "USDA Approved."

The Bureau of Chemistry and others quickly recognized deficiencies in the 1906 act. Among other things, the bureau was concerned that the law did not reach dangerous cosmetics and medical devices. The bureau also was concerned that the 1906 act did not extend to fraudulent statements made in food and drug advertising, as opposed to package labels. Although the bureau and other critics initially believed amendments to the existing statute would remedy the 1906 act's failings, they came to the conclusion over time that a completely new statute would be necessary.

THE FEDERAL FOOD, DRUG, AND COSMETIC ACT

In the 1920s and early 1930s, consumers were exposed to increasing numbers of processed and manufactured foods, drugs, cosmetics, and medical devices. Occasionally, these new products had tragic consequences. For example, a depilatory known as "Koremlu Cream," advertised as a cosmetic, contained thallium acetate that caused severe injury to unsuspecting users. Various "slenderizing" compounds, containing powerful pharmacologic agents, could not be regulated as drugs under the 1906 act because obesity was not recognized as a disease. These products were outside the scope of the 1906 act and the government had no means to remove them from the market.

In another notorious example, "Radiothor" was labeled accurately as "radium-containing water." Because that statement was true and the label made no fraudulent therapeutic claims, the government could not take action against the manufacturer. The agency could only warn consumers not to use "Radiothor," even as people were dying from radiation poisoning.

Further, the 1906 act prohibited fraudulent advertising only if attached to, or packaged with, the product. Thus, both consumers and honest manufacturers were susceptible to the deceptive advertising practices of the unscrupulous producer (and the 1906 act provided for only the mildest criminal penalties).

The 1906 act prohibited fraudulent advertising only if attached to, or packaged with, the product.

By 1933, critics of the 1906 act included consumer advocates, politicians, reporters, and other commentators, as well as officials of FDA (the bureau became FDA in 1930).

1938

The FDCA was passed by Congress, containing new provisions:

- *Extending control to cosmetics and therapeutic devices*
- *Requiring new drugs to be shown safe before marketing, starting a new system of drug regulation*
- *Eliminating the Sherley Amendment requirement to prove intent to defraud in drug misbranding cases*
- *Providing that safe tolerances be set for unavoidable poisonous substances*
- *Authorizing standards of identity, quality, and fill-of-container for foods*
- *Authorizing factory inspections*
- *Adding the remedy of court injunctions to the previous penalties of seizures and prosecutions*

Rexford G. Tugwell, who became Assistant Secretary of Agriculture in 1933 under President Franklin D. Roosevelt, assembled a committee of FDA officials, USDA attorneys, and several administrative law professors. Their objective was the complete overhaul of the 1906 act. These efforts resulted in a bill introduced by Senator Copeland of New York in 1933 as S. 1944.

Consistent with New Deal political theory, the bill would have increased greatly FDA's regulation of the food and drug industries. Most contentious was a provision that authorized the Secretary of Agriculture to issue any regulations deemed necessary to enforce the law. (It was generally understood that the Secretary would delegate all authority to FDA to enforce the law unless the law specifically barred such delegation.) The regulations would have the force and effect of law. The Secretary also would have the authority to set the procedures for issuing regulations.

Jurisdiction over medical devices would be established by including them in the definition of "drug." Cosmetics, previously subject to little regulation, would be brought within the jurisdiction of FDA. Factories that manufactured or processed foods, drugs, or cosmetics, and warehouses that stored such goods would be subject to inspection. FDA also by regulation could require permits for manufacturing, processing, and packaging facilities. False advertising of regulated products would also be prohibited.

S. 1944 would have expanded greatly the criteria for "adulterated" or "misbranded" foods, drugs, cosmetics, or devices. For example, in response to various "quack" remedies then on the market, a drug would be adulterated if dangerous when used according to its labeling and misbranded if it claimed to have an effect that general medical opinion did not support. Food would be misbranded if it failed to meet standards of quality, standards of identity, and standards of package fill that the Secretary was to promulgate by regulation. Adulterated or misbranded goods in interstate commerce were subject to seizure, and any person (including corporate officers) responsible for introducing or receiving such goods could be subject to criminal liability. Significantly, the bill established a strict liability standard; a "knowing" violation of these provisions was not necessary (although more severe penalties applied if a person acted with scienter). In addition, the Secretary was authorized to use "publicity" when necessary to protect the public health or prevent consumer fraud.

S. 1944 sparked a five-year legislative battle that reflected, in large part, the ongoing debate over the rise in administrative autonomy under the New Deal. Critics focused on the broad discretionary authority vested in the Secretary of Agriculture and the lack of procedural safeguards to prevent misuse of power. Although the Secretary was authorized to issue many regulations only after "notice and hearing," the Secretary also was given the authority to define "notice" and "hearing" by regulation. Moreover, any findings of fact after such a hearing were deemed to be conclusively established for purposes of judicial review. The false advertising provisions were another major target of criticism. Both advertisers and publishers believed that the definition of false advertising was too vague and the penalties for publishing such advertising were too severe.

S. 1944, introduced in 1933 by Senator Copeland, sparked a five-year legislative battle that reflected the ongoing debate over the rise in administrative autonomy under the New Deal.

As a result, S. 1944 was revised over successive years in attempts to agree with the objectives of the affected industries. The first revision (S. 2000), submitted to the Senate in 1934, attempted to enhance procedural safeguards by establishing two five-member advisory panels, the Committee on Public Health and the Committee on Food. A majority vote of the appropriate committee was required before FDA could propose a regulation. After a hearing, another majority vote was required before FDA could issue the regulation. The bill also gave jurisdiction to the U.S. district courts to enjoin the enforcement of any regulation that would cause substantial harm to the petitioner "if it is shown that the regulation is unreasonable, arbitrary, or capricious, or not in accordance with the law." "False advertising" was required to be "false or misleading in any particular relevant to the purposes" of the act. The bill died in committee, but was amended and resurfaced in the same session as S. 2800.

In a concession to the publishing industry, S. 2800 modified some provisions relating to advertising and specifically exempted publishers from liability for false advertisements. To deflect criticism that the government was attempting to regulate the practice of medicine, the bill contained an explicit statement to the contrary. A drug was still considered misbranded, however, if the labeling contained the name of a disease for which the drug was not a cure, as supported by "substantial medical opinion" or "demonstrable scientific facts." The Senate Committee on Commerce held hearings on S. 2800 and, after further modification, reported it favorably to the Senate but Congress adjourned without action on the bill.

Senator Copeland persisted, and in 1935 he introduced a new bill, S. 5. This bill retained the Committee on Food and the Committee on Public Health and granted them broader authority to formulate and issue regulations. The bill authorized the Secretary to appoint additional advisory committees to include representatives of the food, drug, cosmetic, and advertising industries, and consumers in the regulatory process. S. 5 eliminated the provision granting the Secretary conclusive power with respect to questions of fact and transferred this to the judicial system. Judicial authority to review regulations was made explicit. FDA was given jurisdiction over false advertising. The bill passed in the Senate.

In the House of Representatives, a subcommittee of the Committee on Interstate and Foreign Commerce held hearings on S. 5 and competing legislation sponsored in the House. In May 1936, this subcommittee agreed to a bill. Among other things, this bill granted sole authority for enforcing the false advertising prohibitions to the Federal Trade Commission (FTC). The House bill eliminated the Committees on Public Health and Food and the advisory committees. Rule-making authority was transferred back to the Secretary, with some restrictions.

The bill passed the House and went to conference. However, neither side would yield on the issue of which agency should control advertising, and the bill failed again.

In January 1937, Senator Copeland reintroduced S. 5 in another attempt to achieve a food and drug bill. To address one of the advertising issues, the bill would use injunctions, rather than criminal sanctions, to enforce the prohibition of advertising that was "false or misleading in any particular." Further, the "particulars" that a court could enjoin were enumerated, including statements regarding the identity, strength, quality, purity, safety, dietary, curative, therapeutic, or beneficial effects of a food, drug, device, or cosmetic. Jurisdiction over advertising was placed in FDA on the theory that advertising was an extension of labeling. The FTC would retain jurisdiction over advertising that was an unfair method of competition. With several other amendments (including a separate definition for "device"), the Senate passed S. 5 and the bill was referred to the House Committee on Interstate and Foreign Commerce.

The Elixir Sulfanilamide tragedy led to passage of the 1938 law.

While the bill was in the House committee, a drug manufacturer released a product labeled "Elixir Sulfanilamide," a new dosage form of a sulfa drug. Before the elixir was marketed, the manufacturer tested the product for flavor, but not for safety. One ingredient in the elixir, which was not listed on the label, was diethylene glycol, a solvent used to prepare the elixir. Almost 100 people died from ingesting the drug. FDA immediately initiated a recall, but could base its actions only on a technical violation of the 1906 act: "elixir" could be used only to describe a solution that contained alcohol; as Elixir Sulfanilamide did not contain alcohol, it was misbranded. The manufacturer's failure to test the drug for safety or to list a lethal ingredient on the label did not violate the 1906 act.

This tragedy reinvigorated the efforts to enact a food and drug bill. In addition, the jurisdictional controversy over advertising was resolved early in 1938 by the Wheeler-Lea Amendments to the Federal Trade Commission Act, which gave the FTC jurisdiction over false advertising of food, drugs, devices, and cosmetics as an unfair or deceptive trade practice. The House committee amended S. 5 to specify that foods, drugs, devices, or cosmetics were misbranded if the labeling was false or misleading in any particular. The committee added a list of factors that would be considered to decide whether labeling was misleading, including representations or suggestions of fact and the omission of any material facts. This provision was intended to prevent manufacturers of drugs and devices from making false effectiveness claims. The bill, however, deleted the provision that deemed a drug misbranded if scientific opinion did not support a labeling claim of efficacy.

As a response to the Elixir Sulfanilamide tragedy, the committee added a provision to S. 5 that defined "new drugs" and required manufacturers to apply to FDA before a new drug could be marketed. As part of the application, the manufacturer had to test the new drug for safety and submit full reports of the investigations conducted to establish safety to FDA for review. If FDA did not act within 60 days, the manufacturer could market the drug. If FDA questioned an application's assertion of safety, the agency could initiate a hearing. Whether by oversight or intention, devices were not subject to premarket safety review.

To facilitate judicial oversight of administrative action, an administrative hearing was required before FDA could issue many regulations. The Secretary could issue, modify, or repeal a proposed regulation only on evidence of record at the hearing. The bill required that the Secretary publicize detailed findings of fact before taking action. Within 90 days after a regulation issued, individuals or businesses could challenge the regulation in any district court. If challenged, the Secretary was required to furnish a certified copy of the administrative record. The court could then review the agency's findings of fact and, in appropriate circumstances, could supplement the record with additional evidence.

The Senate disagreed with some of these amendments and another conference committee was convened. The committee decided that judicial review would be more consistent and less burdensome to the agency if it were conducted in the circuit courts of appeal. Further, to the extent that evidence outside the administrative record was to be taken, it would be done in a proceeding before the Secretary. Other amendments clarified certain labeling provisions. Both houses then approved the bill, and President Roosevelt signed the FDCA on June 25, 1938.

President Roosevelt signed the FDCA on June 25, 1938.

Structure of the Federal Food, Drug, and Cosmetic Act of 1938

As enacted, the FDCA is divided into 10 chapters. While each chapter will be explained in greater detail later in this text, the following brief summary of each chapter's subject matter should prove beneficial at this juncture.

The Federal Food, Drug, and Cosmetic Act of 1938
The FDCA remains the basic law governing food and drug regulation.

Chapter I is the short title of the act. Chapter II provides definitions of important terms.

Chapter III sets forth the prohibited acts and penalties. In particular, section 301 states that "[t]he following acts *and the causing thereof* are hereby prohibited" (emphasis added), thus including aiding and abetting. Among other things, the act prohibits the "adulteration" or "misbranding" of food, drugs, devices, tobacco products, and cosmetics in interstate commerce, or the introduction or delivery for introduction of adulterated or misbranded goods into interstate commerce.

The FDCA also established, for the first time, jurisdiction in the district courts to restrain violations of the act by injunction. A violation of any of the prohibited acts in section 301 can be prosecuted as a misdemeanor under a strict liability standard, applicable to both companies and individuals. The Supreme Court upheld this standard in *United States v. Dotterweich*, 320 U.S. 277 (1943), and in *United States v. Park*, 421 U.S. 658 (1975). As in the 1906 act, a person could avoid criminal penalties by showing a supplier's guaranty. The act also provides the accused an opportunity to present oral or written views to FDA before the agency reports the case to the U.S. Attorney for prosecution. The Supreme Court in *Dotterweich*, however, held that failure to provide that opportunity does not preclude prosecution. In addition, the Secretary is authorized to enforce "minor" violations of the act by means of "written notice or warning." All formal enforcement proceedings are brought by the government, meaning that FDA must act through the Department of Justice (DOJ).

As in the 1906 act, violative articles are subject to seizure and condemnation in the district courts. Multiple seizures are authorized for adulterated products, unapproved new drugs, or products previously adjudicated as misbranded.

Chapter IV addresses regulation of foods. The Secretary is authorized to promulgate regulations establishing standards of identity, quality, and fill of containers for foods. In a concession to the agricultural and dairy industries, most fresh or dried fruits and vegetables, as well as butter, are exempt from these regulations. An adulterated food is defined as a food that contains any "poisonous or deleterious substance," or any "filthy, putrid, or decomposed substance," or that was prepared, packaged, or stored "under unsanitary conditions." Food is also adulterated if missing a "valuable constituent," or if any substance has been added to increase its bulk or make it appear to be of greater value (known as "economic adulteration").

Food is deemed misbranded if its labeling is "false or misleading in any particular," if it is an imitation of another food (unless clearly labeled as an imitation), or if it does not meet FDA regulations setting standards of identity, quality, or container fill.

Food is deemed misbranded, among other things, if its labeling is "false or misleading in any particular," if it is an imitation of another food (unless clearly labeled as an imitation), or if it does not meet FDA regulations setting standards of identity, quality, or container fill. Foods for special dietary use must comply with FDA regulations.

The act also provides for FDA to impose emergency permit controls by regulation, requiring a permit to manufacture certain foods where microbial contamination cannot be readily controlled after the fact. FDA is also authorized to set tolerances for poisonous or deleterious substances that cannot be avoided by good manufacturing practices.

Drugs and devices are the subject of Chapter V. A drug or device is deemed adulterated if it is unsafe or unsanitary. Drugs that fall below the standards of strength and purity established in specified official references (unless clearly labeled as such) or that do not meet the standards of strength or purity represented on the label also are adulterated.

A drug or device is misbranded, among other reasons, if its labeling is "false or misleading in any particular"; fails to identify the manufacturer, packer, or distributor; lacks a statement of net contents; does not list the common name of the drug and every active ingredient; does not contain "adequate directions for use" and "adequate warnings"; or is dangerous to health when used according to the labeling.

"New drugs" cannot be introduced into interstate commerce unless an application has been filed with the Secretary that includes reports showing that the new drug is safe for use. The application becomes effective in 60 days unless FDA notifies the applicant to the contrary. An opportunity for hearing is provided, and the applicant can appeal an adverse decision to a federal district court. Drugs for investigational purposes are exempted from these requirements.

Chapter VI describes the adulteration and misbranding provisions for cosmetics and is the shortest chapter. A cosmetic is adulterated if it:

◆ contains any "poisonous or deleterious substance which may render it injurious to users" when used as directed (except that a coal tar hair dye is exempt if it bears a label warning);

◆ is or contains any "filthy, putrid, or decomposed substance";

◆ was "prepared, packaged or held under unsanitary conditions" and became contaminated or rendered injurious to health; or

◆ has a poisonous or deleterious container; or except for a hair dye, contains an unapproved color or one from an uncertified batch.

"Misbranded" as defined in the 1938 act:
A drug or device is misbranded, among other reasons, if its labeling is "false or misleading in any particular"; fails to identify the manufacturer, packer, or distributor; lacks a statement of net contents; does not list the common name of the drug and every active ingredient; does not contain "adequate directions for use" and "adequate warnings"; or is dangerous to health when used according to the labeling.

FDA is authorized to list and batch-certify harmless colors.

A cosmetic is misbranded if its labeling is "false or misleading in any particular," fails to list the manufacturer and quantity of contents on any package label, lacks prominence and conspicuousness for required label statements, or is in a misleading container. FDA is authorized to exempt cosmetics shipped in bulk to be labeled or repacked elsewhere.

FDA's principal enforcement tool is the establishment inspection.

Administrative provisions are the subject of Chapter VII. Section 701(a) authorizes FDA "to promulgate regulations for the efficient enforcement of this Act." No procedures are specified. More formal rulemaking procedures are set out for regulations to implement such rules as food standards; standards of strength, purity, and quality for noncompendial drugs; and listing of habit-forming drugs. FDA must offer an opportunity for hearing and the agency's decision must be based on "substantial evidence of record at the hearing." Within 90 days, any adversely affected party can appeal the order to an appropriate circuit court of appeals.

Chapter VII also spells out the authority and limits of FDA's principal enforcement tool, the establishment inspection. It authorizes the agency to:

◆ Use its own or state agents to conduct examinations and investigations.

◆ Take samples of foods, drugs, cosmetics, or tobacco products. (This is stated in a backhanded way in section 702(b), which requires FDA to give a portion of the sample to the owner "where a sample . . . is collected for analysis.")

◆ Review and copy records of interstate shipment in the possession of a carrier or the recipient of a food, drug, device, cosmetic, or tobacco product. Refusal of a written request is unlawful, but FDA may not use evidence so obtained in a criminal action against the person who provided the evidence.

◆ Enter and inspect, "at reasonable times," any factory, warehouse, establishment, or vehicle where food, drugs, devices, cosmetics, or tobacco products are produced, packed, or held for introduction into interstate commerce, or after such introduction. FDA inspectors must first obtain permission, but refusal is a prohibited act. The inspection may extend to the facilities, vehicle, equipment, finished and unfinished materials, container, labeling, and, with the exception of cosmetics, all records except for financial data, nontechnical or nonpertinent professional personnel data, or research unrelated to product approvals and other reporting requirements.

◆ Publish reports of formal actions under the act and disseminate information where FDA believes there is an imminent danger to health or "gross" consumer deception.

Chapter VIII governs imports and exports of products. The Secretary of the Treasury is ordered to deliver samples of food, drugs, devices, cosmetics, or tobacco products offered for import as requested by the Secretary of Agriculture. Section 801 states: "If it appears from the examination of such samples or otherwise that" the products violate the FDCA, such products may be refused admission. The refused article must be exported or destroyed. Significantly, no direct right to judicial review is provided.

Articles intended for export are exempt from the adulteration or misbranding provisions of the act only if they comply with the foreign purchaser's specifications, do not violate foreign law, are labeled on the shipping package for export only, and have not been offered in domestic commerce. Unapproved new drugs cannot be exported.

Chapter IX, added in 2009 by the Family Smoking Prevention and Tobacco Control Act (with the previous Chapter IX renumbered to Chapter X), authorizes FDA to set performance standards for tobacco products, require the disclosure of tobacco product ingredients, and regulate "modified risk" tobacco products. In addition, FDA can restrict tobacco sales, distribution, and marketing, and can require stronger health warnings on packaging and in advertisements. The Tobacco Products Scientific Advisory Committee was also established, charged with making recommendations regarding the use of menthol in cigarettes, dissolvable tobacco products, and other issues.

Chapter IX, added in 2009 by the Family Smoking Prevention and Tobacco Control Act, authorizes FDA to set performance standards for tobacco products, require the disclosure of tobacco product ingredients, and regulate "modified risk" tobacco products.

Finally, Chapter X exempts meat and meat food products, biologics, and certain other products from the provisions of the act because they are governed by other statutes. It also specifies the "mission" of FDA and formally exempts the practice of medicine from FDA's authority, among other things.

Amendments to the FDCA

Since 1938, there have been numerous amendments of the FDCA; however, there has been no general overhaul of the entire regulatory scheme comparable to the 1938 act's relationship to the 1906 act. Early amendments primarily were aimed at overcoming omissions and shortcomings in the law, often following court decisions. These statutes generally broadened FDA's regulatory authority and left implementation largely to FDA. More recent amendments have required FDA to focus on commercial and economic issues, frequently specifying precisely how and when FDA must implement the FDCA. In 1997 and 2007, Congress enacted laws that represented the most comprehensive efforts to "reform" the agency and improve regulation of all products since 1938.

There have been numerous amendments of the FDCA since 1938, but there has been no overhaul of the entire regulatory scheme comparable to the 1938 act's relationship to the 1906 act.

Significant Amendments from 1938 to 1962

Scientific developments, as well as the demands of World War II, led to a number of new laws directed at specific drugs. In December 1941, Congress amended the FDCA to require batch certification of the strength, quality, and purity of insulin in order "to adequately ensure safety and efficacy of use." Congress was persuaded of the need to ensure uniformity among batches because of the difficulties in making this drug. Significantly, this law gave FDA, for the first time, specific authority to regulate the efficacy of a particular drug.

Batch certification subsequently was required for penicillin (1945); streptomycin (1947); aureomycin, chloramphenicol, and bacitracin (1949); and all antibiotics (1962). By 1982, however, FDA was convinced that the quality of these drugs was now adequate to permit them to be regulated the same as other new drugs, and the agency ceased requiring batch certification in most instances. These provisions on batch certification of insulin and antibiotics were repealed in the Food and Drug Administration Modernization Act of 1997.

In 1948, after an appellate court held that the FDCA did not reach products after shipment in interstate commerce, Congress amended the FDCA to hold expressly that a product may be in violation of the act while "held for sale (whether or not the first sale) after shipment in interstate commerce." This brought local warehouses and retailers within FDA's jurisdiction.

◆ The Durham-Humphrey Amendment

1951

The Durham-Humphrey Amendment

The Durham-Humphrey Amendment defined the kinds of drugs that cannot be safely used without medical supervision and restricted their sale to prescription by a licensed practitioner.

In 1951, in the Durham-Humphrey Amendment, Congress for the first time defined prescription drugs for purposes of FDA regulation. Prescription and over-the-counter (OTC) status previously were determined by state law or by industry, although FDA had used the misbranding provision requiring "adequate directions for use" to impose prescription limits on some drugs. As amended, the FDCA defines a prescription drug to include habit-forming drugs; drugs that are dangerous for use except under the supervision of a (state) licensed practitioner because of their "toxicity or other potentiality for harmful effect, . . . method of use, or the collateral measures necessary to [their] use"; and those that are limited to prescription dispensing by approved New Drug Applications (NDAs). OTC drugs are not defined but comprise all those drugs that do not meet the prescription drug criteria.

For several years, FDA used this definition (as well as the misbranding and new drug provisions) to prohibit sales of stimulant, depressant, and hallucinogenic drugs, which, unlike narcotics, were not subject to specific laws outlawing their abuse. During the 1950s and 1960s, FDA criminally prosecuted manufacturers, distributors, importers, physicians, truck stop operators, and others engaged in the illicit diversion of these drugs. In the late 1960s, FDA prosecuted a few students for distribution of LSD and other hallucinogens. Congress subsequently passed several controlled substances laws that ultimately were transferred to DOJ and are now enforced by the Drug Enforcement Administration (DEA).

In 1953, after a court restricted FDA's inspectional authority, Congress amended section 704 of the act to make clear that FDA had the right to inspect without the permission of the owner or operator of the establishment.

In 1954, and again in 1958, Congress attended to problems relating to chemical contamination of foods. In 1954, Congress set tolerances for pesticide chemicals in or on raw agricultural commodities, including a complex pre-market approval system based on a demonstration of safety for use of pesticides in foods intended for human use (FDCA §§ 201(q), (r), 402(a)(2), 408). Authority for establishing the tolerances subsequently was transferred to the Environmental Protection Agency, with FDA retaining the authority to proceed against foods that contain unapproved or unsafe levels of pesticides.

◆ The Food Additives Amendment of 1958

Congress subsequently enacted the Food Additives Amendment of 1958, which gave FDA authority to require premarket approval for safety of components added to foods (FDCA §§ 201(s), (t), 402(a)(2), 409). This followed several years of hearings on the appropriate regulatory mechanism to ensure the safety of food ingredients.

1958
Food Additives Amendment
The Food Additives Amendment required manufacturers of new food additives to establish safety. The Delaney Provision prohibited the approval of any food additive shown to induce cancer in humans or animals.

Under this law, a food additive is defined as any substance intended or reasonably expected to become a food component or to affect a food's characteristics that is "not generally recognized [by] qualified experts" as safe (GRAS) for its intended use based on "scientific procedures" or, for substances marketed prior to 1958, based on experience from common use in food (FDCA § 201(s)). A food additive is deemed unsafe unless FDA has reviewed data proving its safety and issued a regulation allowing its use. Human safety data is not required. The law established formal rulemaking procedures for the process.

In addition, the law contained an anticancer provision, known as the Delaney Clause after its leading sponsor, Representative James Delaney (D-NY), which prohibited approval of any food additive that has been "found to induce cancer when ingested by man or animal" or found to induce cancer in appropriate tests. As analytic testing has advanced, this "one molecule" approach has affected several widely used food components, such as the artificial sweeteners cyclamate and saccharin and the preservative nitrite. On two occasions, Congress has taken steps to exempt specific substances from the Delaney Clause. In 1962, the FDCA was amended to exempt ingredients of animal feeds (primarily diethylstilbestrol) if no residue is found in edible portions of the animal. In the Saccharin Study and Labeling Act of 1977, Congress put a moratorium on FDA action to ban saccharin, but required labeling of products containing the sweetener. That act was repealed in December 2000. The Delaney Clause was modified in 1996 with respect to pesticides but otherwise remains in place.

◆ The Color Additive Amendments of 1960

1960
Color Additive
Amendments
The Color Additive
Amendments required
manufacturers to establish
the safety of color additives
in foods, drugs, and
cosmetics.

Congress enacted the Color Additive Amendments of 1960 to regulate colors added to foods, drugs, or cosmetics separately from the Food Additives Amendment. A color additive is defined in the amendment as a dye, pigment, or other coloring agent that "is capable (alone or through reaction with other substance) of imparting color" when added to a food, drug, cosmetic, or the human body. Unlike food additives, the definition of color additives does not contain any grandfather protection for a GRAS color. FDA can approve a color for one use and not others. For example, some colors are approved for external use; some are approved for use everywhere but around the eye.

Like food additives, color additives are unsafe unless used in compliance with a regulation issued by FDA. The color also must be "listed" in the FDA regulation for specific uses, and must be batch certified or exempted by FDA regulation. FDA previously had established a provisional listing of "harmless" coal tar colors based on the 1938 act. FDA was authorized to continue this "provisional listing of commercially established colors" for 30 months. The provisional listing, however, lasted until 1981, and several colors still are provisionally regarded as safe by FDA pending receipt of further data.

The amendment also contained a Delaney Clause that prohibited FDA from approving any color additive found to induce cancer when ingested by man or animal, or found to induce cancer "after tests which are appropriate for the evaluation of the safety of additives for use in food." The prohibition thus is slightly narrower than the similar provision for food additives.

◆ The 1962 Drug Amendments

In the late 1950s, Senator Estes Kefauver began a series of investigations of the drug industry for antitrust and price-fixing violations. In the midst of these investigations, there was, as in 1938, a public health tragedy that convinced Congress to enact legislation to protect the public. The incident involved thalidomide, a tranquilizer that was available in the United States only as an investigational drug, but was commercially marketed in other countries. The drug was found to cause birth defects in children whose mothers took the drug during their pregnancy. As a result of the thalidomide tragedy, Congress reexamined the new drug approval process. This led to enactment of the Drug Amendments of 1962, the most comprehensive revision of the drug regulatory law since 1938.

1962

Drug Amendments
Thalidomide tragedy led to passage of major amendment to the law. Since 1962, drugs must be proven effective as well as safe.

Ironically, although thalidomide raised drug safety concerns, the most significant change brought about by the 1962 Drug Amendments was the added requirement to prove *effectiveness* to obtain premarket approval of a new drug. The definition of "new drug" also was amended to include a drug that was not generally recognized by qualified experts as "safe and effective" for its labeled use (FDCA § 201(p)(1)).

In addition, the drug approval provisions were changed substantially:

◆ FDA now must affirmatively approve a product before it can be marketed;

◆ FDA can deny approval for false or misleading labeling;

◆ there must be "substantial evidence" of efficacy, "consisting of adequate and well-controlled investigations, including clinical investigations, by experts qualified by scientific training and experience to evaluate the effectiveness of the drug involved";

◆ new record and reporting requirements were added;

◆ the investigational new drug exemption authority was broadened to authorize FDA to issue regulations to require reports of preclinical tests, investigator agreements, informed consent, and other records and reports; and

◆ the Secretary of the Department of Health and Human Services (DHHS), but not FDA, can suspend a New Drug Application (NDA) immediately if there is an imminent hazard to health.

The 1962 Drug Amendments also broadened FDA's regulatory authority over all drugs in several respects, authorizing:

◆ good manufacturing practice regulations for all drugs,

◆ increased authority over antibiotics,

◆ mandatory use of the generic name in drug labeling,

◆ inspection authority over prescription drug records,

◆ mandatory inspection of drug establishments every two years,

- annual drug establishment registration,

- regulation of prescription drug advertising, and

- a requirement to prove the efficacy of all new drugs approved from 1938 to 1962.

Legislation From 1962 to 1976

In the decade and a half following the Drug Amendments of 1962, there was considerable emphasis on regulation, but the types of legislation affecting FDA were unusually varied. For example, Congress passed the Drug Abuse Control Amendments of 1965, authorizing FDA to act against depressant, stimulant, and hallucinogenic drugs, which previously had been regulated only as adulterated, misbranded, or unapproved new drugs under the FDCA. The statute added felony penalties for selling such drugs, including counterfeit drugs, and authorized FDA personnel enforcing the law to carry firearms, execute and serve search and arrest warrants, seize products under court order, and arrest an individual who violated the law in the investigator's presence or where there was probable cause to believe that the individual had committed or was committing a felony.

FDA established the Bureau of Drug Abuse Control (BDAC), recruiting those FDA inspectors who enjoyed such activity, as well as law enforcement personnel from other federal and state agencies. BDAC was transferred to DOJ in 1968 as part of the Bureau of Narcotics and Dangerous Drugs and, more recently, to DEA.

◆ The Child Protection Act

In 1966, the Federal Hazardous Substances Labeling Act was modified by the Child Protection Act to ban hazardous toys and other articles, broadening FDA's jurisdiction over products not covered by the FDCA. In 1972, jurisdiction was transferred to the newly created Consumer Product Safety Commission (CPSC).

◆ The Fair Packaging and Labeling Act

The Fair Packaging and Labeling Act (FPLA) also was passed that year, requiring truthful and informative labeling for all consumer products in interstate commerce. FDA shared jurisdiction with the FTC, focusing on foods, drugs, cosmetics, and medical devices. FDA used the FPLA to require cosmetics to bear ingredient labeling. Both the FDCA and the FPLA were amended by the Poison Prevention Packaging Act of 1970, which required child-resistant packaging for household substances that could be hazardous to children. CPSC now enforces that act.

◆ The Animal Drug Amendments of 1968

In the Animal Drug Amendments of 1968, Congress established procedures for approving new animal drugs and animal feed containing new animal drugs. This included the certification of antibiotics intended for use in animals.

◆ The Radiation Control for Health and Safety Act

That same year, Congress passed the Radiation Control for Health and Safety Act, which was intended to protect the public from unnecessary exposure to radiation from electronic products. The law authorized FDA to set standards for emissions for such products as microwave ovens, X-ray machines, color televisions, and cathode ray tubes for computers. Civil penalties may be imposed for noncompliance and, since 1990, the criminal penalties applicable to devices under the FDCA apply as well to radiologic products. The Bureau of Radiological Health, a division of the Public Health Service (PHS), originally enforced the act. In 1971, that bureau was transferred to FDA where it ultimately was merged with the Bureau of Devices to become today's Center for Devices and Radiological Health. The law itself was added to the FDCA.

◆ The Drug Listing Act

In 1972, Congress enacted the Drug Listing Act requiring that all marketed drugs be listed with FDA when a company first registers, and that the lists be updated each June and December. The listing must include all labeling and representative advertisements for prescription drugs, and labels, package inserts, and representative labeling for OTC drugs. Like establishment registration, listing does not involve FDA approval, although FDA occasionally does respond to a listing by questioning whether a product is a new drug.

The Medical Device Amendments of 1976

Under the 1938 act, FDA's authority to regulate medical devices was limited to action against adulterated or misbranded devices. FDA could not review or approve medical devices to confirm that they were safe and effective before they could be distributed commercially. FDA reacted by trying to regulate devices as drugs whenever possible in order to obtain the premarket approval authority that existed for new drugs. Thus, FDA regulated absorbable sutures and injectable liquid silicone as drugs, although they were chemically inert.

Under the 1938 act, FDA's authority to regulate medical devices was limited to action against adulterated or misbranded devices.

1976 Medical Device Amendments

The Medical Device Amendments were passed to ensure the safety and effectiveness of medical devices, including diagnostic products. The amendments required manufacturers to register with FDA and follow quality control procedures. Some products must have premarket approval by FDA; others must meet performance standards before marketing.

After the 1962 Drug Amendments, greater attention was given to regulation of devices. This came from industry, health professionals, some patient groups, and even Congress. Concerns arose over the dangers of some devices, such as the Dalkon Shield, an intra-uterine device that was associated with a number of injuries to women.

In response to these pressures, in 1969 the Secretary of Health, Education and Welfare appointed a departmental study group on medical devices, chaired by Dr. Theodore Cooper, director of the National Heart and Lung Institute. The Cooper Committee issued a report in 1970, which concluded that greater device regulation was needed, but should not follow the drug regulatory scheme. The report recommended, among other things, nongovernmental expert reviews and varying degrees of regulation based on risks of different types of devices. The Cooper Committee report was influential in shaping the Medical Device Amendments of 1976 (MDA), the first comprehensive federal regulatory framework for medical devices in the United States.

Among other things, the MDA revised the definition of "device" to distinguish it from "drug," thereby clarifying some of the confusion that existed in the 1938 act. Specifically, a "device" is intended for the same therapeutic use as a drug, but is

> ... an instrument, apparatus, implement, machine, contrivance, implant, in vitro reagent, or other similar or related article. . . which does not achieve its primary intended purposes through chemical action within or on the body of man or other animals and which is not dependent upon being metabolized for the achievement of its primary intended purpose [FDCA § 201(h)].

Devices that previously had been regulated as drugs were to be returned to device status as "transitional devices."

The MDA established a comprehensive system for classifying and clearing medical devices, based on risk, for introduction in interstate commerce. The MDA distinguished between devices on the market before and after enactment of the 1976 law (i.e., "pre-amendment" or "predicate" devices, and "post-enactment" or "post-amendment" devices). Any device not marketed before the enactment date is automatically placed in the highest risk class of devices (Class III) unless it is "substantially equivalent" to a predicate device already on the market and classified at a lower risk to the public health. To enable FDA to determine if such substantial equivalence exists, the MDA added section 510(k), which requires a person who proposes to market such a device to notify FDA at least 90 days in advance of introduction of the device (commonly referred to as "the 510(k)"). A Class III device requires premarket approval, similar to new drug approval. Class I devices are regulated by general controls. Class II devices may require performance standards.

FDA also was given broad regulatory powers by the MDA, including the authority to:

◆ require registration of device establishments and listings of device products;

◆ prescribe good manufacturing practice regulations;

◆ ban worthless or dangerous products;

◆ require notification, repair, replacement, and/or refund for defective devices;

◆ require records and reports on devices;

◆ define by regulation "restricted devices," which go beyond prescription devices and for which FDA may inspect records;

◆ detain suspected violative devices for 20 days pending the filing of a formal action; and

◆ recall dangerous devices.

Several of these powers are unique to device regulation.

The MDA elevated the importance of device regulation within FDA, and reflected the increasing significance of devices in medical practice.

The MDA elevated the importance of device regulation within FDA, and reflected the increasing significance of devices in medical practice.

Legislation from 1977 to Present

◆ The Orphan Drug Act

In 1982, after much lobbying by patient groups and some manufacturers, Congress concluded that the pharmaceutical industry was not sufficiently committed to the development of drugs to treat rare diseases. Because of the limited market for such drugs, and because patents for them often had expired, manufacturers could not expect to recoup their research and development costs through sales. In 1983, Congress responded with a package of economic incentives embodied in the Orphan Drug Act.

The act applied to drugs "for a rare disease or condition," which initially was defined as one that "occurs so infrequently in the U.S. that there is no reasonable expectation" of recovering development costs. This definition proved unworkable and the act was amended in 1985 to include diseases that affect fewer than 200,000 people in the United States. Sponsors of orphan drugs qualify for tax credits to offset their research costs and may be eligible for FDA research grants. Most important, the sponsor is granted seven years of "market exclusivity," which prevents FDA from approving a competitor's version of the identical drug for the same disease. This is separate from any patent protection and has been a major economic benefit for some companies.

◆ The Drug Price Competition and Patent Term Restoration Act

Several factors during the 1970s and early 1980s led Congress to address more broadly competitive issues in the drug market. These included concerns over the cost of drugs to patients, the development of the generic drug industry, the increasing number of important drugs whose patents were due to expire, and the need to encourage pharmaceutical research. These factors led to the Drug Price Competition and Patent Term Restoration Act of 1984, commonly called the Hatch-Waxman Act after its two principal sponsors, Representative Henry Waxman (D-CA) and Senator Orrin Hatch (R-UT). The act was designed as a compromise to promote competition by encouraging the development of low-cost generic drugs, and to encourage research by granting certain competitive benefits to innovators.

The act required FDA to approve generic drugs that are shown to be "bio-equivalent" to a previously approved drug that is "listed" in an FDA publication, without requiring new proof of safety or effectiveness. By filing this "Abbreviated" New Drug Application (ANDA), the generic manufacturer is spared the cost of conducting clinical studies and can offer the product to consumers at a reduced price.

In return, the act granted brand-name manufacturers two important benefits to encourage drug research. The first is the opportunity to extend the patent term to make up for time lost while a drug is undergoing development and FDA review. The second benefit is a period of "market exclusivity" granted to a sponsor that develops a new chemical entity or a new use for a previously approved drug. For a new chemical entity, the act grants five years of exclusivity against approval of an ANDA or other application that lacks clinical data. For a new use for a previously approved drug, in a new full NDA or a supplement that contains clinical tests "essential" to approval, the act grants three years of exclusivity against an ANDA. FDA also must honor a patent and withhold approval of a generic drug until the patent expires or is held invalid by a court.

The Hatch-Waxman Act has resulted in an explosion of generic drug approvals. There also have been a number of lawsuits brought to interpret some of its provisions. The act was followed by FDA's worst scandal, involving bribes to FDA generic drug staff and submission of false information in several ANDAs.

1984

Drug Price Competition and Patent Term Restoration Act

This act expedited the availability of less costly generic drugs by permitting FDA to approve applications to market generic versions of brand-name drugs without repeating the research done to prove them safe and effective. At the same time, the brand-name companies could apply for up to five years' longer patent protection for the medicines they developed to make up for time lost while their products were going through FDA's approval process.

◆ The Generic Animal Drug and Patent Term Restoration Act

In 1988, Congress passed the Generic Animal Drug and Patent Term Restoration Act, extending to veterinary products the same benefits given to human drugs under the Hatch-Waxman Act. Companies are authorized to produce and sell generic versions of animal drugs using Abbreviated New Animal Drug Applications for previously approved drugs based on evidence demonstrating their safety and efficacy.

◆ The Prescription Drug Marketing Act of 1987

In the mid-1980s, Congress became concerned about diverted or counterfeit drugs in the marketplace. The response was the Prescription Drug Marketing Act of 1987 (PDMA), which was intended to address "an unacceptable risk that counterfeit, adulterated, misbranded, subpotent, or expired drugs will be sold to American consumers." In addition to attempting to regulate diversion of legitimate prescription drugs and counterfeits in domestic commerce, the law prohibited the re-import of exported drugs as U.S. goods returned except to the original manufacturer or for emergency use.

1987
Prescription Drug Marketing Act
Addressed the unacceptable risks associated with counterfeit, adulterated, misbranded, subpotent, or expired drugs.

The PDMA banned the sale or purchase of or trade in prescription drug samples and established comprehensive storage, handling, and recordkeeping requirements for such samples. The PDMA also prohibited, with certain exceptions, the resale of prescription drugs purchased by hospitals, healthcare entities, and charitable institutions, and regulated prescription drug wholesale distributors by requiring states to license them in accordance with federal guidelines. Manufacturers must report loss or theft of samples and the conviction of their sales representatives for illegal diversion. There is a substantial civil penalty for a manufacturer's failure to take appropriate steps to prevent diversion (up to $1,000,000 per violation after two convictions of the firm's representatives). There is also a bounty for whistle-blowers of one-half the criminal fine, up to $125,000.

◆ Safe Medical Devices Act of 1990

The Safe Medical Devices Act of 1990 (SMDA) was the first major revision of the medical device requirements of 1976. The SMDA increased FDA's regulatory authority over the medical device industry, particularly in the areas of post-marketing requirements and the premarket notification and approval process. The SMDA was particularly intended to expedite device premarket clearances and approvals by shifting some of FDA's emphasis from premarket reviews to postmarket regulation and surveillance.

The SMDA defined substantial equivalence, essentially codifying FDA's substantial equivalence decision-making structure. Under the SMDA, to determine that a device is substantially equivalent (and therefore, subject to 510(k) clearance), FDA must find that it has the same intended use as the predicate device. The SMDA gave FDA authority to order special controls for Class II devices beyond the performance standards allowed under the MDA, including postmarket surveillance, patient registry, development and dissemination of guidelines, and other appropriate actions deemed necessary by FDA. The SMDA also included provisions enabling FDA to implement postmarket surveillance, civil penalties, temporary suspension of premarket approval (PMA) applications, required reports of removals and corrections, user and distributor reporting, and medical device tracking. Perhaps the most important postmarketing provision was the requirement of notification to FDA and the manufacturer of all incidents that contribute to serious injury, death, or illness that may have been associated with the use of a medical device. Under the SMDA, anyone who is aware of or has knowledge of an incident that reasonably suggests that a medical device has caused or contributed to the death, serious injury, or serious illness of a patient, visitor, or staff member of a healthcare facility must report the incident to FDA.

◆ The Generic Drug Enforcement Act of 1992

1992

Generic Drug Enforcement Act
The Generic Drug Enforcement Act imposed debarment and other penalties for illegal acts involving approval of ANDAs.

In 1992, following a notorious scandal in which officials of FDA's Generic Drugs Division were convicted of taking bribes and a number of generic drug industry personnel were convicted of bribing FDA officials or submitting false data to the agency, Congress enacted the Generic Drug Enforcement Act (GDEA). The act authorized FDA to "debar" firms and individuals convicted of felonies in connection with the drug approval process from participating in that process for periods ranging from one to 10 years for firms and as long as lifetime for individuals. Despite its name, the law applied to both generic and brand-name drug companies. FDA also can bar a "high managerial agent" who had actual knowledge of a violation, and failed to take steps to report or prevent the violation. FDA can temporarily deny approval of an ANDA submitted by a person under criminal investigation for bribery or false statements.

The GDEA also imposed civil penalties for false statements, bribes, destruction of documents, failure to disclose a required material fact, obstruction of an investigation, use of a debarred person to help prepare a drug application, or work on an application by a debarred person. The fines are severe: up to $250,000 per violation for an individual and $1,000,000 for others. The penalty can be levied by FDA via an administrative proceeding or through a court proceeding brought by DOJ. In either case, there is a right of appeal. Informants are entitled to an award of the lesser of $250,000 or one-half the penalty collected.

◆ The Prescription Drug User Fee Act of 1992

As FDA became more engrossed in approving generic drugs, the research-based industry began to push Congress to give FDA more resources to review full NDAs. The political and economic climate, however, was not conducive to enlarging the budget of any government agency. Instead, there developed a philosophy of applying marketplace principles to government activity. In particular, the administration and Congress began to look to the beneficiaries of government services to pay for those services rather than putting a greater burden on taxpayers.

1992

Prescription Drug User Fee Act
PDUFA added more resources to FDA's review process for drugs and biologics.

The Prescription Drug User Fee Act of 1992 (PDUFA) established requirements for drug and biologics manufacturers to pay fees for applications and supplements that require FDA to review clinical studies. These user fees are intended to enable FDA to hire more reviewers to assess the clinical studies in these applications. In return, FDA pledged (but was not statutorily committed) to speed up the review of NDAs. The act also included annual establishment fees and annual product fees for companies with approved NDAs. The PDUFA was scheduled to expire on September 30, 1997, but has been extended multiple times. The current iteration, PDUFA V, was reauthorized in 2012 as part of the Food and Drug Administration Safety and Innovation Act of 2012 to continue through the end of fiscal year 2017. At the time of this writing, bills to reauthorize PDUFA have passed committees in both houses of Congress and are awaiting floor action.

◆ The Nutrition Labeling and Education Act of 1990

In the mid-to-late 1980s, increased consumer interest and advances in studies of nutrition and health led some major food companies to begin to experiment with nutritional claims in advertising and labeling. In particular, one manufacturer launched a labeling and advertising program for cereal that claimed the product could be useful in a high-fiber diet to help prevent cancer. The claim had been reviewed and approved by the National Cancer Institute and the FTC. FDA was more critical but ultimately took no regulatory action.

Congress also became interested in this subject, enacting the Nutrition Labeling and Education Act of 1990 (NLEA), the first comprehensive revision of the food labeling requirements of the FDCA since 1938. Building on FDA's much earlier voluntary nutrition labeling requirements and more recent proposals to permit health claims for food products, the NLEA ordered FDA to encourage the food industry to "assist consumers in maintaining healthy dietary practices." Among other things, the NLEA provides for mandatory nutrition labeling in a uniform format, including serving size, number of servings per container, and the nutrition content of the food per serving based on a common household measure.

1990

Nutrition Labeling and Education Act

Health claims on foods are regulated under the Nutrition Labeling and Education Act of 1990.

The NLEA authorized, for the first time, the use of a "health claim" in food labeling. This is a claim "that characterizes the relationship of [a] nutrient ... to a disease or a health-related condition." Such health claims were permitted only in compliance with FDA regulations. Congress, however, ordered FDA to consider issuing regulations pertaining to the relationship of calcium and osteoporosis, fiber and cancer, lipids and cardiovascular disease, lipids and cancer, sodium and hypertension, fiber and cardiovascular disease, folic acid and neural tube defects, antioxidant vitamins and cancer, zinc and immune function in the elderly, and omega-3 fatty acids and heart disease. Regulations must be based on "significant agreement" of qualified experts that "the totality of publicly available scientific evidence" supports the claims.

The NLEA imposed federal preemption for any food labeling requirements mandated by the FDCA, preempting any state regulation not identical to the FDA requirements. This does not apply to actions against false or misleading labeling or to food advertising.

◆ The Dietary Supplement Health and Education Act of 1994

1994

Dietary Supplement Health and Education Act

Addressed the regulation of dietary supplements by exempting them from some regulatory requirements.

Manufacturers of dietary supplements and other "health foods" felt that the NLEA did not address adequately their interests. After considerable lobbying and a great deal of grass-roots support, Congress was persuaded to enact the Dietary Supplement Health and Education Act of 1994 (DSHEA). In doing so, Congress expressly recognized, defined, and allowed specific claims for dietary supplements, exempting them from some regulatory requirements applicable to other foods.

Among other things, the DSHEA provided a definition of dietary supplement that includes vitamins; minerals; herbs or other botanicals; amino acids; dietary substances used by man to supplement the diet by increasing the total dietary intake; and any concentrate, metabolite, constituent, extract, or combination of any of these ingredients. The law expressly stated that such dietary supplements are foods. Dietary supplements are exempt from the "food additive" provisions of the law, thus placing the burden on FDA to demonstrate that dietary supplements are unsafe. New dietary ingredients, not marketed in the United States before October 15, 1994, must contain only ingredients that have been used in the food supply before that time, or have a history of use elsewhere or other evidence of safety.

The DSHEA also permitted dissemination of published scientific information and labeling statements pertaining to nutritional claims for dietary supplements, subject to certain specified conditions. FDA was required to issue regulations for nutrition labeling for dietary supplements and for Good

Manufacturing Practices (GMPs) for these products, which are required to be modeled after FDA's food GMPs.

The DSHEA also established a Commission on Dietary Supplement Labels and an Office of Dietary Supplements within the National Institutes of Health to study label claims for dietary supplements and report to the President and Congress with recommendations for legislation and changes in regulations. The office was created to study the potential role of dietary supplements as part of the effort to improve U.S. healthcare, and to promote scientific study of dietary supplements to maintain health, prevent chronic disease, and for other health-related conditions.

In November 1997, the commission issued its report, which included several recommendations to FDA for distinguishing unauthorized disease claims from permissible claims that describe the effect of a dietary supplement on the structure or function of the body ("structure-function" claims). The commission's report served as a basis for FDA's final rule in January 2000 regarding permissible label claims for dietary supplements.

◆ Export Reform and Enhancement Act of 1996

The Export Reform and Enhancement Act of 1996 (EREA) amended the FDCA to alter FDA's role in regulating the trade of drugs, biologics, and medical devices, and eased import and export restrictions on drugs and medical devices. Under the EREA, manufacturers may export both approved and unapproved medical products to certain foreign countries, and may import the components and raw materials necessary to manufacture products intended for export.

◆ The Food and Drug Administration Modernization Act of 1997

Over the years, FDA's regulatory role has expanded considerably from that of removing unsafe or misbranded products from the marketplace, to determining whether drugs and medical devices are safe and effective for their intended use. Critics, including members of Congress, industry, patient groups, and others, became convinced that FDA's ability to accomplish the duties embodied in this expanded role had not kept pace with the agency's statutory responsibilities, resulting in an overly burdensome and inefficient regulatory system. The requirements for the clinical testing and premarket review of new products had become increasingly complex, time-consuming, and costly, with the result that patients had been denied timely access to safe and useful drugs and medical devices.

1997
Food and Drug Administration Modernization Act FDAMA, enacted in 1997, broadened FDA's authority and reformed several areas of regulation.

The Food and Drug Administration Modernization Act of 1997 (FDAMA) was the culmination of a comprehensive legislative reform effort designed to streamline regulatory procedures within FDA and to improve the regulation of drugs, medical devices, and foods. Passed with wide bipartisan support, the legislation was the broadest amendment of the basic law since 1938. The FDAMA was principally designed to ensure the timely availability of safe and effective drugs, biologics, and medical devices by expediting the premarket review process for new products, while maintaining FDA's "gold standard" for product approval.

Building on the reauthorization of the Prescription Drug User Fee Act of 1992, the FDAMA improved FDA's public accountability, required an FDA mission statement to define the scope of the agency's regulatory responsibilities, and required FDA to publish a compliance plan, in consultation with appropriate scientific and academic experts, healthcare professionals, representatives of patient and consumer advocacy groups, and the regulated industry. This was intended to eliminate backlogs in the drug and medical device approval process and ensure the timely review of applications. As part of the agency's new mission statement, FDA must promptly and efficiently review clinical research and take appropriate action on the marketing of regulated products so that innovation and product availability are not impeded or discouraged.

The FDAMA included a unique provision, which amended the FDCA to encourage drug manufacturers to study their drugs in pediatric populations.

The FDAMA included a unique provision, which amended the FDCA to encourage drug manufacturers to study their drugs in pediatric populations. This new provision granted the sponsor of a pending or approved NDA for a drug with current exclusivity under the Hatch-Waxman Act or the Orphan Drug Amendments an extra six months of market exclusivity for performing certain studies in pediatric populations. Pediatric exclusivity attaches to an active moiety and not to a specific drug product, allowing a manufacturer's entire product line containing the active moiety to receive six months of additional market protection. Although this authorization was subject to a sunset provision on January 1, 2002, Congress reauthorized the sunset provision in 2002 and 2007, and eliminated it entirely in 2012.

The FDAMA also created a statutory fast-track approval process for drugs for serious or life-threatening diseases and conditions (based on existing FDA regulations), established a data bank of information on clinical trials for such conditions (with the help of the National Institutes of Health), authorized the use of expert scientific panels to review clinical investigations of drugs, and expanded the rights of drug and device manufacturers to disseminate treatment information.

The FDAMA also broadened FDA's authority over OTC drugs by extending the agency's inspection authority over OTC drug records to the same extent allowed for prescription drugs. Ingredient labeling requirements were also expanded to include inactive ingredients. The FDAMA preempted labeling for OTC drugs (and cosmetics) from state regulation where federal requirements are in place.

The FDAMA reformed the regulation of medical devices with regard to the review of applications, standards, and data requirements. For example, the law mandates priority review for breakthrough technologies in medical devices and grants FDA the authority to contract with outside scientific experts to review medical device applications.

The FDAMA provided streamlined procedures and greater flexibility in FDA regulations regarding nutrient content and health claims for foods. Such claims may be permitted on food labels, without the need for FDA to issue a regulation, if a scientific body of the U.S. government has published an authoritative statement endorsing the claim. The law also established a "notification" procedure for the marketing of indirect food additives.

The FDAMA provided streamlined procedures and greater flexibility in FDA regulations regarding nutrient content and health claims for foods.

◆ Fiscal Year 2001 Agricultural Appropriations—Drug Import Provisions

The Fiscal Year 2001 Agricultural Appropriations included two provisions that amended the FDCA to allow the importation of prescription drugs into the United States from foreign countries. The Medicine Equity and Drug Safety Act of 2000 (MEDS Act) allowed wholesalers and pharmacists to import prescription drugs from specified foreign countries, provided certain documentation and testing information, to be defined in FDA regulations, is included with the drugs. The Prescription Drug Import Fairness Act of 2000 prevented FDA from issuing warning notices to individuals, not in the business of importing drugs, who import drugs for personal use. The purpose was to try to lower the costs of prescription drugs in the United States. However, on December 26, 2000, the outgoing Secretary of the Department of Health and Human Services declined to implement the MEDS Act, and this decision was reaffirmed by the new Secretary of the Department of Health and Human Services on July 9, 2001.

◆ Best Pharmaceuticals for Children Act

The Best Pharmaceuticals for Children Act, *inter alia*, renewed FDA's authority to grant six months of exclusivity for pediatric studies, eliminated the user fee waiver for pediatric use supplements, gave priority review status for pediatric supplements, and authorized government contracts for pediatric studies of drugs that lack patent protection or marketing exclusivity. The law also allowed ANDAs for generic drugs with added pediatric information. In addition, the law directed the Secretary of the Department of Health and Human Services to establish an Office of Pediatric Therapeutics within the FDA Commissioner's office to coordinate all FDA pediatric activities.

◆ The Bioterrorism Act

BIOHAZARD

In June 2002, the Public Health Security and Bioterrorism Preparedness and Response Act of 2002 (Bioterrorism Act) amended the FDCA and the Public Health Service Act to increase the capacity of government at all levels to detect and respond effectively to public health emergencies related to bioterrorist attacks. Among other things, the Bioterrorism Act provided for accelerated approval, licensing, or clearance, as a "priority countermeasure," for a drug, biologic product, medical device, vaccine, vaccine adjuvant, antiviral, or diagnostic test, intended to treat, identify, or prevent infections or diagnose conditions caused by biological agents or toxins. The act required the creation of a national database of biological agents and toxins that could pose a severe threat to human, animal, or plant health; development of security safeguards and mandatory registration for the possession, use, or transfer of such agents and toxins; and inspections, with limited exceptions for clinical or diagnostic laboratories and certain investigational, approved, or licensed products. Prescription drug user fees were extended through the year 2007 with only minor changes.

The Bioterrorism Act also provided for:

- *maintenance of certain manufacturing and shipping records*
- *administrative detention of adulterated foods*
- *pre-importation notifications*
- *prohibition against port shopping*
- *debarment for repeated violations*

Most importantly, the Bioterrorism Act granted FDA significant new authority with respect to foods, including dietary supplements and animal feeds. Domestic and foreign facilities that manufacture, process, pack, or hold food for U.S. consumption must register with FDA. Inspections are permitted upon "a reasonable belief that a food article is adulterated and presents a threat of serious adverse health consequences or death to humans or animals." The Bioterrorism Act also provided for maintenance of certain manufacturing and shipping records; administrative detention of adulterated foods; pre-importation notifications; prohibition against port shopping; and debarment for repeated violations.

The existing "import for export" requirements were broadened to include submission of information and data upon importation of drug components, device components or accessories, food additives, color additives, and dietary supplements (including those in bulk form) that are intended for further processing or incorporation into a regulated product and for subsequent export.

◆ Medical Device User Fee and Modernization Act of 2002

Following the trend to seek user fees from regulated industry, the Medical Device User Fee and Modernization Act of 2002 was enacted to amend the FDCA to subject medical device manufacturers to medical device user fees.

Following the trend to seek user fees from regulated industry, the Medical Device User Fee and Modernization Act of 2002 (MDUFMA) was enacted to amend the FDCA to subject medical device manufacturers to medical device user fees for certain applications, reports, application supplements, and submissions sent to FDA for evaluation. The law also established certain performance goals for FDA to meet. In addition, the law included provisions for device establishment

inspections by accredited third parties, established new regulatory requirements for reprocessed single-use devices, and provided for modular (i.e.,
discrete sections) review of PMAs.

◆ Rare Diseases Orphan Product Development Act of 2002

Stating its concerns over 25 million Americans suffering from more than 6,000
rare diseases, and recognizing the role of the National Organization for Rare
Diseases, Congress passed the Rare Diseases Orphan Product Development Act
of 2002 to amend the Orphan Drug Act by reauthorizing the Orphan Products
Research Grant program to authorize appropriations for Fiscal Years 2002-2006
for grants and contracts for the development of orphan drugs. Fiscal Year 2003-
2006 appropriations were set at $25 million per year.

◆ Animal Drug User Fee Act of 2003

Congress added user fees for veterinary products in the Animal Drug User Fee
Act of 2003, directing FDA to assess and collect user fees for animal drug applications. The law was scheduled to sunset at the end of Fiscal Year 2008, but was
reauthorized and extended until 2013, and then again until 2018.

◆ Medicare Prescription Drug, Improvement, and Modernization Act of 2003

Title XI of the Medicare Prescription Drug, Improvement, and Modernization
Act of 2003, titled "Access to Affordable Pharmaceuticals," was the culmination
of several years of congressional attempts to reduce the cost of drug products
to consumers. To accomplish this goal, the changes in Title XI targeted two issues: generic drug approvals (including government review of marketing agreements between companies) and the importation of prescription drugs from
Canada into the United States. The generic drug revisions in the law primarily
amended provisions of the FDCA that were added in 1984 by the Drug Price
Competition and Patent Term Restoration Act.

Title XI of the Medicare Prescription Drug, Improvement, and Modernization Act of 2003 was the culmination of several years of congressional attempts to reduce the cost of drug products to consumers.

The provisions on importation of prescription drugs from Canada recognized
that Americans increasingly have sought to purchase drugs from Canada and
other foreign countries. This law authorized importation from Canada, under
specific conditions, if the Secretary of the Department of Health and Human
Services certifies to Congress that the imports will not pose any additional risk
to the public health and will result in a significant savings to American consumers. To date, the Secretary has declined to provide such certification.

◆ Pediatric Research Equity Act of 2003

To encourage drug research for pediatric use, Congress enacted the Pediatric Research Equity Act of 2003 amending the FDCA to require that applications for a new active ingredient, new indication, new dosage form, new dosing regimen, or new route of administration for drugs and biological products include a pediatric assessment (unless waived or deferred), and that sponsors of marketed drugs and biologics conduct such an assessment by a specified date (unless waived) under certain circumstances. This law essentially codified FDA's 1998 "Regulations Requiring Manufacturers to Assess the Safety and Effectiveness of New Drugs and Biological Products in Pediatric Patients" (commonly referred to as the "Pediatric Rule"), which had been invalidated by a federal district court for exceeding FDA's authority under the act.

◆ Minor Use and Minor Species Animal Health Act of 2004

A sponsor of a new animal drug for a minor use or use in a minor species may petition FDA to declare its product a "designated new animal drug," similar to the status of human drugs under the Orphan Drug Act.

Concerned over lack of animal drugs for marginal uses, Congress enacted the Minor Use and Minor Species Animal Health Act of 2004 to encourage the development of new animal drugs intended for a minor use (i.e., an indication that occurs infrequently in a few animals, or in limited geographic areas and in a small number of animals annually) or for a use in a minor species (i.e., other than cattle, horses, swine, chickens, turkeys, dogs, and cats). It provided a conditional approval mechanism under which existing safety requirements must be met but the effectiveness standard is "a reasonable expectation of effectiveness" rather than "substantial evidence of effectiveness." In addition, a sponsor of a new animal drug for a minor use or use in a minor species may petition FDA to declare its product a "designated new animal drug," similar to the status of human drugs under the Orphan Drug Act.

◆ Food Allergen Labeling and Consumer Protection Act of 2004

The Food Allergen Labeling and Consumer Protection Act of 2004 required food labels to declare any major food allergen present. The major food allergens are milk; eggs; fish; crustacean shellfish; tree nuts (e.g., almonds, pecans, or walnuts); wheat; peanuts; and soybeans, as well as any protein derived from those allergens, unless it is a "highly refined oil." Tree nuts, fish, and crustacean shellfish must be identified by specific type or species.

The Anabolic Steroid Control Act of 2004 addressed the abuse of steroids by professional athletes and the widespread use of steroids and steroid precursors among students.

◆ Anabolic Steroid Control Act of 2004

Congress enacted the Anabolic Steroid Control Act of 2004 to address the abuse of steroids by professional athletes and the widespread use of steroids and steroid precursors among students. The act amended the Controlled Substances Act (CSA), *inter alia,* to revise the definition of "anabolic steroid" to eliminate the requirement that the substance promote muscle growth and to expand the list of regulated steroids. While the act applies only to DEA and PHS activities, it also narrowed the exemption from CSA regulation only to OTC non-narcotic drug products containing controlled substances that are regulated by FDA under the FDCA.

◆ Project BioShield Act of 2004

Passed largely in response to the terrorist attacks in the fall of 2001, the Project BioShield Act of 2004 provided industry with incentives to develop new chemical, biological, radiological, and nuclear medical countermeasures. The act also granted FDA the authority to allow the interim emergency use of investigational drugs, biological products, and devices to respond to domestic emergencies.

◆ Medical Device User Fee Stabilization Act of 2005

Congress revisited the medical device user fees established in the Medical Device User Fee Stabilization Act of 2005. Among other things, the law set the Premarket Approval Application fees for Fiscal Years 2006 and 2007, increased the annual gross receipts or sales threshold below which businesses are eligible for reduced user fees or a user fee waiver, and added a provision holding any reprocessed single-use device to be misbranded unless it identifies the manufacturer.

◆ Regulation of Contact Lenses as Medical Devices (2005)

Because FDA had previously regulated some non-corrective, decorative contact lenses as cosmetics, Congress amended the FDCA to deem all contact lenses to be medical devices in this very succinct statute.

Congress amended the FDCA to deem all contact lenses to be medical devices.

◆ Stem Cell Therapeutic and Research Act of 2005

The Stem Cell Therapeutic and Research Act of 2005 provided "for the collection and maintenance of human cord blood stem cells for the treatment of patients and research." It amended the Public Health Service Act to authorize the C.W. Bill Young Cell Transplantation Program, which is intended to increase "the number of transplants for recipients suitably matched to biologically unrelated donors of bone marrow and cord blood."

◆ Sanitary Food Transportation Act of 2005

The Sanitary Food Transportation Act of 2005 authorized FDA to promulgate regulations establishing sanitary food transportation practices, including sanitation, packaging, recordkeeping, and isolation, among other things. In addition, the act authorized FDA to issue regulations specifying those nonfood products that may not be shipped with food products.

◆ Pandemic and All-Hazards Preparedness Act of 2006

To address some of the shortcomings of the BioShield Act of 2004, Congress enacted the Pandemic and All-Hazards Preparedness Act of 2006. Among other things, the act required FDA to establish a team of manufacturing and regulatory experts to provide chemical, biological, radiological, and nuclear countermeasure manufacturers with technical assistance, and it allowed DHHS to convene meetings with industry under specified circumstances that would otherwise violate federal antitrust laws.

◆ Dietary Supplement and Nonprescription Drug Consumer Protection Act of 2006

The Dietary Supplement and Nonprescription Drug Consumer Protection Act of 2006 required manufacturers, packers, or distributors of dietary supplements and OTC drugs to submit to FDA all serious adverse event reports associated with the use of their products in the United States. The act also required dietary supplements and OTC drugs to bear either a domestic telephone number or domestic street address where consumers can call or write to report serious adverse events.

◆ Food and Drug Administration Amendments Act of 2007

The Food and Drug Administration Amendments Act of 2007 reauthorized and amended several drug and medical device statutory provisions that were scheduled to sunset, provided FDA with new funding and drug safety oversight responsibility, and addressed virtually all *regulated product categories.*

In what has been described as the broadest amendment of the FDCA in recent memory, the Food and Drug Administration Amendments Act of 2007 (FDAAA) reauthorized and amended several drug and medical device statutory provisions that were scheduled to sunset, provided FDA with new funding and drug safety oversight responsibility, and addressed *virtually all* regulated product categories. The law includes 11 titles, the first five of which reauthorize drug and medical device user fee and pediatric-related programs through Fiscal Year 2012, including PDUFA, MDUFMA, the Best Pharmaceuticals for Children Act, and the Pediatric Research Equity Act. Title III also amended the FDCA to provide new incentives to medical device manufacturers to develop devices for pediatric patients and to give FDA new authority to review and regulate such devices. Titles VI-VIII established a new private-public partnership intended to modernize medical product development and enhance product safety, amend the FDCA with respect to certain conflict-of-interest issues among FDA advisory committee members, and establish databases for clinical trial registries and results.

Title IX, perhaps the farthest-reaching provision of the law, authorized various programs intended to improve the postmarket safety of drugs, including giving FDA the authority to impose risk evaluation and mitigation strategies. Title IX modified the citizen petition process with respect to petitions having the potential to delay approval of generic drug products. The section also prohibited the sale of any food that contains an approved drug, an approved biological product, or a "drug [or biological product] for which substantial clinical investigations have been instituted and for which the existence of such investigations has been made public," unless the food containing the drug or biologic had been marketed prior to such approval or testing. This provision, in particular, might have a significant impact on the development of functional food ingredients.

Title IX, perhaps the farthest-reaching provision of the law, authorized various programs intended to improve the postmarket safety of drugs, including giving FDA the authority to impose risk evaluation and mitigation strategies.

Title X concerned food safety, requiring the creation of a reportable food registry for foods "for which there is a reasonable probability that the use of, or exposure to, such article of food will cause serious adverse health consequences or death to humans or animals." Title X also included a provision requiring FDA to establish ingredient and processing standards and definitions for pet food and update standards for the labeling of pet food. FDA must also establish early warning and surveillance and notification systems "to identify adulteration of the pet food supply and outbreaks of illness associated with pet food." Finally, Title XI included several miscellaneous provisions intended, among other things, to improve antibiotic access and innovation.

◆ Animal Drug User Fee Amendments of 2008/Animal Generic Drug User Fee Act of 2008

In a single piece of legislation, Congress enacted the Animal Drug User Fee Amendments of 2008, which amended and reauthorized the Animal Drug User Fee Act of 2003 (ADUFA I) through Fiscal Year 2013, and the Animal Generic Drug User Fee Act of 2008 (AGDUFA). To support FDA's continuing efforts to address antimicrobial resistance, ADUFA II required that animal drug sponsors submit annual reports to FDA on certain products containing antimicrobial active ingredients and for FDA to make summaries of these reports available to the public.

AGDUFA established a user fee for generic new animal drugs, including abbreviated application, product, and sponsor fees.

The legislation also included technical corrections to FDAAA, in particular, to clarify that consideration of a citizen petition seeking to delay generic approval must be "separate and apart from review and approval of any application."

◆ Patient Protection and Affordable Care Act

The broad healthcare reform law, the Patient Protection and Affordable Care Act (PPACA), signed into law by President Barack Obama on March 23, 2010, while focusing primarily on healthcare and insurance industries, the medical community, and healthcare consumers, included some provisions concerning the FDCA, affecting both drugs and food.

With respect to drugs, the PPACA amended the FDCA to permit FDA to approve an ANDA notwithstanding certain changes in the labeling of the reference listed drug (RLD) approved within 60 days of the anticipated ANDA approval. Changes to "Warnings" in the RLD are excepted, and FDA may decide against the ANDA approval for safety reasons. The ANDA applicant must agree to submit revised labeling quickly. This amendment essentially created an exception, albeit limited, to the requirement that labeling for a generic drug be identical to that of the RLD.

The PPACA also creates a new pathway for the approval of applications for biological products shown to be biosimilar to or interchangeable with a licensed reference product. It amended the FDCA to make user fees under PDUFA applicable to biosimilar and interchangeable biological products.

For foods, the PPACA amended the FDCA to require restaurants and similar retail food establishments with 20 or more locations doing business under the same name and offering substantially the same menu items to disclose on menus and menu boards the calorie content for standard menu items and information on suggested daily caloric intake. The establishments must also make other nutrition information, e.g., sodium and sugar content per serving, available on the premises. An owner or operator of 20 or more vending machines also must disclose calorie content for the products, unless a prospective buyer, before purchase, can examine the nutrition facts panel or, at the point of purchase, obtain nutritional information about the products. The PPACA also directed FDA to issue regulations implementing the new law. Those regulations preempt state requirements that are not identical to the federal laws, but states may impose non-identical menu-labeling requirements for restaurateurs and vending machine operators not subject to the law unless they choose to subject themselves to the federal requirements.

◆ The Family Smoking Prevention and Tobacco Control Act

Ending a contentious legal and political battle and radically changing the relationship between the federal government and the tobacco industry, the Family Smoking Prevention and Tobacco Control Act (FSPTCA), enacted on June

22, 2009, provided FDA with regulatory authority over almost every aspect of tobacco products. The law specifically applied to cigarettes, cigarette tobacco, roll-your-own tobacco, and smokeless tobacco. FDA has the authority to apply the law to other tobacco products by regulation. The law does not apply to producers of tobacco leaves, including "tobacco warehouses."

Following the basic structure of the FDCA, the FSPTCA provided essential definitions, established the conditions that cause tobacco products to be adulterated or misbranded, and established a comprehensive statutory framework for FDA's oversight of tobacco products. FSPTCA added a new Chapter IX to the FDCA, causing old Chapter IX to be renumbered as Chapter X.

Significant provisions of the FSPTCA include the requirement for FDA premarket review of new products, authority for FDA to subject advertising for modified risk products (those marketed as being less harmful) to premarket approval, and mandatory annual registration for any owner or operator of a domestic establishment engaged in the manufacture, preparation, compounding, or processing of tobacco products. Owners or operators must also submit a list of all products they manufacture, prepare, or process, as well as labeling of certain products. Manufacturers and importers of tobacco products must submit "health information" about their current and future tobacco products. The FSPTCA gave FDA the authority to require reports on adverse events, corrective actions, and product removals.

Although the FSPTCA did not authorize FDA to ban certain tobacco products (including cigarettes), it did provide FDA with authority to establish tobacco product standards and to impose restrictions on promotion and distribution of tobacco products. Several provisions aim at reducing smoking by youth (e.g., prohibition of all flavors, herbs, or spices (except menthol) in cigarettes). In addition, tobacco products introduced after February 15, 2007, are subject to premarket review modeled after the process for medical devices. This gives tobacco products already on the market as of February 15, 2007 ("grandfathered products"), a distinct advantage over products introduced after that date ("new tobacco products").

◆ Food Safety Modernization Act

The FDA Food Safety Modernization Act (FSMA), signed into law on January 4, 2011, was the most significant update of U.S. food safety laws since the 1938 original enactment of the FDCA. Spurred by *Escherichia coli* and *Salmonella* outbreaks, FSMA provided FDA with more power to recall tainted products, strengthen inspections of food and produce processors, and require tougher standards for keeping food safe.

Ending a contentious legal and political battle and radically changing the relationship between the federal government and the tobacco industry, the Family Smoking Prevention and Tobacco Control Act provided FDA with regulatory authority over almost every aspect of tobacco products.

The FDA Food Safety Modernization Act was the most significant update of U.S. food safety laws since the 1938 original enactment of the FDCA.

The three main goals of FSMA were to: 1) shift the emphasis from response to prevention, 2) improve the government's capacity to detect and respond to food safety problems, and 3) address the challenge posed by the nation's increased reliance on food imports.

FSMA provided FDA with a legislative mandate to require comprehensive, science-based preventive controls across the food supply and to establish science-based minimum standards for the safe production and harvesting of fruits and vegetables. Food facilities are required to implement a written preventive control plan, monitor the performance of those controls and take specified corrective actions when necessary. FSMA enhanced FDA's authority to inspect food establishment records, imposed biennial food facility registration, authorized FDA to impose requirements to protect against intentional adulteration, and authorized the collection of re-inspection fees, among other things.

FSMA also increased FDA's capacity to detect and respond to food safety problems. It mandated increased frequency of inspections, provided for accreditation of food-testing laboratories, mandated the collection of information on food traceability, conferred mandatory recall authority on FDA, greatly enhanced FDA's administrative detention authority, and amended the reportable food registry to require grocery stores to notify consumers.

Another focus area of FSMA was the safety of imported food, providing FDA with new tools to ensure that imported foods meet U.S. standards and are safe. Among other things, FSMA required importers to verify that the food they import meets certain legal requirements, gave FDA the authority to require certification that an imported food complies with the FDCA, directed FDA to implement a voluntary qualified importer program to speed the importation process, and provided for accreditation of third-party auditors.

The addition of whistle-blower protections for food facility employees to the FDCA provided an extra incentive for food facilities to comply with the law.

FSMA required FDA to undertake more than a dozen rulemakings and issue at least 10 guidance documents, as well as prepare a host of reports, plans, strategies, standards, notices, and other tasks.

◆ Food and Drug Administration Safety and Innovation Act of 2012

After numerous hearings, Congress enacted the Food and Drug Administration Safety and Innovation Act (FDASIA). Among its 140 pages and 11 titles, FDASIA reauthorized and extended user fees for prescription drugs (PDUFA V) and medical devices (MDUFA III), and established new user fee programs for human generic drugs (GDUFA I) and biosimilar biological products (BsUFA I).

FDASIA made substantial changes to the FDCA, including, in Title V, making the Best Pharmaceuticals for Children Act (BPCA) and the Pediatric Research Equity Act (PREA) permanent. Title VI made a number of changes related to medical devices, intended to improve the regulatory process. Title VII gave FDA broader authority with respect to inspections and drug supply chains. Title VIII enacted the Generating Antibiotic Incentives Now (GAIN) Act in an effort to address the availability of new drugs to treat infectious diseases. Title IX created additional incentives for various categories of new drugs, including "fast-track products" and "breakthrough therapies." Title X attempted to assist FDA, physicians, and patient groups by requiring additional notice regarding anticipated drug short-ages. Finally, Title XI included a variety of provisions concerning, among others, the regulation of medical gases, controlled substances, nanotechnology, and prescription drug abuse.

◆ Animal Drug and Animal Generic Drug User Fee Reauthorization Act of 2013

Congress reauthorized and extended user fees for both innovator and generic animal drugs until 2018 (ADUFA III and AGDUFA II).

◆ Drug Quality and Security Act

In November 2013, the Drug Quality and Security Act (DQSA) combined two legislative goals into one statute. Prior to its enactment, a patchwork of state laws existed regarding drug product tracking systems. The law explicitly pre-empted those state laws and established a national standard for an electronic drug product track-and-trace system, including requirements for manufactur-ers, wholesalers, repackagers, and dispensers (e.g., pharmacies) of prescription drugs. The DQSA also clarified FDA's regulatory authority regarding advertise-ments by drug compounding pharmacies and established a new category of facilities that require FDA registration—"outsourcing facilities," which are regulated similarly to drug manufacturers. As distinct from compounders engaged in more traditional compounding for individual patients based on individual prescriptions, outsourcing facilities are permitted to compound and ship interstate large volumes of sterile drugs without first obtaining individual prescriptions. Among other things, they are subject to voluntary registration (with fees), GMP compliance, FDA risk-based inspections, six-month reporting requirements on products compounded, and adverse event reporting.

Outsourcing facilities are permitted to compound and ship interstate large volumes of sterile drugs without first obtaining individual prescriptions.

◆ 21st Century Cures Act

In December 2016, President Obama signed into law the long-awaited 21st Cen-tury Cures Act (Cures Act) after years of partisan gridlock. The act made several significant amendments to the FDCA, and noted new policies for FDA.

61

The Cures Act emphasized patient-focused drug and biologic development, with FDA to develop policies and guidance documents regarding the collection of patient experience data and the use of such data in drug development. The Cures Act also encouraged greater facilitation of developing drugs for rare diseases by extending FDA's Rare Pediatric Disease Priority Review Voucher program and expanding the Orphan Drug Grant program to allow designed observational studies and other natural history analysis. The Cures Act also created a priority review voucher program for a material treatment medical countermeasure application.

The Cures Act amended the FDCA to create a process and requirements for designation of a drug as a regenerative therapy in order to expedite development and review of the drug and possible accelerated approval.

The Cures Act also made several significant changes to the FDCA provisions related to medical devices. Specifically, the Cures Act required FDA to establish a program to provide priority review for medical devices designed to treat or diagnose certain conditions. The Cures Act also directed FDA to review Class I and Class II devices in order to consider whether they may be declared 510(k) exempt with reasonable assurance of safety and effectiveness. In order to address a long-held industry position that FDA's Center for Devices and Radiological Health (CDRH) does not comply with the statutory requirement to review only the data necessary to make a determination of substantial equivalence or device effectiveness and to use the "least burdensome means" of doing so, the Cures Act required each CDRH reviewer to receive training on the meaning and implementation of the "least burdensome" requirements. Similarly, the Cures Act directs FDA to consider the least burdensome appropriate means necessary to demonstrate assurance of device safety and effectiveness for premarket approval (PMA) determinations. The Cures Act also modified the definition of "device" to remove a number of categories of software from FDA's jurisdiction.

THE HISTORY OF THE FOOD AND DRUG ADMINISTRATION

FDA is the oldest federal regulatory agency, dating back to its initial establishment in 1848 as the Agricultural Division of the Patent Office.

FDA is the oldest federal regulatory agency, dating back to its initial establishment in 1848 as the Agricultural Division of the Patent Office. The agency has had several, essentially accumulating, roles. For its first six decades, it was a scientific and technical advisor to other agencies. It added a law enforcement function in 1906. In 1938, the agency was given responsibility for approving the marketing of new drugs, and that premarket licensing function has been broadened by subsequent legislation. Today the agency is regarded as a science-based law enforcement agency responsible for ensuring safe foods and cosmetics, and safe and effective drugs and medical devices in the U.S. marketplace.

More than half of FDA's existence was spent in the USDA, beginning with the transfer of the Agricultural Division to USDA upon the department's creation in 1862. The division's chemical laboratory became known as the USDA Chemical Division. The agency became the Division of Chemistry in 1890 and the Bureau of Chemistry in 1901. Until 1906, the agency had no statutory enforcement duties but primarily provided information and advice to other USDA offices and other agencies, such as the Treasury Department, responsible for enforcing the few relevant federal laws during that time.

Although there were six Commissioners of the agency from 1862 to 1883, it was the seventh Commissioner, Harvey W. Wiley, MD, who is generally acknowledged as the "father of the FDA." Dr. Wiley strengthened and transformed the staff of the division into an advocacy organization and, ultimately, a law enforcement agency. He crusaded for the creation of a national food and drug law, and was credited with a major role in the passage of the 1906 act. Political and personal differences with his superiors, however, led to the establishment of a three-person Board of Food and Drug Inspection, including Dr. Wiley, to approve all legal actions recommended by the bureau. Dr. Wiley frequently was outvoted, and he ultimately resigned under pressure in 1912.

For the next 53 years, until 1965, FDA was directed by career employees, only a few of whom were physicians. Moreover, there were only seven Commissioners or top officials of FDA from 1883 to 1965. Since then, there have been 16 Commissioners in slightly more than 50 years, all but three of whom had never previously worked for the agency (Dr. Herbert Ley, 1968-1969, Dr. Lester Crawford, July-September 2005, and Dr. Scott Gottlieb, appointed in May 2017).

When the 1906 act passed, the Bureau of Chemistry had six field laboratories (San Francisco, New York, Boston, Philadelphia, Chicago, and New Orleans). Seventeen more were opened from 1907 to 1911. The agency's budget in that period was less than $1,000,000, and the agency employed fewer than 100 people.

In 1914, the agency's second "modern" commissioner, Dr. Carl Alsberg, reorganized the agency. He established the Division of Food Control and delegated control of the field laboratories, which were reduced from 23 to 16 to save money, to three food and drug inspection districts (Eastern, Central, and Western). This decentralized the agency's inspection activities, joined the enforcement functions more closely with the scientific functions, and remained the basic organization for the agency until 1948.

In 1927, the agricultural research and the enforcement functions of the Bureau of Chemistry were separated, with the latter becoming the Food, Drug, and Insecticide Administration (FDIA). The Drug Control Laboratory, which was responsible

FDA did not officially exist by statute until the Food and Drug Administration Act of 1988.

for surveillance of proprietary drugs, was included in the FDIA. In 1930, the FDIA became the Food and Drug Administration, although the agency did not officially exist by statute until the Food and Drug Administration Act of 1988.

FDA remained a part of USDA until 1940 when it was transferred to the Federal Security Agency, which also included such agencies as the Public Health Service, the Office of Education, the Civilian Conservation Corps, and the Social Security Administration. The move was in part due to the differing missions and inherent conflict between FDA and its parent, USDA. At the same time, the head of FDA became known as the Commissioner of Food and Drugs, the present title of the post, although no commission existed. The Federal Security Agency became the Department of Health, Education and Welfare in 1953, and subsequently DHHS in 1979, when a separate Department of Education was established.

In 1948, due to concerns over lack of uniformity and efficiency among the three operating districts, the agency was reorganized to centralize authority in Washington, D.C. Commissioner Paul B. Dunbar, whose career with the agency dated to 1907, dismantled the three districts, moving many of the staff to Washington, D.C. to join the divisions of Field Operations, Regulatory Management, and Program Research. The 16 field stations became district offices and reported directly to the Commissioner. There were some morale and related problems, as the districts had developed different enforcement styles over the years.

In 1963, following several years of increasing statutory authority and wider jurisdiction, a tripling of the agency's enforcement budget, and two citizen advisory committee reports (in 1955 and 1962), then Commissioner George P. Larrick reorganized the agency to try to emphasize scientific research, education, and voluntary compliance. He added a Bureau of Education and Voluntary Compliance, and divided the previously existing scientific bureau into the Bureau of Scientific Research and the Bureau of Scientific Standards and Evaluation. These three bureaus joined the Bureau of Medicine and the Bureau of Regulatory Compliance.

Congressional criticism led, in 1966, to the appointment of the first outsider, and the first physician in more than 40 years, as the Commissioner of Food and Drugs.

Despite this reorganization, congressional criticism led, in 1966, to the appointment of the first outsider, and the first physician in more than 40 years, as the Commissioner of Food and Drugs, Dr. James L. Goddard. Dr. Goddard came from the Communicable Disease Center of the Public Health Service, and had a reputation as a reformer and aggressive regulator. He was given a mandate to reform FDA. In 1966, he extensively reorganized FDA, essentially reversing the 1963 changes. Among other things, the two separate science bureaus were recombined as the Bureau of Science and the district offices reported directly to the Commissioner rather than the Bureau of Regulatory Compliance. A new Bureau of Drug Abuse Control was added, following the Drug Abuse Control Amendments of 1965. (This was transferred to the Department of Justice in 1968.) In addition, the Bureau of Veterinary Medicine was created.

Dr. Goddard's brief stay (less than two and one-half years) marked the beginning of what has been called the period of often "short-term," outsider Commissioners. Since then, FDA has had 15 Commissioners: Herbert Ley Jr., MD (7/1/1968–12/12/1969), Charles Edwards, MD (12/13/1969–3/15/1973), Alexander M. Schmidt, MD (7/20/1973–11/30/1976), Donald Kennedy, PhD (4/4/1977–6/30/1979), Jere E. Goyan, PhD (10/21/1979–1/20/1981), Arthur Hull Hayes Jr., MD (4/13/1981–9/11/1983), Frank E. Young, MD (7/15/1984–12/17/1989), David A. Kessler, MD (11/8/1990–2/28/1997), Jane E. Henney, MD (1/17/1999–1/19/2001), Mark B. McClellan, MD, PhD (11/14/2002–3/26/2004), Lester M. Crawford, DVM, PhD (7/18/2005–9/23/2005), Andrew C. von Eschenbach, MD (12/13/2006–1/20/2009), Margaret Hamburg, MD (5/18/2009–4/4/2015), Robert M. Califf, MD (2/24/16–1/20/17), and Scott Gottlieb, MD (5/11/2017–Present). Most of these 15 Commissioners were appointed from outside the agency, and most were physicians. At times, the post of Commissioner was vacant and temporarily filled by an acting Commissioner. (Full biographies of all FDA Commissioners since Harvey W. Wiley, MD are available on FDA's website at https://www.fda.gov/AboutFDA/WhatWeDo/History/Leaders/Commissioners/default.htm.)

In addition, more professionals began to join the agency in positions of authority, often as political appointees. There also has been increasing scrutiny and involvement in FDA's activities by Congress, its parent department, and the White House.

In 1968, FDA was placed by the Department of Health, Education and Welfare under the Public Health Service, then combined with other agencies in the new Consumer Protection and Environmental Health Service (CPEHS). This placed another official above the Commissioner, but CPEHS was abolished less than two years later and FDA again became part of the Public Health Service.

FDA was reorganized in 1970, with the regulatory and voluntary compliance bureaus combined into the Bureau of Compliance and with the establishment of 10 Regional Food and Drug Directors, paralleling the department regional structure. The agency also reorganized along product lines, establishing a Bureau of Drugs and a Bureau of Foods, Pesticides, and Product Safety. Almost 30 years later, FDA still follows that basic organization, although the bureaus have all become Centers with the following names: the Center for Drug Evaluation and Research (CDER), the Center for Biologics Evaluation and Research (CBER), the Center for Devices and Radiological Health (CDRH), the Center for Food Safety and Applied Nutrition (CFSAN), and the Center for Veterinary Medicine (CVM). Each Center has undergone its own changes and reorganizations, but the general organization remains the same.

Reorganization
FDA's current structure stems from the 1970s' reorganization along product lines.

On August 19, 2009, FDA established its first new Center in several years, the Center for Tobacco Products (CTP), to implement the newly enacted Family Smoking Prevention and Tobacco Control Act.

Also in 2009, FDA reorganized its executive-level management, creating, among others, the Office of Foods and the Office of Medical Products and Tobacco, each of which is headed by a Deputy Commissioner reporting directly to the Commissioner of Food and Drugs. From the outset, CFSAN reported to the Commissioner through the Deputy Commissioner in the Office of Foods. In 2013, CVM was formally placed in the renamed Office of Foods and Veterinary Medicine, thus bringing CFSAN and CVM under the same administrative reporting umbrella. The human product Centers—CDER, CBER, CDRH, and CTP—all report through the Deputy Commissioner in the Office of Medical Products and Tobacco.

Over the years, FDA has had to contend with tight budgets and battles with Congress and other agencies over resources and authority. FDA has grown from a budget of some $12,000 in 1890 to a requested budget of $5.1 billion for Fiscal Year 2017 (including $2.3 billion in user fees), and from a handful of employees to more than 14,000 employees. The products regulated by FDA are estimated to account for some 25 cents of every dollar spent by U.S. consumers. The agency has an immense, if often unsung, effect on the economy and the public's health, safety, and well-being.

Chapter 3

The Philosophy of Food and Drug Law

Richard M. Cooper & Benjamin M. Greenblum, Williams & Connolly LLP, Washington, D.C.

Key Points

- Food and drug law is primarily about physical things.
- The overriding purpose of the Federal Food, Drug, and Cosmetic Act (FDCA) is to protect the consuming public.
- As new risks have been recognized, the FDCA has been amended to make it more protective.
- Expansion of Food and Drug Administration (FDA) authority has coincided with expansion of administrative tools throughout the federal government.
- There has been a substantial transfer of power from the courts to FDA.
- FDA has been, and will continue to be, a scientific regulatory agency that protects the public from medical products that are unsafe or ineffective.
- The review process must be rigorous enough to ensure that new products meet the statutory standards, but also must not unduly impede innovation.
- FDA technically does not regulate the practice of medicine; however, its regulations do bear directly on physicians conducting FDA-regulated clinical investigations.
- Consumers now have greater opportunity and necessity to make informed decisions about matters that affect their own health.
- FDA is accountable to the Department of Health and Human Services, the Office of Management and Budget, the President, Congress, and the courts, as well as practically to the scientific and medical communities, the press, and the public.
- FDA takes an expansive view of its mission and authority.
- FDA is increasingly facing issues raised by international trade in the categories of products it regulates.

INTRODUCTION

Food and drug law is primarily about physical things—food, drugs (including biological products such as blood and vaccines), medical devices, cosmetics, tobacco products, and radiation-emitting products. It is only secondarily about the companies and people who manufacture, distribute, and sell those things.

This focus on things is reflected in many aspects of the law and practice under it. The main segments of the governing statute—the Federal Food, Drug, and Cosmetic Act (FDCA)—are organized by type of product: food (Chapter IV); drugs, devices, and electronic products (Chapter V); cosmetics (Chapter VI); and tobacco products (Chapter IX). The agency that administers the statute—the Food and Drug Administration (FDA)—is also organized by product type. Its main operating units include the Center for Food Safety and Applied Nutrition (which also regulates cosmetics), the Center for Drug Evaluation and Research, the Center for Biologics Evaluation and Research, the Center for Devices and Radiological Health, the Center for Veterinary Medicine (which regulates foods and drugs for animals), and the Center for Tobacco Products.

Principal types of FDCA violations:
- *"adulterated" products*
- *"misbranded" products*
- *products marketed without required permission from FDA*

In general, the principal types of violation of the statute are defined so as to make a product "adulterated" or "misbranded" or distributed in interstate commerce without a required FDA permission for such distribution. In identifying a violation by a company or individual, it is generally (although not universally) necessary to identify a product that violates the statute in one of those three ways.

When the government goes to court under the FDCA, the remedy it often seeks is a seizure and condemnation of a product it claims is in violation of the statute or an injunction against shipment of one or more products in interstate commerce. Indeed, the official legal title of such a seizure action is of the form, "United States v. [an estimated number of units of a particular kind of product]." In such a case, the units of the product literally are the defendants. Anyone who claims to own them may enter the lawsuit to defend on their behalf; but, if no one does, the government wins by default, and the products generally are condemned and destroyed.

The reason for this primary focus on things is that the overriding purpose of the FDCA is to protect the consuming public from regulated products that are un-safe (food, drugs, devices, cosmetics, radiation-emitting products), ineffective (drugs and devices), or deceptively or otherwise inadequately labeled (food, drugs, devices, and cosmetics). The general standard applicable to tobacco products is that their marketing be "appropriate for the protection of the public health" (and that they be properly manufactured and labeled). Where a product is violative, FDA's first objective is to protect the public from the product, itself, by bringing about its removal from commerce. Accordingly, the most common informal remedy for a violative product is a recall, which is a more or less volun-tary alternative to a seizure by the government.

In some cases, FDA, acting through the Department of Justice (DOJ), may pursue an additional objective. It may seek to prevent future violations through an injunction against those likely to cause a violation in the future. In addition or in the alternative, it may seek punishment of companies and individuals for past violations, through criminal prosecution in the courts or an administrative proceeding for civil penalties or another administrative remedy.

The FDCA's main judicial remedies—seizure, injunction, and criminal prosecution—are very forceful. Upon the filing of a complaint for seizure by DOJ—before any defense is presented—the products proceeded against are legally seized by U.S. Marshals; and, in general, they are released from seizure only if a claimant appears, and the government fails to persuade the court that the products are violative of the FDCA. If the government obtains an injunction due to concern about product quality, it generally shuts down a manufacturing facility unless and until FDA is satisfied that the facility can manufacture products that comply with the statute. A company or an individual can be convicted of a misdemeanor (an offense punishable by fine and imprisonment for not more than one year) under the FDCA merely for causing or being responsible for the shipment of a product in violation of the FDCA—even without an intent to violate the statute, and even without knowledge that a violation was occurring. Where there is intent to defraud, a violation may be treated, under the FDCA or the general criminal law, as a felony (which is punishable by a higher fine and longer term of imprisonment). Such treatment may lead to severe adverse consequences beyond a particular product and a particular criminal conviction.

A company or an individual can be convicted of a misdemeanor under the FDCA merely for causing or being responsible for the shipment of a product in violation of the statute— even without an intent to violate, and even without knowledge that a violation was occurring.

The law's enforcement scheme is so severe because its purposes, as the Supreme Court commented in 1943, "touch phases of the lives and health of people which, in the circumstances of modern industrialism, are largely beyond self-protection." In explaining why the FDCA imposes strict misdemeanor liability on individuals involved in violations, the Supreme Court stated in 1975 that the FDCA "imposes not only a positive duty to seek out and remedy violations when they occur but also, and primarily, a duty to implement measures that will insure that violations will not occur. The requirements of foresight and vigilance imposed on responsible corporate agents are beyond question demanding, and perhaps onerous, but they are no more stringent than the public has a right to expect . . . ."

This overriding concern to protect the public is, of course, also fully reflected in the statutory standards applicable to regulated products. For example, a food additive may be approved only if its sponsor affirmatively shows that there is a reasonable certainty that it will not harm any consumers. In general, the sponsor of a new drug or medical device must affirmatively show that its product is effective for some appropriate medical use, and that the benefits provided by that effectiveness outweigh the risks to health presented by the product. For a medical product (i.e., a drug or medical device) to be considered "safe," it need not be without risks; rather, its benefits must outweigh its risks. By contrast, for a food or color additive to be "safe," it must be without significant risk. Where there are reasonable scientific or medical doubts about whether these standards have been met, the product is not approved. Categories of products that generally present only low risk, e.g., most foods and cosmetics, are not subject to premarket review.

Food and drug law, however, was not always this protective. As new risks to the public health have been recognized, Congress has amended the law scores of times to make it more protective.

The first general federal food and drug statute, the Pure Food and Drugs Act of 1906, was much simpler than today's law. It applied only to foods and drugs, and did not require any governmental review of any such product before it was put onto the market. If a product was distributed in violation of the statute, the government had to find out about it and bring a court action against the product or against those who were distributing it. Over time, it became clear that the scope of the statute was too narrow, and that the statutory scheme did not adequately protect the public.

The FDCA was enacted in 1938. It extended food and drug law coverage to medical devices and cosmetics. It also established a mechanism for FDA to regulate research on drugs, and required FDA review of new drugs to ensure that they were safe before they could be distributed. This "premarket review" was limited to safety, and did not apply to devices, cosmetics, or foods (except that FDA was authorized to impose a permit requirement on certain classes of foods that can present a severe risk to health if not processed properly). The 1938 act also gave FDA authority to inspect establishments where regulated products are manufactured, processed, packed, or held.

Although the original FDCA was a marked improvement over the 1906 statute, it, too, proved deficient in protecting the public.

Although the original FDCA was a marked improvement over the 1906 statute, it, too, proved deficient in protecting the public. Consequently, the statute has been strengthened by a series of amendments, among the most important of which were these: premarket review for safety was extended to food additives (1958) and color additives (1960); premarket review of drugs was extended to effectiveness as well as safety (1962); premarket review for safety and effectiveness and FDA regulation of research were extended to devices (1976). Numerous other aspects of FDA regulation have been strengthened in other amendments, including enactments to strengthen FDA's ability to prepare for and respond to bioterrorism and other emergencies. In 2009, Congress amended the FDCA and other statutes to give FDA jurisdiction over tobacco products. Congress also has authorized FDA to accredit private parties to conduct inspections of device manufacturers and to recommend initial classification of devices (classification determines the level of rigor of FDA regulation of devices).

The philosophy of premarket review of medical products is simple: to the extent reasonably possible, the most significant benefits and risks of a product should be identified and assessed before the product is distributed. If the risks are not justified, the product should not be distributed. If the risks are justified only if the product is used in accordance with certain conditions, or if certain conditions can reduce even the justified risks, those conditions should be identified and disclosed in the product's labeling. Similarly, the philosophy of premarket review of food and color additives is that, if they present significant risk, they should not be used.

The extension of the premarket review requirements from 1958 to 1976 coincided with a vast expansion throughout the federal government of the use of administrative tools rather than court actions to impose regulatory requirements. Prior to this change in method of governing, FDA had established new interpretations of the statutory standards for regulated products principally through judicial opinions in court actions. Through the DOJ, FDA would file court actions against regulated products and manufacturers or other distributors of such products; it would argue in court that the general words of the statute should be interpreted to impose particular detailed requirements, and that those requirements had been violated; and generally the courts would accept FDA's interpretations and embody them in judicial opinions, on which FDA could rely in later cases. Manufacturers and other distributors interested in learning what the applicable requirements were would consult the statute and the judicial decisions interpreting it. FDA supplemented these sources principally with so-called "trade correspondence" and announcements.

Through its new premarket approval authority and the use of rulemaking (the issuance of regulations of general applicability) and administrative adjudication (the deciding of individual cases in administrative rather than judicial proceedings), FDA developed much more efficient ways (faster, less expensive, more systematic, more coherent, more within the agency's control) to establish binding regulatory requirements. Thus, today, the court cases FDA initiates serve principally not to create new regulatory requirements but, rather, to enforce regulatory requirements already established through administrative means. Consequently, during the last 50 years there has been not only a large increase in regulatory requirements but also a substantial transfer of power over such requirements from the federal courts to FDA. The courts still have the final say on the validity of regulatory requirements, but in practice the courts defer to FDA's views most of the time. Today, someone seeking to learn the requirements applicable to a particular product would consult the statute, the regulations in Title 21 of the Code of Federal Regulations, regulations not yet codified and other issuances in the *Federal Register*, FDA guidance documents, letters (including rulings on citizen petitions), speeches, and congressional testimony, which generally are available on FDA's website (www.fda.gov), and judicial decisions.

The philosophy of premarket review is simple: to the extent reasonably possible, the most significant benefits and risks of a product should be identified and assessed before the product is distributed.

There has been a substantial transfer of power from the courts to FDA. The courts, however, still have the final say on the validity of regulatory requirements, but in practice the courts defer to FDA's views most of the time.

Premarket review and the increased use of administrative techniques to establish regulatory requirements and policy have substantially changed the nature of food and drug law and FDA. In its early years, FDA was essentially a law enforcement agency. The operating units that are now called "Centers" were then called "Bureaus." Science in the agency was a handmaiden to enforcement: its role was to identify problems in the marketplace, and help the agency react to the problems and win in court.

FDA is a scientific regulatory agency.

More recently, currently, and for the foreseeable future, FDA has been, is, and will continue to be, essentially a scientific regulatory agency. It protects the public health principally by screening out unsafe or otherwise inadequate products in premarket review, and by establishing, on the basis of scientific knowledge and agency experience, general regulatory requirements for the design, manufacture, testing, labeling, and, as to prescription medical products, advertising, of marketed products. The vast bulk of public protection is achieved through these preventive activities. They are backed up, of course, by the agency's continued ability and willingness to react to violations through administrative actions and by having DOJ file court actions against violative products and those who manufacture or distribute them. Thus, today, court enforcement is a handmaiden to scientific regulation.

This change in the nature of FDA's role has created or sharpened a number of issues central to the philosophy of food and drug regulation, including these:

◆ the general relationship between FDA and the industries it regulates, the agency's roles with respect to health promotion and health protection, and the relative importance of enforcement and voluntary compliance;

◆ the relation between FDA's regulation of medical products and the practice of medicine and other health-related professions;

◆ the relation between FDA's regulation of medical products and reimbursement for those products under federal healthcare programs (and private health insurance programs);

◆ the extent to which FDA should or, as a practical matter, must rely on consumers to protect their own health, and the role of FDA's regulation of product labeling in that connection;

◆ with its greatly increased regulatory authority, to whom and through what means FDA is ultimately accountable;

◆ in what ways, and to what extent, FDA should adapt its regulatory role to the international market, particularly the increasing volumes of imported products subject to FDA's jurisdiction;

♦ how FDA will be able to maintain protection of the public during what is likely to be a prolonged period of stringency in the federal budget; and

♦ to what extent FDA's activities should be paid for by special fees from the firms FDA regulates rather than by revenues from taxation of the general population.

The remainder of this chapter will address these issues.

THE TENSION BETWEEN PREVENTION OF HARM AND PROMOTION OF BENEFIT

Public health is improved when safe and effective drugs and devices are made available, and when those that are unsafe or ineffective are kept off the market. Clearly, it is part of FDA's mission to protect the public from medical products that are unsafe or ineffective. Under legislation enacted in 1997, it is also part of the agency's mission to "promote public health by promptly and efficiently reviewing clinical research and taking appropriate action on the marketing of regulated products in a timely manner." How should FDA harmonize those objectives? To what extent and in what ways should FDA's premarket review of new drugs and devices be made more searching, more detailed, and more deliberate in order to detect inadequacies that would make a product unsafe or ineffective or to develop additional information that would make product use more safe or more effective; and to what extent and in what ways should FDA review be simplified, streamlined, and speeded up in order to ease entry to the market for new products that may improve health? How, for example, should FDA deal with laboratory-developed tests, which commonly serve limited patient populations, some of which play important roles in healthcare, and whose developers may be unable to bear the cost of regulatory compliance? More generally, should FDA's relationship with the research-based corporations that develop most new drugs and devices be at arm's length and hierarchical (regulator/regulated firm) or should there be a significant cooperative and collegial element? To what extent should FDA, in deciding how to apply the statutory standards for premarket review of medical products, take into account the costs of complying with alternative interpretations of those standards?

Part of FDA's Mission: "promote public health by promptly and efficiently reviewing clinical research and taking appropriate action on the marketing of regulated products in a timely manner."

Plainly, there are no simple answers. In our free-enterprise system, although much basic research is sponsored by government, most new medical technologies and the products that embody them are developed by private firms operating for profit. Under the FDCA, the responsibility for testing new products also rests with private firms, not with FDA. FDA's role is to review proposed new products on the basis of information on effectiveness and safety developed and presented by private firms that have a financial interest in marketing the products, and to determine on the basis of that information (and general scientific and medical knowledge) whether the products meet statutory requirements for distribution in commerce.

The review process must be rigorous enough to ensure that new products meet the statutory standards, and that the information submitted is sufficient to make possible the writing of adequate directions for prescribing and use. The review process must not be so demanding, however, that the availability of good products is prevented or unduly delayed.

Similarly, FDA must not abdicate its regulatory role, its responsibility to ensure that no product is approved unless it satisfies the statutory standards, or its legal duty to review all products independently, objectively, and impartially. These objectives might be compromised if FDA reviewers became too deeply involved in product development or interacted too collegially with employees of private firms, so that the FDA reviewers came to have an emotional stake in product approval. Particularly in times of rapid scientific and technological progress, however, the development of beneficial products will be hindered if FDA reviewers do not work collaboratively with knowledgeable counterpart physicians, scientists, engineers, and statisticians at private companies to develop appropriate test protocols and criteria for review, to identify appropriate medical uses for new products, and to draft maximally useful guidance for prescribers and patients.

FDA and AIDS: AIDS caused FDA to establish a trade-off between the interests of current patients and future patients.

A striking example of an adjustment in the review process in response to urgent need was FDA's reaction to acquired immunodeficiency syndrome (AIDS). Under political pressure for rapid development and approval of drugs to treat persons infected with human immunodeficiency virus (HIV), the agency adopted an actively cooperative role, adopted lenient interpretations of the statutory criteria, drastically reduced its normal demands for test data, and greatly streamlined its review process. The result was swift market entry of any drug that appeared beneficial in the treatment of AIDS. The cost of this success was, in most cases, a lack of the usual quantity and quality of data to support solid conclusions about the detailed benefits and risks presented by particular products and to provide the basis for adequate directions to physicians for use of the products. This overall approach involved a trade-off between the interests of current patients and those of future patients. Because, at the time, there was no effective treatment and the disease was considered fatal in all cases, this was a fully understandable but nevertheless difficult trade-off.

Another example is more recent. In September 2016, FDA granted accelerated approval to Exondys 51 (eteplirsen), the first drug to treat Duchenne muscular dystrophy (DMD) in a limited class of patients who have a particular genetic mutation. DMD is a rare, severely debilitating disease of boys, which often starts in early childhood and leads to death in two to three decades. Accelerated approval of a drug is based on a surrogate or intermediate clinical endpoint rather than on a demonstrated clinical benefit; but, after the approval, the sponsor of the drug must conduct further studies to demonstrate clinical effectiveness. FDA's Office of New Drugs and, despite vocal patient advocacy, the relevant agency advisory committee opposed the approval of Exondys 51, on the ground that the evidence of its effectiveness was inadequate. The Director of FDA's Center for Drug Evaluation and Research, supported by the Commissioner, nevertheless decided to grant accelerated approval; and the Director explained: "In rare diseases, new drug development is especially challenging due to the small numbers of people affected by each disease and the lack of medical understanding of many disorders. Accelerated approval makes this drug available to patients based on initial data, but we eagerly await learning more about the efficacy of this drug through a confirmatory clinical trial that the company must conduct after approval."

This decision has been criticized as lowering FDA's approval standards, establishing a bad precedent, giving false hope to patients and their families, creating unjustified healthcare costs (*Fortune* magazine stated that "[t]he treatment will reportedly cost $300,000"), and possibly discouraging the development of more effective DMD drugs. Like the initial drugs to treat AIDS, Exondys 51 presents the issue of whether, and if so to what extent, the normal standards of proof of effectiveness and safety should be lowered in the case of a fatal or severely debilitating disease or condition for which there is no other accepted treatment. Several provisions of the 21st Century Cures Act, enacted in late 2016, address "patient-focused drug development," and call for standardization of FDA's consideration, in reviewing applications for approval of drugs, of "patient experience data," i.e., data that "are intended to provide information about patients' experiences with a disease or condition, including . . . the impact of such disease or condition, or a related therapy, on patients' lives; and . . . patient preferences with respect to treatment of such disease or condition." These provisions amended a statutory provision, enacted in 2012, that called for FDA to "develop and implement strategies to solicit the views of patients during the medical product development process and consider the perspectives of patients during regulatory discussions." Thus, FDA is required to decide, case by case, what weight to give to patient perspectives when conducting its scientific reviews to decide whether evidence sufficiently shows that a drug is "effective" and "safe" (i.e., that its therapeutic benefits outweigh the risks it presents). Of course, FDA does not decide the relative weights of benefits and risks for individual patients; prescribers and patients do that. Rather, in approving a drug, FDA, in effect, decides that, in at least some circumstances, prescribers and patients, informed by the drug's FDA-approved labeling and other relevant factors, reasonably could decide to use the drug.

In the area of enforcement, FDA necessarily is a cop; but it cannot, itself, continuously patrol every factory, whether in the United States or abroad, where the products it regulates are made, or test the actual quality of every unit of every such product that is on the market in the United States. Thus, the agency has had to develop strategies that maximize the effectiveness of its limited resources in inducing compliance by regulated firms. The agency has had to blend elements of strict enforcement with technical assistance in the form of guidelines, development of consensus implementation standards, and random and for-cause inspections and sampling of products to induce more or less voluntary compliance.

For example, FDA regulations require that foods, drugs, and devices be manufactured in accordance with "current good manufacturing practices." The regulations set forth only very general standards, such as that buildings and facilities shall be clean and sanitary, equipment shall be suitable for its purposes, and employees shall be adequately qualified and trained. Introduction into commerce of a product made in violation of these requirements is technically unlawful. Detailed elaborations of the general requirements in the regulations are set forth in guidance documents created by FDA, in consensus documents developed by experts from FDA and the regulated industries, and in a substantial literature developed by private experts. Additional elaboration is set forth in documents resulting from FDA compliance and enforcement activities— reports of violations observed during FDA inspections, FDA Warning Letters, and judicial decisions resulting from court cases initiated by FDA through DOJ.

Of course, to some extent, an additional incentive for compliance is provided by the state laws of products liability and consumer protection. Where a consumer claims to have been harmed by an FDA-regulated product, violation of an FDA requirement generally may be considered as evidence that the product was defective and that its manufacturer was negligent.

FDA's control over warnings and other information in drug and device labeling and regulatory decisions the agency makes can have a significant effect on products liability litigation.

FDA's control over warnings and other information in drug and device labeling and regulatory decisions the agency makes can have a significant effect on products liability litigation. Issues have been raised as to whether, and if so how, FDA should take account of this effect in carrying out its regulatory responsibilities; and as to whether FDA approval of certain aspects of a product and the product's compliance with the conditions for FDA approval should preempt the imposition of products liability that is based on a theory that such approval and compliance were insufficient under state law.

In the past, the agency generally attempted to be neutral as between injured plaintiffs and defendant manufacturers, and regarded products liability as a useful adjunct to regulation, and therefore generally opposed arguments that its regulatory requirements preempt different or additional requirements under state law. During the administration of President George W. Bush, however, the agency asserted that certain aspects of its regulation of medical products do preempt different or additional state law requirements. Moreover, concerns about liability have contributed to a recognized insufficiency of medical products in certain categories (e.g., drugs to treat illnesses in pregnant women, products for neonates, and contraceptives). There is ongoing debate about what degree of preemption best serves the public health in the long term. During the administration of President Barack Obama, FDA proposed to allow manufacturers of generic drugs to change the safety information in their FDA-approved labeling in response to new information, thereby subjecting them to potential liability under state law for failure to do so—a risk of liability that, under a recent Supreme Court decision, they otherwise would not face.

An area of FDA activity that includes, but also extends beyond, the agency's purely regulatory authorities relates to shortages of medically necessary prescription drugs (including medically necessary prescription biological products). Most such shortages are of sterile injectables. The most common causes of shortages are manufacturing-quality problems and capacity-related delays, unavailability of ingredients, unexpected increases in demand, and business decisions to terminate production, especially as to a drug that is manufactured by one or very few firms. The number of new and continuing shortages increased significantly between 2005 (when FDA began tracking them) and 2012, and, as reported by the Government Accountability Office in July 2016, has been relatively stable since then. An Executive Order in 2011 and legislation in 2012, building on a 1997 statute and FDA's implementation of that statute, expanded a program in which FDA seeks to prevent or mitigate shortages of most types of drugs that are life-supporting or life-sustaining or are intended for use in the prevention or treatment of a debilitating disease or condition, including such drugs used in emergency medical care or surgery. In general, a manufacturer of such a drug is required to notify FDA at least six months before a discontinuation of production or an interruption that is likely to lead to a non-negligible disruption of supply of the drug, or, if such advance notification is impossible, as soon as practicable. The penalty for noncompliance is publication on FDA's website of a noncompliance letter from FDA and the response thereto—a congressional requirement to use the power of publicity.

After receiving such a notification, FDA determines whether and to what extent a national shortage exists, or is likely, and whether the drug is medically necessary. If so, it can take a variety of actions to address the problem, including: finding out whether other manufacturers (domestic or foreign) can supply enough to prevent, mitigate, or end the shortage and encouraging them to do so; expediting FDA's inspections and review of submissions from the manufacturer(s) experiencing the disruption of production and from other manufacturers that seek to provide additional supply; relaxing the normally applicable manufacturing quality standards or other regulatory requirements and developing risk-mitigation measures, e.g., use by hospitals of filters to screen out contaminants in injectable drugs, to permit the shipment of batches that are substandard but nevertheless can be used effectively and safely (FDA calls such actions the exercise of "enforcement discretion" or "regulatory flexibility"); and posting shortage-related information on its website. FDA recognizes that, "if the use of enforcement discretion signals to industry that FDA is willing to exercise flexibility to ensure the availability of any critical product, this could create a long-term disincentive for manufacturers to invest in manufacturing upgrades or other quality improvements to avoid disruptions in supply, exacerbating the risk of shortages over the long term."

FDA sees itself as "responsible for ensuring that safe, effective drugs are available for US patients." It describes part of its efforts to prevent or mitigate shortages as "[w]orking with firms to resolve manufacturing issues" and "[h]elping firms with getting new sources of raw materials." The agency states that, although it "is not able to force a company to continue making a medication . . . FDA can look for alternative manufacturers and work with [them] to bring the product back to the market." Plainly, FDA's work in preventing and reducing shortages makes a significant contribution to healthcare. The types of FDA-firm interactions that these activities embrace, however, differ sharply from the types of interactions that are typical of FDA's regulatory and enforcement activities. One may wonder whether, and, if so how and to what extent, FDA's experiences in working collaboratively with firms to address shortages affect the agency's dealings with those firms in other contexts, and whether any such effects are proper and/or desirable.

FDA AND THE PRACTICE OF MEDICINE

FDA technically does not regulate the practice of medicine.

Although FDA's product-approval decisions and other regulatory actions have a large effect on healthcare, FDA technically does not regulate physicians, dentists, nurses, pharmacists, or other members of the healing professions, except when they conduct clinical trials within FDA's jurisdiction and when they become involved in the manufacture, distribution, or promotion of products within that jurisdiction. For example, when pharmacists compound drugs outside the scope of traditional compounding, they are subject to FDA regulation. Beyond those exceptions, the healthcare professions are regulated by the states.

FDA's regulations do bear directly on healthcare professionals when they conduct FDA-regulated clinical investigations to develop information for product approval. In general, when a healthcare professional's relationship with a patient is also that of a scientific investigator with a research subject, FDA's role is to confirm that the research is scientifically adequate for its purpose and to protect the rights and welfare of the subject by ensuring that risks to the subject have been reduced to the practical minimum and that the subject's informed consent to participation in the investigation has been properly obtained, to ensure that the remaining risks entailed by use of an investigational drug or device are justified by the likelihood that the investigation will yield useful scientific data, and to ensure that the investigational product is not used outside the investigational protocol. Pursuant to regulations, FDA is assisted in the subject-protection aspects of this role by Institutional Review Boards, which review and monitor clinical trials within FDA's jurisdiction.

Use of a lawfully distributed drug or device by a healthcare professional treating a patient is outside FDA's jurisdiction. When FDA approves a drug or approves (or clears) a device, it approves (or clears) it for use only in specific medical circumstances (e.g., to treat certain diseases or other bodily conditions (called "indications"), in certain patient populations). The manufacturer or distributor of an approved (or cleared) product may advertise and otherwise promote it only for use in the circumstances specified in the labeling FDA has approved (or cleared). Physicians and others authorized by state law to prescribe medical products, however, may prescribe the product for any indication or other circumstance they choose (e.g., for the FDA-approved or -cleared indication but for a patient population different from the one for which FDA approved (or cleared) the indication, or for a different indication altogether), subject only to the requirements of state law with respect to medical licensure and malpractice and to third-party payers' standards for reimbursement.

Over time, many products develop medically accepted indications, or uses in patient populations, that are outside the FDA-approved (or -cleared) labeling (so-called "off-label uses"); some off-label uses may even become the standard of care. Unless a manufacturer submits to FDA data adequate to support approval (or clearance) of an additional indication or use, it will remain unapproved (or uncleared). Consequently, it commonly occurs that a drug or device has a medically significant indication or other use outside its approved (or cleared) labeling; but, under FDA policy, the product's manufacturer is generally prohibited from advertising or otherwise promoting that indication or use to physicians and other healthcare providers (although FDA policy permits

Many products develop medically accepted indications, or uses in patient populations, that are outside the FDA-approved (or -cleared) labeling (so-called "off-label uses").

79

a manufacturer to discuss an off-label use when necessary to respond to an unsolicited inquiry by a provider). Organizations that are independent of the manufacturer and distributors of a product are not subject to any such prohibition, and are free to meet any marketplace need for information about off-label uses of an FDA-regulated product.

Manufacturers have nevertheless objected to this restriction on their freedom to disseminate information about their products. Historically, FDA has responded that, if manufacturers were free to disseminate information about unapproved (or uncleared) indications or uses, they would have much less incentive to seek FDA approval (or clearance) of additional indications and uses and to develop the scientific data required for such approval (or clearance). Thus, on this issue, our society's general commitment to free competitive dissemination of truthful information collides with FDA's role as decision-maker about the distribution of new drugs and devices and about manufacturers' statements in the marketplace concerning their FDA-regulated products. A limited compromise of the competing views was included in FDA reform legislation enacted in 1997, but has now expired. In a guidance document published in January 2009, near the end of the Bush administration, FDA endorsed (with certain conditions) dissemination by manufacturers of reprints of medical journal articles and medical and scientific publications relating to unapproved (or uncleared) uses of their approved (or cleared) medical products. FDA issued a revised draft guidance document on the same subject in February 2014. The debate persists.

Historically, FDA has responded that, if manufacturers were free to disseminate information about unapproved (or uncleared) indications or uses, they would have much less incentive to seek FDA approval (or clearance) of additional indications and uses and to develop the scientific data required for such approval (or clearance).

In 2012, the United States Court of Appeals for the Second Circuit held that truthful off-label promotion of an FDA-approved drug is protected by the First Amendment. The government did not seek review of that decision in the Supreme Court. In January 2017, FDA issued a final rule on when products made or derived from tobacco are regulated as drugs, devices, or combination products; a guidance document on medical product communications that are consistent with FDA-required labeling; and a memorandum on public health interests and First Amendment considerations related to manufacturer communications regarding off-label uses of approved or cleared medical products. These publications set forth FDA's positions on the statutory concept of "intended use" and other topics relevant to the lawfulness of manufacturer communications about off-label uses. In February 2017, groups representing medical product manufacturers petitioned FDA, under the new Trump administration, to stay the final rule and to reconsider the interpretation of "intended use" stated therein. Thus, the scope of "intended use" as well as the constitutionality of the government's restrictions on off-label promotion remain unresolved.

The issues concerning manufacturers' communications about their medical products extend beyond purely medical information. As economic considerations have come explicitly to play a much larger role in decisions about healthcare, and as important elements of healthcare decision-making have shifted from individual physicians to managed-care organizations and third-party payers, the demand for economic information about the performance of drugs and medical devices also has increased. The managed-care organizations and third-party payers want to know not only whether a drug or device is effective and safe and for which indications in which patient populations, but also whether it is cost-effective as compared to alternative products and other treatments (such as surgery).

When manufacturers, who obviously have a commercial interest, undertake to provide such information, should the information be subject to approval by FDA before the manufacturers can disseminate it? Even if the recipients are sophisticated organizations? Is such a role for FDA an appropriate or an inappropriate extension of its established role as reviewer of information on product effectiveness and safety? Legislation enacted in 1997, and expanded in 2016, provides that healthcare economic information that relates to an FDA-approved drug indication, that is provided to a payer, a formulary committee, or other similar entity, and that is based on competent and reliable scientific evidence shall not be considered false or misleading. Such information also is exempt from the special requirements for proof of effectiveness and safety of drugs. The information must include "a statement describing any material differences between the healthcare economic information and the labeling approved for the drug" by FDA. In January 2017, FDA issued a draft guidance on drug and device manufacturer communications with formulary committees and similar entities.

FDA AND REIMBURSEMENT

FDA has no authority to regulate the cost of an approved drug or of an approved or cleared medical device. Economic aspects of such products are the province of other agencies.

Whether new medical products approved by FDA are actually available to patients depends to a considerable extent, however, on whether third-party payers (Medicare, Medicaid, other governmental health programs, private insurers) will reimburse for their cost. What role, if any, should FDA play in decisions about reimbursement? How should FDA reviewers of medical products interact with other federal and state officials who review the same products for purposes of reimbursement under a governmentally supported healthcare program, and with private parties that engage in parallel reviews? FDA's Center for

Devices and Radiological Health, for example, is expanding its efforts to facilitate the coordinated development by product sponsors of information needed to support both FDA authorization for distribution and reimbursement by third-party payers; and the Center is exploring ways it can provide information on product effectiveness and safety to decision-makers about reimbursement.

THE RESPONSIBILITIES OF CONSUMERS

As a result of vastly increased knowledge in the health-related sciences and changes in the healthcare delivery system, consumers now have greater opportunity—and necessity—than in recent decades to make informed decisions about matters that affect their own health. These changes are most clearly reflected by the labeling of foods and over-the-counter (OTC) drugs.

FDA encourages competition in product innovation.

As to both types of products, FDA has implemented a philosophy of encouraging competition in product innovation by increasing manufacturers' communications about their products to consumers. The result has been a plethora of new products in food stores and drug stores, and new claims and information on product labels and in advertisements. Congress has particularly encouraged this development with respect to foods.

Increased scientific understanding of human nutrition and of the role of diet in general health has led to fundamental revision of food labels, so as to provide increased information to consumers, and incentives to food processors to produce more healthful foods. Food labels now contain more easily usable information about the nutrient content of foods and, as permitted by FDA pursuant to statutory criteria, claims about the relationship between particular food products and particular diseases.

FDA's strategy in overseeing food labels is to enable consumers to make informed choices in the construction of a healthful overall diet. One might ask, however, how well such a strategy actually serves a population that includes many people who never see such information (in institutions where meals are served (schools, nursing homes, prisons, etc.), who cannot understand or use such information (because, e.g., their language is other than English, or they are functionally illiterate or innumerate) or simply do not have, or do not spend, the time and energy to use it.

In recent years, many medically significant drugs have been switched by FDA from prescription to OTC status.

In recent years, many medically significant drugs have been switched by FDA from prescription to OTC status. Pharmaceutical manufacturers seek such switches when they see attractive marketing opportunities for OTC sales (e.g., after profits from prescription sales have been reduced by generic competition). Such switches make drugs more accessible to consumers and reduce the overall cost of using them by eliminating the requirement of contact with a prescriber. They also shift the cost of the drugs from the healthcare system to the drugs' users because most insurance and other third-party-payer systems that cover prescription drugs do not also cover OTC drugs.

Even where consumers do consult a physician, they are more likely now than in the past to use an OTC rather than a prescription drug. Because managed care systems generally do not cover OTC drugs, the systems have a financial incentive to induce their physicians and other prescribers to direct patients to OTC, rather than prescription, drugs when suitable OTC drugs are available; and the widening range of OTC drugs available expands the opportunities for prescribers to do so. Thus, FDA policy combines with the incentives facing pharmaceutical manufacturers and managed care systems to lead to greater usage of OTC drugs.

Increased societal reliance on OTC drugs means increased reliance on consumers to deal with their own medical needs: increased consumer autonomy, but also increased consumer responsibility. The economics of healthcare drives in this direction, as, perhaps, does the demand of sophisticated consumers. There are important issues of how far and how fast the shift from prescription to OTC should go, and as to what extent, and at what cost, society can or should protect those who cannot cope with the increased personal responsibility.

Great progress in the understanding of the human genome and its relation to specific diseases and medical conditions indicates that personalized medicine will play an increasing role in healthcare. As knowledge about genomics spreads among consumers, and private firms develop new products based on such knowledge, FDA will need to make many decisions about the appropriate role of consumers in personalized medicine.

FDA ACCOUNTABILITY

In making decisions critical to the health of the American people, to whom is FDA accountable? Within the government, FDA is triply accountable.

First, it is part of the Public Health Service in the Department of Health and Human Services (DHHS), and thus part of the executive branch. The agency and its head, the Commissioner of Food and Drugs, are answerable to the Secretary of Health and Human Services, the Office of Management and Budget, and,

FDA is accountable to:
- *executive branch: the President, DHHS, Public Health Service*
- *Congress*
- *the courts*
- *scientific and medical communities*

ultimately, the President. The agency's major regulatory and personnel decisions, budget, congressional testimony, and legislative proposals all are reviewable by one or more of these officials or offices.

Second, the agency is overseen by Congress. The Senate Committee on Health, Education, Labor and Pensions and the House Committee on Energy and Commerce have jurisdiction over the FDCA and other statutes that FDA administers; authorize the agency's budget; and conduct frequent hearings (in the House, through the Subcommittee on Oversight and Investigations and the Subcommittee on Health) on the agency's performance. Because FDA originated as the Bureau of Chemistry in the Department of Agriculture (before it was transferred to what is now DHHS), however, FDA's appropriations are determined by agricultural subcommittees of the Appropriations Committees in the House and Senate. Thus, those committees, too, have a continuing interest in FDA, which is reflected in FDA's annual appropriations hearings. From time to time, other Senate and House committees also take an interest in FDA.

Regulated firms, public interest groups, and others dissatisfied with an FDA action (or inaction) can seek recourse in the courts.

Third, FDA is overseen by the courts. The agency's enforcement program is conducted mostly in the courts, although Congress has given it authority to impose civil monetary penalties and certain other sanctions administratively. Regulated firms, public interest groups, and others dissatisfied with an FDA action (or inaction) can seek recourse in the courts. Because FDA can appear in court only through the DOJ, that department can also impose some check on the agency.

As a practical matter, FDA is also accountable to the scientific and medical communities, and particularly to their academic components. Most of the principal decision-makers at FDA are physicians or scientists, to whom the respect of their professional peers is of great importance. Particularly when FDA makes decisions about cutting-edge technologies or other matters at the scientific frontier (as it often does), the agency's decision-makers want to make decisions that will be respected as sensible in the relevant scientific and medical disciplines. Routinely, the agency, when faced with such a decision, formally seeks the advice of one of its advisory committees, which are composed principally of leading academic physicians and scientists. FDA generally follows their advice.

Like all governmental agencies, FDA is also accountable to public opinion, as shaped by the press. The agency's relations with all the constituencies with which it deals—other governmental bodies, regulated firms, trade associations, scientific and medical groups, organizations representing patients, public interest groups, and others—are all influenced significantly by the agency's standing with the public.

The 21st Century Cures Act includes several provisions that increase FDA's accountability by requiring the agency to issue guidance documents and to make certain additional kinds of information publicly available on its website or otherwise.

Nevertheless, in a large and critical part of its work—review of new products—FDA is largely insulated from effective outside oversight. Such reviews are based on trade secret data generally not otherwise disclosed elsewhere, except to similar regulatory bodies in other countries. The reviews are highly technical, require highly specialized competence in several disciplines, and are extremely labor-intensive. Probably no other governmental institution currently is equipped to oversee the quality of FDA's performance of this distinctive function on an ongoing basis.

Because, over time, FDA's new-product decisions are critical to the fate of many regulated firms, they are extremely reluctant to challenge any particular FDA product-review decision in another forum. Resort to the courts to challenge an FDA denial of approval (or clearance) of a new product is particularly unappealing for several reasons:

♦ the technical nature of the subject matter;

♦ prevailing doctrines of administrative law, which lead to deference to administrative agencies on scientific and technical matters;

♦ the institutional limits on the judiciary, which is not well equipped to make ultimate judgments about scientific and technical matters (as distinct from ascertaining the status of scientific opinion); and

♦ the unattractiveness of trying to market a product that FDA has initially refused to approve.

The result is that in an important area the exercise of governmental power is, to a considerable extent, unaccountable.

FDA is held accountable, however, on infrequent occasions when the press or a segment of the public takes a particularly strong interest in a pending review of a proposed new product or when a past approval of a product has turned out to be a serious mistake. In such circumstances, extraordinary public attention focuses on FDA's decision-making process, and the agency is called to public account for its decision.

FDA is held accountable, however, on infrequent occasions when the press or a segment of the public takes a particularly strong interest in a pending review of a proposed new product or when a past approval of a product has turned out to be a serious mistake.

For example, organized groups representing patients, such as those with the AIDS virus or Alzheimer's disease, have brought public pressure on FDA to approve proposed new drugs. News media sometimes have championed particular drugs or devices under review. When an approved product has turned out to be much more harmful than was anticipated when FDA approved it, FDA has been called before a congressional committee to explain its decision.

These two types of scenarios create conflicting pressures on FDA. The agency may be subjected to public pressure to hasten the approval of an apparently promising new product, but the agency knows it is likely to be criticized severely if its approval turns out to have been a mistake. Few products, however, attract public support before approval, and few FDA approvals turn out to have been mistaken. In the general run of decision-making about approvals of new products—including decisions about what indications and claims for a product will be permitted and how other information will be presented in the product's official labeling—FDA is largely unaccountable as a practical matter. The Food and Drug Administration Safety and Innovation Act, enacted in 2012, makes a modest effort to render FDA's review of applications for approval of new drugs more transparent by requiring "a structured risk-benefit assessment framework."

Ultimately, FDA's accountability is a function not only of how other governmental bodies and other constituencies view the agency, but also of other, competing demands on the attention and resources of those to whom FDA is accountable.

Ultimately, FDA's accountability is a function not only of how other governmental bodies and other constituencies view the agency, but also of other, competing demands on the attention and resources of those to whom FDA is accountable. The variability in effective oversight of the agency presents a persistent philosophical issue for FDA: what should be its basic stance toward the statute it administers? Should FDA officials view the statute as a set of detailed instructions from Congress to be carried out in a manner as faithful as possible to what congressional drafters presumably intended? Or should the statute be viewed as basically a set of authorities for FDA to use to advance its own views of what promotes the public health, through whatever means FDA can use without being overridden by some governmental body or group to which the agency is formally accountable?

For example, if the agency views a particular statutory limitation on its authority as reflecting a congressional compromise inimical to the public health, should the agency respect the limitation faithfully or seek ways to evade it through other statutorily permitted means? To what extent should the agency seek to expand its powers in the face of inertia, distraction, or dysfunction in other centers of power? To what extent should the agency be creative and aggressive in asserting its power to advance policies it considers beneficial to the public health? Alternatively, should the agency seek to discern and carry out the policy preferences of its political superiors in the executive branch and in Congress?

In sum, what is the appropriate role of a subordinate executive-branch agency entrusted with a mission to protect the public health?

Over the decades, different FDA decision-makers have responded differently to this set of issues. In general, the agency has taken an expansive view of its mission and its authorities, and has used its statutory tools aggressively to advance its institutional views of what is good for the public health. The most striking example was FDA's assertion of jurisdiction over tobacco products without an express delegation of statutory authority—an assertion of authority that the Supreme Court held to be invalid, but that later led to the enactment of legislation giving the agency that authority.

FDA takes an expansive view of its mission and its authorities.

FDA in the International Community

Before the advent of today's global economy, FDA's concerns were focused almost entirely on protecting consumers in the United States. FDA viewed itself as having only limited responsibility toward consumers abroad, and only a limited role in facilitating the marketing of American products abroad. The agency also devoted relatively little effort to monitoring imports. Amendments to the FDCA and globalization have required FDA to rethink the proper role of the American national food and drug regulator in the international economy.

What is America's responsibility with respect to FDA-regulated products exported from this country to a foreign country? Should the United States be an international nanny? Should its attitude toward foreign consumers be "let the buying country beware"? Should its role be something in between—and, if so, what? Does it matter whether the importing country does or does not have its own sophisticated regulatory system? Does it matter whether products exported from the United States may be re-exported from the original importing country to a third country? (Products re-exported back to the United States clearly are within FDA's legitimate concern.) If the United States does have some responsibility toward consumers in foreign countries, does it follow that the very same standards of safety, effectiveness, labeling, and product quality that apply to domestically distributed products should also apply to exported products, even when they are going to countries that are very different in population characteristics, healthcare systems, healthcare needs, and general economic level? If different standards should apply, what are they, how should they be ascertained, and what degree of deference should FDA give to the views of governments in the importing countries? What level of effort and resources should FDA allocate to reviewing products to be exported, under any standard? To these difficult questions, there are no simple, obviously correct answers.

What is America's responsibility with respect to FDA-regulated products exported from this country to a foreign country?

In general, FDA would prefer that American firms not export products it regulates whose effectiveness and safety for the ultimate consumers have not been demonstrated. FDA recognizes, however, that standards of effectiveness and safety appropriate for the affluent United States, with its sophisticated health-care system, may not be appropriate for countries that are much poorer and have only rudimentary healthcare systems. Moreover, FDA owes respect to the authority and responsibility of foreign governments to decide what products may be distributed to their own people. In addition, the limitations on FDA's resources and the undesirability of driving export manufacturing facilities abroad constrain FDA's ability to act, and the willingness of Congress to have FDA act, as the protector of all the world's consumers. Nevertheless, Congress has amended the export provisions of the FDCA to address important aspects of this set of issues.

Similarly, the increasing dependence of the United States on imports of medical products and foods and, since 9/11, concerns about bioterrorism have raised serious issues about FDA's ability to protect American consumers from products that are fraudulent or adulterated, have been tampered with, or are otherwise defective. For example, FDA stated in a July 1, 2016 *Federal Register* document: "The number of FDA-regulated products imported into the United States has grown steadily, from approximately 6 million import lines in 2002 to over 35 million import lines in 2015. In 2014, FDA-regulated products imported or offered for import were manufactured in more than 322,500 foreign facilities and arrived in the United States from more than 100 countries." On October 19, 2016, the Comptroller General stated in a presentation: "About 80 percent of the manufacturers producing active pharmaceutical ingredients for the U.S. market are located abroad. Nearly 40 percent of finished drug products and about 50 percent of all medical devices are made overseas." Plainly, if such imports do not materially decrease, FDA, in cooperation with Congress and through agreements with foreign governments, will have to upgrade its programs for protection against unlawful imports, as it has already been doing. This effort will, of course, require the allocation of significantly increased resources, as well as the development and implementation of significantly improved monitoring and inspection systems and expanded interaction with foreign governments. Congressional enactments have increased FDA's responsibilities in these areas, yet Congress has been unwilling to provide FDA the resources it needs for inspection programs adequate to provide confidence in the quality of imported products within FDA's jurisdiction. This serious problem is likely to persist and to increase as imports of FDA-regulated products increase and the stringency of federal budgets for regulatory programs becomes more severe.

To facilitate the international movement of foods, drugs, and devices, FDA has made a major effort to harmonize its regulatory requirements and standards with those of foreign counterpart agencies.

To facilitate the international movement of foods, drugs, and devices, FDA has made a major effort to harmonize its regulatory requirements and stan-dards with those of foreign counterpart agencies. For example, in March 2017, FDA and the European Medicines Agency announced that they had entered into an agreement under which each would be able to utilize the other's good manufacturing practices inspections of pharmaceutical manufacturing facilities. A host of issues relate to the extent to which FDA should compromise with foreign regulators in order to promote international uniformity in data development to support the approval of new products, product labeling, manufacturing systems and practices, factory inspection standards, and other matters. A further issue relates to the level of effort and resources that FDA should devote to assisting U.S. manufacturers to meet importation requirements of foreign governments.

How FDA Should Be Funded

Finally, an issue that arose in the 1990s is whether, and if so to what extent, FDA's activities should be funded by "user fees" from regulated firms rather than by the federal government's general revenues (collected principally from taxpayers). Plainly, from the perspective of the national budget and the interest of taxpayers, any shift of the burden of payment to regulated firms is desirable, although the shift will be reflected in increased costs and, consequently, prices for the products of the regulated firms that pay the fees. Does such a shift raise legitimate concerns?

An issue that arose in the 1990s is whether, and if so to what extent, the activities of FDA should be funded by "user fees" from regulated firms.

Is product review (or inspection of a manufacturing facility) properly viewed as a service provided by FDA to regulated firms, for which it is appropriate that those firms pay a fee? Were not the systems of product review and factory inspection established for the benefit of the consuming public rather than the regulated firms, even though regulated firms benefit generally from the existence of regulatory systems that give the public confidence in the safety and quality (and, as relevant, effectiveness) of their products? Are there likely to be adverse practical consequences of re-conceptualizing product review as a service to regulated firms?

If regulated firms are paying for a particular FDA activity (e.g., review of applications for approval of new drugs), is there a risk that the fact of payment by the firms will affect the performance of the function and the interaction between the agency personnel performing it and the personnel of the paying firms? Over time, might the firms become more assertive in their dealings with the agency, and might FDA personnel feel that they "owe" the paying firms more? If such consequences do occur, are they necessarily undesirable?

Is there a risk that particular FDA functions paid for by regulated firms will receive disproportionate financial support as compared to agency functions funded by the taxpayers, so that, over time, an imbalance will occur between, e.g., product review (paid for by firms) and enforcement (paid for by the taxpayers)? Has such an imbalance already occurred, and with undesirable consequences? Can the political process, including congressional oversight and the appropriations process, be relied on to maintain a reasonable balance?

If FDA functions are paid for by private firms rather than from the public treasury, is there a risk that there will be a natural bureaucratic tendency for the firm-supported functions (and FDA jobs) to proliferate unnecessarily? Or can it reasonably be expected that firms and their trade associations will have sufficient political capital with Congress and the administration to maintain checks on such a development?

The political system has been unwilling to provide, from general revenues, an adequate level of resources for timely FDA reviews of new products.

These questions raise fundamental issues about the principles underlying the regulatory system FDA administers. The risks just described may be real; but it is also undeniable that the political system has been unwilling to provide, from general revenues, an adequate level of resources for timely FDA reviews of new products and inspections of factories, and that the additional resources from user fees can accelerate product reviews and approvals and increase factory inspections, to the general benefit of the public. Whether the advantages of this approach outweigh the disadvantages over the long term will depend principally on the quality of FDA management and the ability of outside constituencies (principally Congress and the news media) to find an effective way to monitor the quality of FDA's performance despite the relative imperviousness of FDA product reviews to public scrutiny. As funding of FDA by user fees extends beyond particular product reviews and types of inspections to other functions, these concerns and the need for effective management and oversight of FDA will increase.

Conclusion

Food and drug law is a fascinating microcosm of old and new issues in political and social philosophy, including many facets of social justice among different groups affected by regulatory decisions. These issues influence day-to-day administration of the law and the large controversies that erupt from time to time.

Chapter 4

The Food and Drug Administration— How It Is Organized and Works

Fred H. Degnan & Smitha Stansbury, King & Spalding, LLP, Washington, D.C.

Key Points

- Although the Food and Drug Administration (FDA) is not an independent agency, it makes every effort to operate as if it were one. It is unique among its sister agencies within the Department of Health and Human Services (DHHS) because of the variety of products and scientific issues it confronts and because of the extensive regulatory and enforcement authority it wields, not to mention the latitude it has been given to police the domestic and international commerce of the products it regulates.
- The agency's evolution from a small bureau in the U.S. Department of Agriculture in 1906 to a very visible and active component of DHHS reveals the development of a highly specialized agency that can adapt and adjust to increased regulatory burdens.
- The fundamental structure and organization of FDA for decades has remained unchanged: the Office of the Commissioner, substantive Centers, and field offices form the nucleus of agency activity and initiatives. Always a national presence, the agency now has a global face as well with offices in key overseas regions.
- Because of the complexity, variety, and importance of the issues within its responsibilities, FDA has been forced to lead the way in developing and employing regulatory tools, such as rulemaking and advisory committees, and has forged generally strong collaborative working arrangements with sister agencies and state authorities. As a result, the agency has enhanced its ability to function efficiently and in a substantively and scientifically sound way.

INTRODUCTION

Although perhaps the most visible and well-known of all public health organizations, the U.S. Food and Drug Administration (FDA) is not an independent agency. Rather, it is a component of the U.S. Department of Health and Human Services (DHHS).

Moreover, and perhaps even more surprising, only very limited statutory authority (e.g., authority with respect to dispute resolution regarding the timeliness of agency review of drug, device, or biological combination product applications) is directly vested in the Commissioner of Food and Drugs. The governing core legislation, the Federal Food, Drug, and Cosmetic Act (FDCA), is designed to be administered almost exclusively by the Secretary of Health and Human Services. In fact, until 1988, the Commissioner, for all practical purposes, served at the pleasure of the Secretary. The FDCA was modified in 1988 to require that the Commissioner be appointed by the President and confirmed by the Senate. Although now in a more favorable political position, the Commissioner, nevertheless, remains answerable to the Secretary of Health and Human Services, as well as to others in the political system.

The routine administration of the FDCA is conducted by FDA.

Notwithstanding the language of the FDCA, the Secretary has delegated the majority of authority under the act to the Commissioner. In turn, the Commissioner has re-delegated the bulk of the authority received from the Secretary to the Directors of FDA's Centers and regional offices. Delegations and re-delegations under the act can be found in Part 5 of FDA's regulations (21 C.F.R. §§ 5.10, 5.20). Thus, as a practical matter, the routine administration of the FDCA is conducted by FDA. The Secretary, however, has not delegated—and, in fact, has specifically reserved—the authority to approve FDA regulations that present significant public issues involving the quality, availability, marketing, or cost of foods, drugs, cosmetics, medical devices, biologics, or any other article subject to regulation by FDA. This hierarchy is important to understanding the role of various parts of the government in highly visible and important FDA activities.

FDA is unique among its sister agencies within DHHS because of the variety of products and scientific issues it confronts, because of the extensive regulatory and enforcement authority it wields, and due to the latitude it has been given to police the domestic and international commerce of the products it regulates. In large part because of the complexity, variety, and importance of the issues within its responsibility, FDA frequently has restructured itself in an effort to enhance its efficiency. And, to be successful in its public health mission, the agency has led the way in developing and employing regulatory tools such as rulemaking and advisory committees, and has forged generally strong, collaborative working arrangements with sister agencies and state authorities. In the process, the agency attempts to maintain a workable balance with Congress and its overseers in the executive branch, DHHS, and the Office of Management and Budget (OMB).

Because the volume of imported food and medical products is ever increasing, FDA has in recent years dramatically expanded its overseas presence. The agency has established offices in China, India, Latin America, and Europe in an effort to provide greater access for FDA inspections and to improve understanding and cooperation between FDA and foreign manufacturers as well as between FDA and foreign counterpart regulatory agencies.

How FDA Is Organized: Headquarters and the Field

In 1906 the Bureau of Chemistry of the U.S. Department of Agriculture (USDA), FDA's first lineal ancestor, faced real challenges. At issue was how best to regulate the safety and labeling of foods and drugs in interstate commerce. Right from the start there was recognition that such regulation, to be effective, required not only policy guidance and decision making from a central organization (the Bureau of Chemistry), but also a strong presence throughout the diverse regions of the United States. As a result, "field" laboratories in New York, Boston, Philadelphia, Chicago, New Orleans, and San Francisco were established to provide critical reports and information needed to enforce what were viewed as the sweeping provisions of the Pure Food and Drugs Act of 1906.

With the passage of time, the complexity of the challenges confronting FDA has increased dramatically. The agency's regulatory authority extends far beyond the food and drug products subject to the 1906 act. Moreover, whereas the tasks and responsibilities that faced the Bureau of Chemistry in 1906 centered primarily around ensuring against the adulteration and misbranding of food and drugs, the tasks and responsibilities confronting the agency today include the development of scientific and regulatory policy; the expert and prompt scientific review of premarket applications; the comprehensive investigation of an array of diverse manufacturers; the even-handed enforcement of statutory prohibitions and standards; the security of regulated products from tampering and terrorist activity; and the coordination of international policies and regulation to foster trade, yet protect domestic consumers from harmful or bogus products.

The fundamental structure of the agency continues to embrace the concept of a national headquarters for policy and decision making and an extensive, professional field force throughout the country to provide informed, consistent public health decision making and regulatory enforcement.

The agency's structure must accommodate these diverse and broad-ranging initiatives and goals. Although restructuring, or at least tinkering with existing structures, has occurred frequently, the fundamental structure of the agency continues to embrace the concept of a national headquarters for scientific evaluation, policy and decision making, and an extensive, professional field force throughout the country to provide informed, consistent public health decision making and regulatory enforcement.

HEADQUARTERS: THE OFFICE OF THE COMMISSIONER

FDA is a highly centralized administrative agency.

FDA is a highly centralized administrative agency. The Office of the Commissioner is structured with the goal of coordinating agency enforcement activity and public policy and ensuring consistency of approach between various agency components in their interpretation of scientific understanding, application of regulatory requirements, and exercise of discretion and judgment (see Figure 1). Simply put, the Office of the Commissioner is involved in every significant agency activity.

It is not uncommon for the Commissioner's office to be reorganized to reflect a particular administration's or a particular Commissioner's perception of a rather dramatic agency and preferred way of conducting business. For example, in July 2011, the restructuring included reshaping the office to allow it to better support the agency's core scientific and regulatory functions. To this end, the Commissioner established four "directorates" to report on and oversee the agency's core functions and responsibilities. The concept behind the restructuring was to unite programs that share common regulatory and scientific foundations. The substantive areas of focus for the four directorates are medical and tobacco products, globalization and import safety, foods, and administrative functions. Subsequent restructuring has confirmed the role of the directorates. The directorates are headed, respectively, by the Deputy Commissioner for Medical Products and Tobacco, the Deputy Commissioner for Global Regulatory Operations and Policy, the Deputy Commissioner for Foods, and the Chief Operating Officer. The directorates reflect the importance of Commissioner-level oversight of the agency's regulation of drugs, medical devices, tobacco, and foods; of the agency's efforts with respect to enforcement and globalization; and of the practical reality that such regulation requires critical decision making with respect to the use of available resources.

FDA's six Centers:
- *Center for Biologics Evaluation and Research (CBER)*
- *Center for Devices and Radiological Health (CDRH)*
- *Center for Drug Evaluation and Research (CDER)*
- *Center for Food Safety and Applied Nutrition (CFSAN)*
- *Center for Tobacco Products (CTP)*
- *Center for Veterinary Medicine (CVM)*

The Office of Regulatory Affairs (ORA) coordinates FDA's enforcement activities nationwide. The role of the deputy position for medical products and tobacco, like that of the similar position for foods, is described as "both an advocate and a support for Center directors." FDA Centers conduct the bulk of FDA's scientific and regulatory evaluations and interpret and apply FDA's statutory authority over food, drugs, tobacco, cosmetics, devices, and radiological products. The Centers are: the Center for Biologics Evaluation and Research (CBER), the Center for Devices and Radiological Health (CDRH), the Center for Veterinary Medicine (CVM), the Center for Drug Evaluation and Research (CDER), the Center for Food Safety and Applied Nutrition (CFSAN), and the Center for Tobacco Products (CTP). Enhancing the communication lines between the Office of the Commissioner and the Centers helps ensure that scientific issues are fully aired and understood.

Figure 1

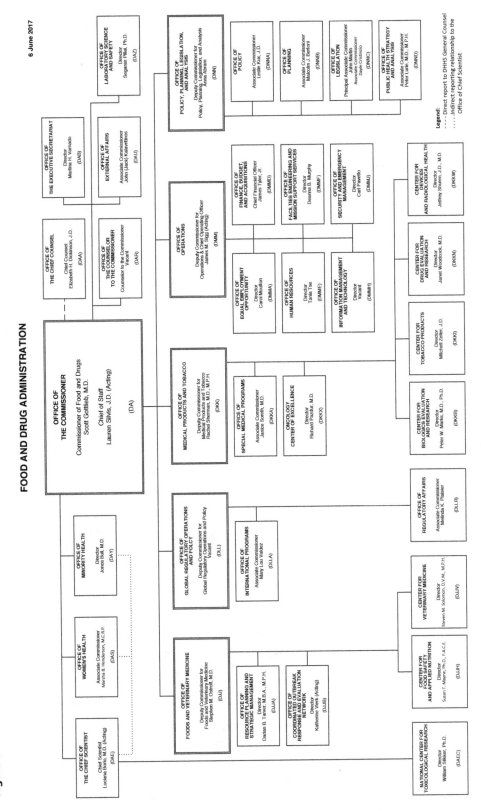

FOOD AND DRUG ADMINISTRATION

6 June 2017

A Closer Look at the Operation of FDA's Six Substantive Centers

Each substantive Center possesses the machinery of an administrative agency. Each Center has a Director and related hierarchy of managers. Moreover, each Center has a focal point for policy guidance, programs, and enforcement actions, as well as the necessary scientific capabilities to support policy and compliance activities.

Centers are active in responding to policies and programs suggested by the Office of the Commissioner or the executive branch. Nonetheless, the mainstay of most Centers' initiatives involves reviewing premarket applications; developing scientific and regulatory policy in the form of guidance documents or regulations; proactively and reactively addressing issues of potential public health concern; preventing, intervening, and responding to food-related risks; and ensuring compliance with the food adulteration and misbranding provisions of the FDCA. Thus, as a practical matter, the first stop in dealing with FDA is usually with the Center whose jurisdiction covers the substantive matter at issue. The Office of the Commissioner is unlikely to act in the absence of substantive input from a Center but, particularly in light of current restructuring in the Office of the Commissioner, the Commissioner may, although rarely, disagree with a Center's science-based analysis of an issue.

"The Field"

Although the field offices report to the Office of the Commissioner, they have traditionally served—and continue to serve—rather specialized functions related to enforcement of the FDCA and its implementing regulations. The "field" is divided into five regions, each responsible for a distinct part of the country. There are more than 20 "district" offices and over 100 additional resident inspection posts within the regions (see Figure 2).

A regional field office is responsible for agency activities within its boundary.

A regional field office is responsible for agency activities within its boundary. Its primary focus is to ensure that regulated industry within a given region complies with the laws and regulations enforced by the agency. Regional directors report to the Associate Commissioner of ORA who, in turn, reports to the Deputy Commissioner of Operations.

The district offices, as well as the much smaller resident inspection posts, perform the nuts-and-bolts, hands-on work. They inspect the facilities in which regulated products are prepared, packed, manufactured, processed, or held, and perform the initial task of evaluating compliance with agency criteria, standards, and regulations. These offices also work cooperatively with state, local,

Figure 2

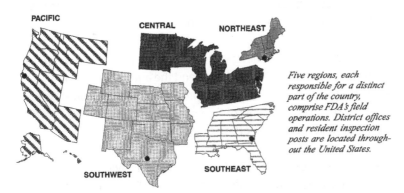

Five regions, each responsible for a distinct part of the country, comprise FDA's field operations. District offices and resident inspection posts are located throughout the United States.

and other federal agencies; encourage local consumer protection programs in areas related to agency-enforced laws and regulations; and provide valuable consumer education.

Field offices are also an important source of information for headquarters. They are often the first to identify new or emerging problems and trends, future program needs, and priorities. Moreover, they refine and improve existing analytical methodologies and explore and develop new monitoring systems (e.g., techniques to detect a specific contaminant in a food or drug product). The field offices also play a major role in managing product recalls, conducting follow-up checks to determine the effectiveness of a recall, and preventing recurring violations of the FDCA. The field recommends legal action to headquarters and to the Office of the Chief Counsel or, as necessary, to the U.S. Attorney in its area. A key role for the field involves providing extensive factual and evidentiary support in civil or criminal proceedings.

In May 2017, the Office of Regulatory Affairs announced a "program alignment" designed to mirror for regional and field offices the organizational model of the agency's Centers and the industries FDA regulates. In the new model, the entire reporting chain beginning with the field's inspection and compliance staff and ending with assistant commissioners in headquarters will specialize in and be dedicated to the regulation of the specific commodity (e.g., food, drugs, etc.) at issue.

The Office of the Chief Counsel

Although integral to the functioning of the agency, the Office of the Chief Counsel is not part of FDA. Rather the office is, technically, the Food and Drug Division of DHHS's Office of General Counsel. Nevertheless, for all practical purposes, the Office of the Chief Counsel generally has served as FDA's law firm

Although integral to the functioning of the agency, the Office of the Chief Counsel is not part of FDA.

and the Chief Counsel as the Commissioner's lawyer. The Chief Counsel position is currently a career, as opposed to a political, post. The position, however, has on occasion in the past been a political position.

The Office of the Chief Counsel reviews and evaluates the propriety of proposed agency actions to enforce the FDCA, helps defend the agency in litigation, works closely with the Centers in developing proposed and final regulations, and generally advises all components of the agency on the requirements of the law and the legal implications of an action or inaction.

The fundamental role of the Office of the Chief Counsel is to measure agency decision making by the prevailing legal standard.

Basically, the role the Office of the Chief Counsel serves in advising various components of the agency is to identify issues of law, policy, and fact that are likely to arise in the context of a given initiative and assess the lawfulness of—or perhaps, more precisely, the probability that the agency will prevail in—such issues. Simply put, the fundamental role of the Office of the Chief Counsel is to measure agency decision making by the prevailing legal standard.

So . . . How Does It All Work? A Hypothetical

The interplay among the various components of FDA perhaps can be made more concrete by resort to a hypothetical. Assume a producer of fresh-cut and packaged salad greens fails to follow good agricultural, good manufacturing practices, or preventive controls in the production of a large lot of product. Assume further that the failure causes an indeterminable number of packages of salad greens to be contaminated with a potentially harmful microorganism. Packages from the lot of salad greens at issue are shipped to retail stores in three states. In time, a few people who have consumed salad greens from packages from the lot in question begin to suffer adverse reactions.

Working independently, two healthcare providers send stool specimens to different clinical laboratories for analysis. In both cases, a strain of *Escherichia coli (E. coli)* is isolated. Both laboratories send the *E. coli* strain to separate public health laboratories that perform DNA finger-printing and submit the pattern to pulse-field gel electrophoresis (PFGE). Additional people become ill and similar testing occurs.

Connecticut is the first state to identify a cluster of *E. coli* cases with matching PFGE patterns. Connecticut health authorities notify the Centers for Disease Control and Prevention (CDC). CDC looks for the strain in other reports of possible outbreaks and quickly confirms matching patterns in the two other states. CDC contacts FDA's Office of Crisis Management, which begins coordinating the agency's internal and external investigational, scientific, and communication activities.

CFSAN, ORA, the Office of Public Affairs, and the two district offices having jurisdiction in the respective states all become involved. CDC works with the states and FDA to create a standard questionnaire and to develop a process for identifying and reporting cases. Working in cooperation with CDC, FDA districts coordinate investigations to gather information related to the illnesses and identify the possible source of contamination. Meanwhile the Commissioner's office has been preparing for media, consumer, and legislative inquiries and has designated an official in the Office of the Commissioner as the primary contact for CFSAN with respect to any new developments concerning the outbreaks.

CFSAN experts, working with CDC experts, identify an apparent association between a number of the outbreaks and consumption of the producer's salad greens. The applicable district office sends investigators to visit the producer's facility and inspect its records, equipment, processing line, and overall harvesting, shipping, cooling, and related practices. While that inspection is going on, an FDA laboratory analyst identifies a strain of *E. coli* in one of the open packages of salad greens retrieved by an agency investigator from the home of one of the outbreak victims. The strain matches the infectious strain reported by the state public health laboratories.

Officials in CFSAN immediately contact the chief executive officer (CEO) of the producer, inform him or her of the confirmatory laboratory results, and request the CEO to cease production of product and to begin a recall of all salad green products currently marketed. The CEO requests a short time to consider the information. CFSAN officials consult with the Office of the Chief Counsel, which in turn advises that based on the facts at hand, the Center is justified in immediately issuing a public alert on its own initiative and also, working through the FDA District Director in the district where the producer is located, to automatically detain the producer's salad greens in light of the credible evidence indicating that the food presents a threat of serious adverse health consequences. Notified of these developments, the CEO agrees to stop distribution and implement a recall immediately, accompanied by a press release. FDA investigators at the company's facility verify that the product was shipped to only three states and that, therefore, there is no need to alert public health counterparts in other states or in Canada and Mexico.

The immediate threat to health now avoided, officials in CFSAN and the Office of the Commissioner study the implications of the episode particularly in light of similar past episodes involving these products. Learnings from the episode may affect agency efforts to implement and enforce the preventive controls requirements of the Food Safety Modernization Act of 2011 and, accordingly, have the potential to influence agency rulemaking, guidance, and enforcement activities.

Meanwhile, the district, in a follow-up inspection of the facility, finds evidence that the producer had reason to suspect the contamination of its products but opted to distribute them. Working closely with the Office of the Chief Counsel and the Office of Criminal Investigations, the district helps develop a criminal action against the producer.

This hypothetical, although bereft of specifics, nevertheless reveals the coordinated approach that FDA routinely applies in handling such public health issues. Field, Center, Commissioner's office, and the Office of the Chief Counsel work together, combining their respective expertise to address not only the immediate problem but also long-term solutions to avoid or deter comparable threats to public health.

FDA's Administrative and Regulatory Tools and How It Uses Them

Rulemaking

Like all agencies, FDA has finite resources that force it to ask hard questions about the best way to regulate. Before 1970 most regulatory agencies like FDA answered the question in a traditional manner, emphasizing enforcement litigation against products, companies, or individuals in violation of the FDCA. There is merit to this approach—particularly for FDA. Because FDA has broad litigation authority, the agency can rely on that authority to bring an array of regulatory actions. It can invoke, for example, the seizure provisions of the act to promptly and efficiently withdraw violative products from the marketplace. In addition, the agency has statutory authority to enjoin manufacturers from producing and marketing violative products. Moreover, FDA has broad authority to recommend that the Department of Justice (DOJ) criminally prosecute, either as a misdemeanor or felony, or both, individuals involved in the interstate commerce of violative products.

As a regulatory tool, however, there can be practical drawbacks to enforcement litigation. It is time-consuming and resource intensive. It is reactive to a situation or problem. It can encourage a "cop" mentality as opposed to an objective, fact-driven assessment of how best to accomplish statutory and regulatory goals.

By the 1970s the complex issues accompanying the variety of products and the distinctive manufacturing disciplines FDA was charged to police prodded the agency to consider, in addition to litigation, proactive means of encouraging and accomplishing compliance. The primary tool the agency chose for this purpose was "informal" rulemaking. In the process FDA "pioneered" rulemaking as a regulatory tool.

FDA pioneered rulemaking as a regulatory tool.

FDA's statutory authority to conduct rulemaking is found in sections 701(a) and 701(e) of the FDCA. Section 701(e) contains "formal" rulemaking authority—authority that involves issuing regulations on the basis of a rulemaking record that may be tested in a quasi-judicial administrative proceeding. Simply put, elaborate procedural safeguards are built into section 701(e) of the act—in fact, the provisions in section 701(e) may be the most elaborate rulemaking procedures under which any federal agency operates.

In stark contrast to section 701(e), section 701(a) is a model of brevity. It reads, in full, as follows: "The authority to promulgate regulations for the efficient enforcement of this Act, except as otherwise provided in this section, is hereby vested in the Secretary."

Under this authority, FDA recognized it could achieve compliance by publishing regulations prescribing how firms interested in being in compliance in the first place could so conform. For example, instead of relying exclusively on seizing misbranded products, the agency recognized that it could publish regulations prescribing how to label a product—e.g., how to name a product; how to craft a principal display panel; how to phrase declarations concerning net weight, sodium content, etc. Instead of relying exclusively on injunctions to force manufacturers to manufacture a food or drug in an appropriate manner, the agency could promulgate regulations containing basic procedures to follow in manufacturing such a product and which, if followed, would enhance the likelihood that a product would not be found to be adulterated or misbranded. Instead of case-by-case consideration of the procedures used by a new drug developer for evaluating data, the agency could issue regulations describing the attributes of a well-controlled investigation, identifying requirements for informed consent, oversight by Institutional Review Boards, etc.

FDA's concept of rulemaking as a regulatory tool was premised on the fundamental notion that regulated industries would, if not welcome, at least follow guidance as to how to manufacture and market compliant, nonviolative products. The notion that an aggressive regulatory agency could enhance its ability to protect the public health by issuing guidance-based regulations was novel in the 1970s. What made the use of rulemaking truly "pioneering," however, was the weight that courts accorded to the agency's regulations.

An agency can issue interpretative or substantive rules.

This is an especially critical point. There are basically two kinds of regulations that an administrative agency can issue. One is "interpretative," the other "substantive." Interpretative rules or regulations are, for purposes of this discussion, synonymous; they contain the agency's view of what the statute means.

101

Enforcement, therefore, is hinged on whether the agency can establish that a particular statutory requirement has been violated. Although an interpretative rule may add persuasive insight to a court's interpretation of the statute, it lacks the force of law and courts are free to disagree with it. A substantive rule or regulation is quite different. It expands an existing substantive provision of law and specifies what that provision requires. If held to be a valid extension of the statutory scheme, a substantive regulation has the force and effect of law—thereby rendering an administrative agency, to an extent, a legislative power.

A string of court cases has recognized the substantive force of a regulation issued under section 701(a). The most notable of these is *Weinberger v. Hynson, Westcott & Dunning*, 412 U.S. 609 (1973), in which the Supreme Court upheld as substantive FDA's regulations defining the fundamental elements of what constitutes "substantial evidence" of effectiveness. By permitting FDA to adopt substantive rules delineating the contours of what constituted an adequate and well-controlled investigation, the court converted controversial questions of scientific fact that normally would be the subject of extensive litigation into the very narrow objective issue of whether a manufacturer complied with the regulation.

The validity of any FDA regulation may be tested in court.

The validity of any FDA regulation may be tested in court. In determining whether a regulation is appropriate, courts focus on whether the statutory scheme and the specific provisions cited by the agency justify the promulgation of the regulation. Such an inquiry focuses on not only the statutory language and purpose but also such practicalities as the types of enforcement problems that may be encountered and the type of supervision required to accomplish the goals of the FDCA. Moreover, a hallmark of any rulemaking is the "administrative record" compiled by the agency in support of the regulation. The administrative record includes comments received from the public on the agency's initial notice of its proposed regulation. In finalizing a rule, the agency must respond with a reasonable explanation as to why the regulation is legitimate, lawful, and supported by the facts.

One of FDA's most creative exercises of its substantive rulemaking authority involved its efforts to regulate the nutrition labeling of food. The FDCA did not mention the word "nutrition" until the passage in 1990 of the Nutrition Labeling and Education Act (NLEA). Nevertheless, nearly 20 years earlier, FDA had embarked on rulemaking initiatives that specifically defined when nutrition food labeling would be necessary, the required format for such information, and the criteria by which the adequacy of certain claims (e.g., "low sodium") would be judged. The promulgation of FDA's nutrition labeling regulations in the 1970s effectively prescribed—with the force and effect of law—how an entire industry had to label its products and formulate product claims. This type of rulemaking, as should be readily apparent, is far more efficient industry-wide as an enforcement tool than are individual lawsuits.

Today, FDA continues to rely on its substantive rulemaking authority. The internal process of issuing regulations is somewhat more cumbersome than it was in the 1970s. While the essential elements of informal notice and comment remain the same, the layers of review in the Office of the Commissioner, the Office of the Secretary of Health and Human Services, OMB, and, on occasion, in the White House are more numerous. Moreover, concerns such as environmental impacts, economic burdens, and paperwork reduction must now be taken into account in every major new regulatory proposal. Nevertheless, the point is as true today as it was decades ago: FDA's ability to issue substantive regulations has changed dramatically how it operates as an administrative agency.

Agency Guidance Documents

Although rulemaking in many ways remains the tool of choice to provide guidance to the regulated community and to gauge regulatory compliance, FDA more and more frequently today resorts to issuing less formal "guidance documents" to assist manufacturers in efficiently dealing with it on matters of mutual interest and concern. The purposes of such "guidance documents" are: 1) to provide assistance by clarifying requirements that have been imposed by Congress or issued by FDA in regulations, 2) to explain how compliance with those statutory and regulatory requirements may be achieved, and 3) to outline specific review and enforcement approaches so as to ensure that the agency acts in an effective, fair, and consistent manner.

Guidance documents are less formal and assist manufacturers by clarifying requirements, explaining compliance, and outlining specific review and enforcement approaches.

A guidance document, for example, may define what the agency considers to be the important characteristics of preclinical and clinical test procedures, manufacturing practices, and scientific protocols. Other guidance documents explain FDA's views on how to comply with relevant statutes and regulations, and how to avoid enforcement actions. CFSAN, for example, has issued guidance documents on issues such as how to submit a food additive petition, the types of changes that constitute a "major change" in an infant formula and thus require documented premarket notification and—with the passage of the NLEA—how to avoid misbranding a product. One of the most successful guidance documents is the agency's "Questions and Answers" publication addressing some of the more common issues raised by the agency's implementation of the NLEA.

FDA distinguishes between "Level 1" and "Level 2" guidance documents. Level 1 guidance documents include documents that set forth initial interpretations of statutory or regulatory requirements, or set forth changes in interpretation or policy that are of more than a minor nature (including complex scientific issues or highly controversial issues). Level 2 guidance documents set forth existing practices or minor changes in the interpretation of a policy.

Before FDA prepares a draft of a Level 1 guidance document, the agency often seeks or accepts early input from individuals or groups outside the agency via public meetings and workshops. After FDA prepares a draft Level 1 guidance, the agency publishes a notice in the *Federal Register* announcing that the draft guidance is available and inviting comment on it. If it wishes, FDA may hold public meetings on the draft guidance or present it to an advisory committee for review. After receiving and reviewing comments, the agency will prepare the final version of the document and publish a notice in the *Federal Register* announcing that the guidance document is available.

No such procedures attend the issuance of a Level 2 guidance. FDA may post and immediately implement a Level 2 guidance document and may request and accept comment.

Guidance documents do not establish legally enforceable rights or responsibilities, and are not legally binding on the public or the agency.

Guidance documents do not establish legally enforceable rights or responsibilities, and are not legally binding on the public or the agency. Rather, they explain how the agency believes relevant statutes and regulations apply to certain regulated activities. Because a guidance document represents the agency's current thinking on a given subject, FDA has formally committed to ensure that its staff does not deviate from it unless there is an appropriate justification and "appropriate supervisory concurrence." Agency guidances are available by request or over the Internet. When dealing with a Center on a particular issue, it is critical to ask whether a relevant guidance document exists.

In between regulations and guidance documents are "guidelines." For years, FDA relied on guidelines to refine and explain the principles and details in an existing regulation. Guidelines also have been used by the agency to lay out clinical test procedures, manufacturing practices, product standards, scientific protocols, ingredient specifications, and other technical or policy criteria. Because, however, the agency's position has been that a guideline represents the formal position of FDA and obligates the agency to follow it, the agency in recent years has placed far more time and resources into the preparation of guidance documents that do not carry such obligatory force.

Meetings

FDA officials want the agency to be as "transparent" as practicable.

FDA officials want the agency to be as "transparent" as practicable. This posture clearly has evolved over the years as the agency broadened from mere enforcement to helping ensure maximum voluntary compliance on the part of industry. This is not to say that FDA is not an aggressive enforcer when the situation merits; it is. But, in recent years the agency has made real efforts to communicate guiding criteria and standards to help industry steer clear of conduct that could give rise to enforcement-related concerns. In addition to regulations and guidance documents, meetings and correspondence are valuable ways the agency attempts to respond to industry questions, issues, and concerns. Meetings can be initiated either by industry or the agency. They may be private or public.

Before a meeting takes place, FDA generally wants the company or group to provide an agenda and a list of attendees. Minutes of every private meeting are prepared and placed on public review in the administrative file of the proceeding. Rather comprehensive regulations govern the conduct of any meeting with the agency. See 21 C.F.R. § 10.65.

Hearings

Another valuable regulatory tool is the administrative "hearing." FDA has extensive regulations governing the conduct of administrative hearings. Formal hearings involving the approval or withdrawal of a licensed product (e.g., a drug, a food additive, etc.) are conducted generally like formal trials (formal evidentiary public hearings, 21 C.F.R. Part 12) or like scientific boards of inquiry (public hearings before a public board of inquiry, 21 C.F.R. Part 13). Traditionally, these hearings, like most any form of litigation, have been both time consuming and resource intensive, and, as a result, have become increasingly rare as FDA and industry look to more efficient dispute resolution mechanisms.

Another valuable regulatory tool is the administrative "hearing."

Regulations also govern the procedures to be followed at hearings before the Commissioner or his or her delegate. Public hearings before the Commissioner have served, particularly in the last 15 years, to permit the agency to hear directly from public and industry sectors alike in various locations nationwide, and to collect informed scientific opinion regarding possible agency initiatives or requirements. In implementing the NLEA, for example, FDA held a series of nationwide hearings regarding the purpose of the food label, and the nature and extent of the nutrition information that should be required to appear on it. The agency also has held hearings on the risks presented by microbial contamination in the manufacture of food and possible procedures designed to prevent such contamination. This type of hearing provides a valuable mechanism for industry and the public to have input in agency policies and practices well before they have been decided.

AGENCY INTERACTION WITH OUTSIDE EXPERTS

Although FDA is a science-based organization possessing a great deal of expertise, outside expert advice has become increasingly critical to its decision making. In part, this is due to the fact that some of the laws administered by the agency (e.g., the Medical Device Amendments of 1976) require the use of outside expert advisory committees. But, in addition, the increasing complexity associated with advances in science and reduced internal resources for developing "in-house" expertise creates the need to include advice from "outside" experts. This heightened role of outside experts seems likely to increase in the future.

Two key sets of regulations govern FDA's "advisory" committees.

Two key sets of regulations govern FDA's "advisory" committees. The General Services Administration has published regulations that apply to all government advisory committees. See 41 C.F.R. Parts 105-154. These regulations set forth basic policies and procedures regarding the establishment, operation, termination, and control of advisory committees.

FDA's own regulations deal with basic administrative aspects that apply to the conduct of an advisory committee. See 21 C.F.R. Part 14. The regulations delineate meeting procedures: what portions of the committee proceedings can be "closed" to the public; the rules of general conduct for a hearing; the preparation of minutes and reports; the maintenance of transcripts; and the handling of public inquiries and requests for advisory committee recommendations. FDA's regulations require that members of an advisory committee must have diverse interests, education, training, and experience. They also describe the procedures for nominating voting and nonvoting members to "technical" and "nontechnical" committees. FDA treats all of its current advisory committees as technical committees, which is important because technical committees may have consumer or industry members. In any event, however, only technical experts can serve as voting members. On technical committees, nonvoting members are meant to serve as liaisons between the groups or constituencies they represent and the committee.

The responsibilities and powers of nonvoting members and voting members are similar. The primary difference between them is that a nonvoting member may vote only on procedural matters, such as the adoption of rules or the approval of minutes and future meeting dates. Moreover, a nonvoting member who represents industry, for example, may have access to data and information that constitute a trade secret, or confidential or commercial financial information, only if that member has been appointed as a special government employee.

While most members are physicians, committee memberships also generally include registered nurses, statisticians, epidemiologists, pharmacists, and pharmacologists.

FDA pays its advisory committee members a fixed daily rate when the committee meets, and also reimburses for travel, food, and lodging. While most members are physicians, committee memberships also generally include registered nurses, statisticians, epidemiologists, pharmacists, and pharmacologists. In addition to the expert members, one consumer representative and usually one industry representative serve on each committee.

Professional members are recruited through notices published at least once a year in the *Federal Register* and through other means, such as contacting professional organizations and medical schools. Nominations are reviewed by FDA staff and the Commissioner of Food and Drugs. A list of candidates is then submitted to the Secretary of the Department of Health and Human Services for final selection. Committee chairpersons are appointed from among the nominees; they are not elected by their committees. Committee members are subject to federal laws that prohibit them from taking part in any official action in which they have a financial interest. Members must file financial disclosure forms and declare in advance of a meeting any conflict of interest that exists.

FDA'S STANDING ADVISORY COMMITTEES
Office of the Commissioner
Science Board
Risk Communication Advisory Committee
Pediatric Advisory Committee
Center for Biologics Evaluation and Research
Allergenic Products Advisory Committee
Cellular, Tissue, and Gene Therapies Advisory Committee
Blood Products Advisory Committee
Transmissible Spongiform Encephalopathies Advisory Committee
Vaccines and Related Biological Products Advisory Committee
Center for Drug Evaluation and Research
Anesthetic and Life Support Drugs Advisory Committee
Antimicrobial Drugs Advisory Committee
Antiviral Drugs Advisory Committee
Arthritis Drugs Advisory Committee
Bone, Reproductive, and Urologic Drugs Advisory Committee
Cardiovascular and Renal Drugs Advisory Committee
Dermatologic and Ophthalmic Drugs Advisory Committee
Drug Safety and Risk Management Committee
Endocrinologic and Metabolic Drugs Advisory Committee
Gastrointestinal Drugs Advisory Committee
Medical Imaging Drugs Advisory Committee
Nonprescription Drugs Advisory Committee
Oncologic Drugs Advisory Committee
Peripheral and Central Nervous System Drugs Advisory Committee
Pharmaceutical Science and Clinical Pharmacology Advisory Committee
Pharmacy Compounding Advisory Committee
Psychopharmacologic Drugs Advisory Committee
Pulmonary-Allergy Drugs Advisory Committee
Center for Food Safety and Applied Nutrition
Food Advisory Committee
Center for Devices and Radiological Health
Device Good Manufacturing Practice (GMP) Advisory Committee
National Mammography Quality Assurance Advisory Committee
Medical Device Advisory Committee

– Anesthesiology and Respiratory Therapy Devices Panel
– Circulatory System Devices Panel
– Clinical Chemistry and Clinical Toxicology Devices Panel
– Dental Products Panel
– Ear, Nose, and Throat Devices Panel
– Gastroenterology and Urology Devices Panel
– General and Plastic Surgery Devices Panel
– General Hospital and Personal Use Devices Panel
– Hematology and Pathology Devices Panel
– Immunology Devices Panel
– Medical Devices Dispute Resolution Panel
– Microbiology Devices Panel
– Molecular and Clinical Genetics Panel
– Neurological Devices Panel
– Obstetrics and Gynecology Devices Panel
– Ophthalmic Devices Panel
– Orthopaedic and Rehabilitation Devices Panel
– Radiological Devices Panel
Radiation-Emitting Products Advisory Committee
Technical Electronic Product Radiation Safety Standards Committee
Center for Tobacco Products
Tobacco Products Scientific Advisory Committee
Center for Veterinary Medicine
Veterinary Medicine Advisory Committee
National Center for Toxicological Research
Contaminants Committee (Ranch Hand Committee)
Science Advisory Board

The size of FDA committees ranges from nine to 15 members. The committees vary in the extent to which they are used. The average number of meetings per year per advisory committee is less than two, but that is misleading as one committee could have six meetings and another none.

Committee agendas are created by FDA staff. Most commonly, committees are asked to recommend whether a product should be approved. They also may be asked for advice on policy. A *Federal Register* notice announcing the meeting is published in advance of the date, along with the products or issues to be considered.

Companies prepare extensively to present to advisory committees because the outcome of the committee vote is extremely important to the fate of the product at issue. In the case of a product review, usually both FDA and the manufacturer present their data or analysis. Any member of the public who has so requested also may make a presentation. The presentations, the committee's deliberations, and the final vote—in short, every aspect of the meeting—are on the record. A transcript of the record is made available.

Companies prepare extensively to present to advisory committees because the outcome of the committee vote is extremely important to the fate of the product at issue.

Once a committee has voted and submitted its advice to FDA, the agency is free to follow, or not follow, the advice. In 2007, in an effort to maximize the integrity, consistency, and utility of advisory committee voting results, FDA issued a guidance recommending that advisory committees adhere to a process of simultaneous voting in which all members vote at once. According to the guidance, the results of the vote should be announced immediately and how each voted should become part of the public administrative record.

In recent years, the integrity of advisory committees has become increasingly a matter of public focus and attention. The reason is obvious: in the wake of public concern over issues involving the safety of FDA-approved products (e.g., Vioxx), it is considered essential that the input from the agency's expert advisory committees help ensure the credibility of agency decision making. As a result, the disclosure of financial interest information has received legislative as well as agency attention. Effective in October 2007, section 712(c)(2) of the FDCA prohibits advisory committee members from participating in a committee matter if they or any immediate family members have a financial interest that could be affected by the advice proffered. Disqualification may be avoided if FDA grants a waiver. Section 712 and 18 U.S.C. § 208 specify the circumstances under which FDA may grant participation. Section 712 of the FDCA also requires that FDA disclose on its website the type, nature, and magnitude of the financial interests of each advisory committee member who has received a waiver.

Advisory committee members are prohibited from participating in a committee matter if they or any immediate family members have a financial interest that could be affected by the advice proffered.

Based on section 712, FDA issued a guidance detailing procedures for determining whether a conflict of interest exists and, as a result, the eligibility of a candidate to participate in an advisory committee's consideration of a particular matter. The guidance sets out a rather stringent policy for considering eligibility for participation than is permitted under the current legal authorities. Under the approach recommended in the guidance, a member possessing a conflict of interest may participate only in the narrowest of circumstances: where the potential conflict is minimal and the member's expertise is needed for the committee's deliberations.

Specifically, if an individual has a disqualifying financial interest, the combined value of which exceeds $50,000, the member "generally" would not be permitted to participate in an advisory committee meeting on the particular matter in which the conflict arises regardless of the need for the member's expertise. If the disqualifying financial interests are $50,000 or less, the member would be eligible to participate only if he or she meets the applicable statutory standard for participation—the need for his or her services outweighs the potential conflict. Third, if the standard for participation is met, the individual's participation is to be limited to nonvoting. Moreover, in cases where there may be a perception of a conflict of interest, FDA reserves the right to limit participation even though full participation would be permitted under the applicable laws.

In addition to standing advisory committees, FDA has submitted with some regularity over the last two decades projects or problems to outside experts for their consideration and recommended resolution. The agency on occasion has used such highly regarded bodies as the National Academy of Sciences, the National Research Council, and the Life Sciences Research Office of the Federation of American Societies for Experimental Biology. Requests for such outside help, as well as all the supporting, nonproprietary information reviewed by the outside group, and the final recommendations of such a group, are publicly available and open to public comment.

Agencies with which FDA works closely:

- *U.S. Department of Agriculture*
- *Environmental Protection Agency*
- *Federal Trade Commission*
- *Consumer Product Safety Commission*
- *Drug Enforcement Administration*
- *National Institute on Drug Abuse*
- *Department of State*
- *U.S. Customs Service*
- *Department of Justice*

How FDA Deals and Interacts With Other Federal Agencies

Introduction

Although the laws that FDA administers provide generally comprehensive authority to regulate products, the agency's authority is not always exclusive. In some cases its jurisdiction may overlap with other federal agencies. In other cases, the agency's jurisdiction may simply be complementary. And, in still other cases, its statutory authority may conflict with that of other agencies.

Although these circumstances easily could lead to chaos, they have not. For decades, FDA has relied on agreements and memoranda of understanding (MOUs) to clarify regulatory responsibilities, areas of primary jurisdiction, reciprocal regulatory and information-based roles, and funding responsibilities with other agencies involved in aspects of food and drug regulation.

U.S. Department of Agriculture

Historically, no agency is closer to FDA than USDA. As noted earlier, FDA's predecessor, the Bureau of Chemistry, originated in USDA and undertook its food and drug responsibilities upon enactment of the Pure Food and Drugs Act of 1906.

Although the bureau eventually evolved into the Food and Drug Administration in 1930, it remained part of USDA until 1940. Thereupon, FDA became part of the Federal Security Agency which, in turn, became the Department of Health, Education and Welfare and then, as it is now, DHHS.

USDA continues to have broad authority over the food supply, including the inspection of meat and poultry and the labeling of food products containing meat or poultry. USDA also inspects and grades fresh fruits, vegetables, and grains.

USDA has broad authority over the food supply, including the inspection of meat and poultry and the labeling of food products containing meat or poultry.

FDA and USDA have entered into scores of MOUs. For example, while FDA has broad authority over the safety and labeling of food, including fresh fruits and vegetables, USDA's Agricultural Marketing Service (AMS) carries out a number of functions designed to aid in the efficient marketing of agricultural products. AMS develops commercial grade standards and specifications for foods, and the rendering of inspection and grading services to producers, processors, shippers, buyers, or other interested parties.

MOUs between the two agencies commit AMS to advising FDA of all the food processing and packaging plants operating under AMS supervision, and to report to FDA, for possible enforcement, any processor or packer that has not corrected objectionable conditions found to exist by FDA and who otherwise, based upon AMS's first-hand information, may not have the capability to consistently produce and market quality food. In turn, FDA agrees to work closely with AMS inspectors and cooperate with them in their efforts to grade and inspect produce. Similar agreements exist between FDA and USDA's Animal and Plant Health Inspection Service, Food Safety and Inspection Service (FSIS), and, concerning public education initiatives, the USDA itself.

FSIS and FDA also coordinate efforts in the meat and seafood industries to curtail the contamination of meat, poultry, and fish products from harmful microorganisms. The agencies have worked extensively to develop consistent, forward-looking Hazard Analysis and Critical Control Point (HACCP) procedures designed to ensure the safest possible food supply. In accomplishing these ends, there has been a significant exchange between the agencies of scientific data and information, as well as expertise.

USDA, FDA, and the Environmental Protection Agency (EPA) coordinate the agencies' respective regulatory authorities over products developed by plant biotechnology, and USDA and FDA coordinate their respective authorities with respect to products developed by animal biotechnology techniques. In 1986 the agencies established the Coordinated Framework for regulating genetically engineered organisms and products. This coordination has been essential in the overall efforts of the federal government to encourage new technologies while at the same time to ensure that every aspect of the use of such technology, from initial investigation to the ultimate production of a consumer product, is carefully and appropriately regulated.

In light of the numerous "overlapping" opportunities in the regulation of food, the notion of vesting one agency with all federal responsibility for food regulation has been considered frequently. Regardless of how this organizational issue is eventually resolved, the cooperative efforts between FDA and USDA have unquestionably formed a foundation for meeting future regulatory challenges involving the evaluation of scientific data, the accommodation of new innovations, and how the public health goals of the country's various food safety laws can be applied in a meaningful fashion.

To this end, key provisions of the FDA Food Safety Modernization Act (FSMA) underscore the need for coordination and communication between FDA and USDA if nationwide, and in fact global, food safety concerns are addressed and the nation's infrastructure for assuring food safety is strengthened. FSMA calls for numerous collaborative efforts between FDA and USDA in order to ensure FDA's scope of regulation is as comprehensive and meaningful as possible. For example, section 418 of the FDCA now requires FDA to consult with USDA before conducting a study of the incidence of foodborne illness. Similarly, in section 419, FDA is instructed to coordinate with USDA prior to establishing science-based, minimum standards for the safe production and harvesting of produce. And, in furtherance of this purpose, FDA is to consult with USDA prior to establishing good agricultural practices and guidances with respect to the safe production of fresh fruits and vegetables. Section 420 provides that FDA must, upon consultation with USDA, promulgate regulations to protect against the intentional adulteration of food. Moreover, FDA must work with USDA to develop and submit to Congress a comprehensive "food defense" strategy to ensure an efficient response to agriculture and food emergencies. Clearly, a strong working relationship between FDA and USDA and information sharing, collaboration, and meaningful communication between the two agencies are critical to the country's national and global goals of food safety.

Environmental Protection Agency

EPA administers two laws that have direct impact on the food supply: the Federal Insecticide, Fungicide, and Rodenticide Act (FIFRA) and the Safe Drinking Water Act (SDWA). FIFRA governs the registration of pesticides. Without such registration, a pesticide cannot be sold lawfully for use in the United States. A major part of the registration process for food use pesticides involves tolerance setting, which is conducted under section 408 of the FDCA. EPA was vested with this tolerance-setting authority in 1970 pursuant to a reorganization plan. As a result, EPA determines the safety of pesticide residues in food, while FDA takes enforcement action under the FDCA for products violating the standards established by EPA.

Under the SDWA, EPA controls contaminants in drinking water that may have adverse effects on the public health. The SDWA gives exclusive control over the safety of public water to EPA. FDA, however, always has considered drinking water to be a food under section 201(f) of the FDCA. Through an MOU both parties agreed that the passage of the SDWA in 1974 implicitly repealed FDA's authority under the FDCA over water used for drinking purposes (although section 410 of the FDCA makes clear that FDA retains exclusive control over bottled drinking water). The MOU goes on to establish that EPA in essence controls all aspects related to the safety of water prior to the water coming out of a public tap, and that water used as an ingredient in food or in food processing remains subject to the FDCA.

FDA and EPA also share authority over chemical additives. The Toxic Substances Control Act (TSCA) gives EPA authority to regulate mixtures of chemical substances and articles containing such substances or mixtures. EPA can require testing of a chemical substance or a mixture based on possible unreasonable risk of injury to health or the environment. Under TSCA, for example, EPA regulates the addition of direct and indirect additives to drinking water. The agencies have agreed that the appropriate interpretation of TSCA excludes from the definition of "chemical substance" products regulated under the FDCA.

The commonality of safety concerns presented by the products regulated by each agency (the toxicity of pesticides, chemical substances, and additives to food or water) has resulted in significant efforts between FDA and EPA to coordinate their scientific approaches to assessing the safety of such substances. MOUs provide general guidance and encouragement to the agencies in accomplishing such harmonization. Nevertheless, differences in opinion as to how most accurately to assess risks do exist between the two agencies. For example, only recently, after years of debate, FDA decided to accept EPA's use of "scaling factors" in extrapolating the results of data from laboratory animals to assess their significance and relevance to the health of people.

The Federal Trade Commission

FDA and the Federal Trade Commission (FTC) possess concurrent jurisdiction over the labeling and advertising of foods, over-the-counter drugs, veterinary drugs and related products, and cosmetics. The two agencies have agreed that the FTC should exercise primary responsibility concerning the advertising of such products, and that FDA will do likewise for matters relating to product labeling. Accordingly, under the Federal Trade Commission Act (FTC Act), the FTC investigates and prosecutes "unfair methods of competition" including "unfair or deceptive practices" and "methods of competition." The FTC's goal

FTC and FDA
FTC and FDA work together under a 1971 liaison agreement.

is to protect consumers from unfair and deceptive advertising and marketing practices, and to prohibit unfair trade practices that could impact on competitive markets and business relationships. FDA's jurisdiction over product labeling is more consumer oriented, and is designed to ensure that products and all the printed graphic or related material that may accompany their sale do not mislead consumers and are presented in a truthful, unambiguous manner.

By virtue of a "liaison agreement" entered into in 1971, the agencies coordinate their activities, and share information and expertise. The arrangement, however, is complicated by the fact that substantiation requirements for labeling under the FDCA are more stringent than those for advertising under the FTC Act. Thus, on occasion, the FTC is placed in the position of appearing more lax in its enforcement posture when compared to FDA. The FTC's unique enforcement powers, however, which include adjudication by the five FTC commissioners as well as the ability to issue cease and desist orders enforceable by injunctive, civil penalty, and criminal contempt proceedings, compensate for whatever lesser substantiation standard the agency may possess.

In many cases, the FTC's follow through in enforcing advertising is important, if not essential, to FDA initiatives over labeling. For example, FDA's comprehensive efforts to implement the NLEA and limit the type of health-related information that may be communicated about the relationship between a component of a diet and the prevention of a disease or health-related condition would be severely diluted if the FTC did not endorse a comparable regulatory philosophy with regard to the advertising of such food components. Working together on this issue the two agencies have developed a comprehensive approach to regulating and ensuring the comparability of health claims on food.

The FTC has also played an important role in helping FDA adapt to judicial precedent requiring FDA to consider the commercial speech implications of any regulatory effort with respect to product misbranding. The FTC's history of relying upon 1) consumer survey data to show that a given advertising claim has the potential to mislead and 2) disclaimers to cure any such potential has provided a helpful framework for FDA in considering enforcement and regulatory policy concerning the lawful contours of product promotion.

Consumer Product Safety Commission

The Consumer Product Safety Act protects the public from unreasonable risks of injury associated with consumer products.

The Consumer Product Safety Act protects the public from unreasonable risks of injury associated with consumer products. The Consumer Product Safety Commission (CPSC) was formally established in 1973. A major component was FDA's Bureau of Product Safety, established in the early 1960s to administer provisions of the Federal Hazardous Substances Act relating to the labeling of products presenting consumer hazards.

In spite of, or perhaps because of, the etiology of CPSC, disputes arose quite ear-ly between the two agencies over jurisdictional points. Whereas FDA believed that a container having a food contact surface should be regulated by FDA as a "food additive" (i.e., because of the potential for migration of a component to the food), CPSC considered such an article within its jurisdiction as a consumer commodity. After much discussion, the agencies agreed to draw the jurisdic-tional line on the basis of whether an article could cause contamination or spoil-age of food as a result of migrating to or otherwise becoming a component of food. Under this approach, home canning equipment that fails to provide a seal adequate to keep air from passing into stored food is regulated by CPSC, as are pressure cookers, slow cookers, refrigerators, or freezers that fail to perform at proper temperatures thereby rendering food unfit to eat. A food container that presents the possibility of components migrating into the food itself (e.g., lead leeching from the soldered lining of a tin can into the food or beverage) would be regulated by FDA as a food contaminant or additive.

This focus on the "mechanical" versus "component" nature of a hazardous sub-stance has come to form the fundamental distinction between CPSC and FDA jurisdiction. Thus, FDA retains its basic jurisdiction over foods, medical devices, drugs, and cosmetics except in those cases where the container of such articles possesses a defect such as sharp edges or a propensity to explode or break. Such situations are regulated by CPSC.

Disputes between the two agencies continue on occasion, and are resolved either informally or through the somewhat time-consuming process of issuing an advisory opinion. In close-call situations, FDA generally prevails, perhaps be-cause of its more efficient and successful track record in enforcement litigation.

The Drug Enforcement Administration, the National Institute on Drug Abuse, and the U.S. Department of State

Federal regulation of drugs of abuse is a shared enterprise among four distinct entities: FDA, the Drug Enforcement Administration (DEA), National Institute on Drug Abuse (NIDA), and the U.S. Department of State (DoS). One area of joint en-terprise is establishing "schedules" for drugs of abuse. The "schedules" establish the level of control in the manufacture, importing, prescribing, or handling of drugs of abuse.

FDA, DEA, NIDA, and DoS share in the federal regulation of drugs of abuse.

Acting on behalf of the Secretary of the Department of Health and Human Services, FDA has the authority to make domestic drug scheduling recom-mendations, which, in turn, determine the level of control that will accom-pany an addictive substance under the Controlled Substances Act. DEA, however, conducts the relevant scheduling proceedings and administers the scheduling, amendment, or repeal of any domestic classification. NIDA, by formal agreement with FDA, provides FDA with recommendations and views regarding the addictive potential of a drug substance. FDA, DEA, and DoS collaborate on issues relating to the administration of international treaties governing the scheduling and classification of narcotics and psychotropic drugs. FDA, NIDA, and DEA also collaborate in administering provisions of the Narcotic Addict Treatment Act that establishes a basis for control of narcotic addict treatment programs to prevent the diversion of narcotic drugs, and to ensure proper treatment of narcotic addicts. All of these relationships are spelled out in MOUs.

Responsibility among the agencies in these areas is generally well defined. FDA and NIDA limit their focus to scientific factors relating to the safety, pharmacology, and addiction potential. DEA implements the scientific findings of FDA and NIDA, and conducts comprehensive enforcement of the control, distribution, and diversion of scheduled substances. In the context of narcotic addict treatment programs, including methadone, FDA and DEA work closely together, with FDA obtaining DEA approval prior to authorizing any treatment program. Both FDA and DEA maintain the authority to deny or revoke approval of a treatment program independent of each other.

U.S. Customs Service

Perhaps in no other area of food and drug regulation does FDA have broader authority than it does over imported products.

Perhaps in no other area of food and drug regulation does FDA have broader authority than it does over imported products. FDA exercises that authority in conjunction and cooperation with the U.S. Customs Service. Section 801(a) of the FDCA permits FDA to refuse admission to an imported article if "it appears" that the article is in violation of the act. FDA has no burden to prove that a product for import actually violates the act. The fundamental test for refusal merely rests upon the "appearance" of a violation—a standard that, when considered literally, is impossible for the agency not to meet should it believe a product to be violative.

Customs' authority over imports arises under the Tariff Act of 1930 as well as under section 801. Section 801 vests the Secretary of the Treasury with the authority to deliver samples of imported products to FDA for analysis. In actual practice, FDA personnel at most ports collect the samples, issue the appropriate notice of sampling and, where applicable, having determined that an article is in violation and may not be brought into compliance, issue a refusal notice. If FDA does not have the personnel to carry out these functions, Customs will do so in close cooperation with agency officials.

In 1979, Customs and FDA entered into an MOU formalizing this process, and delegating to FDA the authority to collect samples, issue notices of sampling, and issue notices of refusal of admission. The MOU permits designation of FDA employees as Customs officers. If an importer wishes to recondition a violative product or to contest a refusal of admission, a bond must be filed. Only Customs can issue the bond. Although FDA can admit a product to import, Customs still must release the product for entry into the market.

Policing the safety of imported food is perhaps FDA's most daunting job. Currently, more than $65 billion worth of food products is imported annually. The sheer volume precludes inspection of every imported product and, as a practical matter, demands the cooperation FDA and the Customs Service has forged. The problems presented by potentially violative products being introduced through import regularly invite congressional scrutiny of FDA actions and consideration of ways, usually through greater resources, to augment FDA's and the Customs Service's abilities to protect the public from risks presented by imported products.

Notably, in 2002 Congress passed legislation designed to help reduce the ability of international terrorists to contaminate foods imported into the United States. The legislation requires food importers to provide FDA with advance notice of shipments of human and animal food imported or offered for import into the United States. This advance information permits FDA, in conjunction with U.S. Customs, to channel resources and target inspections—a necessity in light of the fact that every day FDA receives approximately 25,000 notifications with respect to incoming shipments of food. The legislation also authorizes FDA to ask Customs to institute a temporary hold for 24 hours on any food offered for import if FDA has credible evidence or information indicating that the food presents a threat of serious adverse harm and FDA is unable to immediately inspect or examine the food.

In sum, as a legal—and practical—matter, import issues demand daily cooperation between FDA and Customs. The case can be made that, in light of the volume of FDA-regulated products imported annually, coordination between the two agencies is more crucial to the public health than the coordination between FDA and any other agency.

Department of Justice

FDA does not possess independent authority to represent itself in judicial proceedings. As is the case with most other federal agencies, FDA is represented in court by DOJ. DOJ's Office of Consumer Litigation is the primary overseer of agency-related litigation—litigation that may be either

Going to Court
FDA cannot go to court itself; it is always represented by the Department of Justice.

enforcement-based (i.e., brought by the government) or defensive in nature. Because of the frequent science-based expertise that comes into play in FDA-related litigation, DOJ has historically and continues to welcome participation by lawyers from FDA's Office of the Chief Counsel in the conduct of such litigation. Although occasionally characterized by differences in litigation strategy or assessments of legal empowerment, FDA and DOJ generally have worked well together in defending agency actions and in enforcing the provisions of the FDCA—as the agency's successful litigation track record bears out.

Centers for Disease Control and Prevention

FDA's sister agency, CDC, plays an important complementary and nonregulatory public health role.

Although FDA unquestionably has the lead responsibility within DHHS for ensuring the safety of food and the safety and effectiveness of drugs and devices, FDA's sister agency, CDC, has an important complementary and nonregulatory public health role. As the lead federal agency for conducting disease surveillance, CDC monitors the occurrence of illness and outbreaks in the United States attributable to food and other FDA-regulated products. The disease surveillance systems coordinated by CDC constitute an essential information network for early warnings about dangers presented by regulated products.

With respect to food in particular, CDC's surveillance systems are helpful in measuring federal, state, and local initiatives to reduce foodborne illness. Moreover, CDC's surveillance systems are critical indicators of new and changing patterns of foodborne illness. CDC, time and again, has been able to promptly alert FDA of products implicated in foodborne disease and has provided both agencies with expert scientific opinion on the effectiveness of foodborne disease prevention strategies.

Recognizing the unique expertise of CDC, FSMA provides explicit direction to CDC to take a lead role in food safety surveillance of foodborne illness outbreaks.

Recognizing the unique expertise of CDC, FSMA provides explicit direction to CDC to take a lead role in food safety surveillance of foodborne illness outbreaks. Section 205(a) of FSMA defines "food-borne illness outbreak" in as broad terms as possible: "the occurrence of two or more cases of a similar illness resulting from the ingestion of a certain food." Paragraph (b) requires CDC to "enhance food-borne illness surveillance systems" and to improve the collection, analysis, reporting, and usefulness of data on foodborne illnesses. As a practical matter, CDC has performed these functions for years without the specific authorization FSMA now provides. CDC is now statutorily empowered to take the lead in coordinating federal, state, and local foodborne surveillance systems, including complaint systems, and increasing participation in national networks of public health and food regulatory agencies and laboratories. CDC is also required to facilitate the sharing of surveillance information, develop improved epidemiological tools, obtain quality exposure data and microbiological methods for classifying cases, augment such systems to improve attribution of a foodborne illness outbreak to a specific food, and expand the capacity of such systems to identify new or rarely documented cases of foodborne illness.

CDC's role in providing critical expertise with respect to disease control and prevention will only increase in the coming years. With that increased role, however, comes the potential for the two agencies to hold inconsistent or divergent positions. Ultimately, any FDA regulatory action based on a potential public health threat identified by CDC must be evaluated in light of the governing legal standards FDA is charged to enforce.

Because it is not a regulatory agency, however, CDC is unconstrained by statutory burdens of proof and is free to opine on the extent and severity of potential hazards it defines. Apparent, or real, conflicts between the two agencies can arise. Consider, for example, the use of the compound Bisphenol A (BPA) in plastic bottles. FDA initially advised that the food contact uses of BPA were "safe" within the meaning of existing regulatory standards. CDC, on the other hand, took the more aggressive public position that more study and investigation are needed to assess whether BPA, which may have hormone-like effects on the reproductive system, is not, in fact, injuring consumers. Upon additional review, FDA concluded that BPA is safe at the levels currently being used in foods. The upshot of the difference in views between CDC and FDA and the attending publicity was public confusion and concern. The extent to which the two agencies work together to harmonize discordant views and, where such views remain at odds, to help educate consumers as to why each view is responsibly held, is a coordination goal worthy of attention.

Other Agencies

Other agencies play critical roles in FDA's ability to efficiently exercise its jurisdiction. FDA has developed MOUs or agreements with these agencies to ensure cooperation, including the exchange of scientific information and investigative evidence. These other agencies and their areas of overlapping interests include the Nuclear Regulatory Commission (licensing and regulation of the nuclear industry, and knowledge and information regarding radiation); the Federal Bureau of Investigation (Federal Anti-tampering Act implementation); the National Marine Fisheries Service (voluntary seafood inspection program); the Department of Homeland Security (bioterrorism concerns); and the Bureau of Alcohol, Tobacco and Firearms (the regulation of alcoholic beverages and tobacco).

FDA and Congress

For any federal agency, Congress basically has three distinct functions: legislative (the development, modification, or repeal of legislation); oversight (overseeing how the agency is administering its legislative authority); and appropriations (funding agency programs).

Particularly within the last two decades, FDA has paid increasing attention to managing its relations with Congress. The Office of Legislation (OL) in the Office of the Commissioner is the agency's primary liaison with Capitol Hill. OL initiates, coordinates, and provides in-depth analyses of agency legislative needs and prepares supporting documents and position papers not only for the Commissioner and agency officials but also for Congress and OMB. A large part of OL activities also involves responding to congressional and legislative inquiries—inquiries that from time to time may involve sensitive correspondence critical of agency action or inaction. In cooperation with the FDA Centers, OL coordinates hearings before Congress and coordinates briefings with congressional members and staff.

FDA decisions affect, sometimes dramatically, discrete constituencies. As a result, FDA issues are often lightning rods for congressional attention. The resulting congressional oversight hearings can be contentious affairs that can affect the course of agency regulation and decision making. Saccharin, infant formulas, AIDS treatments, dietary supplements, the pace of product approvals, tobacco, and numerous other issues have been the subject of high-publicity, high-profile, and intense congressional scrutiny. FDA takes these encounters seriously and treats them with enormous care. A large part of FDA's role at any congressional hearing involves education—concise, clear explanations of the roles scientific data, public policy, and legal requirements have in the melding of its positions, decisions, and practices.

Several House and Senate committees have a degree of jurisdiction over FDA activity. As a vestige of FDA's days as part of USDA, the Agricultural Subcommittees of the House and Senate Appropriations Committees continue to review and determine FDA's annual appropriation. The agency's authorizing committees, however, are the House Committee on Energy and Commerce and the Senate Committee on Labor and Human Resources. The House Subcommittee on Oversight and Investigations and the Subcommittee on Health and the Environment traditionally have been very active in surveying and directing agency activity. Other committees with FDA-related responsibilities include, in the Senate, the Committee on Agriculture, Nutrition, and Forestry and the Committee on Governmental Affairs and, in the House of Representatives, the Committee on Agriculture, the Committee on Government Operations, the Committee on Merchant Marine and Fisheries, the Committee on Science, Space and Technology, and the Committee on Small Business.

Another feature of FDA's congressional relations involves the Government Accountability Office (GAO), formerly known as the General Accounting Office. Since the early 1970s, GAO has been called upon by Congress to investigate and report back to Congress on an array of FDA-related matters. As a result, a significant part of FDA's congressional activity is spent in cooperation with GAO in its investigations. OLA coordinates agency responses and serves as the primary liaison with GAO.

FDA and Its Relations With the States

FDA's ability to efficiently regulate hinges to a certain extent on its relationship with state and local authorities. Although FDA possesses the lion's share of regulatory authority, states nevertheless play an important role in public health protection. Every state has a food and drug act, in most cases patterned quite closely upon the FDCA. Moreover, local authorities may have specific regulations or ordinances governing product labeling, weight, and related attributes.

Every state has a food and drug act, in most cases patterned quite closely upon the FDCA.

The Association of Food and Drug Officials of the United States and the Association of Official Analytical Chemists generally work closely with FDA to accomplish the public health protection goals of both the FDCA and its state counterparts. State food and drug officials often are trained by FDA and, in return, provide valuable service to FDA in enforcing provisions of the FDCA. In the food area, for example, an extensive array of model codes governing the sanitation of milk and other retail foods characterize the cooperation between FDA and state officials. In general, FDA prepares the model codes and ensures that they contain the latest and best scientifically based advice about food safety issues. The agency also helps implement the codes at the state level. These codes recognize that thousands of local and state agencies assume the frontline responsibility for inspecting and enforcing food safety laws.

In recent years FDA has intensified these initiatives with the development of a model Food Code designed to prevent foodborne illness. Although neither federal law nor federal regulation, the Food Code provides the states with FDA's best advice for a uniform system of regulation to ensure that food is safe and properly protected at the retail and food service level.

FDA's substantive licensing decisions concerning food additives, drugs, and medical devices generally are deferred to by the states. From time to time a state (e.g., California, under its ballot referendum legislation Proposition 65)

FDA's substantive licensing decisions concerning food additives, drugs, and medical devices generally are deferred to by the states.

may wish to impose an additional requirement, such as a warning, on an FDA authorized product—but this is rare.

Under the NLEA and the Safe Medical Device Amendments of 1990, FDA possesses express preemption authority over inconsistent state requirements. The agency also has extensive implied preemption authority under the Supremacy Clause and the Commerce Clause of the U.S. Constitution. The agency, however, rarely seeks to exercise its preemptive authority over state actions. The agency's policy regarding preemption reflects a general presumption against preemption, and favors working together with state authorities to make the state and federal schemes at issue consistent with one another. On occasion these efforts have not been successful and the agency has preempted with regular success, thereby rendering null and void inconsistent state requirements or activities (e.g., state efforts to regulate imitation food labeling in a manner inconsistent with FDA's nationwide efforts have been found, by two U.S. Courts of Appeals, to be preempted).

Part of FDA's deference to and willingness to work with states, and thereby avoid preemption, is grounded in the recognition that states provide FDA needed support in conducting regulated facility and manufacture inspections, in accomplishing significant product recalls, and in collecting valuable enforcement- and compliance-related information (the nature and extent of these various state activities are contained in scores of MOUs with the agency). These examples of state assistance provide very real deterrents to actions by FDA—like preemption—that could be viewed as being meaningfully at odds with long-term federal and state relations.

FDA's International Relations

For years FDA has inspected foreign new drug manufacturers who wish to market their products in the United States, processed and granted approvals for the export of investigational new drugs, negotiated MOUs on regulatory matters and agreements with foreign governments, and conducted international training programs and conferences. Although FDA continues these important activities, its most fundamental international function today involves efforts to "harmonize" international enforcement and trade-related matters. The initial impetus for this focus arose from the Uruguay Round Agreement on Tariffs and Trade (also referred to as GATT), the Agreement on the Application of Sanitary and Phytosanitary Measures and the Agreement on Technical Barriers to Trade.

Recognizing the importance of assisting appropriate foreign governmental entities in understanding and implementing measures to provide for the safety of food regulated by FDA and exported by such countries to the United States, Congress, in passing FSMA, required that FDA establish offices in foreign countries. In addition to envisioning the educational role such offices are to perform, Congress contemplated that the offices would also conduct "risk-based inspections" of imported foods and would support inspections by foreign government entities. The new requirement reinforced FDA's prior decision to expand its overseas presence in an effort to provide greater access for FDA inspections and for greater engagement with foreign industry and foreign counterpart agencies. As noted earlier in this chapter, FDA has opened offices in China, India, Latin America, and Europe. Operating from its headquarters, FDA has also opened offices focused on Africa and the Middle East.

FDA's most fundamental international function today involves efforts to "harmonize" international enforcement and trade-related matters.

For years, FDA's Office of International Programs (OIP) has been the focal point for the agency's international efforts. OIP has been dedicated to achieving FDA's mission of ensuring the integrity of all imported regulated products by collaborating with international health and regulatory partners with respect to the proper operation of foreign facilities engaging in technical cooperation and training. Overseas presence not only helps achieve the goal of compliant imported regulated products but also builds stronger cooperative relationships.

As might be expected, FDA's international affairs staff in the Office of the Commissioner works closely with the Office of the U.S. Trade Representative and various trade groups in dealing with issues arising from these agreements. FDA also participates with the Codex Alimentarius Commission to develop international standards regarding the safety and sanitation of food. Moreover, FDA works closely with foreign governments to harmonize international technical requirements for pharmaceuticals and biologics, international vaccines, and cosmetics and veterinary drugs.

Although FDA activities in this area are largely overseen by the Office of the Commissioner, experts in each of the agency's Centers are actively involved. Moreover, FDA publishes for comment in the *Federal Register* the procedures it proposes to follow and the criteria it believes appropriate on which to base harmonization decisions.

FDA AND THE EXECUTIVE BRANCH

FDA is a component of DHHS. Thus, it is part of the executive branch. Accordingly, the agency's activities are not only subject to oversight from or by the Secretary of Health and Human Services but also from OMB. Thus, the agency's major regulatory initiatives and rulemaking proposals, legislative proposals, congressional appearances and testimony, and budgetary requests are subject to review, scrutiny, and approval by OMB. OMB's oversight of FDA budget requests is not new, but OMB's oversight and review of agency rulemaking and related initiatives begun under the Carter administration in the late 1970s was increased under the Reagan administration, and continues through today.

The DHHS Office of Inspector General has the authority to investigate fraud and "abuses" of FDA's substantive program authority.

One additional source of FDA oversight resides in the Inspector General (IG) of DHHS. The IG has the authority to investigate fraud and "abuses" of FDA's substantive program authority. In the late 1980s and early 1990s the IG was involved in a number of issues concerning the agency, most notably a series of matters arising from the agency's administration of its generic drug approval program.

CONCLUSION

Over the years, the fundamental structure of FDA, however, has remained unchanged: the Office of the Commissioner, the substantive Centers, and the field offices form the nucleus of agency activity and initiatives. Relations with sister agencies are generally positive and based on years of collaboration and compromise, with only an occasional incident of controversy. The agency also has developed tools, such as rulemaking and advisory panels, to enhance its ability to function efficiently and in a substantively and scientifically sound way.

The agency's evolution from a small bureau in USDA to a very visible and active component of DHHS reveals the development of a highly specialized agency that can adapt and adjust to increased regulatory burdens. By and large, the processes and structures put into place by both Congress and FDA have provided regulation that is commensurate with the risks to be prevented and the goals to be achieved.

Among the more intractable problems that confront the agency today is the issue of resources.

Among the more intractable problems that confront the agency today is the issue of resources. The pressure placed upon an agency with as many public health responsibilities as FDA to address and resolve complex public health issues with ever-diminishing resources is enormous. As a result, the agency's cooperative efforts with sister agencies, state authorities, and international governments appear likely to increase over time. Moreover, reliance on outside expertise and substantive transparent efforts by industry at voluntary compliance are likely to be key components of any agency effort to continue to function effectively.

Chapter 5

The Drugs/Biologics Approval Process

Geoffrey M. Levitt,* Pfizer Inc, New York, NY

Key Points

- The New Drug Application (NDA) and Biologics License Application (BLA) processes follow a series of defined phases, including:
  1) preclinical investigation (laboratory and animal testing);
  2) clinical investigation (human testing);
  3) Food and Drug Administration (FDA) review of the application;
  4) postmarketing.
  Each of these phases involves varying levels of FDA oversight.
- At the preclinical phase, there is little direct FDA oversight. If proper practices and guidelines are not observed, however, the applicant's ability to use preclinical data in support of its application may be jeopardized.
- Clinical investigation is carried out under much closer FDA supervision. During this phase, the applicant must file an Investigational New Drug Application (IND) with FDA before beginning new clinical studies, and must operate under rules and procedures designed to protect the rights and safety of human subjects. In addition, the applicant normally consults closely with FDA on the design of human studies (particularly in the later stages) with the goal of ensuring that the studies will support approval of its NDA or BLA.
- The FDA review phase is initiated by submission of the NDA or BLA. This phase is typically characterized by an ongoing dialogue between the applicant and FDA, wherein the applicant answers the agency's questions and tries to satisfy its concerns. If FDA concludes the drug is safe and effective for its intended use or uses, this phase culminates in approval; if not, the NDA or BLA may be denied (or more often, withdrawn for an overhaul).
- The Abbreviated New Drug Application (ANDA) is an important variant of the NDA. With an ANDA, the applicant must pass all the same hurdles as for a full NDA, with one critical exception: the ANDA applicant does not have to demonstrate the safety and efficacy of its drug. Instead, the ANDA relies on the proven safety and efficacy of an already approved drug to which it refers (the "reference drug"). Therefore, the ANDA applicant, instead of showing safety and efficacy, must show that its drug will work the same in the body (i.e., will be "bioequivalent") to that reference drug.

*The author gratefully acknowledges the assistance of Archana Kannan of Pfizer in preparing this updated chapter.

> ## Key Points, continued
>
> - The biosimilar application is an analogous variant of the BLA. The biosimilar applicant must show that its product is "highly similar" to its reference approved biological product and that there are no "clinically meaningful differences" between the biosimilar and the reference product in terms of safety, purity, or potency. In contrast to an ANDA, the standards for approval of a biosimilar are more flexible and rely more heavily on FDA's scientific judgment. As the biosimilars authority is still relatively new, there is still a great deal of room for development of these standards in practice.
> - There are various forms of exclusivity that are of concern to both NDA/ANDA and BLA/biosimilar applicants, including patent protection, statutory exclusivity, potential generic or biosimilar exclusivity for qualifying ANDA or biosimilar applicants, and orphan exclusivity.
> - Various mechanisms exist to expedite patient access to a new drug or biologic, including treatment Investigational New Drug Applications (under which an investigational product is distributed more widely than otherwise, and for more treatment-oriented purposes) and several forms of expedited approval generally applicable to products that show potential to address unmet therapeutic needs for serious or life-threatening diseases. These mechanisms are worth bearing in mind for the new drug or biologic applicant as a way of obtaining wider and/or faster access to the market.

INTRODUCTION

Before a new drug or biologic may be lawfully marketed in the United States, it must be approved by the Food and Drug Administration.

Before a new drug or biologic may be lawfully marketed in the United States, it must be approved by the Food and Drug Administration (FDA). In reality, there is not one single FDA approval framework that covers all drugs and biologics, but rather a set of distinct frameworks, each of which applies to a specific category of product. These include new drug approvals, abbreviated new drug approvals, the over-the-counter (OTC) review process, biologics, and biosimilars.

All these frameworks have some important elements in common, but also some key differences. The new drug approval process is, in many ways, the standard model and provides a basic framework for understanding the other processes.

FDA Drug Review: The New Drug Application

What Is a "Drug"? What Is a "New Drug"?

Under section 201(g)(1) of the Federal Food, Drug, and Cosmetic Act (FDCA), a "drug" includes: 1) articles recognized in the U.S. Pharmacopoeia, the U.S. Homeopathic Pharmacopoeia or the National Formulary; 2) articles "intended for use in the diagnosis, cure, mitigation, treatment, or prevention of disease"; 3) articles (other than food) "intended to affect the structure or any function of the body"; and 4) articles intended for use as a component of any of the above. "New drug," as defined in section 201(p) of the FDCA, means virtually any drug that first came onto the market, or is offered for entry onto the market, after the enactment of the FDCA in 1938 (which includes the overwhelming majority of drugs in existence today), unless the drug is "generally recognized as safe and effective"—a category whose main practical importance is in the context of OTC drugs. A "new drug" must have an approved New Drug Application (NDA), or one of the recognized variants of an NDA, such as an Abbreviated New Drug Application (ANDA), to be marketed lawfully in the United States.

Although the specifics of product development and FDA review may differ for each new drug product, the process of bringing a new compound onto the market generally follows a series of defined phases: preclinical investigation, clinical trials, submission and review of the NDA, and postmarketing.

Preclinical Investigation

The first stage in a drug's regulatory life cycle is preclinical investigation. The basic goals of preclinical investigation are: 1) to identify the potential effects in the body of the chemical substance being investigated, through laboratory experimentation and animal testing; and 2) to gather enough evidence on the potential new drug to determine if it is reasonably safe to begin preliminary trials in humans.

The first stage in a drug's regulatory life cycle is preclinical investigation.

Unlike human clinical trials, prior notification to FDA is not required to begin a preclinical investigation, although the preclinical phase is subject to specific FDA regulations known as Good Laboratory Practice (GLP) regulations. Unapproved new drugs shipped interstate as part of a preclinical investigation are exempted from the FDCA's general prohibition on interstate shipments of unapproved drugs as long as the drugs are appropriately labeled and adequate records of shipment and receipt are maintained. FDA may, however, terminate a preclinical investigator's ability to ship unapproved drugs if it determines that continuing the investigation is unsafe or otherwise contrary to the public inter-est, or that the drugs are being used for purposes other than bona fide scientific investigation.

Direct FDA involvement in a preclinical investigation ordinarily comes at the conclusion of the investigation, when the agency reviews the Investigational New Drug Application (IND) that the drug sponsor submits prior to beginning human clinical trials. FDA then evaluates the soundness of the data the sponsor has gathered through preclinical investigation, as well as the adequacy of the methods used to gather those data. The agency's evaluation focuses in particu-lar on the preclinical data the sponsor relied on to reach the conclusion that it was reasonably safe to conduct the proposed human clinical investigations. This primarily involves data regarding what effects the drug actually has in the body (pharmacology) and how toxic it is at various possible dose levels (toxicology).

FDA's GLP regulations, which are codified in Part 58 of Title 21 of the Code of Federal Regulations (C.F.R.), govern the laboratory work and facilities associated with any nonclinical study intended to support a marketing application for an FDA-regulated product, including drugs and biologics. These regulations estab-lish certain minimum requirements for different aspects of a testing laboratory's practices, subject the laboratory to FDA inspectional oversight, and provide penalties for noncompliance.

The Good Laboratory Practice regulations specify minimum standards in such areas as personnel, facilities, equipment, and operations.

The GLP regulations specify minimum standards in such areas as person-nel, facilities, equipment, and operations. The regulations typically set these standards through procedural and structural safeguards, rather than through specific substantive requirements.

For example, in the area of personnel, the GLP regulations require that individu-als involved in preclinical studies be sufficiently trained to conduct the study appropriately, but do not specify what such training must encompass. The personnel controls also require the designation of a study director to oversee, monitor, and certify the study and require the establishment of a separate quality assurance unit charged with independently monitoring the progress and scientific soundness of any study. This quality assurance unit, among other tasks, must maintain copies of study schedules and written protocols; conduct periodic inspections to ensure compliance with all regulations and specifica-tions; submit regular status reports to the management of the testing facility; and prepare and sign a written statement outlining quality assurance efforts, which is to be included in the final study report.

The GLP regulations also require facilities to be of suitable size and construction, including proper animal care facilities, as applicable. The regulations provide that any study to be submitted to FDA in support of an IND (or other official application) must be conducted with a detailed protocol specifying the study's objectives and methodologies, and that all relevant records and data from the study must be retained for specified periods. FDA may inspect any GLP-covered facility and its records to determine its compliance with applicable standards.

A testing facility's failure to conform to applicable GLP requirements can result in various sanctions. If the violation adversely affected the validity of a preclinical study and FDA considers lesser regulatory actions inadequate, the violation can result in the facility's being disqualified from carrying out any preclinical testing. In addition, any studies undertaken at a disqualified testing facility that are submitted in support of a subsequent product application may be excluded from consideration. FDA also may disregard a preclinical laboratory study done at a nonconforming facility, even if the nonconformance would not warrant disqualification of the facility. Exclusion of a preclinical study under either of these circumstances may lead, in extreme cases, to the termination or withdrawal of approval of the application.

A testing facility's failure to conform to applicable GLP requirements can result in various sanctions.

Although the direct burden of GLP compliance is on the testing facility, the GLP regulations create strong incentives for sponsors who plan to rely on preclinical studies for subsequent FDA applications to take an active role in overseeing those studies.

Clinical Investigation

The primary purpose of the preclinical investigation is to gather sufficient evidence about the proposed new drug to proceed to the next regulatory stage—testing the product in people. The primary goal of human clinical investigation, in turn, is to gather sufficient information about the safety and efficacy of the drug to support an NDA. In contrast to the preclinical stage, clinical trials involve much more active FDA oversight, designed both to protect the health and safety of the human test subjects and to ensure the integrity and usefulness of the clinical study data.

The Investigational New Drug Application

Unlike the preclinical stage, commencement of clinical trials requires formal notification to FDA. At least 30 days before the drug's sponsor wishes to begin such trials, the sponsor must submit an IND to the agency (basic IND requirements are set out at title 21 C.F.R. Part 312 and in section 505(i) of the FDCA). If FDA does not object to the IND within 30 days, it automatically becomes effective and clinical trials may begin. If FDA finds a problem with the application, however, it may impose a "clinical hold," barring commencement of the investigational studies proposed in the application until the problem is resolved to the agency's satisfaction.

The specific contents of an IND depend both on the nature of the drug and the scope of the proposed trials. All INDs, however, must include the following basic elements: 1) a detailed cover sheet; 2) a table of contents; 3) an introductory statement and general investigative plan; 4) an investigator's brochure, except in the case of sponsor-investigator INDs (i.e., where the investigator herself or himself is the sponsor); 5) a set of comprehensive investigative protocols; 6) information on the proposed drug's chemistry, manufacturing, and controls; 7) pharmacology and toxicology information; 8) a summary of previous human experience with the drug; and 9) any additional information FDA deems necessary.

An IND includes:
- *information on the study drug itself*
- *information on the proposed clinical investigation*

Thus, the IND covers two basic categories of information: information on the study drug itself, and information on the proposed clinical investigation. As to the study drug, the sponsor must provide the pharmacological and toxicological data upon which the sponsor concluded it was reasonably safe to propose clinical trials involving humans. The IND also must include information describing the manufacturing and control of the study drug, as well as comprehensive information on the drug's chemical composition, structural formula, proposed dosage form, and proposed route of administration. Information on any prior human experience with the drug also is required, including any relevant foreign experience, as well as any history of the drug's being withdrawn from investigation or marketing.

As to the information on the proposed investigation, the application must include proposed study protocols, with varying levels of detail depending on the phase of the clinical trial being undertaken. Generally, protocols must identify the objectives and purpose of the study, names and qualifications of investigators, patient selection criteria, study design and methodologies, and the study's measurement criteria, including clinical or laboratory monitoring. The IND also must identify the person(s) with overall responsibility for monitoring the study, as well as outside contract research organizations.

In addition, the application must include a detailed "investigative plan" addressing, among other things, the rationale behind the planned clinical research, an outline of the proposed approach, the types of clinical trials to be conducted, an estimate as to the number of patients involved, and a discussion of any significant anticipated patient risks based on toxicological data. Further, the application must contain a commitment from the sponsor to conduct clinical trials under the supervision of an Institutional Review Board (IRB), and to follow all applicable rules and regulations, including those pertaining to informed consent.

• Informed Consent and Institutional Review Boards

A fundamental goal of regulatory requirements for informed consent and review of clinical studies by IRBs is to ensure the protection of the rights and welfare of human subjects. FDA investigators regularly check for compliance with these regulations, and an institution or sponsor's noncompliance can result in the temporary suspension or formal termination of a clinical study, as well as other administrative sanctions or legal proceedings.

The thrust of the informed consent regulations, which are codified at 21 C.F.R. Part 50, is to ensure that patient participation in clinical trials is entirely voluntary and knowing. Potential participants in clinical trials must be informed adequately about risks, possible benefits, and alternative courses of treatment *before* making the decision to participate in the experimental research. Such consent must be documented, and research subjects cannot be forced to waive any potential future claims for negligence against the study's investigator, sponsor, or institution. Furthermore, when prisoners are enrolled as research subjects, additional restrictions and requirements exist to ensure truly voluntary participation in light of the inherently more coercive prison environment. FDA is permitted to waive informed consent requirements if obtaining informed consent is not feasible or is contrary to the best interests of prospective human subjects, or if the proposed clinical testing poses no more than minimal risk to human subjects and includes appropriate safeguards to protect the subjects' rights, safety, and welfare.

Potential participants in clinical trials must be informed adequately about risks, possible benefits, and alternative courses of treatment before making the decision to participate in the experimental research.

The regulations pertaining to IRBs, codified at 21 C.F.R. Part 56, require IRB oversight of a clinical study in order to ensure that the rights of the human test subjects are adequately protected, while, at the same time, rigorous scientific and medical standards are maintained. The IRB is essentially a committee designated by an institution (e.g., university medical center, contract research organization, or hospital) to review biomedical research involving human subjects. The IRB must approve a proposed clinical study before the study can begin and must continue to monitor the research as it progresses. IRB approval of a proposed clinical study can be given only if certain conditions are met, including that the proposed research appropriately minimizes patient risks and that such risks are reasonable in relation to anticipated benefits.

The regulations also set up relatively detailed requirements for an IRB's internal "housekeeping." Thus, the IRB must establish written procedures detailing, among other things, its review processes and criteria, and its procedures designed to ensure the prompt reporting of changes in ongoing clinical research or in informed consent documents. Moreover, IRB members must come from sufficiently diverse disciplines to enable the IRB to review the study not only in terms of specific research issues but also in terms of the study's acceptability under community and legal standards, as well as professional conduct and practice norms. The IRB also must keep detailed records of its activities; those records are subject to FDA inspection.

◆ The Phases of a Clinical Investigation

Clinical investigations are typically divided into three phases.

Clinical investigations are typically divided into three phases, which often overlap in practice.

Phase 1 studies ordinarily involve the initial administration of the drug to a small number (typically 20 to 80) of healthy test subjects or patients. Such studies are designed to determine the metabolism and pharmacologic actions of the drug in humans and the side effects associated with increasing doses, and, if possible, to gain early evidence on effectiveness. The drug's sponsor also must derive sufficient pharmacological data from Phase 1 trials to devise appropriate Phase 2 studies. In the case of more toxic drugs intended to treat serious or life-threatening conditions, such as many cancer drugs, Phase I trials may take place in patients with the target condition.

Phase 2 investigations involve an expanded patient group (up to several hundred patients) afflicted with the disease or condition being studied. The thrust of Phase 2 trials is to obtain evidence of the drug's effectiveness against the targeted disease, to explore further risk and side effect issues, and to confirm preliminary data regarding optimal dosage ranges. At the end of Phase 2 trials, the sponsor typically meets with FDA to discuss specific regulatory or scientific concerns the sponsor must address in designing and conducting its Phase 3 studies. While such conferences are technically optional, they are almost always advisable as they can provide an invaluable opportunity to address agency concerns that might otherwise impede review of the application.

The sponsor may request a formal meeting with responsible FDA officials to reach a binding agreement on the size or design of clinical or bioequivalence trials. After testing begins, such agreements may be changed only with the written consent of the sponsor or if the director of the responsible FDA division issues a written decision identifying a substantial scientific issue "essential to determining the safety or effectiveness of the drug" that would not otherwise have been addressed.

Phase 3 clinical trials may commence, with appropriate notification to FDA, once the drug's sponsor has gathered preliminary evidence that suggests the drug may be effective. Such studies may involve up to several thousand patients. They frequently take place at multiple locations and involve more clinical investigators than in earlier phases. The primary goal of a Phase 3 clinical trial, or "pivotal" trial, is to collect the data necessary to meet the safety and efficacy standards required for FDA approval.

◆ Obligations of Clinical Sponsors and Investigators

Throughout all phases of a clinical investigation, both the sponsor of the study and the individual investigators have responsibilities and duties designed to ensure patient safety as well as the integrity and soundness of the data derived from the investigation. Noncompliance with these requirements may result in FDA regulatory actions including Warning Letters, exclusion of a disqualified investigator's study results, suspension of an IND or NDA predicated on discredited study data, or even civil or criminal proceedings.

The study sponsor is responsible for ensuring patient safety and appropriate scientific conduct, and has the primary responsibility to keep FDA informed of the progress of the study and of any significant safety-related events. The sponsor also bears responsibility for selecting appropriate investigators, ensuring adherence to proper protocols and practices, recordkeeping, and shipping and handling of investigational product. In addition, sponsors are responsible for compliance with regulations on informed consent and IRBs.

Obligations of clinical sponsors:
- *ensuring patient safety*
- *ensuring appropriate scientific conduct*
- *keeping FDA informed*
- *selecting appropriate investigators*
- *adhering to proper protocols and practices*
- *recordkeeping*
- *shipping and handling of product*
- *reporting any adverse event*
- *obtaining valid informed consent*

The sponsor is also responsible for reporting to FDA and to participating clinical investigators any potential serious risk, from clinical trials or any other source, as soon as possible but in any case within 15 calendar days after determining that the information qualifies for reporting. If an unexpected life-threatening or fatal event occurs, the sponsor must notify FDA within seven calendar days of receiving the information.

Under the Food and Drug Administration Amendments Act of 2007 (FDAAA), the sponsor is required to register on a public database certain summary information about controlled clinical trials, other than Phase I investigations, of products subject to FDA regulation. The sponsor is required to register such trials within 21 days after the first patient is enrolled in the trial. FDAAA also requires sponsors to submit basic results for these trials for posting on the same public database (www.ClinicalTrials.gov) within one year of the completion date of the trial. Sponsors are required to certify to FDA that they have complied with these requirements at the time they submit any "application" under section 505 of the FDCA (for drugs) or section 351 of the Public Health Service Act (for biologics). Per FDA guidance updated in 2017, the certification requirement applies to various types of applications including INDs, NDAs, Biologics License Applications (BLAs), and efficacy supplements to approved NDAs and BLAs. FDAAA also provides for further expansion of the database by regulation. Such regulations were issued in September 2016.

Clinical investigators are required, among other things, to obtain valid informed consent from any participating subjects, to follow study protocols, to ensure that other study personnel follow the required protocols, and to report significant adverse events. An investigator may be disqualified from conducting studies for repeated violations of the regulations, or may be subject to further administrative, civil, or criminal proceedings. If an investigator disqualification occurs, the study's sponsor will be required to establish that the study's overall viability is not threatened by the investigator's misconduct. Investigator misconduct also may result in an FDA determination that the IND can no longer remain in effect, or, in extreme cases, that an NDA predicated upon the investigator's data must be withdrawn.

✦ FDA Oversight: Clinical Holds

Through the imposition of a "clinical hold," FDA may forestall a proposed clinical investigation or suspend an existing one.

Through the imposition of a "clinical hold," FDA may forestall a proposed clinical investigation or suspend an existing one. A clinical hold can be imposed for a number of reasons, including an unreasonable and significant risk to patients, the use of improperly qualified investigators, a deficient or disregarded investigative protocol, or any other serious deficiency in an IND or a particular clinical trial. FDA must communicate the imposition of a clinical hold by telephone or other form of rapid communication, and must provide the drug sponsor, within 30 days, with a written explanation of the basis for the clinical hold. As a general rule, until the agency's consent to lift a clinical hold is obtained, any clinical trial or trials subject to the hold cannot commence or resume. Under the Food and Drug Administration Modernization Act of 1997 (FDAMA), a sponsor faced with a clinical hold may submit a written request to FDA that the hold be removed. FDA must respond to such a request in writing within 30 days.

✦ IND Withdrawal

As with the imposition of a clinical hold, FDA can halt further use or distribution of an investigational drug through withdrawal or suspension of an IND. Similar concerns, such as undue patient risk or serious deficiencies in the application or the clinical protocol, trigger both types of agency action, with withdrawal obviously reserved for the more serious cases.

Where the continuation of a clinical study poses, in FDA's judgment, an immediate and substantial danger to human subjects, the agency may order immediate termination of an IND, subject to possible reinstatement. Where no such immediate risk is present, however, if FDA proposes to withdraw an IND, the agency will notify the sponsor in writing and provide 30 days to submit any corrections or explanations. The sponsor's failure to respond within the specified time frame results in the termination of the IND. The sponsor, however, may request a formal hearing if FDA refuses to accept a submitted correction or explanation.

The New Drug Application: Standards and Procedures

Once Phase 3 clinical trials are completed, the applicant prepares to submit its NDA. This preparation process ordinarily includes a pre-NDA meeting with FDA staff, with the goal of helping to ensure that the application will contain all required data.

✦ Contents of the New Drug Application

The regulatory requirements that govern the contents of an NDA, codified at 21 C.F.R. Part 314, are intended to give FDA enough information to make a meaningful evaluation of the drug. Specific NDA data requirements are lengthy and detailed, covering seven broad categories: 1) preclinical data, such as animal and laboratory studies, evaluating the drug's pharmacology and toxicology; 2) human pharmacokinetic and bioavailability data; 3) clinical data (i.e., data obtained from administering the drug to humans, which must include adequate tests to demonstrate that the drug is safe under the proposed conditions of use, as well as "substantial evidence" that the drug is effective under such proposed conditions); 4) a description of proposed methods by which the drug will be manufactured, processed, and packed; 5) a description of the drug product and drug substance; 6) a list of each patent claiming the drug, drug product, or method of use, or a statement that there are no relevant patents making such claims; and 7) the drug's proposed labeling. The applicant also must provide a summary of the application, concluding with a presentation of both the risks and benefits of the new drug. In addition, the NDA must contain various regulatory certifications covering such matters as financial ties between the sponsor and clinical investigators and compliance with clinical trial registry requirements.

Data requirements in an NDA cover seven broad categories.

Unless an application is publicly disclosed or acknowledged, FDA will keep the application's existence a secret until the agency sends an approval letter. Similarly, the contents of an application generally are kept secret until an approval letter is sent, even if the existence of the application is known. Following approval of the NDA, material in the application that contains trade secrets or confidential commercial information continues to be protected from disclosure, at least in theory. FDAAA added the requirement that FDA must publish on its website within 48 hours of approval of a new drug or biologic a summary review documenting conclusions about the drug from all reviewing disciplines, noting any critical issues or disagreements that arose during the review and how they were resolved. In addition, FDA must publish on its website, within 30 days of approval, the action package for approval of any new drug or biologic that is a new chemical entity; for any other new drug or biologic, the action package must be published within 30 days of receipt of the third Freedom of Information Act request for the package.

◆ Risk Evaluation and Mitigation Strategy

An additional element that may be required as part of an NDA is the risk evaluation and mitigation strategy (REMS), as provided under the FDAAA. FDA may require a sponsor to include a REMS in its NDA when the agency deems it "necessary to ensure that the benefits of the drug outweigh the risks of the drug."

A REMS must contain, at a minimum, a timetable for submission to FDA by the sponsor of REMS assessments at set intervals (18 months, three years, and in the seventh year after approval), subject to possible variations in frequency and possible elimination of the assessment requirement altogether if, after the initial three-year period, FDA determines that the drug's serious risks have been adequately identified and are being adequately managed (FDCA § 505-1(d)). A sponsor may also submit an assessment of an existing REMS to FDA at any time, along with a proposed modification of the REMS. A proposal to modify a REMS strategy is not, however, required to be included with an assessment and also can be submitted to FDA at any time. In addition, a sponsor must submit a REMS assessment:

- ◆ when submitting a supplemental application for a prescription drug for a new indication;

- ◆ when specifically required under the REMS;

- ◆ as specified by FDA if the agency determines that new safety or efficacy information indicates that any REMS element should be modified or added; or

- ◆ within 15 days if the Secretary of the Department of Health and Human Services determines there may be cause to withdraw the drug's NDA under section 505(e) of the act.

In addition to the required periodic assessments, a REMS may also be required to provide for the distribution of a Medication Guide or a patient package insert to each patient when the drug is dispensed if FDA determines that such a requirement may help "mitigate a serious risk of the drug." A communication plan aimed at healthcare professionals may also be required if FDA determines that such a plan may support implementation of an element of the REMS.

A more stringent set of REMS elements may be required if FDA determines them necessary to "assure safe use of the drug, because of its inherent toxicity or potential harmfulness." These elements may require:

- ◆ that healthcare professionals who prescribe or dispense the drug have particular training or experience or are specially certified;

- ◆ that the drug be dispensed only in specified settings such as hospitals;

- ◆ that patient testing, monitoring, and/or enrollment in a registry be required in connection with dispensing the drug.

Whenever a REMS assessment is submitted, FDA must initiate discussion with the sponsor within 60 days, except for assessments required because the Secretary of the Department of Health and Human Services has determined there may be cause to withdraw the NDA, in which case such discussions must begin within 30 days after submission. For proposed REMS modifications submitted as part of an NDA or supplement, FDA must describe the final REMS or any modification to the REMS, as applicable, in the action letter on the application. For proposed REMS modifications submitted as part of a REMS assessment, FDA must describe the final REMS, in most cases, within 90 days of the beginning of the required discussions with the sponsor. Detailed dispute resolution processes apply if FDA and the sponsor disagree on a REMS or REMS modification.

Generic drugs referencing a drug approved with a REMS are subject to all elements of the REMS except the requirement to submit assessments and proposed modifications. For those REMS elements involving restrictions on distribution and use, the generic drug applicant and the reference drug applicant are to use a single, shared system, unless FDA determines that the burdens of such a system outweigh the benefits, or that any aspect of the REMS elements in question is patent-protected or proprietary and the ANDA applicant is not able to obtain a license. In this connection, the law prohibits an NDA sponsor from using any REMS element required to assure safe use in order to "block or delay" approval of an ANDA.

◆ Submitting and Filing the New Drug Application

When an NDA arrives at FDA, the agency considers it to be "received," not "filed." The application is considered "filed" only when formally accepted for review by FDA. The agency must determine whether or not to file an application within 60 days of its receipt. If no grounds for refusing to file the application exist, FDA must file it; the filing date will be 60 days after the date of receipt.

FDA will refuse to file an NDA if:
- *it is incomplete*
- *it is in improper form*
- *it omits critical data*
- *it fails to make required certifications*

FDA will accept an application for filing only if it is sufficiently complete to permit a substantive review. FDA has the authority to refuse to file an application on several grounds, for example: 1) if the application is incomplete or in improper form, or omits data critical to assessing safety, efficacy, or adequate directions for use; or 2) if the application fails to make required certifications regarding how the preclinical and clinical trials were conducted.

Although its refusal to file (RTF) authority sounds quite broad, FDA typically uses that authority only for obvious deficiencies in the application, not in cases that involve "matters of subtle judgment." The agency's RTF guidance document states: "It is important ... that [RTF] be reserved for applications ... plainly inadequate, non-reviewable without major repair, or that make review unreasonably difficult." Applications that contain deficiencies this severe will be subject to refusal, because FDA believes that accepting applications in need of extensive repair is unfair to new drug sponsors whose submissions were complete and properly formatted. (One notable exception to the normal requirement for a complete NDA submission is the category of "fast-track" drugs, discussed later in this chapter. FDAMA explicitly permits FDA to review applications for fast-track drugs on a "rolling" basis.)

There are three circumstances where FDA is especially likely to use its RTF power: 1) omission of a required section of the NDA, or presentation of a section in so haphazard a manner as to render it incomplete on its face; 2) clear failure to include evidence of effectiveness that can meet the statutory and regulatory standards; and 3) omission of critical data, information, or analyses needed to evaluate safety and effectiveness, or to provide adequate directions for use. Because the agency's RTF power is discretionary, it can choose not to use this procedure for particularly critical drugs even if specific grounds for invoking it exist. In practice, potential RTF issues usually are addressed and resolved before the NDA is submitted. The pre-NDA meeting often provides a forum for this process.

If FDA chooses to use its RTF authority, it will notify the applicant, which can then request an informal conference. After the conference, the applicant can request that FDA file the application, with or without amendments to correct the deficiencies. The agency then will file the application "over protest." As a practical matter, however, an applicant has little or no incentive to ask the agency to do this. If FDA believes the application contains deficiencies egregious enough to warrant an RTF response, there is little chance of subsequent favorable FDA action on the application. Therefore, requests to file an application "over protest" are extremely rare.

◆ Substantive Standards for Review

"Safe" and "effective" have special meanings in the new drug approval context.

FDA reviewers must find that an application meets several substantive requirements before the agency will approve the NDA. The most basic requirement is that the drug be both "safe" and "effective." These words have specialized meanings in the new drug approval context.

The FDCA, as enacted in 1938, did not require a sponsor to address efficacy as part of its application to market a new drug—only safety. The Drug Amendments of 1962 added the requirement that a new drug must be supported by "substantial evidence" that the drug will have the effect it purports to have under the indicated conditions of use. "Substantial evidence" is defined in the law as evidence from adequate and well-controlled clinical studies. Although FDA has traditionally required two independent pivotal studies to demonstrate efficacy, FDAMA provided that one "adequate and well-controlled" study accompanied by confirmatory evidence could constitute substantial evidence of effectiveness if FDA determines, "based on relevant science," that data from the study are sufficient to establish effectiveness.

In addition, a drug may not be approved unless there are "adequate tests by all methods reasonably applicable to show whether or not such drug is safe for use under the conditions prescribed, recommended, or suggested in the proposed labeling thereof." In applying this standard, FDA recognizes that there is no such thing as an absolutely safe drug; in addition to the benefits it provides, every drug will present some risks. Therefore, FDA's safety assessment requires consideration of a product's efficacy. As the agency said in its 1995 statement on the efficacy standard, "FDA weighs the product's demonstrated effectiveness against its risks to determine whether the benefits outweigh the risks." This risk/benefit analysis takes account of information such as the seriousness of the disease, the adequacy of any existing remedies, and adverse reaction and any other safety data. In addition, FDA is required under the 2012 Food and Drug Administration Safety and Innovation Act (FDASIA) to implement a structured risk/benefit assessment framework that will facilitate the review of drug risk and benefit considerations. A draft five-year plan describing FDA's proposal to implement and develop such a framework was released in 2013 and is scheduled to be updated in 2018. In addition, FDA plans to publish a draft guidance on benefit-risk assessments for new drugs and biologics in 2020.

In addition to evidence of safety and effectiveness, there also must be adequate manufacturing controls in place before FDA will approve a drug. In particular, the methods used in, and the controls and facilities used for, manufacturing, processing, packing, and holding the drug substance and finished product must comply with FDA's current Good Manufacturing Practice (cGMP) requirements, and must be adequate to maintain the drug's purity, quality, strength, identity, and bioavailability. A pre-approval inspection of the applicant's facilities typically will be conducted to verify compliance with these requirements.

In addition to evidence of safety and effectiveness, there also must be adequate manufacturing controls in place before FDA will approve a drug.

An additional prerequisite to approval is that the drug's labeling must meet applicable statutory and regulatory requirements. The labeling cannot be false or misleading, and must comply with general requirements concerning content and form, including such matters as presentation of clinical data, warnings, and dosage and administration information. The labeling review is usually the final step in the approval process.

Under the Pediatric Research Equity Act of 2003 (PREA) (made permanent by FDASIA in 2012), an NDA or BLA for a new drug or biologic must include an assessment of the safety and efficacy of the product in all relevant pediatric subpopulations (as defined by FDA in consultation with the sponsor), as well as data to support dosing and administration for each pediatric subpopulation for which the product is to be deemed safe and effective. The applicant must first, however, submit an initial pediatric study plan prior to submission of the assessment. Upon meeting with or receiving comments on the initial pediatric study plan from FDA, the applicant must document its agreement with the plan, which may be amended at any time. FDA then must confirm its agreement with the plan and provide its recommendation in response to requests for deferral, partial waiver, or waiver as described below. The content of and process for submitting initial and amended pediatric study plans is described in a draft guidance released by FDA in March 2016. A 2017 amendment gave FDA the authority to require a sponsor of an adult cancer drug with a molecular target that FDA determines is relevant to a pediatric cancer to conduct a "molecularly targeted" pediatric cancer investigation to inform potential pediatric labeling as to dosing, safety, and preliminary efficacy.

Assessment requirements may be deferred for various reasons, including an FDA finding that the product is ready for approval for use by adults before pediatric studies are complete. The requirement may also be waived partially or entirely on a variety of grounds, including that 1) the necessary studies are impossible or highly impractical; 2) there is evidence strongly suggesting that the product would be ineffective or unsafe in children; 3) the product does not represent a meaningful benefit over existing therapies for children and is not likely to be used in a substantial number of children; or 4) for a partial waiver applicable to a specific age group, reasonable efforts to produce a pediatric formulation necessary for that age group have failed. FDA also has authority under PREA to require pediatric assessments for marketed products if FDA finds that 1) the product is used in a substantial number of children for the labeled indications and adequate pediatric labeling could confer a benefit on pediatric patients; 2) there is reason to believe the product would represent a meaningful therapeutic benefit over existing therapies for pediatric patients for one or more claimed indications; or 3) the absence of adequate pediatric labeling could pose a risk to pediatric patients. PREA was amended by FDASIA to permit the extension of deferrals by FDA on its own initiative or in response to an applicant's request for a new deadline. The request for a new deadline must be submitted to FDA 90 days prior to the expiration of the existing deadline. FDA is also required to issue non-compliance letters to any applicant that fails to submit or defer a required assessment, or if the applicant does not submit a request for approval of a pediatric formulation. FDA's non-compliance letters, together with applicant responses to these letters, are made available to the public on FDA's website.

◆ Advisory Committee Review

Although the primary review of an NDA is carried out by the appropriate division within the Center for Drug Evaluation and Research (CDER), FDA may also seek the advice of its expert advisory committees. These committees may review studies of the drug under consideration, as well as its proposed labeling, and provide recommendations on issues pertaining to approval of the drug. Each review division within CDER has access to one or more advisory committees. Advisory committees are composed primarily of prominent research and clinical specialists, but also must include a representative of consumer interests, a representative of the drug manufacturing industry not directly affected by the matter before the panel, and at least two specialists in the disease or condition for which the drug under review is to be indicated.

Advisory committees respond to specific questions posed by the agency regarding safety and efficacy, and evaluate whether additional studies are needed to support approval. FDA typically has been more likely to use advisory committee review if the new drug is particularly significant therapeutically, or if review of the drug involves evaluation of complex scientific data. The FDAAA, however,requires FDA to refer any BLA or any NDA for a new chemical entity to an advisory committee for review prior to approval or to summarize in the action letter why it did not do so. In an effort to ensure that advisory committees reflect the most current expert advice, conflict-of-interest rules were amended under FDASIA to improve outside expert recruitment by FDA and to expand the number of experts who can qualify for nomination to serve on an advisory committee.

In addition to advisory committees, FDA also has discretion to consult outside expert reviewers from the scientific community and may consider the view of patient representatives. Under FDASIA, for example, FDA is required to maintain a list of experts who can provide consultation related to the review of drugs and biological products for rare diseases or that are genetically targeted. In addition, FDASIA requires FDA to implement strategies that enhance patient involvement in medical product development and regulatory discussions.

Advisory committee and outside review recommendations, however, are not binding on the agency. Under FDAMA, FDA must make a final decision on a matter reviewed by an advisory committee and notify the affected parties, or explain why no decision has been reached, within 90 days after the advisory committee's recommendation.

Advisory Committees
Important issues raised by an NDA (or BLA) may be reviewed by FDA advisory committees made up of outside experts.

Advisory committees respond to specific questions posed by the agency regarding safety and efficacy, and evaluate whether additional studies are needed to support approval.

The New Drug Application: FDA Action and Time Frames

The FDCA provides that within 180 days after the filing of an NDA "or such additional period as may be agreed" between FDA and the applicant, FDA must either approve the application or give the applicant notice of an opportunity for a hearing as to whether the application is approvable (essentially, a procedural step required before FDA may formally reject an NDA). Because FDA rarely is in a position to reach a final yes-or-no decision on an NDA within 180 days after it is filed, the agency has created a procedural framework that allows it to engage in multiple rounds of review of an NDA that may stretch on much longer than 180 days without running afoul of the statutory deadline.

First, as described above, FDA has by regulation established a 60-day period following actual receipt of the NDA during which the agency decides if the application is sufficiently complete to allow it be "filed." Only after this determination is made does the statutory "filing clock" start to run.

While the filing step effectively extends the 180-day statutory deadline by 60 days, even this additional amount of time is usually insufficient for FDA to reach a final decision on an application. Accordingly, the primary mechanism by which FDA ensures itself the timing flexibility it needs to complete its review of an application without violating the statutory deadline is to rely on the "or such additional period as may be agreed" language of the statute to create a system in which the NDA applicant in effect agrees to allow the review of the application to continue until FDA is either ready to approve it or makes clear that the application is not approvable in its current form, in which case the applicant typically withdraws the application on its own. (Situations in which an applicant forces FDA to provide a formal hearing on approvability, as the statute contemplates, are quite rare.)

This mechanism in turn is premised on the concept of the review cycle, formerly referred to in FDA regulations as the "review clock." FDA regulations state that within 180 days of the receipt of an NDA, FDA will review it and send the applicant either an approval letter or a "complete response" letter describing the deficiencies that must be satisfactorily addressed before the application can be approved. This 180-day period is called the "initial review cycle." Significantly, however, the regulations also provide that the initial review cycle "may be adjusted by mutual agreement between FDA and an applicant or as . . . the result of a major amendment" (amendments to the NDA are discussed below).

A key vehicle for expressing applicants' agreement to extending the initial review cycle is FDA's performance goals under the Prescription Drug User Fee

Act (PDUFA), which are negotiated between industry and FDA and formally presented to Congress. First enacted in 1992 with the intent of providing additional resources for FDA drug review and accelerating drug review times, PDUFA is reauthorized on a five-year cycle, with the most recent reauthorization (PDUFA VI) taking place in 2017 as part of the FDA Reauthorization Act (FDARA). The FDARA reauthorization will sunset on October 1, 2022. PDUFA applies only to NDAs and BLAs, not to generic drug applications. Generic drug applications are subject to user fees under the Generic Drug User Fee Amendments (GDUFA), which was first enacted as part of FDASIA in 2012 (the fees for generic drug applications are discussed below).

Two categories of user fees are established under PDUFA VI: application fees, which are collected from an applicant when a new drug or biologic application is submitted; and program fees, which are collected on an annual basis from all applicants who have applications pending before FDA, with certain limited exceptions. The legislation provides that 20 percent of total annual user fee revenue is to be derived from application fees and 80 percent from program fees. In exchange, FDA commits to the PDUFA performance goals, which provide for specific review times for NDAs and BLAs. Though technically not legally binding, these performance goals represent FDA's side of a three-way bargain under which industry agrees to pay the user fees and Congress authorizes FDA to collect the fees and use them for drug reviews and related tasks. As such, the performance goals are taken very seriously by the agency.

Under PDUFA, FDA collects substantial user fees in the form of application fees and program fees. In exchange, FDA commits to the PDUFA performance goals.

In its PDUFA performance goals under the 2017 reauthorization, FDA committed to review and act on 90 percent of standard original NDA and BLA submissions (i.e., submissions for drugs similar to existing treatments) within 10 months of receipt of the 60-day filing date, and 90 percent of priority original NDA and BLA submissions (i.e., submissions for drugs that represent significant advances over existing treatments) within six months of the 60-day filing date. Additional performance goals apply to non-NME (New Molecular Entity) NDAs, Class 1 and 2 resubmissions, Original Efficacy Supplements, and Class 1 and 2 Resubmitted Efficacy Supplements. By signing on to the PDUFA performance goals, industry has effectively agreed to an extension of the initial review cycle for standard NDA and BLA applications from six months to 10 months. Under PDUFA VI, FDA also committed to a program for enhanced review transparency and communication that will apply to all NME NDAs and original BLAs, including applications a sponsor submits following a refusal-to-file action, that the agency receives between October 1, 2017 and September 30, 2022. FDA is seeking to improve review transparency and communication through pre-submission meetings, both mid- and late-cycle communications to discuss application status, GCP, GLP, and GMP inspection completion goals, and FDA review team performance goals for applications that are reviewed under this program.

As noted above, at the conclusion of the initial review cycle, FDA will send the applicant either an approval letter or a complete response letter. Because outright approval at the end of the initial review cycle is relatively rare, in most cases the applicant will receive a complete response letter outlining the additional steps that need to be taken before the application can be approved. Upon receipt of a complete response letter, the applicant must resubmit the application, addressing the deficiencies noted in the letter; withdraw the application; or ask FDA to provide an opportunity for a hearing on the approvability of the application. Under FDA regulations, the applicant that receives a complete response letter automatically agrees to an extension of the statutory review deadline until it takes any of these actions. Failure to take any of the specified actions within one year after the issuance of a complete response letter will be considered a request by the applicant to withdraw the application, unless the applicant has requested an extension. If FDA considers the applicant's failure to take action within one year to be a request to withdraw the application, the agency will give the applicant written notice and a 30-day period in which to explain why the application should not be withdrawn and to request an extension of time to resubmit it.

Resubmissions of an application following receipt of a complete response letter fall into two categories. A Class 1 resubmission is one that contains relatively minor information such as final printed labeling, draft labeling, certain safety or stability updates, postmarketing study commitments, assay validation data, final release testing on lots used to support approval, or minor re-analyses of previously submitted data. Under FDA's regulations, a Class 1 resubmission constitutes an agreement by the applicant to start a new two-month review cycle beginning on the date FDA receives the resubmission. A Class 2 resubmission is one that includes any item not specified as part of a Class 1 resubmission, including any item that would require presentation to an advisory committee. A Class 2 resubmission constitutes an agreement by the applicant to start a new six-month review cycle beginning on the date FDA receives the resubmission.

Submission by the applicant of an amendment to a pending application can also affect the review timelines. If the applicant submits a "major amendment" within three months of the end of a review cycle, FDA's regulations state that this constitutes an agreement by the applicant to extend the review cycle by three months. In its PDUFA performance goals under the 2017 reauthorization, however, FDA noted that a major amendment at any time during the review cycle may extend the goal date by three months, with only one extension given per cycle. A major amendment may include, for example, a new clinical safety report, reanalysis of a previously submitted study, or the submission of a REMS including elements to assure safe use that were not included in the original application or that were significantly amended. Submission of an amendment that is not major at any time during a review cycle will not extend the cycle, although FDA also may defer review of such an amendment to the next cycle.

The Postmarketing Period

An applicant's responsibilities with respect to its NDA do not cease upon approval. The postapproval stage brings with it its own set of obligations for the NDA holder.

✦ Changes Affecting an Approved Application

Changes affecting an approved drug are grouped into three categories, each of which carries different procedural requirements. For some changes, the sponsor must submit a supplement to its NDA, and FDA must approve that supplement, before the sponsor can implement the desired changes. This is a "prior approval" supplement. A second group of changes also requires supplementing the NDA, but the sponsor can implement the changes before FDA approves the supplement. These supplements are commonly referred to as "change being effected" supplements. A third category of changes need only be listed in the annual report that the sponsor must file with FDA concerning the drug covered by the NDA.

Changes affecting an approved drug are grouped into three categories, each of which carries different procedural requirements.

Prior approval supplements are required for any change to the drug or its manufacturing processes, equipment, or facilities that has "a substantial potential to have an adverse effect" on the drug's identity, strength, quality, purity, or potency as these factors may relate to its safety or effectiveness. On the manufacturing side, this may include changes in the drug's qualitative or quantitative formulation or approved specifications; changes that may affect the sterility assurance of the drug; and changes in the synthesis of the drug substance that may affect its impurity profile or its physical, chemical, or biological properties. All changes in labeling—including new indications, dosing regimens, populations, and the like—require a prior approval supplement, with limited exceptions that will be discussed below.

"Change being effected" supplements are utilized for changes with only a moderate potential for an adverse effect on the performance of the drug. These supplements fall into two subcategories. The first subcategory requires the sponsor to wait 30 days after submitting the supplement before starting distribution of the drug product incorporating the change in question—the so-called "CBE-30." CBE-30s are to be used, for instance, for a change in the drug's container-closure system that does not affect its quality, or for relaxation of an acceptance criterion or deletion of a test to comply with an official compendium that is consistent with FDA statutory and regulatory requirements. When an applicant submits a CBE-30, it may not distribute the drug incorporating the change in question if within the 30-day period following submission FDA informs it that the change requires prior approval or that required information is missing from the supplement. For the second subcategory of CBE changes,

"Change being effected" supplements are utilized for changes with only a moderate potential for an adverse effect on the performance of the drug.

the applicant may begin distribution of the affected drug product immediately upon receipt by FDA of the supplement. These CBEs are often referred to as CBE-0s. CBE-0s may be used for changes involving addition to a specification or changes in methods or controls to provide increased assurance that the drug will have the characteristics it purports to possess, or a change in labeling that adds or strengthens a contraindication, warning, precaution, or adverse reaction; adds or strengthens dosage and administration information to increase safe use of the product; or deletes false or misleading information.

Finally, changes in conditions with only a minimal potential for an adverse effect on the drug's performance need only be described in the annual report submitted by the applicant. Examples of such changes include editorial or minor changes in labeling, deletion or reduction of an ingredient that only affects the product's color, and changes in the drug's container size or shape without changes in the closure system (for nonsterile solid dosage forms).

◆ Postmarketing Safety-Related Label Changes

A key FDAAA provision aimed at strengthening FDA's safety oversight powers provides FDA with new authority to compel a sponsor to make safety-related changes in drug labeling after approval of the drug. Under this authority, if FDA becomes aware of "new safety information" about a serious drug risk that the agency believes should be included in the drug's labeling, the agency must promptly notify the sponsor. The sponsor then has 30 days to either submit a labeling supplement reflecting the new safety information or explain why it does not believe a labeling change is warranted. If the agency disagrees with the sponsor's conclusion, it must initiate discussions with the sponsor that may not take more than 30 days from the due date of the sponsor's response, unless extended by the agency. Within 15 days of the conclusion of these discussions, FDA may issue an order requiring the sponsor to make those labeling changes FDA deems appropriate to address the new safety information. Violations of any of these requirements by the sponsor will subject the sponsor to misbranding charges and potential civil money penalties.

◆ Adverse Reaction Reporting

"Adverse drug experiences" are somewhat circularly defined under FDA's regulations as any adverse events associated with the use of a drug in humans. An applicant holding an approved NDA or ANDA must promptly review reports of adverse drug experiences associated with its drug, regardless of the source from which such reports are obtained. If a reaction is both serious (e.g., fatal, life threatening, or permanently disabling) and unexpected (not listed in labeling, or differing from reactions listed in the labeling due to greater severity or specificity), it must be reported to FDA in an "alert report" within 15 calendar days of the applicant's receipt of the information. All adverse reactions that are not serious and unexpected must be reported at quarterly intervals for three years after an application is approved, and annually thereafter.

◆ Withdrawal

Although FDA rarely invokes its statutory authority to withdraw NDAs, there are several circumstances under which it can initiate such action. As might be expected, the conditions that can trigger NDA withdrawal generally relate to serious problems with the drug or the application. For instance, FDA can withdraw an NDA if the drug is unsafe for use under the conditions of use for which the application was approved. Similarly, FDA can use its withdrawal authority if new clinical evidence shows that the drug is not safe under approved conditions, or if the drug is not effective. Additionally, FDA can seek withdrawal of an application if the drug's labeling is false or misleading, or if there are inadequate assurances that the drug's quality, strength, and purity are as claimed. The agency also can withdraw an NDA if the sponsor fails to file required patent information in a timely manner, or if the NDA contains false statements of material fact.

Withdrawal
Although FDA rarely invokes its statutory authority to withdraw NDAs, there are several circumstances under which it can initiate such action.

If FDA seeks to withdraw an NDA, usually it must give the applicant notice and the opportunity for a hearing. If the drug in question presents an "imminent hazard," however, the Secretary of the Department of Health and Human Services can summarily suspend approval of the application and give the applicant the opportunity for an expedited hearing. The Secretary cannot delegate the authority to summarily suspend NDAs in this fashion, but can and has delegated to FDA the authority to hold the expedited hearing. In practice, FDA rarely invokes its authority to withdraw or summarily suspend NDAs.

◆ Phase IV Studies

Although clinical studies are a prerequisite to approval, they also are performed after approval as "Phase IV" studies. Such studies can be designed to: 1) obtain additional safety data, 2) obtain additional efficacy data, 3) detect new uses for or abuses of a drug, or 4) determine effectiveness for labeled indications under conditions of widespread usage.

Phase IV
After a new drug is approved, FDA often requires additional studies to obtain more information.

There are at least two reasons FDA may be interested in Phase IV studies. First, such studies allow FDA to grant approval of a new drug on the condition that the applicant complete studies that shed additional light on the drug's safety and efficacy subsequent to approval. Phase IV studies also can be used to facilitate FDA's postapproval monitoring of an approved drug.

The FDAAA added to FDA's postmarketing study toolkit new authority to outright require a sponsor to complete a previously agreed postmarketing study or to impose a new requirement to conduct and complete a postmarketing study on a marketed drug to 1) assess a known serious risk related to use of the drug; 2) assess signals of serious risk related to use of the drug; or 3) identify an unexpected serious risk when available data indicate the potential for such risk. This new authority comes with several restrictions, including that FDA may require a postmarketing study only if adverse event reporting and active surveillance would not be sufficient to fulfill the purpose of the study, and that the required study may take the form of a clinical trial only if a less burdensome kind of study (e.g., a patient registry or an epidemiological study) would not be adequate. Failure to comply with a postmarketing study requirement imposed under this new authority carries with it a potential misbranding charge and substantial civil monetary penalties.

Marketing Protection

The three main statutory market protections in addition to standard patent protection are:

- *the patent extension provisions;*
- *statutory exclusivity for new chemical entities and approvals requiring new clinical studies; and*
- *exclusivity for orphan drugs.*

An issue virtually every drug sponsor faces at some point is what kind of market protection, if any, its product is eligible for, or, conversely, how its product can overcome a competitor's exclusivity in order to enter the market. There are three main statutory routes to securing market protection for qualifying new drug products outside of, or in addition to, standard patent protection: 1) the patent term extension provisions; 2) nonpatent statutory exclusivity provisions for new chemical entities and approvals requiring new clinical studies; and 3) nonpatent exclusivity for orphan drugs.

◆ Patent Term Extension

Congress amended the patent law as part of the 1984 amendments to the FDCA to allow extensions of a product's patent term in certain situations.

The statutory patent term extension provision, codified at section 156 of Title 35 of the United States Code (U.S.C.), recognizes the reality that many pharmaceutical products receive patents long before they are approved for marketing. Because the premarketing regulatory review period may last for a large portion of the product's patent life, Congress amended the patent law as part of the 1984 amendments to the FDCA to allow extensions of a product's patent term in certain situations.

A drug is eligible for a patent term extension if its patent has not expired and has not been extended previously, and if the drug has been subject to a regulatory review period prior to commercial marketing or use. Only one patent per product is eligible for extension.

The length of the extension is based on the length of the regulatory review period. This includes a "testing period," which begins on the date the IND became effective and ends on the date the NDA was submitted, and an "approval period," which covers the time from the submission of the NDA to its approval. In determining the patent extension, each of these two periods will be reduced by: 1) any portion of the period that took place prior to the patent's issuance, and 2) any amount of time during which the applicant did not act with "due diligence" in pursuing regulatory review. After each component of the review period has been calculated and adjusted, the patent will be extended for one-half of the "testing" period and all of the "approval" period, up to a maximum of a five-year extension and a total of 14 years of extended patent life postapproval.

A drug patent owner seeking an extension must submit an application to the Commissioner of Patents and Trademarks within 60 days of receiving NDA approval. FDA assists the Patent and Trademark Office (PTO) in reviewing the application, because only FDA has the information necessary to calculate the regulatory review period and make the due diligence determination. At the end of the review process, the PTO issues or denies the extension.

- **Statutory Exclusivity for New Chemical Entities and Approvals Based on New Studies**

In addition to patent term extension, the FDCA contains provisions that authorize various periods of statutory exclusivity independent of a product's patent status. The goal of these exclusivity provisions is to give innovator drug companies a monetary incentive to invest in the research and testing needed to develop new products, while simultaneously affording consumers broader access to drug products by making available generic products that rely on studies conducted by an innovator company.

Under the FDCA's exclusivity provisions, if an NDA is approved for a drug containing an active ingredient never before approved under an NDA (or "new chemical entity"), then no application for a generic drug that references the drug may be submitted for five years from the date of approval of the drug. Thus, the law in this situation effectively delays generic competition for five years from NDA approval plus the time it takes FDA to review and approve the first generic application. An exception to this five-year rule allows a generic applicant to submit its application beginning four years from the date of NDA approval if that applicant is challenging a patent covering the reference drug (such patent challenges are discussed in more detail below). Another form of statutory market protection is the three years of exclusivity for an NDA or NDA supplement for a previously approved active ingredient if the application contains reports of new clinical studies essential to approval. A second applicant who wishes to market its drug sooner than these exclusivity provisions allow can always do its own clinical studies and submit a full NDA for its version of the product, instead of a generic application, although in practice few companies choose this route because of the cost involved.

Orphan Drugs
Orphan drugs are drugs for diseases that affect 200,000 people or less in the U.S., or that affect more than 200,000 persons and for which there is no reasonable expectation that the manufacturer will recover from U.S. sales the cost of developing and making the drug available in the U.S.

• Orphan Drug Exclusivity

The goal of the Orphan Drug Act of 1983 was to motivate pharmaceutical manufacturers to develop and bring to market drugs for orphan diseases—that is, diseases thought to be too rare to attract the commercial interest of pharmaceutical manufacturers in the ordinary course of business. A "rare" disease is defined in the statute as any disease that affects fewer than 200,000 persons in the United States, or that affects more than 200,000 persons and for which there is no reasonable expectation that the manufacturer will recover from U.S. sales the cost of developing and making the drug available in the United States. Although the Orphan Drug Act created a series of incentives for manufacturers to develop drugs for these rare diseases—including FDA assistance with clinical protocols, available grant assistance for clinical development, and a tax credit for a portion of research and development expenses—by far the most important incentive under this act is the seven-year market exclusivity awarded to the first applicant to obtain marketing approval of a designated orphan drug for a particular disease or condition. To obtain this exclusivity, the applicant must request orphan drug designation for the drug before the submission of the marketing application, and the drug must be so designated before approval of the application. Upon approval of the drug, and assuming that these conditions are met, FDA may not approve another sponsor's application for the same drug for the same disease or condition until seven years from the date of the first applicant's approval, unless: 1) the drug's orphan designation is revoked, 2) its marketing approval is withdrawn, 3) the orphan exclusivity holder consents to the approval of another applicant's product, 4) the orphan exclusivity holder is unable to assure the availability of a sufficient quantity of the drug, or 5) the subsequent sponsor shows that its drug is "clinically superior" to the first sponsor's drug. Clinical superiority may be shown by greater efficacy, greater safety, or a major contribution to patient care.

• Pediatric Exclusivity

Under the Best Pharmaceuticals for Children Act, patent terms, statutory exclusivities, and orphan exclusivity are all eligible for a six-month extension (for an NDA-approved drug only) if the NDA sponsor completes a pediatric study for the drug in response to a written request from FDA.

Under the Best Pharmaceuticals for Children Act (BPCA) (made permanent by FDASIA in 2012), patent terms, statutory exclusivities, and orphan exclusivity are all eligible for a six-month extension (for an NDA-approved drug only) if the NDA sponsor completes a pediatric study for the drug in response to a written request from FDA. Exclusivity can only be granted for the completion of studies that are the subject of a written request, which may include studies that were previously conducted under PREA. If the written request does not require studies in neonates, FDA must include its rationale for not requesting such studies. FDA has 180 days to review studies submitted in response to a written request in order to determine whether the studies comply with the terms of the request, and that determination must be made no later than nine months prior to the expiration of any exclusivity the sponsor wishes to extend. Thus, in practice, a sponsor wishing to qualify for an extension of a particular exclusivity (patent, statutory, or orphan) now must submit its pediatric studies in response to a written request not less than 15 months (180 days plus nine months) prior to the expiration of that exclusivity.

+ **Qualified Infectious Disease Products**

Under the Generating Antibiotics Incentives Now Act (GAIN Act), which was enacted in 2012 as part of FDASIA, a drug designated by FDA to be a Qualified Infectious Disease Product (QIDP) will be granted an extension of exclusivity by five years. QIDPs are also eligible for priority and fast-track review (described below). A QIDP is defined as an antibacterial or antifungal drug that is intended to treat serious or life-threatening infections, including infections that are caused by an antibacterial- or antifungal-resistant pathogen or qualifying pathogens listed by FDA. The additional five-year period of exclusivity may be granted for QIDPs that are approved as part of an NDA, ANDA, supplements to an NDA or ANDA, or for orphan drugs. This extension of exclusivity is also available in addition to any prior granting of pediatric exclusivity by FDA.

FDA Regulation of Drugs: Variations on the Standard Model

Non-NDA Routes to Market: Historical Development

Meeting the safety and efficacy standards required to obtain approval of an NDA entails substantial expense, effort, and expertise. These factors create significant barriers to market entry, a situation that, as in any area of economic activity, can lead to higher prices to consumers. This situation in turn sets up an inherent tension between maintaining the regulatory standards needed to protect the public health and safety, on the one hand, and mitigating the economic burdens imposed by drug prices, on the other. When the need to offer adequate financial incentives to induce companies to undertake the formidable task of new drug development is added to this mixture, the policy equation becomes complex indeed.

Since the passage of the FDCA in 1938, Congress and FDA have made periodic efforts to readjust the balance between each of these goals. Such efforts generally result in further moves to re-level the economic playing field.

◆ "Not New" Drugs

Before the enactment of the FDCA in 1938, there were no significant regulatory barriers to generic competition in the drug market.

Before the enactment of the FDCA in 1938, there were no significant regulatory barriers to generic competition in the drug market. With the statutory establishment of the "new drug" category, however, a drug could not be marketed unless it was either "generally recognized as safe" or its NDA was allowed to become effective absent FDA disapproval, which was the standard approval process under the 1938 version of the act until the 1962 Drug Amendments added the requirement for affirmative FDA approval, as well as the substantive efficacy standard. This process was minimal by today's standards, but it was not cost-free, and as a result imposed certain barriers to entry.

Thus, to facilitate generic competition for post-1938 drugs, FDA established an informal practice whereby, on request, it would inform an interested party whether a particular drug was generally recognized as safe, and consequently not a "new drug" subject to a premarket application. The factual basis for such a "general recognition" decision was typically a history of safe marketing of the pioneer version of the drug in the United States. This policy continued under the 1962 amendments (modified to consider general recognition of both safety and efficacy), but at a slower pace, until the practice was discontinued in 1968 and all such "not new drug" letters were formally revoked by the agency.

◆ The Drug Efficacy Study Implementation Review

DESI Review examines all available data on drugs approved between 1938 and 1962 and makes recommendations as to their efficacy.

The 1962 Drug Amendments contained a provision for the retroactive evaluation of the efficacy of drugs approved as safe (or which had been subject to a "not new drug" letter) between 1938 and 1962. The Drug Efficacy Study Implementation (DESI) Review, established by FDA in 1968, designated the National Academy of Sciences/National Research Council to establish expert panels to review available data on all marketed post-1938 drugs, and to make recommendations as to their efficacy. FDA was then to act on those recommendations by withdrawing drugs found ineffective and by notifying potential generic manufacturers of what information would be required for approval of a generic version of a marketed drug (other than proof of safety and efficacy, which were deemed to have been established by the DESI Review panel).

In response, the agency created a new form of NDA, the ANDA, for which approval was based on sameness of active ingredients and on bioequivalence rather than on safety and efficacy data. This ANDA process for DESI drugs later was codified by statute in the 1984 drug amendments.

◆ **The "Paper NDA" Policy**

As the patent terms on post-1962 drugs began to expire in the 1970s and the early 1980s, it became evident that under existing law there were no feasible means to get competing versions of approved drugs on the market without costly and repetitive testing for safety and efficacy. Because such repeat testing would unnecessarily put more human test subjects at risk, and would waste scarce clinical and agency resources, FDA sought a way to expand the concept of the DESI Review and ANDA policy to generic versions of certain post-1962 drugs. The result was the "paper NDA" policy which, although short-lived, provides a historical and conceptual bridge between the "old drug" and "general recognition" bases for generic drug marketing and the modern statutory ANDA approval process.

The paper NDA policy permitted competing versions of approved new drugs to be approved based on the submission of publicly available reports of well-controlled studies demonstrating the drug's safety and efficacy. The policy was challenged and ultimately upheld in court (*Burroughs Wellcome Co. v. Schweiker*, 649 F.2d 221 (4th Cir. 1981)). Because adequate published studies documenting safety and efficacy were available for only a few post-1962 drugs, however, and because FDA review of such paper NDAs was not significantly easier than for full NDAs, the policy made only a marginal contribution to fostering generic competition. It survives today in modified form as the "505(b)(2)" application, discussed below.

Generic Drugs and the Abbreviated New Drug Application Process

◆ **Legislative Background**

In the late 1970s and early 1980s Congress began to consider legislative options in response to the lack of a viable generic drug approval process for post-1962 drugs. During that time, other legislative efforts were underway to restore the part of drug patents' effective life lost due to increasingly lengthy FDA review times. In 1983, a patent term restoration bill was narrowly defeated in the House of Representatives, and it became apparent that neither an ANDA bill nor a patent term restoration bill could pass Congress independently. As a result, leaders of the generic and innovator sides of the pharmaceutical industry agreed to cooperate in crafting a bill incorporating both the ANDA mechanism sought by generic manufacturers, and patent restoration protections desired by research-based companies. The resulting legislation—the Drug Price Competition and Patent Term Restoration Act—was enacted in 1984.

In the late 1970s and early 1980s Congress began to consider legislative options in response to the lack of a viable generic drug approval process for post-1962 drugs.

153

The dual purposes of this legislation were to expedite the availability of safe and effective, but less expensive, generic versions of approved drugs, while simultaneously encouraging the costly research and development efforts that lead to the discovery of therapeutically important new drugs. The amendments created an abbreviated process whereby a generic company could gain approval of its version of a drug without repeating the expensive and lengthy clinical trials already performed for the drug. As previously discussed, innovator companies received restoration of patent rights to compensate for the time expended in the FDA review process, as well as nonpatent exclusivity for qualifying drug products.

The 1984 amendments also provided protection for the generic drug industry in the form of a provision establishing that it is not an act of patent infringement for a nonpatent holder to make, use, or sell a patented drug during the term of the patent, as long as such activity is reasonably related to the contemplated submission of an application to FDA. This provision, which specifically overruled the early 1984 decision of the newly created Court of Appeals for the Federal Circuit in *Roche Prod., Inc. v. Bolar Pharmaceutical Co.* (733 F.2d 858 (Fed. Cir. 1984)), was necessary to allow generic applicants to have their ANDAs submitted and approved in time to begin marketing on the date of patent expiration. If the court's ruling had stood, development of ANDAs could not have begun until patent expiration. As a result, *de facto* market exclusivity would have extended well beyond the term of the patent. The protection provided by the statutory provision overruling the *Bolar* decision was counterbalanced by a provision allowing an innovator to sue an ANDA applicant upon submission of an ANDA challenging the innovator's patent.

◆ The Statutory ANDA Requirements

The required contents of an ANDA are set forth in section 505(j) of the FDCA and in agency regulations (21 C.F.R. § 314.94). The statute requires that an ANDA contain:

◆ information showing that the proposed conditions of use for the drug have previously been approved for a drug that is listed by FDA as approved for safety and efficacy;

◆ proof that the active ingredient(s) are the same as in the listed drug;

◆ proof that the generic drug will use the same route of administration, dosage form, and strength as the listed drug;

◆ proof that the generic drug is bioequivalent to the listed reference drug;

◆ information showing that the proposed generic labeling is the same as the labeling approved for the listed drug, except for differences related to an approved "suitability petition";

♦ the basic technical information required of a full NDA, including a list of components, statement of the composition of the drug, and description of the methods and facilities used in the production of the drug;

♦ samples of the generic product and proposed labeling; and

♦ a patent certification informing FDA of the patent status of the listed reference drug relied upon by the ANDA.

Although the statutory requirements for an ANDA appear relatively straightforward on their face, many of these requirements have been the basis of contentious administrative and judicial battles.

The Prior Approval and Current Listing Requirements

Two threshold requirements for a drug to be ANDA-eligible are: 1) that the drug's active ingredient has been approved already by FDA for the conditions of use proposed in the ANDA, and 2) that nothing has changed to call into question the basis of approval of the original drug's NDA.

The 1984 amendments require FDA to publish a monthly list of all approved drugs. That publication, commonly known as the *"Orange Book"* (officially titled *Approved Drug Products and Therapeutic Equivalence Evaluations*), serves as the crucial point of reference for many aspects of the ANDA process. In particular, an ANDA may only be submitted if the drug it copies is currently listed in the *Orange Book* as a "reference" listed drug. Such a listing signifies that the drug has been approved, and that as of the date of the *Orange Book* edition consulted, the drug has not been withdrawn from the market over issues of safety or efficacy. Although it is rare for approved drugs later to be found unsafe, an approved drug is on occasion withdrawn from the market voluntarily by the manufacturer. In such cases, FDA must make a determination of whether the drug was withdrawn for safety or effectiveness reasons 1) before approving any ANDA that refers to the listed drug, 2) if any ANDAs that reference the drug have already been approved, or 3) if an interested person petitions FDA to make such a determination.

> *An ANDA may only be submitted if the drug it copies is currently listed in the* Orange Book *as a "reference" listed drug.*

The other situation in which a current listing in the *Orange Book* is significant is when FDA withdraws approval of an NDA pursuant to FDCA section 505(e), as discussed above. This rare occurrence will prevent approval of any pending ANDA for the product and also will serve to withdraw approval of any existing approved ANDAs.

"Suitability Petitions" for Different Active Ingredient(s), Routes of Administration, Dosage Forms, and Strengths

Although a product approved under an ANDA presumptively must have the same active ingredient(s), route of administration, dosage form, and strength as the listed drug it seeks to copy, the FDCA also permits generic products to incorporate differences from those requirements where such differences ultimately will not affect the safety and efficacy of the generic product. (The potential for approval of a generic drug with a different active ingredient from the reference drug only applies to a combination drug for which the generic applicant proposes to substitute a different active ingredient for one of the active ingredients in the reference drug.)

To market a generic product with any of these differences, however, the generic applicant must first submit, and FDA must approve, an ANDA "suitability petition." FDA must act upon a suitability petition within 90 days of receipt and is required to approve any such petition unless it finds that investigations must be conducted in order to demonstrate the safety and efficacy of the generic drug in question.

Bioequivalence

A primary requirement for approval of an ANDA is that the proposed generic drug be shown to be "bioequivalent" to the innovator drug it purports to copy.

A primary requirement for approval of an ANDA is that the proposed generic drug be shown to be "bioequivalent" to the innovator drug it purports to copy. For generic products that meet the bioequivalence requirement, the FDCA allows the presumption that the generic version of the drug will be as safe and as effective as the original version.

The core of the bioequivalence concept, as interpreted by FDA in regulations, is an "absence of a significant difference" in the extent to which, and the rate at which, two different drug products' active ingredients "become available at the site of drug action when administered at the same molar dose under similar conditions in an appropriately designed study." For the typical solid oral dosage form drug, this concept means that one version of the drug provides the same total and peak blood concentrations of the active ingredient as another version. FDA regulations and policy, however, provide a number of different methods for assessing bioequivalence.

FDA regulations require ANDAs to contain either 1) "evidence" of bioequivalence of the ANDA product to the listed reference drug, or 2) "information" showing bioequivalence that is sufficient to allow FDA to waive the "evidence" requirement. In practice, this means that an ANDA must contain either results of human studies showing bioequivalence, or other facts on which FDA can conclude that the ANDA product will be bioequivalent to its reference listed drug.

The regulations regarding "evidence" of bioequivalence specifically state that FDA may accept such evidence based on human (*in vivo*) testing, laboratory (*in vitro*) testing, or both. Those regulations also set out, in rank order of acceptability, types of *in vivo* and *in vitro* tests that may be used to establish bioequivalence. Those tests include *in vivo* blood concentration tests, *in vitro* tests that have been correlated to such *in vivo* blood tests, urinary excretion tests, measurement of observable pharmacological effects over time, comparative clinical trials of safety and efficacy, FDA-accepted *in vitro* dissolution tests, or the catchall "any other approach deemed adequate by FDA" to establish bioequivalence. Consistent with these options, the regulations permit FDA, "for good cause," to "waive a requirement for the submission of evidence of *in vivo* bioavailability if waiver is compatible with the public health." In addition to the *in vivo* and *in vitro* methods referenced in the regulations, FDA draft guidance released in 2013 recommends pharmacokinetic and other study designs ANDA applicants can employ to establish bioequivalence for a variety of drug dosage forms intended for oral and non-oral administration.

Bioequivalence issues associated with generic versions of innovator drugs have created considerable debate and litigation between and among innovator and generic drug companies and FDA. This debate has been particularly focused on drugs that are not "systemically effective"—that is, whose active moiety is not delivered to the site of drug action by systemic blood flow (e.g., drugs that are inhaled, topically applied, or locally active in the gastrointestinal tract, such as antiparasitics).

Bioequivalence issues associated with generic versions of innovator drugs have created considerable debate and litigation between and among innovator and generic drug companies and FDA.

Patent Certification

The final procedural requirement for an ANDA is a patent certification with respect to each patent that covers the reference listed drug the ANDA seeks to copy, or that claims a use for the listed drug. The statute sets out four types of certifications that can be made by a generic applicant in relation to a patent on the reference listed drug:

(I)   that information on the patent has not been filed with FDA by the patent owner;

(II) that the patent already has expired;

(III) a statement of the date on which the patent will expire; or

(IV) that the patent is invalid or will not be infringed by the manufacture, use, or sale of the generic applicant's drug.

FDA by regulation has expanded the paragraph IV certification to include an allegation of unenforceability as well as invalidity or non-infringement and has added a fifth type of certification: a statement that there are no patents that claim the listed drug. It is also possible for a generic applicant to "carve out" a

It is possible for a generic applicant to "carve out" a listed method-of-use patent by stating that it is not seeking approval for the particular indication covered by that patent.

listed method-of-use patent by stating that it is not seeking approval for the particular indication covered by that patent (the so-called "section viii statement," after the statutory subparagraph that addresses it).

If a paragraph I or II certification, or a certification of no relevant patents, is filed, FDA may make approval of the ANDA effective immediately upon completion of its review. If a paragraph III certification is filed, the approval may be made effective on the patent expiration date specified in the ANDA, although a tentative approval may be issued before that time. If the ANDA contains a paragraph IV certification, however, a complex series of events will be triggered, the outcome of which will determine the effective date of approval of the ANDA.

This process begins when a generic company submits an ANDA containing a paragraph IV certification and, as required, notifies the patent owner and the NDA holder that it has submitted such a certification, which is done once FDA has formally accepted the ANDA for review (typically 30 to 60 days after the ANDA is initially submitted, unless the ANDA is refused for filing [see discussion above under "Submitting and Filing the New Drug Application"]). The notification must set forth in detail the factual and legal bases for the ANDA applicant's belief that the listed patent is invalid or will not be infringed by the ANDA applicant's drug.

After receiving this paragraph IV notification, the patent/NDA holder must evaluate the legal and factual arguments asserted by the ANDA applicant. If the patent/NDA holder so decides, it may file a lawsuit against the applicant for patent infringement. The lawsuit must be filed within 45 days of receipt of the paragraph IV notification, or FDA may make approval of the ANDA effective immediately upon the conclusion of the review process. If a lawsuit is brought, an automatic statutory injunction prohibits FDA from making approval of the ANDA effective for 30 months, unless the court rules in favor of the generic company prior to that time or unless the 30-month injunction is shortened or lengthened by the district court in response to undue delay by either party.

Filing a paragraph IV certification is an "artificial act" of patent infringement created by the 1984 amendments to allow the courts to decide whether the patent is valid, or if the proposed future manufacture and sale of the generic version would infringe the patent. Without making the paragraph IV certification itself an act of infringement, it was believed that the courts would be barred under the Constitution from issuing what would otherwise amount to an advisory opinion about potential future infringement by the generic competitor. Once a patent suit based on a paragraph IV certification is brought, the only issues to be decided are whether the proposed generic marketing of the drug will infringe the patent, or whether the patent is otherwise invalid or unenforceable.

Although a paragraph IV challenge is often costly and difficult, the 1984 amendments included an incentive for a generic company to bring such a challenge in the form of a 180-day delay in FDA approval of other companies' ANDAs to the benefit of a generic company that first challenges a listed drug patent. The original version of this incentive provision was ambiguous in several respects and gave rise to frequent litigation, creating uncertainty that seriously undermined its effectiveness. In December 2003 Congress amended the 180-day exclusivity provision, resolving a good deal of the previous uncertainty in favor of an approach aimed at balancing the exclusivity incentive with the interest of getting generic drugs onto the market more quickly and reliably. In particular, the December 2003 amendments established a mechanism whereby a first paragraph IV challenger could forfeit its right to the 180-day exclusivity under a variety of circumstances, including the failure to put its generic drug on the market within a specified period following approval.

> *Although a paragraph IV challenge is often costly and difficult, the 1984 amendments included an incentive for a generic company to bring such a challenge in the form of a 180-day delay in FDA approval of other companies' ANDAs to the benefit of a generic company that first challenges a listed drug patent.*

◆ The Abbreviated New Drug Application: FDA Action and Time Frames

GDUFA was first enacted as part of FDASIA in 2012 and was reauthorized in 2017 as part of FDARA. Under the 2017 reauthorization, FDA is authorized to collect user fees, which are intended to provide the agency with the additional resources it needs to review generic drug applications. Similar to PDUFA, the enactment of GDUFA was accompanied by a commitment by FDA to meet performance goals for the review of ANDAs that has been continued with the 2017 reauthorization. The 2017 reauthorization of GDUFA (GDUFA II) will sunset on October 1, 2022.

> *FDA is authorized to collect user fees, which are intended to provide the agency with the additional resources it needs to review generic drug applications.*

Under GDUFA II, FDA collects Drug Master File fees, ANDA and prior approval supplement filing fees, Generic Drug/Active Pharmaceutical Ingredient Facility fees, and program fees, which are assessed on a sliding scale depending on the number of approved ANDAs owned by the applicant. These fees are each required to constitute a fixed percentage of the total user fee revenue collected. FDA also collected a one-time backlog user fee for pending ANDAs that did not receive tentative approval by October 1, 2012 (this authority was extended under GDUFA II but will expire on October 1, 2022). In exchange, FDA commits to act on pending ANDAs, ANDA amendments, and ANDA prior approval supplements within specified time frames. GDUFA II also contains provisions intended to enhance competition and supply in the generic drug marketplace, including the establishment of 1) a new category of priority ANDAs, which may be subject to shorter deadlines for FDA action, for generic drugs for which there are no more than three approved drug products and which are not subject to any blocking patents or exclusivities, and 2) a new category of "competitive generic therapies," meaning generic drugs for which FDA determines there is inadequate generic competition, that may receive enhanced FDA review and senior management attention and that enjoy a 180-day period of protection against approval of a second generic application for the same drug, subject to certain limitations.

Amendments to ANDA applications, which are grouped by FDA under three tiers, are subject to a separate set of performance goals that can result in the addition of time to a review goal date. Tier 1 amendments include all solicited first major and the first five minor amendments. All unsolicited amendments that are viewed by FDA to be the result of delaying actions or that otherwise would eventually be solicited are also considered Tier 1 amendments. Tier 2 amendments include all unsolicited amendments that FDA determines are not the result of delaying actions. Tier 3 amendments include any solicited major amendment that follows the first major amendment and any solicited minor amendment subsequent to the fifth minor amendment.

The Modern "Paper NDA"—Section 505(b)(2) Applications

The 505(b)(2) application provides for NDAs submitted by an applicant in reliance on safety and efficacy data supplied by another applicant, and to which the 505(b)(2) applicant has no right of reference.

In addition to codifying procedures for ANDAs, the 1984 amendments also established a new category of NDA under section 505(b) of the FDCA—the "505(b)(2) application." This type of application, like the earlier paper NDA, provides for NDAs submitted by an applicant in reliance on safety and efficacy data supplied by another applicant, and to which the 505(b)(2) applicant has no right of reference. Unlike with the old paper NDA, however, the 505(b)(2) applicant is not restricted to reliance on published studies, but may also rely on previous FDA findings of safety and efficacy for another applicant's drug based on unpublished data in FDA's files that is no longer legally protected.

There are several scenarios where a 505(b)(2) application may come into play. One involves an applicant that seeks to market its version of an established drug for a new therapeutic indication or with some other modification requiring new clinical studies, and seeks to rely on relevant safety findings on the drug in a previously approved NDA. Another scenario is where an ANDA suitability petition for a significantly different version of an approved drug—such as a different dosage form or route of administration—is inappropriate because clinical studies are required, but prior studies on the original drug product are still relevant to showing the overall safety and efficacy of the new version of the drug.

The 505(b)(2) application also is similar to an ANDA in that the applicant is required to certify as to the patent status of the drug for which the referenced investigations were conducted, by stating either that the relevant patent information has not been filed by the original applicant (as evidenced by the lack of a listing in the *Orange Book*), that such patent has expired, the date on which the patent will expire, that there are no patents that cover the listed drug, or that the patent is invalid, unenforceable, or will not be infringed by the manufacture, use, or sale of the proposed 505(b)(2) drug. Also, as with ANDAs, the 505(b)(2) applicant that files a paragraph IV patent certification of invalidity or non-infringement must notify the patent holder, who then has 45 days to decide whether to sue the applicant for patent infringement and trigger an automatic 30-month statutory injunction while the courts decide the substantive patent issues involved. Unlike the ANDA situation, however, no 180-day exclusivity is available in connection with a 505(b)(2) application.

Over-the-Counter Drugs

◆ The OTC Review

As noted above, in order to avoid regulation as a new drug, a drug ordinarily must be deemed generally recognized as safe and effective (GRAS/GRAE). The test for general recognition of safety and effectiveness, as it has been applied by FDA and the courts, is a stringent one. In brief, it requires 1) that the drug be "generally recognized, among experts qualified by scientific training and experience to evaluate the safety and effectiveness of drugs, as safe and effective for use under the conditions prescribed, recommended, or suggested in the labeling thereof"; 2) that such general recognition be based on adequate published data demonstrating the drug's safety and efficacy (*Weinberger v. Bentex Pharm., Inc.*, 412 U.S. 645, 652 (1973)); and 3) that the drug have been used "to a material extent" and "for a material time" under the labeled conditions. The courts have stipulated that general recognition of effectiveness for an individual drug product must be supported by the same level of evidence as required for an NDA, including adequate and well-controlled investigations demonstrating efficacy (*Weinberger v. Hynson, Westcott & Dunning, Inc.*, 412 U.S. 609, 629-32 (1973)).

Although it is exceedingly difficult for a drug product to qualify as GRAS/GRAE on an individual basis, the GRAS/GRAE concept has provided FDA with a key legal tool to regulate over-the-counter (OTC) drugs, namely the OTC review. Starting in 1972, FDA instituted a system to review the safety and efficacy of active ingredients (as opposed to individual drug products) in each category of OTC drugs. For each such category, FDA issues a call-for-data notice that is published in the *Federal Register*. These notices ask manufacturers to submit clinical/marketing data for the individual active ingredients contained in their products. The agency then convenes expert advisory panels that are responsible for reviewing the data submissions for the active ingredients in each category.

Once each panel is finished with its review of the active ingredients and the submitted data, it is responsible for providing a final report to FDA. This report reviews each ingredient and places it into one of three categories. Category I ingredients are deemed GRAS/GRAE; Category II ingredients are considered either unsafe or ineffective, or both; and Category III ingredients are viewed

In order to avoid regulation as a new drug, a drug ordinarily must be deemed generally recognized as safe and effective.

The test for general recognition of safety and effectiveness requires:
- *that the drug be "generally recognized, among experts qualified by scientific training and experience to evaluate the safety and effectiveness of drugs, as safe and effective for use under the conditions prescribed, recommended, or suggested in the labeling thereof;"*
- *that such general recognition be based on adequate published data demonstrating the drug's safety and efficacy; and*
- *that the drug have been used "to a material extent" and "for a material time" under the labeled conditions.*

as having insufficient data to determine safety and/or efficacy. The report is published by FDA in the *Federal Register* as an advance notice of proposed rule-making with an opportunity for public comment. FDA then reviews the report, takes into account any public comment and publishes in the *Federal Register* its interpretation of the report, sometimes disagreeing with the panel's interpretations and making changes as necessary. This action, which is also open for public comment, is referred to as the Tentative Final Monograph, and is technically a notice of proposed rulemaking.

FDA then undertakes a final review of the ingredients, again taking into account any public comments, which could include new or additional data. On this basis, the agency publishes in the *Federal Register* a rule establishing a Final Monograph. Following the effective date of the Final Monograph (usually a year after publication), continued marketing is permitted only for drug products with active ingredients, labeling claims, dosage strengths, and other specified conditions included in the Final Monograph.

Occasionally, companies petition FDA to re-open or amend an OTC monograph, or FDA sees a need to re-open the review of a particular category of drugs. The agency will publish a notice in the *Federal Register* to that effect. This action is considered a proposed monograph amendment (technically a notice of proposed rulemaking) and is open for public comment. The review process then proceeds as explained above.

While most OTC drug categories have been finalized by FDA, the OTC drug review process technically remains open, with certain categories of drugs still under review. Until a Final Monograph is published in the *Federal Register* and takes effect, all products containing active ingredients under review in a particular category and meeting certain other conditions regarding labeling claims and other product attributes may continue to be marketed although FDA may take regulatory action against an individual ingredient or product over safety or efficacy issues.

◆ Rx-to-OTC Switches

There are three ways to make an Rx-to-OTC switch:
- *the manufacturer supplements an existing NDA*
- *FDA creates or amends an OTC monograph*
- *the manufacturer can petition FDA for the switch*

A rapidly increasing proportion of the OTC market is made up of products that originally were approved as prescription drugs and subsequently were switched to OTC status, a transition commonly referred to as an "Rx-to-OTC switch." There are three ways to accomplish such a switch: a drug manufacturer can supplement the drug's existing NDA; FDA may create or amend an OTC monograph; or the manufacturer may petition FDA to make the switch.

Currently, by far the most common way to accomplish the Rx-to-OTC switch is by supplementing the drug's NDA. This is in large part due to the opportunity this route affords the drug's sponsor to obtain marketing exclusivity for the switched product. In particular, if the Rx-to-OTC switch supplement involves a change to the drug that is supported by "new clinical investigations" that are "conducted or sponsored by [the applicant]" and are "essential to the [supplement's] approval," the applicant will gain three additional years of marketing exclusivity for the OTC product, as discussed above. There is no set formula for determining what kinds or changes will meet the exclusivity requirements; such changes can relate to such matters as active ingredient, dosage form, route of administration, conditions of use, or dosing regimen.

Procedurally, an applicant seeking to switch a product must file a supplemental application to the drug's NDA and must include a statement explaining why its studies meet the requirements for exclusivity, as described above. Next, FDA will decide whether to approve the switch, and subsequently will make the exclusivity determination. Generic manufacturers of the switched product, however, may file citizen petitions or take other administrative or legal actions to encourage FDA to deny exclusivity. Conversely, a manufacturer who is unhappy with an agency denial of exclusivity may challenge that denial in court.

Expedited Availability

As discussed above, one major response to concerns about drug approval delays has been the establishment of the user fee system. Separate and apart from that system, however, a number of special pathways have been created both by FDA and Congress to expedite the availability of drugs for seriously ill patients. This section provides a brief review of those pathways.

◆ Treatment INDs

The treatment IND mechanism, established by regulation in 1987 and codified by FDAMA, allows an investigational drug to be provided outside controlled clinical trials to treat patients with serious or immediately life-threatening diseases for which no comparable or satisfactory alternative therapy is available. The standard for FDA clearance of a treatment IND for a "life-threatening disease" is whether the available scientific evidence, taken as a whole, provides a reasonable basis for concluding that the drug "may be effective for its intended use" and would not expose patients to an "unreasonable and significant risk of illness or injury." For a "serious" disease, the standard is whether there is "sufficient evidence of safety and effectiveness" to support treatment use. Most IND procedural requirements apply to treatment INDs, including informed consent requirements and prohibitions on pre-approval promotion or other commercialization of experimental treatments (although companies may charge patients enough to cover costs). In addition, the drug sponsor is expected to continue conventional clinical trials and to pursue marketing approval of the drug with "due diligence."

The treatment IND mechanism, established by regulation in 1987 and codified by FDAMA, allows an investigational drug to be provided outside controlled clinical trials to treat patients with serious or immediately life-threatening diseases for which no comparable or satisfactory alternative therapy is available.

✦ Individual Patient Access to Investigational Drugs for Serious Diseases

Under the expanded access mechanism established by FDAMA in 1997, a patient acting through a physician may request an investigational drug, and a manufacturer may provide such a drug, if the patient's physician determines that the patient has no comparable or satisfactory alternative therapy, and that the risk to the patient from the investigational drug is no greater than the risk from the disease or condition. For a drug to qualify for this mechanism, FDA must determine that there is sufficient evidence of safety and effectiveness to support its use and that provision of the investigational drug will not interfere with clinical investigations in support of marketing approval. In addition, the sponsor or clinical investigator must submit to FDA a protocol describing the use of the drug in a single patient or small group of patients. Under the 21st Century Cures Act of 2016, the sponsor of an investigational drug is required to publish its policy on handling such patient requests.

✦ Emergency Access

FDAMA also codified current regulations permitting the shipment of investigational new drugs for the diagnosis, monitoring, or treatment of a serious condition or disease in emergency situations as determined by FDA.

✦ Fast-Track Approval

Fast-track designation is available for drugs or biologics, whether alone or in combination with one or more drugs, that demonstrate the potential to address unmet medical needs for serious or life-threatening diseases or conditions.

Under the fast-track authority established by FDAMA, and broadened by FDASIA, the fast-track designation is available for drugs or biologics, whether alone or in combination with one or more drugs, that demonstrate the potential to address unmet medical needs for serious or life-threatening diseases or conditions. A QIDP-designated drug under the GAIN Act is also eligible for fast-track review.

Under FDA's 2014 guidance describing expedited programs for serious conditions, the first step in the fast-track program is that the sponsor requests FDA to designate its drug as a fast-track product. FDA recommends that sponsors request fast-track status no later than the date of the sponsor's pre-NDA or pre-BLA meeting with the agency. If the drug is given fast-track status, the sponsor will have the opportunity to participate in FDA-sponsor meetings that can result in an expedited review process. In addition, FDA may review portions of a drug application prior to submission of the sponsor's complete application. This rolling review process may occur only after FDA conducts a preliminary assessment of the sponsor's clinical data and determines that the drug may be effective. FDA's acceptance of a sponsor's application sections does not, however, obligate the agency to commence its review or to meet its review performance goals prior to receipt of the sponsor's complete application. In addition, FDA can withdraw a drug's fast-track designation if the drug is found to no longer address an unmet medical need or if a study is conducted in a manner that does not show the drug's ability to treat a serious condition and fulfill an unmet medical need.

♦ Accelerated Approval

Under its accelerated approval authority, FDA may approve a product for a serious or life-threatening disease or condition, including a fast-track product, if it is found to have an effect on a surrogate endpoint that is reasonably likely to predict a clinical benefit. FDA may also approve a product under accelerated approval authority if it is found to have an effect on a clinical endpoint that can be measured earlier than an effect on irreversible morbidity or mortality (also referred to as an intermediate endpoint).

FDA may approve a product for a serious or life-threatening disease or condition, including a fast-track product, if it is found to have an effect on a surrogate endpoint that is reasonably likely to predict a clinical benefit.

According to FDA's 2014 guidance on expedited programs, a surrogate endpoint, for accelerated approval purposes, may be a laboratory measurement, radiographic image, or other type of measure that could be used to support a prediction of a clinical benefit. An intermediate clinical endpoint under accelerated approval would need to measure a therapeutic effect that is reasonably likely to predict the clinical benefit of a drug on irreversible morbidity or mortality. The evidence to support accelerated approval may be epidemiological, pathophysiological, therapeutic, pharmacologic, or based on the use of biomarkers. Accelerated approval can be withdrawn if, for example, a sponsor's study fails to confirm a drug's predicted effect on morbidity or mortality or other clinical benefit, or if the product is determined not to be safe or effective. Approval is also subject to pre- and postapproval submission of product promotional materials.

In its draft guidance, FDA noted that although accelerated approval will generally apply to drugs that provide a meaningful therapeutic benefit in comparison to existing treatments, FDA may also grant accelerated approval to drugs that, despite the lack of a comparative therapeutic benefit, may demonstrate a clinically important improvement from a patient and public health standpoint. This may occur, for example, if approved therapies for a condition are characterized by modest response rates or are heterogeneous in their response.

♦ Breakthrough Therapy

The breakthrough therapy designation was established under FDASIA to expedite the development and review of a drug, whether alone or in combination with one or more drugs, to treat a serious or life-threatening disease or condition and preliminary clinical evidence indicates that the drug may demonstrate substantial improvement over existing therapies on one or more clinically significant endpoints. Preliminary clinical evidence may be early evidence of both a clinical benefit and an effect on a mechanistic biomarker (i.e., a biomarker with activity that is conducted through a theoretical mechanism of action for a disease). A finding of substantial improvement should evidence a drug's advantage over an available therapy that may, for example, only show a moderate response. A clinically significant endpoint for breakthrough therapy purposes will measure an effect on irreversible morbidity or mortality or on serious symptoms.

A request for breakthrough designation can be made with the submission of an IND or at any time following submission of an application as an amendment to an IND. In draft guidance, however, FDA noted that a breakthrough designation request should occur no later than the end of Phase 2 meeting. A drug that qualifies for designation as a breakthrough therapy will also qualify for fast-track status. As development and review of a breakthrough therapy may occur over a short period of time when compared to other drug development programs, FDA will likely meet with sponsors on a regular basis to discuss clinical trial designs that will yield the information that is needed to facilitate an accelerated review and approval process.

◆ Priority Review

A drug application will receive a priority review designation if it treats a serious condition and, if approved, would provide significant improvement in safety or effectiveness.

A drug application will receive a priority review designation if it treats a serious condition and, if approved, would provide significant improvement in safety or effectiveness. FDA must review and take action on a priority review application within six months of its receipt date. Every drug application submitted to FDA is subject to consideration for priority review, even if the applicant does not request this designation. An application may also receive priority review by statute. For example, under FDASIA, priority review (in addition to fast-track review) applies to QIDP drugs as well as to applications that are submitted with a rare pediatric disease priority review voucher. This voucher is issued to an applicant upon the approval of a drug for the treatment of a rare pediatric disease.

The Combination Drug Policy

FDA's combination drug policy provides that:

(a) Two or more drugs may be combined in a single dosage form when each component makes a contribution to the claimed effects and the dosage of each component (amount, frequency, duration) is such that the combination is safe and effective for a significant patient population requiring such concurrent therapy as defined in the labeling for the drug. Special cases of this general rule are where a component is added:

(1) To enhance the safety or effectiveness of the principal active component; and

(2) To minimize the potential for abuse of the principal active component.

21 C.F.R. § 300.50.

Although this regulation on its face reads as a permissive policy, it was actually promulgated to require additional evidence of efficacy for many fixed combination drug products already on the market. For an NDA for a combination drug containing two (or more) active ingredients, the combination policy means that evidence of safety and efficacy would be required not only for the drug as a whole, but also for each of the components. In other words, each component must be shown to contribute individually to the claimed overall effects of the product. This contribution, however, need not relate to efficacy—a component also may be added if it is shown to increase the safety of the other component or components. Of key importance under the combination drug policy is the principle that prior efficacy (or safety) results on individual active components cannot be extrapolated to a proposed combination drug; rather, that combination drug must undergo its own clinical investigations to demonstrate safety, efficacy, and the contribution of the active components. Like many such principles in the drug approval setting, however, this one is not necessarily absolute, and FDA may exhibit more (or less) flexibility in individual cases.

BIOLOGICS

In simple terms, biological products (sometimes referred to as "biologics" or "biologicals") are medical products derived from living organisms. Such products are regulated under section 351 of the PHSA (42 U.S.C. § 262), as well as under various provisions of the FDCA. Legally, biological products are defined under section 351 of the PHSA as including "a virus, therapeutic serum, toxin, antitoxin, vaccine, blood, blood component or derivative, allergenic product, protein (except any chemically synthesized polypeptide), or analogous product, or arsphenamine or derivatives of arsphenamine (or any other trivalent organic arsenic compound) applicable to the prevention, treatment, or cure of a disease or condition of human beings." To be lawfully marketed in interstate commerce, a biological product must be the subject of a biologics license, issued by FDA on the basis of a demonstration that the product is "safe, pure, and potent," and that the facility in which the product is manufactured meets standards to assure that it continues to be safe, pure, and potent.

In simple terms, biological products (sometimes referred to as "biologics" or "biologicals") are medical products derived from living organisms.

Originally, the regulatory scheme for biologics was quite distinct from that for nonbiologic drugs.

Originally, the regulatory scheme for biologics was quite distinct from that for nonbiologic drugs. The most prominent difference was that whereas drugs must obtain NDAs in order to be lawfully marketed, biological products were the subject of a bifurcated approval system under which a product had to obtain a product license, by means of a product license application (PLA), *and* the establishment where the product was manufactured had to obtain an establishment license, through an establishment license application (ELA), before the product could be lawfully marketed.

In 1997, however, FDAMA amended section 351 of the PHSA to establish the single biologics license in place of the former product and establishment licenses for all biological products. FDAMA also stipulated that the FDCA applies to a biological product, with the sole exception that a product for which a license has been approved under PHSA § 351 is not required to have an approved NDA. Finally, Congress stated directly in FDAMA that FDA "shall take measures to minimize differences in the review and approval" of new drugs and biologics. For most practical purposes, therefore, the regulation of human therapeutic biologics in both the pre-approval and postapproval periods is closely similar to that of new drugs.

The regulation of human therapeutic biologics in both the pre-approval and postapproval periods is closely similar to that of new drugs.

Thus, as in the new drug model previously discussed, to gain marketing approval for a therapeutic biologic, the sponsor of that biologic must demonstrate its safety and efficacy for its recommended uses. Along the road to that approval, the IND requirements applicable to new drugs also apply to the investigation of therapeutic biologics. Similarly, in the postapproval world, biologics manufacturers must report adverse events under a scheme similar to that for drugs (21 C.F.R. Part 600, Subpart D).

Biosimilars

In March 2010—more than 25 years after the enactment of the law establishing the modern ANDA system for approval of generic drugs, and following a lengthy period of policy and legislative debate—Congress enacted the Biologics Price Competition and Innovation Act of 2009 (BPCIA), establishing a pathway for abbreviated approval of biologics, or so-called biosimilars. The BPCIA was part of a comprehensive package of healthcare reform legislation, the Patient Protection and Affordable Care Act. While the fundamental concept of creating an abbreviated approval pathway for subsequent-entry products is common to both ANDAs and biosimilars, the requirements for these two categories of products are fundamentally different in a number of respects, reflecting the scientific differences between drugs and biologics.

◆ Application and Approval Requirements

The BPCIA amended section 351 of the PHSA by adding a new subsection (k) establishing requirements for biosimilar applications and approval. Under subsection (k), a biosimilar application must include information demonstrating that: 1) the biological product that is the subject of the application is "biosimilar" to a reference product; 2) the biosimilar product and reference product use the same mechanism(s) of action for the condition(s) of use prescribed, recommended, or suggested in the proposed labeling, to the extent the mechanism(s) of action are known for the reference product; 3) the condition(s) of use prescribed, recommended, or suggested in the labeling proposed for the biosimilar product have been previously approved for the reference product; 4) the biosimilar product has the same route of administration, dosage form, and strength as the reference product; and 5) the facility in which the biosimilar product is manufactured, processed, packed, or held meets standards designed to assure that the product continues to be safe, pure, and potent.

FDA must license a biosimilar if: 1) the agency determines that the information in the application is sufficient to show that the biological product is biosimilar to (or, if sought by the applicant, interchangeable with) the reference product; and 2) the applicant or other appropriate person consents to inspection of the facility that is the subject of the application.

For purposes of this statute, "biosimilarity" means that the biological product in question is "highly similar" to the reference product "notwithstanding minor differences in clinically inactive components" and that there are no clinically meaningful differences between the biological product and the reference product in terms of safety, purity, or potency. The biosimilar application must establish biosimilarity on the basis of data from 1) analytical studies showing that the biosimilar and its reference product are "highly similar" notwithstanding minor differences in clinically inactive components; 2) animal studies, including an assessment of toxicity; and 3) a clinical study or studies (including an assessment of immunogenicity and pharmacokinetics or pharmacodynamics) sufficient to show the safety, purity, and potency of the proposed product for one or more "appropriate" conditions of use for which licensure is sought and for which the reference product is licensed. FDA may, however, waive any of these application requirements if it determines they are unnecessary for a finding of biosimilarity.

> *"Biosimilarity" means that the biological product in question is "highly similar" to the reference product "notwithstanding minor differences in clinically inactive components" and that there are no clinically meaningful differences between the biological product and the reference product in terms of safety, purity, or potency.*

◆ Interchangeability

While a generic drug approved under an ANDA is presumptively the "same" as, and therefore interchangeable with, its reference product, this is not the case for

A biosimilar applicant that wishes its product to be considered interchangeable with the reference product must separately seek and obtain an interchangeability determination from FDA.

biosimilars. Rather, a biosimilar applicant that wishes its product to be considered interchangeable with the reference product must separately seek and obtain an interchangeability determination from FDA. The agency must reach such a determination if it finds that the information submitted in the application shows that: 1) the biological product is biosimilar to the reference product, and 2) the biological product can be expected to produce the same clinical result as the reference product in any given patient. If the product will be administered more than once to an individual, FDA must also find the risk in terms of safety or diminished efficacy of alternating or switching between the two products is not greater than the risk of using the reference product without such alternation or switching. A product that qualifies as interchangeable under the statute may be substituted for its reference product without the intervention of the prescriber.

As a counterpart of the 180-day exclusivity available to the first ANDA applicant to challenge a listed patent covering the reference drug, the first biosimilar product determined to be interchangeable with a particular reference product for any condition of use receives a period of exclusivity protection during which no other product may be deemed interchangeable to that reference product for any condition of use. The exclusivity period terminates on the earlier of: 1) one year after the first commercial marketing of the first interchangeable biosimilar product; 2) 18 months after either a final court decision on all patents in suit, or the dismissal with or without prejudice of an action brought by the reference product sponsor against the biosimilar applicant under the patent resolution provisions of the BPCIA (discussed below); 3) 42 months after approval of the first interchangeable biosimilar product, if the applicant has been sued under section 351(l)(6) and the litigation is still ongoing; or 4) 18 months after approval of the first interchangeable product, if the applicant has not been sued under section 351(l)(6). For this purpose "interchangeable" means that the biosimilar "may be substituted for the reference product without the intervention of the health care provider who prescribed the reference product."

◆ **Exclusivity**

FDA may not make approval of a biosimilar application effective until 12 years after the date on which the reference product was first licensed. A biosimilar application may not be submitted until four years after the date on which the reference product was first licensed under section 351(a). A supplement to the reference product application is not eligible for these exclusivity periods, nor is a subsequent application filed by the same sponsor or a related entity for 1) a change (not including a structural modification) that results in a new indication, route of administration, dosing schedule, dosage form, delivery system, delivery device, or strength, or 2) a structural modification that does not result in a change in safety, purity, or potency. The available exclusivity periods may be extended by six months if the sponsor satisfies the statute's pediatric testing requirements. These requirements incorporate by reference the key provisions of the Best Pharmaceuticals for Children Act, which sets forth the basic scheme for pediatric exclusivity for new drugs (discussed above).

◆ Patents

In lieu of the *Orange Book* patent listing process under the Drug Price Competition and Patent Term Restoration legislation, under the BPCIA the reference product sponsor and biosimilar applicant privately exchange information about relevant patents as a prelude to possible patent infringement litigation. The statute's mechanism for resolving patent disputes may be altered by agreement between the parties.

Under the BPCIA the reference product sponsor and biosimilar applicant privately exchange information about relevant patents as a prelude to possible patent infringement litigation.

Under the BPCIA mechanism, within 20 days after FDA notifies the biosimilar applicant that the application has been accepted for review, the applicant must send the reference product sponsor a copy of the application and information describing the processes used to manufacture the biosimilar. Outside counsel and one in-house counsel for the reference product sponsor are entitled to confidential access to the application and accompanying information, provided those attorneys do not engage in formal or informal patent prosecution related to the reference product. If the biosimilar applicant fails to provide the required information to the reference product sponsor, the sponsor may bring an action against the biosimilar applicant for a declaration of infringement, validity, or enforceability of any patent that claims the biological product or a use of that product.

Within 60 days after receiving this information, the reference product sponsor must provide the biosimilar applicant with a list of patents for which the sponsor believes it (or a patent owner that has granted it an exclusive license) could reasonably assert a claim of patent infringement, and must identify which patents it would be prepared to license to the applicant. Within 60 days of receiving this list, the biosimilar applicant may provide to the reference product sponsor its own list of patents for which it believes the reference product sponsor (or a patent owner that has granted it an exclusive license) could reasonably assert a claim of patent infringement. It must also provide, for each patent listed by the reference sponsor or itself, either: 1) a detailed statement that describes, on a claim-by-claim basis, the factual and legal basis of its opinion that the patent is invalid, unenforceable, or will not be infringed by the commercial marketing of the biosimilar product; or 2) a statement that it does not intend to begin commercial marketing of its product until after expiry of the patent. The biosimilar applicant must also provide a response regarding each patent that the reference product sponsor has stated it is prepared to license to the applicant.

Not more than 60 days after receiving this information, the reference product sponsor must provide the biosimilar applicant with a detailed statement describing on a claim-by-claim basis, as to each patent that the biosimilar applicant claims to be not infringed, why the sponsor believes the patent will be infringed by the commercial marketing of the biosimilar, and, as to each patent the biosimilar applicant claims to be invalid and not enforceable, a response to the biosimilar applicant's claim.

Following these exchanges, the parties must engage in good faith negotiations to agree which patents will be the subject of an action for patent infringement pursuant to the expedited process provided in the statute. If the parties do not agree on such a list of patents within 15 days, the parties will simultaneously exchange lists of patents each believes should be the subject of a patent infringement action. (The reference sponsor's list may not contain more patents than the biosimilar applicant's list, except that if the biosimilar applicant does not list any patents the reference sponsor may list one.)

If the parties agree on a list of patents to be litigated, the reference product sponsor must bring the infringement action within 30 days after the agreement.

If the parties agree on a list of patents to be litigated, the reference product sponsor must bring the infringement action within 30 days after the agreement. If the parties do not agree, the reference product sponsor must bring an infringement action within 30 days after the exchange of lists as described above. Failure to adhere to these deadlines will limit the reference product sponsor's remedy to a reasonable royalty. Not more than 30 days after being served with a complaint in such an infringement action, the biosimilar applicant must provide a copy of the complaint to FDA, which will then publish notice of the complaint in the *Federal Register*.

♦ If the reference product sponsor should have included a patent in its initial list but failed to do in a timely fashion, the patent owner may not bring a patent infringement action with respect to the biosimilar.

♦ After the list of patents has been initially provided to the biosimilar applicant, a patent newly issued to or exclusively licensed by the reference product sponsor that the sponsor reasonably believes could be asserted in an infringement action must be provided to the biosimilar applicant in a supplement to the initial list not more than 30 days after the issuance or licensing.

♦ The biosimilar applicant must provide notice to the reference product sponsor not less than 180 days before the first commercial marketing of the biosimilar product. The reference product sponsor then may seek a preliminary injunction against the marketing of the biosimilar product until the court has reached a finding as to any patent that was in its initial list but not subject to expedited litigation under the statute.

◆ Guidance Documents

Section 351(k) provides that FDA may issue general or specific guidance on the licensure of biosimilars. If the agency issues guidance, it must follow the requirements of section 701(h) of the FDCA (which addresses FDA's authority to issue nonbinding guidance documents generally), and must offer the public an opportunity to comment before finalizing the document. FDA must also establish a process for the public to provide input on priorities for issuing guidance.

FDA may issue general or specific guidance on the licensure of biosimilars.

Significantly, the issuance or non-issuance of guidance does not preclude the review of, or action on, an application submitted under section 351(k).

If FDA issues a product class-specific guidance, that guidance must include a description of the criteria FDA will use to determine whether a biological product is highly similar to a reference product in that product class, as well as the criteria, if available, that FDA will use to determine whether a biological product in that class meets the standards for interchangeability. FDA may indicate in a guidance that science and experience, as of the date of the guidance, do not allow approval of section 351(k) applications with respect to a particular product or product class, not including recombinant proteins.

FDA has issued a number of draft and final guidances on biosimilar topics, including formal meetings between FDA and sponsors (2015); scientific considerations in demonstrating biosimilarity (2015); quality considerations in demonstrating biosimilarity (2015); clinical pharmacology data to support a demonstration of biosimilarity (2016); reference product exclusivity (2014); and considerations in demonstrating interchangeability (2017).

◆ The Biosimilar Application: FDA Action and Time Frames

The Biosimilar User Fee Act of 2012 (BsUFA), which was enacted under FDASIA concurrent with the reauthorization of PDUFA and enactment of GDUFA, authorizes FDA to collect user fees to support the review of biosimilar applications, and is expected to follow a five-year reauthorization cycle. BsUFA was reauthorized in 2017 (BSUFA II) and is scheduled to sunset on October 1, 2022.

FDA collects four types of biosimilar user fees. The Biosimilar Development Program fee includes an initial fee with the submission of a biosimilar product meeting request or clinical protocol and an annual fee. There is also a Biosimilar Biological Product Application and Supplement fee, a Biosimilar Biological Establishment fee, and a Biosimilar Biological Product fee. Similar to its performance commitments under PDUFA, FDA has committed to specific goals for the review of biosimilar original applications. Application resubmissions and supplements are also subject to these performance goals.

The BsUFA performance goals also include information and timelines in connection with proprietary name review, major dispute resolution, clinical holds, and special protocol assessments, and establish five meeting categories for the discussion of biosimilar development matters with FDA. Thus, in addition to requesting an initial advisory meeting to assess the feasibility of 351(k) licensure for a product, applicants and sponsors may also meet with FDA to discuss stalled drug development (Type 1 Meeting), to request advice on a specific question or issue (Type 2 Meeting), to discuss the format and content of an application (Type 4 Meeting), or to conduct an in-depth data review (Type 3 Meeting). The procedures that apply to these five meeting types are discussed in FDA guidance that was issued in November 2015.

Case Studies

Case Study: Court Enforcement of FDA Approval Deadline

The futility of trying to enforce the statutory 180-day filing clock deadline in court seemed to have been confirmed by a 1991 case in which a disgruntled drug company, Barr Laboratories, Inc., sued FDA for not completing the review of its drug applications within the deadline. The court agreed that FDA's delay violated the statute, but refused to do anything about it on the ground that it was up to the agency, not the court, to set drug review priorities, and that to order FDA to meet the deadline on the plaintiff's applications would disadvantage other, equally worthy applicants. *In re Barr Lab., Inc.*, 930 F.2d 72 (D.C. Cir. 1991), *cert. denied*, 502 U.S. 906 (1991).

In 2005, however, a section 505(b)(2) NDA applicant challenged the conventional wisdom, with unexpected results. Sandoz, Inc. had submitted its NDA for the recombinant human growth hormone product Omnitrope in July 2003, relying in part on FDA's prior approval of Pfizer's recombinant human growth hormone product Genotropin. In April 2004, Pfizer objected to the Omnitrope application. In August 2004, FDA informed Sandoz that although the agency had completed its review of Omnitrope, it was deferring a decision because of the application's "nature and complexity." *Sandoz v. Leavitt et al.*, Civ. No. 05-1810 (RMU), D.D.C. April 10, 2006, at 3.

In September 2005 Sandoz sued FDA, asserting that the agency had violated the statutory 180-day action deadline. FDA did not dispute that assertion, but argued that the statutory deadline was "aspirational" and had effectively been modified by the subsequent user fee action date structure agreed upon with Congress. The court brushed this defense aside and granted summary judgment for Sandoz, concluding that the statutory requirement was clear, unambiguous, and unchanged, and that to hold otherwise would be to "accept governmental mediocrity and vitiate the statute's mandatory language." The court distinguished the *Barr* case on the grounds that FDA had approved a number of other subsequently filed NDAs, including 505(b)(2) NDAs, for both naturally sourced and recombinant biologic drugs since Sandoz had submitted its application, so that it was evident that ordering FDA action on Sandoz's NDA would not "directly bottleneck other NDAs." Further, with additional resources now available to FDA under PDUFA, the court felt the agency should be held to a higher standard. Accordingly, the court ordered FDA to comply with the statutory requirement and either approve the application or provide Sandoz with the required notice and opportunity for a hearing on the approvability of the application. To the surprise of some, FDA chose in response to approve Sandoz's application.

For better or worse, however, thus far the *Sandoz* case has led neither to a meaningful change of FDA's NDA review practices nor to a wholesale legal assault on those practices by drug sponsors. For one thing, the specific facts of the case are relatively unique, in particular FDA's written acknowledgment to the sponsor that it had completed its substantive review of the application but was nonetheless refusing to take final action, presumably at least in part because of Pfizer's objections, without any clear end in sight. This left FDA with a glaring legal vulnerability the agency would be unlikely to take on again. More broadly, under the user fee system, it remains the case that sponsors typically have much more to gain by working with FDA within the framework of their action dates to move the application forward than by taking the agency on in court. Nonetheless, the *Sandoz* case illustrates that there are limits to FDA's discretion under the user fee system and that the statutory filing clock deadline retains at least some life still.

> *More broadly, under the user fee system, it remains the case that sponsors typically have much more to gain by working with FDA within the framework of their action dates to move the application forward than by taking the agency on in court.*

Case Study: Early Access to Investigational Drugs

Evidently unsatisfied with the existing mechanisms for expedited availability of experimental drugs described above, the patient advocacy group Abigail Alliance sued FDA over the agency's refusal to allow dying patients unrestricted access to unapproved drugs. After an unexpected ruling by a panel of the D.C. Circuit Court of Appeals in 2006 that the Due Process Clause of the U.S. Constitution protects terminally ill patients' rights to have access to "potentially life-saving" investigational drugs that have passed successfully through Phase I studies, FDA sought reconsideration by the full court. In August 2007 the court rejected the panel's conclusion and ruled that "there is no fundamental right . . . of access to experimental drugs for the terminally ill." *Abigail Alliance v. von Eschenbach*, 495 F.3d 695, 697 (D.C. Cir. 2007).

Case Study: Bioequivalence for Non-Systemically Absorbed Drugs

As noted above, NDA sponsors have frequently challenged FDA's application of bioequivalence requirements to ANDAs referencing their products, particularly for non-systemically absorbed drugs that do not lend themselves to standard *in vivo* blood-level testing to determine equivalence. A prominent early example of conflict over bioequivalence involved the asthma drug albuterol administered by metered dose inhaler (MDI). The NDA holder for the drug, Schering-Plough, submitted a petition to FDA arguing that the statutory bioequivalence requirement, which specifies only measurements of "rate and extent of absorption," categorically precluded FDA from approving any ANDAs for non-systemically absorbed drugs, including, of course, MDI albuterol. FDA denied the petition on the basis that the statute specifically contemplates determinations of bioequivalency based on evidence other than rate and extent of absorption. Schering-Plough then sued FDA in federal district court, but the court agreed with FDA's interpretation and dismissed the complaint. (*Schering Corp. v. Sulli-van*, 782 F. Supp. 645, 647 (D.D.C. 1992), *vacated*, 995 F.2d 1103 (D.C. Cir. 1993).) On appeal, the substance of the district court's holding was affirmed. The appellate court stated that although the FDCA's definition of bioequivalence is "ambiguous," FDA's interpretation of that definition, on the basis of which the agency proposed to approve generic MDI albuterol products, was "reasonable." (*Schering Corp. v. FDA*, 51 F.3d 390, 400 (3d Cir. 1995), *cert. denied*, 116 S. Ct. 274 (1995).).

A more recent challenge to FDA's bioequivalence standards involving a variation on the standard approach was brought by ViroPharma Inc., holder of the NDA for vancomycin, a non-systemically absorbed drug to treat severe gastrointestinal (GI) infections. Citing FDA's response to a citizen petition filed by the sponsor of a different locally acting GI drug in which the agency stated that it could accept *in vitro* studies to show bioequivalence for such drugs, ViroPharma brought suit against FDA alleging that this agency response had effectively amended the bioequivalence regulations without the required notice-and-comment rulemaking. In April 2011, the district court dismissed ViroPharma's case on standing grounds, *ViroPharma Inc. v. Hamburg,* 777 F. Supp. 2d 140 (D.D.C. 2011), and so did not reach the question of regulatory interpretation posed by the plaintiff. The district court's decision was affirmed on appeal in March 2012. *ViroPharma Inc. v. Hamburg,* 471 Fed. Appx. 1 (D.C. Cir. 2012). In April 2012, FDA denied a citizen petition originally filed by ViroPharma in March 2006 to stay approval of vancomycin ANDAs submitted under bioequivalence recommendations permitting *in vitro* testing in lieu of *in vivo* data for vancomycin. FDA also approved three ANDAs for generic vancomycin on the same day that it denied the citizen petition. ViroPharma subsequently filed a motion for preliminary injunction with the district court to require the withdrawal of the vancomycin ANDA approvals until ViroPharma's claims could be ajudicated on the merits. Applying *Chevron* analysis, the district court found that ViroPharma was not likely to succeed on the merits of its claims, in part, because FDA's interpretation of its own bioequivalence regulations were controlling. Thus, FDA's approval of the ANDAs was allowed to stand. *ViroPharma Inc. v. Hamburg,* 898 F. Supp. 2d 1 (D.D.C. 2012). In January 2013, ViroPharma filed a motion for summary judgment requesting that the district court consider additional information to adjudicate its claims on the merits. The district court again, however, found that FDA acted within its discretion when it approved the vancomycin ANDAs. *ViroPharma Inc. v. Hamburg,* 916 F. Supp. 2d 76 (D.D.C. 2013).

Case Study: Notice and Information Requirements for Biosimilar Applications

In a case of first impression under the 2009 Biosimilars Price Competition and Innovation Act, the U.S. Supreme Court was asked to interpret two key procedural provisions of the BPCIA in the case of *Sandoz Inc. v. Amgen Inc. et al.,* 582 U.S. _____ (2017) (Slip op. No. 15-1039, June 12, 2017). The first such provision concerned the requirement that the biosimilar applicant provide the reference product sponsor with a copy of the application and a description of the biosimilar's manufacturing processes within 20 days of FDA's acceptance of the biosimilar application for review. In this case, the biosimilar applicant, Sandoz, had failed to provide the reference product sponsor, Amgen, with the required information, and Amgen sought injunctive relief to compel Sandoz to furnish the information. The Supreme Court held that the statutory right of the reference product sponsor to bring an action against the biosimilar applicant for a declaration of infringement, validity, or enforceability in such circumstances is the sole remedy provided under federal law, and that no federal injunctive relief is available. The Supreme Court, however, remanded the case to the Federal Circuit to determine whether injunctive relief would be available under state law.

The second provision at issue was the BPCIA's requirement that the biosimilar applicant provide the reference product sponsor with 180 days' notice prior to the first commercial marketing of the biosimilar. Sandoz provided such notice to Amgen a day after FDA accepted Sandoz's biosimilar application for review, but Amgen asserted that under the statute, such notice could not be given until after FDA had licensed the biosimilar for commercial marketing. The Supreme Court held that the required notice of commercial marketing may be given either before or after FDA approval, so that a biosimilar applicant does not need to await licensure before providing the notice.

Chapter 6

A Pharmacovigilance Primer

Edward John Allera, Genevieve M. Spires, Tina Hu-Rodgers, & Alexandre Gapihan, Buchanan Ingersoll & Rooney PC, Washington, D.C.

Key Points

- Pharmacovigilance includes all activities directed toward detecting, assessing, understanding, and preventing adverse events or other product-related problems.
- The regulatory framework for pharmacovigilance has been in place for decades, imposing postapproval requirements on all categories of drugs.
- Any adverse experience that is not listed on a drug's current label is considered an "unexpected" drug experience.
- There are five basic types of postmarketing reports, whose requirements are dictated by the seriousness of the adverse experience.
- Congress, in the Food and Drug Administration Amendments Act of 2007, created a statutory mechanism in recognition of the importance of pharmacovigilance: risk evaluation and mitigation strategy.
- Pharmacovigilance reporting requirements are designed to safeguard public health and safety by creating a system for improving the labeling of drug products.

INTRODUCTION

Pharmacovigilance encompasses all postapproval scientific and data-gathering activities relating to the detection, assessment, understanding, and prevention of adverse events or any other product-related problems. Interestingly, no statutory definition of the practice exists under the Federal Food, Drug, and Cosmetic Act (FDCA) or the Food and Drug Administration's (FDA's) regulations. FDA has created the regulatory framework for pharmacovigilance indirectly under its authority to regulate all drug labeling as well as its authority to require maintenance of records for new drugs.

Pharmacovigilance has played a role in the safe use of pharmaceuticals for decades. For example, the declaration of phenformin as an "imminent hazard to health" in the 1970s was based on pharmacovigilance information. The role of pharmacovigilance has dramatically increased in recent years as public policy considerations, public perceptions, and acceptance of risk have shifted.

It has long been accepted by FDA and industry that the risk analysis that occurs during the drug development process has to be thorough and rigorous. In recent years, there has been increased recognition of the need and importance of monitoring a drug's safety after approval, while in actual medical use. As a result, the discipline of pharmacovigilance has become increasingly central to the regulatory life cycle of drugs.

It is well recognized that not all safety concerns will be identified during the clinical trial process.

It is well recognized that not all safety concerns will be identified during the clinical trial process. Even drugs intended for chronic use are seldom tested in more than 3,000 to 5,000 patients prior to approval. In contrast, postapproval patient exposure to a new drug increases by orders of magnitude. Of particular concern are patients with co-morbid conditions and those who are taking other drugs.

Heavy publicity about postapproval adverse events allegedly associated with drugs such as Vioxx and Avandia have heightened both public and political awareness of the important role that pharmacovigilance plays in protecting public health. In the Food and Drug Administration Amendments Act of 2007 (FDAAA), Congress recognized the importance of pharmacovigilance and created a statutory mechanism—the risk evaluation and mitigation strategy (REMS)—as a safety strategy to manage known or potential serious risks of a drug following its approval. Further, the Centers for Medicare & Medicaid Services (CMS) has issued regulations to facilitate gathering data from the Medicare Part D drug program to aid, in part, pharmacovigilance. All of these factors magnify the importance of pharmacovigilance.

BACKGROUND

The regulatory framework for pharmacovigilance has been in place for decades. Specific FDA regulations impose postapproval pharmacovigilance requirements on all categories of drugs: grandfathered drugs (21 C.F.R. § 310.305); drugs approved under a New Drug Application (NDA) (21 C.F.R. § 314.80); drugs approved under an Abbreviated New Drug Application (ANDA) (21 C.F.R. § 314.98); and biologics (21 C.F.R. § 600.80). Additional regulations exist for postapproval testing requirements (21 C.F.R. § 310.303), highlighting the need for congruency between the information gathered during the pre-approval phase with information collected postapproval. The symmetry of the pharmacovigilance process is further confirmed in 21 C.F.R. § 314.70(c)(6)(iii)(A) where supplemental applications are required to add or strengthen a contraindication, warning, precaution, or adverse reaction. Supplements are subject to a 30-day pre-implementation FDA review and approval of the proposed language.

Reporting Requirements

Overview

Even before the current focus on pharmacovigilance, two principles for adverse event reporting were set forth in FDA's regulations: timeliness and accuracy. Each has weaknesses given the partially voluntary nature of the reporting system, the limitations on the data and clinical information available, and the need for data interpretation.

Even before the current focus on pharmacovigilance, two principles for adverse event reporting were set forth in FDA's regulations: timeliness and accuracy.

With regard to timing, the current environment of an ever-increasing number of reports to FDA, faster FDA review cycles for NDAs, more complex new drug submissions, and the greater use of drugs by an aging population have placed more pressure on FDA, and as a consequence, manufacturers, to develop sophisticated infrastructures that will help them to quickly and aggressively obtain and report adverse effects.

The accuracy of reporting, however, represents a unique challenge. The accurate interpretation of reported information can be difficult, especially considering the common usage of gross or crude terms, ranging from various lexicons to differences in human perception (i.e., different clinicians and patients may define specific adverse effects vastly differently).

Because crises involving drug safety always permit cynical hindsight and second-guessing of pharmacovigilance data, the timeliness of submitting adverse event reports to FDA is also critical. FDA has vast experience in adverse events, drug safety reports, and safety evaluation not only concerning the drug in question, but also identical, similar, and related drugs. This database affords FDA a perspective on risk that is unavailable to any single applicant because no single report or series of reports is dispositive; it is only a piece of the greater safety picture. For a manufacturer, not only is thorough and timely reporting of adverse events necessary but also it is important that the manufacturer maintain an active dialogue with FDA about the reports, trends, and any other data that may affect the labeling or status of the drug. Significantly, U.S. courts have viewed such collaborative efforts by manufacturers with FDA to be a basis for limiting product liability.

Definitions

FDA has developed a glossary of terms to deal with pharmacovigilance (21 C.F.R. §§ 310.305, 312.32, 314.80, and 600.80). An "adverse drug experience" is defined as any adverse event associated with the use of a drug in humans, whether or not drug related, in the course of professional practice, including intentional or unintentional overdosage, drug abuse, drug withdrawal, or the failure of the drug to have its intended effect.

"Disability" is a substantial disruption in a person's ability to conduct normal life functions.

"Life-threatening" is an adverse drug experience that places the patient at the immediate risk of death, but does not include an adverse experience that, had it occurred in a more severe form, might have caused death.

A "serious adverse experience" is one occurring at any dose of a drug that results in death, a life-threatening experience, inpatient hospitalization, or prolongation of an existing hospitalization, a persistent or significant disability or incapacity, or a congenital anomaly or birth defect. Other events that do not cause the foregoing are also deemed serious if they may jeopardize the patient and require medical or surgical intervention to prevent those events.

Any adverse experience that is not listed in the current labeling of the drug is regarded as an unexpected drug experience.

The role of labeling surfaces in the definition of unexpected drug experiences. Any adverse experience that is not listed in the current labeling of the drug is regarded as an unexpected drug experience. These include events that may be symptomatically and pathophysiologically related to an event listed in the labeling but differ due to greater severity or specificity. FDA interprets "unexpected" as relating to the actual observation rather than the theoretical pharmacological possibility.

For unapproved drugs, approved drugs, and approved biologics these terms are considered to be identical, and reporting should be handled consistently. Attempts to create different systems within a company only increase the likelihood of failing to comply with FDA's regulations and expectations.

Reports

Five basic types of postmarketing reports exist, and their reporting requirements are dictated by the seriousness of the adverse experiences: 15-day Alert Reports, 15-day Follow-Up Reports, Periodic Adverse Experience Reports, Field Alerts, and Annual Reports.

♦ 15-day Alert Report

An applicant is required to report each adverse drug experience that it becomes aware of that is both serious and unexpected, whether foreign or domestic, as soon as possible but not later than 15 calendar days from initial receipt of the information. For an unapproved drug, any person whose name appears on the label, whether as its manufacturer, packer, or distributor, has the filing obligation. Thus, the obligation applies to any adverse reaction that does not appear on the label and is serious by virtue of either its increased severity or incidence. Information from scientific literature or from abroad is subject to the 15-day Alert reporting requirement if the information is found in scientific or medical journals as case reports or as the result of a clinical trial. A copy of the published article is to be filed with the report.

These reports are designed to quickly provide FDA with relevant data from participants in the healthcare delivery system about a potentially adverse event related to a drug. The focus is on new or potentially new adverse experiences. While the adverse reports system in the United States has been termed voluntary in the general sense (with respect to healthcare providers and others in the healthcare distribution system), it is mandatory for any drug manufacturer, packer, or distributor whose name appears on the label.

While the adverse reports system in the United States has been termed voluntary in the general sense (with respect to healthcare providers and others in the healthcare distribution system), it is mandatory for any drug manufacturer, packer, or distributor whose name appears on the label.

◆ 15-day Alert Report Follow-Up

The obligation for follow-up falls directly on every person identified on the label of the drug product whether the holder of the approved application, the manufacturer, the packer, or the distributor of either approved drugs or those drugs marketed without approvals. The reports must be prominently identified as to their content (e.g., "15-day Alert Report" or "15-day Alert Report Follow-Up"). The format for submission has historically been FDA Form 3500A, or a computer-generated version that provides an equivalent in all elements of data and is agreed to by FDA.

The holder of the application is obligated to conduct a comprehensive follow-up investigation. This point is critical. FDA's regulations impose an additional 15-calendar-day requirement on the report of new information or as requested by the agency. FDA's regulations require records of the steps taken in the investigation to be maintained even if no new information is detected. If new information is detected, it is subject to a new 15-day reporting requirement. Normally, however, FDA will be in contact with the company, and a thorough report will be prepared in accord with a time frame agreed to by the parties. Similar obligations apply to the manufacturer of the drug, whether approved or unapproved. To reduce duplicative reporting, companies listed on the labeling can fulfill their obligations by providing notice to the applicant or manufacturer within five calendar days of the receipt of the adverse experience. In the contemporary environment, there appears to be no restriction on persons listed on the label from fulfilling these obligations in lieu of the holder of the approval or the manufacturer.

Persons or companies included on the labeling who report the adverse experience to the manufacturer or holder of the approval must maintain records of their adverse experience reporting, including the following: the date the adverse event was reported to them; the date it was reported to its business cohort (e.g., the manufacturer); and the name and address of the applicant or manufacturer.

As expected, confusion often arises regarding who is responsible for reporting. This has occurred, in large part, as a result of pharmaceutical industry operations becoming more "virtual" in recent years. The subcontracting by pharmaceutical companies of key operations, such as manufacturing, distribution, marketing, and recordkeeping, has become commonplace. While it is commonly recognized that such arrangements require the creation of defined contractual obligations, this does not always take place in practice, creating reporting vulnerabilities where there is the absence of precise delegation of responsibilities among the parties. Confusion can arise about fulfillment of the legal obligations under the FDCA, resulting not only in the failure to comply with obligations of the act but also the potential for substantive commercial liabilities among the parties. The specific issues associated with follow-up are discussed below because they are the basis for the Periodic Adverse Experience Reports.

◆ Periodic Adverse Experience Report

For the first three years after approval of an application, the applicant must submit quarterly reports of all adverse events that do not fall within the 15-day Alert Reports (i.e., those reported adverse events that are already noted within the product labeling or are not deemed to be "serious and life threatening"). The reports must be filed within 30 days of the end of the quarter, and the annual report must be filed within 60 days of the date of the NDA or ANDA approval. The reports must contain a narrative summary and analysis of the available information, an analysis of the 15-day Alert Reports (which are to be fully referenced), and a description of any action taken by the manufacturer since its receipt of the most recent report of the adverse event.

Generally, except for information regarding 15-day Alert Reports, adverse drug experience information from postmarketing studies, reports from the scientific literature, and foreign marketing experience are exempt from the periodic reporting system. Should an applicant conclude, however, that an adverse event is associated with a recently approved drug being further studied under a new investigational NDA, FDA regulations provide that the applicant should include this event in its periodic report but should also clearly mark this incident as being distinct from those experiences that are being spontaneously reported. All submitted records must protect the privacy of the patients involved, and therefore should not include the specific names and addresses of the individual patients. Unique identifiers of no more than eight characters that are assigned by the reporter should be created. The applicant should also include the name of the reporter. Under FDA's regulations the names of the patients, healthcare professionals, hospitals, and geographical identifiers are not publicly releasable.

Further, the agency has a regulation that states that the submission of a report does not necessarily reflect a conclusion by the filer or FDA that the report or information constitutes an admission that the drug has caused or contributed to an adverse event. The regulation leaves open the ability of the applicant or other filer not to admit or deny that any report constitutes an admission.

The submission of a report does not necessarily reflect a conclusion by the filer or FDA that the report or information constitutes an admission that the drug has caused or contributed to an adverse event.

Limitations exist with any reporting system—whether spontaneous, mandatory, or voluntary—and FDA recognizes them: passivity, under reporting, variable quality and incompleteness, duplicate reporting, and inability to determine accurately the incidence rate because the numerator is uncertain and the denominator must be projected. More than 90 percent of the adverse experience reports are manufacturer reports, and the majority of them are periodic reports, although the rate of 15-day reports is increasing. Fewer than 10 percent of the reports are direct reports from healthcare professionals.

Acknowledging these limitations, FDA has issued guidelines intended to improve both the accuracy and the consistency of adverse experience reporting, thus hoping to further improve the public health value of pharmacovigilance. Optimally, FDA prefers reports to contain a description of the adverse event or disease experience, including the time to onset of signs and symptoms. Suspected and concomitant therapy details should be provided. A listing of over-the-counter, nutrient supplement, and discontinued medications that were being taken concomitantly should also be included in the description as well as, to the extent possible, patient characteristics. In essence, the agency is seeking important baseline patient information that is relevant to the detection and diagnosis of the adverse event, as well as the methods used in making the diagnosis and the clinical course of the event and outcome. Relevant therapeutic measures and laboratory data are also sought, both at baseline and during the event, if available. Any information about response to dechallenge or rechallenge should also be submitted.

FDA has developed principles to assess submitted reports. Some of the questions that it poses include: Did the event occur within an expected time frame? Was there an absence of symptoms prior to drug exposure? Was there a positive challenge or dechallenge? Is the event consistent with the pharmacological effect of the drug or the class of drugs administered? Was the event identified in clinical trials? Is there an absence of alternative explanations?

FDA does not presently recommend any specific categorization of causality, although commentators have used the categories of probable, possible, and unlikely.

Currently, there is no internationally agreed-upon standard or criteria for assessing causality. Moreover, confounded cases are common, and it is rarely possible to know with a high level of certainty that a specific event was specifically caused solely by a drug product. Of critical importance, FDA does not presently recommend any specific categorization of causality, although commentators have used the categories of probable, possible, and unlikely.

For both 15-day Alert Reports and Periodic Reports, a 10-year requirement exists for maintaining raw material and records, although the periodic reporting requirement does not apply to unapproved drugs.

◆ Field Alerts

The notification may be provided by telephone or other method of rapid communication, and a prompt written follow-up is required that is plainly marked "NDA-Field Alert Report." These reports are filed directly with the local field office, and by regulation are applicable only to approved products. There is no specific requirement in FDA's regulations for manufacturers of unapproved drugs to make such filings.

These reports have the shortest time requirement—three days. The clock is normally considered to start after the completion of the investigations into the potential manufacturing deficiencies. For marketed approved applications, whether NDAs or ANDAs, Field Alerts can be the most critical filings. These reports normally concern manufacturing problems and they often relate to more imminent public health risks. Accordingly, many consider such filings an integral part of current Good Manufacturing Practices (cGMPs) that are applicable to all drugs, whether approved or marketed without an approval. As previously noted, within three working days of the receipt of information about distributed drugs or drugs about to be distributed, the application holder is to notify the district office that is responsible for the manufacturing facility should it believe that or become aware that its drug product is mislabeled or adulterated; that the drug product's labeling is not correct; and/or that the drug product could be mistaken for and/or erroneously used in place of another product. Some specific types of circumstances that require notification within three days include bacterial contamination; significant chemical, physical, or other change; deterioration in the distributed drug product; or any failure of one or more distributed batches to meet the specifications established for it in its applications.

◆ Annual Reports

Within 60 days of the anniversary date of the application's approval, the applicant is required to file an annual report with the FDA reviewing division that was responsible for its approval. Two copies are required, accompanied by a transmittal Form FDA 2252. The report is to contain a summary of all significant new information that might affect the safety, effectiveness, or labeling of the drug product subject to the application. The description is to include any actions taken or that the applicant intends to take as a result of any new information gathered during the year (e.g., labeling changes, new studies). A description of steps taken to evaluate pediatric use of the product should also be included.

Drug advertisements and promotional labeling are submitted independent of the annual report. Specimens of mailing pieces and other labeling or advertising devised for promotion of the drug product must be submitted at the time of the initial dissemination of the labeling and at the time of the initial publication of the advertisement.

Distribution data according to National Drug Code number, the number of units, and quantities distributed for domestic and foreign use are to be reported. Patient, professional, and package inserts are to be supplied, including all text, tables, etc. A summary of any labeling changes should also be included. Also to be filed are chemistry, manufacturing, and controls changes, but only for new information that may affect the agency's previous conclusions about the drug product's safety or effectiveness. Any change that does not require a supplemental filing should be included in the annual report. It should last be noted that electronic submissions are now available.

Clinical data submissions are essential. Published clinical trials of the drug, or abstracts that include trials on the safety and effectiveness of the drug, must be submitted. Clinical trials on new uses, biopharmaceutics studies, pharmacokinetics, and clinical pharmacology studies must also be submitted. Reports of clinical experience pertinent to safety, such as epidemiologic studies or analyses of experience in monitored patients, must be filed whether they are conducted by the applicant or otherwise obtained by it. Summaries of completed unpublished clinical trials are to be filed. The status of postmarketing study commitments must be filed as well as a log of outstanding regulatory commitments.

The various pharmacovigilance reporting requirements are designed to safeguard public health and safety by creating a system for improving the labeling of drug products. The annual report is the most comprehensive and lucid document intended for this purpose. Each report is designed to highlight the occurrence of new, unexpected adverse events or an increase in the incidence of adverse events. In contemporary terms, FDA's various pronouncements in speeches and guidelines define the mission of pharmacovigilance as

The various pharmacovigilance reporting requirements are designed to safeguard public health and safety by creating a system for improving the labeling of drug products.

to facilitate the safe and effective use of drug products by promptly gathering and evaluating drug safety data and identifying "safety signals" that in turn allow for the most accurate labeling of drug products and their safe use.

A safety signal detection system is, simply stated, a key component of an effective risk management program. FDA uses the term "safety signal" to refer to a concern about an excess number of adverse events compared to what one would expect to be associated with a drug's use. The importance of strong pharmacovigilance activities was underscored by Congress, which specifically created a statutory "signal of a serious risk" in the FDAAA. The term pharmacovigilance and related term "signal of a serious risk" are analogous to terms such as cGMPs and current Good Clinical Practices. The terms are not static. They are evolving and have the potential for retroactive application by adversaries attempting to prove that the labeling of the drug product failed to contain all the relevant information.

A "safety signal" is an apparent excess of adverse events that can be found in a single well-documented case report, preclinical findings, or experience with other similar products in the drug's pharmacological class.

According to both contemporary guidance and FDAAA, a "safety signal" is an apparent excess of adverse events that can be found in well-documented case reports, preclinical findings, or experience with other similar products in the drug's pharmacological class. It can also come from literature or risk management programs. Such signals should be assessed in terms of magnitude, population at risk, changes in risk of time, biological plausibility, and interactions.

FDA expects companies to develop and maintain effective pharmacovigilance signal detection and reporting systems. Generally, such systems search available case reports, adverse experience databases, the literature, and FDA's adverse experience review system to look for product-related data. Data searches are often carried out using sophisticated database-mining systems, with updated coding terminology like that of the *Medical Dictionary for Regulatory Activities*. The goal is to identify potential product-event linkages that may be considered signals and calculate the rate of risk (i.e., the reporting rates versus the actual incidence rate). Effective risk management systems will not only help detect these signals but also help manage them and reduce the risks.

When a signal is detected, investigation is considered appropriate through observational studies, either randomized or non-randomized. Types of non-randomized studies include pharmacoepidemiologic studies, surveys, and registries. Signals that may warrant further investigation include new unlabeled adverse events (especially if serious); an apparent increase in the severity of a labeled event; the occurrence of serious events presently thought to be rare; new interactions; identification of previously unrecognized at-risk populations; confusion about the product's name or use; or inadequacies that are detected relative to current risk minimization efforts.

FDA's policies relative to pharmacovigilance activities are constantly evolving to reflect changes in technology as well as the growing sophistication of drug products. In this regard, it is important to note that retrospective data reviews, as well as reviews of currently reported data, can both play an important role in drug product safety. Thus, manufacturers must constantly be evaluating available data, both old and new, to safeguard the public health. Such a landscape, especially where the guidelines are broad and constantly evolving, also represents a challenge to drug manufacturers, who can potentially face significant liability risks despite vigilant efforts to maintain effective pharmacovigilance programs.

Supplemental Applications—Closing the Loop

The goal of pharmacovigilance is to ensure that labeling of drug products is comprehensive and contains the most contemporary description of the drugs' safe and effective data. This allows the risks associated with the drugs' use to be intelligently weighed, and for healthcare providers and patients to make informed decisions about the drugs' usage. Based upon the information gathered by pharmacovigilance plans and submissions to FDA, informed decisions can be made about any changes necessary to the product's current labeling. The pharmacovigilance process is continuous, as is the need to improve the labeling of a product during its entire life cycle.

The pharmacovigilance process is continuous, as is the need to improve the labeling of a product during its entire life cycle.

It is unquestioned that the holder of an approved NDA must satisfy the fundamental requirements of pharmacovigilance. Until generic competition arrives, the holder of the approved application is the focal point of all the relevant data. Today, generic drug products constitute more than 70 percent of the drug units sold in the U.S. market. Once an ANDA is approved for a drug, generic penetration can reach 90 percent in just 90 days. After a period of years, the generic version unquestionably will become the market leader, and the evidence on the drug's use gleaned from the market for reporting may be primarily about generic versions of the drug. FDA's regulations setting forth obligations of holders of approved NDAs are incorporated by reference into the agency's regulations imposing obligations on holders of approved ANDAs (see 21 C.F.R. §§ 314.70 (c), 314.97, and 314.98). As the role of generic drugs grows, the obligations of the holders of approved ANDAs in the area of pharmacovigilance may increase dramatically. Holders of these approvals must be aware of the current and evolving environment.

If the pharmacovigilance data lead one or more holders of an approval to conclude that a labeling change may be appropriate, the critical question becomes the proper approach for implementing the change. Theoretically, FDA's regulations permit the holder of an approved application, either NDA or ANDA, to file a supplemental application to implement the change within 30 days to strengthen a contraindication, warning, precaution, and adverse experience. That interpretation is often proffered in product liability litigation, and the failure of companies to implement the change is alleged to be negligence or a breach of the appropriate standard of care. However, the obligations of ANDA holders are in flux due to recent case law and a proposed rule issued by FDA.

Recent case law has created some inconsistencies and issues between FDA regulation and product labeling based on pharmacovigilance that affect companies in the market. A series of cases in the last several years has established that although the holder of an approved New Drug Application generally may not modify a drug label without FDA approval, it nonetheless can unilaterally make certain post-NDA labeling changes in order to add or strengthen a warning to improve drug safety, without FDA approval of the change. The NDA holder is responsible for its label regardless of FDA's concerns, and bears responsibility for the content of its label at all times, even if FDA disagrees or cannot decide on the appropriate warning.

Changes to generic drug labels are permitted only when a generic drug manufacturer is attempting to match an updated brand-name label or to follow FDA's instructions.

This unilateral authority to effect labeling changes is not available to manufacturers of generic drug products. Because the listed drug product is the basis for generic drug approval, the generic drug's labeling must always be the same as that of its brand-name predecessor. Accordingly, changes to generic drug labels are permitted only when a generic drug manufacturer is attempting to match an updated brand-name label or to follow FDA's instructions. Unilateral labeling changes to strengthen a warning, and "Dear Doctor" letters containing any substantial new warning information, are considered to be violations of a generic manufacturers' duty of "sameness."

At present, generic drug manufacturers only have the option of proposing to FDA that stronger warning labels are needed. If a generic drug manufacturer believes new safety information should be added to a product's labeling, it should convey that to FDA, and the agency will determine whether the labeling for the generic and listed drugs should be revised. If FDA agrees that a label change is necessary, it can work with the brand-name manufacturer to create a new label for both the brand-name and generic drug.

This scenario may be changing, however. FDA has issued a Proposed Rule that would allow generic manufacturers to independently revise their product's labeling through a "changes being effected" (CBE) process. The rule has not yet been finalized, but it could potentially have a significant impact on the labeling landscape for generic manufacturers. Currently, ANDA holders can only use the CBE supplement process to update their product labeling to conform with approved labeling for the reference listed drug or to respond to FDA's specific request to submit a labeling change. Under the proposed rule, however, a generic drug manufacturer that has newly acquired information about a drug product (i.e., data from new clinical studies, adverse event reports, etc. that reveal risks not previously revealed in submissions to FDA) would be permitted to unilaterally update its product labeling via a CBE-0 supplement, regardless of whether the resulting revised labeling differs from that of the reference listed drug. Additionally, the ANDA holder would be permitted to distribute a "Dear Health Care Provider" letter addressing this labeling change and presenting the important new drug safety information that warranted the CBE-0 supplement.

Although this proposed change in existing labeling regulations would create increased parity between NDA holders and ANDA holders, it is not without potential problems. FDA has acknowledged that the proposed rule may create confusion in instances where multiple ANDA holders submit CBE-0 supplements with labeling changes that differ from each other and from the reference listed drug. FDA also recognized that issues may arise at the patient-care level, as healthcare providers are unlikely to review product labeling for each of the generic drugs that may be substituted for the prescribed product when making treatment decisions with their patients. The agency proposes to address these concerns by creating a publicly accessible, dedicated Web page to aggregate and list all labeling changes proposed in a CBE-0 supplement pending FDA review.

FDA's intent in creating this proposed new labeling rule is to ensure that generic drug companies actively participate with the agency in ensuring the timeliness, accuracy, and completeness of drug safety labeling in accordance with current regulatory requirements. It is hoped that implementation of the proposed regulatory change may eliminate the preemption of certain failure-to-warn claims with respect to generic drugs. It is crucial, therefore, for generics manufacturers to keep an open line of communication with FDA at all times.

The most appropriate way for a company to protect itself is to maintain a dialogue with FDA on the issues associated with pharmacovigilance and to be as meticulous as possible in filing necessary reports. We are entering a new era when pharmacovigilance will be the foundation for improved drug product labeling and potential litigation. FDA, CMS, and other agencies, such as the U.S. Department of Veterans Affairs, are committed to improving their skills in keeping electronic records in this area. In the current atmosphere the courts have been receptive to limiting liability when proper dialogue and diligent filing are followed. Following the principles that apply to pharmacovigilance is one step toward following the standards of care that are evolving in the industry.

The most appropriate way for a company to protect itself is to maintain a dialogue with FDA on the issues associated with pharmacovigilance and to be as meticulous as possible in filing necessary reports.

Chapter 7

Approval of New Animal Drugs

Joseph W. Cormier, J.D., Ph.D., Hyman, Phelps & McNamara, PC, Washington, D.C.

Key Points

- The requirements for a New Animal Drug Application (NADA) vary significantly depending on the intended use and target species of the drug.
- For NADAs, "phased review" does not refer to clinical phases, as in the human drug context; rather, it refers to the process of sponsors submitting, and the Food and Drug Administration (FDA) reviewing, NADA technical sections before the NADA has been submitted.
- FDA's regulatory mandate over new animal drugs includes evaluation of the effects of animal drugs on human and animal food supplies; because animal drugs are used in food-producing animal species, the requirements to demonstrate food safety are extensive.
- Because unapproved drug products compose a substantial percentage of the animal drug industry, FDA takes a more deliberative and open view toward the marketing of unapproved animal drug products.
- There are several important variants to the NADA: the Abbreviated New Animal Drug Application (ANADA) for generic versions of approved animal drugs, conditional approval and indexing under the Minor Use and Minor Species Animal Health Act, and NADAs for genetically engineered animals.
- FDA's authority over animal drugs is broad, in contrast to its limited authority over veterinary devices and veterinary biologics. As a result, FDA will sometimes take the position that a product is a new animal drug when other Centers within FDA would take a different position in the human context.
- There are several forms of market incentives granted to animal drugs, including exclusivity, patent protection, and specific incentives for companies to develop products that are intended to treat a rare animal disease or a species of animal that is not typically the focus of animal drug development.

INTRODUCTION

New drugs intended for use in animals other than humans must be approved by the Food and Drug Administration (FDA) prior to their commercial use. Although there are many similarities between the human and animal drug approval processes, the approval and regulation of new animal drugs present unique issues that can sometimes result in outcomes different from those expected in the human approval context.

Although it goes almost without saying, one specific fact differentiates FDA regulation of human and animal drugs: a human drug is intended for use in one biological species, *Homo sapiens*, whereas an animal drug may be intended for use in one or more of the many animal species (other than humans). FDA has approved new animal drugs to treat dogs, cats, horses, chickens, pigs, cows, goats, honeybees, white-tailed deer, and numerous fish species among others.

Because new animal drugs are used in a wide variety of species, the nature of these products as well as their dosage forms and routes of administration can be complex and, at times, challenging to both manufacturers and FDA.

Because new animal drugs are used in a wide variety of species, the nature of these products as well as their dosage forms and routes of administration can be complex and, at times, challenging to both manufacturers and FDA. It is helpful to think of animal drugs with various types of descriptors. For example, is the target species a species traditionally consumed as food (e.g., swine, cattle, poultry, or fish) or one that has not traditionally been consumed as food in the United States (e.g., dogs, cats, or horses)? Another descriptor differentiates products by whether the proposed indication is for a therapeutic use (i.e., to treat a disease) or a production indication (i.e., to increase food animal production efficiency). Still a third descriptor is based on the route of administration, including whether the drug will be administered directly to the animal or whether it will be mixed and diluted in animal feed.

As a thought experiment, consider regulating an oral versus intravenous chemotherapy for dogs, or a drug mixed into animal feed to increase feed efficiency in cattle, or a drug administered to honeybee larvae via dusting onto the backs of adult honeybees.

As we will see, these and other factors will have a significant affect on the specific regulatory requirements for a given product.

THE NEW ANIMAL DRUG APPLICATION

As mentioned in Chapter 5, the statutory definition of a "drug" is exceedingly broad, including any "article" that: 1) is recognized in the U.S. Pharmacopoeia, U.S. Homeopathic Pharmacopoeia, or the National Formulary; 2) is intended to diagnose, cure, mitigate, treat, or prevent disease; 3) other than food is intended to alter the structure or any function of the body; and 4) is a component of any of the first three items.

Section 201(v) of the Federal, Food, Drug, and Cosmetic Act (FDCA) defines a "new animal drug," in relevant part, as "any drug intended for use for animals other than man, including any drug intended for use in animal feed." While there are some exceptions included in the definition, which are discussed in more detail below, the scope of FDA's regulatory authority over animal drugs is substantial.

Unlike unapproved human drugs, unapproved animal drugs are deemed to be adulterated under FDCA §§ 512(a) and 501(a) unless and until FDA has approved a New Animal Drug Application (NADA) or one of its variants, such as an Abbreviated New Animal Drug Application (ANADA), or conditional approval or indexing of drugs for minor uses or minor species. This statutory nuance has subtle consequences for veterinary products. (For example, when exporting an unapproved new animal drug, manufacturers export under FDCA § 801(e) rather than under FDCA § 802.)

Unlike unapproved human drugs, unapproved animal drugs are deemed to be adulterated under FDCA §§ 512(a) and 501(a) unless and until FDA has approved a New Animal Drug Application (NADA) or one of its variants.

The Center within FDA that is responsible for the regulatory oversight of animal drugs is the Center for Veterinary Medicine (CVM). The specific requirements and process for obtaining approval from CVM varies, sometimes substantially, based on the drug product. To understand some of these variations it is helpful to first consider the general theme.

Therapeutic NADAs Intended for Non-Food Animals

Just as with human products, obtaining regulatory approval for a new animal drug can take several years and requires a substantial financial investment.

The approval of new animal drugs intended to treat diseases in animals not traditionally consumed as food presents the most straightforward NADA. This is by no means to suggest that the product development and regulatory path is simple or easy; just as with human products, obtaining regulatory approval for a new animal drug can take several years and requires a substantial financial investment.

♦ **The Preclinical Phase**

Prior to introducing a new animal drug into its target species, various studies and tests are performed to identify potential safety concerns in the target species as well as to gather the first evidence that the drug could, in theory, have the intended clinical effect.

While some of the preclinical information will not be submitted to FDA, for those data that will, FDA's regulations provide a specific exemption from the prohibition against interstate shipment for testing conducted *in vitro* or on research animals, provided certain conditions are met. Among other things, the new animal drug must provide specified product labeling, the receiving investigator must be qualified to conduct the testing, and adequate records must be generated and kept for at least two years after shipment of the product. This exemption does not apply to new animal drugs intended for use as part of laboratory-based diagnosing or treating of disease.

All research animal studies of new animal drugs are required to meet FDA's regulations governing Good Laboratory Practice (GLP).

All research animal studies of new animal drugs are required to meet FDA's regulations governing Good Laboratory Practice (GLP). The GLP regulations, found at 21 C.F.R. Part 58, detail, among other things, the organization and personnel employed, as well as the facilities, equipment, testing controls, and records required for eventual submission to FDA. Because nonclinical testing of new animal drugs must follow the same GLP regulations as nonclinical testing of human drugs, and because Chapter 5 provides a detailed summary of the GLP requirements, this chapter will not repeat that information. Rather, for more detailed information regarding GLPs, please see the "Preclinical Investigation" section in Chapter 5.

All animal studies are overseen and monitored by Institutional Animal Care and Use Committees (IACUCs). As Institutional Review Boards oversee human studies, IACUCs oversee animal studies with a particular focus on the ethical and humane care and use of study animals.

◆ **The Technical Sections, the INAD, and Phased Review**

An NADA consists of as many as eight technical sections:

◆ Target Animal Safety;

◆ Effectiveness;

◆ Chemistry, Manufacturing, and Controls (CMC);

◆ Human Food Safety;

◆ Environmental Impact;

◆ Labeling;

◆ Freedom of Information (FOI) Summary; and

◆ All Other Information.

Applications for drugs intended to treat non-food animals must complete seven of these eight sections. The three most significant sections are the Target Animal Safety, the Effectiveness, and the CMC technical sections.

In brief, the Target Animal Safety and the Effectiveness technical sections contain full reports of all studies that show that the new animal drug is safe for the target species and effective for its intended use. The CMC technical section contains complete information regarding the manufacture and quality of the new animal drug, including its active ingredient and the new animal drug product (i.e., the drug in its final dosage form and packaging).

The collection of the data and information necessary for these technical sections requires the opening of an Investigational New Animal Drug file (INAD). The opening of an INAD provides an exemption from the statutory prohibition against interstate shipment of an unapproved new animal drug, i.e., the investigational animal drug may be shipped although it has not been approved. An investigational new animal drug must meet several regulatory requirements, including requirements concerning the label, use, and disposal of the drug. FDA also requires that the sponsor of an INAD keep FDA informed about the quantities of the drug that are shipped under the INAD.

The opening of an INAD also is necessary to conduct the clinical trials to support an NADA. Additionally, FDA has established a process under which a sponsor may submit full data for the NADA technical sections under the INAD. Under this process, referred to as "phased review" (not to be confused with the human drug IND phases), FDA reviews portions of what would ordinarily be the NADA prior to the filing of the NADA. Sponsors engage FDA and receive feedback, both formal and informal, regarding their submissions. Once FDA considers the data and information for a given technical section as meeting the NADA standard for approval, FDA issues a "technical section complete letter." Phased review, thus, is the process of collecting the seven or eight applicable technical section complete letters. Once all the technical section complete letters have been received, sponsors file an "Administrative NADA" with FDA. This is called an Administrative NADA because the content of the NADA merely is the proposed product labeling, copies of the various technical section complete letters, and a letter of reference to the INAD.

Under "phased review," FDA reviews portions of what would ordinarily be the NADA prior to the filing of the NADA.

- ◆ **Clinical Studies**

All clinical studies from which data will be submitted to FDA must be conducted in conformity with Good Clinical Practices (GCPs). For animal drugs, GCPs are a compilation of international quality standards that are intended to assure that: 1) study integrity is maintained; 2) the welfare of the subject animals has been considered; 3) risks to personnel conducting the study are minimized; 4) the environmental impacts of the study have been evaluated; and 5) the human and animal food chains have been protected. The GCP standards are developed by relevant regulatory agencies in Japan, the European Union, and the United States, considering the animal husbandry practices in those countries and in Australia and New Zealand.

GCPs detail specific requirements regarding a number of critical aspects of clinical development. They discuss the responsibilities of study investigators, the study sponsor, and the individuals who monitor the execution of the study. GCPs include the sponsor's responsibilities when sponsors outsource the conduct of the study to a contract research organization (CRO). Of particular importance, GCPs discuss study documentation and recordkeeping and development of a study protocol and study report.

The study sponsor is primarily responsible for the design, implementation, and oversight of the clinical study.

The study sponsor is primarily responsible for the design, implementation, and oversight of the clinical study. FDA expects study sponsors to keep the agency informed regarding planned, ongoing, and completed studies. Sponsors also are responsible for ensuring that all personnel involved in the study are appropriately trained to carry out the study according to the pre-specified study protocol. Although sponsors may delegate certain responsibilities to CROs, the study sponsor is ultimately responsible for regulatory compliance, including IACUC oversight.

The IACUC plays a central role in ensuring the ethical treatment of study subjects.

Because target animal studies are conducted in animal subjects, which cannot provide informed consent, the notions of informed consent are substantially different. The IACUC plays a more central role in ensuring the ethical treatment of study subjects. In the event that study subjects are animals that are not owned by the sponsor or the CRO, consent must be obtained from the animal's owner prior to enrollment in the study.

If FDA determines that a clinical study or studies have not been conducted in conformity with the INAD regulations (e.g., GCPs and proper IACUC oversight), FDA may elect to place one or more studies on clinical hold, halting further investigation until the issues are resolved. If issues are not resolved, FDA may elect to terminate the INAD by notifying the sponsor and providing the sponsor with an opportunity for a formal hearing.

◆ Approval

Simultaneous with the approval of a new animal drug, FDA promulgates a specific regulation that details the active ingredient, the product's specifications, the sponsor, and the conditions, indications, and limitations of use.

One notable difference between human and animal drugs is that, simultaneous with the approval of a new animal drug, FDA promulgates a specific regulation that details the active ingredient, the product's specifications, the sponsor, and the conditions, indications, and limitations of use (including any withdrawal periods).

NADAs for Other Types of Products

◆ Therapeutic Drugs in Food Animals

The difference between use of a drug to treat a condition in dogs, a non-food-producing animal, and use of the same drug to treat the same condition in cows, a food-producing animal, is substantial. In addition to the obvious differences between the species, because cows are food-producing animals additional regulatory requirements apply. For species that are used to make products that are consumed by humans as food, a host of additional regulatory requirements come into play. These requirements flow from FDA's food safety mandate and are intended to ensure the safety and security of the country's animal and human food supply.

FDA's INAD regulations prohibit the introduction of study animals into the human or animal food supply without prior authorization from FDA. This regulatory requirement can substantially increase the costs associated with studies of food-producing animals. Given the expense of raising livestock and the value that each animal has at slaughter, it is common for INAD sponsors to seek a food use authorization from FDA. These requests must include information regarding the pharmacology of the new animal drug in the target species, including the presence of drug in the edible products of the target species (most often muscle, liver, kidneys, milk, and eggs). In the event that FDA authorizes the food use, it will generally include conditions on the number of animals that may be placed into the food supply during a given period and a maximum on the total number of animals introduced into the food supply. Perhaps most significantly, a food use authorization will almost invariably include a requirement that the drug not be administered to the animal for a specified, often lengthy, period of time before the animal's introduction into the food supply. This period of time is referred to as a "withdrawal period." Violations of the conditions of the food use authorization are taken seriously by FDA and can have substantial legal consequences for sponsors.

A food use authorization will almost invariably include a requirement that the drug not be administered to the animal for a specified, often lengthy, period of time before the animal's introduction into the food supply.

NADAs for animals that produce products traditionally consumed as food also must complete all eight technical sections, including the technical section for Human Food Safety. The Human Food Safety section includes data relating to the toxicology of the drug and its metabolites in humans, drug residue chemistry, and, if the new animal drug has anti-infective properties, microbial food safety. Sponsors must also propose a tolerance level for safe human exposure to drug residues and/or an appropriate withdrawal period for the drug. Additionally, because FDA and the U.S. Department of Agriculture (USDA) monitor the presence of animal drug residues in the human and animal food supplies, sponsors must submit a method for determining the quantity, if any, of the new animal drug in or on food, and any substance formed in or on food because of the drug's use.

◆ Drugs with Non-Therapeutic Indications

Although this has been an area of controversy for FDA, and FDA slowly has been reducing the number of animal drugs approved for non-therapeutic uses, the agency has approved, and continues to approve, new animal drugs for uses that do not involve the prevention, diagnosis, mitigation, or treatment of disease in animals. These drugs typically are used to increase the efficiency of food animal production, often by increasing the efficiency by which an animal converts consumed food into marketable weight gain.

FDA has jurisdiction over, and approves, these New Animal Drug Applications under the so-called "structure/function" clause of the drug definition. Recall that the statutory definition of a drug includes "articles (other than food) intended to affect the structure or any function of the body of . . . animals." Because non-therapeutic veterinary products are intended to increase production efficiency, at a minimum they alter the structure of the animal's body, if not also its function.

NADA-related studies generally are larger in size due to the difficulty in demonstrating a statistically significant effect (which tends to be much smaller in size and must be teased out from a more highly variable control population).

FDA has been in the process of re-evaluating all approved drugs with production claims to determine whether the claimed effect is supported by appropriate data and whether the risk-benefit calculation still argues in favor of continued availability.

FDA has been in the process of re-evaluating all approved drugs with production claims to determine whether the claimed effect is supported by appropriate data and whether the risk-benefit calculation still argues in favor of continued availability. This process, as it relates to the use of antibiotics as growth-promoting animal drugs, has also been the subject of proposed legislation in Congress.

◆ Medicated Animal Feed

Some new animal drugs are intended to be added to animal feed, rather than administered directly to a given animal. The bulk drug product, undiluted by animal feed, is referred to as a Type A Medicated Article. Type A Medicated Articles are not intended to be directly administered to an animal, and are only approved to be diluted in animal feed. Once diluted into animal feed, the Type A Article is referred to as a Type B Medicated Feed. Type B Medicated Feeds generally may be either fed to animals or diluted further. Diluted Type B Medicated Feeds are referred to as Type C Medicated Feeds.

Although FDA has regulatory authority over animal feed and animal feed mills that mix and produce animal feeds, FDA generally leaves the regulation of animal feed mills to the individual states.

Although FDA has regulatory authority over animal feed and animal feed mills that mix and produce animal feeds, FDA generally leaves the regulation of animal feed mills to the individual states. Accordingly, when approving a Type A Medicated Article or a Medicated Feed, sponsors are required to submit a so-called "blue bird label" for Type B and Type C Medicated Feeds manufactured with the Type A Medicated Article and information detailing a specific analytical method that can be used to determine the amount of drug product in a given amount of animal feed. Because the drug amounts are often at very low levels, these methods must be highly sensitive and thoroughly validated. Prior to accepting a sponsor's regulatory method, FDA will usually conduct a method trial of its own in order to ensure that the method is robust enough for FDA and state laboratories. Once approved, FDA makes these analytical methods publically available.

The other significant difference between Medicated Articles and Feeds versus other NADAs is that the required manufacturing standards are different. Drug current Good Manufacturing Practice (cGMP) regulations are found at 21 C.F.R. Part 211, whereas the cGMP regulations for Medicated Feeds and Medicated Articles are found at 21 C.F.R. Parts 225 and 226, respectively.

Standards of Review

◆ Target Animal Safety

A new animal drug must be "safe for use under the conditions prescribed, recommended, or suggested in the proposed labeling." Section 512(d)(2) of the FDCA details specifically what factors FDA must consider when making the safety determination. Those include: 1) whether and how probable it is that the drug will be later consumed in or on food; 2) the cumulative effect, considering all chemically related compounds, of the drug on man or animals; 3) the margin of safe use of the drug; and 4) whether the conditions of use in the product labeling are likely to be followed in practice.

When determining animal drug safety, studies are conducted where animals are given one, three, and five times the highest proposed label dose. The study animals are given the assigned dose for a period of time that exceeds the longest treatment duration on the proposed label, generally three times the duration. Animals are tested extensively, including full necropsies. Safety studies may also include drug or dosage-form specific studies.

When determining animal drug safety, animals are tested extensively, including full necropsies.

◆ Effectiveness

Sponsors must demonstrate that there is "substantial evidence" that the drug will have the effect that it is purported or represented to have under the conditions of use contained in the product labeling.

Section 512(d)(3) of the FDCA defines what constitutes substantial evidence for an animal drug: studies in the target species; laboratory animal studies; field studies; a bioequivalence study; or an *in vitro* study. FDA's regulations require that the number of studies be sufficient to demonstrate the drug's effect is both reliable and repeatable. In effect, animal drug sponsors may, theoretically, meet the effectiveness requirement with a single study and supporting evidence from laboratory animals, or even from published literature alone.

Section 512(d)(3) of the FDCA defines what constitutes substantial evidence for an animal drug: studies in the target species; laboratory animal studies; field studies; a bioequivalence study; or an in vitro study.

Because the effectiveness standard is so malleable, FDA has issued a number of guidance documents that provide specific guidance regarding effectiveness trials for specific classes of drugs, and even for specific species using specific classes of drugs. Here, the use of pre-submission conferences with FDA provides invaluable information and guidance for drug sponsors.

- **Chemistry, Manufacturing, and Controls**

As a part of the NADA, the CMC technical section includes detailed information regarding the chemistry of the new animal drug as well as how the active ingredient and the drug product is manufactured, formulated, and tested both during and after manufacture.

A new animal drug must be manufactured in conformity with cGMPs such that, as required by section 512(d) of the FDCA, "the methods used in, and the facilities and controls used for, the manufacture, processing, and packing of [the new animal drug] are []adequate to preserve its identity, strength, quality, and purity." For animal drugs that are not Type A Medicated Articles or Type B or Type C Medicated Feeds, the manufacturing standards are identical to those required for human drugs. FDA has promulgated specific cGMP regulations governing the manufacture of Medicated Articles and Medicated Feeds. Prior to approval, FDA will often conduct a pre-approval inspection (PAI) of a new drug facility. The approval of an NADA can be delayed pending the outcome of a PAI.

The CMC section must also contain information regarding the controls that are put into place throughout the manufacturing process, before product is released for commercial distribution, and after the product has entered commerce. The CMC section is often the last of the three (or four for food animals) technical sections completed prior to approval.

- **Human Food Safety**

The goals of the Human Food Safety technical section are to identify a no-observed adverse effect level (NOAEL), establish an acceptable daily intake (ADI) for humans potentially consuming drug residues, and determine what product labeling requirements are necessary to ensure that the established ADIs are not exceeded. The battery of tests that encompass the Human Food Safety technical section include repeat-dose toxicity, pharmacology, immunotoxicity, neurotoxicity, carcinogenicity, genotoxicity, reproductive and developmental toxicity studies, and residue depletion studies.

As discussed above, product labeling may include a specific withdrawal period prior to introduction of the animal into the human or animal food supply. All animal drug withdrawal periods are codified in FDA's animal drug regulations and published in the *Federal Register*.

OTHER TYPES OF NEW ANIMAL DRUG APPLICATIONS

Generic Animal Drugs

In 1988, Congress passed the Generic Animal Drug and Patent Term Restoration Act. This law, among other things, directs that generic animal drugs are subject to the same regulatory oversight as innovator animal drugs, are subject to the same postmarketing requirements, and must be manufactured to the same standards that apply to their referenced innovator drugs.

Generic animal drugs must open an investigational file with FDA, referred to as a Generic Investigational New Animal Drug (JINAD), and then file an ANADA. The ANADA does not need to include information regarding safety, human food safety, or effectiveness of the generic drug, as it relies on FDA's finding of safety, human food safety, and effectiveness for the referenced innovator drug. An ANADA, however, must meet all of the CMC requirements for new animal drugs, and must demonstrate that the drug is bioequivalent to the reference drug. Sponsors may request a waiver from needing to submit *in vivo* bioequivalence data, though such requests are generally limited to specific types of reference drugs, such as oral dosage forms.

An ANADA must meet all of the CMC requirements for new animal drugs, and must demonstrate that the drug is bioequivalent to the reference drug.

Although FDA relies on the finding of human food safety from the reference drug, FDA may request that an ANADA sponsor submit a tissue depletion study to demonstrate that the generic version is removed from specific tissues in the same manner as the reference drug.

Minor Use and Minor Species

The Minor Use and Minor Species Animal Health Act of 2004 (the MUMS Act) was intended to make more medications legally available to veterinarians and animal owners to treat minor animal species and uncommon diseases in the major animal species. In this regard, the MUMS Act was intended to function much the same way as the Orphan Drug Act for human drugs—drugs that receive designation as a MUMS drug are granted an additional seven years market exclusivity, and MUMS drugs are exempt from certain user fees.

The MUMS Act defines a "minor species" as any species that is not a "major species." The statute defines "major species" as one of seven groups of animal species—dogs, cats, horses, cattle, pigs, turkeys, and chickens. The definition of "minor use" is not defined by statute, but has been delegated to FDA. FDA regulations set the upper limit for the potential number of animals in a major species that have a given condition for the indication to be eligible as a minor use. Those limits are:

♦ 50,000 horses;

♦ 70,000 dogs;

♦ 120,000 cats;

♦ 310,000 cattle;

♦ 1,450,000 pigs;

♦ 14,000,000 turkeys; and

♦ 72,000,000 chickens.

In addition to the designation benefits that are analogous to orphan drug designation for human drugs, the MUMS Act also provides for conditional approvals and drug indexing.

Conditional approval under MUMS is available once a product has met the safety and manufacturing standards of approval, but has only demonstrated a "reasonable expectation" of effectiveness. Conditionally approved MUMS drugs are required to complete and submit the required data regarding the effectiveness studies during the time that the drug is conditionally approved. Sponsors must renew their request for conditional approval each year after the conditional approval, and may do so four times, for a total of up to five years of conditional approval. If the required data are not submitted by the end of the conditional approval period, the conditional approval automatically terminates. In addition, the conditional approval is withdrawn if FDA approves any new animal drug for the conditionally approved indication.

MUMS drugs for species or indications that are considered too rare to conduct adequate and well-controlled studies are eligible for listing on an index of legally marketed unapproved drugs. Importantly, indexing is only permitted for minor species, and then only for non-food-producing minor species and for early life stages of food-producing minor species. Indexed drugs do not receive any of the marketing exclusivity advantages granted to designated MUMS drugs and indexed drugs are not permitted to be used outside the scope of the indexed use. Although a drug may not be indexed if it or another compound is approved for the same use in the same species, more than one compound may be indexed for the same use in the same species.

Genetically Engineered Animals

In the mid-2000s, FDA asserted its authority to regulate animals that have been produced by genetic engineering. Under FDA's theory, the intentionally altered genomic DNA in the animal is an article that alters the structure and/or function of the animal, and, therefore, meets the statutory definition of an animal drug. Because once the animal has been engineered FDA cannot physically exercise its jurisdiction over the rDNA present in each cell of the resulting animal and its offspring, FDA asserts jurisdiction over the entire animal itself, as the animal "contains a new animal drug."

FDA asserts jurisdiction over the entire animal itself, as the animal "contains a new animal drug."

Although this interpretation of FDA's animal drug authorities has not been directly challenged in court, the U.S. District Court for the District of Columbia implicitly affirmed FDA's reading in a case that challenged FDA's decision to exercise its enforcement discretion and not require an NADA for ornamental zebra fish engineered to glow in the dark. *See Int'l Ctr. For Tech. Assessment, et al. v. Thompson, et al.*, 421 F. Supp. 2d 1 (D.D.C. 2006).

Importantly, FDA's review process for genetically engineered animals is dramatically different from that for "conventional" new animal drugs. The process requires a close relationship with the FDA review teams charged with reviewing these applications, as review times can vary significantly. For example, the first approval of a genetically engineered animal was a goat genetically engineered to produce a human biologic in its milk. At the time of its approval in 2009, FDA touted the speed with which the NADA for the engineered goats was approved. On the other hand, the second approval of a genetically engineered animal, Atlantic salmon engineered to grow to market size in half the time as non-engineered salmon, took more than 20 years to receive its approval.

FDA's review process for genetically engineered animals is dramatically different from that for "conventional" new animal drugs.

POSTAPPROVAL RESPONSIBILITIES

Although the regulatory process of seeking and obtaining an approval can be a marathon, the legal requirements for animal drugs continue long after the approval order. Sponsors of approved animal drugs have a number of ongoing responsibilities throughout the lifetime of the approval, a few of which are discussed below.

Changes to the Approved Application

The FDCA implicitly acknowledges that it is unrealistic to expect that an approved application will remain the same over time.

◆ Manufacturing Changes

The most common changes are in the way that a product is manufactured. As manufacturing technologies improve, sponsors look for ways to increase the efficiencies of their processes; as labor markets change, sponsors may elect to move manufacturing to different locations throughout the globe; equipment can fail or become obsolete; corporate governance changes can result in the consolidation of dispersed activities into central locations. These are just a few of the many ways that product manufacturing will, inevitably, change the content of the approved application.

To address these manufacturing changes, FDA has established a risk-based system for the review of such changes.

To address these manufacturing changes, FDA has established a risk-based system for the review of such changes. Because these changes are made via different types of submissions at differing times, it is helpful to think of the differences between the various types of supplements as relating to when FDA would want to know about the changes. For some changes, FDA will want to review and approve the changes before a sponsor sells product manufactured under the changed application. For others, FDA may only want some notice of the change, but will not insist on sponsors waiting for FDA review. Still others, FDA may not feel it is necessary to be notified of the change until some time after the change has been implemented.

The highest risk changes, for example, moving manufacturing from one facility to a new facility, require that sponsors seek affirmative approval before implementing those changes. These changes are submitted via a "Prior Approval Supplement." Here, the application is not changed unless and until FDA agrees to the change.

For lower risk changes, for example, a change to the vial or cap that contains a sterile drug product, FDA requires that sponsors give FDA 30 days' notice prior to implementing the change. These changes are submitted via a "Changes Being Effected in 30 Days," or CBE-30, supplement. During these 30 days, FDA may notify the sponsor that it is converting the submission to a prior approval supplement, effectively halting the implementation while FDA completes its review. Importantly, even if FDA does not convert the supplement to a prior approval supplement, if, after FDA's review, FDA concludes that the change is not acceptable, the sponsor may be required to stop production and recall product manufactured under the changed application. In this regard, although submitting a CBE-30 speeds the time to implementation of a change, the sponsor runs the risk that FDA will not agree with the change. Unless FDA objects, the change is considered a part of the approved application 30 days after submission.

For still lower risk changes, for example, changing a manufacturing control such that there is greater assurance of product quality, sponsors may implement those changes as soon as they notify FDA. Here, sponsors submit a "Changes Being Effected," or immediate CBE or CBE-0, supplement to FDA. Again, sponsors run the risk that FDA will disagree with the change, but sponsors are able to more quickly execute such a change. The application is changed as of the date that FDA is notified of the change.

For changes classified as having the "lowest risk" (for example, tightening of the drug product specifications), FDA permits sponsors to implement these changes immediately and report them to FDA in an annual report, referred to as the "Minor Changes and Stability Report," or MCSR. Each year, within 60 days of the anniversary of the product approval date, sponsors must submit an annual report that includes all of the minor manufacturing changes implemented during the previous year. Here, the changes to the application are effective as of the date the sponsor implements them.

+ **Withdrawal**

FDA's regulations permit the agency to withdraw approval of an application. As one would expect, FDA may initiate such an action only under specified circumstances, including sponsor fraud in the application or an FDA finding that new information shows that the drug is either unsafe or ineffective under the approved conditions of use. Not surprising, given the various legal, not to mention constitutional, issues implicated by such actions, FDA rarely invokes this authority, and, even when doing so, must go through a lengthy process with the sponsor.

When initiating a withdrawal action, FDA must provide the sponsor with notice and the opportunity for a formal hearing. The formal hearing process can take years to complete when including time for appeals through the administrative review process, not to mention any judicial court proceedings that may also result from a sponsor seeking relief from the federal courts. Accordingly, FDA will typically work informally with the sponsor either to address its concerns through labeling changes, or to convince the sponsor to voluntarily withdraw the application.

When initiating a withdrawal action, FDA must provide the sponsor with notice and the opportunity for a formal hearing.

The sponsor of an approved application, may, at any time and on its own initiative, request that the approved application be withdrawn on the grounds that the drug is no longer being marketed. Such voluntary withdrawals may not be requested if FDA has formally notified the sponsor of its intent to withdraw the application and has offered the sponsor the opportunity for a formal hearing on the matter.

OTHER ISSUES

The number of issues that are related to the approval of new animal drugs are too numerous to cover in detail here. There are several, however, that are worth noting and discussing briefly.

User Fees

Like human drugs, biologics, and devices, animal drugs—both innovator and generic—are subject to statutory fees. The Animal Drug User Fee Act (ADUFA) and the Animal Generic Drug User Fee Act (AGDUFA) were modeled after the human drug user fees and operate in a similar manner. Sponsors are required to pay fees during both the INAD and NADA phases of approval, as well as annual fees once a product has received approval. Some of these fees are incurred by each drug sponsor or by each individual drug, while others are levied when specified submissions are sent to FDA.

Although the fees for animal drugs are substantially less than those for human drugs, some of the fees present a substantial burden on an industry that operates with far lower profit margins than its human drug cousin.

Although the fees for animal drugs are substantially less than those for human drugs, some of the fees are hundreds of thousands of dollars and present a substantial burden on an industry that operates with far lower profit margins than its human drug cousin. Accordingly, FDA has established, and is relatively generous with granting, partial or full waivers from various fees. These waivers can be for a number of reasons, including that being subject to a user fee would present a barrier to innovation. Typically, FDA will grant user fee waivers for first-time sponsors during the INAD phase, where making the "barrier to innovation" argument is most compelling.

Unapproved Animal Drugs

Within the veterinary community, the use of unapproved drugs is common.

Within the veterinary community, the use of unapproved drugs is common. In some cases, unapproved drugs are considered the standard of care. Although unapproved animal drugs are defined, by statute, to be adulterated and mis-branded, FDA takes a risk-based approach when establishing its enforcement priorities. Members of FDA's staff have discussed the agency's philosophy with respect to unapproved new animal drugs during various public meetings, stating that:

♦ Standard-of-care unapproved drugs will not suddenly become unavailable;

♦ FDA's goal is to increase the availability of approved animal drugs and decrease reliance on unapproved animal drugs;

♦ FDA is working with sponsors to bring unapproved animal drugs into the approval process;

♦ FDA is using its existing authority to find legal homes for essential veterinary drugs that are not currently approved; and

♦ FDA will use enforcement actions judiciously in a manner consistent with its approach to unapproved new animal drugs.

Of course, because, as a matter of law, an unapproved new animal drug violates the FDCA, FDA can, at any time, take any enforcement action it deems necessary against individuals or entities that introduce such drugs into interstate commerce. Despite such potential legal liability, a thriving unapproved animal drug market nonetheless persists.

Marketing Protections

Just as with human drug products, there are mechanisms that protect the marketing of a new animal drug. Sponsors of a new animal drug receive protection from generic competition for three years where approval required new clinical or field investigations. If the new animal drug is a compound that has not been approved as an animal drug for any indication, then the sponsor is granted five years marketing exclusivity.

Just as with human drug products, there are mechanisms that protect the marketing of a new animal drug.

Additionally, as discussed in the above section regarding the MUMS Act, designation as a Minor Use or Minor Species drug affords sponsors seven years of additional market exclusivity as an incentive to drug companies to develop such products.

From a patent extension perspective, a patent for a new animal drug is extended by the time that FDA reviewed the administrative NADA and half the time that the INAD file was open, subject to certain limitations that are beyond the scope of this chapter.

Veterinary Devices and Veterinary Biologics

FDA has jurisdiction over medical devices and certain biologics that are intended for veterinary use. With respect to veterinary devices, it is notable that although FDA has jurisdiction over these products, Congress has not granted FDA any authority for premarket review. Consequently, the burden is on FDA to demonstrate that a veterinary device is adulterated or misbranded or otherwise in violation of the FDCA.

With respect to veterinary biologics, FDA shares jurisdiction with the USDA. FDA and USDA have entered into an agreement that spells out when a product will be regulated as a veterinary biologic by USDA's Center for Veterinary Biologics (CVB), and when a product will be regulated as an animal drug by

With respect to veterinary biologics, FDA shares jurisdiction with the USDA.

FDA's Center for Veterinary Medicine. In general, the requirements for licensure through CVB are less burdensome to industry than those for receiving approval through CVM.

Because products that are veterinary devices or are veterinary biologics regulated by CVB have lower barriers for marketing than if those same products were regulated as animal drugs, sponsors seek to argue that their products fit into these other two categories, whereas CVM will tend to argue that they are drugs that require premarket approval of an NADA.

Combination Products

For combination products that contain a fixed combination of two animal drugs, FDA requires approval of an NADA for each specific combination.

Combination products that are drug/device or drug/biologic combinations are treated differently in the animal context than for human products. FDA takes the position that section 503(g) of the FDCA, as well as its implementing regulations, do not apply to veterinary products. Accordingly, FDA does not feel bound by the analysis required by those statutory and regulatory provisions that call for a detailed analysis of the primary mode of action and regulation of a product according to that mode of action.

FDA will usually assert its animal drug authority over any combination product that contains a drug component.

As a result, FDA will usually assert its animal drug authority over any combination product that contains a drug component. This is not a surprising result given FDA's lack of oversight of veterinary devices and veterinary biologics. To date, no one has challenged FDA's interpretation of its statute and implementing regulations on this issue.

Chapter 8

The Medical Device Approval Process

Steve Kanovsky, GE Healthcare, Waukesha, WI and Edward C. Wilson, Jr. & Michael S. Heyl, Hogan Lovells US LLP, Washington, D.C.

Key Points

- Medical devices include thousands of healthcare products, from simple articles (such as thermometers, tongue depressors, and heating pads) to more complex products (such as heart pacemakers, kidney dialysis machines, and proton beam therapy systems).

- Generally, medical device manufacturers must obtain clearance of a 510(k) premarket notification or approval of a Premarket Approval Application (PMA) for any device intended to be distributed commercially for the first time in the United States, unless the device is exempt from such requirements.

- There are three classifications of medical devices depending on the level of risk, with Class I devices posing the least amount of risk and Class III devices posing the greatest risk.

- The 510(k) premarket notification process refers to section 510(k) of the Federal Food, Drug, and Cosmetic Act (FDCA) and is used for devices that are *substantially equivalent* to a legally marketed Class I or II (low- to moderate-risk) device. The 510(k) premarket notification process is shorter than the PMA process because the Food and Drug Administration (FDA) usually requires less data and other information in 510(k) notifications to demonstrate that the 510(k) device is substantially equivalent to a predicate device.

- High-risk devices and devices that are not substantially equivalent to a legally marketed predicate device require PMA approval. The PMA process is lengthy because FDA generally requires clinical data demonstrating the safety and effectiveness of the PMA device for its intended use.

- The FDCA permits device manufacturers to ship devices solely for investigational use without an approved PMA or cleared 510(k) notice if the requirements of FDA's investigational device exemption (IDE) regulations are met.

OVERVIEW

The Food and Drug Administration's (FDA's) regulation of medical devices is extremely complex. As new technologies emerge, the challenges of determining how medical devices will be regulated and navigating the premarket clearance and approval process are complicated and often daunting.

Once products are cleared or approved to market, companies face rigorous regulatory requirements to maintain that status. Congress did not enact specific legislation governing the regulation of medical devices until 1976. Prior to that date, protection from defective devices depended on FDA's enforcement of limited provisions in the Federal Food, Drug, and Cosmetic Act of 1938 (FDCA) and on judicial interpretations that extended FDA's regulatory authority over drugs to devices. This patchwork of sources for regulatory oversight proved cumbersome.

The Medical Device Amendments of 1976 expanded FDA's statutory authority over devices.

By the mid-1970s, it was clear that, due to significant and rapid scientific advances, and because some unsafe, ineffective, and even fraudulent devices were occasionally marketed, an increase in federal regulation was required. In 1976, Congress passed the Medical Device Amendments (MDA), which vastly expanded FDA's statutory authority over devices. Since then, Congress has enacted several pieces of legislation to help ensure the safety and effectiveness of medical devices. Among other things, amendments to the FDCA have further expanded FDA's authority to clear or approve medical devices prior to marketing. For example, FDA is now authorized to collect user fees from applicants of medical device submissions. Congressional amendments have also required FDA to increase the transparency of the medical device clearance and approval process. As FDA's medical premarket clearance and approval processes have evolved over time, this chapter will provide a practical summary and perspective regarding the premarket clearance and approval requirements applicable to most medical devices.

What the Statute and Regulations Say

FDA defines "medical device" as:

> … an instrument, apparatus, implement, machine, contrivance, implant, in vitro reagent, or other similar or related article, including any component, part, or accessory, which is: (1) recognized in the official National Formulary, or the United States Pharmacopoeia, or any supplement to them, (2) intended for use in the diagnosis of disease or other conditions, or in the cure, mitigation, treatment, or prevention of disease, in man or other animals, or (3) intended to affect the structure or any function of the body of man or other animals, and which is not dependent upon being metabolized for the achievement of its primary intended purposes.

In contrast, products that accomplish their principal objectives by chemical action or by being metabolized by the body are considered drugs. Devices range from simple devices, such as thermometers, tongue depressors, and heating pads, to more complex products, such as intrauterine contraceptive devices, heart pacemakers, kidney dialysis machines, and total hip replacements. It is not always easy to determine if a product would be considered by FDA to be a drug or a device; some products are considered "combination products"—meaning they are a combination of a device *and* a drug or a biologic.

CLASSIFICATION OF DEVICES

Medical devices available on the market on or before May 28, 1976 (called "pre-amendment devices"), and devices similar to them, are distinguished from devices introduced after that date. Unless significantly modified, pre-amendment devices are permitted to remain on the market without FDA review, pending final classification or other action by FDA.

On the other hand, devices introduced after the MDA enactment date are subject to FDA review depending on the amount of control necessary to ensure their safety and effectiveness. Those medical devices are assigned to one of three regulatory classes based on the level of control necessary to ensure their safety and effectiveness. Medical devices with the highest level of risk require the highest level of FDA review and approval. Class I devices are generally subject only to "general controls" as they present the least potential harm to the user. Class II devices are normally subject to general controls and "special controls." Special controls are usually device-specific and include performance standards, postmarket surveillance, patient registries, and special labeling requirements. Finally, Class III devices are the most regulated and require premarket approval in addition to general and special controls. FDA has established classifications for approximately 1,700 different types of devices and grouped them into 16 medical specialties, such as hematology, ophthalmology, obstetrical and gynecological, cardiovascular, radiology, and general surgery.

Medical devices are assigned to one of three regulatory classes based on the level of control necessary to ensure their safety and effectiveness.

Class I devices include elastic bandages, examination gloves, and certain hand-held surgical instruments; barring the exemptions discussed below, Class I devices are subject only to general controls. These controls include requirements for facility registration and product listing with FDA; premarket notification (unless exempt); maintenance of records and filing reports regarding device marketing experience; adherence to Good Manufacturing Practices (GMPs), known as the Quality System Regulation (QSR) (unless exempt); and any distribution and use limitations FDA may impose. In addition, general controls authorize FDA to ban devices that present substantial deception or significant risks, as well as to detain devices that are alleged to violate the FDCA (pending legal action). Finally, FDA may require manufacturers to notify purchasers and users of devices that present unreasonable risks and to impose corrective action in certain situations.

The Food and Drug Administration Modernization Act of 1997 (FDAMA) exempted all Class I devices from FDA's premarket notification requirements, except those Class I devices that are intended for a use that is of substantial importance in preventing the impairment of human health or that present a potentially unreasonable risk of injury or illness (Class I reserved devices). Several dozen devices fall into the Class I reserved category, such as blood bank supplies, keratomes, cannulas, cardiovascular surgical instruments, and positron cameras. Many Class I devices are exempt from the design control provisions of the QSR requirements.

Class II devices are those devices for which general controls alone are insufficient to ensure their safety and effectiveness. Class II devices are subject to both general and special controls (e.g., performance standards, postmarket surveillance, patient registries, and FDA guidelines). Examples of Class II devices are powered wheelchairs, infusion pumps, and surgical drapes.

The 510(k) premarket notification process is the process under which a manufacturer notifies FDA of its intent to market a device that is identical to, or substantially similar to, a marketed device.

Most Class II devices require 510(k) clearance. The 510(k) premarket notification process is one under which the manufacturer notifies FDA of its intent to market a device that is substantially equivalent to a legally marketed device. The manufacturer must submit data demonstrating the equivalence; FDA clears for marketing those devices that meet the criteria. Under FDAMA, however, FDA exempted some Class II devices from 510(k) requirements. FDA may continue to add additional Class II devices to the exemption list on its own initiative or in response to a petition from an interested person. It is important to note that there may be limitations to the 510(k) exempt status of otherwise exempt Class I and Class II devices. These exemption limitations are noted in the device classification provisions of the Code of Federal Regulations (C.F.R.).

Generally, Class III devices are those devices that must receive premarket approval by FDA to ensure their safety and effectiveness. They are life-sustaining, life-supporting, and implantable devices, or new devices that have been found not to be substantially equivalent to legally marketed devices. Class III devices require FDA approval of a Premarket Approval Application (PMA) or a Product Development Protocol (PDP) (discussed at the end of this chapter).

Examples of Class III devices include heart valves, silicone gel-filled breast implants, drug-eluting stents, and certain bone growth stimulators. Class III devices that were on the market prior to the MDA may be marketed via the 510(k) notification route until FDA requires PMAs for these devices by publishing a notice in the *Federal Register*.

Certain devices ordered by healthcare professionals to conform to special needs of them or their patients are considered "custom devices." This term is distinguished from "customized" devices, which are required to be customized to meet each individual's specific needs. Custom devices are not subject to premarket approval and clearance requirements, though they remain subject to other provisions of the FDCA, such as the prohibitions against adulterating or misbranding products that are placed into interstate commerce. Importantly, custom devices are subject to FDA's GMP requirements for devices and Medical Device Reporting requirements. Due to ambiguities in FDA's definition of the custom device requirements, there has historically been a disparity between FDA's interpretation and enforcement of the custom device exemption versus industry's application of the exemption. For example, FDA's position as to the number of custom devices a company could make in any given year was not always consistent. To help address this issue, Congress redefined the term "custom devices" in the 2012 Food and Drug Administration Safety and Innovation Act (FDASIA). The new definition adopted existing FDA and federal court interpretations while adding new limitations to the applicability of the custom device exemption.

Custom devices are exempt from otherwise applicable performance standards or premarket approval and clearance requirements. Strict requirements must be met, however, for a device to be considered "custom."

In comparison, *customized* devices are subject to the full array of FDA regulatory requirements, including the premarket clearance and approval requirements.

Congress provided a mechanism for changing the classification of a device if new information emerges regarding its safety and effectiveness. FDA reclassified hundreds of devices from Class III to Class II or from Class II to Class I. In most cases, FDA exempted Class I devices from its 510(k) requirements; it has also exempted some Class II devices. When FDA reclassifies a device, it reclassifies the "generic type" of device, not the specific device for which a reclassification petition was submitted. Thus, a manufacturer may expend significant resources preparing a reclassification petition and indirectly benefit competitors that manufacture devices within the same generic type.

FDA can also use its enforcement discretion in determining whether certain devices require 510(k) clearance (e.g., convenience kits comprising legally marketed devices that are simply being assembled in kit form for "convenience" of the purchaser or user). Historically, convenience kits were subject to 510(k) review. FDA determined, however, that under certain circumstances, premarket clearance for convenience kits is not necessary. Therefore, FDA published a list of generic types of convenience kits that are exempt from FDA's 510(k) requirements, but not exempt from the registration, listing, prohibition against misbranding, and QSR. To be subject to the policy, all components of the kit must be legally marketed (e.g., subject to a cleared 510(k) notification, exempt from FDA's premarket notification requirements, or have pre-amendments status), and further processing of the kit cannot significantly affect the safety or effectiveness of the kit or its components.

The intended use of a device is a significant factor in determining its classification.

The intended use of a device is a significant factor in determining its classification. For example, lasers that are used for most dermatological and urological procedures are regulated as Class II devices. If the same laser (with certain modifications) is capable of performing ophthalmic procedures, such as LASIK, then the device would be a Class III device and require PMA approval for that indication.

How is the classification of a medical device determined? 21 C.F.R. Part 800 identifies, describes, and classifies thousands of products by device type (e.g., ophthalmic devices are covered in 21 C.F.R. Part 886). If a device has the same intended use and meets the general description of the device described in the classification regulation, the "new" device will likely fall under that regulation.

If a "new" device is not classified, the sponsor may look to the regulatory pathway used by competitors with similar products. Certain information about cleared 510(k) notifications and approved PMAs is publicly available after FDA has taken final action on a submission. This information is helpful in determining how FDA will likely regulate a device.

Where an unclassified device is determined not to be substantially equivalent, and thus Class III, a company can request reclassification based upon the low level of risk of the device.

Another means for determining the likely device classification is to have a pre-submission meeting with FDA to discuss the device's description, technological characteristics, and intended uses. Alternatively, a person may submit a written request under FDCA section 513(g), which requires FDA to identify the classification of a device and applicable premarket requirements. In addition, a manufacturer may petition FDA to down-classify a Class III device to Class I or Class II. FDA's guidance for submitting reclassification petitions explains the procedures and requirements for a reclassification petition and includes a Classification Questionnaire Form.[1] Finally, a person may submit a 510(k) premarket notification for a device and see if FDA clears the submission or finds the device not substantially equivalent (NSE) to a predicate device. If an NSE determination is made, the company could either submit a new 510(k) notice with additional data to support clearance or submit a *de novo* petition for down-classification (discussed in more detail below). If FDA does not agree that a device could be cleared to market via the 510(k) or *de novo* pathway,

FDA will require the submission and approval of a PMA (or the far less popular PDP) to market the device. Although the foregoing process is still available to 510(k) applicants, under FDASIA, a company may submit *de novo* petitions for down-classification without having to submit a 510(k) notification and receiving an NSE decision.

MEDICAL DEVICE USER FEE

Under the Medical Device User Fee and Modernization Act of 2002 (MDUFMA), FDA established user fees for the review of certain premarket submissions. The revenue generated by those user fees is intended to provide financial stability for FDA's medical device review program in return for improved and predictable performance by FDA in the review of new marketing submissions. Under MDUFMA, user fees were required for the review of premarket notifications (510(k)), PMA applications, Biologic License Applications (BLAs), premarket reports (PMRs), PDPs, panel-track PMA supplements, BLA efficacy supplements, and real-time PMA supplements.

FDA established user fees for the review of certain premarket submissions.

The Food and Drug Administration Amendments Act of 2007 (FDAAA), among other things, extended FDA's authority to collect user fees until 2012. FDAAA restructured the fee schedule to provide manufacturers with more predictability and stability in the payment of medical device user fees. FDAAA also added the user fee provisions to additional types of submissions. For example, FDA may collect user fees for 30-day notices (for PMAs), PMA annual reports, and 513(g) requests for designation. Fees are also required for initial and annual establishment registrations for each facility engaged in covered activities, such as manufacturing, importation, specification development, and contract sterilization. As before, revenues generated from FDA's user fee program were to be used to expedite the medical device review process in accordance with FDA performance goals.

Through the passage of FDASIA, the Medical Device User Fee Amendments (MDUFA III) reauthorized medical device user fees through September 30, 2017. MDUFA III permits FDA to collect at least $595 million, with higher fees required for PMAs, 510(k) notifications, establishment registration fees, and requests for PMA supplements, annual reports, and product classification requests. MDUFA III also expanded the number of facilities required to register and list their devices. Revenues from the user fee program will be used, in part, to increase the number of new reviewers to help meet significant new performance goals.

Investigational Device Exemptions

Purpose of an Investigational Device Exemption

An investigational device exemption (IDE) allows an unapproved device to be shipped in interstate commerce for purposes of conducting supportive clinical research.

Devices used on human subjects to investigate the device's safety and effectiveness for a certain intended use not yet cleared or approved by FDA are considered "investigational devices" under section 520(g) of the FDCA. These devices have not been approved for commercial distribution by FDA for their investigational use. An investigational device exemption (IDE) allows an unapproved device to be shipped in interstate commerce for purposes of conducting clinical research that can be submitted in support of a 510(k) or PMA submission. Without this exemption, shipment of an unapproved device in interstate commerce would violate the FDCA. Notably, although an approved IDE application exempts a device from certain provisions of the FDCA, it does not exempt it from other federal, state, or local regulations. For example, an investigational device that emits radiation may be subject to radiological health regulations, including product performance standards for equipment such as lasers and diagnostic x-rays. Investigational devices must also comply with applicable FDA advertising and labeling requirements.

Significant Risk and Nonsignificant Risk Devices

IDE regulations describe two types of devices: 1) significant risk and 2) non-significant risk. A significant risk device is defined as an investigational device that: 1) is intended as an implant and presents a potential for serious risk to the health, safety, or welfare of a subject; 2) is purported or represented to be for use in supporting or sustaining human life and presents a potential for serious risk to the health, safety, or welfare of a subject; 3) is for a use of substantial importance in diagnosing, curing, mitigating, or treating disease, or otherwise preventing impairment of human health and presents a potential for serious risk to the health, safety, or welfare of a subject; or 4) otherwise presents a potential for serious risk to the health, safety, or welfare of a subject (21 C.F.R. § 812.3(m)).

Some examples of significant risk studies include clinical trials on cardiac pacemaker/pulse generators, balloon dilation catheters for benign prostatic hyperplasia, implantable prostheses (ligament, tendon, hip, knee, and finger), and intraocular lenses.

A nonsignificant risk device study does not pose a significant risk to patients. Some examples of nonsignificant risk studies include clinical trials on daily wear contact lenses, denture repair kits, and general urological catheters.

Significant risk device studies must meet all regulatory requirements set forth in 21 C.F.R. Part 812, including requirements that the sponsor obtain IDE approval from FDA and approval of the investigational plan from each participating Institutional Review Board (IRB) before commencing the study. If the investigation does not present a significant risk to patient health, the sponsor may begin without obtaining FDA approval of the study provided that each reviewing IRB agrees that the study poses a nonsignificant risk and approves the study (nonsignificant risk studies are deemed to have IDE approval by FDA). Each subject must provide informed consent and the study protocol must be approved by the IRB, regardless of whether an investigation involves a significant or nonsignificant risk study device.

Initially, the sponsor makes the assessment of whether a device study presents a nonsignificant risk, in which case the sponsor provides the IRB with the study proposal, an explanation of why the study is a nonsignificant risk study, and other supporting information (e.g., any reports of prior investigations). The sponsor or investigator must also advise the IRB whether the study subjects must undergo a procedure as part of the investigational study (e.g., a surgical procedure), so the IRB can evaluate any harm that could be caused by the procedure in addition to any potential harm that could be caused by the device. In making this initial determination, a sponsor and IRB should consider FDA's guidance under "Information Sheet Guidance For IRBs, Clinical Investigators, and Sponsors Significant Risk and Nonsignificant Risk Medical Device Studies" (*see* http://www.fda.gov/downloads/regulatoryinformation/guidances/ucm126418.pdf).

Institutional Review Boards (IRBs)

IRBs are committees, either independent or affiliated with medical institutions, composed of qualified experts who review and approve biomedical research, as well as conduct a continuing review of ongoing research, to help ensure the protection of the rights and welfare of human subjects. In deciding whether a study (whether nonsignificant risk or significant risk) is approvable, an IRB must be assured that: 1) risks to subjects are minimized and are reasonable in relation to anticipated benefits and knowledge to be gained, 2) subject selection is equitable, 3) informed consent materials and procedures are adequate, and 4) provisions for monitoring the study and protecting the privacy of subjects are acceptable. To help ensure that risks to the subjects are reasonable in relation to the anticipated benefits, the risks and benefits of the investigation are compared to the risks and benefits of alternative devices or procedures. If the reviewing IRBs agree that the study presents a nonsignificant risk and is approvable, the investigation may proceed without FDA approval of an IDE application. If any reviewing IRB determines that the study poses a significant risk, the

An IRB must be assured that:

1) risks to subjects are minimized and are reasonable in relation to anticipated benefits and knowledge to be gained,

2) subject selection is equitable,

3) informed consent materials and procedures are adequate, and

4) provisions for monitoring the study and protecting the privacy of subjects are acceptable.

sponsor must notify FDA that a significant risk determination has been made and an IDE application must be submitted to and approved by FDA before beginning the study. Moreover, at any time, FDA may overrule a nonsignificant risk determination by an IRB and require the sponsor to submit an IDE application to FDA for approval.

IDE Exempt Investigations

Clinical investigations of devices to support a market application are generally subject to the IDE requirements.

Clinical investigations of devices to support a market application are generally subject to the IDE requirements. There are, however, limited exemptions from the IDE regulations. For example, per 21 C.F.R. § 812.2(c), a diagnostic device that complies with the labeling requirements in 21 C.F.R. § 809.10(c) is exempt from the IDE regulations if the testing: 1) is noninvasive, 2) does not require an invasive sampling procedure that presents significant risk, 3) does not by design or intention introduce energy into a subject, and 4) is not used as a diagnostic procedure without confirmation by another medically established diagnostic product or procedure. Any such exempt studies, however, still must comply with FDA's IRB and informed consent requirements.

Certain other studies also are exempt from FDA's IDE regulations, including evaluation of a device for consumer product testing, a device that is legally marketed provided it is used in accordance with its cleared labeling (or labeling in effect prior to MDA, for pre-amendment devices), or a custom device unless the device is being studied to determine its safety or effectiveness for commercial distribution.

Content of an IDE

Per 21 C.F.R. § 812.20(b), the sponsor of the proposed human clinical investigation that is not exempt per 21 C.F.R. § 812.2(c) must include the following information in an IDE application:

(1) name and address of sponsor;
(2) report of prior investigations, including published and unpublished information relevant to the evaluation of the safety and effectiveness of the device;
(3) investigational plan, including a description of the objectives and duration of the study, analysis of risk, justification, patient population, monitoring procedures, and the protocol;
(4) device description and description of methods, facilities, and controls for manufacturing;
(5) example of investigator agreement;

(6) certification that all investigators who will participate in the study have signed the investigator agreement;

(7) names, addresses, and chairpersons of IRBs;

(8) participating institutions;

(9) statement of noncommercialization;

(10) labeling; and

(11) informed consent materials.

IDEs that do not contain the required elements will not be accepted under FDA's Center for Devices and Radiological Health (CDRH) "refuse to accept" policy. Furthermore, the *IDE Refuse to Accept Procedures* (Blue Book Memorandum D94-1, May 20, 1994) states that the CDRH Office of Device Evaluation (ODE) may reject IDE submissions for three primary reasons: (i) an IDE is not required for the investigation; (ii) the application omits a required section; or (iii) the application fails to address scientific/technical issues clearly described in publicly available, general, device-specific, and cross-cutting guidances. Moreover, ODE's reviewing divisions use the IDE refuse to accept checklist to determine whether to proceed with the review of an IDE application. If an IDE application does not contain all of the necessary elements, it will be returned to the sponsor for revision before FDA begins a substantive review.

An IDE application that does not contain all required information will be returned to the sponsor for revision before FDA begins a substantive review.

IDE Review Process

FDA has 30 days to review an IDE application. An IDE application is considered approved 30 days after it has been received by FDA, unless FDA notifies the sponsor prior to the expiration of the 30 days that the IDE is approved with conditions or disapproved. In practice, however, sponsors generally wait for an approval notification from FDA so as not to begin studies that might have to be stopped or modified. If FDA disapproves an IDE, the sponsor may respond to the deficiencies and/or request a regulatory hearing under 21 C.F.R. Part 16. If FDA approves the IDE with conditions, the sponsor has 45 days in which to address the conditions of approval.

Notably, sponsors of Class III or implantable device clinical studies may submit an investigational plan (including the clinical protocol) to FDA for review, in order to reach agreement on the proposed plan. In practice, FDA also typically agrees to review investigational plans for Class I and II non-implantable devices. Neither Blue Book Memorandum #D95-1 *(Goals and Initiatives for the IDE Program)* nor IDE Guidance #99-1 *(Pre-IDE Program: Issues and Answers)* make distinctions with respect to class or type of device. The plan can be submitted prior to the actual official submission of the IDE application or prior to seeking IRB approval. Any agreement between the sponsor and FDA must be made part of the administrative record and may be changed only: 1) with written agreement of the sponsor or 2) pursuant to an FDA decision identifying a substantial scientific issue essential to determining the safety or effectiveness of the device. Any agency determination must be documented after providing the sponsor with an opportunity for a meeting during which the substantial scientific issues are documented.

Informal, nonbinding guidance is also available via a pre-submission process to allow FDA to provide guidance and feedback on development of supporting preclinical data or the investigational plan for incorporation into the IDE application. These meetings can take many forms, including conference calls, video conference calls, or face-to-face meetings. *See* FDA's pre-submission draft guidance document available at https://www.fda.gov/downloads/MedicalDevices/DeviceRegulationandGuidance/GuidanceDocuments/UCM311176.pdf.

IDE Supplements

Sponsors of significant risk studies are required to obtain FDA approval of an IDE supplement before making a change in the investigational plan that may affect scientific soundness or the rights, safety, or welfare of subjects.

Pursuant to FDA's IDE regulations, sponsors of significant risk studies are required to obtain FDA approval of an IDE supplement before making a change in the investigational plan that may affect its scientific soundness or the rights, safety, or welfare of subjects. Under FDAMA section 201, FDA promulgated new regulations that allow study sponsors to make modifications to investigational devices and study protocols without submitting IDE supplements to FDA. The regulations set forth several specific changes that no longer require IDE supplements: 1) developmental changes in the device (including manufacturing changes) that do not constitute a significant change in design or basic principles of operation and that are made in response to information gathered during the course of investigation and 2) changes or modifications to clinical protocols that do not affect: a) the validity of data or information resulting from the completion of an approved protocol or the relationship of likely patient risk to benefit relied upon to approve a protocol; b) the scientific soundness of an investigational plan submitted in the IDE; or c) the rights, safety, or welfare of the human subjects involved in the investigation.

Moreover, the IDE regulations state that these types of changes can be made if the sponsor of the study: 1) determines, on the basis of credible information, that the change or modification meets the specified criteria and 2) submits to FDA, within five days, a notice of the change or modification. The intent of this provision is to place the burden on the study sponsor to determine whether proposed changes necessitate the filing of an IDE supplement. FDA can disagree with the sponsor's determination and require an IDE supplement at its discretion.

Investigational Device Labeling Requirements

Per 21 C.F.R. § 812.5, investigational devices are subject to specific labeling requirements. The labeling of investigational devices must include:

(1) name and place of business of the manufacturer, packer, or distributor;
(2) the quantity of contents;
(3) the statement, "CAUTION—Investigational device. Limited by federal (or United States) law to investigational use;"
(4) all relevant contraindications, hazards, adverse effects, interfering substances, or devices, warnings, and precautions;
(5) no false or misleading statements; and
(6) no representation that the device is safe or effective for the purposes for which it is being investigated.

Note that a manufacturer may include a statement that the product has an approved IDE.

Sponsor and Investigator Responsibilities

Per IDE regulations, sponsors of IDE investigations and the investigators participating in IDE investigations have various responsibilities. Investigators are responsible for: 1) ensuring that the study is conducted according to investigational plan and applicable FDA regulations; 2) obtaining informed consent from study subjects; 3) supervising the use of the device; and 4) returning unused investigational devices to the sponsor or disposing of them as the sponsor directs. Sponsors are responsible for: 1) selecting qualified investigators and providing them with the information they need to conduct the study properly; 2) properly labeling the device; 3) obtaining IRB review and approval; 4) ensuring proper monitoring of the study; 5) investigating any unanticipated adverse events that occur during the study and taking appropriate action; and 6) informing FDA and IRBs about significant new information (21 C.F.R. § 812.40).

In addition to the above responsibilities, both sponsors and investigators are subject to recordkeeping responsibilities. Per 21 C.F.R. § 812.140(a), investigators must keep records of: 1) correspondence with the sponsor, FDA, IRB, and other investigators and monitors; 2) receipt and disposition of investigational devices; 3) study subjects' case histories and exposure to the device; 4) documentation of informed consent; and 5) the protocol and any deviations. Sponsors are responsible for maintaining records of the following per 21 C.F.R. § 812.140(b): 1) correspondence with investigators, FDA, IRB, and other sponsors and monitors; 2) shipment and disposition of investigational devices; 3) signed investigator

Sponsors and investigators each have independent recordkeeping and reporting responsibilities.

statements; 4) name and address of each investigator; and 5) name and address of each IRB that has reviewed the study.

Finally, both sponsors and investigators are subject to reporting responsibilities. For investigators, per 21 C.F.R. § 812.150(a), the following must be reported: 1) unanticipated adverse effects reports (if occurring during the study, should be submitted to the sponsor and IRB within 10 working days after the investigator first learns of the event); 2) deviations from the investigational plan or informed consent process; 3) progress reports (should be submitted to the sponsor and IRB, and the investigator should monitor progress reports on the study at regular intervals — at least yearly); and 4) final reports (should be submitted to the sponsor and IRB within three months of the end of the study).

Sponsors' reporting requirements include: 1) evaluating reports of unanticipated adverse effects from the investigator and reporting results to FDA, all reviewing IRBs, and participating investigators within 10 working days after sponsor first receives notice; 2) submitting a current investigator list to FDA every six months; 3) submitting progress reports at regular intervals (at least yearly) to all IRBs and, for a significant risk study, to FDA; 4) in the instance of IRB or FDA withdrawal of approval, notification of all reviewing IRBs and all participating investigators within five working days; and 5) for significant risk studies, notifying FDA of termination of the study within 30 days and submitting final reports to FDA, all reviewing IRBs, and participating investigators within 30 days of the end of the study. For nonsignificant risk studies, a final report must be submitted to all reviewing IRBs within six months of study termination (21 C.F.R. § 812.150(b)).

Disqualification of Investigators

An investigator can be disqualified by FDA from performing clinical research for failure to comply with regulatory requirements or for repeated or deliberate submission of false information to a sponsor.

Per 21 C.F.R. § 812.119, an investigator can be disqualified by FDA from performing clinical research for failure to comply with regulatory requirements or for repeated or deliberate submission of false information to a sponsor. If a study investigator is disqualified, FDA typically will examine the investigator's study data to determine whether it is reliable. If found unreliable, this can be a basis for withdrawing approval of any IDE or marketing application that included the unreliable data.

Registration Requirements for Clinical Trials

FDAAA established registration requirements for "applicable clinical trials." An applicable device clinical trial is defined as:

(1) a prospective clinical study of health outcomes comparing an intervention with a device subject to [510(k), PMA, and

Humanitarian Device Exemptions premarket requirements] against a control in human subjects (other than a small clinical trial to determine the feasibility of a device, or a clinical trial to test prototype devices where the primary outcome measure relates to feasibility and not to health outcomes); and

(2) a pediatric postmarket surveillance [requirement].

"Applicable clinical trials" must meet registration requirements established by the Food and Drug Administration Amendments Act of 2007 (FDAAA).

Thus, per FDAAA, studies being conducted under an approved IDE and even studies that have NSE designations may need to be registered with the Clinical-Trials.gov data bank.

To register a study, required information includes (but is not limited to) the study title; a brief summary of the study written for the lay public; the study design; the primary purpose of the study; the study phase; the study type; the disease or condition being studied; the intervention name and type; the start date; the expected completion date; the sample size; and the primary and secondary endpoints. The sponsor also must provide recruitment information including eligibility criteria, gender, age limits, policies on accepting healthy volunteers, recruitment status, and individual site status. In addition, contact information for the sponsor's facility, as well as certain administrative information (e.g., the unique protocol identification number, the name and contact information for the individual responsible for the study, etc.), must be provided.

Product submissions, including 510(k)s, PMAs, and humanitarian device exemption applications, must be accompanied by a certification that the applicant has complied with the clinical trial registration requirements. FDA has created a certification form (Form FDA 3674, available on FDA's website) to provide the required certifications. Guidance is available on the ClinicalTrials.gov website to assist sponsors with the determination of whether a study meets the definition of an applicable trial and, therefore, is subject to the reporting requirements.

The humanitarian device exemption applies to devices that:
- *are designated to treat or diagnose a disease or condition that affects fewer than 4,000 persons per year,*
- *are not available otherwise and there is no comparable device available,*
- *do not expose patients to unreasonable or significant risk, and*
- *the benefits to health outweigh the risks.*

HUMANITARIAN DEVICE EXEMPTIONS

To encourage the discovery of devices that benefit a small number of patients in the United States, FDA may grant a humanitarian device exemption (HDE) from the effectiveness requirements of the FDCA after finding that: 1) the device is designated to treat or diagnose a disease or condition that affects fewer than 4,000 individuals per year; 2) the device is not available otherwise and there is no comparable device available to treat or diagnose the disease or condition; 3) the device will not expose patients to unreasonable or significant risk; and 4) the benefits to health from its use outweigh the risks.

Two distinct steps are necessary to obtain approval to market a humanitarian device. First, the sponsor must submit a request to FDA's Office of Orphan Products Development (OOPD) seeking a determination that the disease or condition that the device is intended to treat or diagnose affects or is manifested in fewer than 4,000 individuals in the United States per year. This request for humanitarian use designation (HUD) should provide the following: 1) the precisely defined proposed indication for use based upon current medical and scientific knowledge; 2) a brief description of the device, including illustrations and a discussion of its principle of operation; and 3) documentation of the target population demonstrating that the rare disease or condition affects or is manifested in fewer than 4,000 people in the United States per year. FDA must approve, disapprove, or return the HUD request for additional information within 45 days of the request.

Second, if OOPD determines that the device is eligible for a humanitarian designation, an HDE application must be submitted to the relevant Center within FDA (Center for Biologics Evaluation and Research (CBER), Center for Drug Evaluation and Research (CDER), or CDRH). The application is similar in both form and content to a PMA; it is not required, however, to contain the results of scientifically valid clinical investigations demonstrating that the device is effective for its intended purpose. Importantly, FDA will only grant an HDE if there are no other devices on the market to diagnose or treat the same condition or disease.

The HDE application must also estimate the number of patients who would be required to generate data to support a full PMA and an explanation of why such a study is not feasible or why the cost of conducting such a study could not reasonably be expected to be recovered. Such application must also include a description of all pediatric subpopulations that suffer from the disease or condition that the device seeks to address and the approximate number of affected pediatric patients. Finally, as previously stated, all HDE applications must include certification that the applicant has complied with the clinical trial registration requirements. FDA is required to send the applicant an approval order, approvable letter, or order denying approval within 75 days of receipt of an HUD request accepted for filing and for which there were no major amendments.

If the amount to be charged for the device is greater than $250, the application must contain a report by an independent certified public accountant or attestation from a responsible individual in the organization verifying that the amount charged does not exceed the costs of the device's research, development, fabrication, and distribution. Manufacturers of pediatric devices receiving an HDE, however, are permitted to sell their devices for a profit, provided that the devices meet all other HDE requirements. Despite this, the number of pediatric devices distributed during a year may not exceed the annual distribution number specified by FDA when the HDE was granted.

The use of an HUD must initially and continually be reviewed by an IRB. The IRB does not, however, have to approve each use of an HUD, but rather the general use of the HUD at a facility.

HDEs will be granted for an unlimited time frame. Nevertheless, FDA may require the sponsor of the HDE device to demonstrate continued compliance with the HDE regulations if FDA believes that such a demonstration is necessary to protect the public health or if FDA has reason to believe that the criteria for the HDE are no longer met. FDA can suspend or withdraw the HDE only after providing the holder of the HDE an opportunity for an informal hearing.

510(k) PREMARKET NOTIFICATION PROCESS

Overview

The 510(k) process involves a comparison between a new device and one or more legally marketed devices (i.e., predicate device(s)). A predicate device is a legally marketed Class I or Class II device, or a Class III device for which PMAs are not yet required. A manufacturer is required to file an FDCA section 510(k) premarket notification prior to: 1) initial marketing of a device; 2) making a change or modification to a cleared device that could significantly affect the safety or effectiveness of the device; or 3) making a major change or modification to the intended use of a previously cleared device. The regulations require manufacturers to submit a 510(k) notification at least 90 days prior to the intended introduction into the market of a device that requires premarket clearance. A device that requires 510(k) clearance may not be marketed until the applicant receives an "order" from FDA stating that the new device is substantially equivalent to a legally marketed predicate device (21 U.S.C. § 360(k)).

The 510(k) process involves a comparison between a new device and one or more legally marketed devices (i.e., predicate device(s)).

For a new device to be found "substantially equivalent" to one or more legally marketed predicate devices, the new device must have 1) the same intended use as a predicate and 2) either a) the same technological characteristics as the predicate device *or* b) different technological characteristics, but the information submitted must not raise new questions of safety and effectiveness and must demonstrate substantial equivalence. Technically, a device that is the subject of a 510(k) notification may have multiple predicate devices, as certain features of the device may be substantially equivalent to features of certain predicate devices, while other features may be substantially equivalent to

To be "substantially equivalent," a new device must have:

- *the same intended use as a predicate; and*
- *either the same technological characteristics as the predicate device or different technological characteristics, but the information submitted must not raise new questions of safety and effectiveness and must demonstrate substantial equivalence.*

features of other predicates (21 U.S.C. § 360c(1)(I)(a)). While FDA has previously questioned the approach of using combination predicates to demonstrate substantial equivalence, FDA's current position is that there should be a primary predicate device for substantial equivalence. Secondary predicates may be used to identify specific technologies, the risks of which have been controlled through separate clearances. FDA has developed a decision tree to facilitate the substantial equivalence determination. FDA generally limits its determination as to whether the product is substantially equivalent based on the device's proposed labeling included in the 510(k) filing. To help prevent cleared devices from being used outside the scope of the FDA-cleared indications for use, FDA has occasionally requested that companies place a boxed warning on device labels with respect to specific off-label uses.

Initially, FDA required proof of equivalence to an actual pre-amendments device (i.e., one that was on the market prior to MDA). The Safe Medical Devices Act of 1990 (SMDA) made it clear, however, that a post-amendments Class I or Class II device may be found substantially equivalent to any legally marketed Class I or Class II device or Class III device for which FDA has not yet called for PMAs. The predicate device, therefore, need not be a pre-amendments device, but it cannot be a device that was removed from the market by FDA or determined to be misbranded or adulterated by judicial order (21 U.S.C. § 360c(I)(2)).

Contents of a 510(k) Premarket Notification

The format and information required in a 510(k) premarket notification are specified in 21 C.F.R. §§ 807.87, 807.90, 807.92, and 807.93. The contents of a 510(k) premarket notification include:

- ♦ **Device Name.** The device name, both the trade or proprietary name and the classification name, must be included.

- ♦ **Identification.** The applicant's name and street address must be included.

- ♦ **Registration Number.** If applicable, the FDA establishment registration number of the owner or operator submitting the premarket notification should be included.

- ♦ **Classification.** The applicant should include the class of the device (i.e., Class I, II, or III) and, if known, the appropriate classification panel.

- ♦ **Description.** The 510(k) notification should include a physical description of the new device, together with an explanation of its intended use, principles of operation, power source, composition, and other information necessary to understand the device.

♦ **Substantial Equivalence Comparison.** Applicants should make a comparison of the new device to its predicate as easy as possible for the FDA reviewer. The 510(k) notification should, therefore, include a discussion of the similarities and differences between the device and its predicate device(s) and should make use of comparative tables whenever possible.

Applicants should make the comparison of the new device to its predicate as easy as possible for the FDA reviewer.

♦ **Software.** Applications for computerized devices must follow the appropriate CDRH guidance.[2]

♦ **Standards.** The applicant should identify any mandatory or voluntary standards met by the device.

♦ **Performance.** Performance data to help demonstrate that the proposed device is as safe and effective as the predicate device should be included.

♦ **Biocompatibility.** Submissions for devices that directly contact the body must include a description of the characteristics of their materials. This description should compare the device to its predicate in sufficient detail to determine biocompatibility, as well as the kind of tests needed to determine biocompatibility. Any material differences between the new device and the claimed predicate device must be stated explicitly. Manufacturers need to provide biocompatibility test data for any materials found in the new device that are not present in the predicate device.

In practice, FDA biocompatibility experts may point out that even with the same raw material, biocompatibility requirements can change. For example, additives, the formulation or manufacturing process, and device design could change a biocompatibility profile.

♦ **Sterility.** Submissions for devices that are labeled sterile must cite the sterilization method as well as the method used to validate the sterilization cycle and the sterility assurance level.

♦ **Labeling.** Although applicants may submit drafts of their device labeling, the submission should be representative of the final version.

♦ **Class III Certification and Summary.** All 510(k) submissions for Class III devices must include a statement certifying that the applicant has searched for all available information regarding the device's safety and effectiveness and citations to any adverse safety and effectiveness data.

♦ **510(k) Summary or Statement.** A premarket notification must include either a summary of the 510(k) safety and effectiveness information upon which the substantial equivalence determination is based or a statement that this information will be made available by the 510(k) applicant to any person within 30 days of a written request.

♦ **Truthful and Accuracy Statement.** All 510(k) applicants must include a statement certifying that all information in the application is truthful and accurate and that no material fact has been omitted.

The FDA guidance document "Refuse to Accept Policy for 510(k)s: Guidance for Industry and Food and Drug Administration Staff" (December 31, 2012) requires the use of a detailed checklist to ensure that all necessary elements are included in the 510(k). Each type of submission (traditional, special, or abbreviated 510(k)) has a corresponding checklist. In addition, ODE has issued many device-specific guidance documents that contain requirements for data and information to be submitted, such as engineering testing data, information regarding applicable national and international standards, or human clinical data. These documents are posted on FDA's website, which should be consulted frequently as documents are added and removed from the site as necessary.

510(k) Premarket Notifications Supported with Clinical Data

A 510(k) notification that includes clinical information to demonstrate substantial equivalence is referred to as a "hybrid 510(k)" or "mini-PMA."[3]

For such submissions, FDA requires that the 510(k) notification be supported by clinical data demonstrating equivalence of the new device to its predicate device(s) and/or the current standard of care. In addition to determining safety and effectiveness generally, the data collected is intended to validate that any technological differences between the device under consideration and the predicate device(s) and/or standard of care do not raise questions of safety and effectiveness.

In cases in which a PMA or 510(k) includes clinical data, FDA requires study sponsors to either disclose certain financial interests of the clinical investigators or certify that the clinical investigators do not hold disclosable financial interests. Under FDAAA, any 510(k) that contains clinical data must be accompanied by a certification that the applicant has complied with the clinical trial registration requirements.

Device Modifications

One of the most difficult decisions for 510(k) holders is when to submit a new premarket notification for changes the holder intends to make to one of its legally marketed devices.

One of the most difficult decisions for 510(k) holders is when to submit a new premarket notification for changes that the holder intends to make to one of its legally marketed devices. As stated above, FDA's regulations require that a new 510(k) notification be cleared by FDA before the holder makes a change or modification to the device that "could significantly affect the safety or effectiveness of the device, e.g., a significant change or modification in design, material, chemical composition, energy source, or manufacturing process" or makes a major change or modification in the intended use of the device.[4]

In 1997, FDA issued guidance entitled "Deciding When to Submit a 510(k) for Changes to An Existing Device."[5] In this guidance, FDA provides decision trees to assist manufacturers in determining whether a 510(k) is needed for a specific device modification. A manufacturer is responsible for making the initial determination as to whether a device modification requires a new 510(k) notice. The modified device should be compared to the manufacturer's most recently cleared device rather than the version of the device that is currently being marketed, because the sum of many incremental changes can have a significant cumulative effect on safety and effectiveness.

In 2011, as part of the agency's efforts to change the 510(k) process, FDA disseminated a draft guidance to assist manufacturers in determining what modifications require the submission of new 510(k) notices,[6] replacing the 1997 guidance. Industry largely opposed the draft guidance, because it likely would have required the submission of a new 510(k) even for routine design modifications. Responding to these concerns, FDASIA included requirements that led to FDA's eventual withdrawal of the 2011 draft guidance. Accordingly, when making 510(k) modification determinations, companies should continue to follow the 1997 guidance.

Although the 510(k) holder is responsible for making the initial determination as to whether a change or modification could significantly affect safety or effectiveness, FDA may review the company's decision. If FDA disagrees with the company's decision not to file a new 510(k) notification for a device modification or change, FDA may require the company to file a 510(k) notification and discontinue marketing the device while the 510(k) is pending. FDA may also take enforcement action against a company for failure to obtain clearance of the modified device before introducing it into interstate commerce. As a practical matter, if a company makes a good faith effort to document the reasons it did not submit a new 510(k) for the device change, if the reasons appear genuine, and if there are no demonstrated safety problems with the modified device, FDA may use its enforcement discretion to allow the company to continue marketing the device while the new 510(k) notification is pending, though there is never a guarantee that FDA will exercise its enforcement discretion in any particular situation.

"The New 510(k) Paradigm"

To streamline the evaluation of 510(k)s, FDA developed "The New 510(k) Paradigm" (March 20, 1998), which offered manufacturers three alternative approaches for seeking 510(k) clearance.[7] The paradigm retained the traditional methods of demonstrating substantial equivalence (through adequate device descriptions, appropriate preclinical testing, and, occasionally, clinical trials).

The New 510(k) Paradigm
- *Traditional 510(k)*
- *Special 510(k): Device Modification Option*
- *Abbreviated 510(k)*

In addition, under the 510(k) Paradigm, the device manufacturer has the option of submitting a "Special 510(k)" for certain types of device modifications or an "Abbreviated 510(k)."

Under the Special 510(k): Device Modification Option, a manufacturer intending to modify its own legally marketed, cleared device may conduct the necessary verification and validation activities to demonstrate that the design outputs of the modified device meet the design input requirements. Special 510(k)s are usually processed by the ODE within 30 days of receipt. Modifications that affect the intended use or alter the basic fundamental technology of the device are not eligible for this type of submission, but may be eligible for the Abbreviated 510(k) route.

While not frequently utilized, device manufacturers may submit an Abbreviated 510(k) when: 1) a device-specific guidance document exists; 2) a special control has been established; or 3) FDA has recognized a relevant consensus standard. Abbreviated 510(k)s include summary information that describes how special controls have been used to address the risks associated with the device type and a declaration of conformity with any relevant recognized standards.

Review Process

FDA responds to a 510(k) notification in one of three ways. FDA can: 1) decide that a device is substantially equivalent to a legally marketed device that does not require premarket approval; 2) decide that it is not substantially equivalent (NSE); or 3) notify the applicant that additional information is required to determine whether the device is substantially equivalent. A decision that a device is substantially equivalent to a predicate device gives the 510(k) holder the right to commercially market it in the United States. A finding that a device is not substantially equivalent to the predicate device means FDA needs additional data to determine if the device is substantially equivalent or if it is a "new" Class III device, requiring approval of a PMA before being marketed (unless FDA down-classifies the entire device category from Class III to either Class I or Class II or clears the device through the *de novo* classification process). It generally takes four to 12 months to obtain 510(k) premarket clearance, but the process can take longer if FDA requires additional information.

In making a request for information, FDA is directed to consider the "least burdensome means of demonstrating substantial equivalence."

In requesting information, FDA is directed to consider the "least burdensome means of demonstrating substantial equivalence." FDA defined the least burdensome concept as "a successful means of addressing a premarket issue that involves the most appropriate investment of time, effort, and resources on the part of industry and FDA."[8] FDA has also developed a number of principles for applying the least burdensome concept, which may serve as a useful starting point in discussions with reviewers. First, information unrelated to the regulatory decision should not be part of the decision-making process. Second, alternative approaches to all regulatory issues should be considered to optimize time, effort, and resources. Third, all reasonable mechanisms to lessen review times should be used. It is advisable to at least raise with FDA least burdensome arguments, but note the agency ultimately determines the amount and type of information necessary to support marketing applications.

Although FDA's response to section 510(k) applications establishes whether a particular device can be marketed without a PMA, FDA does not "approve" a premarket notification in the same way that it approves a PMA. FDA's response to section 510(k) notifications makes clear that its findings under this provision extend only to whether a device is substantially equivalent to a predicate device and not whether if it is safe and effective for its intended use.

If FDA determines that a device is not substantially equivalent, the applicant may:

♦ submit another 510(k) with new data or new indications for use,

♦ request a Class I or II designation through the *de novo* process,

♦ file a reclassification petition,

♦ submit a Premarket Approval Application (PMA), or

♦ appeal the NSE determination to the CDRH ombudsman.

Third-Party Review

On August 1, 1996, FDA began a voluntary Third-party Review Pilot Program for selected medical device 510(k)s to 1) provide manufacturers of eligible devices with an alternative 510(k) review process that could yield more rapid marketing clearance decisions and 2) enable FDA to use its scientific review resources for higher-risk devices, while maintaining confidence in the review by third parties of low- to moderate-risk devices.

FDA-accredited third parties can conduct initial review of 510(k)s for low- to moderate-risk devices.

In 1997, with the passage of FDAMA, Congress codified and expanded the pilot program. FDAMA directed FDA to accredit third parties (Accredited Persons) in the private sector to conduct the initial review of 510(k)s for low- to moderate-risk devices; specified that an Accredited Person may not review any Class III device, "Class II devices that are permanently implantable, life-supporting, or life sustaining," or Class II devices for which clinical data are required; and set limits on the number of Class II devices that may be ineligible for Accredited Person review because clinical data are required. In 2001, FDA clarified that all

Class I devices and all Class II devices that are not permanently implantable, life sustaining, or require clinical data *are* eligible for third-party review.

Within 30 days of receiving the written classification and substantial equivalence recommendation from the accredited party, FDA must make its decision as to whether the device is substantially equivalent. If the agency does not adopt the recommendation of the accredited party, FDA must provide the 510(k) applicant and the reviewer a detailed statement explaining its reasons.

Evaluating the 510(k) Pathway

Although the current 510(k) pathway provides flexibility to tailor the premarket review process to address the specific characteristics of the device under review, industry, consumers, healthcare providers, as well as FDA staff and Congress have questioned whether the 510(k) process functions as initially intended. Consumer advocacy groups have characterized the 510(k) pathway as a "fast-track process" and have expressed concern that the process allows devices with unproven safety and effectiveness onto the market. In addition, FDA staff has raised concerns regarding the pathway's effectiveness. Meanwhile, industry has complained that increased scrutiny by some reviewers at FDA is hindering medical device development.

In response to the concerns raised by industry, consumers, FDA staff, and increasing congressional pressure, CDRH commissioned reviews of the 510(k) process to evaluate how well the process was facilitating innovation and assuring that medical devices are safe and effective.

In response to these concerns, CDRH commissioned reviews of the 510(k) process to evaluate how well the process was facilitating innovation and assuring that medical devices are safe and effective. The evaluations were conducted by the 510(k) Working Group and the Task Force of the Utilization of Science in Regulatory Decision Making, with each group issuing preliminary reports. The 510(k) Working Group report evaluated how well the current 510(k) pathway is meeting the public health goals of facilitating innovation and assuring that medical devices are safe and effective.[9] The Task Force of the Utilization of Science in Regulatory Decision Making addressed how CDRH can better incorporate new science into its regulatory decision-making.[10]

These preliminary reports outlined 55 recommendations for improving the 510(k) program. In follow-up to public comments received on the recommendations, CDRH announced a plan to implement 25 initiatives to improve the 510(k) process.[11] These proposals included 1) streamlining the *de novo* classification process via a draft guidance; 2) providing additional guidance on pre-submission communications; 3) issuance of new draft guidance regarding modifications to 510(k) devices; 4) providing additional guidance on the use of multiple predicates to establish substantial equivalence; 5) establishment of a

Center Science Council to oversee development of a procedure for responding to new scientific information and periodically audit 510(k) decisions; 6) issuance of additional guidance on clinical data requirements; 7) establishment of a network of external experts; and 8) providing notice to industry when FDA has modified the regulatory expectations for devices based on new scientific evidence. FDA has acted on a number of these initiatives (e.g., new pre-submission process and a direct *de novo* process).

PMA APPROVAL PROCESS

An approved PMA is a license granted to the applicant to market a medical device. Under section 515 of the FDCA, a PMA must be filed if a proposed device is not substantially equivalent to a legally marketed Class I or Class II device or if it is a pre-amendments Class III device for which FDA requires PMAs.

A PMA differs significantly from a 510(k) premarket notification in the amount of information (particularly clinical data) that must be submitted to FDA. In contrast to 510(k) notices, which must demonstrate that the new device is "substantially equivalent" to a predicate device, a PMA must be supported by valid scientific evidence to demonstrate the "safety and effectiveness" of the device for its intended use. PMAs typically include the results of extensive clinical trials, bench tests, laboratory studies, animal studies, and references to any standards relevant to a device's safety or effectiveness. The PMA must contain a complete description of the device and its components; a detailed description of the methods, facilities, and controls used to manufacture the device; the proposed labeling and advertising literature; and any training materials. All published and unpublished literature concerning the prior use of the product must be included, as well as a bibliography of all published reports that were not submitted and were known to the applicant concerning the device's safety and effectiveness. Because of the amount of information submitted in a PMA, PMA review time is significantly longer than for 510(k) notifications.

A PMA differs significantly from a 510(k) premarket notification in the amount of information that must be submitted to FDA.

The following table summarizes the major distinctions between 510(k) notices and PMAs.

	510(k) Premarket Notification	Premarket Approval (PMA)
Devices Subject to Requirement	Few Class I, most Class II, and some Class III pre-amendments devices	All Class III post-amendments devices and some Class III pre-amendments devices
Clinical Data Requirements	Most are not supported by clinical data; Hybrid 510(k) notifications include clinical data	Clinical studies almost always required to support submission
Evidence of Safety and Efficacy Required	Information and data to support the "substantial equivalence" of the device to a legally marketed predicate device	Clinical data and/or scientific evidence supporting "safety and efficacy" claims
Marketing Rights	No exclusivity	Like a Product License
Average FDA Review Time[12]	63 FDA days (ODE) 98 total days (ODE)	225 FDA days (ODE) 284 total days (ODE)
Regulations on Device Changes	Must file new 510(k) if the change "could significantly affect" the safety or efficacy of the device or a major change to the intended use of the device	Must file a new PMA, some form of PMA supplement, or annual report depending on the nature and effect of change on the safety and effectiveness of the device
Advisory Panel Review	No Advisory Panel Review for almost all 510(k) devices	Advisory Panel Review for some but not all PMAs. Generally, no Advisory Panel Review for PMA Supplements

FDA ultimately determines the amount and type of data and information necessary to support marketing applications.

FDA's Least Burdensome Approach policies also apply to PMAs. As with the least burdensome requirements for 510(k)s, while it is advisable to at least raise with FDA least burdensome arguments, the agency ultimately determines the amount and type of data and information necessary to support marketing applications.

Contents of a PMA

The format and information required in a PMA is outlined in 21 C.F.R. § 814.20:

◆ The name and address of the applicant.
◆ A detailed table of contents. A PMA shall include separate sections for non-clinical laboratory studies and for clinical investigations involving human subjects.
◆ A detailed summary to provide the reviewer a general understanding of the data and information in the application. The summary shall contain the following information:
  ◆ *Indications for use.* A general description of the disease or condition the device will diagnose, treat, prevent, cure, or mitigate, including a description of the patient population for which the device is intended.

- *Device description.* An explanation of how the device functions, the basic scientific concepts that form the basis for the device, and the significant physical and performance characteristics of the device. A brief description of the manufacturing process should be included if it will significantly enhance the reviewer's understanding of the device. The generic name of the device as well as any proprietary name or trade name should be included.

- *Alternative practices and procedures.* A description of existing alternative practices or procedures for diagnosing, treating, preventing, curing, or mitigating the disease or condition for which the device is intended.

- *Marketing history.* A brief description of the foreign and U.S. marketing history, if any, of the device, including a list of all countries in which the device has been marketed and a list of all countries in which the device has been withdrawn from marketing for any reason related to the safety or effectiveness of the device. The description shall include the history of the marketing of the device by the applicant and, if known, the history of the marketing of the device by any other person.

- *Summary of studies.* An abstract of any information or report described in the PMA under paragraph (b)(8)(ii) of 21 C.F.R. § 814.20 and a summary of the results of technical data submitted under paragraph (b)(6) of that section. The summary shall include a description of the study objective; a description of the study experimental design; a brief description of how the data were collected and analyzed; and a brief description of the results, whether positive, negative, or inconclusive. This section shall include the following:

  - A summary of the nonclinical laboratory studies submitted in the application;
  - A summary of the clinical investigations involving human subjects submitted in the application, including a discussion of subject selection and exclusion criteria, study population, study period, safety and effectiveness data, adverse reactions and complications, patient discontinuation, patient complaints, device failures and replacements, results of statistical analyses of the clinical investigations, contraindications and precautions for use of the device, and other information from the clinical investigations as appropriate (any investigation conducted under an IDE shall be identified as such).

- *Conclusions drawn from the studies.* A discussion demonstrating that the data and information in the application constitute valid scientific evidence within the meaning of 21 C.F.R. § 860.7 and provide reasonable assurance that the device is safe and effective for its intended use. A concluding discussion shall present benefit and risk considerations related to the device including a discussion of any adverse effects of the device on health and any proposed additional studies or surveillance the applicant intends to conduct following approval of the PMA.

- ◆ A complete description of:
    - ◆ The device, including pictorial representations;
    - ◆ Each of the functional components or ingredients of the device if the device consists of more than one physical component or ingredient;
    - ◆ The properties of the device relevant to the diagnosis, treatment, prevention, cure, or mitigation of a disease or condition;
    - ◆ The principles of operation of the device; and
    - ◆ The methods used in, and the facilities and controls used for, the manufacture, processing, packing, storage, and, where appropriate, installation of the device, in sufficient detail so that a person generally familiar with current good manufacturing practice can make a knowledgeable judgment about the quality control used in the manufacture of the device.
- ◆ Reference to any performance standard under section 514 of the act or the Radiation Control for Health and Safety Act of 1968 (42 U.S.C. 263b et seq.) in effect or proposed at the time of the submission and to any voluntary standard that is relevant to any aspect of the safety or effectiveness of the device and that is known to or that should reasonably be known to the applicant. The applicant shall —
    - ◆ Provide adequate information to demonstrate how the device meets, or justify any deviation from, any performance standard established under section 514 of the act or under the Radiation Control for Health and Safety Act, and
    - ◆ Explain any deviation from a voluntary standard.
- ◆ The following technical sections, which shall contain data and information in sufficient detail to permit FDA to determine whether to approve or deny approval of the application:
    - ◆ A section containing results of the nonclinical laboratory studies with the device, including microbiological, toxicological, immunological, biocompatibility, stress, wear, shelf life, and other laboratory or animal tests as appropriate.
    - ◆ A section containing results of the clinical investigations involving human subjects with the device, including clinical protocols, number of investigators and subjects per investigator, subject selection and exclusion criteria, study population, study period, safety and effectiveness data, adverse reactions and complications, patient discontinuation, patient complaints, device failures and replacements, tabulations of data from all individual subject report forms and copies of such forms for each subject who died during a clinical investigation or who did not complete the investigation, results of statistical analyses of the clinical investigations, device failures and replacements, contraindications and precautions for use of the device, and any other appropriate information from the clinical investigations. Any investigation conducted under an IDE shall be identified as such. Information on clinical investigations involving human subjects shall include the following:

- ◆ A statement with respect to each study that it either was conducted in compliance with the institutional review board regulations in 21 C.F.R. Part 56, or was not subject to the regulations under 21 C.F.R. §§ 56.104 or 56.105, and that it was conducted in compliance with the informed consent regulations in 21 C.F.R. Part 50; or if the study was not conducted in compliance with those regulations, a brief statement of the reason for the noncompliance.
  - ◆ A statement that each study was conducted in compliance with 21 C.F.R. Part 812 concerning sponsors of clinical investigations and clinical investigators, or if the study was not conducted in compliance with those regulations, a brief statement of the reason for the noncompliance.
- ◆ For a PMA supported solely by data from one investigation, a justification showing that data and other information from a single investigator are sufficient to demonstrate the safety and effectiveness of the device and to ensure reproducibility of test results.
- ◆ A bibliography of all published reports not submitted under this section, whether adverse or supportive, known to or that should reasonably be known to the applicant and that concern the safety or effectiveness of the device.
- ◆ An identification, discussion, and analysis of any other data, information, or report relevant to an evaluation of the safety and effectiveness of the device known to or that should reasonably be known to the applicant from any source, foreign or domestic, including information derived from investigations other than those proposed in the application and from commercial marketing experience.
- ◆ Copies of such published reports or unpublished information in the possession of or reasonably obtainable by the applicant if an FDA advisory committee or FDA requests.
- ◆ One or more samples of the device and its components, if requested by FDA. If it is impractical to submit a requested sample of the device, the applicant shall name the location at which FDA may examine and test one or more devices.
- ◆ Copies of all proposed labeling for the device. Such labeling may include instructions for installation and any information, literature, or advertising that constitutes labeling under section 201(m) of the Act.
- ◆ An environmental assessment. However, PMAs are categorically excluded from requiring an environmental assessment (EA) or environmental impact statement (EIS) if the device is of the same type and for the same use as a previously approved device (21 C.F.R. § 25.34(d)). For these types of products, sponsors must include a statement requesting a categorical exclusion in the PMA application.

◆ A financial certification and/or disclosure statement as required by 21 C.F.R. Part 54.

◆ Such other information as FDA may request. If necessary, FDA will obtain the concurrence of the appropriate FDA advisory committee before requesting additional information.

◆ A Benefit/Risk analysis also should be included in a PMA. See FDA's guidance entitled, "Guidance for Industry and Food and Drug Administration Staff – Factors to Consider When Making Benefit-Risk Determinations in Medical Device Premarket Approvals and *De Novo* Classifications," available at https://www.fda.gov/downloads/medicaldevices/deviceregulationand-guidance/guidancedocuments/ucm517504.pdf.

Review Process

FDA may request more information or clarification of information already provided in the application, which extends the review period.

Upon receipt of a PMA, FDA makes a threshold determination as to whether it is sufficiently complete to permit a substantive review. If so, FDA will accept the application for filing. As with 510(k) submissions, FDA can refuse to accept the PMA application if the PMA is submitted without all the necessary elements. Once accepted, FDA begins an in-depth review of the submission. FDA may request more information or clarification of information already provided in the application, which extends the review period. If FDA determines that additional clinical trials are necessary, the PMA review may be delayed for the additional period of time required to conduct the studies and to submit the results in an amendment to the pending PMA.

In 1998, CDRH implemented a "modular approach" for PMA submissions to expedite the PMA review process. Instead of waiting for all sections to be complete, the modular approach allows sponsors to submit parts of their application as soon as they are ready for filing. CDRH and the sponsor must agree which elements will be included in each module. This approach opens communications between the sponsor and CDRH at every step in the application process.

At some point during the review period, FDA may convene an advisory committee (typically a panel of clinicians) to evaluate the application and to recommend whether FDA should approve the device, although FDA is not bound by the recommendation of the advisory panel. During the PMA review process, FDA will inspect the manufacturer's facilities to ensure compliance with applicable QSR requirements. In addition, FDA may conduct a Bioresearch Monitoring audit of clinical data.

If FDA's evaluations of the PMA, the manufacturing facilities, and the integrity of the clinical data are favorable, FDA may issue either an approval letter or an "approvable" letter, which contains a number of conditions that must be met in order to secure final PMA approval. If the manufacturer satisfies those conditions, FDA will issue an approval letter authorizing commercial marketing of the device for specific indications. If FDA's evaluation of the PMA or the manufacturing facilities is not favorable, FDA will deny approval of the application or issue a "non-approvable" letter, which identifies the major deficiencies with the PMA that must be resolved before the application is approved.

Postapproval Requirements

Since 1986, FDA has had authority to impose postmarket approval requirements on any device requiring premarket approval. Postapproval requirements may include:

♦ Restriction of sale, distribution, or use;

♦ Continuing evaluation and periodic reporting on safety, effectiveness, and reliability;

♦ Inclusion in the labeling and advertising of any restricted device of warnings, hazards, or precautions important for safe and effective use;

♦ Inclusion of identification codes on device or its labeling or, for an implanted device, on cards given to patients;

♦ Maintenance of records that will enable the applicant to submit to FDA information needed to trace patients;

♦ Maintenance of records for specified periods of time and organization and indexing of records into identifiable files to enable FDA to determine whether there is reasonable assurance of the device's continued safety and effectiveness;

♦ Submission of periodic reports containing required information;

♦ Batch testing; and

♦ Any other requirements determined by FDA to be necessary to provide reasonable assurance, or continued reasonable assurance, of safety and effectiveness.

A sponsor must also grant FDA access to records and reports and permit authorized FDA employees to copy and verify records and reports. It must also permit FDA to inspect, at a reasonable time and in a reasonable manner, all manufacturing facilities to verify that the device is being manufactured, stored, labeled, and shipped under approved conditions. The failure to comply with any postapproval requirement constitutes grounds for withdrawing a PMA's approval.

Postmarket Surveillance Studies

Recognizing that FDA's PMA review process cannot identify all possible problems with a device, Congress provided in the SMDA that FDA must impose additional postmarket surveillance requirements in certain cases and that it had the discretion to impose such requirements in other cases.

Recognizing that FDA's PMA review process cannot identify all possible problems with a device, Congress provided in the SMDA that FDA must impose additional postmarket surveillance (PMS) requirements in certain cases (i.e., in the form of postmarketing studies) and that it had the discretion to impose such requirements in other cases. The Medical Device Amendments of 1992 (MDA 1992) further amended the FDCA to provide the following:

♦ That a company's failure to comply with the PMS requirements is a prohibited act, subject to criminal and civil penalties; and

♦ A device for which required PMS is not carried out is misbranded and subject to seizure.

Under section 522 of the FDCA (21 U.S.C. § 360l), as amended by MDA 1992, FDA was required to impose PMS requirements on certain devices (mandatory surveillance) and was allowed to impose PMS requirements on any other device for which the agency decides that studies must be conducted to protect the public health or to provide safety and effectiveness data (discretionary surveillance). Under FDAMA, however, FDA is no longer required to mandate that manufacturers of high-risk devices conduct PMS studies.

Instead, FDA may order PMS studies for the following types of Class II and Class III devices: 1) devices whose failure would be reasonably likely to have a serious adverse consequence; 2) devices intended to be implanted in the human body for more than one year; or 3) devices intended to be life-sustaining or life-supporting devices used outside a device user facility.

Upon receiving a PMS order, the manufacturers must, within 30 days, submit a surveillance plan. FDA then has 60 days to evaluate the qualifications of the person designated to conduct the surveillance and determine whether the plan will result in the collection of useful data. The duration of any FDA-required study may not exceed 36 months. A longer study must be mutually agreed upon by the manufacturer and FDA. If no agreement is reached, the dispute resolution process in section 404 of FDAMA is followed.

In a PMA approval letter (or in the substantial equivalence order for 510(k) notifications), FDA will notify the manufacturer if it is required to conduct PMS studies. A manufacturer may also be alerted to the need for PMS studies in the PMA "approvable" letter (and in the case of 510(k) notifications, in correspondence shortly after the 510(k) notification is submitted).

Device Modifications

Approval of a PMA supplement is required before making a change that affects device safety or effectiveness. PMA supplements often require the submission of the same type of information required for the initial PMA, except that the supplement is generally limited to the information needed to support the safety and effectiveness of the proposed modification or clarify safety and effectiveness of an existing device (i.e., new adverse event information, higher than predicted failure rates, etc.). The regulations identify types of changes that require the submission of a PMA supplement if the change affects safety or effectiveness, including 1) new indications for use; 2) labeling changes; 3) use of a different facility or establishment to manufacture, process, or package the device; 4) changes in manufacturing facilities, methods, or quality control procedures; 5) changes in sterilization procedures; 6) changes in packaging; 7) changes in the performance or design specifications, circuits, components, ingredients, principle of operation, or physical layout of the device; and 8) extension of the expiration date of the device based on data obtained under a new or revised stability or sterility testing protocol that has not been approved by FDA. Many of these changes are presumed to affect safety and efficacy, requiring a PMA supplement.

Additionally, when a PMA supplement is required for an incremental change to the design of a device that affects safety and effectiveness, the PMA supplement must be approved by FDA if 1) nonclinical data demonstrate that the design modification creates the intended additional capacity, function, or performance of the device and 2) clinical data from the approved PMA application and any supplement provide a reasonable assurance of safety and effectiveness of the modified device. FDA is allowed to require additional clinical data to evaluate the design modification of the device to provide a reasonable assurance of safety and effectiveness.

There are several types of submissions that may be used to obtain FDA approval for a modification to a PMA device. These include: a new PMA; a traditional PMA Supplement; a 30-day notice; a Special PMA Supplement for Changes Being Effected; or a PMA Manufacturing Site Change Supplement. FDA has disseminated guidance to assist manufacturers in determining which type of PMA Supplement is required for various types of device modifications.[13]

PMA Annual Reports

FDA requires the PMA holder to report a change for which a PMA supplement is not required in a periodic (annual) report. The change may be made

Types of changes requiring a PMA supplement:

1) new indications for use;

2) labeling changes;

3) use of different facility or establishment to manufacture, process, or package;

4) changes in manufacturing facilities, methods, or quality control procedures;

5) changes in sterilization procedures;

6) changes in packaging;

7) changes in performance or design specifications, circuits, components, ingredients, principle of operation, or physical layout of the device; and

8) extension of expiration date of device based on data obtained under a new or revised stability or sterility testing protocol not approved by FDA.

before it is reported to FDA. FDA guidance on PMA changes also allows manufacturers to make certain minor changes to their approved devices by simply documenting the change information in the firm's files. As a practical matter, most companies include in their annual reports general information about all changes that have been made to the device that have not been the subject of an approved supplement in order to put FDA on notice of the changes.

Annual reports must contain a bibliography and a summary of unpublished reports of data from any clinical investigations or nonclinical laboratory studies involving the device or related devices and any reports in the scientific literature concerning the device. The annual report should summarize information pertaining to the original PMA, as well as any subsequent PMA supplements and should include all postapproval reports for PMA supplements. The annual report should also describe any adverse device effects.

The PDP Is an Alternative to the PMA Process

Though rarely used, an alternative to the PMA process is the Product Development Protocol (PDP) (FDCA § 515(f)).

The PDP procedure is optional; FDA cannot require a sponsor to use the PDP process for determining market approval.

Under 21 C.F.R. § 814.19, a device with a completed PDP will be considered to have an approved PMA. The PDP procedure is optional; FDA cannot require a sponsor to use the PDP process for determining market approval. The major distinguishing feature of a PDP from a PMA approach is FDA's early involvement at the design or preclinical testing phase. Thus, the PDP approach involves a close relationship between FDA and the sponsor in designing appropriate preclinical tests and clinical investigations to establish the safety and effectiveness of the device. The requirements for proof of safety and effectiveness are as stringent under a PDP as they are under a PMA; thus, the PDP process offers little advantage if the device already has undergone considerable design investigation and evaluation. Historically, the PDP has proven to be unfeasible for a manufacturer and overly demanding of FDA's resources.

Pediatric Subpopulations

On April 1, 2010, FDA issued a proposed rule and companion direct final rule to require, with certain device submissions, a description and count of pediatric subpopulations suffering from the disease or condition the device was intended to treat. After significant adverse comments, FDA withdrew the direct final rule but later issued supplemental notice of proposed rulemaking. In January 2014, FDA issued a final rule, codified as 21 C.F.R. Part 814, which requires inclusion of the information regarding pediatric uses in accordance with section 515A of FDCA. Unlike the proposed rule, the description and number of pediatric subpopulations must be for known, rather than potential, pediatric uses. This submission requirement applies to PMAs, HDEs, PDPs, and all PMA supplements submitted to FDA. Any additional information that becomes "readily available" regarding pediatric subpopulations should be included as submissions are made. According to the final rule, FDA has followed the definition of "pediatric subpopulations" offered by section 520(m)(6)(E)(i) of the FDCA to include individuals 21 years of age or younger at the time of diagnosis or treatment. As required by section 515A(a)(3) of the FDCA, FDA will submit this information to Congress with its annual reports.

RADIOLOGICAL HEALTH

The Electronic Product Radiation Control provisions of the FDCA, set forth in sections 531 through 542 (originally enacted as the Radiation Control for Health and Safety Act of 1968 and incorporated into the FDCA by the SMDA), give FDA responsibility for all medical *and* nonmedical electronic products that emit ionizing or non-ionizing electromagnetic or particulate radiation or any sonic, infrasonic, or ultrasonic wave. FDA's implementing regulations are codified in 21 C.F.R. Parts 1000 through 1299. These regulations set forth the following types of requirements: 1) performance standards, 2) reporting requirements, and 3) labeling. These products must comply with all of the applicable requirements, unless exempted by regulation.

All medical and nonmedical electronic products that emit any ionizing or non-ionizing electromagnetic or particulate radiation or any sonic, infrasonic, or ultrasonic wave must comply with applicable performance, reporting, and labeling requirements.

FDA has issued radiation performance standards intended to control unnecessary human exposure to potential hazardous ionizing and non-ionizing radiation and to ensure the safe and effective use of such radiation. Performance studies apply to products such as television receivers and diagnostic X-ray systems.

Manufacturers must submit product reports (including supplements and abbreviated reports), annual reports, and notices of defect or noncompliance. Manufacturers must document any actual or possible unexpected exposure during manufacturing, testing, or use of any electronic product in the appropriate report or notice.

Electronic products subject to a standard must bear labeling identifying the name and address of the manufacturer, the date of manufacture, and the manufacturer's statement that the product complies with the Department of Health and Human Services' radiation standards or similar language.

FDA has made available product-specific guidance documents and information packages to assist manufacturers in meeting the reporting requirements for radiation-emitting products.

FDA has made available product-specific guidance documents and information packages to assist manufacturers in meeting the reporting requirements for radiation-emitting products. If the product is a medical device, the requirements are in addition to premarketing or postmarketing requirements that also apply to the device.

CONCLUSION

FDA's regulations on devices are extensive and often complex. This chapter summarizes FDA's premarket requirements for devices. It does not address postmarketing requirements, including QSR compliance, medical device reporting, tracking, or product recalls. While it is not an exhaustive account of what is necessary to comply with premarket device requirements, it does highlight the basic requirements for marketing devices in the United States.

Endnotes

1. Center for Devices and Radiological Health, Food and Drug Administration, Guidance: Changes in Device Classification (Feb. 1997).
2. Office of Device Evaluation, Center for Devices and Radiological Health, Food and Drug Administration, "Guidance for the Content of Premarket Submissions for Software Contained in Medical Devices" (May 11, 2005).
3. If information concerning similarity to a predicate device must be obtained through a clinical trial, the trial is subject to the requirement of the IDE regulation, 21 C.F.R. § 812.22.
4. 21 C.F.R. § 807.81(a)(3)(i).
5. Office of Device Evaluation, Center for Devices and Radiological Health, Food and Drug Administration, "Guidance for Industry and FDA Staff – 510(k) Device Modification: Deciding When to Submit a 510(k) for a Change to an Existing Device" (Jan. 10, 1997).
6. Office of Device Evaluation, Center for Devices and Radiological Health, Food and Drug Administration, "Draft Guidance for Industry and FDA Staff – 510(k) Device Modifications: Deciding When to Submit a 510(k) for a Change to an Existing Device" (July 27, 2011).
7. Office of Device Evaluation, Center for Devices and Radiological Health, Food and Drug Administration, "The New 510(k) Paradigm— Alternate

Approaches to Demonstrating Substantial Equivalence in Premarket Notifications—Final Guidance" (Mar. 20, 1998).

8. *See* Office of Device Evaluation, Center for Devices and Radiological Health, Food and Drug Administration, "The Least Burdensome Provisions of the FDA Modernization Act of 1997: Concept and Principles; Final Guidance for FDA and Industry" (Oct. 4, 2002).

9. Center for Devices and Radiological Health, Food and Drug Administration, 510(k) Working Group Preliminary Report and Recommendations, Aug. 2010.

10. Center for Devices and Radiological Health, Food and Drug Administration, Task Force of the Utilization of Science in Regulatory Decision Making Preliminary Report and Recommendations (Aug. 2010).

11. Center for Devices and Radiological Health, Food and Drug Administration, "510(k) and Science Report Recommendations: Summary and Overview Comments and Next Steps" (Jan. 19, 2011).

12. U.S. Food and Drug Administration, Office of Device Evaluation, Annual Report, Fiscal Year 2009 at 5-9.

13. Office of Device Evaluation, Center for Devices and Radiological Health, Food and Drug Administration, "Guidance for Industry and FDA Staff—Modifications to Devices Subject to Premarket Approval (PMA)—The PMA Supplement Decision-Making Process" (Dec. 11, 2008).

Chapter 9

Combination Products

Suzanne O'Shea, Paula Gray, Sarah Baumann, Gina LaBella Tulin, Dorothy Henckel, & Miles Johnson, all of Navigant Consulting, Chicago, IL

Key Points

- A combination product comprises two or more different types of regulated components. It can be a drug/device, a biologic/device, a drug/biologic, or a drug/device/biologic.
- The Federal Food, Drug, and Cosmetic Act directs the Food and Drug Administration (FDA) to assign review of a combination product to an agency Center based on the product's primary mode of action, the single mode of action that provides the most important therapeutic effect of the combination product.
- A sponsor of a combination product can submit a request for designation where the jurisdiction of the reviewing Center is unclear or in dispute.
- FDA has issued regulations on good manufacturing practices and postmarket safety reporting for combination products. Other combination product issues are the subject of several guidance documents.

WHAT IS A COMBINATION PRODUCT?

A combination product is a product that consists of more than one type of regulated article. It could be a drug/device, a biologic/device, a drug/biologic, or a drug/device/biologic.

Products that combine two products of the same type are not regarded as combination products. For example, a fixed combination drug product comprising two or more drug ingredients in a single dosage unit is not this type of combination product. Similarly, products comprising two or more devices, or two or more biological products, are not combination products. Products comprising a drug and a cosmetic, or a drug and a dietary supplement, are also not considered combination products, although they raise some of the same issues as combination products. The Food and Drug Administration's (FDA's) Office of Combination Products (OCP) provides information about some of these products on its webpage, Other Types of Combinations of FDA Regulated Products (https://www.fda.gov/CombinationProducts/AboutCombinationProducts/ucm101464.htm).

The first statutory reference to combination products occurred in the Safe Medical Devices Act of 1990 (SMDA). The Federal Food, Drug, and Cosmetic Act (FDCA) combination product provisions have been amended from time to time over the years. The 21st Century Cures Act (Cures Act), enacted in 2016, amended several existing combination product provisions of the FDCA, and added several new combination product provisions. The FDCA does not contain a straightforward definition of a combination product, stating only that "The Secretary shall . . . assign a primary agency center to regulate products that constitute a combination of a drug, device or biological product." FDCA § 503(g)(1)(A), 21 U.S.C. § 353(g)(1)(A).

In 1991, shortly after enactment of the SMDA, FDA issued regulations defining combination products. The regulations identify four kinds of combination products:

◆ A product comprising two or more regulated components—i.e., drug/device, biologic/device, drug/biologic, or drug/device/biologic—that are physically, chemically, or otherwise combined or mixed and produced as a single entity (21 C.F.R. § 3.2(e)(1)).

Combination products like this are frequently referred to as "single-entity combination products." Examples include drug-coated stents, an implantable replacement joint coated with a growth factor, and a monoclonal antibody with a therapeutic drug attached. Prefilled autoinjectors and prefilled syringes, some of the most common combination products, are single entity combination products.

◆ Two or more separate products packaged together in a single package or as a unit and comprising drug and device products, device and biological products, or biological and drug products (21 C.F.R. § 3.2(e)(2)).

Such products are referred to as "co-packaged" combination products. An example is a kit containing a drug in a vial, and a single-use injector pen into which the drug in the vial will be placed.

◆ A drug, device, or biological product packaged separately that according to its investigational plan or proposed labeling is intended for use only with an approved individually specified drug, device, or biological product where both are required to achieve the intended use, indication, or effect and where upon approval of the proposed product the labeling of the approved product would need to be changed (e.g., to reflect a change in intended use, dosage form, strength, route of administration, or significant change in dose) (21 C.F.R. § 3.2(e)(3)).

◆ Any investigational drug, device, or biological product packaged separately that according to its proposed labeling is for use only with another individually specified investigational drug, device, or biological product where both are required to achieve the intended use, indication, or effect (21 C.F.R. § 3.2(e)(4)).

Products meeting these two definitions are referred to as "cross-labeled" combination products. An investigational device intended to deliver an individually specified approved drug product in a new way would fit the definition under 21 C.F.R. § 3.2(e)(3). An investigational device intended to deliver an individually specified investigational new drug would also be deemed a "combination product" under 21 C.F.R. § 3.2(e)(4).

PRIMARY MODE OF ACTION AND ASSIGNMENT OF A LEAD AGENCY CENTER

The FDCA addresses the threshold combination product issue: when a product comprises more than one type of product, which Center within FDA will review and regulate it? The FDCA directs FDA to assign combination products to an agency Center based on the product's primary mode of action (PMOA). Specifically, the act states that if the PMOA of a product is that of:

(i) a drug (other than a biological product), the agency center charged with premarket review of drugs shall have primary jurisdiction;

(ii) a device, the agency center charged with premarket review of devices shall have primary jurisdiction; or

(iii) a biological product, the agency center charged with premarket review of biological products shall have primary jurisdiction.

The FDCA addresses the threshold combination product issue: when a product comprises more than one type of product, which Center within FDA will review and regulate it?

FDCA § 503(g)(1)(D), 21 U.S.C. § 353(g)(1)(D).

The SMDA did not include a definition of PMOA. This omission was remedied by the Cures Act. The FDCA now defines PMOA as:

> the single mode of action of a combination product expected to make the greatest contribution to the overall intended therapeutic effects of the combination product.
> FDCA § 503(g)(1)(C), 21 U.S.C. § 353(g)(1)(C).

This statutory definition of PMOA very closely tracks the definition of PMOA found in the regulations, which FDA issued in 2005, to remedy the absence of a definition in the SMDA. The definition of PMOA now found in the FDCA is likely to be interpreted in just the same way as FDA's previous regulatory definition, found at 21 C.F.R. § 3.2(m). The final rule establishing the PMOA regulation was published in the *Federal Register* (70 Fed. Reg. 49,848 (Aug. 25, 2005)).

The preamble to the 2005 final rule provides several examples of PMOA, including a drug-coated vascular stent. A vascular stent provides a mechanical scaffold to keep a blood vessel open while the drug is slowly released from the stent to prevent the buildup of new tissue that would re-occlude the artery. This product has two modes of action—the device mode of action contributed by the stent and the drug mode of action contributed by the drug coating. The stent itself provides the most important therapeutic effect of the product, while the drug augments the effectiveness of the stent. Accordingly, drug-coated stents are generally assigned to the Center for Devices and Radiological Health (CDRH) for review and regulation under the device provisions of the act.

In contrast, a drug-eluting disc, which is surgically implanted and contains a drug that is slowly released for prolonged, local delivery of chemotherapeutic agents to a tumor site, also has device and drug modes of action. In this case, however, the chemotherapeutic drug makes the most important contribution to the therapeutic effect of the product. Products like this are assigned to the Center for Drug Evaluation and Research (CDER) for review and regulation under the new drug provisions of the FDCA.

Where it is impossible to say that one component provides the most important therapeutic action of the product, FDA follows an assignment algorithm set out in the regulations.

In some cases, neither FDA nor the sponsor can determine which constituent part may make the greatest contribution to the therapeutic effect of the combination product. This sometimes occurs when a combination product has two independent modes of action, neither of which is subordinate to the other. To resolve these types of questions, the regulations describe an algorithm FDA will follow to determine the Center assignment in such situations. The first step of the algorithm is to determine whether one agency Center regulates other combination products presenting similar questions of safety and effectiveness with regard to the combination product as a whole. When no agency Center regulates combination products presenting similar questions of safety and effectiveness with regard to the combination product as a whole, the agency proceeds to the second step of the algorithm; the agency considers which Center has the most expertise related to the most significant safety and effectiveness questions presented by the combination product. 21 C.F.R. § 3.4(b).

For example, consider a contact lens combined with drug to treat glaucoma. In this case, a contact lens is placed in the eye to correct vision. The contact lens also contains a drug to treat glaucoma that will be delivered from the lens to the eye. Neither mode of action is clearly primary, and so FDA would turn to the algorithm to determine PMOA. Under the first step of the algorithm, FDA would consider that CDER regulates glaucoma drugs, and CDRH regulates contact lenses, but neither agency Center regulates combination products that present questions of safety and effectiveness similar to those presented by both the contact lens and the glaucoma drug.

FDA would then turn to the second step of the algorithm. In this case, the most significant safety and effectiveness questions are related to the characterization, manufacturing, and clinical performance of the drug component, while the safety and effectiveness questions raised by the vision-correcting contact lens are considered more routine. As a result, the corrective contact lens with a glaucoma drug product would be assigned to CDER for review.

If a second manufacturer were to submit a marketing application for a similar product, the similar product would be subsequently assigned to CDER under the first step of the algorithm.

The Cures Act added some rather confusing language about PMOA to the FDCA. FDCA § 503(g)(1)(E), 21 U.S.C. § 353(g)(1)(E), states: "In determining the primary mode of action of a combination product, the Secretary shall not determine that the primary mode of action is that of a drug or biological product solely because the combination product has any chemical action within or on the human body."

Perhaps Congress intended to direct more combination products to CDRH through this restriction against finding PMOA attributable to a drug or biological product solely because of *any chemical action*. This interpretation of the Cures Act provision suggests that Congress believed that FDA had too frequently determined that the PMOA of combination products was attributed to the drug constituent part because of the drug constituent part's tiny (*any chemical action*) contribution to the overall intended therapeutic effect of the product. If this interpretation is correct, then the provision essentially directs FDA to determine PMOA consistent with the statutory and regulatory definitions (i.e., the greatest contribution to the overall therapeutic effect).

On the other hand, it may be that this provision in the Cures Act was intended as a response to litigation over the definition of a device (*Prevor v. FDA*). The statutory definition of a device states that a device cannot "achieve its primary intended purpose through chemical action within or on the body of man . . . " FDCA § 201(h)(3), 21 U.S.C. § 321(h)(3). One of the issues in the Prevor case was FDA's interpretation and application of the statutory definition of a device. This provision in the Cures Act may have been an attempt to change FDA's interpretation of the definition of a device, though it is not clear that the effort was successful. A full discussion of the *Prevor* line of cases and the definition of a device is beyond the scope of this chapter. Information about the *Prevor* line of cases is available on the OCP webpage (https://www.fda.gov/downloads/combination-products/jurisdictionalinformation/rfdjurisdictionaldecisions/redacteddecision-letters/ucm479168.pdf).

It remains to be seen how FDA will implement this provision of the Cures Act.

REQUESTS FOR DESIGNATION

A Request for Designation (RFD) is the formal process by which the sponsor of a combination product requests that FDA assign the product to a Center for review when it is unclear or in dispute as to which Center has jurisdiction over the product. An RFD is not required for every combination product. If a sponsor feels comfortable that the PMOA of its combination product is clear, it may make a submission to the appropriate Center without an RFD. However, if the FDA Center believes the product presents a jurisdictional question, the Center may direct the sponsor to submit an RFD to the OCP.

A Request for Designation is a formal process by which the sponsor of a combination product requests that FDA assign the product to a Center for review when it is unclear or disputed as to which Center has jurisdiction over the product.

The specific information to be included in the RFD is described in detail in 21 C.F.R. § 3.7(c) and is further clarified in FDA guidance "How to Write a Request for Designation (RFD)" (April 2011). An RFD is limited to 15 pages, and contains summary information about the product and its intended use. FDA recommends that an RFD be submitted as soon as sponsors have enough information about the product to enable FDA to make a decision.

An RFD must also contain the sponsor's assessment of the modes of action of the components of the combination product, as well as the sponsor's description of the product's PMOA. Sponsors may include data on these points if it is useful to the determination of the product's modes of action and PMOA. The sponsor is also given the opportunity to recommend which Center should have jurisdiction over the product.

By statute (FDCA § 563(b), 21 U.S.C. § 360bbb-2(b)), and regulation (21 C.F.R. § 3.8(b)) the agency is allowed 60 days to respond to RFDs. The agency's decision is in the form of a designation letter. Jurisdictional assignments made in an RFD letter are unique in two respects. First, the agency may change these decisions without the consent of the sponsor only for public health reasons based on scientific evidence (FDCA § 563(b), 21 U.S.C. § 360bbb-2(b)) or for other compelling reasons (21 C.F.R. § 3.9(b)). As a practical matter, FDA rarely, if ever, changes jurisdictional assignments made in a designation letter without the consent of the sponsor, and so the letters are considered binding on the agency.

Second, if the agency does not issue a designation letter in response to an RFD within the 60 days, the sponsor's recommendation as to assignment of the product takes effect. (FDCA § 563(c), 21 U.S.C. § 360bbb-2(c). 21 C.F.R. § 3.8(b).) The agency rarely, if ever, fails to issue an RFD letter within 60 days.

In August 2016, FDA's OCP announced a less formal method for gaining information about assignment of combination products to an agency Center, referred to as the Pre-Request for Designation (Pre-RFD) process. A guidance document, "How to Prepare a Pre-Request for Designation (Pre-RFD)," was issued in January 2017. The Pre-RFD process allows manufacturers of products in early-stage development to submit a Pre-RFD packet to OCP when contemplating a specific configuration for their combination product. This early feedback is intended to provide manufacturers with early insights on their product's design before formally submitting an RFD. While the content of a Pre-RFD is similar to a full RFD, there are several items that are not required in this submission that must be present in an RFD submission:

♦ The sponsor is not required to recommend the classification and assignment of the product to OCP, and

♦ The sponsor is not required to identify the classification of currently marketed products that may be similar to their product.

OCP aims to review Pre-RFDs in 60 days and provide a Pre-RFD letter with recommendations to the sponsor. However, there is no statutory or regulatory provision stating that the sponsor's recommendation take effect if FDA misses the 60-day deadline. In addition, Pre-RFD determinations are not subject to the same restrictions on FDA changing its mind in the absence of the sponsor's consent. As a consequence, the recommendations within such responses may have less regulatory significance than feedback provided in an actual RFD.

FDA regulations provide that if a sponsor disagrees with a designation letter, it may request reconsideration within 15 days. No new information may be included in a request for reconsideration, and OCP will respond to a request for reconsideration within 15 days of receipt. (21 C.F.R. § 3.8(c).)

The Cures Act provides additional methods of resolving disagreements with FDA's designation decision. FDCA § 503(g)(1)(F), 21 U.S.C. § 353(g)(1)(F), states that sponsors may request, and FDA must provide, a substantive rationale for a designation decision, and reference scientific evidence provided to FDA by the sponsor. In addition, the sponsor may propose studies to establish the relevance of chemical action in achieving the PMOA of the product, and FDA is to collaborate with the sponsor and seek to reach agreement on the trial design within 90 calendar days. If the sponsor conducts the study, and submits the information to FDA, FDA must consider the data when reevaluating the PMOA determination. FDA's initial PMOA determination remains in effect until a new PMOA determination is made.

Transparency of Jurisdictional Determinations

In 1991, the Center for Biologics Evaluation and Research (CBER), CDER, and CDRH created three Intercenter Agreements (ICAs): a CBER–CDER Intercenter Agreement, a CBER–CDRH Intercenter Agreement, and a CDER–CDRH Intercenter Agreement. Although they differ in content, format, and scope, the ICAs share the common purpose of explaining how various categories of both combination products and single-entity medical products were classified and assigned at the time the agreements were written in 1991. The ICAs constitute guidance that is not binding on the public or the agency.

At the time the ICAs were written, they were the major jurisdictional statements issued by the agency, but their usefulness became increasingly limited as new products were developed that were not envisioned when the ICAs were established. Since 1991, FDA has continued to classify and assign many new products not specifically covered by the ICAs. The body of jurisdictional decisions has therefore grown significantly, and over time, the ICAs have become incomplete statements.

In 2006, the agency published a *Federal Register* notice in which it concluded that while the CDER–CDRH and CBER–CDRH ICAs continue to provide useful nonbinding guidance about the assignment and classification of products, the CBER–CDER ICA was rendered almost completely out of date by the transfer of many therapeutic biological products from CBER to CDER in 2003. For these reasons, the agency proposed to continue the CDER–CDRH and the CBER–CDRH ICAs in effect, and to rescind the CBER–CDER ICA. To date, the CBER–CDER ICA has not been formally rescinded.

FDA has stated that it believes it is very important to provide robust transparency in jurisdictional decision making. Such transparency in jurisdictional decision making should result in greater predictability and consistency of decisions, and decrease ambiguity and uncertainty about agency perspectives. Moreover, as the bases for agency decision making become clearer, the need for formal RFDs and informal inquiries covering specific products may be diminished, which should conserve resources for both industry and the agency. In the past, FDA posted capsular descriptions of jurisdictional determinations, and has posted some RFD designation letters online once the products were approved or cleared. Unfortunately, these efforts have not been maintained by FDA. It can be very challenging for industry to learn specific information about prior jurisdictional determinations.

Consults and Collaboration

Even though one agency Center is designated as the lead, the other Center for the additional constituent part will likely be involved in the review and approval of the combination product.

In 2002, FDA issued a Staff Manual Guide (SMG) for the Intercenter Consultative/Collaborative Review Process. The objective of this SMG is to improve intercenter communication on combination products, as well as the timeliness and consistency of intercenter consultative and collaborative reviews. The SMG describes an intercenter consult as "A review activity in which a reviewer in one Center requests advice from a reviewer in another Center on a specific question or issue raised in the review of a submission. The consultative review will be used to assist the requesting reviewer in making appropriate regulatory/scientific decisions."

Recently, FDA has taken additional steps to improve the intercenter consult process. In 2015, the OCP published the results of an internal review of the intercenter consult process. This internal review resulted in four findings, and five recommendations, including:

♦ Establish clear guidance for the review of common combination product types.

♦ Create new simplified processes for access to CDER and CDRH document archiving systems for reviewers in the other Center.

♦ Update the Intercenter Consultative/Collaborative Review Process Standard Operating Procedures and Policies (SOPP) Manual and Intercenter Consult Request (ICCR) form.

♦ Create and maintain a combination-product-specific organizational chart.

♦ Establish a mechanism for estimating time spent on intercenter consults so resources can be allocated appropriately.

In August 2016, FDA announced a pilot intercenter process intended to improve the review of combination products and intercenter communications. The following four actions have been implemented to improve consultation between CDER and CDRH:

♦ Establishment of timelines, specific to Center and submission type, for identifying products as combination products and issuing and completing consults needed to support the review;

♦ Development of a tiered consult approach that streamlines interactions across Centers and identifies a clear process for identifying the right experts for a consult;

♦ Definition of clear roles and responsibilities for the lead Center, the consulted Center(s), the OCP, and the Combination Products Policy Council for review of a combination product submission; and

♦ Creation of a standard, semi-automated, user-friendly ICCR form that is managed electronically to ensure 1) users always have the most updated version and 2) all forms, and all intercenter combination product consults, are tracked through a single system.

FDA set the goal to implement the improved processes in all Center offices by mid-2017.

In addition, in April 2016, FDA announced the creation of the Combination Products Policy Council. The intent of this senior-level, agency-wide council will be to provide a forum for discussing, resolving, and implementing product and policy issues. The council mission is to:

♦ Modernize the intercenter consultation process and related aspects of combination product and cross-labeled product review;

♦ Promote development of innovative, safe, and effective combination products and cross-labeled products; and

♦ Promote alignment in addressing challenging medical product classification issues.

FDA's Staff Manual Guide describing the Combination Products Policy Council (SMG 2010.17) is clear that the council is intended as a resource to FDA, and does not meet directly with individual sponsors of combination products.

POSTMARKET SAFETY REPORTING

On December 20, 2016, FDA issued a new set of regulations covering postmarketing safety reporting for combination products.

In December 2016, FDA issued regulations explaining how postmarket safety reports (PMSRs) for combination products should be submitted to FDA. These regulations are found at 21 C.F.R. Part 4, Subpart B.

The PMSR regulations distinguish between combination product applicants and constituent part applicants. A *combination product applicant* means the applicant that holds the marketing authorization for the combination product as a whole. For example, the holder of an approved New Drug Application (NDA) that covers a drug and a pen injector is considered a combination product applicant. A *constituent part applicant* means the applicant for a constituent part of a combination product where the constituent parts are marketed under applications held by different manufacturers. For example, the holder of an approved NDA covering a drug product that is a constituent part of a cross-labeled combination product, and the holder of the approved or cleared device marketing application covering the device constituent part of the cross-labeled combination product, would both be considered constituent part applicants. In many cases where there are two constituent part applicants, there will be no combination product applicant. 21 C.F.R. § 4.101.

The combination product PMSR regulations require that combination product applicants and constituent part applicants comply with the postmarket safety reporting requirements associated with the type of marketing application. 21 C.F.R. § 4.102(a).

In addition, the PMSR regulations require combination product applicants to submit additional specified reports based on the constituent parts included in the combination product. 21 C.F.R. § 4.102(c). Specifically, if a combination product contains a device constituent part, and the combination product is approved under an NDA or a Biologics License Application (BLA), then the combination product applicant must also submit:

♦ Device five-day reports (when a reportable event necessitates remedial action to prevent an unreasonable risk of substantial harm to the public health. See 21 C.F.R. § 803.53.);

♦ Device malfunction reports (failure of a device to meet its performance specifications or otherwise perform as intended; and the malfunction would be likely to cause or contribute to death or serious injury if the malfunction were to recur. Must be submitted within 30 calendar days of receipt of information. See 21 C.F.R. § 803.50);

♦ Device correction or removal reports (21 C.F.R. §§ 806.10 and 806.20).

See 21 C.F.R. § 4.102(c)(1).

If a combination product contains a drug constituent part, and the combination product is approved or cleared under a device marketing application or a BLA, then the combination product applicant must submit:

♦ Drug field alert reports (incidents that cause the drug product to be mistaken for another article, and incident of bacteriological contamination or significant deterioration. These are to be reported within three working days of receipt by the applicant. See 21 C.F.R. § 314.81);

♦ Drug 15-day reports (the applicant is required to report adverse drug experience that is both serious and unexpected within 15 days of receipt of information by the applicant. See 21 C.F.R. 314.80.).

See 21 C.F.R. § 4.102(c)(2).

If a combination product contains a biological product constituent part, and the combination product is approved or cleared under a device marketing application or a BLA, then the combination product applicant must submit:

♦ Biological deviation reports (to be reported within 45 days of receipt of information. See 21 C.F.R. § 606.171.)

♦ Biological product 15-day reports (the applicant is required to report adverse drug experience that is both serious and unexpected within 15 days of receipt of information by the applicant. See 21 C.F.R. § 600.80.)

See 21 C.F.R. § 4.102(c)(3).

If a combination product with a drug or biological product constituent part received marketing authorization under a device application, a 15-day report (see 21 C.F.R. § 314.80 or § 600.80) may be submitted within 30 calendar days rather than 15 calendar days. FDA stated that it had determined that it would be able to respond in a timely manner to reports submitted within 30 days rather than 15 days, and that permitting the reports to be submitted within 30 days would permit better alignment with device reporting requirements. 21 C.F.R. § 4.102(c)(2)(ii) and (3)(ii), *Federal Register* of December 20, 2016, 81 Fed. Reg. 92,603, 92,607.

In addition, for combination product applicants for a product that contains a device constituent part, and was approved under an NDA, Abbreviated New Drug Application (ANDA), or BLA, periodic safety reports submitted under 21 C.F.R. § 314.80 or § 600.80 must include a summary and analysis of device five-day reports, and device malfunction reports that were submitted during the report interval. 21 C.F.R. § 4.102(d)(1).

FDA has stated that one purpose of the new PMSR rules for combination products is to avoid duplicative reporting. Combination product applicants may submit a single report that satisfies multiple applicable reporting requirements, including submission deadlines. For example, a combination product applicant that holds an NDA for a drug/device combination product must submit both 15-day reports as described in 21 C.F.R. § 314.80 and device malfunction reports as described in 21 C.F.R. § 803.50 for an event that triggers both reporting requirements. The applicant could satisfy requirements by submitting a single report within 15 days that includes all the information that would be required in both types of reports for this event. If the applicant determines that additional time is needed to investigate the device malfunction, the applicant can submit a follow-up report to the initial 15-day report with additional information. See *Federal Register* of December 20, 2016, 81 Fed. Reg. 92,603, 92,607, footnote 3.

In another example, a combination product applicant that holds a premarket approval (PMA) for a drug/device combination product must submit both drug 15-day reports and device malfunction reports for an event that triggers both requirements. In this case, the applicant could satisfy requirements by submitting a single report within 30 days that includes all the information that would be required in both types of reports for this event. See 21 C.F.R. § 4.101(c)(2)(ii).

Constituent part applicants also have additional requirements. When a constituent part applicant receives information that involves a death or serious injury as described in 21 C.F.R. § 803.3, or an adverse experience as described in 21 C.F.R. § 314.80(a) or 21 C.F.R. § 600.80(a), the applicant must provide the information to the other constituent part applicant(s) for the combination product no later than five calendar days from receipt of the information.

Constituent part applicants must submit reports described in 21 C.F.R. Parts 314, 600, 606, 803, and 806, as applicable, as described in those reports.

Combination product applicants must submit the same reports in the same manner, except that:

♦ For combination products covered by an NDA or ANDA, device five-day reports and device malfunction reports must be submitted as described in 21 C.F.R. § 314.80(g) (electronic submissions). Similarly, for combination products covered by a BLA, device five-day reports and malfunction reports must be submitted as described in 21 C.F.R. § 600.80(h).

♦ For combination products covered by a device application, drug, or biological product, 15-day reports must be submitted in accordance with 21 C.F.R. § 803.12 (electronic format).

GOOD MANUFACTURING PRACTICES

In 2013, FDA issued regulations on current Good Manufacturing Practices (cGMPs) for combination products. 21 C.F.R. Part 4, Subpart A.

cGMPs are intended to ensure that drugs, biological products, devices, and HCT/Ps (human cells, tissues, and cellular and tissue-based products), are manufactured properly. cGMPs for drugs and biological products are contained in 21 C.F.R. Parts 210 and 211; device Quality System Regulations (QSRs) are contained in 21 C.F.R. Part 820. Additional requirements for certain biological products are contained in 21 C.F.R. Parts 600 through 680, and Good Tissue Practices applicable to HCT/Ps are found in 21 C.F.R. Part 1271.

Current Good Manufacturing Practices and Quality System Regulations are intended to ensure that drugs; biological products; human cells, tissues, and cellular and tissue-based products; and devices are made properly.

Each set of regulations is somewhat different because each is tailored to the characteristics of the types of products for which they were designed. Each set of regulations contains certain express or specific requirements that may be only generally expressed in the other set of regulations. For example, the cGMP regulations for drugs and biological products specifically require calculation of yield and stability while QSRs contain more general design validation provisions. Similarly, QSRs have detailed Corrective and Preventive Action (CAPA) provisions, while cGMPs contain more general production record requirements.

The regulations governing cGMPs for combination products do not create new regulations specific to combination products. Instead, as stated in the preamble to the final rule:

> The constituent parts of a combination product retain their regulatory status (as a drug or device, for example) after they are combined. Accordingly, the cGMP requirements that apply to each of the constituent parts continue to apply when they are combined to make combination products. (78 Fed. Reg. 4307 (Jan. 22, 2013)).

Under the regulations, each drug, biological product, or device constituent part of a combination product, taken individually, is subject to its governing cGMP regulations until it is combined with another type of constituent part to form a combination product. (21 C.F.R. 4.4(c) and (d).)

For example, when the constituent parts of a combination product are separately marketed, such as a new device intended for use with an individually specified, already approved drug product marketed by a different manufacturer, the device constituent part is subject only to the QSRs, while the drug constituent part is subject only to the cGMP regulations.

Similarly, if the constituent parts of a single-entity or co-packaged combination product are manufactured at separate facilities, each facility must comply with the cGMPs applicable to that type of product.

However, once the constituent parts of a combination product have arrived at the same facility, or the manufacture of these constituent parts is proceeding at the same facility, then all applicable cGMP requirements must be complied with at that facility, which means that the combination product as a whole may be subject to more than one cGMP regulation. (21 C.F.R. 4.4(a).)

However, the regulations provide for an alternative to running a single facility under two separate cGMP processes. Referred to in the preamble as the "streamlined" approach, described in 21 C.F.R. 4.4(b), this rules allow manufacturers to comply with cGMP requirements by implementing and complying with either the drug cGMPs or the device QS regulation, rather than both, under certain conditions. These conditions include compliance with specified provisions from the other of these two sets of regulations.

The foundation of the streamlined approach is FDA's comparison of the requirements of drug cGMPs and device QSRs. In many cases, the requirements of one system are also requirements of the other system. However, both drug cGMPs and device QSRs include requirements that are not required under the other system. The regulations identify the requirements of each system that do not have corresponding requirements in the other system.

More specifically, if a single-entity or co-packaged combination product includes both a drug and a device and the cGMP operating system is shown to comply with the drug cGMP regulations at 21 C.F.R. Parts 210 and 211, the manufacturing facility would also have to comply with the additional specific provisions of the QS regulation, but not the entire device QS regulation. Similarly, if the manufacturer opts to comply with the device QS regulation, it must also comply with specific drug cGMP regulations once the constituent parts of the combination product are combined.

The following chart identifies provisions of the cGMP and QSRs that must supplement a manufacturer's quality system (either drug cGMPs or device QSRs).

Current Good Manufacturing Practice Provisions to Consider During and After Joining Together Co-Packaged and Single-Entity Combination Products

If the Operating Manufacturing Control System Is Part 820 (QS Regulation), demonstrate compliance with these specific cGMP requirements:		If the Operating Manufacturing Control System Is Part 210/211 (cGMP Regulation), demonstrate compliance with these specific QS requirements:	
Regulation	Title	Regulation	Title
§ 211.84	Testing and approval or rejection of components, drug product containers, and closures	§ 820.20	Management responsibility
§ 211.103	Calculation of yield	§ 820.30	Design controls
§ 211.132	Tamper-evident packaging for OTC drugs	§ 820.50	Purchasing controls
§ 211.137	Expiration dating	§ 820.100	Corrective and preventive action
§ 211.165	Testing and release for distribution	§ 820.170	Installation
§ 211.166	Stability testing	§ 820.200	Servicing
§ 211.167	Special testing requirements		
§ 211.170	Reserve samples		

It should also be noted that if a constituent part is a biological product or an HCT/P, the relevant provisions of 21 C.F.R. Parts 600 through 680, or Good Tissue Practices in 21 C.F.R. Part 1271, also must be met. Due to the complexity of these types of products, the application of the regulations is specific to the function of the product and on a case-by-case basis.

FDA recommends that manufacturers present information to the agency during the development phase about how they intend to achieve compliance with both sets of regulations during and after joining the constituent parts together of proposed combination products that will have constituent parts that are physically, chemically, or otherwise combined, or that will be co-packaged. For example, FDA recommends that a pre-investigational new drug (pre-IND) or pre-investigational device exemption (pre-IDE) meeting include a discussion of the sponsor's implementation of cGMPs, including consideration of risks of the combination product, its technology, and any anticipated postmarket development and postapproval changes. FDA recommends that the sponsor include all critical manufacturers in these discussions and include information on critical steps that may be conducted at source/contract firms and any special testing. FDA's OCP is available as a resource to sponsors in the resolution of cGMP concerns.

The preamble to the final rule (78 Fed. Reg. 4307 (Jan. 22, 2013)) includes a helpful discussion of several specific issues relating to cGMPs for combination products, including point-of-care products, convenience kits, drug container/closures, calculation of yield, and reserve samples. It is recommended that the preamble be consulted for additional information on these topics. In addition, FDA's "Guidance for Industry and Staff: Current Good Manufacturing Practice Requirements for Combination Products" describes and explains the final rule on cGMP requirements for combination products and was finalized in January 2017.

The Cures Act requires FDA to identify variations on compliance with cGMPs that would be deemed acceptable for manufacturers to demonstrate compliance to Good Manufacturing Practices for combination products. This list must be generated within 18 months from the date of issue of the new act (November 25, 2016) and must be updated by FDA periodically. Until such publication is issued, manufacturers must rely on the methods discussed above to demonstrate compliance with GMPs.

Number of Marketing Applications

The statute does not address the statutory provisions under which a combination product is to be regulated. In practice, combination products are almost always regulated under the type of application ordinarily submitted to the Center with jurisdiction over the product. In other words, combination products assigned to CDER are ordinarily reviewed under the new drug provisions of the FDCA, or the biological product licensing provisions of the Public Health Service Act (PHSA); combination products assigned to CDRH are ordinarily reviewed under the device provisions of the FDCA; while combination products assigned to CBER are ordinarily reviewed under the licensing provisions of the PHSA or the device provisions of the FDCA.

Combination products are almost always regulated under the type of application ordinarily submitted to the Center with jurisdiction over the product.

According to FDA regulations, "the designation of one agency component as having primary jurisdiction for the premarket review and regulation of a combination product does not preclude . . . in appropriate cases, the requirement by FDA of separate applications." (21 C.F.R. § 3.4(c).) This regulation suggests that most of the time combination products will be reviewed and regulated under one application.

The Cures Act amended the FDCA to state that FDA "shall conduct the premarket review of any combination product under a single application whenever appropriate." FDCA 503(g)(1)(B), 21 U.S.C. § 353(g)(1)(B). The Cures Act further amended FDCA to state "Nothing in this subsection shall be construed as prohibiting a sponsor from submitting separate applications for the constituent parts of a combination product, unless [FDA] determines that a single application is necessary. FDCA § 503(g)(6), 21 U.S.C. § 353(g)(6).

At the time of writing this chapter, it is not clear how FDA will reconcile the Cures Act provisions.

FDA issued an undated concept paper (https://www.fda.gov/downloads/combinationproducts/requestsforcomment/ucm108197.pdf) intended to clarify the number of marketing applications necessary for approval or clearance of a combination product. At this time, the concept paper may be the most reliable guide to FDA's thinking.

While a combination product is assigned to an agency Center based on the product's primary mode of action, the PMOA does not automatically determine the type of marketing application that will be used. As a practical matter, however, combination products are reviewed under the type of marketing application usually reviewed by the assigned Center.

According to the concept paper, while a combination product is assigned to an agency Center based on the product's primary mode of action, the PMOA does not automatically determine the type of marketing application that will be used. Depending on the type of product, approval or clearance could be obtained either through a single marketing application, or through separate marketing applications for the individual constituent parts of the combination product.

According to the concept paper, for most combination products, a single marketing application should be sufficient to ensure product safety and effectiveness. FDA review of a combination product under a single application addresses the combination product as a whole and its constituent parts.

Although two applications for a combination product have rarely been required, there are some circumstances in which two applications could be necessary to ensure safety or effectiveness of the combination product.

Although two applications for a combination product have rarely been required, the concept paper notes that there are some circumstances in which two applications could be necessary to ensure safety or effectiveness of the combination product. According to the concept paper, two applications might be required in the following circumstances:

♦ when the constituent parts are separate and complex products (e.g., drugs and implantable delivery pumps, devices in combination with a new molecular entity);

◆ when one constituent part has uses beyond the combination product (e.g., a single-dose drug and a reusable delivery device that is used for delivery of other drugs);

◆ when a BLA for further manufacture is appropriate to ensure the identity, safety, purity, and potency of certain biological products (e.g., cell and gene therapy, therapeutic proteins, monoclonal antibodies, blood products) when the product as a whole is being regulated under the drug or device provisions;

◆ to effect labeling revisions for a constituent part that is already approved for uses that do not include the proposed combination product indication (e.g., when a previously PMA-approved drug delivery device is later approved to deliver an additional drug, the labeling of both the additional drug and the device are typically changed in order to reflect their use in combination);

◆ to apply mechanisms necessary to ensure appropriate regulation, or unique regulatory requirements that are not available under a single marketing application (e.g., gene therapy products); to maintain regulatory consistency (for a device co-packaged with a drug covered by a new drug product exclusivity, a separate NDA/ANDA may be necessary for the drug constituent part).

Additionally FDA, under some circumstances, may accept two applications from the manufacturer when one would suffice to ensure the safety and effectiveness of the product. FDA recognizes that certain regulatory mechanisms (such as new drug exclusivity or orphan drug benefits) are associated only with certain types of marketing applications and that sponsors may wish to derive specific benefits that accrue under a particular type of application. In addition, when two manufacturers are involved in the development and manufacture of a combination product, each manufacturer may prefer its own application. The concept paper requests stakeholder perspectives on appropriate FDA responses when sponsors desire to have multiple applications.

Finally, the concept paper states that for single-entity combination products (combination products that are physically, chemically, or otherwise combined, as described in 21 C.F.R. § 3.2(e)(1)), a single marketing application is the only feasible option because drugs and devices are generally approved or cleared only as finished products, not as components for further manufacture. Some manufacturers of "single-entity" combination products would prefer to have their products reviewed and approved or cleared under two marketing applications, to make postapproval changes easier, among other reasons. It is not clear how the recent 21st Century Cures Act amendments will affect FDA's statement in the concept paper that for single-entity combination products, a single marketing application is the only feasible option.

User Fees

Congress first authorized FDA to collect fees from companies that manufacture drugs and biological products under the Prescription Drug User Fee Act of 1992 (PDUFA), and from companies that manufacture devices under the Medical Device User Fee and Modernization Act of 2002 (MDUFMA). FDA has issued a guidance document (https://www.fda.gov/downloads/RegulatoryInformation/Guidances/UCM147118.pdf) describing the assessment of user fees for combination products.

In general, combination products reviewed under one application will be subject to the user fees associated with that type of application.

In general, combination products reviewed under one application will be subject to the user fees associated with that type of application. For example, a biologic/device or a drug/device combination product for which a device PMA application is required would be subject to the PMA fee under MDUFMA.

In instances where one application would suffice but the sponsor(s) elect to submit two applications covering the constituent parts of a combination product, FDA believes that the user fees associated with both applications should be payable. Although sponsors may still be eligible for fee waivers or reductions, FDA assesses the two fees because review of two applications when one would suffice places an extra burden on FDA resources.

On the other hand, when FDA requires two applications for a combination product, sponsors are encouraged to consider submitting a request for user fee waiver or reduction. In particular, according to the guidance, FDA will look closely at whether a PDUFA "barrier to innovation" waiver may be applicable to reduce the additional fee burden associated with FDA's requirement for two marketing applications.

Both PDUFA and MDUFMA provide waivers or reductions of fees associated with the submission of applications by small businesses, although the eligibility standards and amount of the fee waiver or reduction differ. Sponsors of combination products requiring two applications should consider applying for the small business waiver or reduction under PDUFA and/or MDUFMA if they meet the qualification criteria.

Other than certain specific situations, such as marketing applications submitted by small businesses, standard MDUFMA fees are required for nearly all device-marketing applications. In contrast, PDUFA provides for waivers or reduction of fees where:

◆ Such waiver is necessary to protect the public health.

◆ The assessment of the fee would present a significant barrier to innovation because of limited resources or other circumstances.

◆ The fees to be paid by such person will exceed the anticipated present and future costs incurred by the Secretary in conducting the process for the review of human drug applications for such person.

A combination product that incorporates cutting-edge, innovative technology that holds promise for advancing patient care may also be eligible for waiver or a reduction of fees as FDA believes that assessment of two marketing application fees could represent a significant barrier to its development. To be eligible for the "innovative combination product" waiver under PDUFA's "barrier to innovation because of . . . other circumstances" provision, FDA considers the following factors:

◆ the combination product as a whole is innovative;

◆ FDA is requiring two fee-bearing marketing applications for the product;

◆ the applications request approval only of the two components of the combination product for use together (i.e., neither application includes an independent use for that constituent part of the combination product); and

◆ the applicant does not qualify for a small business waiver or has limited resources.

A combination product that incorporates cutting-edge, innovative technology that holds promise for advancing patient care may be eligible for waiver or a reduction of fees as FDA believes that assessment of two marketing application fees could represent a significant barrier to its development.

FDA considers the following factors in determining whether a combination product is innovative for purposes of the waiver application:

◆ the product addresses an unmet medical need in the treatment, diagnosis, or prevention of disease and therefore provides significant, meaningful advantage over alternatives;

◆ factors such as whether one of the two applications includes a new molecular entity, has been designated as a priority drug, is eligible for expedited device review, or has been granted fast-track status; and

◆ the existence of treatment alternatives (which would weigh against deciding that a product is innovative).

For innovative combination products requiring two applications, FDA would expect to reduce PDUFA fees as follows in appropriate situations:

♦ For products requiring a MDUFMA application and a PDUFA application, FDA would expect to reduce the PDUFA fee by the amount of the MDUFMA fee. Thus a sponsor would pay the full MDUFMA fee associated with the MDUFMA application, and a PDUFA fee reduced by the amount of the MDUFMA fee. The total amount paid would be the equivalent of one PDUFA fee.

♦ For products requiring two PDUFA applications (for combination products comprising a drug constituent part and a biological product constituent part), FDA would expect to reduce each PDUFA fee by half. In such a case, the total amount paid would be equivalent to one PDUFA fee.

According to the guidance, the "innovative combination product" waiver provides for a possible waiver only of application fees; the waiver is not applicable to annual product and establishment fees. FDA reviews requests for waivers of product and establishment fees, as well as requests for waivers or reductions of application fees not qualifying for the "innovative combination product" waiver, under criteria applicable to both combination and non-combination products.

POSTAPPROVAL MODIFICATIONS TO COMBINATION PRODUCTS

In January 2013, FDA issued a Draft Guidance for Industry describing principles to determine the type of marketing submission that may be required for post-approval changes for combination products approved under a BLA, NDA, or device PMA.

In general, if a change made to any constituent part of a combination product would have required a postmarket submission to FDA if that constituent part had been a stand-alone product, then a postmarket submission is also required for the combination product. In cases where the regulatory identity of the constituent part differs from the type of marketing application covering the combination product, then FDA is generally satisfied with one postmarket submission to the original application. The type of submission to provide for the change will depend on the type of application used to obtain approval of the combination product. For example, a change to the device constituent part of a combination product approved under an NDA should be submitted in the appropriate postmarket NDA submission and submitted to that NDA.

The Draft Guidance includes two tables:

♦ Table 1: Type of NDA/BLA Submission for a Change in a Device Constituent Part of a Combination Product Approved under an NDA/BLA

♦ Table 2: Type of PMA Submission for a Change in a Biological Product/Drug Constituent Part of a Combination Product Approved under a PMA

These tables should be consulted for additional information on submission of supplements to provide for postapproval changes.

Unfortunately, the draft guidance does not address changes to combination products cleared under a 510(k), or combination products approved under an NDA/BLA when the device constituent part would have been reviewed under a 510(k) if the device constituent part were a stand-alone product.

Medical device manufacturers have relied on FDA's existing guidance, "Deciding When to Submit a 510(k) for a Change to an Existing Device – Draft Guidance for Industry and Food and Drug Administration Staff" (K97-1, January 10, 1997) for many years to make post-clearance decisions on submission requirements for medical devices. Some combination product manufacturers have attempted to develop a "hybrid" approach for evaluation of postapproval changes for combination products when the device constituent part would be covered by a 510(k) as a stand-alone product. If this approach is followed, care should be taken to ensure that combination product attributes are not overlooked or underclassified, leading to regulatory submissions not being filed when they should.

As the industry has become more familiar with both typical changes made to drug/biologic delivery systems and FDA's expectations for evidence provided in combination product regulatory submissions, the International Organization for Standards (ISO) convened a team of industry experts to develop a technical considerations (TC) document for changes related to dose administration combination products. Titled "Change Assessment of Devices Intended for Administration of Medicinal Products," this TC document, drafted in December 2016, provides assessment techniques and recommended testing considerations when changes to a device constituent part are considered for dose delivery systems. While this TC document does not provide a direct link between the type of design change to be made and the type of regulatory submissions to be filed, it does work to bridge the knowledge gap through assessment of device constituent part changes and its impact on existing regulatory submissions.

Outside of the draft ISO standard and FDA's single guidance, no further clarification has been provided regarding FDA's expectations for how manufacturers should evaluate combination products for needed postapproval changes.

FDA's Office of Combination Products

Immediately following formal creation of the combination products category in 1990, the task of designating a lead agency Center for review and regulation of combination products was assigned to the Office of the Chief Mediator and Ombudsman in the Office of the Commissioner. Over the years, a number of concerns were raised about combination products, including concerns about the consistency, predictability, and transparency of the assignment process; issues related to the management of the review process when two or more FDA Centers had review responsibilities for a combination product; and lack of clarity about the postmarket regulatory controls applicable to combination products.

The FDCA gives FDA's Office of Combination Products broad responsibilities covering the regulatory life cycle of combination products.

FDA's Office of Combination Products was established on December 24, 2002, to address such concerns. The law gives OCP broad responsibilities covering the regulatory life cycle of combination products. As outlined by the office, the primary roles of OCP include:

◆ To serve as a focal point for combination product issues for FDA staff and industry,

◆ To develop guidance, regulations, and standard operating procedures to clarify the regulation of combination products,

◆ To classify products as drugs, devices, biological products, or combination products and assign an FDA Center to have primary jurisdiction for pre-market review and postmarket regulation where the jurisdiction is unclear or in dispute,

◆ To ensure timely and effective premarket review of combination products by overseeing the timeliness of and coordinating reviews involving more than one agency Center,

◆ To ensure consistency and appropriateness of postmarket regulation of combination products,

◆ To facilitate resolution of disputes regarding the timeliness of premarket review of combination products,

◆ To update agreements, guidance documents, or practices specific to the assignment of combination products,

◆ To develop annual reports to Congress on the office's activities and impacts, and

◆ To provide training to FDA staff and regulated industry on combination product regulation.

The 21st Century Cures Act gave OCP additional responsibilities, including coordinating intercenter reviews, overseeing the timeliness of such reviews, and overseeing the alignment of feedback regarding such reviews. FDCA § 503(g)(8)(C), 21 U.S.C. § 353(g)(8)(C).

By most accounts, OCP has been successful in meeting these objectives. In particular, the annual Reports to Congress provide a great deal of detail about the activities of the OCP.

Due to ongoing need, OCP continues to issue draft and final guidance documents:

♦ "Classification of Products as Drugs and Devices and Additional Product Classification Issues"

♦ "Interpretation of the Term "Chemical Action" in the Definition of Device Under Section 201(h) of the Federal Food, Drug, and Cosmetic Act"

♦ "Current Good Manufacturing Practice Requirements for Combination Products"

♦ "Human Factors Studies and Related Clinical Study Considerations in Combination Product Design and Development"

A complete listing of FDA's guidance documents to consider when developing a combination product can be found on FDA's Office of Combination Products website (https://www.fda.gov/regulatoryinformation/guidances/ucm122047.htm).

These guidance documents provide additional information on how FDA will classify products, or constituent parts of combination products, as drugs or devices in addition to other technical considerations. A discussion of these guidance documents has been included in this chapter because the documents were issued by the OCP.

The 21st Century Cures Act also identified the expectation for FDA to issue specific guidance for combination products. Within four years after enactment of this act (November 25, 2016), final guidance for the following topics is expected to be released:

♦ Guidance identifying a "structured process" for pre-submission interactions between FDA and combination product sponsors;

♦ Guidance on best practices for feedback from pre-submission interactions on combination products (this guidance must include ensuring that the agency is providing its "best advice" based on such interactions) and

♦ Guidance on meeting requests when a determination of the primary mode of action is necessary, which is expected to specifically include:

o Information that the sponsor must submit for such a meeting,
o How such early-stage meetings with FDA will relate to other types of FDA meetings related to the combination product, and
o How any agreements reached during these meetings will be documented, including the content of such agreements.

Chapter 10

The Cosmetics Regulatory Process

Thomas F. Myers, Personal Care Products Council, Washington, D.C.

Key Points

- The Federal Food, Drug, and Cosmetic Act (FDCA) defines cosmetics as articles applied to the human body to cleanse, beautify, promote attractiveness and alter the appearance, etc.
- The FDCA prohibits "adulterated" cosmetics, which includes not only contaminated ingredients or packaging, but also use of unapproved color additives or banned ingredients.
- The FDCA prohibits "misbranding," which includes false or misleading labeling by claims about the product, inaccurate labeling such as net content declaration, having a misleading container size or amount, and other violations.
- Cosmetics are not subject to premarket approval by the Food and Drug Administration (FDA), but the product and ingredients must be substantiated for safety. If the manufacturer cannot substantiate safety, a warning is required.
- Color additives are the only cosmetic ingredients that must be pre-approved ("listed") by FDA. Color additives are subject to the Delaney Clause, which bars using any color shown to cause cancer "in man or animal."
- Coal tar hair dyes are subject to special regulatory requirements.
- FDA issued draft guidance establishing a maximum level of 10 parts per million (ppm) for lead as an impurity in cosmetic lip products, such as lipsticks, and other externally applied cosmetics.
- FDA monitors compliance through random inspections of cosmetic facilities and self-reporting.
- The cosmetic industry has several self-regulatory programs that work with FDA in assuring ingredient and product safety.
- The "intended use" doctrine states that cosmetic or drug status is determined by claims about the intended use of the product.
- Cosmetic product labeling is governed by the FDCA and the Fair Packaging and Labeling Act (FPLA). Cosmetic labels must state the statement of identity, net contents, ingredients, any required warning, and other information.
- The FDCA prohibits the manufacture and sale of rinse-off cosmetics (including toothpaste) that contain intentionally added plastic microbeads.
- Cosmetics are subject to a host of state reporting requirements and regulatory programs.

LEGAL AND REGULATORY AUTHORITY

Under the Federal Food, Drug, and Cosmetic Act (FDCA), the standards governing cosmetics differ significantly from those governing food, medical devices, drugs, or tobacco products largely because of the relatively few risks associated with their use. Section 201(i) of the FDCA defines a "cosmetic" as:

1) an article intended to be rubbed, poured, sprinkled, or sprayed on, introduced into or otherwise applied to the human body or any part thereof for cleansing, beautifying, promoting attractiveness, or altering the appearance; and
2) an article intended for use as a component of any such article; except that such term shall not include soap.[1]

The FDCA prohibits the introduction into interstate commerce of any cosmetic that is "adulterated." Section 601 of the FDCA is very specific about what makes a cosmetic adulterated:

♦ if it bears or contains any poisonous or deleterious substance that may render it injurious to users under conditions of use prescribed in the labeling thereof, or under such conditions of use as are customary or usual;

♦ if it consists in whole or in part of any filthy, putrid, or decomposed substance;

♦ if it has been prepared, packed, or held under unsanitary conditions whereby it may have become contaminated with filth, or whereby it may have been rendered injurious to health;

♦ if its container is composed, in whole or part, of any poisonous or deleterious substance that may render the contents injurious to health; or

♦ if it is not a hair dye and it is, or it bears or contains, a color additive that is unsafe within the meaning of section 721(a).

FDA regulations provide that the presence of specified ingredients in the formulation render a cosmetic product adulterated.

Further, Food and Drug Administration (FDA) regulations provide that the presence of specified ingredients in the formulation render a cosmetic product adulterated. Examples of such ingredients include the antibacterial agent bithionol; mercury as an eye makeup preservative (except at strict limits); vinyl chloride included as a propellant in cosmetic aerosol products such as hairsprays; certain halogenated salicylanilides; zirconium in aerosol cosmetics; and specified cattle materials.

The FDCA also prohibits the sale of any cosmetic that is "misbranded." Under section 602 of the FDCA, a cosmetic is misbranded:

♦ if its labeling is false or misleading in any particular;

♦ if in package form unless it bears a label containing 1) the name and place of business of the manufacturer, packer, or distributor; and 2) an accurate statement of the quantity of the contents in terms of weight, measure, or numerical count: *Provided* That under the clause (2) of this paragraph reasonable variations shall be permitted, and exemptions as to small packages shall be established, by regulations prescribed by the Secretary.

♦ if any word, statement, or other information required by the act to appear on the label or labeling is not prominently placed thereon with such conspicuousness (as compared to other words, statements, designs, or devices in the labeling) and in such terms as to render it likely to be read and understood by the ordinary individual under customary conditions of purchase and use;

♦ if its containers are so made, formed, or filled as to be misleading;

♦ if it is a color additive and its packaging and labeling are not in conformity with regulations issued under section 721 (this requirement does not apply to color additives marketed and intended for use only in or on hair dyes as defined in section 601(a)); or

♦ if its packaging or labeling is in violation of an applicable regulation issued pursuant to sections 3 or 4 of the Poison Prevention Packaging Act of 1970.

FDA regulations require that a manufacturer substantiate the safety of a finished cosmetic product and each of its ingredients. Because cosmetics are not required to be approved by FDA before marketing, FDA promulgated a labeling requirement for products where safety has not been substantiated before marketing. A product is considered misbranded if safety substantiation is not available, unless the following warning appears on the principal display panel: "*Warning* — The safety of this product has not been determined." (21 C.F.R. § 740.10(a)). FDA has made it clear that the safety substantiation requirement does not require that new testing be conducted in every case "where reasonable scientific opinion would regard the available data as adequate."

FDA regulations require that a manufacturer substantiate the safety of a finished cosmetic product and each of its ingredients. A product is considered misbranded if safety substantiation is not available, unless the following warning appears on the principal display panel: "Warning: — The safety of this product has not been determined."

COLOR ADDITIVES

The only cosmetic ingredients that must be pre-approved ("listed") by FDA to be used in a finished cosmetic product are color additives. Specified color additives also must be "certified," meaning each production batch must be approved by FDA.

FDA approves color additives specifically for use in a cosmetic, a drug, a device, or a food, or any combination of those products (e.g., D&C Green No. 5, FD&C Yellow No. 5). FDA also may put limitations on the cosmetic use of a color additive, such as where it may be used ("externally except eye area"), and may establish maximum allowable use levels (e.g., "Lip products (5% maximum)"). Use of an unapproved color in a cosmetic makes the product adulterated under the FDCA and subject to FDA seizure and other legal action. The requirement for pre-approval of color additives stems from the Color Additive Amendments of 1960.

These amendments prohibited use of a color additive unless a regulation permits the additive's use. The FDCA defines "color additive" as a "dye, pigment, or other substance [which] when added or applied to a food, drug or cosmetic, or to the human body or any part thereof, is capable (alone or through reaction with any other substance) of imparting color thereto . . . ."

The Delaney Clause imposes an absolute ban on any color "if, after tests which are appropriate for the evaluation of the safety of additives for such use, or after other relevant exposure of man or animal to such additive, it is found by the Secretary to induce cancer in man or animal."

The Color Additive Amendments also contain the "Delaney Clause," a provision named for its author, Congressman James Delaney (D-NY). This provision was intended to guard against cancer-causing ingredients and imposes an absolute ban on any color "if, after tests which are appropriate for the evaluation of the safety of additives for such use, or after other relevant exposure of man or animal to such additive, it is found by the Secretary to induce cancer in man or animal." (21 U.S.C. § 379e(b)(5)(B)). The courts ultimately concluded that Congress intended for FDA to deny approval of a color additive if it posed a risk, even a *de minimis* or trivial one, of inducing cancer in animals.

Color additives also have impurity specifications that must be satisfied in order for the additive to be used as a cosmetic ingredient. In December 2016, FDA issued draft guidance on lead as an impurity in cosmetic lip products, such as lipsticks, and other externally applied cosmetics, such as eye shadows, blushes, compact powders, shampoos, and body lotions. The guidance, issued in response to a petition filed by the Personal Care Products Council, establishes a maximum level of 10 parts per million (ppm) for lead. FDA developed the guidance after sampling a variety of finished cosmetic products and assessing the amount of lead levels in the surveyed products. FDA concluded that lipsticks and cosmetics that meet or fall below the 10ppm maximum lead level pose no health risk to consumers. Moreover, 10ppm is also consistent with standards set by the International Cooperation on Cosmetics Regulation (ICCR), and regions such as Canada, Japan, and the European Union.

It is important to note that lead is never used as an intentionally added ingredient in or as an additive to lipstick or other cosmetics. However, because lead is a naturally occurring metal, it is routinely detected in the air, water, and soil. Consequently, it may be found at extremely low levels as a trace contaminant in the raw natural ingredients used to formulate cosmetics, just as it is in thousands of other products.

There is an exemption for coal tar-derived colors used in hair dyes. Section 601(a) of the FDCA states that a cosmetic is adulterated if it contains any deleterious substance that could harm the user when the product is used according to the labeling or customary use. This prohibition, however, does not apply to coal tar hair dyes if their labels bear the following statement:

> Caution This product contains ingredients, which may cause skin irritation on certain individuals, and a preliminary test according to accompanying directions should first be made. This product must not be used for dyeing the eyelashes or eyebrows; to do so may cause blindness.

In addition, the label should have adequate directions for preliminary testing such as patch test directions. If the label lacks the caution statement and patch test directions, FDA can take regulatory action. This exemption applies only to coal tar hair dyes and not to other coloring ingredients in hair dyes, or eyebrow and eyelash dye products.

FDA ENFORCEMENT AUTHORITY

The primary means for FDA to monitor the cosmetics industry is through random inspections of cosmetic facilities. FDA also checks imports at ports of entry and investigates consumer or competitor complaints about specific products. If FDA perceives a violation through information obtained during a facility inspection or an import inspection, it may send the company a "Warning Letter." The Warning Letter typically issues from FDA's district office, which oversees the facility or the place of import in the United States, but may occasionally come from the Center for Food Safety and Applied Nutrition at FDA headquarters.

FDA monitors the cosmetics industry through random inspection of cosmetic facilities, checks imports at ports of entry, and investigates complaints about specific products.

Inspection of cosmetic manufacturing establishments is one of FDA's primary means of cosmetic product oversight. FDA is not required to notify the facility in advance of inspection. The inspection usually is routine, but could be triggered by FDA's belief that a company's product(s) is being manufactured or marketed in violation of the law.

A Cosmetic Facility

FDA's authority during a cosmetic inspection differs from the agency's authority to inspect a biologic or drug facility. A cosmetic manufacturer, for example, is not legally required to provide FDA inspectors with master formula records, batch production records, products or ingredient analyses, safety testing data of any type, and consumer complaint files or adverse experience data. Moreover, companies are not required to produce any financial data or other business records; however, if requested by an FDA inspector, companies are required to provide access to and copies of shipping records showing movement of cosmetics in interstate commerce.

The right of FDA inspectors to take photographs during an inspection is an area of continuing controversy among FDA, industry, and the courts. In its *Inspections Operations Manual* (IOM), FDA takes the position that it has the authority to take photographs. The FDA IOM instructs inspectors not to request permission to take photographs but to take the camera into the firm and use it as necessary, as with any other inspectional equipment. Industry has taken the posture that it may deny inspectors the ability to take photographs, particularly when necessary to protect trade secrets regarding manufacturing equipment, formulations, or processes.

In the course of cosmetic inspections, FDA inspectors frequently take samples of finished and unfinished materials and labeling. FDA frequently samples products to ensure that the cosmetic is using FDCA-approved color additives.

THE COSMETIC/DRUG DISTINCTION

In determining whether a product is a "cosmetic" or a "drug," it is important to examine the definitions for "cosmetic" and "drug" in the FDCA. As noted earlier, the term "cosmetic" means:

1) articles *intended* to be rubbed, poured, sprinkled, or sprayed on, introduced into or otherwise applied to the human body or any part thereof for cleansing, beautifying, promoting attractiveness, or altering the appearance, and
2) articles *intended* for use as a component of any such articles; except that such term shall not include soap. (emphasis added) (FDCA § 201(i); 21 U.S.C. § 321(i))

"Drug" means:

articles *intended* for use in the diagnosis, cure, mitigation, treatment, or prevention of disease in man or other animal; and . . . articles (other than food) intended to affect the structure or any function of

the body of man or other animals . . . ." (emphasis added) (FDCA §
201 (g)(1); 21 U.S.C. § 321(g)(1))

The key words in the cosmetic and drug definitions are "intended for use" and
"intended to be." The manufacturer's intent is critical, though not the only factor, in FDA's evaluation of whether or not a particular product constitutes a drug
or a cosmetic. FDA determines the "intended use" by analyzing, among other
things, the claims stated on the product's labeling, its advertisements, and any
promotional materials. In a guidance document on this topic, FDA notes that its
evaluation can go beyond even the express claims made on a given product;
consumer perception and use of particular ingredients that have a well-known
therapeutic use may render a product a drug instead of a cosmetic. Generally,
however, if the claims refer only to beautifying or promoting attractiveness, the
product is considered "cosmetic" and must be labeled in compliance with FDA
regulations governing cosmetics.

*The key words in the
cosmetic and drug
definitions are "intended for
use" and "intended to be."*

It is possible that products are intended as both cosmetics *and* drugs, for example if the products make both cosmetic and drug claims, such as an antiper-
spirant (drug)/deodorant (cosmetic) product. Cosmetic-drugs must comply with
both the cosmetic and drug regulatory requirements for that product.

As cosmetic products become more sophisticated and offer greater benefits to
consumers, the point at which a product's claims render it a drug becomes even
more critical as drugs are categorically subject to more stringent regulation.
The cosmetic/drug issue is an area of contention between FDA and manufacturers. Three cases from the late 1960s remain the preeminent judicial guidance
on when a "cosmetic" will be considered a "drug." In one case, the court held
that claims associated with a product called "Sudden Change" (represented as
giving a "face lift without surgery"; promising to "lift out puffs") were sufficient
to make the product a "drug." In another case, the court held that claims for the
product "Line Away" (such as "made in a pharmaceutical laboratory"; packaged
under "biologically aseptic conditions"; creates a "tingling sensation" while "at
work"; "tightening" facial skin; and "discouraging new wrinkles from forming")
made this product a "drug." In a third case, involving a product called "Magic
Secret," the court held that claims that the product was "pure protein" and that
it caused an "astringent sensation" were *not* sufficient to cause consumers to
conclude that the product would do anything more than alter their appearance,
which was a cosmetic benefit.

These cases still provide guidance when determining whether a claim is a cosmetic or drug claim. While not carrying the same precedential weight as a court
case, under FDA's regulatory and enforcement authority, the issuance of Warning Letters also provides manufacturers with insight into the agency's approach

to the cosmetic-drug distinction. For example, in 1987, FDA issued regulatory letters to dozens of cosmetic manufacturers challenging manufacturers' claims for skincare products as "drug" claims. While most of those matters were resolved privately, FDA's response to a citizen petition arising out of one of those matters made it clear that the agency relies heavily on the decisions in *Sudden Change*, *Line Away*, and *Magic Secret* when determining the "drug" or "cosmetic" status of a product. At the same time, FDA has declined to establish guidelines for cosmetic claims, stating that each claim or group of claims had to be viewed in context to determine whether it is a cosmetic or drug claim.

The agency has suggested, however, that the mere presence of an ingredient at levels that will "affect the structure or function of the body" may be sufficient to make the product a drug, regardless of the claims in advertising and labeling, a position that represents a divergence from its past practice. An example involves the presence of hormone ingredients in a topical preparation. FDA concluded that the mere inclusion of hormones, even in the absence of drug claims, made the products "cosmetic-drugs" subject to a monograph.[2] Later, however, it withdrew the proposed regulation that advanced this position with respect to a proposed ban on any hormone or estrogen ingredient in cosmetics.

FDA AND INSPECTION OF COSMETIC-DRUGS UNDER FDAMA

FDAMA allows facilities that manufacture products regulated both as cosmetics and drugs (such as skincare products containing sunscreen and antiperspirant/ deodorant products) to be inspected to the same extent as prescription drug manufacturers.

The Food and Drug Administration Modernization Act of 1997 (FDAMA) changed FDA's inspection authority for drugs but *not for cosmetics*. Section 704 of the FDCA, however, as amended by FDAMA, allows facilities that manufacture products regulated both as cosmetics and drugs (such as skincare products containing sunscreen and antiperspirant/deodorant products) to be inspected to the same extent as prescription drug manufacturers. Under such circumstances, FDA has authority to request all records that could determine whether a cosmetic drug is adulterated or misbranded. The following records may be available under the OTC Drug Inspection Authority:

♦ Quantitative formulas, specifications for all active and inactive ingredients and all testing done to ensure that ingredients met those specifications; all records relating to the manufacture of the drug, including batch records, validation records, stability testing data, and all other types of records either required to be maintained under drug good manufacturing practice (GMP) regulations or that bear upon compliance with drug GMP regulations;

♦ all testing of ingredients and finished products relating to microbial content; all release specifications for finished product, all testing of finished products to determine compliance with release specifications, and all records relating to investigations of batches that in any way failed release specifications; all testing and other safety substantiation for inactive and active ingredients, and for finished products;

♦ all data relating to product packaging; all consumer complaints of any type relating to safety and effectiveness;

♦ all testing to support product claims of any type;

♦ all consumer complaints about product performance or other product attributes;

♦ formula records, manufacturing batch records, adverse reaction reports, and evidence of GMP compliance for cosmetic drugs.

This expanded inspection authority does not apply to cosmetic products that are not also drugs.

Labeling Deficiencies

FDA has issued Warning Letters to cosmetic companies in recent years alleging labeling deficiencies. These deficiencies fall into several basic categories. The largest category by far consists of labeling claims that, under the "intended use" doctrine, convert a cosmetic into a drug. FDA scrutinizes not only the claims and representations made about a product but also whether the mandatory labeling information is present (such as listing ingredients). Any resulting Warning Letter for labeling violations would allege that the product is "misbranded" under section 602 of the FDCA.

A recent spate of Warning Letters signals an aggressive new approach by FDA to potential FDCA violations. In 2016, the agency issued more than 30 Warning Letters to personal care companies for allegedly making drug claims about cosmetic products—more than triple the number of similar Warning Letters issued in 2015. This is, in large part, due to increased FDA scrutiny of product claims made on a company's website. Many of these recent Warning Letters have taken the following form:

> This is to advise you that the Food and Drug Administration (FDA) reviewed your website at the Internet address [xxxxx] on [date] and has determined that you take orders there for the products [xxxxxx]. The claims on your website establish that the products are drugs under sections 201(g)(1)(B) and/or 201(g)(1)(C) of the Federal Food, Drug, and

Cosmetic Act (the Act) [21 U.S.C. § 321(g)(1)(B) and/or 21 U.S.C. § 321(g)(1)(C)] because they are intended for use in the diagnosis, cure, mitigation, treatment, or prevention of disease and/or articles intended to affect the structure or any function of the human body . . .

While the increased number of Warning Letters appears to represent a new phase of aggressive enforcement by FDA over the cosmetics industry, one thing is clear: companies should be vigilant to avoid making "drug" claims about their cosmetic products not just on label, but also on websites and on any packaging or promotional materials.

As with other FDA-regulated products, if FDA believes a cosmetic is adulterated or misbranded under the statute, the agency may take several actions including seizure, refusal of entry into the United States if it is a foreign product, going to federal district court to obtain a restraining order to prevent further shipments, or initiating a criminal enforcement action. Examples of products seized as "adulterated" in the past include various eyebrow and eyelash dye products, and nail preparations containing methyl methacrylate.

Industry Self-Regulation

♦ Cosmetic Ingredient Review

CIR was designed to help companies substantiate the safety of ingredients used in cosmetics and the final formulation without duplicating safety testing already done by others.

In 1975, the cosmetic industry requested that FDA establish a program to publicly substantiate the safety of cosmetic ingredients. Due to other resource commitments, FDA declined and suggested that the cosmetic industry establish its own program to evaluate cosmetic ingredient safety.

In response, the cosmetic industry developed and adopted a number of self-regulatory programs, with the Cosmetic Ingredient Review (CIR) becoming the cornerstone of the cosmetic industry's self-regulatory effort. This industry-funded body was established in 1976 by the Cosmetic, Toiletry, and Fragrance Association (CTFA) (now known as the Personal Care Products Council). The CIR was designed to help companies substantiate the safety of ingredients used in cosmetics and the final formulation without duplicating safety testing already done by others.

As part of the ingredient safety assessment, the available scientific data on an ingredient is reviewed by a seven-member expert panel. Panel conclusions are publicly announced by CIR without private review or comment by the industry. The panel's scientists are nominated by consumer, scientific, and clinical groups; government agencies; and industry. They are chosen from several scientific disciplines, such as chemistry, dermatology, and toxicology. The expert panel also has three nonvoting members representing a consumer group, industry, and FDA.

The scientific review of each ingredient goes through several stages. The technical staff of CIR prepares a Scientific Literature Review that summarizes known data gleaned from databases and industry studies. The Literature Review is made available for public comment with a request for any data, published or unpublished, that the review has not included. After 60 days, the comments received (including data submissions), are incorporated into the document for panel consideration. After a series of public meetings, the panel issues a Tentative Report.

The Tentative Report may reach any one of four tentative conclusions: safe as used, safe with certain qualifications, unsafe, or insufficient data available to CIR to support safety. The Tentative Report is available for comment for 60 days. All comments are analyzed and a response developed. The CIR Final Report incorporates any changes based on public comment and is published in the peer-reviewed *International Journal of Toxicology*. Final Reports on ingredient safety also appear in the *CIR Compendium*, which is published annually.

A primary goal of CIR is to minimize duplication of ingredient safety testing; consequently CIR has deferred or excluded review of ingredients that are subject to other safety assessments. Examples include over-the-counter (OTC) drug active ingredients, fragrance ingredients (reviewed by the Research Institute for Fragrance Materials), ingredients in New Drug Applications, color additives reviewed by FDA under section 721 of the FDCA, and those subject to any final FDA regulation. Chemicals considered by CIR for review are ranked for priority according to potential biological activity, frequency of use, concentration of use, route of exposure (e.g., inhalation), area of exposure (e.g., the eyes), and any special group of users (e.g., infants).

A primary goal of the Cosmetic Ingredient Review is to minimize duplication of ingredient safety testing.

◆ Voluntary Registration and Reporting Programs

Since the early 1970s, the cosmetics industry, on its own initiative, has participated in two voluntary, FDA-administered programs. One program involves the voluntary registration of cosmetic facilities, including foreign facilities. Upon registering, a facility is assigned a registration number by FDA. The other program involves the voluntary registration of cosmetic product ingredient statements. FDA has developed an electronic database with industry input into which such information should be reported (and updated where necessary). The facility and formula information is entered into an FDA database that enables the agency to notify and investigate the appropriate entities in the event of an adverse incident involving a cosmetic product. The programs apply only to products sold at retail and exclude products sold for professional use.

♦ **Voluntary Industry Code of Practice**

In 2006, the Personal Care Products Council adopted a Consumer Commitment Code designed to reinforce industry practices already in place and to promote additional actions intended to enhance cosmetic safety. The code incorporates existing practices such as the current reporting of manufacturing establishments and includes a new Safety Information Summary Program that provides FDA with relevant cosmetic product information and makes ingredient safety readily available upon request. The code went into effect on January 1, 2007, and is open to all members of the industry.

INGREDIENTS AND FORMULATION

Plastic Microbeads

On December 28, 2015, President Obama signed The Microbead-Free Waters Act, which amended the FDCA to prohibit the manufacture and sale of rinse-off cosmetics (including toothpaste) that contain intentionally added plastic microbeads. A "microbead" is defined to mean "any solid plastic particle that is less than five millimeters in size and is intended to be used to exfoliate or cleanse the human body or any part thereof."

This new federal law contains a defined schedule of dates to guide manufacturers and retailers in their compliance, and it was intended by Congress to set a national, uniform standard on microbeads. It also was widely supported by the personal care industry, which had already voluntarily begun to replace plastic microbeads with other viable alternatives.

The law specifically prohibits the manufacture of rinse-off cosmetic products containing plastic microbeads by July 1, 2017, and the sale of them by July 1, 2018; for OTC drugs, the dates are July 1, 2018 and July 1, 2019, respectively.

Volatile Organic Compounds

Volatile Organic Compounds (VOCs) are found in a variety of consumer products, including certain cosmetics. VOCs are known to contribute to the formation of ground-level ozone, a criteria air pollutant regulated by the U.S. Environmental Protection Agency. While VOCs do not necessarily give rise to human health or environmental concerns, they react with nitrogen oxides (NOx) in the presence of heat and sunlight to form ground-level ozone—the primary component of "smog." For that reason, VOCs are regulated as "ozone precursors" under the U.S.

Clean Air Act. Many states likewise have promulgated regulations setting stringent VOC emission levels for various consumer product categories.

Cosmetic product formulators must continuously monitor state VOC regulations because the emission limits are constantly being lowered as states struggle to meet federal clean air attainment requirements for criteria air pollutants. California generally has the most stringent VOC emission levels for consumer products in the nation.

STATE REPORTING REQUIREMENTS

A host of state reporting requirements, some specific to cosmetics and some applying to consumer products generally, likewise mandate action by personal care companies. Some of these state laws are simple reporting requirements, while others may directly impact cosmetic formulations. California, perhaps not surprisingly, has the most robust regulatory programs affecting cosmetics.

Safe Cosmetics Act

The California Safe Cosmetics Act was enacted in 2005 ostensibly for the purpose of collecting information on "hazardous" and potentially hazardous ingredients in cosmetic products sold in California and to make this information available to the public. It obligates cosmetic manufacturers to report annually on hazardous materials in their products.

Specifically, the act requires manufacturers to report cosmetic products that contain any level (concentration) of a chemical known or suspected to cause cancer or reproductive harm, excluding incidental ingredients and degradation chemicals. Trade secret information is not exempt from reporting. Companies claiming trade secret or confidential business information must submit supporting written documentation to justify this designation to California's Department of Public Health, which will make the final determination on any trade secret designation.

To assist companies with reporting, the California Department of Public Health developed a list of reportable ingredients, which was compiled from lists from other authoritative bodies (e.g., U.S. Environmental Protection Agency, the National Toxicology Program, the International Agency for Research on Cancer, etc.). This list is published on the agency's website.

In June 2013, California passed a budget "trailer" bill that contained language requiring the Safe Cosmetic Program to develop and launch a fully searchable public database. As of 2017, this database is fully operational and allows consumers and the public to conduct searches by company name, brand name, product category, or ingredient.

"Green Chemistry" Laws

Prior to the recent enactment of comprehensive chemical management reform at the federal level, many states had begun to enact laws to minimize or eliminate the generation, use, and disposal of hazardous substances in consumer products and processes. While these so-called "green chemistry" laws tend to vary by state in scope and application, all require companies to report the use of certain ingredients in their products.

California, Maine, Minnesota, Oregon, and Vermont have enacted green chemistry laws and promulgated implementing regulations, which authorize state agencies to regulate "chemicals of concern" in consumer products through different frameworks. For example, some laws are limited to just children's products and require only the notification and reporting of certain substances. Others, like California, apply to all consumer products, require comprehensive alternatives analyses, and authorize the use of Draconian agency responses, including manufacturing bans and sales restrictions.

California's "Safer Consumer Products" program is the most robust state program. The state's Department of Toxic Substances Control (DTSC) implements the program, and (at the time of this publication) is in the process of identifying the next round of "Priority Products" for regulation. DTSC has stated that it will likely identify a personal care product as a Priority Product for regulation. A company that manufactures a Priority Product containing a "Chemical of Concern," as that term is defined by the regulation, must notify DTSC of this fact in writing and, unless the company agrees to remove the Chemical of Concern, it must conduct an alternatives analysis to determine whether a "safer" chemical could be used instead. The process is intended to encourage chemical substitution or product redesign. DTSC will evaluate the alternative analysis to determine if the chosen alternative creates adverse public health or environmental impacts that require a regulatory response.

LABELING AND PACKAGING REQUIREMENTS

Labeling

FDA regulates cosmetics labeling under two federal laws—the FDCA and the Fair Packaging and Labeling Act (FPLA). FDA has issued labeling regulations under these laws in 21 C.F.R. Part 701. Labeling cannot be false or misleading, and label information must be prominent and conspicuous.

The FDCA requires that label information be placed on the immediate container of a cosmetic. If the retail package consists of an immediate container enclosed in an outside container (e.g., cologne bottle in a box), both the inner and outer containers must display the mandatory information. There are exceptions; for example, a product contained in a see-through transparent package or shrink-wrap would not have to be labeled if it surrounds a container otherwise properly labeled. If the information is easily legible through the outer container then the individual products inside the container can bear all the required labeling information.

Labeling:
The FDCA requires that label information be placed on the immediate container of a cosmetic. The FPLA only requires label information to appear on the outer container of a cosmetic.

A final concept affecting label placement under the FDCA is the distinction between "label" and "labeling." The FDCA defines "labeling" more broadly than "label":

> The term "labeling" means all labels and other written, printed, or graphic matter
> (1) upon any article or any of its containers or wrappers, or
> (2) accompanying such article.

Thus, the term "labeling" includes pamphlets, leaflets, and other written material accompanying a cosmetic product, but not necessarily affixed to it.

Unlike the FDCA, the FPLA requires label information to appear only on the outer container of a cosmetic. Thus, if a retail package consists of an immediate container enclosed in an outside container (e.g., a jar of face cream in a box), the FPLA does not apply to the immediate (or inner) container label. It is sufficient to place the required information on the outer container only. If a cosmetic product is displayed for sale in its immediate container only (e.g., a deodorant in an aerosol can), however, the immediate container must comply with the FPLA.

These interpretations are consistent with the purpose of the FPLA, which is to provide purchasers with certain information at the point of retail sale so that they can compare ingredients in products and make value comparisons prior to purchase.

Only products intended to be displayed to retail purchasers are subject to the requirements of the FPLA. (A "consumer commodity is defined to include any food, drug, device, or cosmetic sold at retail for use by the consumer in the home.") Therefore, shipping containers used to transport bulk quantities of a product need not comply with the FPLA. Similarly, cosmetics intended as free gifts or samples and not for sale, and products sold to salons for application to customers by professional cosmetologists, are not subject to these requirements.

The FPLA requires that specified information appear on the principal display panel (PDP). The PDP is defined as "that part of a label that is most likely to be displayed, presented, shown, or examined under normal and customary conditions of display for retail sale."

The label of a cosmetic must state the identity or name of the product. It is also permissible to include a common or usual name, an appropriately descriptive name, a fanciful name understood by the public, or an appropriate illustration or vignette representing the intended cosmetic use. The statement of identity is required only to appear on the outer container. Most marketers, however, put it on both the inner and outer containers.

The purpose of the quantity statement is to allow consumers to make a value judgment about the products they are purchasing. The net quantity of contents tells the consumer how much of the cosmetic is in the container. The quantity statement must appear on both the inner and outer container under both the FDCA and the FPLA.

Under the 1992 amendments to the FPLA, the net quantity of contents in cosmetic labeling must be expressed in *both* the English and metric systems. The quantity declaration for "English" units is stated in avoirdupois pounds and ounces for weight or mass; and fluid ounces for fluid measure statements. The metric declaration of net contents must be stated in kilograms, grams, or milligrams for solid, semisolid, or viscous cosmetics, and liters or milliliters for liquid cosmetics.

Both the FDCA and FPLA require that the name and the place of business of the manufacturer, distributor, or packer must appear on both the inner and outer cosmetic containers. The place of business must include the city, state, and zip code. A street address is required only if it does not appear in a local telephone directory.

For products not sold at retail and for free samples, ingredient statements are not mandatory.

For products intended for retail sale, FDA requires ingredient labeling under the authority of the FPLA. Consequently, the ingredient declaration must appear on the outer container only. Cosmetic ingredients must be listed "in descending order of predominance" on "an appropriate information panel." For products not sold at retail and for free samples, ingredient statements are not mandatory.

There are two exceptions to the listing of all ingredient names. First, flavors and fragrances may be listed generically rather than by "name." As a result, the term "fragrance" or "flavor" may appear in the ingredient declaration in descending order of predominance. The second exception is when FDA has granted a manufacturer's petition for a trade secret exemption. If trade secret status is granted for the ingredient, the words "and other ingredient(s)" must appear at the end of the ingredient statement.

Ingredients must be listed by established name. FDA regulations identify a priority list of sources to determine the appropriate name for an individual cosmetic ingredient. Unless FDA has established a name by regulation, CTFA's[3] *International Cosmetic Ingredient Dictionary and Handbook* is the primary source for an "adopted name." If an ingredient does not appear in the CTFA dictionary, alternative sources are listed in order of priority such as the U.S. Pharmacopoeia and others. Only if the ingredient does not appear in the recognized sources can the manufacturer choose to use a name generally recognized by consumers or, in the absence of that, a chemical or other technical name.

Warning statements on cosmetic labels are required under the authority of the FDCA "whenever necessary or appropriate to prevent a health hazard that may be associated with the products." Warnings must appear on both the inner and outer containers, be prominent and conspicuous, and meet minimum type-size requirements. FDA regulations require warnings with specific language for cosmetics in self-pressurized containers (e.g., aerosols), feminine deodorant sprays, certain bubble baths, and cosmetics that have not been substantiated adequately for safety. In addition, the FDCA requires a specific warning for coal tar hair dyes. FDA does not require specific flammability warnings for cosmetics, including aerosol or alcohol-based cosmetics, but many companies include such warnings voluntarily.

Warning statements on cosmetic labels are required under the authority of the FDCA "whenever necessary or appropriate to prevent a health hazard that may be associated with the products."

Packaging

There are strict federal prohibitions against misleading packaging in consumer products, and specifically, "nonfunctional slack fill," which is the impermissible empty space between the actual container capacity and the volume of the product contained therein.

The Federal Food, Drug, and Cosmetic Act and the Fair Packaging and Labeling Act both contain general prohibitions against packaging that is made, formed, or filled as to be misleading. The FPLA further states that a package shall be deemed "misleading" if it contains nonfunctional slack fill, which it defines as a package filled to substantially less than its capacity for reasons other than a) protection of the contents, or b) the requirements of machines used for enclosing the contents in such package. (FPLA, § 5(c)(4).) It also authorized FDA to adopt regulations to "prevent the nonfunctional slack fill of packages" containing food, drugs, devices, or cosmetics, and FDA eventually promulgated such regulations in 1994, which included several additional reasons (i.e., "safe harbors") why slack fill might be permissible in a container. (See 21 C.F.R. 100.100.)

California has its own prohibition on the use of nonfunctional slack fill, which became a basis for litigation against manufacturers. As lawsuits began to proliferate against consumer product companies, the cosmetics industry took steps to negotiate slack fill "enforcement" guidelines with the California Attorney General's office, the District Attorneys Association, the California Department of Food and Agriculture, and the California Association of Weight and Measures Officials. On April 21, 1988, new enforcement guidelines went into effect that expanded the number of "safe harbor" exemptions from two to 15; and in 1997, the California legislature codified the enforcement guidelines' exemptions (at Business and Professions Code § 12606 and Health & Safety Code § 110375).

Unfortunately, in 2013, almost 16 years after the enforcement guidelines were codified, companies suddenly face renewed enforcement actions in California for alleged nonfunctional slack fill in their product packaging. The reason for the renewed enforcement efforts were, ostensibly, that packaging with non-functional slack fill was misleading, *per se*, even if it met one of the 15 exemptions, and thus violated the statute. California allows district attorney offices to retain penalties recouped for investigating slack fill violations, further fueling the new spate of lawsuits.

The cosmetics industry, through the Personal Care Products Council, successfully worked with California Senator Correa to introduce, and eventually pass, a new law that clarified the application of the slack fill exemptions already codified in law. It stated that if a package satisfied one of the non-functional slack fill exemptions, the package was not *per se* misleading or deceptive.

Despite this, slack fill lawsuits continue to be filed in California, albeit less frequently; companies doing business in California should be aware of this fact when developing product packaging.

CONCLUSION

In sum, safety substantiation by cosmetic manufacturers of their ingredients and products and proper labeling remain the cornerstones of the regulatory scheme governing cosmetic products. These longstanding requirements, together with the voluntary industry reporting and registration programs, have rendered cosmetics the safest of all of the FDA-regulated product categories.

Endnotes

1. "Soaps" are not considered a cosmetic and, therefore, are exempt from all provisions of the FDCA. Soap products must, however, comply with the Federal Trade Commission's regulations issued under the Fair Packaging and Labeling Act (FPLA).
2. See 21 C.F.R. § 310.530 ("use of the word 'hormone' in the ... ingredient statement is an implied drug claim").
3. The Personal Care Products Council was formerly known as the Cosmetic, Toiletry and Fragrance Association (CTFA). FDA has not updated its regulations to reflect this name change.

Chapter 11

The Regulation of Foods and Food Additives

*Daniel A. Kracov & Raqiyyah R. Pippins, Arnold & Porter Kaye Scholer LLP, Washington, D.C.**

Key Points

- Although the Food and Drug Administration (FDA) has primary authority over the regulation of most foods, the U.S. Department of Agriculture (USDA) regulates meat and poultry products, the Alcohol and Tobacco Tax and Trade Bureau regulates alcoholic beverages, and the Federal Trade Commission (FTC) has jurisdiction over food advertising.

- Adulteration is the central concept underlying FDA's regulation of the safety of food products. There are a number of statutory bases for a food to be adulterated, including the presence of poisonous or deleterious substances, insanitary practices in food processing, or the use of unapproved food additives. The Food Safety Modernization Act, passed by Congress in December 2010, greatly expanded FDA's authority over the safety and security of foods and FDA is implementing regulations related to ensuring the safety of both transported and imported foods.

- Under the Food Quality Protection Act, a special regulatory framework applies to pesticides in food. The Environmental Protection Agency registers pesticide products and sets tolerances for the presence of pesticide residues in food products. These tolerances are then enforced by FDA.

- In July 2017, the National Bioengineered Food Disclosure Standard amended the Agricultural Marketing Act of 1946 to require the Secretary of Agriculture to establish a national disclosure standard for bioengineered foods. The amendment was passed to preempt state legislation related to food biotechnology labeling. The bill provides USDA two years to develop specific rules related to the labeling of food products containing bioengineered or "genetically modified organism (GMO)" ingredients.

- Misbranding is the statutory term for violations relating to the labels and labeling of food products, as opposed to actual composition and safety. The central standard in the Federal Food, Drug, and Cosmetic Act (FDCA) permits FDA to deem a product misbranded if its "labeling is false or misleading in any particular."

* The author wishes to thank Joshua Glasser for his contributions to prior versions of this chapter while an associate at Arnold & Porter LLP.

Key Points, continued

- FDA and USDA administer extensive regulations governing the labeling of food products, including the basic components of the label, mandatory nutrition labeling, and complex rules governing the nutrient content and health claims. In May 2016, FDA published two final rules revising nutritional labeling requirements, which impact both the design (and content) of the Nutrition Facts Label as well as the serving sizes upon which the labeling is based.
- Dietary supplement products are regulated under the FDCA as amended by the Dietary Supplement Health and Education Act of 1994. Those amendments provide a separate definition for dietary supplements, as well as special rules governing the safety and labeling claims for such products.

INTRODUCTION

Foods represent the most basic of the Food and Drug Administration's (FDA's) public health responsibilities: ensuring that what is eaten on a daily basis is both wholesome and fairly represented to the public. This responsibility requires an understanding and careful balance of many factors, including chemical and biological safety risks, evolving information on nutrition and health, food marketing concerns and, more recently, food supply security—all within an increasingly complex statutory framework.

AGENCY JURISDICTION

An article is a "food" if it is used for human or animal food or drink, if it is a chewing gum, or if it is used as a component of any food.

The Federal Food, Drug, and Cosmetic Act (FDCA) gives FDA jurisdiction to regulate most foods in interstate commerce. Under FDCA § 201(f), an article is a "food" if it is used for human or animal food or drink, if it is a chewing gum, or if it is used as a component of any food. This is not necessarily a commonsense definition. For FDCA purposes, a food can include items that are not intended for consumption, such as seeds and rejected eggs. Raw, unprocessed food substances may or may not be foods. For example, although inedible green coffee beans were found to be a food within the statutory definition, *U.S. v. Green Coffee Beans*, 188 F.2d. 555 (2d Cir. 1951), the agency does not consider raw sugar to be a food because it contains certain impurities that can be removed only by the refining process. The agency also construes the term "food" to encompass substances migrating to food from food-contact articles such as containers and cutting surfaces.

In addition to the FDCA, there are other important food regulatory authorities at the federal level. The production and labeling of most meat and poultry products are regulated by the U.S. Department of Agriculture (USDA) under the Federal Meat Inspection Act and the Poultry Products Inspection Act. USDA exercises exclusive jurisdiction over the inspection of meat products until they leave a plant, but FDA and USDA have concurrent jurisdiction over misbranding and adulteration of meat products after inspection. Under an agreement between the agencies, FDA generally informs the USDA's Food Safety and Inspection Service (FSIS) when an apparent violation is encountered involving meat or poultry products, and usually will not initiate action against such products. USDA also regulates the production of eggs and egg products under the Egg Products Inspection Act. FDA has jurisdiction over game meats, such as deer and rabbit, as well as seafood products. FDA also regulates food products containing a relatively small proportion of meat—such as a dressing with bacon bits—interpreted as less than or equal to 3 percent meat.

FDA shares regulatory authority over alcoholic beverages with the Department of Treasury's Alcohol and Tobacco Tax and Trade Bureau (TTB). Although FDA may regulate ingredients used in alcoholic beverages, TTB generally is responsible for regulation of alcoholic beverage labeling, and has primary responsibility for recalls of alcoholic beverages.

The Federal Trade Commission (FTC) has primary responsibility over food advertising. The FTC frequently takes enforcement action in specific cases of deceptive food advertising, particularly with respect to weight loss and health-related claims, and routinely consults with FDA when such advertising raises issues of safety or nutrition.

Food Safety

The regulation of food safety under the FDCA centers around the legal definition of "adulteration." The term is defined by a range of acts specified in the FDCA that cause a food to be adulterated and, therefore, in violation of the statute.

Food safety, under the Federal Food, Drug, and Cosmetic Act, focuses on the legal definition of adulteration.

Poisonous or Deleterious Substances

The first adulteration provision under the FDCA is found in section 402(a)(1), which incorporates two standards under which a food may be deemed adulterated:

> If it bears or contains any poisonous or deleterious substance which may render it injurious to health; but in case the substance is not an added substance such food shall not

be considered adulterated under this clause if the quantity of such substance in such food does not ordinarily render it injurious to health.

This is the primary provision used by FDA to regulate the safety and purity of whole foods as opposed to the discrete ingredients added to foods.

The first part of the standard is much broader than it appears, for the term "added" can include the artificial introduction of a substance into a food by indirect means. Thus, in *United States v. Anderson Seafoods*, 622 F.2d 157 (5th Cir. 1980), the court determined that if a portion of the total amount of mercury found in swordfish resulted from industrial pollution, then all of the mercury in that product could be treated as an added substance subject to the "may render injurious" standard. Although the mere presence of an added poisonous or deleterious substance in a food does not satisfy the "may render" standard for proof of adulteration, FDA typically is given broad deference in its construction of the standard. *United States v. Lexington Mill & Elevator Co.*, 232 U.S. 399 (1914). Any "added" substance potentially could be subject to this standard, including microbial contamination.

The second part of section 402(a)(1), the "ordinarily render injurious to health" standard, is rather narrow in comparison. This provision applies to substances that are inherent in whole foods, such as toxins naturally present in fruits and vegetables. Such substances must be shown to be harmful before they result in food adulteration. As a result of the broad construction of the "may render" standard for "added" substances, this basis for adulteration is rarely invoked.

Unavoidable Contaminants

A food bearing or containing a poisonous substance is not considered adulterated if the quantity of the added substance is within an established tolerance level.

Under FDCA § 402(a)(2), a food is adulterated if it contains any avoidable added poisonous or deleterious substance that is "unsafe" within the meaning of FDCA § 406. An "unsafe" substance under section 406 is "any poisonous or deleterious substance added to any food, except where such substance is required in the production thereof or cannot be avoided by good manufacturing practice."

Section 406 permits FDA to establish tolerances for such "unavoidable contaminants." Such tolerances may limit the quantity of the substance in or on the food to the extent necessary for the protection of public health. If a tolerance is in effect, a food bearing or containing the poisonous substance is not considered adulterated if the quantity of the added substance is within the tolerance level. This tolerance provision permits the agency to take into account not just the presence of the poisonous or deleterious substance in the particular food in question, but the "other ways in which the consumer may be affected by the same or other deleterious substances."

Section 406 tolerances may be developed only through formal rulemaking, a time-consuming and resource-intensive process. As a result, the agency generally has adopted "action levels," which technically are nonbinding enforcement guidelines that identify levels of contamination above which FDA may bring an enforcement action. Both tolerances and action levels are based on the unavoidability of the added substances, and they do not establish a permissible level of contamination where the added substance is avoidable.

The agency also may establish "regulatory limits" through informal rulemaking, representing the level at which the agency would consider a food adulterated under section 402(a)(1). Such a regulatory limit may be appropriate where a substance cannot be avoided by current Good Manufacturing Practices (cGMPs) or there is insufficient information to establish a tolerance.

Filthy, Putrid, or Decomposed Substances

A food may be considered adulterated under FDCA § 402(a)(3) "if it consists in whole or in part of any filthy, putrid, or decomposed substance." As a practical matter, virtually any natural food product will have some level of filth—whether mold or insect parts— that has little or no impact on its safety or quality. The courts have tried to give these statutory terms their "usual and ordinary meaning," but with little consistency. Thus, in *United States v. Tomato Paste*, 22 F. Supp. 515 (E.D. Pa. 1938), the presence of worm fragments rendered tomato paste filthy, while in *United States v. Canned Tomato Paste*, 236 F.2d 208 (7th Cir. 1956), a paste that had a small number of insect fragments, fly eggs, and rodent hairs was not adulterated.

Although FDA does not have authority to set tolerances for decomposition or filth in food, the agency has developed "defect action level" guidances.

The agency does not have authority to set tolerances for decomposition or filth. Nevertheless, to bring some consistency to this area, and based on its enforcement discretion under the FDCA, the agency has developed "defect action levels." Defect action levels are guidances that indicate levels of filth, mold, and other contaminants that are not likely, taken alone, to result in an enforcement action, and can be achieved by applying cGMPs. It is important to note that a defect action level cannot be met by blending highly contaminated food with uncontaminated food, for FDA considers the finished product to be adulterated regardless of the net level of contamination.

Containers

Under FDCA § 402(a)(6), a food may also be adulterated if it is in a container that "is composed, in whole or in part, of any poisonous or deleterious substance which may render the contents injurious to health." This provision has rarely been invoked by FDA, which typically relies upon its other adulteration and indirect additive authorities.

Unfit for Food

A food may also be adulterated "if it is otherwise unfit for food" under FDCA § 402(a)(3). This provision describes a condition in which a food is in an inedible state, and does not necessarily depend upon the presence of filth or decomposition. The "unfit for food" adulteration provision is based on the perception of the average consumer. For example, in *United States v. Herring Roe*, 87 F. Supp. 826 (D. Me. 1949), the court found that in order for a fish roe to be unfit for food, it must be so tough and rubbery that the average consumer under ordinary conditions could not eat it. This statutory basis for adulteration is rarely used, largely because other adulteration provisions are less subjective and easier to prove.

Sanitation/Good Manufacturing Practices

One of the most important adulteration provisions is FDCA § 402(a)(4), which deems a food to be adulterated "if it has been prepared, packed, or held under insanitary conditions whereby it may have been contaminated with filth, or whereby it may have been rendered injurious to health." This provision does not require FDA to prove that a food product has been contaminated or rendered injurious to health. Rather, the mere presence of the insanitary conditions and the possibility that those insanitary conditions may have resulted in the adulteration is enough to bring the charge. Typically, the agency looks for evidence of rodent droppings, insect parts, unscreened windows, or other insanitary practices where food is processed to bring a case under this provision.

FDA determined that one of the most effective ways to ensure sanitary conditions in food production was through controls on food manufacturing operations.

In 1967, FDA determined that one of the most effective ways to implement section 402, and thereby maintain a safe and sanitary food supply, would be through controls on manufacturing operations. That year, the agency published the first set of proposed food cGMP rules. After many revisions and several unsuccessful lawsuits challenging FDA's authority to promulgate the regulations, the cGMP rules have become an established condition of doing business in the food industry, and are found at 21 C.F.R. Part 110. Dietary supplements cGMP rules are found at 21 C.F.R. Part 111. As discussed in the next section, however, FDA currently is implementing additional controls over food processing facilities—specifically, a requirement that food processors and other regulated facilities adopt a hazard-management and preventive controls plan. This requirement, when implemented, is expected to enhance, and not replace, the current food cGMPs.

The food cGMP regulations impose affirmative obligations on manufacturers to control the risk of chemical, microbiological, and other contamination of food. The underlying theory is that effective sanitation requires careful planning and vigilance in every phase of production, and that manufacturers must carry the primary responsibility for maintaining a safe and sanitary food supply. FDA recognizes, however, that manufacturing operations can vary widely and still be safe and sanitary, and the umbrella cGMP rules allow for some flexibility in methods of compliance. The rules are couched in terms of a mandatory result, together with permissive guidelines for methods of compliance.

The umbrella cGMPs touch every aspect of food production, including raw material inspection, employee training, plant design, equipment specifications and cleaning, quality control testing, and distribution of finished products. While recordkeeping requirements exist in other areas, FDA did not impose specific recordkeeping requirements in general food cGMPs. Daily production logs, manuals, and other written records, however, provide proof to an FDA inspector that a company's compliance programs exist. The inspector then can verify that the written program reflects that company's actual, current practices.

"Umbrella" cGMP regulations address:
- *personnel practices*
- *plant design*
- *equipment specifications and cleaning*
- *production controls*
- *quality control testing*
- *product distribution*

The cGMP regulations require plant managers to take precautions to ensure that food products are not contaminated by employees. Four requirements are prescribed with regard to personnel practices: 1) any person with evidence of disease must be excluded from any operation where he or she may come into contact, either directly or indirectly, with food; 2) employees must maintain proper hygiene, including hand washing; 3) employees must be trained in sanitary practices; and 4) employees must be adequately supervised.

Under the food cGMPs, manufacturing facilities must be designed, constructed, and maintained to protect against contamination of food. The regulations provide a partial checklist of points for plant managers to follow, setting forth requirements for the maintenance of grounds, construction of physical plants, adequate lighting and ventilation, pest control, use and storage of chemicals, water supply and plumbing, and waste removal.

The cGMP regulations also govern construction, cleaning, and maintenance of equipment. Manufacturers must use only tools that can be properly cleaned and maintained, and must protect them from corrosion or contamination. Conveyor belts and other manufacturing systems, freezer and cold storage systems, compressed air cleaning systems, and instruments for measuring and regulating manufacturing conditions (e.g., temperature, acidity, and water flow) must be well maintained.

Other cGMP provisions address production controls, including inspection of raw materials, in-process monitoring, and storage and transport. Manufacturers must adhere to adequate sanitation principles in all production procedures, including receiving, inspecting, transporting, preparing, manufacturing, packaging, and storing foods. To meet the prescribed quality control standards, manufacturers must periodically test their products for chemical, microbial, or extraneous material contamination, and either reject or reprocess any products that they determine to be contaminated. Similarly, raw materials must be inspected to ensure that they are clean and suitable for processing, and must be stored properly to avoid contamination and minimize deterioration. Moreover, manufacturers must monitor such factors as time, temperature, humidity, and pH to ensure that mechanical breakdowns, delays, and temperature fluctuations do not contribute to the decomposition or contamination of food. The rule also details specific techniques for preventing and minimizing microbiological contamination of batters and sauces, refrigerated foods, and acidified and dehydrated foods. Finished food must be transported and stored under conditions that will protect it against contamination and deterioration of the food and the container.

Evolution of Food Safety Measures

A primary criticism of FDA's historical regulatory approach to food safety has been that it is primarily reactive and not sufficiently focused on the prevention of food-safety-related incidents. However, recent years have seen major changes in food regulation. Most importantly, a critical new law was enacted in this area: the Food Safety Modernization Act (FSMA), signed into law in January 2011. FSMA was intended to reposition FDA as a proactive regulator focused on food safety prevention rather than remediation. The law greatly expands FDA's authority over the safety and security of regulated foods, and several aspects, such as enhanced registration requirements, an increased focus on inspections and food imports, and new mandatory recall authority, are discussed later in this chapter. However, a critical issue is whether FDA will have sufficient resources to fully implement FSMA's provisions. The law requires FDA to undertake an enormous array of rulemaking and guidance development processes, and then engage corresponding oversight and enforcement activities.

A key feature of FSMA is that food processing, shipping, and other regulated facilities will be required to adopt a comprehensive hazard-management and preventive controls plan.

A key feature of FSMA is that food processing, shipping, and other regulated-facilities will be required to adopt a comprehensive hazard-management and preventive controls plan. See FDCA § 418. It is expected that this new requirement will not replace the "umbrella" food cGMPs discussed above; rather, FDA has stated that the food cGMPs likely will serve as the foundation for a preventive controls plan. In September 2015, FDA issued its final preventive controls for human food rule, which require food facilities to have a written plan in place to identify potential hazards, put in place steps to address them, verify that the steps are working, and outline how to correct any problems that arise.

The requirement for preventive controls parallels Hazard Analysis and Critical Control Points (HACCP), which FDA currently requires of seafood processors (21

C.F.R. Part 123) and juice processors (21 C.F.R. Part 120), and which USDA's FSIS requires of meat and poultry processors. HACCP is a preventive strategy that is based on the development by the food producer of a plan that anticipates food safety hazards and identifies the specific critical points in the production process where a failure would likely result in a hazard being created or allowed to persist. Such critical control points are monitored systematically, and corrective action is taken when control over those points is lost.

Under FSMA, regulated facilities are required to evaluate and prepare written analyses of known or reasonably foreseeable food safety hazards that could affect food manufactured, processed, packed, transported, or held there (such as chemical hazards, pesticides, parasites, and allergens, whether unintentionally or intentionally introduced) at least every three years or sooner, as appropriate. Facilities must then implement preventive controls to minimize or eliminate such hazards, monitor the effectiveness of such controls, take corrective action as needed, and maintain documentation of the controls.

FSMA also imposes requirements applicable to on-farm production. Historically, farms have been exempt from many FDA requirements (including facility registration and cGMP requirements) or otherwise subject to less intensive regulation.

FSMA, however, required FDA to establish science-based minimum standards for safe production and harvesting of fruits and vegetables (raw agricultural commodities) for which FDA determines such standards minimize the risk of serious adverse health consequences or death. See FDCA § 419. In November 2015, FDA issued its final rule on produce safety, which implements section 105 of FSMA. The rule applies to both domestically produced and imported produce, and requires farms that grow, harvest, pack, or hold fruits and vegetables covered by the rule to follow standards designed to prevent microbiological contamination of their produce.

FDA has also taken steps to increase its regulatory oversight of food transportation activities by finalizing the rulemaking process to implement the Sanitary Food Transportation Act of 2005 (SFTA), which shifted authority for the regulation of sanitary food transportation practice from the Department of Transportation to FDA. The SFTA gives broad authority to FDA to regulate the transportation of human and animal food products. See FDCA § 416. In April 2016, FDA issued a final rule on sanitary transport of food, which established requirements to help ensure that human and animal food are not adulterated because they have been transported under insanitary conditions such as inadequate refrigeration and unclean vehicles.

The Sanitary Food Transportation Act of 2005 gives broad authority to FDA to regulate the transportation of human and animal food products.

FOOD ADDITIVES

In the decades after the passage of the FDCA, the number of chemicals added to foods for functional purposes increased enormously, yet there was no mechanism for FDA premarket clearance based on a safety evaluation. To take action against an ingredient in the product, FDA could rely only on its evaluation of the product, already on the market, under its general adulteration standards for added substances. In 1954, congressional hearings before Congressman James Delaney (D-NY) focused on the safety of additives in the food supply, revealing that only 200 of the 1,400 chemicals known to be added to foods had been shown to be safe. This uncertainty suited neither FDA nor food companies, for there were no clear additive safety standards.

The need for food additive regulation led to the passage of the Food Additives Amendment of 1958.

The consensus regarding the need for food additive regulation led to the passage of the Food Additives Amendment of 1958, in which Congress provided the agency with a framework for food additive regulation that mandated proof of safety prior to marketing. Under section 201(s) of the FDCA, the term "food additive"

> ... means any substance the intended use of which results or may reasonably be expected to result, directly or indirectly, in its becoming a component or otherwise affecting the characteristics of any food (including any substance intended for use in producing, manufacturing, packing, processing, preparing, treating, packaging, transporting, or holding food; and including any source of radiation intended for any such use), if such substance is not generally recognized, among experts qualified by scientific training and experience to evaluate its safety, as having been adequately shown through scientific procedures (or, in a case of a substance used in food prior to January 1, 1958, through either scientific procedures or experience based on common use in food) to be safe under the conditions of its intended use.

This definition is quite broad, encompassing any substance that may reasonably be expected to directly or indirectly affect or become a part of a food. Such substances are presumed to be unsafe—and therefore adulterate a food—unless the additive has been the subject of a premarket approval by FDA.

There are significant exceptions to the food additive definition, most notably generally recognized as safe (GRAS) substances, pesticide chemical residues, and dietary supplements. One additional, but relatively small, category of excepted uses of such substances are those that are subject to a "prior sanction." Prior sanctioned substances are those that were the subject of FDA or USDA

safety opinions prior to 1958 and are "grandfathered" as part of the 1958 legislation. Such substances are still subject to the general adulteration standards and,
in large part, have been eclipsed by the premarket approval and GRAS framework over time.

Any food that bears or contains any food additive that is unsafe within the
meaning of FDCA § 409 (i.e., unapproved or used outside the parameters of an
approval) is considered adulterated. Section 409 provides a formal petition process for the approval of food additives by the agency, which applies a science-
based safety standard to review of food additive petitions. At a minimum, a
food additive petition must include the name of the substance; its chemical
identity and composition; the proposed conditions of its use; proposed labeling; physical effects data; technical effects (and levels) data; information on the
manufacturing process, facilities, and controls; methods of detecting and determining the quantity of the additive in the finished food; the results of safety
investigations; and an environmental assessment. 21 C.F.R. Part 171.

Any food that bears or contains any food additive that is unsafe is considered adulterated.

The term "safe" for purposes of food additive approval means that there is a
reasonable certainty in the minds of competent scientists that a substance is
not harmful under its intended conditions of use. The agency considers the
probable levels of consumption of the additive, and the cumulative effect of the
additive and related substances in the diet in arriving at its determination. The
toxicological testing requirements for food additives are the subject of a guidance document, known as the "Red Book." FDA will calculate the exposure to
the additive based upon an estimated daily intake that is within an acceptable
daily intake (ADI) derived from data on toxicological effects and the determination of a "no observable adverse effect level" to which an appropriate safety
factor (typically 1/100) is applied. If FDA finds an additive to be safe, it issues a
regulation specifying the conditions under which the additive may safely be
used. See 21 C.F.R. Parts 172-178.

Although food additives are subject to a general safety standard, there is a significant exception. Section 409(c)(3)(a) of the FDCA contains what is commonly
referred to as the "Delaney Clause," which provides that "[n]o additive shall
be deemed to be safe if it is found to induce cancer when ingested by man or
animal, or if it is found after tests which are appropriate for the evaluation of the
safety of food additives, to induce cancer in man or animal."

Under the Delaney Clause, no additive is deemed safe if it induces cancer when ingested by humans or animals, or is found after appropriate testing to induce cancer in humans or animals.

Due to the absolute nature of the Delaney Clause, FDA has made significant
efforts to avoid it by adopting policies of construction and interpretation. One
statutory exception is the DES Proviso, which provides that the Delaney Clause
does not prohibit the use of a compound if "no residue" of that compound
administered to food-producing animals can be "found" in meat, milk, or eggs

by an approved analytical method. FDCA § 409(c)(3)(A). The agency also may make a scientific determination that a substance does not technically or directly "induce" cancer.

FDA interprets the term "additive" in the Delaney Clause to apply only to the additive as a whole and not its unavoidable, nonfunctional constituents. 47 Fed. Reg. 14,464 (Apr. 2, 1982). If carcinogenic constituents of an additive are detected, FDA conducts a risk assessment under the general safety standard for food additives. FDA first applied this "constituents policy" in its 1982 approval of the color additive D&C Green No. 6, which contains the carcinogenic contaminant n-toluene. The policy has been applied on numerous occasions since then, and has been challenged and upheld in court. Other efforts by FDA to avoid the Delaney Clause, however, such as the argument that it is too rigid and should be subject to a *de minimis* exception, have been rejected by the courts.

The Delaney Clause has consistently been criticized as outdated in light of current methods of assessing the risk of carcinogenicity. Nevertheless, although its applicability to pesticide residues was eliminated as part of the 1996 enactment of the Food Quality Protection Act (FQPA), the Delaney Clause remains in force in the food and color additive areas.

INDIRECT ADDITIVES/FOOD CONTACT SUBSTANCES

The food additive definition is extremely broad, extending beyond substances intentionally added for a functional purpose to include even nonedible items— such as adhesives, packaging, and food contact surface materials—that "may reasonably be expected" to become a component or otherwise affect the characteristics of a food. These migrating indirect additives generally are subject to the same food additive and GRAS frameworks applicable to direct food additives.

FDA has established a process for determining when the likelihood or extent of migration to food of a substance used in a food contact article is so trivial as not to require food additive approval. This "threshold of regulation" exempts from food additive regulation those non-carcinogenic substances in food contact articles that result in a dietary concentration of the substance of 0.5 parts per billion (ppb) or less. Also exempted are regulated direct food additives when used in food contact articles at levels that result in a dietary exposure of 1 percent or less of the ADI for the additive as determined by the agency. 21 C.F.R. § 170.39. Such substances may not have a technical effect in the food, and must be the subject of a submission to FDA documenting eligibility for the terms of the threshold regulation, including an environmental assessment.

The 1997 Food and Drug Administration Modernization Act (FDAMA) created a new statutory classification to encompass indirect additives that does not require premarket approval. This class, referred to as "food contact substances," is defined as "any substance intended for use as a component of materials used in manufacturing, packing, packaging, transporting, or holding food if such use is not intended to have any technical effect in such food." Food contact substances typically consist of materials used in food packaging such as plastics, paper, and adhesives, but can also include substances used in the manufacture of food.

FDAMA created a new statutory classification to encompass indirect additives that does not require premarket approval.

Section 409(a)(3) provides that a food additive will not be deemed unsafe if it is a food contact substance and the substance and its use have been approved in a food additive regulation like any other substance, or it is the subject of a notification that has become effective. Under section 409(h), manufacturers may file a notification with FDA regarding a food contact substance 120 days before its introduction into interstate commerce. The notification must identify the food contact substance and its intended use, as well as a description of the manufacturer's determination that the intended use is safe, including the information that forms the basis for that conclusion. All such information will be kept confidential by FDA for 120 days after receipt, at which time it will be available to the public, except for trade secrets or confidential commercial information.

In May 2002, FDA issued regulations governing this provision and a guidance document for industry on submitting food contact notifications (FCNs). 67 Fed. Reg. 35,724 (May 21, 2002) (codified at 21 C.F.R. Part 170, Subpart D); "Guidance for Industry: Preparation of Premarket Notifications" (May 2002). A manufacturer of a food contact substance is required to submit a FCN for new uses of food contact substances that are food additives. A notification is effective for the manufacturer that submitted the FCN—or anyone who can demonstrate that the food contact substance being marketed has been manufactured or supplied by the manufacturer—where the food contact substance is being used under the conditions that are the subject of the FCN. A notification becomes effective 120 days after receipt by FDA, at which time the food contact substance may be distributed in interstate commerce, unless FDA makes a determination that, based on the data and information before it, the use of the substance has not been shown to be safe and a food additive petition should be filed requesting that a regulation be issued.

Generally Recognized as Safe Substances

In framing the food additive definition, Congress recognized that there was a range of food substances that should not be the subject of the petition requirement. Such substances are not merely safe, they are generally recognized as safe (GRAS). The burden of demonstrating such GRAS status falls upon the proponent of the GRAS use of an ingredient. Moreover, the general recognition of safety is not based on the opinion of the lay population—it is based on the views of experts qualified to evaluate the safety of foods. Although unanimity is not required, GRAS status must at least be a consensus opinion of qualified experts.

The passage of the Food Additives Amendment in 1958 presented a significant transitional problem. Many ingredients, including common foods such as vinegar, vegetable oil, salts, spices, flavors, and gums, did not have a clear regulatory status. FDA clarified the status of those substances by publishing the "GRAS List" to which it subsequently added other categories of substances that the agency deemed to be subject to the GRAS exemption.

In 1970, as a result of banning cyclamate, an artificial sweetener previously considered to be GRAS, due to concern about carcinogenicity, the agency initiated a comprehensive study of substances presumed to be GRAS. In this "GRAS review," FDA evaluated a broad range of substances using contemporary scientific standards. It then issued regulations that affirmed the GRAS status of those ingredients where appropriate. FDA also promulgated a series of regulations setting forth the criteria for determining GRAS status, the category of food substances it considers eligible for GRAS status or GRAS affirmation, and the procedures for petitioning the agency to affirm the GRAS status of other substances. 21 C.F.R. §§ 170.30, 170.35.

Until recent years, a manufacturer could seek, through filing a GRAS affirmation petition, a formal determination from FDA that a given substance is GRAS and therefore appropriate for use in food without being approved as a food additive. See 21 C.F.R. Parts 184 and 186. This nonstatutory process generally proved interminable, and was a low priority for FDA's overburdened staff. FDA has long acknowledged, however, that GRAS status may be determined without formal FDA action (referred to as "self-determination of GRAS status"). Thus, the GRAS exception from the food additive definition creates a separate regulatory category for substances which, although intentionally added to food, are not subject to mandatory premarket review.

In making a GRAS self-determination, a company assumes a risk that FDA may not agree with its determination, and may seek withdrawal of the product through informal means or by resort to its seizure or injunctive authorities. This risk usually is minimized by having the product and its planned use(s) reviewed by independent scientific consultants and legal counsel.

The process of determining whether a substance is GRAS involves evaluation of the same safety issues as are raised with respect to food additives, as well as a determination that the terms for GRAS status have been satisfied. For substances used in food prior to January 1, 1958, GRAS status may be established through "experience based upon common use in food." For all other substances, GRAS status must be established through safety data collected by "scientific procedures"; i.e., studies. Experience data may serve, however, to confirm the findings of these studies, including information on use of the substance abroad.

The process of determining whether a substance is GRAS involves evaluation of the same safety issues as are raised with respect to food additives, as well as a determination that the terms for GRAS status have been satisfied.

"Scientific procedures" are defined by FDA to include "those human, animal, analytical, and other scientific studies, whether published or unpublished, appropriate to establish the safety of a substance." 21 C.F.R. § 170.3(h). The GRAS eligibility regulation further states that general recognition of safety through scientific procedures shall "require the same quantity and quality of evidence" as is required to obtain food additive approval and "shall ordinarily be based upon published studies which may be corroborated by unpublished studies and other data and information." 21 C.F.R. § 170.3(b).

It must be remembered, however, that the safety of a substance is evaluated within the context of its intended use. Thus, while a general purpose food ingredient may be deemed or affirmed as GRAS without any limitation on how it may be used, most GRAS determinations are made in the context of one or more specified uses. GRAS substances must comply with applicable specifications, must perform an appropriate function in the food, and must be present in the food at a level no higher than necessary to accomplish that purpose.

For a substance to be GRAS, the pertinent scientific community must be familiar with the substance and believe it to be safe. In other words, GRAS status depends on showing not only that a substance is safe, but also that it is widely viewed as such by experts in the field. FDA evaluates the qualifications of experts whose opinions are offered in support of GRAS status. The GRAS eligibility regulation repeats the statutory requirement that "general recognition of safety may be based only on the views of experts qualified by scientific training and experience to evaluate the safety of substances directly or indirectly added to food." 21 C.F.R. § 170.30(a). Thus, FDA effectively applies the concept of peer review to the scientist as well as to the science, and it relies on documented credentials as one factor in assessing the validity of studies and the integrity of other scientific evidence offered in support of GRAS status.

In 2016 FDA issued a final rule that amended and clarified the criteria for when the use of a substance in food for humans or animals is not subject to the premarket approval requirements due to GRAS status. The rule replaced the voluntary GRAS affirmation petition process with a voluntary notification procedure under which any person may notify FDA of a conclusion that a substance is GRAS under the conditions of its intended use. 81 Fed. Reg. 54,949 (August 17, 2016). Rather than publishing a regulation with a finding of safety as it purported to do under the prior system, FDA provides a response to the notice within 180 days.

The stated goal of the GRAS notification proposal is to increase the agency's awareness of private GRAS determinations, make the process by which FDA recognizes GRAS status more efficient, and reduce resources devoted to the non-statutory GRAS affirmation process. While FDA's response to such notices does not carry the same weight as a GRAS determination by FDA, it enables manufacturers who make their own GRAS determinations to ascertain the agency's position on the matter quickly. Concurrently, the proposal has intensified commercial pressure on those marketing GRAS ingredients to submit notifications to FDA in lieu of private determinations of GRAS status.

Color Additives

Color additives must be shown with reasonable certainty to pose no risk to human health, to accomplish an intended effect, and to not deceive consumers.

Color additives are subject to a separate statutory approval framework under the FDCA. Section 201(t) defines a "color additive" as any material that, when added to food, is capable of imparting color, except those that the Secretary of Health and Human Services, by regulation, determines are used "solely for a purpose or purposes other than coloring." FDCA § 721 provides a framework for the listing and certification of color additives that is similar to the premarket approval process for food additives. Color additives must be shown with reasonable certainty to pose no risk to human health, to accomplish an intended effect, and to not deceive consumers. Section 721 includes a Delaney Clause, although there is no exclusion for GRAS or prior sanctioned colors. Color additives may be subject to precise specifications, and FDA may subject color additives to batch certification to ensure that specifications are met.

Pesticide Residues

Historically, pesticide residues have presented a major regulatory problem. Until the passage of the FQPA in 1996, the Environmental Protection Agency (EPA) was responsible for setting tolerances for pesticide residue on raw agricultural commodities under FDCA § 408, which incorporated a risk-benefit standard. Although a "flow-through" proviso permitted levels of pesticides in processed foods up to the level permitted in raw agricultural commodities under section 408, EPA also set tolerances for pesticide residues that concentrated in processed foods under section 409 (the food additive provision). Those residues, however, were subject to the food additive Delaney Clause. As a result of the judicial rejection of EPA's policy of applying a *de minimis* standard to these residues, *Les v. Reilly*, 968 F.2d 985 (9th Cir. 1993), a number of tolerances for important pesticides were subject to revocation.

The FQPA redefined "pesticide chemical" in FDCA § 201(q)(1) to include any substance that is a pesticide within the meaning of the Federal Insecticide, Fungicide, and Rodenticide Act (FIFRA), including active and inert ingredients in the pesticide. A "pesticide residue" is defined in section 201(q)(2) as a residue in or on a raw agricultural commodity or processed food of a pesticide chemical, or any other added substance that is primarily the result of the metabolism or other degradation of a pesticide chemical. These changes took all pesticide residues out of the food additive definition and the food additive Delaney Clause. Instead, all tolerances for pesticide residues in a food must be established on the basis of a single safety standard that requires a reasonable certainty that no harm will result from an aggregate exposure to the pesticide chemical residue, including all anticipated dietary exposures and all other exposures for which there is reasonable information. FDCA § 408(b)(2)(A). Specific consideration also is given to exposures to infants and children, and the consideration of pesticide benefits in tolerance-setting is significantly limited to certain "eligible" residues.

All tolerances for pesticide residues in a food must be established on the basis of a single safety standard that requires a reasonable certainty that no harm will result from an aggregate exposure to the pesticide chemical residue, including all anticipated dietary exposures and all other exposures for which there is reasonable information.

The enforcement of tolerances for pesticide residues is now the responsibility of FDA, although EPA may initiate action if a violation of FIFRA is involved. The FQPA provides for civil penalties as an alternative method of taking enforcement action against the sale of a food that is adulterated by unsafe pesticide residues, although such penalties cannot be applied to farmers.

FOOD BIOTECHNOLOGY

The use of organisms to make food products, such as yogurt, represents one of the oldest of food technologies. A major scientific development in food science in the last decade, however, has been the application of new biotechnologies, including recombinant DNA techniques and cell fusion, to go beyond traditional methods and make direct genetic modifications to food sources. Food biotechnology, as well as animal cloning for agricultural purposes, led to a great deal of discussion and inquiries to FDA and state legislatures, leading to state legislation mandating disclosure requirements related to biotechnology.

In response, in July 2017, the National Bioengineered Food Disclosure Standard was signed into law, which amended the Agricultural Marketing Act of 1946 to require the Secretary of Agriculture to establish a national disclosure standard for bioengineered foods. While USDA has two years to issue a regulation to implement the law, the amendment immediately preempted state laws mandating disclosure of the use of biotechnology. FDA will continue to apply its general regulatory authorities to products of food biotechnology until formal guidance is provided by USDA.

FDA Policy Regarding Genetic Modification of Plant Varieties

In 1992, FDA issued a policy under which new plant varieties developed by application of genetic modification are regulated within the existing framework of the FDCA and FDA regulations. 57 Fed. Reg. 22,984 (May 29, 1992).

Food additive petitions are required in cases where the food differs in structure, function, or composition so significantly as to raise safety questions that warrant formal premarket review to ensure public health protection.

In general, FDA regulates foods derived from new plant varieties under the general adulteration standard, which requires the producer of a new food to evaluate its safety and ensure that FDA standards are met. FDA applies the food additive and GRAS frameworks to plant products derived from single gene transfers. Food additive petitions under section 409 of the FDCA are required in cases where the food differs in structure, function, or composition so significantly as to raise safety questions that warrant formal premarket review to ensure public health protection.

FDA has developed a decision tree approach that provides for the assessment of the new plant variety, the characteristics of the host and donor species, the nature of the genetic change, the identity and function of newly introduced substances, and unexpected or unintended effects that accompany genetic changes. Particular concerns that need to be assessed as part of this analysis include:

♦ toxins known to be characteristic of the host and donor species;

♦ the potential that food allergens would be transferred from one food source to another;

♦ the concentration and bioavailability of important nutrients for which a food crop is ordinarily consumed;

♦ the safety and nutritional value of newly introduced proteins; and

♦ the identity, composition, and nutritional value of modified carbohydrates, or fats and oils.

Originally, FDA administered a "voluntary" consultation system in which companies would decide whether to consult with the agency pursuant to the decision tree. FDA has since changed this approach, and companies must consult with the agency regarding their intent to market, at least 120 days before marketing. Based upon this notification FDA may determine that additional testing or labeling is necessary, or that a food additive filing may be required.

In 2006, FDA issued a guidance requesting that developers of new proteins in new plant varieties for food submit a safety evaluation to FDA prior to the stage of development where the protein could inadvertently enter the food supply. "Guidance for Industry: Recommendations for the Early Food Safety Evaluation of New Non-Pesticidal Proteins Produced by New Plant Varieties Intended for Food Use" (June 2006). A safety evaluation need not be submitted where a protein has been previously reviewed as part of a consultation and no safety concerns were identified, or where a protein has been part of a previous safety evaluation with no identified safety concerns and is later introduced into another plant species.

A safety evaluation should focus on whether the new protein is an allergen or a toxin, and should contain information including a description of its purpose or intended technical effect and a list of any identities and sources of the introduced genetic material. The guidance document states that FDA should respond within 120 days with the results of the safety evaluation.

With respect to labeling of genetically modified foods, FDA applies its general analysis under section 403(i) of the FDCA, which requires that the producer of a food product describe the product by its common or usual name, or, in the absence thereof, an appropriately descriptive term. In addition, under section 201(n), all food product labeling must reveal facts that are material in light of representations made or suggested by labeling or with respect to consequences that may result from use. In other words, a new name or a label disclosure is only required when the application of biotechnology alters a food's characteristics or composition to such a degree as to create an important consumer expectation or safety concern. A good example would be the need to disclose the introduction of a peanut protein into a tomato that could result in an allergic reaction in a susceptible population. FDA's historical approach will be augmented by USDA's implementation of the 2017 amendments to the Agricultural Marketing Act, which will require that manufacturers disclose the inclusion of genetically modified organisms in food. As noted above, USDA has two years from the passage of the statute to develop a regulatory scheme to implement the law. In January 2017, FDA issued a statement affirming that its position on bioengineered foods has not changed from the position stated in its 1992 statement of policy, but that in light of the National Bioengineered Food Disclosure Standard signed into law in July 2017, questions regarding future disclosure requirements for bioengineered food products or ingredients should be directed to USDA's Agricultural Marketing Service.

Cloning in Animal Species Used for Food

Animal cloning has raised public concerns, and FDA has conducted an in-depth analysis of animal cloning in the last several years. In 2001, FDA requested that livestock producers and researchers not introduce food from animal clones or their offspring into the food supply until FDA evaluated potential risks to consumers. FDA issued a draft assessment in 2006, and final risk assessment in January 2008, finding that meat and milk from clones of adult cattle, pigs, and goats, and their offspring, are as safe to eat as food from conventionally bred animals.

FDA issued a draft assessment in 2006, and final risk assessment in January 2008, finding that meat and milk from clones of adult cattle, pigs, and goats, and their offspring, are as safe to eat as food from conventionally bred animals.

The result of the FDA risk assessment on animal cloning is that FDA has lifted the voluntary moratorium on products from the offspring of cloned animals. USDA has requested, however, that the voluntary moratorium remain in place temporarily for products from cloned animals (but not the offspring of cloned animals) to provide for an orderly introduction of such products into the food supply. Neither FDA nor USDA is requiring labeling or any other additional measures for food from cattle, swine, and goat clones, or their offspring.

Genetically Engineered Animals Used for Food

On January 19, 2017, FDA released for public comment a draft revised Guidance for Industry (GFI) #187, "Regulation of Intentionally Altered Genomic DNA in Animals." The guidance applies to genetically engineered (GE) animals currently being developed for a number of uses based on the purpose of the genetic modification. In the guidance, FDA explains that a GE animal is an animal that contains an added recombinant DNA segment that is intended to alter the structure or function of the animal and, as such, FDA has taken the position that GE animals contain a new animal drug and will be regulated under the new animal drug provisions of the FDCA. The 2017 draft revised guidance expands the scope of the prior guidance to address animals with intentionally altered genomic DNA developed through use of genome editing technologies, as well as techniques such as rDNA in genetic engineering. Under this framework, in 2015 FDA determined that AquAdvantage® genetically altered salmon met the statutory requirements for approval. The agency found that the salmon are safe to eat, the introduced DNA is safe for the fish itself, and the salmon met the sponsor's claim about faster growth.

Economic Adulteration

The adulteration provisions of the FDCA are not limited to safety issues. "Economic" adulteration under section 402(b) can occur if:

♦ any valuable constituent has been in whole or in part omitted or abstracted; or

♦ any substance has been substituted wholly or in part; or

♦ damage or inferiority has been concealed in any manner; or

♦ any substance has been added or mixed or packed so as to increase its bulk or weight, or reduce its quality or strength, or make it appear better or greater value than it is.

Early cases in this area dealt with coloring foods in a manner that caused economic adulteration, such as the addition of pumpkin to bakery products to give the appearance of egg content. The addition of water to foods was—and remains—a popular approach to adulteration. Perhaps the most prominent example in recent years was the highly publicized case, *United States v. Beech-Nut Nutrition Corp.*, 871 F.2d 1181 (2d Cir. 1989), involving the economic adulteration of apple juice for babies with a substandard ingredient. In general, the economic adulteration provisions of the FDCA are used only when the agency cannot otherwise regulate non-safety-related aspects of food formulation.

In general, the economic adulteration provisions of the FDCA are used only when the agency cannot otherwise regulate non-safety-related aspects of food formulation.

Misbranding

Misbranding is the statutory term for FDCA violations relating to the labels and the labeling of a food product, as opposed to its actual composition and safety. The primary basis upon which a food may be deemed misbranded is if "its labeling is false or misleading in any particular" under section 403(a). A failure to reveal material facts under section 201(n) also can constitute misleading labeling under this standard. Other general bases on which FDA may make a misbranding finding include, in part:

Misbranding is the statutory term for FDCA violations relating to the labels and the labeling of a food product, as opposed to its actual composition and safety.

♦ If a food is "offered for sale under the name of another food." FDCA § 403(b).

♦ "If it is an imitation of another food, unless its label bears, in type of uniform size and prominence, the word 'imitation' and, immediately thereafter, the name of the food imitated." FDCA § 403(c). See later section in this chapter titled "Standards of Identity."

♦ If "its container is so made, formed, or filled as to be misleading." FDCA § 403(d).

315

Food Labeling

Two primary statutory authorities—the FDCA and the Fair Packaging and Labeling Act (FPLA)—govern the regulation of food labeling. "Label" is defined under section 201(k) as a display of written, printed, or graphic matter on the immediate container of any article. Under section 201(m), "labeling" is further defined to include all labels and other written, printed, or graphic matter on any article or any of its containers or wrappers, or accompanying such article. Thus, the FDCA requires information appearing on the label to also be included on the outside container or wrapper of the retail package. In contrast, requirements imposed solely by the FPLA apply only to the outside container or wrapper of the retail package.

Basic Components of the Food Label

Over the years, FDA has developed regulations pertaining to virtually every aspect of food labeling, including specifications for both mandatory and voluntary information. Moreover, a number of exemptions have been recognized to accommodate special packaging and marketing issues, specific product categories, and other attributes that may trigger specific labeling requirements. For example, products with nutrient content claims trigger specific referral and disclosure requirements. Drinks that purport to contain fruit juice must bear information regarding the percentage of juice in the product.

The regulations governing the basic components of the food label are found at 21 C.F.R. Part 101, Subpart A. These regulations specify two areas on a product's label where required information may appear: the Principal Display Panel (PDP) and the Information Panel (IP). The PDP is the part of the label most likely to be displayed, presented, shown, or examined by the consumer under normal and customary conditions of display for retail sale. The IP is that part of the label that is immediately contiguous and to the right of the PDP as observed by the consumer facing the PDP. If there is more than one PDP, each must contain the mandatory label information. Only one IP is necessary, however, even if there is more than one PDP. An IP is not required if all required information is placed on a PDP.

In general, FDA regulations require certain information to appear on the PDP; other information may appear on either the PDP or the IP. For example, the identity and net content statements must appear on the PDP. If an IP is used, all necessary information except the identity and content statements may appear on the IP. If the IP is too small, the information may be split between the IP and the PDP. No one item, however, may be split between the two panels (e.g., part of an ingredient statement on each panel).

Each aspect of the food label is subject to specific requirements. The following are the basic parameters for major components of the food label:

♦ An "identity statement" is the standardized, common, or usual name of the food, or a fanciful name generally used by the public for the particular product. The identity statement should identify accurately or describe either the basic nature of the product or its characterizing properties or ingredients, using simple and direct terms. When the nature of the product is obvious, a fanciful name commonly used by the public may serve as the identity statement.

♦ The "net quantity of contents statement" is the declaration in terms of weight, measure, or numerical count of the unit container and, where carton labeling is necessary, the numerical count and the total package content. The statement should be placed in the bottom 30 percent of the PDP as a distinct item, in the most appropriate units of both the English and metric systems.

♦ The "responsibility statement" states the name, street address, and zip code of the person who manufactures, packs, or distributes the product. In the case of a corporation, the actual corporate name must appear. If the particular business address appears in a current city directory or telephone directory, the street address may be omitted but the zip code must be included. If the principal place of business differs from the place of manufacture, packing, or distribution, only the principal place of business is required.

♦ The "ingredient statement" is a list of the product's ingredients by their common or usual name, in descending order of predominance by weight in the product (except for ingredients under 2 percent of the weight of the product).

♦ "Flavor labeling" details the type of flavoring of the product including natural, artificial, or a combination of the two. These labeling requirements are quite complex and require careful review. In general, if the label, labeling, or advertisement of a food makes any direct or indirect representation regarding a primary recognizable flavor, or if the manufacturer or distributor wishes to designate the flavor of the food by any means other than through the statement of ingredients, that flavor becomes the "characterizing flavor" for the purposes of flavor labeling. The choice of which terms and wording to employ in the flavor labeling depend on the type and number of flavors a product contains. If a food contains any artificial flavor that simulates, resembles, or reinforces the characterizing flavor, the name of the food must be accompanied by the name of the characterizing flavor, together with the word(s) "artificial" or "artificially flavored." Such labeling must precede or follow the characterizing flavor in the product, and is expressed as "artificial," "artificially flavored," etc., depending on the type of flavor(s) used (e.g., artificially orange flavored). The disclosure should appear on the PDP with the identity statement.

♦ Nutrition labeling must appear by way of a prescribed format that provides detailed "Nutrition Facts" on the product. The nutrition labeling requirements are reviewed in detail below.

♦ If any nutrient content claims are made, a disclosure statement referring to nutrition labeling of a specific size relative to the claim must be included along with the claim if there are other food constituents present at certain disclosure levels. Nutrient content claims are subject to specific definitions and are reviewed in detail below.

♦ Every article of foreign origin must be marked in a conspicuous place to indicate the English name of the country of origin.

♦ Ingredient Labeling

A food product is misbranded if the ingredients are not listed in descending order of predominance by weight, as such an ingredient statement is likely to confuse consumers. Ingredients that are present in amounts of 2 percent or less need not be listed in descending order if a qualifying statement such as "Contains _____ percent or less of _____" appears at the end of the ingredient statement, with the second blank filled in with the names of the ingredients present at less than 2 percent.

Each ingredient must be listed specifically by its common or usual name.

Each ingredient must be listed specifically by its common or usual name. Collective terms such as "artificial flavors," "natural flavors," "spices," and "artificial flavors," however, may be listed for those ingredients without further elaboration. FDA provides a definition for each of these terms, and lists those items that may be included under them in an ingredient statement. An ingredient statement for flavors is required in addition to any flavor labeling required in conjunction with the identity statement.

While flavors and spices may be listed generically in ingredient statements, certified colors must be identified individually. Certified colors added to foods are designated in the ingredient statement by a common or usual name (e.g., "FD&C Blue No. 1," "Blue 1," "Blue 1 Lake"). The terms "FD&C" and "No." may be omitted from the name of the color. A collective name, such as "artificial color" or "color added," may still be used to declare noncertified color additives, although many companies choose to list noncertified colors by their common or usual name (e.g., annatto, grape skin extract).

Preservatives must be identified in an ingredient statement, not only by the common or usual name of the preservative, but by a separate description of its function, e.g., "benzoate of soda—a preservative" or "stannous chloride to protect flavor." Incidental additives—those ingredients present in a food at insignificant levels and which do not have any technical or functional effect in the finished food—need not be included in the ingredient statement. There is a specific rule in the case of sulfites. If the sulfites have either a technical or functional effect on the product or are present in an amount greater than 10 parts per 1,000,000, then they are not considered incidental and must be included in the ingredient statement in the same manner as any other ingredient in the product.

The ingredient declaration may appear either on the PDP or the IP, but the entire statement must appear on a single panel.

♦ Allergens

Under the Food Allergen Labeling and Consumer Protection Act (FALCPA) of 2004, all packaged foods labeled on or after January 1, 2006, also must comply with food allergen labeling requirements set forth in FDCA § 403(w). Specifically, a food that is not a raw agricultural commodity and contains a "major food allergen"—defined as milk, egg, fish, crustacean shellfish, tree nuts, wheat, peanuts, and soybeans—is misbranded unless the label identifies, immediately after or adjacent to the list of ingredients, that the food "Contains" the food source from which the allergen is derived. These allergen labeling requirements apply to all foods regulated under the FDCA, including both domestically manufactured and imported products.

♦ Nutrition Labeling

In 1990, Congress passed the Nutrition Labeling and Education Act (NLEA) to require uniform nutrition labeling on most FDA-regulated packaged food products. Extensive regulations are found at 21 C.F.R. § 101.9. USDA has adopted parallel nutrition labeling and nutrient content claims regulations. The statute and regulations provide a number of exemptions from nutrition labeling requirements, which can be lost if claims are made on the label or labeling. The exemptions include:

When Congress passed the Nutrition Labeling and Education Act (NLEA), the act reaffirmed the legal basis for FDA's labeling initiative and established an explicit timetable.

♦ food produced by certain small businesses;

♦ food served in restaurants and in other establishments for immediate consumption, such as schools, hospitals, and airplanes (as discussed directly below, however, a new law, currently being implemented, will require nutrition labeling for certain foods served at "chain" restaurants and similar retail food establishments);

♦ ready-to-eat foods prepared primarily on-site (for example, at bakeries, delicatessens, and candy stores);

♦ raw fruits, vegetables, and fish;

♦ food shipped in bulk, provided that it is not sold in that form to consumers, and is used in the manufacture of foods at another site;

♦ foods that contain insignificant amounts of all nutrients and food components required to be declared on the nutrition label (for example, coffee beans and tea leaves);

♦ foods in small packages that have a total surface area of less than 12 square inches. Such foods are required to bear an address or telephone number that a consumer can use to obtain the required information. A modified label format is also provided for intermediate size packages (40 or less square inches), provided that these foods bear no nutrition claims or other nutrition information;

♦ medical foods;

♦ infant formulas; and

♦ dietary supplements (subject to separate labeling requirements).

Restaurants and similar retail food establishments that are part of a chain with 20 or more locations doing business under the same name (and offering for sale substantially the same menu items) will need to provide calorie and other nutrition information for standard menu items, including food on display and self-service food.

As noted above, the Patient Protection and Affordable Care Act of 2010 amended the FDCA to require restaurants and similar retail food establishments that are part of a chain with 20 or more locations doing business under the same name (and offering for sale substantially the same menu items) to provide calorie and other nutrition information for standard menu items, including food on display and self-service food. See FDCA § 403(q)(5)(H). In December 2014, FDA issued a final rule to implement these new labeling requirements, in which the agency defined the term "restaurant or similar retail food establishment" as an establishment that sells restaurant or restaurant-type food whose primary business activity is the sale of food to consumers. An establishment's primary business activity is considered to be the sale of food to consumers if either: 1) it presents itself as a restaurant, or 2) it uses more than 50 percent of its total floor area for the sale of food. FDA has extended the compliance date for menu labeling from May 2017 to May 2018.

In December 2014, FDA also issued a rule implementing the vending machine food labeling provisions of the Affordable Care Act of 2010. The rule requires operators who own or operate 20 or more vending machines to disclose calorie information for food sold from vending machines, subject to certain exemptions. In August 2016, FDA issued "Draft Guidance for Industry: Calorie Labeling of Articles of Food in Vending Machines" requesting comment on implementation of the rule. While the compliance date for the rule was December 1, 2016, FDA has extended the compliance date to July 1, 2018 for foods sold from glass-front vending machines that have visible front-of-pack labeling.

In May 2016, FDA published two final rules revising nutritional labeling requirements, which impact both the design of the Nutrition Facts Label and the serving sizes upon which the labeling should be based: "Food Labeling: Revision of the Nutrition and Supplement Facts Labels" (Nutrition Facts Rule) and "Food Labeling: Serving Sizes of Foods that can Reasonably be Consumed at One Eating Occasion" (Serving Size Rule). The rules—among other things—place a greater emphasis on calorie count, provide additional information on added sugars, establish a more limited definition for dietary fiber, create new age categories for products specifically intended for infants and children, and account for updates in portion sizes, all in an effort to, in the words of FDA, help "expand and highlight the information [people] most need when making choices."

The Nutrition Facts Rule updates the design of, and nutrition information content on, food labels by implementing larger and bolder fonts to display more prominently calorie count, adding a line detailing the amount of "added sugars," replacing the mandatory disclosure requirements for vitamin A and vitamin C with vitamin D and potassium, removing information on calories from fat, and updating Daily Values for various nutrients. The Serving Size Rule implements new serving size requirements for dozens of foods, to reflect the portion sizes that FDA believes people actually consume. The serving size for some products increased while the serving size for other products, like yogurt, decreased. In addition, the new rule eliminates the flexibility previously given to manufacturers to label a product that contained between 150 and 200 percent of the Reference Amount Customarily Consumed (RACC) of a product as a single-serving requirement. Under the new rule, manufacturers are required to provide single-serving labeling information for a container with less than 200 percent of the RACC, and can voluntarily use a dual-column label for products between 150 and 200 percent of the RACC. If a product contains between 200 percent and 300 percent of the RACC, FDA requires the use of dual-column labeling (based on whether the consumer were to eat the entire container in one vs. multiple sittings).

A potentially controversial component of the updated labeling requirements is the addition of a new line for added sugars. In the past, the food industry strongly objected to an analogous proposal, arguing that added sugars—sugars added to food during processing—are chemically identical to natural sugars in foods. However, citing newer research, the agency took the position that providing this information will help consumers comply with the 2010 Dietary Guidelines for Americans, which recommend reducing calories from added sugars.

The serving size changes are significant. For example, according to FDA, research showed that Americans typically consume significantly more than one half a cup of ice cream, despite the fact that a half cup was listed as the serving size. As a result, under the new rule, the RACC for ice cream has been increased from one-half cup to two-thirds cup, which means the number of calories listed in one serving size of a typical Chocolate Chip Cookie Dough ice cream will now be 375 calories as opposed 250 calories. Similarly, the RACC for beverages, ranging from soda, to juice and coffee, has been raised from 8 fluid ounces to 12 fluid ounces. In contrast, FDA reduced the RACC for all forms of yogurt, including drinkable yogurt, from 225 grams (8 ounces) to 170 grams (6 ounces). The agency believes that these changes will help consumers make more informed decisions.

While the original compliance deadline for companies was July 26, 2018, on June 13, 2017, FDA announced its intention to extend the compliance date for the Nutrition Facts Label final rules. At publication, this date had not yet been set.

The current nutrition labeling regulations can be found at 21 C.F.R. § 101.9 and require manufacturers to include information about certain nutrients on product labels (mandatory nutrients). Information about certain other nutrients may be listed at the manufacturer's discretion (voluntary nutrients). If a claim is made about any of the voluntary nutrients, or if a food is fortified or enriched with any of them, information about that nutrient then becomes mandatory. The mandatory and voluntary nutrients enumerated in the regulations are the only ones permitted to appear on the nutrition panel. Those mandatory nutrients (italicized) and the voluntary nutrients are listed in the following table in the order in which they must appear on the label.

Current Mandatory Nutrients and Voluntary Nutrients*	
Listed in the order in which they must appear on the label. Mandatory nutrients are italicized.	*total calories*
	calories from fat
	calories from saturated fat
	total fat
	saturated fat
	trans fat
	cholesterol
	sodium
	potassium
	total carbohydrate
	dietary fiber
	soluble fiber
	insoluble fiber
	sugars
	sugar alcohols
	other carbohydrate (the difference between total carbohydrate and the sum of dietary fiber, sugars, and sugar alcohol if declared)
	protein
	vitamin A
	vitamin C
	calcium
	iron
	other vitamins and minerals (see 21 C.F.R. § 101.9(c))

*until implementation of the updated Nutrition Facts rules.

Updated Mandatory Nutrients and Voluntary Nutrients	
Listed in the order in which they must appear on the label. Mandatory nutrients are italicized.	*total calories*
	total fat
	saturated fat
	trans fat
	cholesterol
	sodium
	total carbohydrate
	dietary fiber
	soluble fiber
	insoluble fiber
	Total sugars
	Added sugars
	other carbohydrate (the difference between total carbohydrate and the sum of dietary fiber, sugars, and sugar alcohol if declared)
	protein
	vitamin D
	calcium
	iron
	potassium
	other vitamins and minerals (see 21 C.F.R. § 101.9(c))

The regulations go into great detail on the methodology to be used in calculating nutrient content, and discuss specific analytical methods to be used to determine the amount of each dietary component present in foods. In most cases, a food manufacturer is free to use other methods. Where FDA contests the results found by the food manufacturer, however, the agency uses the analytical methods identified in the regulations.

When listing these nutrients, not only their absolute quantitative measure must be identified; the NLEA also requires that reference values for nutrients—the "Daily Value"—be included. The Daily Value is the average amount of a particular nutrient that an individual should consume in a day. A nutrition label must declare the Daily Value and, in some cases, the quantity by weight of all nutrients.

FDA has established a detailed format for the presentation of nutrition information on food products. The nutrient declarations are based upon serving size listed in "common household units" such as cups, tablespoons, or teaspoons, except for beverages, which must be listed in fluid ounces. To determine the appropriate serving size for a food product, a manufacturer must look to the reference amount in FDA's regulations for the relevant product category (21 C.F.R. § 101.12) which, as noted above, were updated in May 2016. The Reference Amount Customarily Consumed represents the amount of food from the product category that is customarily consumed per eating occasion. RACCs are not intended as dietary recommendations, but rather as guides to help manufacturers establish appropriate serving sizes. Manufacturers determine the serving size for a product by calculating what fraction of a sales unit equals the RACC. This is rarely an exact fit, so the regulations contain standards to convert RACCs to appropriate serving sizes. For example, if the sale unit of a product weighs at least 67 percent but less than 200 percent of the reference amount, the serving size of the product is one unit. Underneath the serving size is the "Number of Servings Per Container."

The nutrient declarations are based upon serving size listed in "common household units" such as cups, tablespoons, or teaspoons, except for beverages, which must be listed in fluid ounces.

FDA has recognized that the levels of nutrients in food products generally will not calculate out as even, uniform numbers. The presentation of a wide array of numerical values, including fractions or decimal places, will render the nutrition label unnecessarily confusing to consumers, and make comparison of values among different products more difficult. Therefore, the regulations provide specific rules for rounding nutrient values on nutrition labels up or down, generally to increments of five or 10. The regulations establish different rounding parameters for different nutrients, and the level of adjustment made will vary for different ranges within individual nutrients (e.g., the different rules discussed for rounding caloric values above or below 50).

If standard-size packages (those that have a total surface area available for labeling of more than 40 square inches) cannot fit the nutrition panel onto the Information Panel in the general tabular format, a modified, tabular format, which presents the information in a horizontal, side-by-side display, may be used. If the package lacks sufficient continuous vertical space to utilize even this modified vertical display, the regulations provide for a horizontal format. Small and intermediate-size packages (those which have a total surface area available for labeling of 40 square inches or less) are subject to looser requirements for the presentation of nutrition labeling. The Nutrition Facts label may appear on any label panel, not only the Information Panel. Moreover, if necessary for reasons of package space, the footnotes to the nutrition label may be omitted and replaced with an asterisked statement at the bottom of the label that percent Daily Values are based on a 2,000-calorie diet.

Small packages (those with a total surface area of 12 square inches or less available for labeling) are eligible for an even greater exception to the labeling format requirements. If necessary for reasons of space, small packages may omit the full nutrition labeling and instead merely list an address or telephone number through which to obtain nutrition information. If a manufacturer uses the "telephone number exemption," it may not make any claims in the label as to the nutrient content of the product.

If necessary for reasons of space, small packages may omit the full nutrition labeling and instead merely list an address or telephone number through which to obtain nutrition information.

If a food contains insignificant amounts of seven or more of the mandatory nutrients and total calories, the manufacturer may use a simplified Nutrition Facts format that omits much of the information that appears in the standard display. "Insignificant amount" is defined as an amount that may be declared as zero under the nutrition labeling regulations, or for total carbohydrates, dietary fiber, and protein, a declaration of "less than 1 g" (see the above discussion of rounding rules). Trans fat does not have to be included if the total fat in a food is less than 0.5 gram per serving and the label makes no claims about fat, fatty acids, or cholesterol content. This simplified format contains information on total calories, total fat, total carbohydrate, protein, and sodium only. These five nutrients must be declared, even if they are present in insignificant amounts. If the food product contains calories from fat and/or mandatory nutrients in greater than insignificant amounts, they must be declared on the label. Any nutrients added to the food must be declared as well.

The Nutrition Facts panel must appear on the Principal Display Panel or the Information Panel. There are, however, exceptions to this requirement. For example, FDA gives packages that have a total surface area available for labeling greater than 40 square inches greater flexibility in displaying nutrition information. If the Principal Display Panel and the Information Panel do not provide sufficient space to accommodate all of the required information, the manufacturer may use any alternate panel that can be seen readily by consumers for the nutrition label.

◆ Nutrient Content Claims (Descriptors)

Nutrient content claims on food labels also are governed by NLEA. Manufacturers are permitted to place claims on a label regarding the level of a nutrient in a food, provided that they use only the descriptive terms that FDA has defined by regulation. This enables manufacturers to highlight particular nutritional attributes of their products through a uniform frame of reference.

FDA allows two types of nutrient content claims: absolute claims, which describe the level of a nutrient in a serving of a product, and relative claims, which compare the level of nutrient per serving in a product to that of a reference product.

FDA allows two types of nutrient content claims: absolute claims, which describe the level of a nutrient in a serving of a product, and relative claims, which compare the level of nutrient per serving in a product to that of a reference product. Absolute claims may utilize only the particular descriptive terms approved by FDA, which are listed and defined below. Relative claims only can compare products to appropriate classes of reference foods established by FDA for use as the basis for relative claims. All nutrient content claims, whether absolute or relative, must be based on RACCs. Special rules apply to claims for foods with small RACCs.

Labels containing a relative claim must state, in immediate proximity to the claim, the identity of the reference product and the amount by which the reduced product differs from it, expressed as a percentage or a fraction, e.g., "30 percent fewer calories than regular _____." The label also must bear quantitative information comparing calories per serving to the reference product. This can be accomplished by a statement such as "calorie content of regular is 120 calories per 12 oz. serving; calorie content of diet is 2 calories per 12 oz. serving," or by a chart or graph display of the nutrient levels of the reference product, and the corresponding lower levels in the reduced product. This quantitative information must appear either next to the most prominent reduced calorie claim, or on the nutrition Information Panel.

If a product qualifies for a nutrient content claim, but contains a high level of certain other nutrients, a referral/disclosure statement is required. Specifically, if a food making a nutrient content claim contains more than 13 grams of fat, 4 grams of saturated fat, 60 milligrams of cholesterol, or 480 milligrams of sodium per RACC, then the referral statement must read "See [appropriate panel] for information about [nutrient requiring disclosure] and other nutrients."

A table of FDA-approved nutrient content claims is found at the end of this chapter. The NLEA allows for the submission of petitions requesting that FDA promulgate definitions for new nutrient content claims or accept synonyms for defined terms, or allow the use of implied nutrient content claims in brand names. For example, in response to citizen petition, FDA is currently reconsidering its definition and standard for the term "healthy."

♦ Structure-Function Claims

Conventional foods may also bear "structure-function" claims—claims relating a food or food ingredients to an effect on the structure or function of the body. Such claims have been used on foods for many years, and include statements such as "calcium builds strong bones." One of the important distinctions between conventional foods and dietary supplements lies in this area: FDA takes the position that conventional food claims must be derived from the "nutritive value" of the food, an ambiguous concept that FDA regulations define as "a value in sustaining human existence by such processes as promoting growth, replacing loss of essential nutrients, or providing energy." 21 C.F.R. § 101.14(a)(3).

Conventional foods may also bear "structure-function" claims—claims relating a food or food ingredients to an effect on the structure or function of the body.

♦ Health Claims

In addition to nutrient content claims, NLEA authorizes the use of health claims—defined as a statement that expressly or by implication characterizes the relationship of certain nutrients to a disease or health-related condition—on food labels. Health claims differ from nutrient content claims in that they focus not on the amount of a particular nutrient supplied by the food product in question, but rather on the potential health benefits of consumption of that nutrient, with the food product in question being but one source of that nutrient.

An "authorized health claim" is permitted only if FDA has promulgated a regulation approving the claim and setting forth the conditions under which it may be used. A food is misbranded, and may be considered an unapproved drug, if it bears any health claim other than those authorized by FDA, or if it fails to meet the requirements of the regulation authorizing its use. Food products are permitted to bear authorized health claims for certain relationships between a nutrient or a food and the risk of a disease or health-related condition.

An "authorized health claim" is permitted only if FDA has promulgated a regulation approving the claim and setting forth the conditions under which it may be used.

FDA may issue an authorized health claim regulation on its own, or in response to a petition from manufacturers. Such a claim may be authorized if the agency determines, based on the totality of publicly available scientific evidence (including evidence from well-designed studies conducted in a manner consistent with generally recognized scientific procedures and principles), that the claim is supported by such evidence.

A "qualified health claim" is permitted where a claim is based on credible evidence, but the strength of the scientific evidence falls below the threshold for FDA to issue an authorized health claim regulation based on significant scientific agreement.

In addition, a "qualified health claim" is permitted where a claim is based on credible evidence, but the strength of the scientific evidence falls below the threshold for FDA to issue an authorized health claim regulation based on significant scientific agreement (the SSA standard). FDA established a review process for qualified health claims in response to several court decisions, including *Pearson v. Shalala*, 164 F.3d 650 (D.C. Cir. 1999), which ruled on First Amendment grounds that FDA may not reject a health claim found to be potentially misleading unless the agency also reasonably determines that no disclaimer would eliminate the potential deception.

In 2003, FDA established interim procedures for reviewing petitions for qualified health claims. "Guidance for Industry and FDA: Interim Procedures for Qualified Health Claims in the Labeling of Conventional Human Food and Human Dietary Supplements" (July 2003). Under this interim process, FDA reviews qualified health claim petitions on a case-by-case basis. FDA must respond by letter within 270 days notifying the petitioner whether FDA intends to exercise enforcement discretion with respect to a qualified health claim or to deny the petition. In a letter of enforcement discretion, FDA specifies the nature of the qualified health claim for which FDA has no objections. FDA has developed standardized qualifying language for qualified health claims subject to letter of enforcement discretion, based on the three levels of support used in the evidence-based ranking system.

FDA posts on its website all petitions requesting a qualified health claim for a 60-day public comment period. FDA also posts on its website all letters of enforcement discretion and denial letters for qualified health claim petitions. The posted letters of enforcement discretion give notice to manufacturers regarding how FDA intends to exercise its enforcement discretion on the use of the qualified health claim.

In 2009, FDA issued a final guidance document that sets forth an evidence-based review system for the agency's evaluation of petitions submitted for SSA health claims or qualified health claims. "Guidance for Industry: Evidence-Based Review System for the Scientific Evaluation of Health Claims" (Jan. 2009). Thus, in contrast to previous practice, FDA is now using a single approach for evaluating SSA and qualified health claim petitions. Under this approach, FDA determines whether the scientific evidence meets the SSA standard or, if not, can support a qualified health claim that includes qualifying language that identifies limits to the level of scientific evidence. The guidance explains that the SSA standard is intended to be a strong standard that provides a high level of confidence in the validity of the substance/disease relationship. On the other hand, SSA does not require unanimous agreement within the relevant scientific community.

Per the guidance, FDA will observe the following steps when evaluating the scientific evidence for health claims: 1) identifying scientific studies that evaluate the substance/disease relationship; 2) identifying surrogate endpoints for disease risk; 3) evaluating human studies to determine if scientific conclusions can be made; 4) assessing the methodological quality of each human study; 5) evaluating the totality of the evidence; 6) assessing SSA; 7) analyzing the specificity of claim language for qualified health claims; and 8) reevaluating existing SSA or qualified health claims, as appropriate.

The FDCA, through the passage of FDAMA, also allows a class of health claims and nutrient content claims which are not required, prior to use, to be codified into a regulation as an authorized health claim or be the subject of letter of enforcement discretion as a qualified health claim. These claims, referred to as "authoritative statement" claims, are permitted if:

The FDCA, through the passage of FDAMA, allows a class of health claims and nutrient content claims which are not required, prior to use, to be codified into a regulation as an authorized health claim or be the subject of letter of enforcement discretion as a qualified health claim.

♦ a scientific body of the U.S. government with official responsibility for public health protection or research directly relating to human nutrition (e.g., the National Institutes of Health or the Centers for Disease Control and Prevention) or the National Academy of Sciences or any of its subdivisions, has published an authoritative statement, currently in effect, about the relationship between a nutrient and a disease or health-related condition to which the health claim refers, or which identifies the nutrient level to which the claim refers, as appropriate;

♦ the person intending to make the claim submits to FDA, 120 days before introducing the food into interstate commerce with such a claim, a notice of the claim, including: 1) the exact words to be used and a concise description of the basis for concluding that the authoritative statement relied upon has been made; 2) a copy of the authoritative statement relied upon; and 3) a balanced representation of the scientific literature relating to the relationship that is the subject of the health claim or nutrient content claim;

♦ the claim and the food for which it is made are in compliance with FDA regulations prohibiting claims on foods that contain nutrients in amounts that increase the risk of diet-related diseases or health conditions, and the general provisions on misbranding; and

♦ the claim is stated so that it accurately represents the authoritative statement on which it is based, and it enables the public to understand both the information provided and its relative significance in the context of the total daily diet.

During the 120-day period between notification to FDA and the introduction of the food bearing the claim into interstate commerce, FDA may inform the notifier that it has not submitted all of the information required by the act. As noted, a health claim or nutrient content claim based on an authoritative statement may be made without FDA approval. Such a claim may be continued until either: 1) FDA issues a regulation (and the regulation has become effective) prohibiting or modifying the claim, or finding that the requirements of the act for such a claim have not been met, including a finding that the notification did not include all of the information required; or 2) a federal court determines, in the context of an enforcement proceeding, that the statutory requirements have not been met.

Standards of Identity

Section 401 of the FDCA permits FDA to set a certain definition or standard for a food to "promote honesty and fair dealing in the interest of consumers." Such regulations may include establishing a common or usual name for a food, providing a reasonable definition and standard of identity, setting a reasonable standard of quality, or reasonable standards of fill of container. See 21 C.F.R. Parts 102 (common or usual names for non-standardized foods), 103 (quality standards for foods with no identity standards), 104 (nutritional quality guidelines for foods), and 130-169 (general conditions for standards of identity, and specific standards). The development of standards for most products—to the extent developed at all—is subject to informal, notice-and-comment rulemaking procedures rather than formal rulemaking.

To a large extent a standard of identity can be characterized as a recipe for a food that provides consumers with a consistent expectation as to composition and quality. A food may be considered misbranded if it is represented on its label as a food for which a definition and standard of identity has been established, yet fails to conform to that definition and standard even if it is wholesome and its label is otherwise truthful. See FDCA § 403.

Standards also may pertain to the quality of a food product. Products failing to meet a "standard of quality" must disclose the fact of substandard quality in a label statement. "Standards of fill" also commonly are used to protect against "slack fill" or products with excess water levels.

According to section 403(c) of the FDCA, a food is misbranded "[i]f it is an imitation of another food, unless its label bears, in type of uniform size and prominence, the word 'imitation' and, immediately thereafter, the name of the food imitated." FDA regulations further provide that "imitation labeling" is required if a food is a substitute for and resembles another food but is nutritionally inferior to that food. "Nutritional inferiority" is defined as any reduction in the content of the essential nutrient that is present at a measurable amount, not including caloric or fat content with a measurable amount considered to be 2 percent or more of the daily reference value for protein and potassium, and the referenced daily intake for specified vitamins and minerals. Rather than bearing the term "imitation"—which virtually ensures a food product's demise in the marketplace—products that resemble a standardized food but are not nutritionally inferior may bear an appropriate common or usual name, an appropriately descriptive term, or a fanciful name that is not false and misleading.

Under 21 C.F.R § 130.10, a food may bear the name of a standardized food that does not meet the standard if the deviation from the standard is described by a nutrient content claim on the label. This regulation permits the development of healthful versions of standardized foods without requiring labeling that would prevent consumers from buying the product. Among a number of specific limitations, in order for a food product to comply with this "generic" standard of identity:

A food may bear the name of a standardized food that does not meet the standard if the deviation from the standard is described by a nutrient content claim on the label.

♦ nutrients may be added so that the product is not nutritionally inferior to the standardized food;

♦ the substitute food must possess the same or similar performance characteristics as the standardized food;

♦ deviations from the non-ingredient provisions of the standard are permitted if intended to produce the performance characteristics;

♦ deviations must be the minimum necessary to qualify for the nutrient content claim; and

♦ any significant deviations from the range of performance characteristics for the standardized food must be noted on the label, such as "not recommended for frying."

FOOD SECURITY/SAFETY

FDA has increasingly focused on issues of food security in the last several years, which began in earnest in particular following the passage of the Public Health Security and Bioterrorism Preparedness Response Act (Bioterrorism Act) of 2002. In response to Title III of the Bioterrorism Act, "Protecting Safety and Security of Food and Drug Supply," FDA issued regulations governing facility registration (FDCA § 415), new food import requirements (FDCA § 801(m)),

FDA has increasingly focused on issues of food security in the last several years.

administrative detention authority (FDCA § 304(h)), and recordkeeping and access requirements (FDCA § 414). In addition, in response to the Food and Drug Administration Amendments Act of 2007 (FDAAA), FDA established a Reportable Food Registry through which food facility registrants must notify FDA about foods that may present a risk of serious adverse health consequences or death to humans or animals. See FDCA § 417.

Nevertheless, as previously discussed in this chapter, there have been continuing concerns about FDA's ability to ensure the safety of the nation's food supply. Responding to these concerns, Congress passed FSMA, which greatly expands FDA's authority over regulated foods. In addition to the new requirements discussed above (i.e., food facilities must adopt written preventive controls plans, and FDA must increase regulation over certain farm operations), FSMA includes various other provisions intended to bolster FDA's oversight and enforcement authorities, such as enhanced registration and recordkeeping requirements and administrative detention authority, increased FDA inspections, mandatory FDA recalls, and heightened scrutiny of food imports.

Food Facility Registration

In October 2005, FDA issued a final rule requiring domestic and foreign facilities that manufacture, process, pack, or hold food for consumption by humans and animals in the United States to register with FDA, now set forth at 21 C.F.R. Part 1, Subpart H.

The current food facility regulations require that a food manufacturer separately register each facility once with FDA. The registration for foreign facilities also must include the name of the U.S. agent for the facility. FDA is required to compile and maintain an up-to-date list of registered facilities, which is available on its website.

Foreign facilities are not required to register with FDA where the manufactured food undergoes further processing or packaging at another facility outside the United States. In addition, manufacturers of food contact substances are not required to register with FDA. Other establishments excluded from the registration requirements include farms, restaurants, and other retail food establishments, and nonprofit food establishments.

FSMA enhances the facility registration requirements in FDCA § 415 by requiring registration renewal every two years, and by granting FDA a significant new registration-related authority: suspension. Specifically, the FDA Commissioner can suspend a facility registration based on a determination that the food manufactured, processed, packed, received, or held by the facility has a reasonable probability of causing serious adverse health consequences or death to humans or animals.

Prior Notice of Imported Food

In November 2008, FDA issued a final rule establishing prior notice require-ments for imported foods, now set forth at 21 C.F.R. Part 1, Subpart I.

The prior notice regulations require that prior notice is given to FDA for all food for humans and animals imported or offered for import into the United States for use, storage, or distribution in the United States. These requirements apply to food for trans-shipment through the United States to another country and food for future export, but are not applicable for foods that are imported and then exported without leaving the port of arrival until export. A prior notice may be submitted by any person with knowledge of the required information, and may be transmitted to FDA by a third party, such as a customer, on behalf of the submitter. Prior notices are submitted electronically to FDA through ei-ther 1) the U.S. Customs and Border Patrol (CBP) Automated Broker Interface of the Automated Commercial System (ABI/ACS) or 2) the FDA Prior Notice System Interface (PNSI). Prior notice submissions must contain detailed production, transportation, and recipient information.

Prior notice must be given to FDA for all food for humans and animals imported or offered for import into the United States for use, storage, or distribution in the United States.

The time requirements for submission of prior notice, and confirmation by FDA for review, are as follows: 1) if the article of food is arriving by road, no less than two hours before arriving at the port of arrival; 2) if the article of food is arriv-ing by rail, no less than four hours before arriving at the port of arrival; 3) if the article of food is arriving by air, no less than four hours before arriving at the port of arrival; or 4) if the article of food is arriving by water, no less than eight hours before arriving at the port of arrival. Except where a food is offered for import by international mail, a prior notice may not be submitted more than 15 calendar days before the anticipated date of arrival of the food for submissions through FDA's PNSI and not more than 30 calendar days before the anticipated date of arrival for submissions through CBP's ABI/ACS.

A food may be refused admission into the United States if the prior notice is inadequate—either due to no prior notice, inaccurate prior notice, or untimely prior notice. A refused food must be exported (unless seized or administratively detained by CBP or FDA under other authority), or it must be held within the port of entry unless otherwise directed by CBP or FDA. A request may be made within five days for FDA to review whether a food refused admission is in fact subject to prior notice requirements or whether the information submitted in the prior notice is accurate. If FDA determines that the food is not subject to prior notice requirements or the prior notice submission is accurate, it will notify the requester that the food is no longer subject to refusal of admission.

In May 2013, FDA issued a final rule that amends the prior notice regulations as required by FSMA. 78 Fed. Reg. 32,359 (May 30, 2013). Under the final rule, a person submitting a prior notice of imported food is required to report the name of any country to which the article has been refused entry.

Administrative Detention

Under the new law, FDA may impose administrative detention of food if it has "reason to believe" that an article of food is adulterated or misbranded.

In June 2004, FDA issued a final rule establishing regulations, set forth in 21 C.F.R. Part 1, Subpart K, authorizing the detention of any food found during an inspection, examination, or investigation conducted under the FDCA, when based on credible evidence or information indicating such food presents a threat of serious adverse health consequences or death to humans or animals. 69 Fed. Reg. 31,659 (June 4, 2004). FSMA gives FDA expanded authority in this area by lowering the standard for administrative detention provided in FDCA § 304(h). Under the new law, FDA may impose administrative detention of food if it has "reason to believe" that an article of food is adulterated or misbranded. On February 5, 2013, FDA issued a final rule implementing its expanded detention authority. 78 Fed. Reg. 7994.

An officer or qualified employee of FDA may order an administrative detention, which must be approved by the Secretary or a designated official. The detention period must be reasonable and not exceed 30 calendar days. Any person entitled to claim the food if it were seized may appeal the detention order to the Secretary.

Records

Persons who manufacture, process, pack, transport, distribute, receive, hold, or import food in the United States must maintain and allow FDA access to records.

In December 2004, FDA issued a final rule establishing regulations, set forth in 21 C.F.R. Part 1, Subpart J, requiring persons who manufacture, process, pack, transport, distribute, receive, hold, or import food in the United States to maintain and allow FDA access to records. 69 Fed. Reg. 71,561 (Dec. 9, 2004). Records to be maintained by food firms relate to the identity of the immediate previous source of all food received and the immediate subsequent recipient of all food released, and records must be retained at or reasonably close to the establishment where the activities covered in the records occurred. The record retention period for human foods ranges from six months to two years depending on the food's shelf life, and the retention period for animal food is one year.

The following persons or facilities are not subject to the recordkeeping and access requirements: farms; restaurants; persons performing covered activities when the food is meat, poultry, or egg products subject to exclusive USDA jurisdiction; and foreign persons, except those who transport food in the United States. The records requirements also do not extend to the following information: recipes for food; financial and pricing data, personnel data, research data, or sales data (other than shipment data regarding sales). In addition, certain persons or facilities—including small retail food establishments and certain nonprofit food establishments—are not subject to the record establishment requirements, but are subject to the availability requirements for existing records. FSMA moderately expands FDA's authority to inspect records at food facilities as provided in FDCA § 414. Currently, FDA must provide written notice before accessing records and must have a reasonable belief that an article of food is adulterated and presents a threat of serious adverse health consequences or death to humans or animals. FSMA removes the requirement that FDA must have a reasonable belief that the food is adulterated—if FDA reasonably believes the food will cause serious adverse health consequences or death. The requirement that FDA provide advance notice before accessing records remains in effect.

Reportable Food Registry

In September 2009, FDA established an electronic Reportable Food Registry, as required by FDAAA. A reportable food is a food (other than a dietary supplement and infant formula) for which there is a reasonable probability that the use of, or exposure to, the food will cause serious adverse health consequences or death to humans or animals. A responsible party, defined as a person who submits a food facility registration to FDA for a facility where food is manufactured, processed, packed, or held, is required to notify FDA through the Reportable Food Registry within 24 hours after the party determines that a food is a reportable food.

A reportable food is a food (other than a dietary supplement and infant formula) for which there is a reasonable probability that the use of, or exposure to, the food will cause serious adverse health consequences or death to humans or animals.

FSMA enhances the Reportable Food Registry system in FDCA § 417. Specifically, FDA is required to obtain consumer-oriented information about reportable foods, and to then prepare a one-page summary of the food that will be made available on the Internet and provided to grocery stores.

Inspections

FSMA requires FDA to increase the frequency of inspections of all domestic and foreign food facilities. In particular, FDA is required to identify and allocate resources to inspect "high-risk facilities," which will be identified based on a number of factors, including: known risks of the food, compliance history of the facility, and rigor and effectiveness of the facility's hazard analysis and risk-based preventive controls. See FDCA § 421. The legislation required FDA to inspect all high-risk domestic facilities within five years of enactment of FSMA and no less than every three years thereafter, and to inspect all non-high-risk domestic facilities within seven years of enactment and no less than every five years thereafter.

With respect to foreign facilities, FSMA requires FDA to inspect at least 600 foreign facilities within one year of enactment, and to double those inspections every year for the next five years. FDCA § 421(a)(2)(D). The law provides that if a foreign facility registered with FDA refuses an inspection, its food cannot be imported into the United States. See FDCA § 807(b).

Mandatory Recall Authority

FSMA granted FDA the authority to order mandatory recalls of food (other than infant formula, for which FDA previously had mandatory recall authority). See FDCA § 423. The law grants FDA mandatory recall over food if: 1) there is a reasonable probability that the food is adulterated or misbranded; 2) the use of or exposure to the food will cause serious adverse health consequences or death to humans or animals; and 3) the responsible party has refused to voluntarily cease distribution and recall the products. For any mandatory recall, or for a voluntary recall of food that will cause serious adverse health consequences or death to humans or animals, FDA must set up an incident command operation within 24 hours after initiation of the recall.

Food Imports

In November 2015, FDA issued two final rules to make importers more accountable for food safety and enable FDA to rely on credible third parties to monitor conditions and standards in foreign facilities that process food: the foreign supplier verification programs for importers of food for human and animals rule and the accreditation of third-party certification bodies to conduct food safety audits and to issue certifications rule. The foreign supplier verification rule, which implements section 301 of FSMA, requires importers to perform certain risk-based activities that verify that food imported into the United States has been produced using processes and procedures that provide the same level of public health protection as those required of domestic food producers. The accredited third-party auditor certification rule, which implements section 307 of FSMA, establishes a program for accreditation of certification bodies to conduct food safety audits and issue certifications of foreign facilities and the foods for humans and animals they produce.

FSMA also contains provisions that encourage coordination with foreign countries to ensure imported food safety.

FSMA also contains provisions that encourage coordination with foreign countries to ensure imported food safety. The law requires FDA, in consultation with other executive agencies and stakeholders, to develop a comprehensive plan to expand the technical, scientific, and regulatory capacity of foreign governments and their respective food industries, from which foods are exported to the United States. FDA was required to establish satellite offices in foreign countries to provide assistance to the appropriate foreign government entities in ensuring safety of food and other products regulated by FDA, including by directly conducting risk-based inspections of such articles and supporting inspections by foreign governmental entities.

Intentional Adulteration

Section 106 of FSMA required FDA, in coordination with the Department of Homeland Security and in consultation with USDA, to issue regulations to protect against the intentional adulteration of food. An FDA proposal issued in December 2013 would require that larger food businesses in the United States and abroad take steps to prevent contamination of the food supply. Such facilities would be required to maintain a written food defense plan that assesses their vulnerabilities to intentional adulteration where the intent is to cause public health harm, including acts of terrorism, and identify and implement strategies to minimize or prevent such threats.

MEDICAL FOODS

Medical foods have always been a subject of confusion. Although the category was conceived as a special category of foods administered by physicians for dietary management of a specific disease or disorder, it was not until 1988, with the passage of the Orphan Drug Amendments, that a statutory definition was provided for medical foods:

> A food which is formulated to be consumed or administered enterally under the supervision of a physician and which is intended for the specific dietary management of a disease or condition for which distinctive nutritional requirements based upon recognized scientific principles are established by medical evaluation.

Medical foods are administered by physicians for dietary management of a specific disease or disorder.

This definition was later incorporated into the NLEA.

For many years, FDA discussed the establishment of regulations for medical foods. In 1996, FDA published an advance notice of proposed rulemaking (ANPR) to request comments on its approach to the "broad group of heterogeneous products that are marketed as medical foods." 61 Fed. Reg. 6066 (Nov. 29, 1996). Concerns were expressed about the "medical foods paradox"—while these products are intended for the specific dietary management of a disease or condition for which distinctive nutritional requirements had been established, they could be sold without any nutrition information on their label or labeling and could bear claims that were not evaluated by FDA. Additionally, no mechanism existed to ensure that the formulation of a medical food had been evaluated prior to sale to ensure that it was suitable for the intended patient population. The agency expressed specific concern that such a lack of scrutiny could have adverse public health consequences, especially if claims were not scientifically valid or if product labeling did not disclose information necessary for safe and effective use.

FDA considers the statutory definition of medical foods to be quite narrow and limited to those foods that are specially formulated and processed for a patient who is seriously ill or who requires use of the product as a major component of a disease or condition's specific dietary management. FDA has recently been policing products purporting to be medical foods, and careful attention to the parameters of this category is essential. FDA has issued a guidance on the topic, "Frequently Asked Questions About Medical Foods," found at https://www.fda.gov/RegulatoryInformation/Guidances/ucm054048.htm.

Infant Formulas

An infant formula is deemed adulterated if it does not provide specific nutrients, does not meet quality requirements prescribed by the Secretary, or is not produced in compliance with applicable cGMPs and quality control procedures.

Under FDCA § 201(z), the term "infant formula" means "a food which purports to be or is represented for special dietary use solely as a food for infants for reason of its simulation of human milk or its suitability as a complete or partial substitute for human milk." Special requirements for infant formula are provided under FDCA § 412, which deems an infant formula adulterated if it does not provide specific nutrients, does not meet quality requirements prescribed by the Secretary, or is not produced in compliance with applicable cGMPs and quality control procedures. Records development and retention requirements also apply to infant formula products, and FDA has the authority to review and copy all records containing microbiological testing results of raw materials used in infant formula powder and unfinished infant formula. FDA also maintains requirements for the labeling of infant formulas, including nutrient content, directions for preparation and use, and a "use by" date. Finally, special requirements also apply to procedures for processing consumer complaints relating to infant formulas.

Under FDCA § 412(c), persons introducing any new infant formula into interstate commerce must submit a registration with FDA, at least 90 days before the marketing of a new infant formula, that includes the quantitative formulation of the new infant formula or description of any reformulation or change in processing of the formula. A "new infant formula" includes "an infant formula manufactured by a person which has not previously manufactured an infant formula, and . . . . an infant formula manufactured by a person who has previously manu-factured infant formula and in which there is a major change, in processing or formulation, from a current or any previous formulation produced by such manufacturer." FDCA § 412(c)(2). Preparations for special uses, such as for infants with inborn errors of metabolism, low birth rate, or other unusual medical or di-etary problems, are exempt from the quality factors, quality control procedures, and recordkeeping requirements, subject to terms and conditions established by FDA. Such deviations are based upon an appropriate rationale submitted to the agency that supports the deviation from the general requirements.

In February 2014, FDA issued an interim final rule revising the infant formula regulations to establish requirements for cGMPs, including audits; quality fac-tors; quality control procedures, notification, and record and reporting require-ments. 79 Fed. Reg. 7934 (Feb. 10, 2014).

Persons introducing any new infant formula into interstate commerce must submit a registration with FDA, at least 90 days before the marketing of a new infant formula, that includes the quantitative formulation of the new infant formula or description of any reformulation or change in processing of the formula.

CONCLUSION

Food regulation continues to evolve as new challenges arise. The food law framework, particularly in the areas of food safety and security, has undergone considerable changes in recent years, and increased scrutiny of this framework likely will continue due to the risks of foodborne illness, food bioterrorism, and as part of international harmonization efforts. Concurrently, the line between so-called "functional foods" and disease will continue to change historical notions as to the relative role of foods in the promotion and maintenance of health. Even in this era of increasing complexity, however, the traditional concerns that food must be wholesome and truthfully represented remain the central tenets of federal regulation of the food supply.

Approved Health Claims

Note: The model claim statements are examples. Certain regulations provide additional choices.

Approved Claims	Food Requirements	Claim Requirements	Model Claim Statements
Calcium and Osteoporosis, and Calcium, Vitamin D, and Osteoporosis § 101.72	For calcium and osteoporosis claim – high in calcium For calcium, vitamin D and osteoporosis claim – high in calcium and vitamin D Assimilable (bioavailable) supplements must disintegrate and dissolve, and phosphorus content cannot exceed calcium content	The claim makes clear the importance of adequate calcium intake, or when appropriate, adequate calcium and vitamin D intake, throughout life, in healthful diet, are essential to reduce osteoporosis risk. The claim does not imply that adequate calcium intake, or when appropriate, adequate calcium and vitamin D intake, is the only recognized risk factor for the development of osteoporosis. The claim does not attribute any degree of reduction in risk of osteoporosis to maintaining an adequate dietary calcium intake, or when appropriate, an adequate dietary calcium and vitamin D intake, throughout life.	Calcium and osteoporosis: – Adequate calcium throughout life, as part of a well-balanced diet, may reduce the risk of osteoporosis. – Adequate calcium as part of a healthful diet, along with physical activity, may reduce the risk of osteoporosis in later life. Calcium, vitamin D, and osteoporosis: – Adequate calcium and vitamin D throughout life, as part of a well-balanced diet, may reduce the risk of osteoporosis. – Adequate calcium and vitamin D as part of a healthful diet, along with physical activity, may reduce the risk of osteoporosis in later life.

Sodium and Hypertension
 	
§ 101.74
	Low Sodium	The claim states that diets low in sodium "may" or "might" reduce the risk of high blood pressure
		
		Required terms:
		
		  "Sodium"
		  "High blood pressure"
		
		Indicates that high blood pressure depends on many factors
		
		Includes physician statement (Individuals with high blood pressure should consult their physicians) if claim defines high or normal blood pressure
			Diets low in sodium may reduce the risk of high blood pressure, a disease associated with many factors.

Dietary Fat and Cancer
 	
§ 101.73
	Low fat
	
	Fish & game meats: "Extra Lean"
		The claim states that diets low in fat "may" or "might" reduce the risk of some cancer, without attributing any degree of reduction of risk
		
		Required terms:
		
		  "Total Fat" or "Fat"
		  "Some types of cancers" or "Some cancers"
		
		Indicates that the development of cancer depends on many factors
		
		Does not specify types of fats or fatty acids that may be related to the risk of cancer
			Development of cancer depends on many factors. A diet low in total fat may reduce the risk of some cancers.

Approved Claims	Food Requirements	Claim Requirements	Model Claim Statements
Dietary Saturated Fat and Cholesterol and Risk of Coronary Heart Disease § 101.75	Low saturated fat Low cholesterol Low fat Fish & game meats: "Extra Lean"	The claim states that diets low in saturated fat and cholesterol "may" or "might" reduce the risk of heart disease, without attributing any degree of reduction of risk. Required terms: "Saturated fat and cholesterol" "Coronary heart disease" or "Heart disease" Indicates that the development of heart disease depends on many factors Includes physician statement (Individuals with elevated blood total—or LDL—cholesterol should consult their physicians) if claim defines high or normal blood total and LDL-cholesterol	While many factors affect heart disease, diets low in saturated fat and cholesterol may reduce the risk of this disease.
Fiber-containing Grain Products, Fruits, and Vegetables and Cancer § 101.76	A grain product, fruit, or vegetable that contains dietary fiber, or a food that contains the above. Low fat, and good source of dietary fiber under § 101.54 (without fortification)	The claim states that diets low in fat and high in fiber-containing grain products, fruits, and vegetables "may" or "might" reduce the risk of some cancers, without attributing any degree or reduction of risk. Required terms: "Fiber," "Dietary fiber," or "Total dietary fiber" "Some types of cancer" or "Some cancers" Indicates that development of cancer depends on many factors Does not specify types of dietary fiber that may be related to risk of cancer	Low-fat diets rich in fiber-containing grain products, fruits, and vegetables may reduce the risk of some types of cancer, a disease associated with many factors.

Approved Claims	Food Requirements	Claim Requirements	Model Claim Statements

Fruits, Vegetables, and Grain Products That Contain Fiber, Particularly Soluble Fiber, and Risk of Coronary Heart Disease
§ 101.77
	A fruit, vegetable, or grain product that contains fiber, low saturated fat, low cholesterol, low fat, and at least 0.6 grams of soluble fiber per RACC (without fortification), and soluble fiber content provided on label	States that diets low in saturated fat and cholesterol and high in fruits, vegetables, and grain products that contain fiber "may" or "might" reduce the risk of heart disease, without attributing any degree of reduction of risk.
		
		Required terms:
		    "Fiber," "Dietary fiber," "Some types of dietary fiber," "Some dietary fibers,"
		        or "Some fibers"
		    "Saturated fat" and
		    "Cholesterol"
		    "Heart disease" or
		        "Coronary heart disease"
		Indicates that development of heart disease depends on many factors.
		
		Includes physician statement (Individuals with elevated blood total or LDL-cholesterol should consult their physicians) if claim defines high or normal blood total and LDL-cholesterol
			Diets low in saturated fat and cholesterol and rich in fruits, vegetables, and grain products that contain some types of dietary fiber, particularly soluble fiber, may reduce the risk of heart disease, a disease associated with many factors.

Fruits and Vegetables and Cancer
§ 101.78
	A fruit or vegetable, low fat, and good source (without fortification) of at least one of the following:
	Vitamin A, Vitamin C, or dietary fiber
		States that diets low in fat and high in fruits and vegetables "may" or "might" reduce the risk of some cancers, without attributing any degree of reduction of risk.
		Required terms:
		    "Fiber," "Dietary fiber," or "Total dietary fiber"
		    "Total fat" or "Fat"
		    "Some types of cancer" or "Some cancers"
		Characterizes fruits and vegetables as "Foods that are low in fat and may contain Vitamin A, Vitamin C, and dietary fiber"
		Characterizes specific food as a "Good source" of one or more of the following: Dietary fiber, Vitamin A, or Vitamin C
			Low-fat diets rich in fruits and vegetables (foods that are low in fat and may contain dietary fiber, Vitamin A, or Vitamin C) may reduce the risk of some types of cancer, a disease associated with many factors.
			OR
			Broccoli is high in vitamins A and C, and is a good source of dietary fiber.

Approved Claims	Food Requirements	Claim Requirements	Model Claim Statements
		Does not specify types of fats or fatty acids or types of dietary fiber that may be related to risk of cancer. Indicates that development of cancer depends on many factors.	
Folate and Neural Tube Defects § 101.79	"Good source" of folate (at least 40 mcg folate per serving) Dietary supplements, or foods in conventional food form that are naturally good sources of folate (i.e., only non-fortified food in conventional food form) The claim shall not be made on products that contain more than 100 percent of the RDI for Vitamin A as retinol or preformed vitamin A or vitamin D Dietary supplements shall meet USP standards for disintegration and dissolution or otherwise bioavailable Amount of folate required in Nutrition Label	States that daily consumption of adequate amounts of folate by a woman during childbearing years may reduce risk of spinal bifida or other neural tube defects, without attributing any degree of reduction of risk. Required terms: Terms that specify the relationship (e.g., women who are capable of becoming pregnant and who consume adequate amounts of folate) "Folate," "Folic Acid," "Folacin," "Folate a B Vitamin," "Folic Acid, a B Vitamin," or "Folacin, a B Vitamin" "Neural tube defect," "birth defects, spinal bifida, or anencephaly," "birth defects of the brain or spinal cord anencephaly or spinal bifida," "spinal bifida or anencephaly, birth defects of the brain or spinal cord" Does not imply that the level of folate intake is the only recognized risk factor for neural tube defects. Must also include information on the multifactorial nature and prevalence of neural tube defects, dietary sources of folate, and the safe upper limit of daily intake.	Healthful diets with adequate folate may reduce a woman's risk of having a child with a brain or spinal cord birth defect.

Approved Claims	Food Requirements	Claim Requirements	Model Claim Statements
Dietary Noncariogenic Carbohydrate Sweeteners and Dental Caries § 101.80	Sugar free, and when a fermentable carbohydrate is present, the food must not lower plaque pH below 5.7. The following are eligible substances: 1) sugar alcohol (xylitol, sorbitol, mannitol, maltitol, isomalt, lactitol, hydrogenated starch hydrolysates, hydrogenated glucose syrups, erythritol, or a combination of these); 2) sugar (D-tagatose and isomaltulose); and 3) non-nutritive sweetener (sucralose)	States that noncariogenic carbohydrate sweeteners do not promote dental caries, compared to other carbohydrates, without attributing any degree of reduction of risk. Required terms: "does not promote," "may reduce the risk of," "useful [or is useful] in not promoting," or "expressly [or is expressly] for not promoting" dental caries. "Sugar alcohol," "sugar alcohols," or the name of the sugar alcohols, or D-tagatose, or sucralose (note: D-tagatose may be identified as "tagatose") "Dental caries" or "tooth decay" When the substance that is the subject of the claim is a noncariogenic sugar (i.e., D-tagatose or isomaltulose), the claim shall identify the substance as a sugar that, unlike other sugars, does not promote the development of dental caries. Includes statement that frequent between-meal consumption of foods high in sugars and starches can promote tooth decay. Packages with less than 15 square inches of surface area available for labeling may use a shortened claim.	Frequent between-meal consumption of foods high in sugars and starches promotes tooth decay. The sugar alcohols in [name of food] do not promote tooth decay. (Full claim) OR Does not promote tooth decay. (Short claim—on small packages only)

Approved Claims	Food Requirements	Claim Requirements	Model Claim Statements
Soluble Fiber from Certain Food and Risk of Coronary Heart Disease § 101.81	Meet requirements for low fat (unless due to fat content derived from listed whole oat sources), low saturated fat, and low cholesterol The food product must include one or more of the following whole oat or barley foods: 1) oat bran, 2) rolled oats, 3) whole oat flour, 4) whole grain barley or dry milled barley. The whole oat or barley foods must contain: 1) at least 0.75 g of soluble fiber per RACC of the food product; 2) Oatrim that contains at least 0.75 g of beta-glucan soluble per RACC of the food product; or 3) psyllium husk that contains at least 1.7 g of soluble fiber per RACC of food product. Beta-glucan soluble fiber from the following are eligible sources of soluble fiber: 1) oat bran; 2) rolled oats; 3) whole oat flour; 4) Oatrim; 5) whole grain barley and dry milled barley; 6) barley betafiber; and 7) soluble fiber from psyllium husk with purity of no less than 95%. The amount of soluble fiber per RACC must be declared in nutrition label	States that diets low in saturated fat and cholesterol that include soluble fiber from [source] "may" or "might" reduce the risk of heart disease, without attributing any degree of reduction of risk. Does not imply that low saturated fat and cholesterol diets that include soluble fiber are the sole means of achieving a reduced risk of CHD. Required terms: "Saturated fat" and "cholesterol" "Heart disease" or "coronary heart disease" In specifying the substance the claim uses the term "soluble fiber" qualified by the name of the eligible source of the soluble fiber, which is either whole oat or barley or psyllium seed husk. Claim specifies the daily dietary intake of the soluble fiber source necessary to reduce the risk of CHD Claim specifies the amount of soluble fiber in one serving of the product. For psyllium products — see potential warning/notice statement under 21 C.F.R. § 101.17(f)	Soluble fiber from foods such as [name of source] as part of a diet low in saturated fat and cholesterol may reduce the risk of heart disease. Diets low in saturated fat and cholesterol that include [_____ grams] soluble fiber per day from [source (can include name of food product)] may reduce the risk of heart disease. One serving of [name of food] provides___ grams of this soluble fiber.
Soy Protein and Risk of Coronary Heart Disease § 101.82	Meet requirements for low saturated fat, low cholesterol, and low fat (except that foods made from whole soybeans that contain no fat in addition to that inherent in the whole soybean are exempt from the "low fat" requirement) Shall contain at least 6.25 g of soy protein.	States diets that are low in saturated fat and cholesterol and that include soy protein "may" or "might" reduce risk of heart disease, without attributing any degree of reduction of risk. Required terms: "Heart disease" or "coronary heart disease" "Soy protein" "Saturated fat" and "cholesterol" Does not imply that consumption of soy is the only way to reduce risk of coronary heart disease. Claim specifies daily dietary intake levels of soy protein associated with reduced risk. Claim specifies amount of soy protein in a serving of food.	25 grams of soy protein a day, as part of a diet low in saturated fat and cholesterol, may reduce the risk of heart disease. A serving of [name of food] supplies_____ grams of soy protein. Diets low in saturated fat and cholesterol that include 25 grams of soy protein a day may reduce the risk of heart disease. One serving of [name of food] provides _____ grams of soy protein.

Approved Claims	Food Requirements	Claim Requirements	Model Claim Statements
Plant Sterol/Stanol Esters and Risk of Coronary Heart Disease § 101.83	Must meet requirements for low saturated fat and low cholesterol. Must contain at least 0.65 g of plant sterol esters per RACC of spreads or salad dressings, or at least 1.7 g of plant stanol esters per RACC of spreads, salad dressings, snack bars, and dietary supplements. Spreads and salad dressings that exceed 13 g fat per 50 g must bear the statement *"see nutrition information for fat content"* Salad dressings are exempted from the minimum 10% DV nutrient requirement	States diets low in saturated fat and cholesterol that include plant sterol/stanol esters may reduce the risk of coronary heart disease, without attributing any degree of reduction of risk. Required terms: "Heart disease" or "coronary heart disease" "Plant sterol esters" or "plant stanol esters;" except "vegetable oil" may replace the term "plant" if vegetable oil is the sole source of the sterol/stanol ester Claim specifies the daily dietary intake of plant sterol or stanol esters necessary to reduce CHD risk, and the amount provided per serving. Claim specifies that plant sterol or stanol esters should be consumed in two servings eaten at different times of the day with other foods.	Foods containing at least 0.65 gram per serving of vegetable oil sterol esters, eaten twice a day with meals for a daily total intake of least 1.3 grams, as part of a diet low in saturated fat and cholesterol, may reduce the risk of heart disease. A serving of [name of food] supplies_____ grams of vegetable oil sterol esters. Diets low in saturated fat and cholesterol that include two servings of foods that provide a daily total of at least 3.4 grams of plant stanol esters in two meals may reduce the risk of heart disease. A serving of [name of food] supplies _____grams of plant stanol esters.

General criteria all health claims must meet:

Only information on the value that intake or reduced intake, as part of a total dietary pattern, may have on a disease or health-related condition

Enables public to understand information provided and significance of information in the context of a total daily diet

Complete, truthful, and not misleading

Food contains, without fortification, 10 percent or more of the Daily Value of one of six nutrients (dietary supplements excepted):

Nutrient	10%DV	Nutrient	10%DV
Vitamin A	500 IU	Calcium	100 mg
Vitamin C	6 mg	Protein	5 g
Iron	1.8 mg	Fiber	2.5 g

All information in one place without intervening material (Reference statement permitted)

Uses "may" or "might" to express relationship between substance and disease

Does not quantify any degree of risk reduction

Indicates disease depends on many factors

Disqualifying nutrients in foods contained at less than the levels specified:

Disqualifying Nutrient	Food	Main Dishes	Meal Products
Fat	13.0 g	19.5 g	26.0 g
Saturated Fat	4.0 g	6.0 g	8.0 g
Cholesterol	60 mg	90 mg	120 mg
Sodium	480 mg	720 mg	960 mg

Low Fat
Food: ≤ 3 g per RACC (and per 50 g if RACC is small)
Meals and main dishes: ≤ 3 g per 100 g and not more than 30% of calories from fat

Low Saturated Fat
Food: ≤ 1 g per RACC and ≤ 15% of calories from saturated fat
Meals and main dishes: ≤ 1 g per 100 g and < 10% of calories from saturated fat

Low Cholesterol
Food: < 20 mg per RACC (and per 50 g of food if RACC is small)
Meals and main dishes: < 20 mg per 100 g

Low Sodium
Food: ≤ 35 mg per RACC (and per 50 g if RACC is small)
Meals and main dishes: ≤ 140 mg per 100 g

"Extra Lean"
Seafood or game meat: < 10 g total fat and ≤ 4.5 g saturated fat and < 95 mg cholesterol per RACC and per 100 g
Meals and main dishes: < 10 g total fat, ≤ 4.5 g saturated fat, and < 95 mg cholesterol per 100 g and per LS

High in Calcium
Food: ≥ 200 mg per RACC
Meals and main dishes:
Contains food that is high in calcium and identifies the food

Good Source of Vitamin A
Food: between 90 to 171 mcgs per RACC
Meals and main dishes: Contains food that is a good source of Vitamin A and identifies food

Good Source of Vitamin C
Food: ≥ 9 to 17.1 mg per RACC
Meals and main dishes: Contains food that is a good source of Vitamin C and identifies food

Good Source of Dietary Fiber
Food, meals, and main dishes: if not low in total fat, then must disclose the level of total fat per serving.

ABBREVIATION: DV = Daily Value; RACC = Reference Amount Customarily Consumed per Eating Occasion; LS = Labeled Serving; IU = International Units; RACC small = ≤ 30 g or 2 tablespoons or less

To be labeled as "Healthy," a food must meet the definition of "Low" for fat and saturated fat, and neither cholesterol nor sodium may be present at a level exceeding the disclosure levels in 21 C.F.R. 101.13(h). In addition, the food must comply with definitions and declaration requirements for any specific nutrient content claims.

21 C.F.R. 101.65(d)(2)

Conditions for the Use of "Healthy" [*]

Individual Food	Seafood or Game Meat[5/]	Meal or Main Dish
TOTAL FAT low fat	TOTAL FAT < 5 g fat/RACC & /100 g	TOTAL FAT low fat
SATURATED (sat) FAT low sat fat	SATURATED (sat) FAT < 2 g sat fat/RACC & /100g	SATURATED (sat) FAT low sat fat
SODIUM ≤ 480 mg/RACC and LS; or ≤ 480 mg/50 g, if RACC is small	SODIUM ≤ 480 mg/RACC and LS; or ≤ 480 mg/50 g, if RACC is small	SODIUM ≤ 600 mg/LS
CHOLESTEROL ≤ disclosure level	CHOLESTEROL < 95 mg/RACC & /100 g	CHOLESTEROL ≤ 90 mg/LS
BENEFICIAL NUTRIENTS Contains at least 10% of DV/RACC for vitamins A, C, calcium, iron, protein, or fiber The following are excepted: 1) raw fruits and vegetables; 2) frozen or canned single ingredient fruits and vegetables (may include ingredients whose addition does not change the nutrient profile of the fruit or vegetable); 3) enriched cereal-grain products that conform to a standard of identity in 21 C.F.R. 136, 137, 139.	BENEFICIAL NUTRIENTS Contains at least 10% of DV/RACC for vitamins A, C, calcium, iron, protein, or fiber	BENEFICIAL NUTRIENTS Contains at least 10% of the DV/LS of two nutrients (for a main dish product) or of three nutrients (for a meal product) of vitamin A, vitamin C, calcium, iron, protein, or fiber.
FORTIFICATION Per 21 C.F.R. § 104.20	FORTIFICATION Per 21 C.F.R. § 104.20	FORTIFICATION Per 21 C.F.R. § 104.20
OTHER CLAIMS Food complies with established definition and declaration requirements for any specific nutrient content claim		
NOTE: RACC = Reference Amount Customarily Consumed per Eating Occasion, LS = Labeled Serving, DV = Daily Value RACC small = 30 g or less or 2 tablespoons or less 5/ Raw, single ingredient seafood or game meat once processed becomes an individual food, meal, or main dish.		

* Pending issuance of new rulemaking by FDA.

Rounding Rules for Declaring Nutrients

Nutrient Serving	(M) or (V)*	Core Nutrient	Units	Increment Rounding**	Insignificant Amount	Other Relevant Information***
Calories	M	X	cal	< 5 cal express as zero < 50 cal express to nearest 5 cal increment > 50 cal express to nearest 10 cal increment	< 5 cal	§ 101.9(c)(1)
Calories from saturated fat	M		cal	< 5 cal express as zero < 50 cal express to nearest 5 cal increment > 50 cal express to nearest 10 cal increment	< 5 cal	If < 0.5 g fat: "cal from fat" not required § 101.9(c)(1)(ii)
Total fat	M	X	g	< 0.5 g express as zero < 5 g express to nearest 0.5 g increment > 5 g express to nearest 1 g increment	< 0.5 g	§ 101.9(c)(2)
Cholesterol	M		mg	< 2 mg express as zero 2–5 mg express as "less than 5 mg" > 5 mg express to nearest 5 mg increment	< 2 mg	§ 101.9(c)(3)
Sodium	M	X	mg	< 5 mg express as zero 5–140 mg express to nearest 5 mg increment > 140 mg express to nearest 10 mg increment	< 5 mg	§ 101.9(c)(4)
Total carbohydrate	M	X	g	< 0.5 g express as zero < 1 g express as "Contains less than 1 g" OR "less than 1 g" > 1 g express to nearest 1 g increment	< 1 g	§ 101.9(c)(6)
Dietary fiber	M		g	< 0.5 g express as zero < 1 g express as "Contains less than 1 g" OR "less than 1 g" > 1 g express to nearest 1 g increment	< 1 g	§ 101.9(c)(6)(i)
Soluble & Insoluble fiber	V		g	< 0.5 g express as zero < 1 g express as "Contains less than 1 g" OR "less than 1g" > 1 g express to nearest 1 g increment	< 0.5 g	§ 101.9(c)(6)(i)(A) & (B)
Sugars	M		g	< 0.5 g express as zero < 1 g express as "Contains less than 1 g" OR "less than 1g" > 1 g express to nearest 1 g increment	< 0.5 g	§ 101.9(c)(6)(ii)

Nutrient Serving	(M) or (V)*	Core Nutrient	Units	Increment Rounding**	Insignificant Amount	Other Relevant Information***
Added Sugars	M (unless less than 1 g of sugar per serving and no claims about sugar)		g	< 0.5 g express as zero < 1 g express as "Contains less than 1 g" or "less than 1 g"	< 0.5 g	§ 101.9(c)(6)(iii)
Sugar alcohol	V		g	< 0.5 g express as zero < 1 g express as "Contains less than 1 g" OR "less than 1g" > 1 g express to nearest 1 g increment	< 0.5 g	§ 101.9(c)(6)(iv)
Protein	M	X	g	< 0.5 g express as zero < 1 g express as "Contains less than 1 g" OR "less than 1 g" > 1 g express to nearest 1 g increment	< 1 g	§ 101.9(c)(7)
When declaring nutrients other than vitamins and minerals that have RDIs as a % DV	**M**		**% DV**	express to nearest 1% DV increment	< 1% DV	
Vitamins & minerals (express as % DV)	M		% DV	< 2% of RDI may be expressed as: (1) 2% if actual amount is 1.0% or more (2) zero (3) an asterisk that refers to statement "Contains less than 2% of the Daily Value of this (these) nutrient (nutrients)" (4) for Vit A, C, calcium, iron: statement "Not a significant source of_____(listing the vitamins or minerals omitted)" < 10% of RDI express to nearest 2% increment > 10% – < 50% of RDI express to nearest 5% increment > 50% of RDI express to nearest 10% increment	< 2% RDI	Vitamins and minerals other than Vit. A, C, calcium and iron, listed in (8)(iv), are mandatory if added as nutrient supplement in food or if claim is made § 101.9(c)(8)(iii) & (iv)

Nutrient Serving	(M) or (V)*	Core Nutrient	Units	Increment Rounding**	Insignificant Amount	Other Relevant Information***
Beta-carotene (express as % DV)	V		% DV	≤ 10% of RDI for vitamin A express to nearest 2% DV increment > 10% – < 50% of RDI for vitamin A express to nearest 5% DV increment > 50% of RDI for vitamin A express to nearest 10% DV increment		§ 101.9(c)(8)(vi)

* (M) Mandatory and (V) Voluntary
** To express to the nearest 1 g increment, amounts exactly halfway between two whole numbers or higher (e.g., 2.50 to 2.99 g) round up (e.g., 3 g), and amounts less than halfway between two whole numbers (e.g., 2.01 to 2.49 g) round down (e.g., 2 g).
*** *NOTES FOR ROUNDING % Daily Value (DV) for Total Fat, Saturated Fat, Cholesterol, Sodium, Total Carbohydrate, Fiber, and Protein:*
(1) To calculate % DV, divide either the actual (unrounded) quantitative amount or the declared (rounded) amount by the appropriate RDI or DRV. Use whichever amount will provide the greatest consistency on the food label and prevent unnecessary consumer confusion (§ 101.9(d)(7)(ii)).
(2) When % DV values fall between two whole numbers, rounding shall be as follows:
    —for values exactly halfway between two whole numbers or higher (e.g., 2.50 to 2.99) the value shall round up (e.g., 3%)
    —for values less than halfway between two whole numbers (e.g., 2.01 to 2.49) the values shall round down (e.g., 2%).

Definitions of Nutrient Content Claims

NUTRIENTS*	FREE	LOW	REDUCED/LESS	COMMENTS[1]
	Synonyms for "Free": "Zero," "No," "Without," "Trivial Source of," "Negligible Source of," "Dietarily Insignificant Source of" Definitions for "Free" for meals and main dishes are the stated values per labeled serving	Synonyms for "Low": "Little," ("Few" for Calories), "Contains a Small Amount of," "Low Source of"	Synonyms for "Reduced/Less": "Lower" ("Fewer" for Calories) "Modified" may be used in statement of identity Definitions for meals and main dishes are same as for individual foods on a per 100 g basis	For "Free," "Very Low," or "Low," must indicate if food meets a definition without benefit of special processing, alteration, formulation or reformulation; e.g., "broccoli, a fat-free food" or "celery, a low calorie food"
Calories § 101.60(b)	Less than 5 calories per reference amount and per labeled serving Not defined for meals or main dishes	40 calories or less per reference amount consumed if reference amount is greater than 30 grams (and per 50 g if reference amount is smaller) Meals and main dishes: 120 cal or less per 100 g	At least 25% fewer calories per reference amount than an appropriate reference food (or for meals and main dishes, at least 25% fewer calories per 100 g) Reference food may not be "Low Calorie" Uses term "Fewer" rather than "Less"	"Light" or "Lite": If 50% or more of the calories are from fat, fat must be reduced by at least 50% per reference amount. If less than 50% of calories are from fat, fat must be reduced at least 50% or calories reduced at least 1/3 per reference amount § 101.56 "Light" or "Lite" meal or main dish product meets definition for "Low Calorie" or "Low Fat" meal and is labeled to indicate which definition is met For dietary supplements: Calorie claims can only be made when the reference product is greater than 40 calories per serving

NUTRIENTS*	FREE	LOW	REDUCED/LESS	COMMENTS[1]
Total Fat § 101.62(b)	Less than 0.5 g per reference amount and per labeled serving (or for meals and main dishes, less than 0.5 g per labeled serving) No ingredient that is fat or understood to contain fat except as in note 2	3 g or less per reference amount (and per 50 g if reference amount is small) Meals and main dishes: 3 g or less per 100 g and not more than 30% of calories from fat	At least 25% less fat per reference amount than an appropriate reference food (or for meals and main dishes, at least 25% less fat per 100 g) Reference food may not be "Low Fat"	"_____% Fat Free": OK if food meets the requirements for "Low Fat" 100% Fat Free: Food must be "Fat Free" "Light": See above For dietary supplements: Fat claims cannot be made for products that are 40 calories or less per serving
Saturated Fat § 101.62(c)	Less than 0.5 g saturated fat and less than 0.5 g trans fatty acids per reference amount and per labeled serving (or for meals and main dishes, less than 0.5 g saturated fat and less than 0.5 g trans fatty acid per labeled serving) No ingredient that is understood to contain saturated fat except as in note 2	1 g or less per reference amount and 15% or fewer calories from saturated fat Meals and main dishes: 1 g or less per 100 g and less than 10% of calories from saturated fat	At least 25% less saturated fat per reference amount than an appropriate reference food (or for meals and main dishes, at least 25% less saturated fat per 100 g) Reference food may not be "Low Saturated Fat"	Next to all saturated fat claims, must declare the amount of cholesterol if 2 mg or more per reference amount, and the amount of total fat if more than 3 g per reference amount (or 0.5 g or more of total fat for "Saturated Fat Free") (or for meals and main dishes, per labeled serving) For dietary supplements: Saturated fat claims cannot be made for products that are 40 calories or less per serving

NUTRIENTS*	FREE	LOW	REDUCED/LESS	COMMENTS[1]
Cholesterol § 101.62(d)	Less than 2 mg per reference amount and per labeled serving (or for meals and main dishes, less than 2 mg per labeled serving) No ingredient that contains cholesterol except as in note 2	20 mg or less per reference amount (and per 50 g of food if reference amount is small) Meals and main dishes: 20 mg or less per 100 g	At least 25% less cholesterol per reference amount than an appropriate reference food (or for meals and main dishes, at least 25% less cholesterol per 100 g) Reference food may not be "Low Cholesterol"	Cholesterol claims only allowed when food contains 2 g or less saturated fat per reference amount, or for meals and main dishes products, per labeled serving size for "free" claims or per 100 g for "low" and "reduced/ less" claims Must declare the amount of total fat next to cholesterol claim when fat exceeds 13 g per reference amount or labeled serving (or per 50 g of food if reference amount is small), or when the fat exceeds 19.5 g per labeled serving for main dishes or 26 g for meal products For dietary supplements: cholesterol claims cannot be made for products that are 40 calories or less per serving

NUTRIENTS*	FREE	LOW	REDUCED/LESS	COMMENTS¹
Sodium § 101.61(b)	Less than 5 mg per reference amount and per labeled serving (or for meals and main dishes, less than 5 mg per labeled serving) No ingredient that is sodium chloride or generally understood to contain sodium except as in note 2 "Salt Free" must meet criterion for "Sodium Free"	140 mg or less per reference amount (and per 50 g if reference amount is small) Meals and main dishes: 140 mg or less per 100 g "Very Low Sodium": 35 mg or less per reference amount (and per 50 g if reference amount is small). For meals and main dishes: 35 mg or less per 100 g	At least 25% less sodium per reference amount than an appropriate reference food Reference food may not be "Low Sodium"	"Light" (for sodium reduced products): If food is "Low Calorie" and "Low Fat" and sodium is reduced by at least 50% "Light in Sodium" If sodium is reduced by at least 50% per reference amount. For meals and main dishes, "Light in Sodium" meets definition for "Low in Sodium" "No Salt Added" and "Unsalted" must meet conditions of use and must declare "This is Not A Sodium Free Food" on Information Panel if food is not "Sodium Free" "Lightly Salted": 50% less sodium than normally added to reference food and if not "Low Sodium" so labeled on Information Panel
Sugars § 101.60(c)	"Sugar Free": Less than 0.5 g sugars per reference amount and per labeled serving (or for meals and main dishes, less than 0.5 g per labeled serving) No ingredient that is a sugar or generally understood to contain sugars except as in note 2 Disclose calorie profile (e.g., "Low Calorie")	Not defined. No basis for a recommended intake	At least 25% less sugars per reference amount than an appropriate reference food (or for meals and main dishes, at least 25% less sugar per 100 g) May not use this claim on dietary supplements of vitamins and minerals	"No Added Sugars" and "Without Added Sugars" are allowed if no sugar or sugar containing ingredient is added during processing. State if food is not "Low" or "Reduced Calorie" The terms "Unsweetened" and "No Added Sweeteners" remain as factual statements Claims about reducing dental caries are implied health claims "Sugars" do not include sugar alcohols

NOTES:

[1]Restaurant Foods that bear claims are exempt from certain accompanying information that must be provided by foods from other sources. See specific provisions for more information.

[2]Except if the ingredient listed in the ingredient statement has an asterisk that refers to the statement below the list of ingredients, which states "adds a trivial amount of sugar," "adds a negligible amount of sugar," or "adds a dietarily insignificant amount of sugar."

*"Small Reference Amount" reference amount of 30 g or less or 2 tablespoons or less (for dehydrated foods that are typically consumed when rehydrated with water or a diluent containing an insignificant amount, as defined in § 101.9(f)(1) of all nutrients per reference amount, the per 50 g criterion refers to the prepared form of the food).

Statement "See _____ panel for nutrition information" must accompany all content claims when levels exceed: 13 g Fat, 4 g Saturated Fat, 60 mg Cholesterol, or 480 mg Sodium per reference amount, per labeled serving or, for foods with small reference amounts, per 50 g, disclosure statement is required as part of claim (e.g., "See side panel for information on fat and other nutrients").

Other Nutrient Content Claims	
"Lean"	On seafood or game meat that contains 10 g total fat, 4.5 g or less saturated fat and 95 mg cholesterol per reference amount and per 100 g (for meals & main dishes, meets criteria per 100 g and per label serving). On mixed dishes not measurable with a cup (as defined in 21 C.F.R. 101.12(b) in table 2) that contain less than 8 g total fat, 3.5 g or less saturated fat, and less than 80 mg cholesterol per reference amount.
"Extra Lean"	On seafood or game meat that contains 5 g total fat, 2 g or less saturated fat, and 95 mg cholesterol per reference amount and per 100 g (for meals and main dishes, meets criteria per 100 g and per label serving)
"Good Source," "Contains," or "Provides"	Contains 10% or more of Daily Value (DV) to describe protein, vitamins, minerals, dietary fiber, or potassium per reference amount May be used on meals or main dishes to indicate that product contains a food that meets definition but may not be used to describe meal or main dish itself May not be used for total carbohydrates
"High," "Rich in," or "Excellent Source of"[4]	Contains 20% or more of Daily Value (DV) to describe protein, vitamins, minerals, dietary fiber, or potassium per reference amount May be used on meals or main dishes to indicate that product contains a food that meets definition but may not be used to describe meal or main dish itself May not be used for total carbohydrates
"More," "fortified," "enriched," "added, "extra," or "plus"	10% or more of the DV per reference amount May only be used for vitamins, minerals, protein, dietary fiber, and potassium
"High Potency"	May be used on foods to describe individual vitamins or minerals that are present at 100% or more of the RDI per RACC or on a multi-ingredient food product that contains 100% or more of the RDI for at least 2/3 of the vitamins and minerals with RDIs and that are present in the product at 2% or more of the RDI (e.g., "High potency multivitamin, multimineral dietary supplement tablets")
"Modified"	May be used in statement of identity that bears a relative claim, e.g., "Modified Fat Cheese Cake, Contains 35% Less Fat Than Other Regular Cheese Cake"
Any Fiber Claim	If claim is made and food is not low in total fat, must state level total fat per labeled serving
Antioxidant Claims	Each nutrient for which a claim is made has recognized antioxidant activity (scientific evidence that after absorption from GI tract, the substance participates in physiological, biochemical, or cellular processes that inactivate free radicals or prevent free radical-initiated chemical reactions) An RDI has been established for each antioxidant nutrient present

Other Nutrient Content Claims	
	Each antioxidant nutrient is present in amounts sufficient to qualify for a claim of "high," "good," or "more"
	Beta-carotene may be the subject of an antioxidant claim when the level of vitamin A present as beta-carotene in the food is sufficient to qualify for the claim.
	Claim must identify the particular nutrients for which it is made, and may not use terms such as "complete" or "antioxidant complex"

4 Dietary supplement of vitamins and minerals can not use these claims to describe any nutrient or ingredient (e.g., fiber protein, psyllium, bran) other than vitamins or minerals

Relative Claims

To bear a relative claim about the level of a nutrient, the amount of that nutrient in the food must be compared to an amount of nutrient in an appropriate reference food as specified below.

"Light"/"Lite"	(1) A food representative of the type of food bearing the claim, e.g., average value of top three brands for representative value from valid data base; and (2) A similar food (e.g., potato chips for potato chips)
"Reduced" and "Added" (or "Fortified" and "Enriched")	(1) An established regular product or average representative product and (2) A similar food
"More" and "Less" (or "Fewer")	(1) An established regular product or average representative product and (2) A dissimilar food in the same product category which may be generally substituted for labeled food (e.g., potato chips for pretzels) or a similar food

Accompanying Information for Relative (or Comparative) Claims

For all relative claims, percent (or fraction) of change and identity of reference food must be declared in immediate proximity to the most prominent claim. Quantitative comparison of the amount of the nutrient in the product per labeled serving with that in the reference food must be declared on the Information Panel. A relative claim for decreased levels of a nutrient may not be made if the nutrient content of the reference food meets the requirement for a "low" claim for that nutrient (e.g., 3 g fat or less).

Implied Claims

Claims about a food or ingredient that suggest that the nutrient or ingredient is absent or present in a certain amount or claims about a food that suggest a food may be useful in maintaining healthy dietary practices and which are made with an explicit claim (e.g., "healthy, contains 3 grams of fat") are implied claims and are prohibited unless provided for in a regulation by FDA. In addition, the agency has devised a petition system whereby specific additional claims may be considered.

Claims that a food contains or is made with an ingredient that is known to contain a particular nutrient may be made if the product is "Low" in or a "Good Source" of the nutrient associated with the claim (e.g., "good source of oat bran").

Equivalence claims: "Contains as much [nutrients] as a [food]" may be made if both reference food and labeled food are a "Good Source" of the nutrient on a per serving basis (e.g., "Contains as much vitamin C as an 8 ounce glass of orange juice").

The following label statements are generally not considered implied claims unless they are made in a nutrition context: 1) avoidance claims for religious, food intolerance, or other non-nutrition related reasons (e.g., "100% milk free"); 2) statements about non-nutritive substances (e.g., "no artificial colors"); 3) added value statements (e.g., "made with real butter"); 4) statements of identity (e.g., "corn oil" or "corn oil margarine"); and 5) special dietary statements made in compliance with a specific Part 105 provision.

The term "healthy" and related terms ("health," "healthful," "healthfully," "healthfulness," "healthier," "healthiest," "healthily," and "healthiness") may be used if the food meets the requirements in 21 C.F.R. § 101.65(d)(2).

Claims on Food for Infants and Children Less Than Two Years of Age

Nutrient content claims are not permitted on foods intended specifically for infants and children less than two years of age except:

1) Claims describing the percentage of vitamins and minerals in a food in relation to a Daily Value.
2) Claims on infant formulas provided for in Part 107.
3) The terms "Unsweetened" and "Unsalted" as taste claims.
4) "Sugar Free" and "No Added Sugar" claims on dietary supplements only.

Terms Covered That Are Not Nutrient Content Claims

"Fresh"	A raw food that has not been frozen, heat processed, or otherwise preserved
"Fresh Frozen"	Food that was quickly frozen while still fresh

Chapter 12

The Regulation of Dietary Supplements

James William Woodlee, Cynthia L. Meyer & Anthony L. Young, Kleinfeld, Kaplan and Becker, LLP, Washington, D.C.

Key Points

- The Dietary Supplement Health and Education Act became law in 1994, establishing dietary supplements as a separate category of food with their own safety standards, labeling requirements, and good manufacturing practice requirements.

- Whether a product is a "dietary supplement" is determined by the product's formulation or delivery form, and by the definition of "dietary ingredients." Any "dietary ingredient" intended to supplement the diet may be a dietary supplement, so long as it meets other statutory and regulatory criteria.

- Regardless of the form of a dietary supplement, it may not be represented as a conventional food or for use as the sole item of a meal or of the diet. If claims are made for the cure, mitigation, or treatment of disease, the product will be assumed to be intended for use as a drug.

- The first use of an ingredient determines its eligibility for use as a dietary supplement. If a product is first marketed as a dietary supplement and is later approved as a drug or biologic, it can continue to be marketed as a dietary supplement. If the ingredient is first marketed, however, as a drug or biologic, it is not normally eligible to be regulated as a dietary supplement.

- As a practical matter, safety substantiation for dietary supplements should be similar to that for foods. Careful written documentation by one or more qualified experts supporting the safety of the ingredient for its recommended use will help a manufacturer not only meet its regulatory obligations under the Federal Food, Drug, and Cosmetic Act, but also minimize the risk of product liability exposure in the event that something goes wrong.

- "New dietary ingredients" are those that were not marketed as a dietary ingredient in the United States before October 15, 1994. If a new dietary ingredient has not been present in the food supply as an article used for food in a form in which the food has not been chemically altered, then the marketer must submit a notification to the Food and Drug Administration (FDA) at least 75 days before marketing the product with information demonstrating that dietary supplements containing the ingredient will reasonably be expected to be safe.

Key Points, continued

- Comprehensive good manufacturing practice regulations for dietary supplements are now in place. They establish process controls and documentation requirements to assure dietary supplement quality and are a principal focus of FDA inspections.

- A dietary supplement label must include: a) a statement of identity; b) an ingredient statement; c) a Supplement Facts box; d) the name and place of business of the manufacturer, packer, or distributor; e) a domestic street address or phone number through which adverse event reports can be received; and f) an accurate statement of the quantity of contents.

- Within 30 days of making a structure-function claim, the marketer must notify FDA that it has included such claim on the label or labeling of its dietary supplement and such claims must be linked to a statutorily required disclaimer.

- The Federal Trade Commission (FTC) addresses dietary supplement advertising. The FTC has published a guide to assist in understanding its rules, entitled "Dietary Supplements: An Advertising Guide for Industry."

INTRODUCTION

For many years, U.S. Food and Drug Administration (FDA)-related laws provided only one regulatory option for dietary supplements: they could be marketed and were regulated as "foods." As a result, FDA took the position that ingredients in dietary supplements had to meet the same safety standards as ingredients added to foods—that is, they had to be "generally recognized as safe" (GRAS) or covered by a food additive regulation.

FDA also normally took the position that labeling claims for dietary supplements were governed by the same standards as those for foods. As a result, many health-related claims—even claims that, by today's standards, would be considered relatively benign claims about a dietary supplement's effect on the healthy structure or function of the body—could cause a supplement to be regulated as a drug, and therefore as an unapproved new drug. From shortly after the enactment of the Federal Food, Drug, and Cosmetic Act (FDCA), FDA brought actions against marketers of "dietary supplements" that made very frank drug claims as well as those making claims that would now be considered to be structure-function claims. These reported cases helped shape the rich history of our food and drug law.

In 1994, however, the Dietary Supplement Health and Education Act (DSHEA) amended the FDCA, adopting, for the first time, a legal definition for "dietary supplement" and included provisions specifically applicable to dietary supplements (related primarily to the safety, labeling, and ingredients to be used in such products). As a result, dietary supplements now occupy a unique niche in the framework of food law and the FDCA.

Dietary supplements are still "foods" under the law, and many of the laws and regulations applicable to foods continue to apply. Dietary ingredients in dietary supplements, however, no longer need to be GRAS or covered by a food additive regulation to be legally marketed. In addition, there are some unique health-related claims that are permitted only for dietary supplements and not for conventional foods.

What Is a "Dietary Supplement"?

Statutory Definition

DSHEA codified a new definition for dietary supplements. A product is a "dietary supplement" only if it conforms to section 201(ff) of the FDCA, which establishes various criteria governing 1) ingredients, 2) formulation, 3) intended use, and 4) relationship to drugs and biologics. These criteria are as follows:

A product is a "dietary supplement" only if it meets various criteria governing

- *ingredients*
- *formulation*
- *intended use*
- *relationship to drugs and biologics.*

Ingredients. A dietary supplement must contain one or more of the following "dietary ingredients": 1) a vitamin, 2) a mineral, 3) an herb or other botanical, 4) an amino acid, 5) a dietary substance for use by man to supplement the diet by increasing the total dietary intake, or 6) a concentrate, metabolite, constituent, extract, or combination of any of the ingredients listed above. In addition, a dietary supplement may not be a tobacco product.

If this list of eligible ingredients seems almost all encompassing, it is because of the phrase in the fifth part of the definition. The phrase "dietary substance for use by man to supplement the diet by increasing the total dietary intake" might lead one to conclude that any new substance added to the diet through a dietary supplement would be covered by this phrase because it will increase the dietary intake of that substance to above zero. FDA, however, has interpreted "dietary substance" to mean a substance that is or has been in the diet and used for food, and not a substance that is for the first time intended for use to supplement the diet. The rationale for this position is straightforward; "dietary" means of, or pertaining to, the diet and one cannot increase the total dietary intake of a substance that is not presently in the diet.

It is a historical fact that many synthetic drug ingredients were originally found in and derived from plants (botanicals) and then later synthesized and manufactured as chemical drugs. FDA has taken the position that a synthetic copy of a constituent of a botanical was never part of the botanical and thus cannot be a "constituent" of the botanical that qualifies as a dietary ingredient under section 201(ff)(1)(F) of the FDCA (21 U.S.C. 321(ff)(1)(F)). Similarly, a synthetic version of a botanical extract is not an "extract" of a botanical under section 201(ff)(1)(F) because it was not actually extracted from the botanical.

A dietary supplement may not be represented as a conventional food or for use as a sole item of a meal or of the diet.

Formulation. Dietary supplements must be intended for ingestion and may be formulated either into products that are in capsule, tablet, liquid, powder, soft-gel, gelcap, or gummy form, or into products that are in conventional food form (such as beverages or nutrition bars). Regardless of how it is formulated, however, a dietary supplement may not be represented as a conventional food or for use as a sole item of a meal or of the diet.

If a product looks, smells, and tastes like a conventional food, can it be marketed as a dietary supplement? The answer would appear to be "yes," but only so long as the product is not "represented as" a conventional food. And there's the rub: at this time, from FDA's perspective, it does not take much to "represent" a product as a conventional food. For example, describing a product as a "shake in chocolate and vanilla flavors" or as a "good tasting and satisfying treat," or "snack" may be enough to "represent" it as a conventional food and exclude it from dietary supplement status. As a general rule, if a product can be consumed primarily for its taste or aroma, or if it can be substituted for a conventional food in the diet, then there is a risk that FDA could regulate it as a conventional food and not a dietary supplement. While there have been no court decisions on this issue, FDA has publicly objected to the characterization of soup, yogurt snack products, and candy bar-like products as dietary supplements. In response to the popularity of "energy drinks," many of which are marketed as dietary supplements, FDA has also issued "Guidance for Industry: Distinguishing Liquid Dietary Supplements from Beverages." In addition, it should be noted that—as the statutory language provides—FDA takes the position that products represented as "meal replacements" are ineligible for dietary supplement status.

What does "intended for ingestion" mean? A court opinion states "The ordinary and plain meaning of the term 'ingestion' means to take into the stomach and gastrointestinal tract by means of enteral administration." *United States v. Ten Cartons Ener-B Nasal Gel*, 888 F. Supp. 381, 393-94 (E.D.N.Y.), *aff'd*, 72 F.3d 285 (2d Cir. 1995). As a result, FDA has taken the position that nasal products, topical skin products, sublingual tablets, sprayed products that are absorbed in the mouth, aromatherapy products, gargles, and throat lozenges are ineligible for dietary supplement status because they are not "intended for ingestion." On the other hand, FDA has accepted sublingual and lozenge products that are labeled with directions to be held in the mouth or under the tongue and then swallowed (ingested).

Intended Use. A dietary supplement must be labeled as a dietary supplement and be intended to supplement the diet. As discussed above, it may not be intended for use as a conventional food. Also, it may not be intended for use as a drug; that is, it may not be intended for use in the diagnosis, cure, mitigation, treatment, or prevention of disease. (A dietary supplement, however, is not a "drug" if it is labeled with an authorized health claim, even though that claim may refer to a disease. Health claims are described later in this chapter.)

A dietary supplement may not be intended for use as a conventional food or as a drug.

Relationship to Drugs and Biologics. A dietary supplement may, under some circumstances, include substances that are approved or investigational drugs— if the substances were used first as foods or dietary supplements.

Approved Drugs. Under the statute, a product is eligible for regulation as a dietary supplement if it is or includes an article that was approved as a new drug or licensed as a biologic, so long as the article was lawfully marketed as a dietary supplement or as a food prior to the date it was approved as a drug or biologic (unless FDA has issued a regulation stating otherwise). If the article was not lawfully marketed as a dietary supplement or food prior to the approval date, then it is ineligible for dietary supplement status (unless, again, FDA has issued a regulation stating otherwise).

Investigational Drugs. If an article has been authorized for investigation as a new drug in substantial clinical investigations that have been instituted and whose existence has been made public, and if the article was not lawfully marketed as a dietary supplement or food prior to the date when it was authorized for investigational use pursuant to an Investigational New Drug Application (IND), then it is ineligible for dietary supplement status (unless FDA has issued a regulation stating otherwise). FDA has taken the position that a product labeled and promoted as a dietary supplement was not legally marketed as a dietary supplement before the approval of an IND because the product was adulterated due to the presence of a new dietary ingredient that failed to meet the requirements of the FDCA, i.e., for which no premarket notification had been made to FDA.

In its "Draft Guidance for Industry: Dietary Supplements: New Dietary Ingredient Notifications and Related Issues (August 2016) (Contains Nonbinding Recommendations Draft–Not for Implementation)," FDA discusses these provisions in a question-and-answer format, and this draft guidance should be consulted if there is any approved or investigational drug issue with respect to a dietary ingredient.

An article marketed as a dietary supplement or food before being approved as a new drug is eligible for dietary supplement status.

The Definition of "Article." The rules summarized in the two paragraphs above refer to "articles"; that is, if an "article" was marketed as a dietary supplement or food before being approved as a new drug, it is then eligible for dietary supplement status. But what exactly is an "article"? A court decision suggests that it is any substance that is intended to be in a dietary supplement. For example, if the dietary supplement is formulated to contain an ingredient that has been approved as a new drug, and if it is sold or promoted based on the presence of that ingredient, then that ingredient may be considered the relevant "article" for purposes of determining whether the product is eligible for dietary supplement status. This may be true even if the ingredient is a relatively minor constituent in the overall dietary supplement product.

The court decision dealt with a product containing red yeast rice, called "Cholestin," which was marketed as a dietary supplement to address cholesterol. FDA argued that the red yeast rice was manufactured purposely to contain high levels of lovastatin, an approved cholesterol-lowering drug that was not marketed as a food or dietary supplement prior to approval. FDA also argued that Cholestin was promoted for its lovastatin content. Therefore, FDA considered lovastatin to be the relevant "article" for purposes of determining whether Cholestin was eligible for dietary supplement status. The manufacturer argued that Cholestin simply contained red yeast rice, a traditional Asian product that happens to include some lovastatin as a minor constituent. It considered red yeast rice to be the relevant "article." The court found for FDA, concluding that, in this case, the relevant "article" was lovastatin.

The manufacturer in that case also argued that, even if lovastatin were the relevant "article," it was eligible for dietary supplement status because it had been marketed as a constituent of many traditional foods prior to its having been approved as a drug. The court rejected this argument, however, agreeing with FDA that, for lovastatin to have been marketed in foods prior to approval as a drug, the marketed foods must have been promoted for their lovastatin content, or the lovastatin must have been increased or optimized as a constituent. As a result, Cholestin was determined to be a drug, not a dietary supplement, because it contained lovastatin, an article that was not marketed as a dietary supplement or food before it was approved as a drug. *Pharmanex Inc. v. Shalala*, 35 F. Supp. 2d 1341 (D. Utah 1999), *rev'd and remanded*, 221 F.3d 1151 (10th Cir. 2000).

DIETARY SUPPLEMENT SAFETY

Under the law, all dietary supplements must be safe (i.e., not "adulterated").

Under the law, all dietary supplements must be safe.

♦ A dietary supplement is considered adulterated if either it, or any dietary ingredient contained in it, presents a "significant or unreasonable risk of illness or injury" under conditions of use recommended or suggested in labeling (or if no conditions of use are suggested or recommended in the labeling, under "ordinary" conditions of use).

♦ A dietary supplement also is considered adulterated if either it, or any dietary ingredient contained in it, bears or contains any poisonous or deleterious substance that may render it injurious to health.

There is a parallel between dietary supplements and GRAS food substances: the law leaves the initial determination of safety up to the manufacturer. Unlike GRAS food substances, however, there is no requirement that dietary supplements be "generally recognized" in the scientific community "as safe," or that safety be based on data and information that is published or otherwise generally available to the scientific community.

A comparison of the safety standards for dietary supplements and GRAS food substances is interesting. Whereas dietary supplements may not present a "significant or unreasonable risk of illness or injury," FDA has concluded that GRAS status must be based on "reasonable certainty that the substance is not harmful under the intended conditions of use." 62 Fed. Reg. 18,937 (Apr. 17, 1997). It is possible that, to have some confidence that one's dietary supplement does not present a "significant or unreasonable risk of illness or injury," one would have to have a "reasonable certainty that the substance is not harmful"—but that is entering into the realm of speculation. Suffice it to say that the exact scope of the data needed to support safety has not been as clearly elucidated for dietary supplements as it has been for foods.

The exact scope of data needed to support safety has not been as clearly elucidated for dietary supplements as it has been for foods.

Accordingly, a manufacturer would be well advised to substantiate the safety of dietary supplements in a manner that would be recognized as adequate by the scientific community. As a practical matter, such substantiation would be similar to that used for foods. For well-known dietary ingredients, it might be appropriate to rely on a conclusion based on a general recognition of safety supported by a long period of common use at the levels intended for the target population or supported by adequate studies reported in the scientific literature. Where there is any question, however, about the safety of a particular ingredient or product, or about the interpretation of the scientific literature, it would be prudent to obtain the supporting opinion of qualified experts.

Regardless of how a safety conclusion is reached, the company should document its conclusion in sufficient detail to substantiate that it has addressed the relevant safety issues. Careful documentation of the safety of a dietary supplement will help a manufacturer not only to meet its regulatory obligations under the FDCA but also to minimize product liability exposure in the event that something goes wrong.

It is particularly important that a dietary supplement manufacturer prepare labeling with clear conditions for use and warnings consistent with the safety profile of its dietary supplement. Under the statute, if labeling does not limit the conditions for use, then a dietary supplement may be considered adulterated if it presents a significant or unreasonable risk of illness or injury under all "ordinary" conditions of use—which can be a very broad category of uses. In most cases, then, it is prudent to limit the conditions of use recommended or suggested in labeling through the use of clear directions and warnings. For example, in March 2002, FDA issued a Consumer Advisory with respect to dietary supplements containing the botanical ingredient kava.[1] Following this advisory, many manufacturers and distributors of such products included cautionary information from the advisory on product labels.

FDA bears the burden of proof on each element to show that a dietary supplement is adulterated.

DSHEA offers dietary supplement manufacturers two protections in the event of a legal action by FDA against the safety of a product. First, it specifies that FDA shall bear the burden of proof on each element to show that a dietary supplement is adulterated. Second, the manufacturer has the opportunity to present its views to FDA (i.e., to try to persuade FDA not to refer the case to a U.S. Attorney). The burden of proof on FDA to show that a dietary supplement is not safe was firmly established in 2006 when the Tenth Circuit Court of Appeals held that "Congress expressly placed the burden of proof on the government to determine whether a dietary supplement is adulterated" and further stated that: "The burden remains on the agency to show that the risks associated with a dietary supplement outweigh benefits and are, therefore, unreasonable." *Nutraceutical Corporation v. von Eschenbach*, 459 F.3d 1033.

In reaching its decision, the court relied upon the standard of review for such FDA decisions that has evolved over the past 20 years: "The review of scientific literature is properly the province of the FDA, to which this Court grants deference based on its expertise" (459 F.3d at 1043). Using this standard, and its own review of the record, the court found that FDA had made its case by the "preponderance of the evidence" standard set out in DSHEA.

As a practical matter, the burden of proof provision of DSHEA, as applied by the court in *Nutraceutical Corporation*, means that FDA may, through rulemaking, deem a dietary supplement (or dietary ingredient) to be adulterated. In so doing, FDA has the burden to show by a preponderance of the evidence that the risks are either significant or outweigh the benefits and are, therefore, unreasonable. In such a rulemaking, FDA's review of scientific information would normally be given deference because of the agency's expertise.

New Dietary Ingredients

If a dietary supplement contains a "new dietary ingredient," then: 1) it is subject to an additional safety requirement, and 2) information on the ingredient may need to be reported to FDA prior to marketing the product.

♦ **What is a "new dietary ingredient"?** Any dietary ingredient that was not marketed in the United States in a dietary supplement before October 15, 1994, is a new dietary ingredient. Manufacturers are responsible for determining whether their ingredients meet this definition of "new."

Manufacturers are responsible for determining whether their ingredients meet the "new dietary ingredient" definition.

♦ **What additional safety requirements apply?** There is an additional standard for a "new dietary ingredient": A dietary supplement product is considered adulterated if it is, or contains, a "new dietary ingredient" for which there is inadequate information to provide reasonable assurance that such ingredient does not present a significant or unreasonable risk of illness or injury, when used under the conditions recommended or suggested in the labeling of the dietary supplement. Therefore, manufacturers must ensure that their "new" ingredients are adequately substantiated as being safe when used under the conditions recommended or suggested in the labeling of the dietary supplement in which they are contained. (Of course, as discussed above, all dietary ingredients should be substantiated as being safe.)

♦ **When does information need to be reported to FDA?** If a dietary supplement contains a new dietary ingredient, but the ingredient has been present in the food supply as an article used for food in a form in which the food has not been chemically altered, then it need not be reported to FDA. A report, however, must be submitted if this is not the case; that is, if the ingredient has not been present in the food supply, or if its form has been chemically altered for use in a dietary supplement as compared with its form in the food supply (known as a "reportable new dietary ingredient" or "reportable NDI").

For a reportable NDI, two requirements must be met. First, there must be a history of use or other evidence establishing that the dietary ingredient, when used under the conditions recommended or suggested in the labeling of the dietary supplement, will reasonably be expected to be safe. Second, at least 75 days before being introduced or delivered for introduction into interstate commerce, the manufacturer or distributor of the dietary ingredient or dietary supplement must submit information to FDA, including any citation to and copies of published articles or unpublished reports of safety studies, that is the basis on which the manufacturer or distributor has concluded that a dietary supplement containing such dietary ingredient will reasonably be expected to be safe. (Note that FDA will keep the 75-day notification confidential for 90 days after its receipt; after that time it becomes public, except for trade secrets or confidential commercial information.)

If these two conditions for a reportable NDI are not met, then the dietary supplement is deemed adulterated, and may be subject to FDA enforcement action if and when it is marketed.

In its "Draft Guidance for Industry: Dietary Supplements: New Dietary Ingredient Notifications and Related Issues (August 2016) (Contains Nonbinding Recommendations Draft–Not for Implementation)," which FDA distributed for comment purposes only, FDA discusses the NDI provision in detail.

A docket in which NDI notifications are filed has been established on Regulations.gov.[2] From this docket, it is possible to determine how FDA has addressed each NDI notification that it has received.

A petition process also is available for reportable NDIs: the FDCA permits a petition to be filed proposing the issuance of an order prescribing the conditions under which an NDI reasonably will be expected to be safe. FDA must make a decision on such a petition within 180 days of its filing. To date, there have been no petitions filed under this provision.

Facility Registration

Facilities that manufacture, process, pack, or hold food, including dietary supplements, for consumption in the United States are required to register the facility with FDA.

Under the Public Health Security and Bioterrorism Preparedness and Response Act of 2002, as amended by the Food Safety Modernization Act (FSMA), owners, operators, or agents in charge of domestic or foreign facilities that manufacture, process, pack, or hold food, including dietary supplements, for consumption in the United States are required to register the facility with FDA. Retail establishments are exempt from registration. Food facilities that are required to register with FDA must renew their registrations every two years (between October 1 and December 31 of each even-numbered year).

Foreign facilities that manufacture, process, pack, or hold food, including ingredients intended for use in dietary supplements, or dietary supplements, also are required to register and renew unless food from that facility undergoes further processing (including packaging) by another foreign facility before the food is exported to the United States. If the subsequent foreign facility performs only a minimal activity, however, such as putting on a label, both facilities are required to register.

All facilities are also subject to the recordkeeping requirements of the Bioterrorism Act.

cGMPs

A dietary supplement is adulterated if it has been prepared, packed, or held under conditions that do not meet current Good Manufacturing Practice (cGMP) regulations. FDA promulgated cGMP regulations for dietary supplements on June 25, 2007 (72 Fed. Reg. 34,751; 21 C.F.R. Part 111), and all companies should now be in compliance with the cGMP regulations. The focus of the regulations is the requirement for each manufacturer to implement a system of production and process controls that covers all stages of manufacturing, packaging, labeling, and holding of the dietary supplement to ensure the quality of dietary supplements and that dietary supplements are packaged and labeled as specified in the master manufacturing record required for each product.

FDA did not propose to require expiration dating for dietary supplements because, while "there are current and generally available methods to determine the expiration date of some dietary ingredients, for example vitamin C, we are uncertain whether there are current and generally available methods to determine the expiration dating of other dietary ingredients, especially botanical dietary ingredients." 68 Fed. Reg. 12,157, 12,203-04 (Mar. 13, 2003). In the final cGMP rule, FDA confirmed this decision. Nonetheless, as a practical matter, expiration dating, or shelf-life dating as it is sometimes called, is demanded by retailers. And FDA has made clear that "any expiration date that you place on a product label (including a 'best if used by' date) should be supported by data." (72 Fed. Reg. 34,855-56.) This statement by FDA is not in the cGMP regulations, however, and there is no regulatory requirement that such data be maintained and made available to FDA inspectors.

FDA does not require expiration dating for dietary supplements but it is, for the most part, a market necessity.

FDA Warning Letters to dietary supplement companies regarding cGMP violations provide a rich source of information regarding FDA's interpretation of the cGMP regulations and enforcement observations and may be found on FDA's website.[3]

Under the FDA FSMA, food facilities are required to develop Hazard Analysis and Risk-Based Preventive Controls programs to help ensure food safety. This requirement does not apply to a facility that manufactures, processes, packs, or holds dietary supplements that are in compliance with the cGMP requirements and adverse event reporting requirements (described below). However, these FSMA-mandated requirements apply to the manufacture of the ingredients used in dietary supplements (e.g., dietary ingredients, food additives, GRAS substances, color additives, or other constituents that are used for their technical effect in the supplements). 21 C.F.R. Part 117.

FSMA also requires importers of food to implement foreign supplier verification programs to ensure that imported products meet U.S. legal requirements. There is no statutory exception for dietary supplement manufacturers. However, FDA regulations implementing the foreign supplier verification program requirements include modified requirements for certain dietary supplement firms. 21 C.F.R. 1.511. Similarly, dietary supplement manufacturers are not exempted from FSMA's provision empowering FDA to order recalls if a company refuses to recall in situations where FDA has found a reasonable probability that the product will cause serious adverse health consequences or death to humans.

Third-Party Substantiation of Identity, Purity, and Safety

Prior to the promulgation of cGMPs for dietary supplements, a number of organizations made efforts to establish voluntary criteria for the identity, purity, and safety of dietary supplements. Industry trade associations established voluntary cGMP systems whereby manufacturers could submit to inspections in order to assure customers of the integrity of their facilities and processes. These voluntary programs form the basis for educating the dietary supplement industry with respect to compliance with the FDA cGMP regulations. The U.S. Pharmacopoeia now publishes monographs for dietary supplement ingredients. In addition the National Institutes of Health (NIH), through the Office of Dietary Supplements, provides information on dietary supplements and the safety of ingredients.[4]

Products That Combine an OTC Drug with a Dietary Supplement

A number of companies have considered marketing a combination over-the-counter (OTC) drug and dietary supplement product. For example, a combination of low-dose aspirin and vitamin E, or an OTC cough suppressant and vitamin C, have been considered. In theory, such combination products should be "legal," provided: a) the "drug side" of the product falls under an OTC monograph and is labeled properly; b) the "dietary supplement side" of the product does not make drug claims; and c) the dietary supplement ingredients can be deemed safe and suitable inactive ingredients that do not cause the product to become a "new drug" requiring submission of a New Drug Application.

FDA, however, has strongly advised against the marketing of such products in a series of letters to companies, noting "serious concerns about the marketing of any such combination product," and stating that it would take "appropriate measures" against such products. From FDA's perspective, these combination products raise several public health issues. For example:

FDA advises against the marketing of combination over-the-counter drug and dietary supplement products.

♦ **Safety and Efficacy:** The addition of a new ingredient to a legally marketed drug product could affect/interact with the safety and efficacy of the drug component.

♦ **Potentially Misleading:** Consumers may potentially believe that both components have been subjected to the more stringent drug regulatory requirements, when, in fact, only the drug component may have been reviewed by the agency for safety and effectiveness.

♦ **Consumer Confusion:** It is uncertain under what circumstances the disclaimer required by DSHEA for certain dietary supplement claims (as discussed further below) could appear on a combination product without causing consumer confusion.

These policies remain in effect as FDA firmly seeks to maintain the boundaries between drugs and dietary supplements. FDA has issued Warning Letters to two major OTC drug manufacturers after those companies introduced OTC drug/dietary supplement combination products to the market.[5]

Postmarketing Surveillance and the Dietary Supplement and Nonprescription Drug Consumer Protection Act

In 1993, FDA initiated adverse event monitoring for special nutritional products, including dietary supplements. This database consisted of reports from FDA's MedWatch program; FDA's field offices; other federal, state, and local public health agencies; and letters and phone calls from consumers and health professionals. In 2002, FDA announced that this system was limited and that the information in it was provided in a manner that made it difficult for users to appropriately interpret adverse events. Accordingly, FDA removed this information from its website and the Center for Food Safety and Applied Nutrition (CFSAN) then developed a new system for tracking and analyzing adverse event reports involving foods, cosmetics, and dietary supplements.

As the dietary supplement industry matured, it came to understand that a mandatory system for adverse event reporting would benefit all its various "stakeholders"—industry, consumers, healthcare professionals, and regulators. On December 22, 2006, the Dietary Supplement and Nonprescription Drug

Consumer Protection Act was signed into law. This law requires adverse event reporting and recordkeeping for dietary supplements and nonprescription drugs marketed without an approved New Drug Application. Dietary supplement manufacturers, packers, or distributors must report serious adverse events that may be associated with the use of their dietary supplements to FDA.

The basic requirement of the law is that serious adverse events (those events that report death, a life-threatening experience, inpatient hospitalization, a persistent or significant disability or incapacity, or a congenital anomaly or birth defect; or require, based on reasonable medical judgment, a medical or surgical intervention to prevent a serious outcome) must be reported to FDA within 15 business days of receipt. These reports and records associated with these reports must be kept, along with all other reports of adverse events (i.e., non-serious adverse events), for six years, and made available to FDA inspectors upon request. As with all reports of adverse events to FDA, submission of the report is not regarded as an admission that the dietary supplement involved caused or contributed to the adverse event being reported. To facilitate reporting of adverse events, the law also requires that manufacturers and distributors include a domestic telephone number or domestic address on the label of their products through which they may receive a report of an adverse event.

In December 2016, FDA announced that adverse event data reported by consumers, healthcare professionals, and companies is now available at https://www.fda.gov/food/newsevents/constituentupdates/ucm531519.htm. Data from mandatory reports by industry for the period January 2004 through September 30, 2016 is available in CAERS data files and will be updated quarterly.

Dietary Supplement Labeling

Required Components of the Dietary Supplement Label

The basic required labeling components for conventional foods that are described in FDA regulations at 21 C.F.R. § 101, Subpart A are also applicable to dietary supplements. A dietary supplement label must include:

♦ a statement of identity (e.g., "dietary supplement" or "botanical supplement," but not "sports supplement";

♦ an ingredient statement;

♦ nutrition information;

◆ the name and place of business of the manufacturer, packer, or distributor; and

◆ an accurate statement of the quantity of contents, in terms of weight, measure, or numerical count.

If any of the above information does not appear in the correct format on a dietary supplement label, then the product will be considered misbranded and subject to FDA enforcement action (unless an exemption applies). Additionally, as with conventional food claims, any claims on dietary supplement labels or labeling must be truthful and not misleading in any aspect. False or misleading claims on dietary supplement labels will render the product misbranded.

In April 2005, FDA published a dietary supplement labeling guide that provides plain-language information regarding the labeling of dietary supplements.[6] This guide also notes that the Tariff Act of 1930 requires that every article of foreign origin (or its container) imported into the United States conspicuously indicate the English name of the country of origin of the article.

◆ Nutrition Labeling

Following enactment of the Nutrition Labeling and Education Act (NLEA) some confusion existed as to the type of nutrition information to be included on dietary supplement labels. The NLEA Nutrition Facts box (required for foods) was not easily translated to dietary supplements. DSHEA subsequently clarified this point, requiring that dietary supplements bear nutrition labeling "in a manner appropriate" for these products.

To this end, FDA promulgated regulations set forth in 21 C.F.R. § 101.36 (most recently revised in 2016) that specify the detailed nutritional labeling requirements for dietary supplements. The regulations require a Supplement Facts box that is similar in format and appearance to the Nutrition Facts box required for conventional foods. The Supplement Facts box and its contents must appear on the label in the format set forth in the regulations. The box must state "Supplement Facts" across the top and must include information such as the serving size, servings per container (unless it appears as part of the net contents declaration), a listing of any of the required "(b)(2)-dietary ingredients" that have a reference daily intake (RDI) or a daily reference value (DRV) and their subcomponents (i.e., total calories, total fat, saturated fat, trans fat, cholesterol, sodium, total carbohydrate, dietary fiber, total sugars, added sugars, protein, vitamin D, calcium, iron, and potassium), and the amount per serving and percent daily value (if applicable) of such ingredients. These ingredients are referred to in the regulations as "(b)(2)-dietary ingredients" based on the section of the regulations in which they are defined, section 101.36(b)(2). Certain

The Supplement Facts box required for dietary supplements is similar in format and appearance to the Nutrition Facts box required for conventional foods.

other listed nutrients may be declared with these ingredients, but they must be declared if a claim is made about them. Or, in some cases, if they are added for supplementation.

The regulations also discuss dietary ingredients for which RDIs and DRVs have not been established. In contrast to the (b)(2)-dietary ingredients, these ingredients are referred to as "other dietary ingredients," and if present in the dietary supplement, must be declared with their amounts in a separate section of the Supplement Facts box, just below the (b)(2)-dietary ingredients.

Proprietary blends, botanica ingredients, and sources of dietary ingredients also must be declared consistent with the regulations.

The following is an example of a Supplement Facts box for a dietary supplement containing dietary ingredients with RDIs and DRVs. Other examples are provided in the regulations at 21 C.F.R. § 101.36.

Supplement Facts

Serving Size 1 Gelcap
Servings Per Container 100

	Amount Per Serving	% Daily Value
Vitamin A (as retinyl acetate and 50% as beta-carotene)	900 mcg	100%
Vitamin C (as ascorbic acid)	90 mg	100%
Vitamin D (as cholecalciferol)	20 mcg (800 IU)	100%
Vitamin E (as dl-alpha tocopheryl acetate)	15 mg	100%
Thiamin (as thiamin mononitrate)	1.2 mg	100%
Riboflavin	1.3 mg	100%
Niacin (as niacinamide)	16 mg	100%
Vitamin B_6 (as pyridoxine hydrochloride)	1.7 mg	100%
Folate	400 mcg DFE (240 mcg folic acid)	100%
Vitamin B_{12} (as cyanocobalamin)	2.4 mcg	100%
Biotin	3 mcg	10%
Pantothenic Acid (as calcium pantothenate)	5 mg	100%

Other ingredients: Gelatin, lactose, magnesium stearate, microcrystalline cellulose, FD&C Yellow No. 6, propylene glycol, preservatives (propylparaben and sodium benzoate).

◆ Ingredient Labeling

The declaration of ingredients on a dietary supplement label is required. Under some circumstances, ingredients may be declared in the Supplement Facts box as source ingredients (e.g., in the declaration "calcium (as calcium carbonate)" the source ingredient for calcium is calcium carbonate). Ingredients that are not declared in the Supplement Facts box should appear in a statement of ingredients immediately below the Supplement Facts box or, if there is insufficient space, immediately contiguous and to the right of the box. The detailed requirements for the declaration of ingredients on dietary supplement products can be found at 21 C.F.R. §§ 101.4(g), (h), and 101.36(d).

Label Claims for Dietary Supplements

There are three major categories of optional claims that can be made on dietary supplement labels and labeling: 1) structure-function claims, 2) health claims, and 3) nutrient content claims. In addition, claims of general well-being and claims related to a nutrient deficiency disease may be made.

Three major categories of optional claims can be made on dietary supplement labels and labeling:
- *structure-function claims*
- *health claims*
- *nutrient content claims*

DSHEA added section 403(r)(6) to the FDCA, which sets forth four types of claims for dietary supplements:

◆ Statements that claim a benefit related to a classical nutrient deficiency disease (e.g., scurvy) and discloses the prevalence of such disease in the United States

◆ Statements that describe the role of a nutrient or dietary ingredient intended to affect the structure or function in humans (e.g., "calcium builds strong bones")

◆ Statements that characterize the documented mechanism by which a nutrient or dietary ingredient acts to maintain such structure or function (e.g., "antioxidants maintain cell integrity")

◆ Statements that describe general well-being from consumption of a nutrient or dietary ingredient

Structure-Function Claims

The claims described in the two middle bullet points above are known as structure-function claims. These claims are permitted on dietary supplement labels and labeling so long as certain conditions are met:

◆ **Substantiation.** The manufacturer making the claim must have substantiation that the claim is truthful and not misleading. This means that prior to making a claim, the manufacturer must have substantiation that provides a reasonable basis for the express or implied message being conveyed. FDA has published a guidance document entitled "Substantiation for Dietary Supplement Claims Made Under Section 403(r)(6) of the Federal Food, Drug, and Cosmetic Act" that provides guidelines for proper claim substantiation.[7]

◆ **Notification**. Within 30 days of making a structure-function claim, the manufacturer, packer, or distributor must notify FDA's Office of Dietary Supplement Programs that it has included such a statement on the label or labeling of its product. Details on the information to be included in this notification are set forth in FDA regulations at 21 C.F.R. § 101.93. If FDA objects to the claim, it will send a "Courtesy Letter" to the notifier explaining why the claim is considered by FDA to be unlawful. This Courtesy Letter provides guidance so that the manufacturer or retailer will have fair warning of FDA's position with regard to the claim. If the notifier fails to remove the claim from its labeling following a Courtesy Letter, it may be considered by FDA to be operating in violation of the law; there is a risk that FDA will initiate official enforcement action against the notifier and/or the product in the future. However, note that FDA's failure to send a Courtesy Letter does not indicate "approval" or prevent FDA from challenging the claim in the future.

◆ **Disclaimer**. The following disclaimer in boldface type must accompany a structure-function claim: **"This statement has not been evaluated by the Food and Drug Administration. This product is not intended to diagnose, treat, cure, or prevent any disease."** A slightly modified disclaimer is provided where multiple claims are made. FDA regulations at 21 C.F.R. § 101.93 require that the disclaimer either appear immediately adjacent to the statement or appear elsewhere on the same page as the statement and linked to it by a symbol (e.g., asterisk). If the statement is linked by a symbol, it must be set off in a box.

◆ **Structure-Function Claims Versus Disease Claims**

A structure-function claim cannot state or imply that the dietary supplement treats, cures, mitigates, or prevents disease.

In January 2000, FDA published a final regulation (21 C.F.R. §§ 101.93(f), (g)) in an attempt to define structure-function claims and to clarify how such claims can be distinguished from unapproved health claims or "disease" claims. Notably, a structure-function claim may not state or imply that the dietary supplement treats, cures, mitigates, or prevents disease. If it does, then the product may be subject to enforcement action as a drug, and/or as a dietary supplement that is labeled with an unauthorized health claim. According to FDA, prohibited disease claims include those that assert that the product:

◆ has an effect on a specific disease or class of diseases,

◆ has an effect on the characteristic signs or symptoms of a disease,

◆ has an effect on a condition associated with a natural state, if the condition is uncommon or can cause significant harm,

♦ has an effect on a disease as implied by one or more of the following:

- the name of the product,
- a statement about an ingredient in the product that has been regulated by FDA as a drug,
- citation of a publication on the immediate product label so as to imply disease prevention or treatment,
- use of the term "disease" except in general statements that do not refer to a specific disease or product, or
- pictures, symbols or vignettes,

♦ belongs to a class of products that is intended to diagnose, mitigate, treat, cure, or prevent disease,

♦ is a substitute for a product that is a therapy for disease,

♦ augments a therapy or drug action intended to diagnose, mitigate, treat, cure, or prevent disease,

♦ has a role in the body's response to a disease or a vector of disease,

♦ treats, prevents, or mitigates adverse events associated with a disease therapy, or otherwise suggests an effect on a disease or diseases.

Distinguishing between structure-function claims and "disease" claims is one of the most troublesome issues confronting label writers for dietary supplements. The difficulty in distinguishing such claims is evidenced by a few examples: "helps promote digestion" is a permissible structure-function claim whereas "relieves acid indigestion" is a disease claim, and "helps support healthy cartilage and joint function" is a structure-function claim, whereas "maintains normal bone density in post-menopausal women" is an implied disease claim (implying treatment for osteoporosis). The preamble to FDA's January 2000 final rule (65 Fed. Reg. 1,000 (Jan. 6, 2000)) provides a good discussion of these issues. In addition, FDA has published a guidance document entitled "Structure/Function Claims Small Entity Compliance Guide" that provides simple, straightforward guidance for making these claims.[8]

♦ Health Claims

Health claims either expressly or by implication characterize the relationship of a conventional food or dietary supplement to a disease or health-related condition. Described in more detail in FDA regulations at 21 C.F.R. § 101.14, a health claim generally is not permitted unless FDA has promulgated a regulation setting forth the conditions for use of such claim, including the specific permissible language for the claim. An example of an approved health claim published in FDA regulations is as follows: "25 grams of soy protein a day, as part of a diet low

A health claim generally is not permitted unless FDA has issued a regulation stating the conditions for use of such claim, including the specific permissible language of the claim.

in saturated fat and cholesterol, may reduce the risk of heart disease. A serving of [name of food] supplies X grams of soy protein." 21 C.F.R. § 101.82.

FDA may issue a health claim regulation on its own or in response to a petition from a manufacturer. When FDA receives a petition requesting approval of a new health claim, the claim may be authorized only if FDA determines that there is significant scientific agreement among experts qualified by scientific training and experience to evaluate such claims (based on the totality of scientific evidence), and that the claim is supported by such evidence.

FDA has grappled with the standard for substantiation of health claims (i.e., what represents "significant scientific agreement"). The current approach is described in a January 2009 final guidance entitled "Evidence-Based Review System for the Scientific Evaluation of Health Claims."[9]

"Qualified" health claims may be made for dietary supplements as well as conventional foods.

FDA has accepted certain "qualified" health claims for use in dietary supplement labeling although these qualified health claims do not appear in FDA regulations and the process for the formal regulatory approval of such claims is still evolving.

An example of a qualified claim negotiated by FDA and the industry is as follows: "As part of a well-balanced diet that is low in saturated fat and cholesterol, folic acid, vitamin B6 and vitamin B12 may reduce the risk of vascular disease." A disclaimer immediately adjacent to the claim in the same font size must appear: "FDA evaluated the above claim and found that, while it is known that diets low in saturated fat and cholesterol reduce the risk of heart disease and other vascular diseases, the evidence in support of the above claim is inconclusive."[10] Qualified health claims may also be made for conventional foods.

FDA has also provided a guidance to the industry with respect to submissions in support of qualified health claims entitled "Guidance for Industry: FDA's Implementation of "Qualified Health Claims": Questions and Answers; Final Guidance."[11] FDA publishes its evaluation of qualified health claims on its website.[12]

◆ Nutrient Content Claims

Nutrient content claims are used by manufacturers to highlight specific nutritional attributes of their products through a uniform frame of reference. Examples of such claims are "good source of Vitamin C" or "low in fat." The regulations pertaining to nutrient content claims are set forth at 21 C.F.R. § 101.13 and in Subpart D of Part 101. These regulations apply both to conventional foods and to dietary supplements and specify the types of nutrient content claims that are permissible and their requirements. Generally, to make such claims, the specific language used must be defined in the regulations. If not already defined, a manufacturer may submit a petition to FDA for approval and publication in the regulations. Particular care must be taken with respect to "antioxidant" nutrient content claims, which are limited by the regulation to specific recommended daily intake (RDI) nutrients, e.g., Vitamin C, at specific amounts, e.g., greater than 10 percent of the RDI for the nutrient, which must also be named in the claim. 21 C.F.R. § 101.54(g).

Specific nutrient content claims also are permitted, provided the manufacturer provides notice to FDA at least 120 days prior to making the claim that an authoritative statement is supported by a scientific body of the U.S. government. FDA must then issue a regulation or seek a court order to prohibit the claim. This method was utilized with respect to nutrient content claims for DHA, EPA, and ALA from fish oils. Several years after three petitions were filed with respect to these ingredients, FDA published a proposed regulation in 2007 that would disallow all but one of the claims. However, all three petitions remained in effect, each allowing different specific nutrient content claims, until the final rule became effective January 1, 2016.

The primary difference between the regulation of nutrient content claims for conventional foods and dietary supplements is that, for claims about an ingredient that is not defined in the regulations or for which FDA has not established an RDI or DRV, dietary supplements may make nutrient content claims that characterize the percentage level of a dietary ingredient (e.g., "contains 200% of the lycopene in a tomato"). For conventional foods, any such claims cannot be made without approval by FDA through publication in a regulation or acceptance of an authoritative statement of a scientific government body. For both dietary supplements and conventional foods, a claim may be made that states the level of a nutrient per serving, e.g., "Contains 2 grams Omega-3 fatty acids (EPA/DHA) per serving."

INFORMATION ABOUT DIETARY SUPPLEMENTS THAT IS NOT REGULATED AS "LABELING" (THIRD-PARTY LITERATURE)

The definition of labeling for all FDA-regulated products is found in section 201(m) of the FDCA. It includes "all labels and other written, printed, or graphic matter (1) upon any article or any of its containers or wrappers, or (2) accompanying such article." This definition is important because it means that "labeling" encompasses more than just the label, which is the written material appearing on the immediate product container. "Labeling" has been interpreted broadly by the Supreme Court and may include promotional

"Labeling" has been broadly interpreted by the Supreme Court and may include promotional materials.

materials, such as brochures, letters, and videos, even if they don't physically accompany the product at the time of the sale. Therefore, claims found in these promotional vehicles are subject to FDA's jurisdiction. Websites, according to FDA, may be considered labeling, at least under some circumstances—although the Federal Trade Commission (FTC) also considers them to be advertising.

If a dietary supplement is promoted through its labeling to treat, diagnose, cure, mitigate, or prevent disease, then FDA may consider the product to be a drug that cannot be marketed without prior approval of a New Drug Application. Prior to DSHEA, it was FDA's position that books and other publications disseminated by a dietary supplement manufacturer were labeling, even if they were written by third parties, if that literature discussed a dietary supplement product. DSHEA, however, exempts this type of literature from being regulated as labeling. This exemption often is referred to as the "third-party literature" exemption.

It permits manufacturers, distributors, and retailers to disseminate scientific literature, books, and other publications so long as the criteria set forth in section 403B of the act are met. Such a publication may be used in connection with the sale of a dietary supplement when it meets all of the following criteria:

♦ it is not false or misleading;

♦ it does not promote a particular manufacturer or brand of a dietary supplement;

♦ it presents a balanced view of the information;

♦ it is physically separate from the dietary supplements, if displayed in a store; and

♦ it does not have any information appended to it (e.g., a sticker with a company's name or logo).

As a result, marketers of dietary supplements are permitted to legally disseminate publications that refer to disease treatment and prevention, so long as the above criteria are met. Note that DSHEA's legislative history suggests that this exemption does not apply to a summary of a publication other than an official abstract of a peer-reviewed scientific publication. Significantly, the language of the law does not include this limitation.

It must be noted that this "Third-Party Literature" exemption is narrow, and FDA has taken the position that disseminating a large amount of scientific literature that describes how a dietary ingredient treats, mitigates, or prevents disease may be evidence that demonstrates that the company intends to sell its products containing that ingredient as drugs, and unapproved new drugs, in violation of the FDCA's separate prohibition of such sales.

Dietary Supplement Advertising

The FTC is the federal agency generally responsible for regulating product advertising. With respect to FDA-regulated products, the FTC and FDA have worked together under a longstanding agreement governing the division of responsibilities between the two agencies. FDA has primary responsibility for regulating claims in labeling and the FTC has primary responsibility for regulating claims in advertising. This means that dietary supplement claims found in traditional advertising media such as television, radio, and print will be regulated and enforced primarily by the FTC, whereas claims found on dietary supplement labels and brochures will be regulated and enforced primarily by FDA. Claims found on the Internet and in promotional videos have been considered either advertising or labeling, and therefore both the FTC and FDA have taken enforcement action against false claims appearing in these promotional vehicles.

Dietary supplement claims found in traditional advertising media such as television, radio, and print will be regulated and enforced primarily by the FTC, whereas claims found on dietary supplement labels and brochures will be regulated and enforced primarily by FDA.

In 1998, the FTC published a guide, "Dietary Supplements: An Advertising Guide for Industry."[13] Throughout the guide, the FTC reiterates its basic common-sense principles used to regulate advertising for any product: 1) all advertising must be truthful and not misleading; and 2) before disseminating an advertisement, advertisers must have adequate substantiation for all claims (the Prior Substantiation Doctrine). The guide further explains that, just as with other product health claims, claims for dietary supplements generally will require substantiation with "competent and reliable scientific evidence." This is defined as: "tests, analyses, research, studies, or other evidence based on the expertise of professionals in the relevant area that have been conducted and evaluated in an objective manner by persons qualified to do so, using procedures generally accepted in the profession to yield accurate and reliable results."

While there is no fixed formula for the type and number of studies a manufacturer must have to substantiate its claims, in most cases if the weight of the evidence does not support the claim, it should not be made, even if qualified. Manufacturers and retailers must consider all relevant research relating to the claimed benefit of their dietary supplement and should not focus only on research that supports the effect, while discounting research that does not. To ensure compliance with the FTC guidelines, manufacturers and retailers should: 1) carefully draft advertising claims with particular attention as to how claims are qualified and what express or implied messages are actually conveyed; and 2) carefully review the support for a claim

If the weight of the evidence does not support a claim, the claim should not be made, even if qualified.

to make sure it is scientifically sound, adequate in the context of the surrounding body of evidence, and relevant to the specific product and claim advertised.

In recent years, the FTC has been quite active in taking enforcement action against dietary supplement manufacturers and retailers making false, misleading, or unsubstantiated claims about their products. As a result, some dietary supplement marketers have been required to pay consumer redress of up to $20 million, or more, due to false or misleading advertising claims made in advertising materials challenged by the FTC. In seeking redress, it is the FTC's position that sellers must return all "ill-gotten gains" to consumers. This means the value of the sales to consumers, not the net profits. In the usual case, the FTC requires the production of detailed financial information to track "ill-gotten gains" to assure that they are accounted for. In more than one recent case, the FTC has required the sale of company owners' homes, cars, and boats as part of the resolution of the case.

In addition to the FTC, state attorneys general are also active from time to time in enforcing against false or misleading dietary supplement claims, and such actions often result in the payment of extensive monetary damages.

THE FUTURE OF DIETARY SUPPLEMENT REGULATION

The future of the dietary supplement industry is in its own hands.

Over the more than 20 years since DSHEA became law, the regulatory scheme for dietary supplements has matured with regulations covering labeling, the implementation of cGMP requirements, and a law that mandates the reporting of serious adverse events and the retention in company files of all adverse event information. At the same time, FDA enforcement resources have been stretched and strained as more and more products regulated by the agency come from sources outside the United States. Against this background, the future of the dietary supplement industry may largely be under the control of the industry itself.

The dietary supplement industry is still perceived by many healthcare professionals, the media, and legislators as "unregulated." This is probably because the products come mainly in pill form, which gives them the appearance of drugs, but the products are not approved by FDA prior to marketing. While ephedrine alkaloid-containing dietary supplements remained on the market, the industry was barraged with bad publicity, usually associated with serious adverse events alleged to be associated with the use of products containing this ingredient. That publicity adversely affected the entire product category while often spiking ephedra sales upward. If the industry were to market another product alleged to cause serious adverse events at a level approaching what was reported with ephedra, legislative action to change the present regulatory structure would be a likely consequence. Accordingly, the future of the dietary supplement industry is in its own hands.

CONCLUSION

The Dietary Supplement Health and Education Act of 1994 created a new regulatory scheme for dietary supplements. Since enactment, FDA has promulgated regulations implementing the law. The promulgation of cGMP regulations for dietary supplements and legislation mandating the reporting of serious adverse events associated with the use of dietary supplements have taken this relatively new product category to a higher level of regulation.

Endnotes

1. *See* http://www.fda.gov/Food/ResourcesForYou/Consumers/ucm085482. htm.
2. *See* Docket FDA-1995-S-0039, *available at* http://www.regulations. gov/#!docketDetail;dct= FR%252BPR%252BN%252BO%252BSR;rpp=10;po= 0;D=FDA-1995-S-0039.
3. http://www.fda.gov/ICECI/EnforcementActions/WarningLetters/default. htm.
4. *See* http://ods.od.nih.gov/.
5. http://www.fda.gov/ICECI/EnforcementActions/WarningLetters/2008/ ucm1048456.htm; http://www.fda.gov/ICECI/EnforcementActions/WarningLetters/2008/ucm1048083.htm; http://www.fda.gov/ICECI/EnforcementActions/WarningLetters/2009/ucm188361.htm.
6. *See* https://www.fda.gov/Food/GuidanceRegulation/GuidanceDocuments-RegulatoryInformation/DietarySupplements/ucm2006823.htm.
7. *See* https://www.fda.gov/food/guidanceregulation/guidancedocuments-regulatoryinformation/dietarysupplements/ucm073200.htm.
8. *See* https://www.fda.gov/food/guidanceregulation/guidancedocuments-regulatoryinformation/dietarysupplements/ucm103340.htm.
9. *See* http://www.fda.gov/Food/GuidanceRegulation/GuidanceDocuments-RegulatoryInformation/ucm073332.htm.
10. *See* https://www.fda.gov/Food/IngredientsPackagingLabeling/LabelingNutrition/ucm072855.htm.
11. *See* https://www.fda.gov/food/guidanceregulation/guidancedocuments-regulatoryinformation/ucm053843.htm.

12. *See* links to letters of denial, letters of enforcement discretion, and letters of withdrawal for qualified health claims at https://www.fda.gov/food/ingredientspackaginglabeling/labelingnutrition/ucm2006877.htm.

13. https://www.ftc.gov/tips-advice/business-center/guidance/dietary-supplements-advertising-guide-industry.

Chapter 13

FDA Regulation of Tobacco Products

Joseph A. Page, Georgetown University Law Center, Washington, D.C.

Key Points

- The Family Smoking Prevention and Tobacco Control Act (Tobacco Control Act) subjects the manufacturing, labeling, marketing, and distribution of tobacco products to comprehensive federal regulation.
- The Tobacco Control Act created a new Chapter IX within the Federal Food, Drug, and Cosmetic Act.
- Cigarettes, cigarette tobacco, roll-your-own tobacco, and smokeless tobacco fall within the definition of tobacco product.
- The 2016 deeming rule asserted FDA jurisdiction over all tobacco products, including e-cigarettes, cigars, cigarillos, and pipe and hookah tobacco.
- Adulteration and misbranding are among the many acts prohibited by the Tobacco Control Act.
- Tobacco product manufacturers are required to report registration information, health-related information, records and reports, and test data to the Food and Drug Administration.
- The Tobacco Control Act regulates the production of modified risk tobacco products, which are sold for the purpose of reducing the dangers associated with the consumption of commercially available tobacco products.

INTRODUCTION

Cigarette smoking has long been the number-one cause of preventable deaths in the United States and today accounts for nearly 500,000 annual fatalities. In 2009 Congress enacted a law authorizing comprehensive federal regulation dealing with the health risks associated with tobacco products. The new statute gave FDA broad authority to carry out its directives, most of which were incorporated into the Federal Food, Drug, and Cosmetic Act (FDCA).

A Brief History of Tobacco Product Regulation in the United States

During the early decades of the 20th century, cigarette smoking had become widely prevalent in the United States, and by 1950 adult smoking rates in the United States were well in excess of 40 percent. But at the same time, scientific studies had begun to link cigarette smoking and cancer, and personal-injury lawyers had begun to bring negligence suits against tobacco companies on behalf of consumers who claimed they had suffered smoking-related harm. In response, as subsequently emerging evidence has amply documented, the major cigarette producers colluded to fabricate doubt on the association between smoking and disease and to suppress evidence of the link. They also defended the lawsuits with all the massive resources at their command.

The 1964 Surgeon General's report concluding that smoking is causally related to cancer led to the first advertising and labeling requirements.

In 1964, however, the federal government issued the first Surgeon General's report dealing with smoking and health and deriving from an exhaustive study of the scientific data by a blue-ribbon panel, which concluded that cigarette smoking was causally related to lung cancer. These findings received enormous press coverage, and for a time smoking rates declined. However, the upward trajectory of cigarette consumption soon resumed.

Soon after the issuance of the 1964 report, the Federal Communications Commission (FCC) utilized its so-called "fairness doctrine," which obligated broadcasters to provide free time for the airing of opposing views on matters of public controversy, and to promulgate a rule that required television and radio stations airing cigarette commercials to balance them by furnishing free time for anti-smoking messages.

By this time pressure was beginning to build on Congress to take some action to reduce the harmful effects of smoking. The tobacco industry responded with what turned out to be a masterful tactical stroke, deciding not to block a bill that would require a small warning to appear on cigarette packaging, and in 1965 the Federal Cigarette Labeling and Advertising Act became law. The companies were now able to defend some of the personal-injury lawsuits being brought against them on behalf of smokers by arguing that the mandatory warning labels had made consumers aware of the risks of smoking and that therefore, under the tort doctrine of assumed risks, the industry would not be liable. Moreover, in order to obtain industry acquiescence, proponents agreed to include in the statute a provision preempting states from regulating health-related aspects of cigarette advertising.

The industry also decided that it would be better to have the government ban all electronic advertising of cigarettes rather than to be compelled to air anti-smoking messages, and as a result, Congress enacted the 1969 Public Health Cigarette Smoking Act, which prohibited the advertising of cigarettes on any electronic communications medium after January 1, 1971. This statute also strengthened the preemption provision in a way that led to a ruling by the United States Supreme Court to the effect that the new language barred many tort claims against the tobacco companies.[1]

During the next two decades, the industry managed to exclude tobacco products from several newly enacted consumer protection laws, and found new ways, such as in the promotion of popular sporting events, to promote their products indirectly via the electronic media. On the other hand, anti-smoking activists managed to convince Congress to pass the 1984 Comprehensive Smoking Education Act, which increased the thrust of the warnings required on cigarette packages, and the 1986 Comprehensive Smokeless Tobacco Health Education Act, which mandated that smokeless tobacco products carry warning labels on their packaging and advertising.

During the 1990s, two interrelated developments sharply altered the regulatory landscape for tobacco. Lawsuits against the major tobacco companies by the attorneys general of many states sought reimbursement for the Medicaid costs paid by the states to treat tobacco-related disease, as well as the judicial imposition of restrictions on the advertising, marketing, and promotion of cigarettes. In the reimbursement suits, the states were not subject to allegations that they had assumed the risk of smoking, a defense that provided the primary obstacle in damage suits by smokers. Also, the use of procedural mechanisms that facilitated the discovery of evidence in the suits by the attorneys general began to uncover extensive documentary proof that tobacco industry officials not only had long been fully aware of the dangers and the addictive properties of nicotine, but also that they were actually manipulating nicotine levels in order to keep cigarette smokers addicted, as well as promoting cigarettes to children, misrepresenting the health effects of cigarettes, and suppressing evidence of the dangers and addictiveness of smoking. After congressional hearings had directed public attention to these issues, numerous other states filed similar actions.

In the 1990s states began filing lawsuits seeking reimbursement from the tobacco industry for Medicaid expenses they had incurred for providing health benefits to citizens suffering ill health because of smoking.

Lengthy negotiations between the attorneys general and the tobacco companies then produced a proposed comprehensive settlement (called the Tobacco Resolution) of the state lawsuits in June 1997. This would have imposed numerous restrictions on the advertising, marketing, and promotion of cigarettes and would have conferred on FDA regulatory jurisdiction over cigarettes. However, the Resolution was contingent on the enactment of a federal statute, which the proponents of the agreements were unsuccessful in obtaining from Congress.

The collapse of the Resolution resulted in the reinstatement of the state lawsuits, and after four states settled individually with the major tobacco companies, a new comprehensive settlement agreement, or so-called Master Settlement Agreement, resolved all the remaining lawsuits.

During this period, FDA on its part was in the process of asserting that the FDCA gave it jurisdiction over cigarettes. Up until the 1990s, FDA had taken the position that so long as manufacturers made no disease prevention claims, cigarettes did not meet the legal definition of "drug" under the FDCA and hence the agency had no authority to regulate them as such. Information developed in discovery in the state lawsuits and in congressional hearings, however, soon attracted the attention of David Kessler, Commissioner of FDA, and further investigation by the agency convinced him to reverse its position and assert that it actually did have legal authority over cigarettes. In 1996, after a lengthy rulemaking process, the agency published regulations based on findings that 1) nicotine met the definition of a "drug" under the FDCA because it was "intended to affect a function of the human body," and 2) that cigarettes are medical devices under the FDCA because they are designed and intended to deliver nicotine. The regulations then put a number of restrictions on the marketing of cigarettes to minors.

Seeking judicial review of the regulations, the industry argued that FDA's original position had been correct. The issue reached the United States Supreme Court in 2000 in the case of *Food and Drug Administration v. Brown & Williamson Tobacco Corporation*,[2] where the Court ruled against the government. A majority of the Justices found that although nicotine met the literal definition of a "drug" under the act and cigarettes met the literal definition of a device for the delivery of nicotine, Congress had over a number of years repeatedly passed legislation based on the assumption that cigarettes were not subject to FDA jurisdiction; therefore, it would not be appropriate for FDA to regulate cigarettes in the absence of express congressional authorization. The Court also pointed out the contradiction of attempting to regulate a lethal product with no therapeutic function under the statutory standards for drug and device approval, which required proof of safety and effectiveness.

In each congressional session between 2001 and 2008, efforts were made to enact a statute providing FDA with authority over tobacco products, but with no success. While Congress continued to consider such legislation, a massive lawsuit initiated by the Department of Justice in 1999 against the major tobacco companies went to trial in the United States District Court for the District of Columbia. Largely based on documents produced in the cases brought by the state attorneys general, the government's complaint alleged that the major tobacco companies had engaged in a conspiracy under the Racketeer Influenced and Corrupt Organizations Act (RICO) to defraud the public about the dangers of cigarette smoking, and asked that the court require disgorgement of the profits the companies had made as a result of their misconduct. After a trial of enormous length and complexity, the court ruled in the government's favor.[3] It also issued an opinion running to nearly 1,000 pages, which spelled out in meticulous detail how the major cigarette companies had conspired to 1) conceal the fact that cigarettes caused fatal disease; 2) conceal the fact that nicotine was addictive; 3) target children in the advertising, marketing, and promotion of cigarettes in order to addict them before they reached the age of majority; 4) misrepresent that "light" cigarettes were less dangerous than other cigarettes; 5) misrepresent the fatal consequences of secondhand smoke to non-smokers; and 6) suppress research and scientific information at variance with their marketing strategy. In 2009 the United States Court of Appeals upheld these findings, but ruled that under RICO the government could pursue only remedies that were forward-looking and thus it could not order disgorgement of the fruits of past wrongdoing, as the government had asked the court to do.[4] The final formulation of the remedies in the case remains in litigation.

The issuance of these exhaustively documented judicial findings, combined with the election of an administration willing to grant FDA regulatory jurisdiction and the tactical acquiescence of Philip Morris USA, the largest domestic tobacco company, led to the enactment of the 2009 Tobacco Control Act, which enjoyed the support of a large bipartisan majority in both houses of Congress.

Public attitudes and policies toward smoking had already undergone a profound change by the time the Tobacco Control Act became law. The revelations of industry misconduct documented in discovery in the state attorneys general litigation gave impetus to regulatory efforts at the state, local, and federal levels. Sharp increases in both federal and state tobacco taxes, the cigarette price hikes due to the settlement payments to the states under the Master Settlement Agreement, restrictions on the advertising, marketing, and promotion of cigarettes incorporated in the Agreement, revelations that smoking causes not only lung cancer but also dozens of other fatal diseases, enactment of clean indoor ordinances in many cities and states, public education programs designed to inform consumers of the consequences of smoking, and recognition of the misconduct of the tobacco companies, had all contributed to a dramatic reduction in tobacco usage both among adults and adolescents between the mid-1990s and the enactment of the Tobacco Control Act in 2009. Thus, the federal statute reflected a substantial change in public attitudes, under which smoking, once viewed as normal and benign, became increasingly seen as dangerous and anti-social.

Public attitudes and policies toward smoking had already undergone a profound change by the time the Tobacco Control Act became law.

A PRELIMINARY LOOK AT THE TOBACCO CONTROL ACT

The same enforcement mechanisms the government might use against manufacturers of food, drugs, cosmetics, medical devices, and dietary supplements are for the most part available in proceedings against the makers of tobacco products.

The statute eventually signed into law by President Barack Obama brought all tobacco products within the purview of the FDCA and gave administrative responsibility over them to FDA, on the ground that the agency was the most logical choice within the existing federal regulatory universe. Hands-on authority to administer the new statute was then assigned to a newly created entity located within FDA and called the Center for Tobacco Products (CTP). The Center could recommend enforcement actions, use informal rulemaking to issue regulations that had the force of law, issue guidance documents to advise interested parties about how it viewed industry practices and interpreted the law, and educate the public about the hazards caused by tobacco products. The same enforcement mechanisms the government might use against manufacturers of food, drugs, cosmetics, and medical devices would for the most part be available in proceedings against the makers of tobacco products.

The Tobacco Control Act, which bristles with detail, created a new Chapter IX within the FDCA. It constructed a regulatory regime with elements that are in part novel and in part borrowed from pre-existing statutory language applicable to other products, and it incorporated elements of FDA's proposed 1996 rules as well. In addition, it left standing and amended the Federal Cigarette Labeling and Advertising Act and the Comprehensive Smokeless Tobacco Health Education Act.

The Preamble to the Tobacco Control Act

The initial six sections of the Tobacco Control Act amount to a preamble, and do not appear as part of the FDCA. They include factual justifications for the new law, a statement of its purposes, and limitations on its scope and effect, as well as a severability provision and modifications of deadlines that other sections of the statute impose on FDA.

Findings

The findings listed in section 2 of the act are lengthy and detailed. Several themes emerge. Subsections (1) to (29) spell out the scope and dimensions of the health problems caused by tobacco products, and do so in a way that amounts to an understated yet unmistakable indictment of the misbehavior of the tobacco industry, especially in purposefully addicting minors to nicotine. Subsections (30) to (32) give reasons why the restrictions the act places on the advertising and promotion of tobacco products do not violate the free speech guarantee of the First Amendment to the Constitution. Subsections (33) to (35) insert miscellaneous facts, such as the chronic nature of tobacco dependence, the need to achieve smoking cessation because it is the only safe alternative to smoking, and the link between the illicit trade of tobacco products and both organized crime and terrorist activity. Subsections (36) to (43) stress the importance of risk reduction as a goal of the regulation of tobacco products. Subsections (44) and (45) indicate why Congress decided to give FDA the task of administering the act. Subsection (46) explains why manufacturers should not be allowed to include in labeling or advertising any statement to the effect that FDA regulates the product. The last three subsections (47, 48, and 49) return to the backdrop of industry blameworthiness and cite findings of fact made in the exhaustive 2006 opinion by a United States District Court judge, to the effect that tobacco companies had not stopped targeting young people as potential smokers, and that they "designed their cigarettes to precisely control nicotine delivery levels and provide doses of nicotine sufficient to create and sustain addiction while also concealing much of their nicotine-related research."[5]

Purposes

The Tobacco Control Act's purposes, set out in section 3, justify the selection of FDA to take charge of regulating tobacco products and the creation of what the act called "new and flexible enforcement authority" to enable the agency to perform its duties. At the same time, they betray traces of internal inconsistency, with subsection (9) calling for the promotion of the cessation of smoking and subsection (7) directing FDA to continue to allow adults to purchase tobacco products. Subsection (6) speaks to a need to inform consumers about the ill effects that flow from the use of tobacco products, a goal that would not seem to have any impact on persons so helplessly addicted to nicotine that they are in no position to make free choices. Accurate information would be useful only to non-addicted adults willing and able to stop using tobacco products or non-users capable of making a choice about whether or not to begin using a tobacco product.

Perhaps what Congress had in mind was the preservation of a libertarian value, the right of competent adults to decide to engage or continue to engage in risky conduct that endangers no one but themselves. However, neither the stated findings nor the goals make this point nor do they explain how massive market manipulation on the part of the tobacco industry may dilute individual freedom.

Broad Limitations on FDA Authority

The Tobacco Control Act particularizes the scope of FDA's new regulatory authority by both detailing the powers delegated to the agency and by placing express limitations on them. On a broad level, Congress subjected FDA to two important restrictions. First, the act defines terms in ways that limit the scope of the statute. Second, it excludes from FDA's regulatory reach certain specified entities engaged in tobacco-related activity.

Definitions

"Tobacco Product." Section 201(rr) of the FDCA spells out the meaning of the key phrase "tobacco product." The term encompasses "any product made or derived from tobacco that is intended for human consumption, including any component, part, or accessory of a tobacco product (except for raw materials other than tobacco used in manufacturing a component, part, or accessory of a tobacco product)."

An item that would otherwise fall within the definition of "tobacco product" is excluded from that category if it also falls within the definition of "drug" or "medical device."

Section 901(b) provides that Chapter IX applies to cigarettes, cigarette tobacco, roll-your-own tobacco, and smokeless tobacco. Thus, these items fall automatically within the definition of "tobacco product." The subsection goes on to give FDA authority to promulgate regulations that sweep other items within the definition of "tobacco products." Thus, section 901(b) is a barrier that blocks FDA from regulating these other items, such as cigars, pipe tobacco, and electronic cigarettes, under Chapter IX until the agency first goes through the administrative process of promulgating a regulation that deems them (thus the terms "deeming rule" or "deeming regulation") to be "tobacco products." In addition, an item that might otherwise fall within the definition of "tobacco product" is excluded from that category if it also falls within the statutory definition of "drug" or "medical device," a proviso that eliminates the possibility of dual classification. Moreover, once an item is by definition a "tobacco product," it cannot legally be combined with and sold with any other product regulated under the FDCA.

E-Cigarettes and the Deeming Regulation. Shortly after the Tobacco Control Act took effect, FDA tried to bypass the need for a deeming regulation for electronic (or e-) cigarettes, which vaporize a liquid nicotine mixture in such a way as to enable users to inhale it. The agency argued that they should be considered a drug-device combination subject to FDA approval, and therefore would not fall within the definition of "tobacco products." FDA reasoned that electronic cigarettes were not traditional tobacco products like cigarettes and smokeless tobacco, and the manufacturers not only intended them to affect the structure or function of the body, but also meant them to be useful in the prevention, mitigation, or treatment of a smoker's symptoms associated with nicotine withdrawal, which would bring them within the legal definition of a "drug." Hence, they would be subject to the strict regulations that restrict the marketing of pharmaceutical products.

Two distributors successfully enjoined FDA from barring the importation of electronic cigarettes, when a United States District Court judge ruled that these products were not drug-device combinations, but instead were by definition "tobacco products," and had to be regulated as such.[6] On appeal, a three-judge panel of the United States Court of Appeals agreed with the judge and rejected FDA's position.[7]

A judicial decision held that e-cigarettes were by definition "tobacco products" and could not be regulated as a "drug-device combination."

The result of this decision was to place e-cigarettes outside FDA jurisdiction unless and until the agency issued a deeming regulation subjecting them to the provisions of the Tobacco Control Act, a process that would permit the government to regulate them as tobacco products. Momentous consequences ensued. At the time of the decision, e-cigarettes had virtually no presence in the United States. Had they been subjected to FDA regulation as drug-device combinations, it would have been expensive and time-consuming for manufacturers to bring them to market. In the absence of regulation, however, the market for e-cigarettes burgeoned rapidly. Moreover, rather than promptly issuing a regulation asserting jurisdiction over e-cigarettes, FDA did not propose a rule doing so until April 2014, and did not finalize the rule until May 2016. In addition, many regulatory provisions included in this regulation would not take effect until 2017 or 2018. Thus, the marketing of e-cigarettes would go unregulated for nearly six years. (A further extension of the effective date is mentioned at the end of this chapter.)

Assertion of Jurisdiction Over Other Tobacco Products. In addition, FDA did not assert jurisdiction over cigars, cigarillos, pipe tobacco, hookah, or other tobacco products until it issued the proposed deeming rule in 2014 and the final deeming rule in 2016. The deeming rule purported to assert FDA jurisdiction over all tobacco products other than those that had been subject to jurisdiction since the enactment of the Tobacco Control Act in 2009 (i.e., cigarettes, cigarette tobacco, roll-your-own tobacco, and smokeless tobacco).

Cigars. When FDA issued the proposed deeming rule in 2014, it provided two alternative versions for dealing with cigars. One would have subjected all cigars to FDA regulation and another would have exempted "premium cigars." The term "cigar" covers a wide range of products. With the advent of the Master Settlement Agreement in 1998 and sharp increases in state taxes on cigarettes that began to take effect about the same time, some manufacturers found it advantageous to make small changes in their tobacco products in order to have them classified as cigars rather than cigarettes. With the enactment of the Tobacco Control Act in 2009, the incentives for manufacturers to classify their products as cigars or little cigars rather than cigarettes increased. These products escaped immediate regulation by FDA. Moreover, cigar makers began taking further advantage of this loophole by flavoring some of their products, which made them appealing to young people. Cigars were just as addictive and as dangerous as cigarettes and often were designed to have smoke that was likely to be inhaled. Prior to the deeming rule FDA sought to assert jurisdiction over several such products on the ground that they met the definition of "cigarettes." The deeming rule extending FDA jurisdiction to cigars would eliminate at least some of the incentives for claiming that these tobacco products were cigars rather than cigarettes.

In response, manufacturers of large premium cigars argued that their products were quite different from the smaller products marketed as cigars. They insisted that their products did not appeal to children, were priced at levels too high to make them popular with adolescents, were not designed to have their smoke inhaled, and were often smoked only occasionally by their users; consequently, it was inappropriate for FDA to deem them tobacco products. Some public health organizations, however, pointed out that such cigars contained high levels of nicotine and all the same toxicants and carcinogens as cigarettes, and that it was not clear that adolescents did not use them. Furthermore, there were ongoing disagreements about how to define a class of "premium cigars" that could be exempted from regulation.

The final deeming regulation released in May 2016 brought e-cigarettes and other tobacco products under FDA jurisdiction.

In the final deeming rule, FDA rejected any exemption for premium cigars and asserted jurisdiction over all cigars. Subsequently, manufacturers of premium cigars brought suit against FDA's assertion of jurisdiction over their products, arguing that the agency's action was arbitrary and capricious under the Administrative Procedure Act (APA), and hence invalid.[8] This litigation is still pending.

The Effects of the Deeming Regulation. The consequences of the deeming rule have been far-reaching, because FDA regulation under the Tobacco Control Act can affect many aspects of the marketing of tobacco products. These include the prohibition of sales of tobacco products to minors; restrictions on advertising and labeling; requirements for FDA orders before new products can be marketed; and restrictions on the making of claims that a tobacco product is less dangerous than other such products. The effect of the deeming rule with respect to each of these areas of regulation will be discussed in sections dealing with each such area.

The most controversial aspects of the deeming rule are those relating to marketing restrictions. Prior to the issuance of the deeming rule, manufacturers of e-cigarettes, cigars, and other tobacco products had been free to introduce new products into the market or change the contents of their product without regulatory supervision. The deeming rule would require manufacturers to obtain FDA marketing orders in order to continue selling their products, to change them, or to introduce new products.

In order to permit manufacturers of the newly deemed products to adjust to the new regulatory regime, FDA established a phased schedule for implementation. Manufacturers of newly deemed products were permitted to continue to introduce new products without FDA marketing orders until August 8, 2016. Since that date, however, the provisions of the Tobacco Control Act requiring marketing orders for products not on the market as of that date have gone into effect. With respect to newly deemed products that had been commercially marketed on or before August 8, 2016, the deeming rule established a delayed-compliance schedule that permits such products to remain on the market for designated periods pending the filing of applications for marketing orders and, if such orders are filed, pending the disposition of such applications.

In order to permit manufacturers of the newly deemed products to adjust to the new regulatory regime, FDA established a phased schedule for implementation.

In addition, the deeming rule subjects the newly deemed products to most of the other provisions of the Tobacco Control Act, including, but not limited to, submission of ingredients lists, product testing requirements, prohibition of free sampling, prohibition of modified-risk claims in the absence of an FDA order, textual (but not graphic) warning label requirements, reporting and inspection of manufacturing facilities, and numerous other requirements. In addition, it subjects the newly deemed products to any product standards the agency may have promulgated, restrictions on labeling, restrictions on marketing and advertising, and good manufacturing practices.

Opposition to the Deeming Rule. Manufacturers of both cigars and e-cigarettes have filed lawsuits in various federal courts to enjoin the enforcement of its provisions, principally those requiring FDA marketing orders prior to the sale of such products and parts of the rule permitting FDA to issue standards governing the contents of the products. The first of these cases to be filed, *Nicopure Labs LLC v. FDA*,[9] was a lawsuit brought by an e-cigarette manufacturer that argued that the promulgation of the rule was, *inter alia*, arbitrary and capricious and hence in violation of the APA. At the time of this writing, the case is awaiting decision. In several other cases the government has been granted extensions to make filings defining its position. The latest of these extensions, granted in three cases on May 1, 2017, were 90-day extensions issued after the government announced plans to reconsider the effects of the deeming rule on both cigars and e-cigarettes. At this writing, the government's position in those cases remains unclear.

At the same time legislation has been introduced in Congress, both in the form of proposed amendments to bills for funding the operation of the government and in the form of separate bills that would limit the jurisdiction of FDA to regulate e-cigarettes and premium cigars. It is uncertain whether such legislation will be enacted. (The agency's response, a new approach to the regulation of tobacco products, is described at the end of this chapter.)

"Smokeless Tobacco." Section 900(18) defines "smokeless tobacco" as "any tobacco product that consists of cut, ground, powdered, or leaf tobacco, and that is intended to be placed in the oral or nasal cavity." Products that fall squarely within this definitional category include snuff and chewing tobacco.

FDA has issued a statement asserting its authority to regulate dissolvable tobacco products as "smokeless tobacco." These items would include nicotine lozenges meant to be placed in the mouth, where they gradually dissolve, allowing the ingestion of nicotine. To meet the definition, such products would also need to consist of "cut, ground, powdered, or leaf tobacco," which seems to be the case with most of these items, since they are made from compressed tobacco. The broad requirement that they be "intended to be placed in the oral cavity" would logically encompass pellets designed to dissolve in the mouth.

Similarly, another potential class of tobacco products that could fall within the meaning of smokeless tobacco are heatless, smoke-free tobacco inhalers that contain cut, ground, powdered, or leaf tobacco, provided that such a product, or a component, part, or accessory (for example, a mouthpiece) must be placed in the oral or nasal cavity in order to be consumed.

Exclusion for Raw Tobacco

The Tobacco Control Act explicitly exempts raw tobacco and those who produce it.

The Tobacco Control Act explicitly exempts raw tobacco and those who produce it. The definition of "tobacco product" in section 201(rr)(1) embraces "any product made or derived from tobacco," which would not logically include the raw tobacco itself. Section 901(c)(2)(A), moreover, removes from the scope of Chapter IX "tobacco leaf that is not in the possession of a manufacturer of tobacco products," as well as "the producers of tobacco leaf, including tobacco growers, tobacco warehouses, and tobacco grower cooperatives . . . ." Congress also added section 901(c)(2)(C), which declares that no exercise of statutory construction should permit the agency "to promulgate regulations on any matter that involves the production of tobacco leaf or a producer thereof, other than activities by a manufacturer affecting production."

Prohibited Acts

Adulteration

The Tobacco Control Act sets out eight distinct ways by which FDA might consider a tobacco product to have been adulterated. Three of them relate to actual or potential contamination caused by a direct exposure to a harmful substance or condition. Four relate to what might be termed indirect adulteration caused by the failure to conform to regulatory requirements designed to protect against actual or potential contamination. One has very little, if anything, to do with contamination.

The Tobacco Control Act sets out eight distinct ways by which FDA might consider a tobacco product to have been adulterated.

Actual or Potential Contamination. Section 902(1) of the FDCA provides that a tobacco product is adulterated if "it consists in whole or in part of any filthy, putrid, or decomposed substance, or is otherwise contaminated by any added poisonous or added deleterious substance that may render the product injurious to health." The first clause is copied verbatim from section 501(a)(1), dealing with adulterated drugs and devices. The second is less straightforward, taken from the "may-render-injurious" standard for added substances in food found in section 402(a)(1). Neither the courts nor FDA have elaborated on the meaning of this language, mainly because of the multitude of special provisions Congress has inserted into the FDCA to regulate specific added food substances. This section seems to deal with health risks that are marginal, certainly when compared to the inherent dangers posed by tobacco products, so that FDA is not likely to assign a high priority to its enforcement.

Subsections (2) and (3), dealing with insanitary conditions and packaging composed of poisonous or deleterious substances, copy verbatim the standards for the adulteration of drugs and medical devices.

Indirect Adulteration. The Tobacco Control Act authorizes FDA to set standards, review certain tobacco products before they can be marketed, promulgate rules that specify good manufacturing practices, and regulate modified risk tobacco products. These provisions aim in part to prevent tobacco products that might carry with them risks even greater than the hazards inherent in them from entering the stream of commerce. Section 902 classifies as adulterated any tobacco products that have been marketed but do not comply with regulations designed to protect consumers from these additional risks, without regard to whether the products in question were actually harmful, or had been exposed to actual insanitary conditions, or had come into contact with any actual or potentially harmful substance.

Technical Adulteration. Section 902(4) deals with tobacco products whose manufacturer has violated provisions of section 919 requiring the payment of user fees. The link between user fees and the factual contaminating of a product is highly tenuous, perhaps based on the supposition that a manufacturer's refusal to pay the fees might in some way hinder FDA in its efforts to prevent the marketing of tobacco products that subject consumers to the risk of adulteration.

Misbranding

Section 903 takes a multipronged approach to misbranding, which, like adulteration, is a prohibited act. First, it contains a general prohibition against false or misleading labeling or advertising of a tobacco product. Second, the section specifically lists certain information that must appear on the labels of tobacco products, and provides that a label not bearing this information will be deemed misbranded. Third, with respect to advertising as well as labeling, the section categorizes as misbranding failures to conform to certain of the act's requirements identifying information that must be conveyed to potential consumers and customers.

A tobacco product can be misbranded due to:
- *false or misleading labeling or advertising*
- *failure to list certain factual information on the labeling*
- *failure to include required identifying information with respect to both labeling and advertising*

In addition to the substantive requirements that certain information appear on labels and labeling, section 903 speaks to the method by which this information is to be conveyed. Subsection (a)(3) provides that mandated information must be prominent and conspicuous and must be comprehensible to the ordinary consumer under ordinary conditions of purchase and use; if not, the product may be deemed misbranded.

General Prohibition Against False or Misleading Statements. Section 903(a)(1) begins with a general proposition, found elsewhere in the FDCA, to the effect that the labeling of a tobacco product is misbranded if it is "false or misleading in any particular." Section 903(a)(8) applies this rule to advertising as well.

The prohibition against misbranding covers not only untrue affirmations but also omissions that create misimpressions.

The language in section 201(n) to the effect that the failure to reveal material facts may be relevant in determining whether labeling or advertising is false or misleading in any particular also applies to tobacco products. Hence, the prohibition against misbranding covers not only untrue affirmations but also omissions that create misimpressions.

As a general proposition, FDA may use its informal rulemaking authority to declare as misleading the failure to disclose information not specifically required by other sections of Chapter IX. Therefore, the extensive jurisprudence that section 201(n) has generated in cases involving other product categories may be relevant in cases involving tobacco products.

Specific Requirements Contained in Section 903. Section 903(a)(2) requires that the labels of tobacco products in package form bear certain factual information, such as the name and place of business of the manufacturer. Section 903(a)(8) imposes a similar mandate for advertisements.

Specific Requirements Contained in Other Sections. Section 903 puts teeth into provisions found in other sections of the Tobacco Control Act and requires that specific information designated either by those provisions or by FDA regulations appear on the labeling or advertisements of tobacco products. These include sections 920(a) (origin labeling for tobacco products other than cigarettes), 905 (registration information), and 907 (labeling required by a tobacco product standard).

In addition, section 903 designates as misbranding the failure to comply with certain statutory or regulatory requirements imposed elsewhere in Chapter IX of the act and having nothing to do with the communication of information to consumers. These mandates encompass restrictions on the sale and distribution of tobacco products, the failure to comply with requirements to furnish health information to FDA, the failure to comply with FDA orders that notices of risks be given or recalls undertaken, and the failure to keep required records and reports and provide them to FDA when requested.

Other Prohibited Acts

In addition to applying the concepts of adulteration and misbranding to the manufacture and marketing of tobacco products, the Tobacco Control Act adds a number of particularized items to the long list of prohibited acts in section 301 of the FDCA. These include: failure to comply with recordkeeping and reporting requirements mandated by sections 909 and 920; failure to furnish health information, as required by section 904; and failure to comply with substantive obligations as they relate to labeling (section 903(b)), tobacco product standards (section 907), notification (section 908), modified risk tobacco products (section 911), and advertising (section 913). Other miscellaneous prohibitions relate to the shipping of a detained product, the sale of tobacco products in violation of a no-sale order, the counterfeiting of tobacco products, their charitable distribution, and the failure on the part of a manufacturer or distributor to report knowledge of the illegal trade of tobacco products.

Finally, section 301(tt) contains an explicit prohibition against any representation in the labeling or advertising of tobacco products to the effect that FDA approves or endorses them, or considers them safe. There is also an explicit prohibition against any representation in the labeling or advertising of tobacco products to the effect that FDA approves or endorses them, or considers them safe, or that tobacco products are safe and less harmful because they are regulated by FDA. However, the advantage of this section is that it dispenses with the need for the government to prove that such statements amount to deception.

ENFORCEMENT

The enforcement options that the government can invoke against the commission of prohibited acts relating to tobacco products fall into three categories: 1) they may be identical to mechanisms applicable to food, drugs, medical devices, and cosmetics; 2) they may be identical to mechanisms applicable only to certain products regulated by the FDCA; and 3) they may be unique to tobacco products.

Common Mechanisms. The rules that govern criminal penalties and injunctions in enforcement actions dealing with food, drugs, cosmetics, and medical devices also apply to tobacco products. This means that the case law and rules interpreting the imposition of these mechanisms in proceedings involving these products will also govern proceedings affecting tobacco products. Moreover, tobacco establishments registered with FDA are subject to mandatory biennial inspections governed by section 704, which also authorizes inspections of food, drug, medical device, and cosmetics establishments. Finally, section 705, giving FDA authority to generate publicity, also covers tobacco products.

Selective Mechanisms. Equally applicable to tobacco products are the substantive and procedural rules governing judicial actions to seize medical devices and administrative proceedings to detain them. Moreover, section 303(f)(5), containing procedural rules for the imposition of civil penalties, applies to all products, including tobacco products, implicated in statutory violations for which these sanctions might be imposed.

Unique Mechanisms. The Tobacco Control Act creates a special section authorizing the assessment of civil penalties for statutory violations in cases involving tobacco products. This provision specifies the amounts of penalties that may be awarded, and the effect of a defendant's efforts to correct a violation.

The act also permits the government to impose a no-tobacco-sale order on retail outlets found to have committed repeated violations of regulations promulgated under section 906(d), dealing with restrictions on the sale and distribution of tobacco products.

Reporting Requirements

The Tobacco Control Act requires all tobacco product manufacturers to report certain information to FDA. These mandates help the agency accomplish a principal goal of the act, the imposition of appropriate regulatory controls on the tobacco industry, a task that will require FDA access to data that only the industry can provide. The statute itself particularizes some of these reporting requirements. In other instances, it authorizes FDA to promulgate rules mandating the submission of additional information.

All tobacco product manufacturers are required to report certain information to FDA so as to allow the agency "to impose appropriate regulatory controls on the tobacco industry."

Section 905 calls for the annual registration of entities engaged in the manufacture of tobacco products. Section 904 obliges the submission of health-related information to FDA. Section 909 authorizes FDA to issue regulations requiring the maintenance of records and the submission of reports deemed necessary for assuring that tobacco products are not adulterated or misbranded, and for otherwise protecting the public health. Section 915 directs FDA to finalize rules requiring tests and the disclosure of test results when the agency deems this necessary to safeguard the public.

The act also places limitations on reporting requirements, in order to protect the tobacco industry from data requests that are either quantitatively or qualitatively unreasonable. Moreover, some reporting obligations apply only to certain tobacco products, such as those intended to modify risks.

Registration

Section 905, dealing with annual registration, applies to existing domestic manufacturers, new domestic manufacturers, and foreign manufacturers whose tobacco products will be imported into the United States. Domestic manufacturers must report their names, places of business, and all other tobacco-related establishments they operate. Foreign establishments will be subject to registration requirements established by FDA regulations.

Registration requirements for tobacco product manufacturers closely track the language of FDCA § 510, which sets out the registration requirements for producers of drugs and devices.

These mandates closely track the language of section 510, which sets out the requirements for the registration of producers of drugs and devices. Thus, subsection 905(b) copies section 510(b) by requiring the registration of all establishments engaged in "manufacture, preparation, compounding or processing"; in language taken directly from sections 510(a) and (b), section 905(a) includes repackagers, and subsection (b) requires that in the case of partnerships the "name" include each partner, and in the case of corporations, the "name" include each corporate officer, director, and the state of incorporation.

The information that must accompany registration includes not only names and places of business, but also "a copy of all consumer information and other labeling" and a sample of advertisements for the product. The act does not define the somewhat vague term "consumer information." Its linkage to the phrase "other labeling" suggests strongly that it incorporates information that has the same characteristics as labeling. Hence, it would seem to embrace any material that a tobacco company communicates to consumers, even if it does not fall within the sweep of the terms "labeling" and "advertising."

Health-Related Information

Section 904(a) obligates tobacco companies to submit to FDA a list of all ingredients in their products, as well as a description of the content, delivery, and form of nicotine contained therein, a list of all product constituents determined by FDA to be hazardous, and all documents concerning the health, toxicological, behavioral, or physiological effects of their tobacco products.

Section 904(b) expands even further the duty to report health-related information. It gives FDA authority to promulgate regulations requiring the submission of all documents incorporating research done, supported by or in the possession of tobacco companies, and relating to the health, toxicological, behavioral, or physiological effects of tobacco products, or relating to the existence of technology that might reduce health risks associated with tobacco products, and all documents relating to marketing research and its effectiveness.

Records and Reports

Section 909(a) gives FDA broad authority to issue regulations requiring the maintenance of records and the making of reports deemed necessary to protect the public health. The only example specifically provided targets "information that reasonably suggests that . . . marketed tobacco products may have caused or contributed to a serious unexpected adverse experience associated with the use of the product or any significant increase in the frequency of a serious, expected adverse product experience."

The Tobacco Control Act does not explain the meaning of the term "serious adverse experience," a curious omission because the expression "serious adverse drug experience" is defined in Chapter V of the FDCA. Since the ordinary use of tobacco products can cause death or certain kinds of serious bodily harm, the term must refer to other types of serious bodily harm, or an increase in the rate of death or serious bodily harm normally caused by these products.

Subsection 909(a) requires FDA to provide reasons for the reporting rules it is imposing. It also contains some specific limitations on FDA's authority to promulgate regulations dealing with records and reports. For example, they must not be "unduly burdensome," and FDA must balance the cost of complying with them against the health benefits they are expected to produce. Curiously, this is the only Tobacco Control Act provision that directs FDA to take into account financial burdens that a regulation might impose on tobacco companies.

FDA must provide reasons for the reporting rules it imposes.

A further reporting requirement is contained in section 909(b), which calls on FDA to issue regulations mandating that the agency be notified whenever a tobacco producer takes corrective action on its own to remove a tobacco product from the market in order to reduce a health risk or because the product violates some provision of Chapter IX.

Test Data

Section 915(b) directs FDA to finalize regulations that will require the tobacco industry to test product ingredients and additives by brand and sub-brand and to report the results; and to make public disclosures of the results of tests on tar, nicotine, and other constituents as determined by the agency. Section 915(c) permits FDA to conduct or to require tests on constituents, including constituents of smoke, and to require the public disclosure of results.

TOBACCO PRODUCT STANDARDS

Although section 907 bears the title "Tobacco Product Standards," it in fact conflates the concepts of standards and bans by authorizing (or barring) the prohibition of certain types of tobacco products having certain specified characteristics, while at the same time legalizing the regulatory imposition of requirements relating to their composition, design, labeling, or marketing. Thus, the section gives FDA authority to set the latter type of standard, and at the same time creates self-executing rules specifically prohibiting the inclusion of certain flavors as the characterizing ingredients in cigarettes and certain pesticide residues in tobacco. Violations of these rules and standards would amount to prohibited acts.

Self-Executing Rules

Consistent with a major purpose of the Tobacco Control Act—the protection of minors from the perils of cigarette smoke—section 907(a)(1)(A) prohibits the inclusion of flavors, herbs, and spices as constituents or additives amounting to ingredients that characterize cigarettes. They may be artificial or natural, and might include strawberry, grape, orange, clove, cinnamon, pineapple, vanilla, coconut, licorice, cocoa, cherry, or coffee—all flavors that might be appealing to young people. FDA may use this version of its standard-setting authority to set rules for artificial or natural flavors, herbs, or spices not enumerated in section 907(a)(1)(A). Tobacco flavor receives a permanent exemption from this ban.

Exception for Menthol. Menthol receives special treatment because of its special appeal to African-American smokers, more than three-quarters of whom use cigarettes spiced with it, and because of increased risks of harm associated with them. Section 907(a)(1)(A) permits FDA to ban menthol cigarettes, but only after first obtaining a report and recommendation from its Tobacco Products Scientific Advisory Committee (TPSAC) and then promulgating a regulation under section 907(a)(3). On March 25, 2011, the committee recommended that FDA take appropriate action to remove menthol cigarettes from the marketplace. The report was advisory only and did not require FDA to take any particular action. The major tobacco manufacturers vigorously disputed the conclusions in the report and issued their own separate reports. They also filed suit in the United States District Court for the District of Columbia seeking to disqualify from service on the committee members who had testified in lawsuits against the tobacco manufacturers, and to prohibit FDA from using the report as the basis for any regulatory action. Although the district court ruled in favor of the manufacturers, the district court's opinion was reversed on appeal by the United States Court of Appeals for the District of Columbia, on the ground that the manufacturers had not established that they had suffered any injury from the alleged violation, and therefore had no legal standing to bring the suit.[10] By the time the case was resolved, none of the committee members whose participation was challenged remained on the committee.

Subsequent to and independent of the TPSAC report, FDA commissioned its own report on the effect of menthol in cigarettes and issued it in 2013. That report concluded that the weight of the evidence indicated that menthol in cigarettes is likely associated with greater addiction, that menthol smokers show greater signs of nicotine dependence and are less likely to successfully quit smoking, and that the cooling and anesthetic properties of menthol, coupled with the marketing of menthol cigarettes, "make it likely that menthol cigarettes pose a health risk above that seen with non-menthol cigarettes."

Following the release of the report, FDA commenced an Advance Notice of Proposed Rulemaking seeking public comment on a potential product standard for menthol in cigarettes. Since receiving comments, the agency has taken no further action.

Flavoring in Other Tobacco Products

The act's prohibition on characterizing flavors in cigarettes does not extend to other tobacco products and smokeless tobacco products, which were also made subject to the Tobacco Control Act as of the effective date of the legislation, and have continued to feature many characterizing flavors. The most controversial issues regarding flavoring in tobacco products, however, have concerned the newly deemed products, particularly e-cigarettes and cigars.

Flavoring of E-Cigarettes. The massive growth of e-cigarette sales, particularly among underage users, has been accompanied by an explosion of the use of characterizing flavors. At the time the deeming rule was promulgated, there were literally thousands of flavored e-cigarette products on the market. Industry critics have argued that many such flavors, such as gummy bear and cotton candy, are clearly targeted to appeal to underage users, and in comments submitted to FDA on the proposed deeming rule they have called on FDA either to prohibit the use of such characterizing flavors or to require evidence that such flavors do not promote youth usage of such products as a condition of remaining on the market. When FDA developed the final deeming rule, it sent to the Office of Management and Budget (OMB) a rule that would have limited applicability of the discretionary compliance periods to unflavored products or flavored products that had demonstrated they were not targeted at underage users. In the version of the final rule that was published, however, no such distinction was made. Nevertheless, FDA may consider the effects of such flavors on the actual usage of these products when it reviews marketing applications submitted pursuant to the rule.

The massive growth of e-cigarette sales, particularly among underage users, has been accompanied by an explosion of the use of characterizing flavors.

Flavoring of Cigars. Critics of the industry have also argued that the flavoring of cigars has contributed to the increased prevalence of cigar usage among youth, and have called on FDA to issue a product standard prohibiting the use of characterizing flavors in cigars. When FDA promulgated the deeming rule in 2016, it stated that it would issue an additional rule regarding the use of characterizing flavors in cigars. However, no such rule has yet emerged from the agency.

The broad issue of flavoring in tobacco products remains a prime subject of contention between the industry and its critics. (FDA deals with the problem in its new regulatory approach to tobacco products, described at the end of this chapter.)

Promulgation of Standards for Tobacco Products

In addition to creating the special, self-executing rules in subsection (a)(1), section 907 gives FDA the power to develop tobacco product standards. The act spells out with considerable detail the types of standards that might be adopted, the factors FDA must take into account in promulgating a standard, and the procedure the agency must use.

Types of Standards. Although the act nowhere defines the term "tobacco product standard," section 907(a)(4) gives a number of examples of standards that might be appropriate for the safeguarding of the public health. They all relate to the composition, design, testing, and marketing of tobacco products, and hence cover broad ground. Thus, standards may set levels of nicotine yields or lessen or eliminate the presence of other constituents. They also may affect the construction, components, ingredients, additives, constituents, and properties of a tobacco product. Finally, standards may impose requirements for testing, sale, and distribution, and labeling necessary to assure the proper use of the product.

FDA is prohibited from issuing a regulation that bans cigarettes, smokeless tobacco products, cigars, pipe tobacco, and roll-your-own tobacco products, or that reduces nicotine yields to zero.

Section 907(d)(3) places an important limitation on FDA's authority to set standards. It prohibits FDA from issuing a regulation that bans cigarettes, smokeless tobacco products, cigars, pipe tobacco, and roll-your-own tobacco products, or that reduces nicotine yields to zero. The reason given is the importance of such a regulation, most likely in the sense that it implicates the sort of policy decision that should be left to the legislative and executive branches, given the public health, cultural, and law enforcement ramifications that a total prohibition might produce.

Considerations. In order to justify the setting of a tobacco-product standard, FDA must make a finding that it would be "appropriate for the protection of the public health." Section 907(a)(3)(B)(i) requires the agency to take into account scientific evidence establishing the risks and benefits of the standard to both consumers and affected third parties; any increase or decrease in the odds that current consumers will stop using the tobacco product involved; and any increase or decrease in the danger that non-consumers will begin to use it.

Noticeably absent here is any express mandate that FDA take into account the extent of any economic burden with which a standard might saddle the tobacco industry. Other consumer protection statutes explicitly require the consideration of the costs of compliance with standards. Moreover, an executive order issued by OMB directs federal agencies to consider the costs and the benefits of all possible regulatory options and to choose regulatory options that maximize societal benefits. Since the act forbids FDA from banning cigarettes and other tobacco products, it seems clear that FDA could not promulgate a standard that would impose such heavy costs that it would amount to a de facto ban.

In addition to determining the appropriateness of a proposed standard in terms of public health, FDA must also consider whether compliance with the standard is technologically achievable and whether the standard might have any countervailing (or negative) effects on the health of young users, adult users, and non-users.

Standard-Setting Procedures. Section 907(c) sets out the procedures FDA must follow when proposing to set, amend, or revoke a tobacco product standard. They generally track the informal processes the agency normally utilizes in promulgating regulations under section 701(a), except that here the statute specifies certain requirements, such as the providing of a justification to support the necessary finding that the standard will appropriately protect the public health, an invitation to interested parties that they submit a competing proposal for a standard, and consultation with the Secretary of Agriculture.

Section 907(d) provides for the promulgation of a final rule, along with the findings that subsection (c) directs FDA to make. It also requires the consideration of a number of factors relevant to the establishment of an effective date for the regulation. These include the technical feasibility of complying, the existence of patents that might make compliance impossible, and alterations in the methods of growing tobacco domestically.

Appellate Review. Section 912(a) provides for judicial review of the establishment, amendment, or revocation of a tobacco product standard by a United States Court of Appeals in accordance with section 706(2)(a) of the APA, which directs the setting aside of agency actions if they are "arbitrary, capricious, an abuse of discretion, or otherwise not in accordance with the law." In this respect, tobacco product standards differ from medical device performance standards, motor-vehicle safety standards, and consumer product safety standards, all of which must be justified by substantial evidence in the record as a whole.

Tobacco product standards differ from medical device performance standards, motor-vehicle safety standards, and consumer product safety standards, all of which must be justified by substantial evidence in the record as a whole.

On the other hand, as has been demonstrated, the act spells out in great detail the numerous findings FDA must make in support of standards the agency promulgates. Compliance with these requirements will not only strain FDA resources but also may heighten judicial scrutiny when industry challenges regulations in court.

Proposed Standard on NNN in Smokeless Tobacco Products. In the eight years that have passed since the Tobacco Control Act went into effect, FDA has proposed only one product standard, which would establish a maximum level for nitrosonornicotine (NNN), a virulent carcinogen found in smokeless tobacco products. To justify the standard, FDA noted an association between NNN levels and oral cancer, and concluded that compliance with the standard was technologically feasible because one manufacturer, Swedish Match, was already producing and marketing smokeless tobacco products that met the standard. The FDA proposal was published on January 23, 2017, and will not go into effect unless and until FDA issues a final rule.

REGULATION OF LABELING

The Tobacco Control Act uses the misbranding provision to require manufacturers to place a considerable amount of factual information on the labeling of tobacco products.

The Tobacco Control Act uses the misbranding provision to require manufacturers to place a considerable amount of factual information on the labeling of tobacco products. Normally, labeling conveys directions for the safe use of a product, as well as hazard-related communications that enable both actual and potential consumers to make informed choices about whether or not to expose themselves to risks attributable to the use of a product. What makes tobacco product regulation unique is that the most widely marketed items, such as cigarettes and smokeless tobacco, are inherently dangerous, and there is no way to consume them in a safe way. Moreover, the deadly risks to which they expose consumers, when compared to the benefits they provide, would seem to suggest only one rational choice—non-consumption.

This section will first touch on some general labeling requirements applicable to all tobacco products. Then it will consider how the law mandates the disclosure of information on labeling for the purpose of discouraging non-smokers, especially those who have not reached adulthood, from becoming consumers of cigarettes. It will also cover labeling obligations applicable to tobacco products other than cigarettes. Finally, it will survey briefly labeling requirements that are less directly related to consumer protection.

General Labeling Requirements

Section 903(a)(1) provides that a tobacco product will be deemed misbranded "if its labeling is false or misleading in any particular." In addition, section 903(b) provides that FDA may issue a regulation mandating prior approval of statements appearing on the label of a tobacco product to make certain that the statements do not violate either the general prohibition against misbranding or any other provision of the act. The failure to comply with a directive issued under the section would amount to a prohibited act under section 301(q)(1)(A).

Cigarette Labeling

In dealing with the placement of cautionary statements on the labeling of cigarettes, the Tobacco Control Act amended the 1965 Federal Cigarette Labeling and Advertising Act (FCLAA) and also inserted additional provisions relating to labeling into the FDCA. The result, in the case of cigarettes, is a highly complex system of labeling regulation.

Under the amendments, the FCLAA now requires more explicit warnings about the risks related to smoking. The Tobacco Control Act also authorizes FDA to promulgate regulations providing for graphic warnings on packages, and to make substantive revisions of these new cautionary statements. It requires FDA to use notice-and-comment rulemaking to determine whether to mandate the label disclosure of the tar and nicotine yields of cigarettes. Finally, it directs FDA to re-promulgate a substantial portion of its invalidated 1996 regulations, except for two subsections dealing with cigarette and smokeless tobacco packages.

Amending FCLAA. Section 201(a) of the Tobacco Control Act amends the FCLAA, and requires the placement of one of nine health-warning statements that describe in stark terms the dangers of smoking. It specifies where on the package the warning must appear, the size of the type, and the color of the print and background (white on black, or black on white). It also exempts manufacturers and distributors who are not marketing their products in the United States, and retailers, if they meet certain requirements.

However, at this point the Tobacco Control Act differs from its predecessors, in that it vests in FDA the authority to revise the statutorily required warnings, and even to add to them. This may represent a congressional deferral to agency expertise, and also a recognition that warnings may become ineffective or dated, especially in the light of advances in scientific knowledge, and agencies may be better able to adjust to these changes in a timely fashion.

FDA-Mandated Warnings. Section 201(d) authorizes FDA to promulgate regulations requiring graphic displays to accompany the warning statements on cigarette packages, and to illustrate the adverse health effects caused by cigarettes, and to use informal rulemaking to promulgate regulations changing both the way warnings are conveyed and their textual substance, if the agency could find that "such a change would promote greater public understanding of the risks associated with the use of tobacco products."

On June 22, 2011, FDA promulgated regulations that required color images to accompany each of the statutorily mandated warnings. Industry then judicially challenged both the statutory authority enabling FDA to do this and the agency's implementation of this authority. The ensuing litigation is discussed *infra* in the section on "Constitutional Issues."

Tar and Nicotine Levels. Section 206 of the Tobacco Control Act amends the FCLAA to give FDA authority to determine, via informal rulemaking, whether cigarette packages should also include information about tar and nicotine levels.

Labeling of Smokeless Tobacco and Other Tobacco Products

Section 204 of the Tobacco Control Act amends the 1983 Comprehensive Smokeless Tobacco Health Education Act (CSTHEA) in a way that parallels the changes it makes to the FCLAA. It sets out four different mandatory warnings, which must appear individually and on a rotating basis on the packages of smokeless tobacco products; specifies the size and form of the type; and gives FDA authority to promulgate rules that adjust the format and type sizes. Section 205 amends the CSTHEA to enable FDA to use rulemaking to revise the warning statements on the label, conditioned on a finding that "such a change would promote greater public understanding of the risks associated with the use" of such products.

In addition to smokeless tobacco, several other particular categories of tobacco products are subject to special labeling requirements. These include tobacco products for which standards have been set, new tobacco products, and modified risk tobacco products.

Miscellaneous Labeling Requirements

Section 903(a)(2) requires the labels of tobacco products sold in package form to bear the name and place of business of the manufacturer, packer, or distributor; an accurate statement of the quantity of contents; and, in a bow to economic protectionism, the percentage of both domestic- and foreign-origin tobacco in the product. The label must also carry the established name of the product in prominent type, as required by FDA regulations.

REGULATION OF ADVERTISING

The Tobacco Control Act makes applicable to cigarette and smokeless tobacco advertisements the warnings requirements applicable to the labels of those products. Secondly, it directs FDA to promulgate a final rule that incorporates advertising regulations the agency issued in 1996, with some limitations. In addition, it authorizes FDA to develop regulatory restrictions on the advertisement of any tobacco product upon a finding that "such regulation would be appropriate for the protection of the public health." With respect to advertisements and other descriptive printed material issued by the manufacturer, packer, or distributor, section 903(a)(8) mandates the inclusion of certain specific information. Finally, section 903(a)(7)(A) provides that a tobacco product is misbranded if its advertising is false or misleading in any particular.

Warnings

In forcing cigarette ads to bear the same cautionary statements as mandated for labeling, the Tobacco Control Act makes allowances for different types of advertising and foreign language publications, and authorizes FDA to use informal rulemaking to make appropriate adjustments in these requirements. Advertisers must rotate warnings quarterly for each brand of cigarettes they advertise, in accordance with a plan submitted to and approved by FDA. Smokeless tobacco advertisements must bear the same warning statements as those required for labels, with similar adjustments. The act also bans radio and television advertisements for those kinds of products. These provisions coordinate the regulation of labels and advertisements, as well as the labeling and advertising requirements imposed on cigarettes and smokeless tobacco.

Provisions of the Tobacco Control Act coordinate the regulation of labels and advertisements.

Implementation of FDA Regulations

The Tobacco Control Act directs FDA to publish as a final rule, and with certain designated exceptions and changes, the portion of the 1996 regulations that places restrictions on the sale, distribution, and use of cigarettes and smokeless tobacco for the protection of minors. It also specifies the procedure that the agency must use in promulgating the rule.

Advertising and Promotional Media. The 1996 regulations list media where advertising of cigarettes and smokeless tobacco may be disseminated: newspapers, magazines, and other publications; billboards, posters, and placards; non-point-of-sale promotional material; point-of-sale promotional material; and audio or visual formats delivered at point of sale. To disseminate this type of advertising in media not specifically listed requires prior notice to FDA.

Limitations on Form and Content. The rules provide that advertising (as well as labeling) must use only black text on a white background. Exempted from this restriction are ads in facilities where machines and self-service displays are permitted, and in publications whose readership is primarily adult. Audio formats may have only words, with no music or sound effects. Video formats may have only static black text on a white background. Industry objected to these restrictions as violating the First Amendment and challenged them in court. The judicial resolution of the lawsuit will be discussed *infra* in the section on "Constitutional Issues."

Indirect Promotion. The rule also prohibits the promotion of cigarettes or smokeless tobacco by marketing other products or services that carry the brand name, logo, symbol, motto, or any other indicia of product recognition of a particular brand of cigarette or smokeless tobacco. It forbids the offering of any other item in exchange for the purchase of cigarettes or smokeless tobacco. This eliminates both point-of-sales and non-point-of-sales rewards programs. In addition, the regulation prohibits tobacco companies from sponsoring "any athletic, musical, artistic, or other social or cultural event," or any team or entry bearing any indication of product identification with any brand of cigarettes or smokeless tobacco.

Outdoor Advertising. The 1996 regulations provided that outdoor advertising of cigarettes and smokeless tobacco could not be situated within 1,000 feet of a public playground or playground area in a public park. The Tobacco Control Act directs FDA to modify this rule in accordance with governing First Amendment case law. The FDA regulation implementing the 1996 rules opted for further consideration of constitutional objections that have been directed at restrictions on outdoor advertising.

General Authority to Regulate Advertising

The Tobacco Control Act gives FDA broad authority to promulgate rules putting restrictions on the advertising and promotion of tobacco products upon a finding that "such regulation would be appropriate for the protection of the public health." The act requires that any limitations be consistent with the First Amendment. FDA would have to consider "the risks and benefits to the population as a whole," the likelihood or improbability that existing consumers would stop using the products, and the likelihood or improbability that non-consumers would begin using the products.

Inclusion of Specific Information

The act also provides that a tobacco product is misbranded if advertisements (as well as other descriptive printed matter issued by the manufacturer, packer, or distributor) do not include the product's established name, a brief indication of its intended uses, and warnings, precautions, side effects, and contraindications relevant to the product.

DISTRIBUTION CONTROLS

One reason for FDA's original choice to regulate cigarettes as medical devices was the availability of existing statutory provisions that empowered the agency to regulate distribution of devices, authority that would not have been available if FDA had classified cigarettes as "drugs." Moreover, the 1996 rules were meant to protect minors, which would have been very difficult to do without restricting how these products might get into the hands of underage consumers.

The Tobacco Control Act shares this goal, and hence places a number of limitations on the distributors and retailers who form the links between manufacturers and consumers. It does so in several ways. First, as in the case of advertising, it directs FDA to promulgate the distribution requirements and restrictions that the 1996 regulations would have imposed, if the Supreme Court in *Brown & Williamson* had ruled that FDA had jurisdiction over cigarettes. Second, it puts limitations on the distribution of free samples. Third, it requires FDA to develop new regulations governing non-face-to-face contacts between retailers and consumers. And finally, it authorizes FDA to promulgate rules placing additional restrictions on the distribution and sale of tobacco products.

Implementation of the 1996 Regulations

The Tobacco Control Act directed FDA to promulgate its 1996 regulations dealing directly or indirectly with the distribution and sale of cigarettes and smokeless tobacco products to minors. The agency did this in 2010. These rules made the following changes:

Federal Restriction on Sales to Minors. Sales of tobacco products to persons under the age of 18 became illegal under federal law, and sales to persons under the age of 26 would require prior photo identification of the purchaser. Although the Tobacco Control Act prohibits FDA from raising the minimum age, states and their political subdivisions retain the authority to do so, and in recent years some have increased the minimum age to 21.

Non-Face-to-Face Sales. Retailers may sell to customers only in face-to-face exchanges, and therefore vending machines and self-service displays of tobacco products are prohibited. However, the act provided an exception for the use of vending machines and self-service displays if the responsible retailer can assure that persons younger than 18 will not have access to them.

Free Samples. The 1996 FDA regulations contained a flat ban on the distribution of free samples of cigarettes and smokeless tobacco. The Tobacco Control Act directs FDA to re-promulgate this ban but adds to it an exception for smokeless tobacco in a "qualified adult-only" facility, defined so as to ensure that minors would have no access to the samples.

Use of Tobacco Product Brand Names. Manufacturers and distributors are prohibited from marketing or selling products other than tobacco products that bear the brand name, logo, or symbol of any tobacco product. This prohibition applies, for example, to items of apparel and other merchandise carrying such names and symbols.

Sponsorship of Events. Manufacturers, retailers, and distributors are prohibited from sponsoring any athletic, musical, artistic, or other social or cultural events that use the brand name, logo, or symbol of any brand of cigarettes or smokeless tobacco.

The sponsorship rules and the regulations dealing with free samples and tobacco product brand names faced a legal challenge from industry. The litigation will be discussed *infra* in the section on "Constitutional Issues."

Authority to Go Beyond the 1996 Regulations

The act also gives FDA broad authority to promulgate other restrictions on the sale and distribution of tobacco products. It provides that FDA may do this if it can justify a finding that such rules "would be appropriate for the protection of the public health." However, the act prohibits FDA from requiring a doctor's prescription for the purchase of tobacco products.

FDA has not utilized this authority, other than to extend some of the same restrictions to newly deemed tobacco products.

In addition, the act directs FDA to promulgate new regulations governing non-face-to-face transactions for the purchase of tobacco products. However, the agency has not yet done so.

New Tobacco Products

The Tobacco Control Act distinguishes between tobacco products already on the market and new tobacco products. Existing tobacco products can remain on the market indefinitely unless they fail to comply with a product standard issued by FDA or otherwise fail to comply with the law. By contrast, a new tobacco product cannot be legally sold unless FDA has granted premarket approval, based on specific standards and procedures spelled out in the act. From a commercial perspective, therefore, it is highly advantageous for a tobacco product to be considered existing rather than new. Note, however, that both existing and new tobacco products must comply with any applicable product standards.

Definition of a "New Tobacco Product"

The law defines an existing tobacco product as a product that was commercially marketed in the United States on February 15, 2007, a date approximately 28 months prior to the effective date of the statute (June 22, 2009). "Commercial marketing" does not include test marketing, and a product that was sold only in test markets on February 15, 2007, is not an existing tobacco product.

Even if a product was commercially marketed on February 15, 2007, it cannot be an existing product if it has been "modified" in any way. Examples of modification include any change in overall design; the change of a component, part, or constituent; a change in the content, delivery, or form of nicotine; or any other additive or ingredient. FDA has interpreted "modification" to include any change in the physical characteristics of the product. The agency originally construed "modification" to include certain changes in the packaging or labeling of the product, but in a lawsuit challenging this interpretation, the United States District Court for the District of Columbia ruled that changes in packaging or labeling that do not affect the physical characteristics of the product do not qualify as modifications and do not disqualify the product from being an existing tobacco product.[11] However, a change in packaging that can affect the physical characteristics of the product, such as the use of materials that can leech into the contents of the package, does constitute a modification and would make the product statutorily "new."

A "new tobacco product" is defined as a tobacco product either not commercially available in the United States before February 15, 2007, or a tobacco product marketed before that date and subject to modification after that date.

Exemptions from Requirement of Premarket Approval

There are two ways by which a manufacturer can avoid having to secure premarket approval of a "new tobacco product." First, it can make a showing that the product is substantially equivalent to a tobacco product marketed before February 15, 2007. This approach is modeled after the system of premarket notification in the medical device section of the act. Second, the manufacturer can demonstrate that the product falls within a special exemption.

A manufacturer can market a new tobacco product as substantially similar to an existing product by demonstrating that the new product has the same characteristics as the predicate product.

Substantial Equivalence. Under section 905(j), a manufacturer wishing to market a new tobacco product deemed substantially similar to a tobacco product in commercial distribution before February 15, 2007, must submit to FDA a report explaining the basis for that determination. Section 910(a)(3)(A) defines the latter term as requiring the possession of the same characteristics as the predicate tobacco product, that is, the product to which the new tobacco product is substantially similar. Subsection (B) defines "characteristics" as "materials, ingredients, design, composition, heating source, or other features of a tobacco product." If the product characteristics are different, substantial equivalence may still be found if the new tobacco product does not raise questions of public health that are different from those raised by the predicate product. The burden of determining substantial equivalence is on the applicant.

In general, requirements for determining "substantial equivalence" are considerably less onerous and extensive as those applicable to new-product applications, and focus on demonstrating the similarities between the new product and the predicate product. Section 910(a)(3)(C) bars a finding of substantial equivalence if FDA had removed the predicate tobacco product from the market, or if a court decision had found it to be adulterated or misbranded.

The act created two categories of substantial-equivalence applications. A manufacturer that had commercially marketed a product on or before March 22, 2011 and that filed a substantial-equivalence application by that date could continue marketing the product unless and until FDA denied the application. Such applications are referred to as "provisional SE applications" because the manufacturer is provisionally entitled to continue marketing the product. A manufacturer that filed an application after March 22, 2011 could not market the product unless and until FDA granted the application. Such applications are referred to as "regular SE applications."

FDA received more than 3,000 applications by March 22, 2011, nearly all of which were filed within a few days of the deadline. A much smaller number of regular applications have been filed since that date. FDA gave priority to processing the latter. It found that many such applications were incomplete or non-compliant, and many were withdrawn by the manufacturer. After an initial delay in rendering decisions on regular applications, FDA has largely eliminated the backlog of regular applications and has granted several hundred of them.

By contrast, FDA placed a lower priority on processing the "provisional" applications and more than six years since they were filed, FDA still has not yet acted on the large majority of them. In the interim, manufacturers have remained free to keep the products covered by these applications on the market.

The standards applied by FDA in processing substantial-equivalence applications were significantly altered by the decision of the United States District Court for the District of Columbia in *Philip Morris USA v. Food and Drug Administration*.[12] Initially, FDA took the position that the "characteristics" of a product included the product's name and labeling and that a change in either the name or the labeling of a product was a modification rendering the product a new tobacco product. Subsequently, FDA determined that the label was not part of the product but that changes in the name of a product, and certain changes in product labeling nevertheless constituted a modification rendering the product a "new tobacco product"—even if the physical aspects of the product remained the same. As a consequence, such products were subject to the requirement of obtaining a marketing order. However, the court in *Philip Morris* rejected this analysis and held that changes in the name of the product and changes in the labeling of the product—in the absence of changes in the physical aspects of the product—did not make the product a "new product" and did not trigger the requirement for a marketing order. Furthermore, the court held that the term "characteristics" in the definition of substantial equivalence referred only to the physical characteristics of the product and not to its name or its labeling. The court noted that FDA had jurisdiction over product labeling but that the exercise of such jurisdiction was subject to the requirements of a different section of the Tobacco Control Act.

FDA had also taken the position that the "same characteristics" branch of the definition of substantial equivalence required that the characteristics of the new product be identical to the characteristics of the predicate product. The court in *Philip Morris* rejected that position as well, holding that a new product could be found to have "the same characteristics" as a predicate product so long as the physical characteristics of the product were not "significantly different" from those of the predicate product. The court did not elaborate on the distinction between changes that are "significant" and changes that are not, and the contours of any such distinction are unclear. Subsequent to the decision, FDA announced that it would not appeal and indicated that it would provide additional guidance to implement the decision. As of May 2017, no such guidance had been issued.

In reviewing substantial-equivalence applications, FDA has taken the position that a new product had to be shown to be substantially equivalent to a single predicate product and rejected attempts by manufacturers to show that products were substantially equivalent to a group of predicate products. This requirement remains in place.

FDA has also created a process for manufacturers to have products classified as "existing tobacco products" by demonstrating that they had been marketed on February 15, 2007. Such a showing not only permits a manufacturer to market the product without obtaining a marketing order but it also permits the product itself to serve as a predicate in a subsequent substantial-equivalence application. As of May 2017, more than one thousand products had been classified as existing products.

Applicability of Marketing Order Rules to Newly Deemed Tobacco Products

The deeming rule requires manufacturers of newly deemed products that were not commercially marketed on February 15, 2007 to obtain marketing orders in order to keep them on the market.

The deeming rule requires manufacturers of newly deemed products that were not commercially marketed on February 15, 2007 to obtain marketing orders in order to keep them on the market. Thus, it creates periods during which products can continue to be marketed pending the filing of an application. The compliance periods were recently extended by three months. For products as to which an application for an exemption for substantial equivalence is filed, the compliance period now extends until November 8, 2018; for products as to which a substantial-equivalence application is filed, the compliance period now extends until May 8, 2019; and for products as to which a new product application is filed, the period extends until November 8, 2019. Moreover, if an application is filed, the manufacturer is permitted to keep marketing the product for up to one year after these dates unless FDA earlier denies the application. FDA may grant an extension of the time period.

These compliance periods apply only to newly deemed products that were on the market on August 8, 2016. Newly deemed products that were not on the market by that date cannot be marketed unless a marketing order has been granted. The staggered compliance periods established in the deeming rule reflect the fact that new-product applications are more time consuming to prepare than substantial-equivalence applications, and substantial-equivalence applications are more time consuming to prepare than applications for exemptions from substantial equivalence. Manufacturers have complained that the compliance period established for new product applications is insufficient for their preparation.

Moreover, each class of newly deemed products faces its own set of challenges. Few, if any, e-cigarette products were commercially marketed on February 15, 2007. Thus, all or substantially all e-cigarette products are new tobacco products. FDA has promulgated a draft guidance directed specifically to applications for newly deemed products. This guidance makes clear that applications for new product marketing orders will require extensive information, and that it will be expensive for manufacturers to develop applications suitable for filing. Moreover, FDA has classified vape shop retailers who mix e-cigarette liquids as "manufacturers" of tobacco products and therefore subject to the marketing requirements of the statute. E-cigarette manufacturers have argued that it is economically prohibitive for them to file new product applications. The deeming rule provides an avenue for such manufacturers to purchase liquids from manufacturers that have obtained new product orders for "master files." This in essence converts a vape shop retailer from a manufacturer to a reseller of a product for which an order has been issued, and alleviates the burden of making a large and expensive regulatory filing before the marketing of a product.

E-cigarette manufacturers have also argued that using February 15, 2007, as the demarcation date between existing products and new products is inappropriate in the context of e-cigarettes, because virtually no e-cigarette products were commercially marketed on that date; therefore, there will be few if any e-cigarette products that do not require a marketing order. They have argued that a much later demarcation date should be applied, with many taking the position that the date should be August 8, 2016, when introduction of new e-cigarette products without marketing orders became illegal under the deeming rule. They have argued that application of the February 15, 2007 date leads to an anomalous result, whereby thousands of cigarette brands may be marketed without a marketing order but virtually no e-cigarette brands would qualify.

Those opposed to changing the date point to the fact that creating such a rule would permit the sale of thousands of products introduced with no premarket requirements. They point to the fact that e-cigarette manufacturers have known for years that FDA would apply the new product rules to them and that the fact that they have had years in which they have operated with no regulation presents no argument for freezing in place their preferred position.

In any event, FDA has interpreted the statute—which expressly designates February 15, 2007 as the demarcation date between existing products and new products—to create a legal requirement to maintain this deadline. Lawsuits brought by e-cigarette companies to challenge the deeming rule argue that the statute gives FDA discretion to change the date and argue that the drafters of the statute did not foresee the consequences of applying this date to their products. However, a departure from that date would require FDA to override the specific statutory language.

Cigar manufacturers also dispute the application of the demarcation date to their products and challenge its use in their lawsuits seeking to invalidate portions of the deeming rule. They argue that although the marketing of cigars long predates the demarcation date, they lack the detailed information about the products marketed on that date that would make it possible to establish which cigars qualify as existing products. Opponents of changing the date argue that the cigar manufacturers have known for years that FDA would apply the statute to cigars, and that manufacturers wishing to claim that their products qualify as existing products should have made provision for asserting such a claim. (A description of relevant date changes contained in FDA's new approach to tobacco product regulation appears at the end of this chapter.)

Premarket Approval

If a manufacturer of a new tobacco product cannot establish the requisite substantial equivalence and cannot qualify for an exemption, the only remaining recourse is to apply to FDA for premarket approval.

What an Application Must Include. Section 910(b)(1) mandates the submission of an application containing full reports of information showing the health risks linked to the product and an indication that these risks are less serious than those attributable to other tobacco products; a full description of the components, ingredients, additives, and properties of the new tobacco product and a description of how it operates; a full account of how it is manufactured, processed, and, if relevant, packed and installed; a reference to any applicable tobacco product standard and information to demonstrate that either the new product conforms to it or why any deviation from the standard is justifiable; product samples; and any other information FDA might request.

Standards for Denial. Under section 910(c)(2), FDA must deny the application if there is no proof that letting the product on the market would be appropriate for the protection of the public health; if the methods used to manufacture, process, or pack the product do not conform to the good manufacturing practice requirements of section 906(e); if the proposed labeling is false or misleading in any particular; or if the new product does not meet an applicable product standard.

Meaning of "Appropriate for the Protection of the Public Health." The critical part of the standard for the approval for new tobacco products is the meaning of the phrase "appropriate for the protection of the public health." This is the same test FDA must meet in order to justify regulations placing restrictions on the advertising, promotion, and distribution of tobacco products under section 906(d)(1), and when promulgating tobacco product standards under section 907(a)(3). The agency must consider whether it is more or less likely that existing consumers of tobacco products will stop using those products, and that non-consumers will begin to use them.

As a practical matter, these stringent requirements have discouraged manufacturers from filing new product applications, and only a handful have been submitted. The only new product application granted to date has been for Swedish snus (smokeless tobacco) products manufactured by Swedish Match North America. The product had a decades-long history of use in Sweden that demonstrated not only the physical consequences of consuming the product, but also the effect of its marketing on non-tobacco consumers.

The stringent requirements have discouraged manufacturers from filing new product applications, and only a handful have been submitted.

Procedures for Withdrawal. Section 910(d) sets out procedures for the withdrawal or temporary suspension of new tobacco products previously approved by FDA. The agency must first submit the issue to the TPSAC, and then provide an opportunity for an informal hearing. On the basis of the facts before it, including the recommendation of the Advisory Committee and any additional information and argumentation that surfaced at the hearing, FDA will then make its determination.

Standards for Withdrawal. FDA may then withdraw its approval order if the agency can conclude that keeping the product on the market would no longer be appropriate to protect the public health; the application contained an untrue statement of a material fact; the applicant's conduct fell below standards set out elsewhere in the act; or that certain new information has surfaced, justifying the withdrawal.

Temporary Suspension. Section 910(d)(3) enables FDA, after giving an opportunity for an informal hearing, to suspend on a temporary basis a premarket approval order, if the continued marketing of the product "would cause serious adverse health consequences or death, that is greater than ordinarily caused by tobacco products on the market."

MODIFIED RISK TOBACCO PRODUCTS

Amid the lengthy list of findings of fact in the Tobacco Control Act are eight findings that express serious congressional concern about the marketing of tobacco products for which manufacturers make assertions that they reduce risks or exposures to risks inherent in similar products, and about the harm this can cause to the public health if the claims made for them do not come to fruition or consumers misunderstand them. In response to these preoccupations, the act includes a set of comprehensive, richly detailed directives that create a system of premarket approval for what are termed "modified risk tobacco products." (Since claims involve speech, industry eventually sought to invalidate the requirement of premarket approval here as a violation of a right protected by the First Amendment. The litigation incorporating this challenge is discussed *infra* under "Constitutional Issues.")

Premarket Authorization

The act first defines "modified risk tobacco products," to which the requirement of premarket approval will apply. It then sets out the procedures that applicants and FDA must follow and the substantive standards the agency must apply in passing judgment on the application. Finally, it establishes a special exception applicable to certain modified risk products.

FDCA § 911(b)(1) defines a "modified risk tobacco product" as one that is "sold or distributed for use to reduce harm or the risk of tobacco-related disease associated with commercially marketed tobacco products."

Definition. Section 911(b)(1) defines a "modified risk tobacco product" as one that is "sold or distributed for use to reduce harm or the risk of tobacco-related disease associated with commercially marketed tobacco products." Subsection (b)(2) then refines the definition by limiting it to situations in which the manufacturer represents that the product presents a lesser risk of a tobacco-related disease or is less harmful than one or more commercially available tobacco products, or presents a reduced exposure to or does not contain a substance or substances recognized as harmful. The representation may be made through a label, labeling, advertising or, after the enactment of the Tobacco Control Act, by any other action directed by the manufacturer to consumers.

The definition makes it clear that whether a product is a "modified risk" product depends entirely on the claims made about it. A new product or an existing product is not a "modified risk" product unless and until FDA grants an application permitting a modified risk claim to be made about the product. Thus, FDA might grant a new product application yet not permit modified risk claims to be made about the product.

In addition, the modified risk definition would apply if the label, labeling, or advertising uses the descriptive terms "light," "mild," "low," or a similar adjective. In effect, this provision required manufacturers to remove these terms from their labels and advertising when the regulation went into effect, since they would have been unable to meet the statutory requirements for the grant of an application. Manufacturers have substituted non-verbal color designations for these terms. Although industry critics have asserted that these were simply different means of conveying the same misleading information and have called on FDA to take action to prevent such practices, FDA has done nothing to stop this.

Application Process. Section 911(d) mandates submissions of applications that contain a description of the product and the proposed labeling and advertising; the conditions for its use; its formulation; sample labels and labeling; all health-related documents (favorable or unfavorable, and including scientific data) relating to the capacity of the product to reduce risk or exposure and relating to human health; data concerning how consumers actually use the product; and any other information FDA may require. The agency must make this information available to the public, subject to protections normally afforded trade secrets and otherwise confidential commercial information. It must also solicit comments about this material and about the label, labeling, and the increased or decreased likelihood that existing tobacco product users who would otherwise stop using those products will switch to the product that is the subject of the application; the increased or decreased likelihood that non-users of tobacco products will begin using the product; and the risks and benefits to persons from the use of the product relative to the use of products approved as drugs for smoking cessation under the FDCA. The burden of proof here falls on the applicant. All modified risk applications must be submitted for review by the TPSAC, which makes a recommendation to FDA. FDA is not bound to follow TPSAC's recommendation.

Standard for Grant of a Modified Risk Order. The test FDA must use to determine whether or not to approve an application to market a modified risk tobacco product is whether it will "significantly reduce harm and the risk of tobacco-related disease to individual tobacco users," and will "benefit the health of the population as a whole taking into account both users of tobacco products and persons who do not currently use tobacco products." The statute directs FDA, in making this determination, to take into account the relative health risks of the product to individuals; the increased or decreased likelihood that existing users who would otherwise stop using tobacco products would switch to the product; the increased likelihood that persons who do not use tobacco products will start using the product; and the risks and benefits of the product compared to those of smoking cessation products regulated as drugs under Section V of the FDCA.

The standard for approval of a modified risk application is whether the product will "significantly reduce harm and the risk of tobacco-related disease to individual tobacco users," and will "benefit the health of the population as a whole taking into account both users of tobacco products and persons who do not currently use tobacco products."

Special Rules for Certain Products. Section 911(g)(2) creates an exception for applicants unable to meet the requirements for modified risk tobacco products. To qualify, FDA must determine that: 1) an approval order would promote the public health; 2) what makes the label, labeling, and advertising qualify the product for modified risk treatment arises from explicit or implicit representations that the product or its smoke does not contain, or contains a reduced level of, a substance or presents a reduced exposure to a substance in tobacco smoke; 3) the only available evidence to show this would have to derive from long-term epidemiological studies; and 4) the only other scientific evidence available indicates that "a measurable and substantial reduction in morbidity or mortality among individual users is reasonably likely in subsequent studies." This provision is based on the recognition that the impossibility of obtaining long-term epidemiological studies for new products should not prohibit a claim that a product does not contain or has a reduced level of a hazardous substance if the claim is otherwise supportable.

Conditions of Marketing for Special Cases. Section 911(g)(2)(C) provides that approval under these special rules will last only for a five-year term, subject to renewal; and the applicant must conduct postmarket surveillance and studies, and submit results of them to FDA annually.

Additional Conditions for Marketing All Modified Risk Products. Section 911(h) spells out additional preconditions for the marketing of modified risk tobacco products. They include proof that the advertising and labeling of the product will enable the public to understand the information conveyed about modified risk and the relative importance of this information in relation both to overall health and the tobacco-related diseases and conditions. In addition, FDA may exercise regulatory oversight over comparative claims and quantitative comparisons, and require additional label disclosures and labeling about conditions of use.

Postmarket Obligations. Under section 911(i), FDA must require postmarket surveillance and studies, and annual submissions of results. The required focus here is on consumer perception, behavior, and health, for the purpose of enabling FDA to review the soundness of its premarket approval.

Withdrawal of Authorization. If FDA determines that it has grounds to withdraw its approval of an application to make modified risk claims, section 911(j) provides that it must first give the applicant the opportunity for an informal hearing. The agency must then decide whether to take the product off the market. The grounds for withdrawal are: new information indicating that FDA can no longer make the findings it had to make under section 911(g); the subsequent discovery of the absence of material information, or the inclusion of any untrue statement of a material fact, in the application; a finding that a representation that the product reduces risk or exposure is no longer valid; or the applicant's failure to conduct required postmarket surveillance or submit results of it or of any other required studies.

Swedish Match Application. Swedish Match North America has filed the most highly publicized modified risk application. It involves snus (smokeless tobacco), a product that the company had long marketed in Sweden and Norway and as to which there was substantial epidemiological evidence supporting a claim that the products were less hazardous than other tobacco products. In fact, the evidence of such effects was sufficiently strong that FDA later granted orders authorizing the marketing of these products as new tobacco products, the only such orders issued to date.

Despite such evidence, FDA denied the Swedish Match modified risk application because the company sought to use the modified risk process to alter the warning labels required by statute rather than to make affirmative claims of its own. The company sought to remove two of the four statements from warning labels, i.e., the statement that "WARNING: Smokeless tobacco products may cause oral cancer" and the statement that "WARNING: Smokeless tobacco products may cause gum disease and tooth loss." In addition, Swedish Match sought to change the existing warning that "WARNING: This product is not a safe alternative to cigarettes" and to substitute language stating "No tobacco product is safe but this product presents significantly lower risks to health than cigarettes." FDA denied the application as to the tooth warning because the evidence did not support such a change. It denied the application as to the oral cancer claim because it found that making such a change would by implication indicate that the product could not cause oral cancer, a conclusion FDA found insupportable. It denied the application seeking a change in the warning that the product is not a safe alternative to cigarettes because, *inter alia*, there was insufficient evidence to show that the modified risk information would be sufficiently comprehended by the public.

Modified Risk Claims and the Deeming Rule. Numerous manufacturers of e-cigarette products have made modified risk claims in the advertising, marketing, and promotion of their products. Under the deeming rule, products as to which such claims are made can no longer be manufactured in the absence of an FDA order permitting them.

DRUGS INTENDED TO TREAT TOBACCO DEPENDENCE

Regulation of drugs to treat tobacco dependence falls under the jurisdiction of the Center for Drug Evaluation and Research (CDER) rather than the CTP, and Section V of the FDCA, rather than the Tobacco Control Act, regulates these pharmaceuticals.

Section 918 directs FDA to consider classifying new drug products for smoking cessation, including nicotine-replacement products, as fast-track research and approval products within the scope of section 506. It also mandates that FDA give thought to authorizing the prolonged use of nicotine-replacement products, such as patches, gums, and lozenges, for the treatment of tobacco dependence and of evidence for additional indications for nicotine-replacement products, such as for relief of craving and relapse avoidance. Finally, it calls on FDA to prepare and submit to Congress a report on how best to regulate, promote, and spur the development of innovative products and treatment to

FDCA § 918 directs FDA to consider classifying new drug products for smoking cessation, including nicotine-replacement products, as fast-track research and approval products within the scope of section 506.

achieve total abstinence from tobacco use, reductions in tobacco consumption, and reductions in the harm caused by continued tobacco use.

Although FDA has submitted its report and CDER has taken some limited steps to encourage the development of drugs to treat tobacco dependence, manufacturers still face regulatory obstacles to the development of effective medications. Toward the end of 2016, FDA promulgated a rule designed to clarify the relationship between the CDER and the CTP, but the new administration has postponed implementation of the rule pending further consideration.

POSTMARKETING CONTROLS

The Tobacco Control Act creates two types of postmarketing controls that FDA might exercise over all tobacco products. Section 908 permits the agency to notify the public of a risk discovered after a tobacco product has entered the stream of commerce or to order a recall of the product. Section 909 requires manufacturers and importers to notify FDA about adverse reactions that they have discovered after the products linked to them entered the marketplace. In addition, section 911 imposes extra postmarketing mandates on manufacturers of modified risk tobacco products.

Notice Requirements

Section 908(a) mirrors language in section 518(a) dealing with medical devices. It enables FDA to order the issuance of warnings relating to product-related risks that have come to light after the initial marketing of the product. FDA must make two factual findings: the product must "present an unreasonable risk of substantial harm to the public" and notification must be both "necessary" and "the most practicable means" for eliminating that risk. Once the agency has made these determinations, it may then require that notification be given "in an appropriate form by the persons and means best suited under the circumstances involved, to all persons who should properly receive such notification in order to eliminate such risk." One method of notice is specifically mentioned as an option—public service announcements.

The Tobacco Control Act borrows liberally from the medical device section of the FDCA to give FDA authority to mandate recalls of tobacco products.

Recalls

As in the case of notification, the Tobacco Control Act borrows liberally from the medical device section of the FDCA to give FDA authority to mandate recalls of tobacco products. The agency must first make a finding that "serious adverse health consequences or death" would with reasonable probability result from "a manufacturing or other defect not ordinarily contained in tobacco products on the market." An order based on this finding must target an "appropriate person (including the manufacturers, importers, distributors, or retailers of the tobacco product)," and must call for an immediate cessation of distribution. The act then gives any person subject to the order an opportunity for an informal hearing within 10 days of the issuance of the directive. At issue in the hearing would be whether the actions required by the order are appropriate and whether the order should be amended to include a recall.

If FDA opts to go ahead with a recall, the agency must develop a timetable and require progress reports. Recalls may not reach down to the level of individual purchasers and must include notification to persons put at risk by the use of the product. If these individuals cannot be found, FDA is authorized to contact them through the use of its authority to generate publicity, as spelled out in section 705(b), which contains a further limitation to the effect that the product put consumers in "imminent danger to health."

MISCELLANEOUS PROVISIONS

Good Manufacturing Practice Requirements

Section 906(a) directs FDA to promulgate regulations that require manufacturers of tobacco products to conform to current Good Manufacturing Practice (GMP) or Hazard Analysis and Critical Control Point (HACCP) methodology. Affected parties may apply for permanent or temporary exemptions or variances. In the drafting stage of GMP rules, the agency must solicit input from the TPSAC as to whether or not to grant an exemption or variance. Interested parties must be given an opportunity for an oral hearing before a GMP regulation is promulgated as a final rule, and petitioners for exemptions or variances must be given an opportunity for an informal hearing after issuing an order either approving or denying the petition. Despite these provisions, FDA has not yet proposed regulations or published a guidance on this subject.

Tobacco Products Scientific Advisory Committee

Section 917 directs FDA to set up a 12-member entity to be known as the Tobacco Products Scientific Advisory Committee. The responsibilities of the committee are to furnish FDA with advice, recommendations, and information as specifically provided for in the act, on the effects of reducing nicotine levels in tobacco products, on the possibility of finding a nicotine level that will not produce tobacco dependence, and on any other issues as requested by FDA. Members of the committee must have technical qualifications relating to tobacco products and represent various specified interest groups. They are subject to the conflict-of-interest rules in section 712.

The provisions of the act that call for input from the committee include sections 906(e)(1)(B)(i) (GMP requirements), 907(d)(1) and (5) (tobacco product standards), 907(e)(1) (menthol cigarettes), 910(b)(2) (new tobacco products), and 911(f) (modified risk tobacco products).

User Fees

Section 919 establishes a schedule of user fees to be assessed against the manufacturers and importers of tobacco products. According to subsection (b)(3), fees are to be calculated according to the type of product being made or imported and the percentage of market share based on the total volume of domestic sales of the class of product during the fiscal year. Failure to pay user fees will cause a manufacturer's or importer's products to be considered adulterated under section 902(4). The Tobacco Control Act is unique in that user fees completely pay for the administration and enforcement of the statute.

The Tobacco Control Act is unique in that user fees completely pay for the administration and enforcement of the statute.

Prevention of Illicit Trade

Although the Tobacco Act explicitly bars FDA from banning cigarettes and other specific tobacco products and from mandating that nicotine yields of a tobacco product be reduced to zero, the act does prohibit the sale of many kinds of flavored cigarettes. It also imposes on manufacturers a number of obligations that will increase the costs of production, which could in turn cause them to discontinue the marketing of certain tobacco products or to increase prices; in the latter instance, some consumers may no longer be able to afford these items. Both unavailability and unaffordability could give rise to illegal commerce. To deal with this possibility, the Tobacco Control Act includes several provisions aimed at discouraging the illegal trade of tobacco products.

Origin Labeling. Section 902(a) requires that all tobacco products bear on their labels, packaging, and shipping containers the legend "sale only allowed in the United States." The purpose of this obligation is to facilitate the detection of tobacco products manufactured abroad and then sold illegally in this country.

Recordkeeping. Section 920(b) directs FDA to promulgate recordkeeping regulations that will make it easier to monitor the commercial movement of tobacco products in order to aid in the suppression of illicit trade. These rules may include the requiring of label codes. The agency's authority here is limited to "the establishment and maintenance of records by any person," which suggests that it may be directed at an individual rather than on an industry-wide basis. Another limitation, aimed at protecting the privacy of individual purchasers, prohibits FDA from mandating the production of records of individual purchases for personal consumption.

Inspection of Records. Section 920(c) gives FDA access to certain records if the agency has a reasonable belief that a tobacco product is part of an illegal trade or smuggling operation or is a counterfeit. The language of the section contains a troublesome ambiguity since it does not limit this access to persons involved in the manufacture or marketing of the specific tobacco products suspected of being involved in an illicit operation. However, logic would seem to dictate the implication of this constraint. Records inspections must take place "at reasonable times and within reasonable limits and in a reasonable manner, upon presentation of appropriate credentials and a written notice." The refusal to permit access to or the copying of any record as required by section 920(c) is a prohibited act under section 301(e).

FDCA § 920(c) gives FDA access to certain records if the agency has a reasonable belief that a tobacco product is part of an illegal trade or smuggling operation or is a counterfeit.

Awareness of Illegal Transactions. Under section 920(d), manufacturers and distributors of tobacco products have an obligation to notify the Attorney General or the Secretary of the Treasury promptly if they have reason to know that one of their products that has left their control is being marketed by a person who is not paying the required duties or taxes or is involved in an illicit sales operation. The requisite state of mind here is either actual knowledge or "the knowledge which a reasonable person would have had under like circumstances or which would have been obtained upon the exercise of due care." The latter amounts to a negligence test. The failure to make a report as required by this section is a prohibited act under section 301(e).

PREEMPTION

The Tobacco Control Act specifically addresses how much space the new federal law leaves for state and local governments to impose additional restrictions on the manufacture and marketing of tobacco products. It amends the FCLAA and the CSTHEA to allow states and localities to regulate the time, place, and manner of cigarette and smokeless tobacco advertising. In addition, it creates a limited preemption scheme that applies to the regulation of tobacco products generally.

Time-Place-Manner Regulation

Sections 203 and 205(b) of the Tobacco Control Act permit states and localities to pass laws and promulgate regulations putting bans or limitations on the "time, place, and manner, but not content, of the advertising or promotion of

The Tobacco Control Act permits states and localities to pass laws and promulgate regulations putting bans or limitations on the "time, place, and manner, but not content, of the advertising or promotion of any cigarette" or of any smokeless tobacco product.

any cigarette" or of any smokeless tobacco product. This means that how these products are marketed, but not the actual substance of the advertising, might be subject to regulation at the state or local level.

New Preemption Rules

In a rather awkward way, section 916 of the FDCA spells out a new set of preemption rules applicable to all tobacco products. They erect a preemption barrier for certain kinds of regulation by entities other than FDA, and for tobacco products other than cigarettes and smokeless tobacco. The section first details the kinds of regulatory activity that will not be preempted. It then spells out exceptions. It then specifies exceptions to the exceptions. Finally, it places product liability lawsuits outside the reach of federal preemption.

What Others Can Do. Section 916(a)(1) applies not only to states and their subdivisions, but also to federal agencies and Indian tribes. These entities may adopt and enforce laws, administrative rules, or other measures that are in addition to or more stringent than requirements imposed under the Tobacco Control Act. More specifically, they can take action "relating to or prohibiting the sale, distribution, exposure to, access to, advertising and promotion of, or use of tobacco products by individuals of any age, information reporting to the State, or measures relating to fire-safety standards for tobacco products." Moreover, no part of the act may "limit or otherwise affect any State, tribal or local taxation of tobacco products."

What Others Cannot Do. After bestowing authority on other government entities to impose additional or stricter rules on sales, distribution, advertisements, and promotion, as well as reporting and fire safety, section 916(a)(2)(A) then imposes a broad preemption rule that will govern specific aspects of regulation under the Tobacco Control Act: "tobacco product standards, premarket review, adulteration, misbranding, labeling, registration, good manufacturing standards, or modified risk products."

What Others Can Do (Revisited). In a disconcerting reversal of direction, section 916(a)(2)(B) then posits that the prohibitions in subsection (A) will not govern "requirements relating to the sale, distribution, possession, information reporting to the State, exposure to, access to, the advertising and promotion of, or use of, tobacco products by individuals of any age, or relating to fire safety standards for tobacco products." What this seems to suggest, for example, is that a state might regulate the advertising of a modified risk product.

Products Liability. Section 916(b) makes clear that tobacco regulation under the act will not preempt "any action or the liability of any person under the product liability law of any State." This leaves the door open for state tort claims that in the exercise of due care a tobacco company should have included additional or more dramatic cautionary statements on the labeling or in the advertising of a tobacco product.

CONSTITUTIONAL ISSUES

A decade or so before Congress passed the Tobacco Control Act, the Commonwealth of Massachusetts attempted to limit both outdoor and indoor advertisements of smokeless tobacco and cigars. Industry objections to these restrictions ultimately reached the United States Supreme Court, which ruled that the promotional materials under scrutiny amounted to constitutionally protected commercial speech.[13] A majority of the Court found that the limitations Massachusetts sought to impose on billboards and outdoor advertising constituted an undue infringement on the right of defendants to communicate with adult smokers. In reaching this conclusion, the Court used the test it had adopted in *Central Hudson Gas & Electric Corporation v. Public Service Commission of New York*,[14] which applied to speech that was neither false nor misleading. To restrict it, *Central Hudson* required the government to show that it has a substantial interest in doing so, that the restriction directly advances that interest, and that it is not more extensive than would be necessary to promote the interest. Given this backdrop, it was inevitable that elements of the tobacco industry would raise constitutional objections to both the new law and FDA regulations issued under its authority.

Challenges to Marketing Restrictions

Since the Tobacco Control Act gave the government extensive power not only to curb but also to influence the marketing of cigarettes, the industry not surprisingly mounted constitutional counter-attacks on both the statutory provisions bestowing this authority on FDA and the agency's effort to implement them. Shortly after the act became law, a group of cigarette manufacturers brought suit to prevent FDA from giving substance to several of the marketing-related provisions of the act, including the grant of authority to the agency to require graphic images on cigarette packaging, on the ground that they violated the First Amendment to the Constitution. Subsequently, once FDA acted under the authority some of these provisions gave to the agency, another group of manufacturers suing in the United States District Court for the District of Columbia challenged the constitutionality of agency regulations mandating that certain highly graphic images appear on cigarette packs. The results produced by these lawsuits did not conflict, but the reasoning that underpinned them did, a situation that might well eventually require resolution by the United States Supreme Court.

The first of these cases involved a broad effort to nullify several different marketing restrictions in addition to the speech compelled by the graphic-image requirement. A U.S. District Court ruled in plaintiffs' favor on various counts.[15] Industry appealed, and in *Discount Tobacco City & Lottery Inc. v. United States*,[16] (the name of the case had changed on appeal) a three-judge panel of the Court of Appeals for the Sixth Circuit affirmed several rulings of the district court and reversed several others. The discussion that follows will treat first the Sixth Circuit's disposition of the issues not involving graphic images, and then the court's rejection of the constitutional challenge to the act's grant of authority to mandate graphics. The latter holding will be compared with the decision of the United States Court of Appeals for the District of Columbia in *R.J. Reynolds Tobacco Company v. Food and Drug Administration*,[17] which invalidated the FDA regulations requiring graphic images on cigarette packs.

Ban on Color and Imagery in Advertisements. Plaintiffs in *Discount Tobacco City* challenged the act's requirement that labeling and advertising use only black text on a white background, with no imagery, as well as the narrowness of the exceptions to the rule. The court rejected the government's claim that all uses of color and imagery are likely to attract minors, and held that to avoid invalidation on constitutional grounds, restrictions should confine themselves to speech necessary to carry out the goal of protecting young people. In the court's view, the act's ban on color and imagery was "vastly overbroad," and hence violated plaintiff's commercial-speech rights.

Brand-Name Event Sponsorship and Merchandise. On the other hand, the panel upheld the regulatory ban on the use of brand names to sponsor events to which children might be exposed, or to distribute items such as caps and T-shirts or corporate logos, on the ground that it was not more than necessary to reduce youth exposure to brand names or possession of branded merchandise.

Premarket Review of Risk Reduction Claims. Plaintiffs also took aim at the statutory requirement that harm reduction claims made by a modified risk tobacco product be subject to premarket review by FDA, so that a manufacturer who made such claims before FDA preclearance would violate the act. The companies asserted that this would prevent them from participating in public health debates about tobacco harm reduction, and hence would infringe upon their right to free speech. The court, however, ruled that the act sought to prohibit only commercial speech embodied in the labeling and advertising of specific products, a restriction justified by the industry's long history of using misleading health claims to market reduced risk cigarettes; the prohibition would not apply to non-commercial speech in any public health debate.

Cigarette Package Warnings. Section 201 of the Tobacco Control Act updates the warnings cigarette packs must bear, specifies their size and location, and authorizes FDA to mandate additional, graphic warnings. The Sixth Circuit rejected the companies' claim that consumers are already aware of smoking risks and in fact overestimate them. By a 2-1 vote, the panel also ruled that FDA's authority to require graphic images was not in itself unconstitutional, since they can convey factual information reasonably related to the act's goal of preventing consumer deception. In so doing, the majority applied a rule fashioned by the United States Supreme Court in *Zauderer v. Office of Disciplinary Counsel*,[18] which refused to overturn a state regulation that compelled certain disclosures by attorneys advertising contingent-fee services. Under this test, a speech requirement would be constitutional if it was reasonably related to the state's interest in protecting consumers against deception.

Graphic Warning Labels. In the 1960s the United States became the first country to require warning labels on cigarette packs and cigarette advertisements. However, the mandatory cautionary statements were small, inconspicuously placed warnings and outdated, having last been modified in 1985. By 2009 their effectiveness was generally regarded as dubious at best. In the intervening years many other countries had required much larger graphic warnings on cigarette packs, and advertising illustrating the grisly dangers of smoking.

The Tobacco Control Act mandated several changes in warning labels on cigarette packs. It required that cigarette packs bear nine new, more explicit textual warnings, to be used in rotation; that the warnings be in 17-point type and be placed on the top of both the front and the back of the pack; and that they occupy 50 percent of the space on both the front and back. More important, the law directed FDA to include graphics as part of the warning labels and to promulgate regulations requiring such graphics no later than June 22, 2011, to be effective 15 months thereafter.

The Tobacco Control Act mandated several changes in warning labels on cigarette packs.

Very soon after the enactment of the statute and before FDA had selected any graphics, a group of cigarette manufacturers and retailers brought suit in the United States District Court for the Western District of Kentucky, and alleged that the requirements for graphic warning labels were unconstitutional on their face as a violation of the manufacturers' freedom of speech. The district court rejected this contention and the United States Court of Appeals, by a 2-1 vote, affirmed the court's decision.[19] The court ruled that FDA's statutory authority to require graphic images was not in itself a violation of the First Amendment, since they can convey factual information reasonably related to the act's goal of protecting consumers against deceptive practices.

Meanwhile, FDA proceeded through notice-and-comment rulemaking to select graphics for use on the warning labels. In conformity with the statutory mandate, FDA promulgated the final rule on June 22, 2011. A group of manufacturers then brought suit against the agency in the United States District Court for the District of Columbia, alleging that the specific graphics selected by FDA were a violation of their First Amendment right of free speech. The manufacturers also argued that the requirement that the warnings occupy 50 percent of the front and back of the cigarette packs also violated their constitutionally protected rights. They did not challenge the truth or the appropriateness of the text of the new warnings.

The district court, applying the most stringent standard of review, found that the graphic warnings required by the FDA's order were unconstitutional. On review, by a 2-to-1 majority, the Court of Appeals, applying a standard of review generally applied in commercial speech cases, held that FDA's order was unconstitutional because the government had not demonstrated that the graphic warning labels selected would advance a permissible governmental interest.[20] In reaching this conclusion, the court relied on the regulatory impact statement that accompanied the rule that had concluded that the warning labels would not cause large numbers of smokers to quit. FDA declined to seek Supreme Court review, and the government publicly announced that the agency would develop new graphic warning labels and promulgate a rule to fulfill its obligations under the statute.

In the meantime, the United States Court of Appeals for the District of Columbia Circuit had occasion to consider how *Zauderer* would apply in a different compelled-speech context, involving a Department of Agriculture regulation that mandated country-of-origin labeling for certain meat products. In an *en banc* decision, the majority ruled that the *Zauderer* test applies to government-required disclosures aimed at other interests in addition to preventing deception in commercial speech.[21] In so doing, the court specifically overruled language in *R.J. Reynolds* indicating otherwise. This may create uncertainty that will require eventual resolution by the Supreme Court.

By 2016, more than four years after the Court of Appeals decision and more than five years after the statutory deadline for promulgation of graphic warning labels, FDA had neither promulgated new warning labels nor listed promulgation of new warning labels on the interagency calendar of expected agency actions. In October 2016, a group of public health advocacy organizations brought suit against FDA in the United States District Court for the District of Massachusetts, alleging that FDA's failure to promulgate graphic warning labels was a violation of its statutory duty under the Tobacco Control Act, and that the failure to promulgate graphic warning labels constituted agency action unlawfully withheld within the meaning of the APA.[22] The plaintiffs sought an order requiring FDA to comply with its statutory obligations. At the time of publication, the lawsuit is pending.

New Regulatory Approach to Tobacco Products

Just before this edition went to press, FDA announced the results of a rethinking of how it would deal with the risks imposed by tobacco products. What amounts to a new regulatory approach by the agency makes the addictive property of nicotine its central focus, and seeks to enhance the scientific soundness of the regulatory process to be pursued. It sets out as goals:

What amounts to a new regulatory approach by the agency makes the addictive property of nicotine its central focus.

♦ the consideration of a cigarette standard that will lower the amount of nicotine to a level that will render the product minimally or non-addictive;

♦ the extension of deadlines for the submission of tobacco product review applications for newly deemed tobacco products (to August 8, 2022 for e-cigarettes, and to August 8, 2021 for cigars, pipe tobacco, and hookah tobacco);

♦ advance notices of proposed rulemaking to solicit public comments on the contribution of flavors (including menthol) to the seducing of young people to join the ranks of tobacco product consumers, and on the risks posed by premium cigars; and

♦ the improvement of the regulatory process as it governs FDA approval of medicinal nicotine products, premarket tobacco product applications, modified risk tobacco products, and substantial-equivalence claims.

Endnotes

1. Cipollone v. Liggett Group, Inc., 505 U.S. 504 (1992).
2. Food and Drug Administration v. Brown & Williamson Tobacco Corp., 529 U.S. 120 (2000).
3. United States v. Philip Morris, USA, Inc., 449 F. Supp. 2d 1 (D.D.C. 2006).
4. United States v. Philip Morris, USA, Inc., 566 F.3d 1095 (D.C. Cir. 2009).
5. United States v. Philip Morris, USA, Inc., 449 F. Supp. 2d 1 (D.D.C. 2006).

6. Smoking Everywhere, Inc. v. U.S. Food and Drug Administration, 680 F. Supp. 2d 62 (D.D.C. 2010).
7. Sottera, Inc. v. FDA, 627 F.3d 891 (D.C. Cir. 2010).
8. Cigar Ass'n of America v. United States Food and Drug Administration, U.S. District Court, D.C., No. 1:16-cv-01460, July 15, 2016.
9. No. 1:16-cv-878 (D.D.C. May 10, 2016).
10. R.J. Reynolds Tobacco Co v. FDA, 810 F.3d 827 (D.C. Cir. 2016).
11. Philip Morris USA Inc. v. FDA, 202 F. Supp. 3d 31 (D.D.C. 2016).
12. *Id.*
13. Lorillard Tobacco Co. v. Reilly, 533 U.S. 525 (2001).
14. 447 U.S. 557 (1980).
15. Commonwealth Brands, Inc. v. United States, 678 F. Supp. 2d 512 (W.D. Ky. 2010).
16. 674 F.3d 509 (6th Cir. 2012).
17. 696 F.3d 1205 (D.C. Cir. 2012).
18. 447 U.S. 557 (1980).
19. Discount Tobacco City Lottery, Inc. v. United States, 647 F.3d 509 (6th Cir. 2012).
20. R.J. Reynolds Tobacco Co. v. FDA, 695 F.3d 1205 (D.C. Cir. 2012).
21. American Meat Institute v. United States Dep't of Agriculture, 760 F.3d 18 (D.C. Cir. 2014).
22. American Academy of Pediatrics v. United States Food and Drug Administration, U.S. District Court, Massachusetts, No. 1:16-cv-11985, Oct. 4, 2016.

Chapter 14

Regulation of Promotion and Distribution

Wayne L. Pines, APCO Worldwide Inc., Washington, D.C.

Key Points

- The promotion of medical products is central to their proper use. The Food and Drug Administration (FDA) regulates medical product promotional materials, including traditional paid product advertising as well as other promotional materials that are product-specific and that are issued by a company or an agent of that company.
- A few basic principles apply to FDA's regulation of advertising and promotion: materials must be truthful and not false or misleading, must contain a fair balance of benefits and risks, and must provide for full disclosure of prescribing (drugs) or usage (devices) information.
- FDA is especially concerned about the promotion of uses not included in the approved labeling or not supported by "substantial evidence," the pre-approval promotion of new medical products, the lack of fair balance and adequate risk information, and unsupported comparative claims of superiority.
- FDA does not prohibit any communication techniques from being used to promote medical products, but there are nuances of policy that apply to each technique.
- FDA generally enforces the law by issuing letters to companies in violation. The letters cite the alleged violation and seek remedy. Enforcement actions generally stem from FDA's review of materials submitted by companies or from complaints from competitors or physicians.
- Other statutes also apply to marketing medical products.
- Settlements under the False Claims Act and anti-kickback statute have changed the way that pharmaceutical and medical device companies market their products.
- Court decisions have raised fundamental questions about FDA's oversight of promotional activities by medical products companies.

OVERVIEW

The promotion of medical products is central to their success and optimum use. Promotion encompasses a variety of objectives: informing consumers about new and existing products that may be of value in improving their health; educating healthcare providers about new and existing products and how to use them; providing information needed by those who finance or pay directly for medical products, such as managed care organizations or hospitals; and positioning products to differentiate them from those of competitors.

There is also the need to keep other audiences informed about research and new products. The public demands such information; everyone wants to know about medical progress. Investment capital for new companies is dependent on understanding research progress, as well as the potential market value of new products. Maintaining investment community interest in a company hinges upon focused communications. Healthcare providers need to know, on a continuing basis, what kinds of advances are being made in their specialty areas.

These forms of communication, when initiated, controlled, or influenced by a medical products company or by one of its agents (e.g., an advertising or public relations agency), are regulated by the Food and Drug Administration (FDA). Promotional materials issued by medical products companies or their agents are among the most regulated of all forms of communication in the United States. FDA's concerns about product communications that are controlled (directly as well as indirectly) by drug or device companies center primarily upon communications that promote the products for "off-label" uses, make claims that are false and/or misleading, make unsupported comparisons with other products, and/or overstate efficacy or minimize risk.

"Off-label" means that the claims made in the promotional materials or statements are not included in or are not consistent with the officially approved labeling for the product, or are not supported by "substantial evidence."

"Off-label," in particular, has become a controversial term. Basically it means that the claims made in the promotional materials or statements are not included in or are not consistent with the officially approved labeling for the product, or are not supported by "substantial evidence." FDA's underlying concern with "off-label" promotional efforts is that they may result in patients being prescribed unproven therapies or ones that may be less effective or more risky than therapies approved for that use by FDA. The agency also is concerned that "off-label" promotion can undermine companies' incentive to conduct additional studies that will establish safety and efficacy for the new use.

One of the issues that arises in most debates is FDA's reliance on the product labeling as the basis of what can be communicated. There are arguments that information that is generally accepted as being medically truthful and not misleading should be permitted to be communicated by companies, even if that information is not included in the official FDA-approved labeling or does not meet FDA's definition of "substantial evidence." Denying the right of companies to communicate truthful and non-misleading information, many contend, is in fact contrary to the interests of patients and the public health in general.

Others argue that advertising and promotion should be regulated more aggressively. Some contend that physicians should receive medical information primarily from traditional scientific sources, such as peer-reviewed medical journals, not from drug or device companies with an interest in selling a product. Abuses of promotion and marketing efforts by companies over the years have reinforced this view.

Concerns also have been raised about the extent of FDA's jurisdiction. FDA has assumed regulation of all product-specific communications by a medical products company, even before the product is approved and available. FDA also assumes jurisdiction over conversations that take place between a company's sales representative and a physician, and the sales information provided to financial managers at a managed care organization. FDA also regulates what is said by a practicing or academic physician who receives compensation from a drug or device company to promote a product, even when the physician is describing his or her own research or clinical experiences.

One ambiguous facet of the issue is that FDA does accept the need for and value of communicating legitimate and accurate product information in the period before a product or new use is approved and there is no labeling to provide parameters. FDA's own regulations establish the legitimacy of "scientific exchange"—the well-recognized need for scientists to communicate with each other about research findings, and for companies to communicate research information. It is when such "exchange" crosses over into "commercialization"—and FDA has never defined that line with precision—that FDA regulators become concerned.

"Scientific exchange" has never been defined with precision.

In its enforcement actions and in a draft guidance, FDA also seems to draw a distinction based on who within the company is involved in the communication of "non-promotional," scientific information. The basis for FDA enforcement actions is generally the content of what is said, not who says it. FDA has indicated, however, that it is less suspicious when medical personnel deal with "off-label" information. For example, in a December 2011 draft guidance on how companies should respond to unsolicited requests for "off-label" information, FDA "recommends that questions or requests about off-label uses be referred to the firm's medical or scientific representative or department. FDA recommends that medical or scientific personnel have specialized backgrounds in responding to unsolicited requests for information." At the same time, it must be recognized that medical personnel who use the opportunity to promote a product "off-label" or before approval are subject to the same restrictions as all other company employees.

Because of nuanced issues like this, the regulation of promotional materials is one of the most challenging areas of FDA regulation. The agency's approach is continually evolving to meet new communications technologies and creative programming by marketing staffs. At the same time, medical products companies generally have learned to work within the agency's regulatory framework. Larger companies have full-time regulatory staffs dedicated to assuring compliance with FDA promotional requirements. Smaller companies often rely on consultants to keep them up to date on FDA policies.

Drawing a line between violative and permitted activities usually requires experienced judgment. Within companies, FDA promotional policies often are a source of conflict between the marketing and public relations staffs on the one hand, and regulatory and legal staffs on the other. The marketing and public relations teams want their companies to be appropriately aggressive based on their understanding of the rules; regulatory and legal staffs want to make sure the company is in compliance, even when the rules are sometimes vague and evolving. Each company's management must decide its own policies and internal processes in designing and implementing marketing and communications programs, and whether to seek FDA review in advance for certain materials.

What the Law Requires

The 1962 amendments gave FDA authority over prescription drug advertising after Congress heard testimony of alleged abuses by pharmaceutical companies in seeking to market their products to physicians.

The legal basis for FDA's authority to regulate medical product communications dates from the 1962 Drug Amendments. Before 1962, promotional activities for prescription drugs were regulated by the Federal Trade Commission (FTC). The 1962 amendments gave FDA authority over prescription drug advertising after Congress heard testimony of alleged abuses by pharmaceutical companies in seeking to market their products to physicians. The concern about marketing abuses by medical products companies has been a recurring theme and frequently has been the subject of hearings before Congress or media stories.

The pharmaceutical advertising section of the Federal Food, Drug, and Cosmetic Act (FDCA), as enacted in 1962, consists of a single paragraph in the section of the law that defines a "misbranded" product (FDCA § 502(n); 21 U.S.C. § 352(n)). It requires that the generic name of the drug appear "prominently" in promotional materials, that the drug's formula appear, and that a "brief summary" relating to side effects, contraindications, and effectiveness appear in all advertising. It also prohibits FDA from requiring that advertising materials be approved in advance, except in "extraordinary circumstances." FDA issued detailed regulations in the 1960s and 1970s to establish specific requirements for paid advertising for prescription drugs.

Similar requirements for medical devices (FDCA § 502(r); 21 U.S.C. § 352(r)) have evolved from the requirements of the 1962 Drug Amendments, as well as guidances and enforcement actions that affect the marketing of all FDA-regulated medical products—human drugs and biologicals, veterinary drugs, and medical devices.

FDA regulations that apply to the promotion of medical products are contained in several sections of the Code of Federal Regulations (Title 21). Among the applicable sections are Part 200 and, most particularly, Part 202 for pharmaceutical promotion, Part 510 for veterinary drugs, Part 601 for biological products, and Part 801 for medical devices. The sections that deal with human prescription drugs generally set the policies for prescription veterinary drugs.

Since 1962, there have been fundamental changes in how medical products are marketed, in the audiences that need and want to know about them, and in communications technology generally. No longer are medical products promoted just to healthcare providers. No longer is the printed medical journal or the visit by the company's sales representative the primary vehicle of communicating product information. FDA has adapted to this continuously evolving environment.

FDA regulation has adapted to the continuously evolving environment.

The formal FDA regulations provide only a small measure of the information needed to comply with FDA requirements. The regulations are most helpful when it comes to understanding the requirements for traditional paid advertising directed at physicians—the oldest form of marketing now being practiced and the regulatory objective of the 1962 amendments. For more recently introduced communications methods, FDA policy is set forth in other FDA documents, most prominently in guidances and enforcement action letters issued by the agency. To keep up with evolving policies, careful attention must be paid to the Warning Letters and other correspondence that involve specific companies or products. Further, policies have been elucidated in the meetings and symposia where FDA regulators speak.

Underlying Principles

A few basic principles underlie FDA's regulations, guidances, and regulatory actions regarding promotion and advertising. Essentially, any medical product that fails to adhere to these principles in its promotional practices could be viewed as "misbranded" by FDA and subject to an enforcement action. The basic principles that underlie FDA's advertising and promotion policies, and that apply to all medical products categories, are:

It's Basic!
A few basic principles underlie all of FDA's regulation of promotion and advertising.

◆ **Product-specific promotional information issued by medical products companies is regulated.** While the 1962 amendments envisioned that FDA primarily would regulate advertising directed at physicians, because that was the principal means of promoting prescription drugs at the time, over the years FDA has expanded the horizons of its jurisdiction to include all promotional information. While some attorneys dispute FDA's expanded view of its jurisdiction, as a practical matter FDA does assume regulatory authority over not just prescription drug advertising but also sales materials, information directed at consumers, press materials, information provided to the investment community, sales materials for managed care organizations and hospitals, and oral statements made by any company employee or representative that discuss a specific product.

◆ **FDA regards promotional materials issued by drug companies as either "advertising" or "labeling/promotional labeling."** "Advertising" consists of traditional paid advertising (e.g., when a company pays to place an advertisement). "Labeling," or more precisely "promotional labeling," to distinguish the term from being confused with the package insert, includes everything else (e.g., brochures, booklets, direct mail pieces, press releases, letters to formulary committees, slide kits, and audio-visual materials). "Advertising" and "promotional labeling" must meet the same general standards for truthfulness, accuracy, and balance.

There is one disclosure requirement that differentiates "advertising" and "promotional labeling." When paid advertising appears, the risk disclosure requirements can be met with the inclusion of a "brief summary" of risk information, whereas materials classified as "promotional labeling" generally must be accompanied by the full package insert.

All information in promotional materials issued by or on behalf of a drug or device company must be truthful and not false and/or misleading.

Sometimes materials issued by or on behalf of a medical products company that do not mention a specific product, such as information about a disease, may be regarded as "labeling" or "promotional labeling" if the materials are intended to be used in conjunction with the promotion of a product or if a reasonable person would be able to identify the product based on the implicit claim.

◆ **Under FDA's regulations, all information in promotional materials issued by or on behalf of a drug or device company must be truthful and not false and/or misleading.** FDA, however, imposes requirements above and beyond simple accuracy and truthfulness. For example, a press release may accurately and truthfully describe new research on an unapproved use of an approved product, but if it also does not include a "fair balance" of risk factors and provide for "full disclosure" of risk information, then it could be regarded by FDA as violative. Further, if the issuance contains information inconsistent with FDA-approved labeling, even if that information is medically accurate, truthful, and well accepted by experts in the medical field, that information may be regarded by FDA as violative.

♦ **Information must be fairly balanced with risk information.** FDA defines "fair balance" as a "balanced presentation of benefits and risks." This means that, in an advertisement, to the extent that a particular benefit is described, the medical risks associated with that benefit also must be described. In a press release, when benefits are described, FDA expects that the major adverse experiences and side effects also will be described. "Fair balance" also may mean that a product's limitations must be delineated. "Fair balance" is hard to define with any better precision because it differs for each individual product.

FDA defines "fair balance" as a "balanced presentation of benefits and risks."

Television advertising that is product-specific must also meet the "fair balance" requirement by including risk information within the advertising itself. Further, television advertising must also meet the "brief summary" requirement. It does so by making "adequate provision" for the recipient of the information to obtain prescribing information.

"Adequate provision" for television advertising directed to a consumer audience can be met through mechanisms set forth by FDA (initially in an August 1997 draft guidance, and then again two years later in a final guidance). It was the 1997 draft guidance that basically opened the door to product-specific direct-to-consumer (DTC) television advertising. FDA stated that the "adequate provision" requirement could be met for television by including in the commercial an 800 number that the consumer can call to ask for further information to be mailed, faxed, or read; a referral to an Internet site; a referral to information in an advertisement in a current issue of a print publication that included the brief summary; or provision of information that healthcare professionals can provide to patients.

The "net impression" of a promotional piece is a major consideration for FDA in evaluating its compliance. In May 2009 FDA issued a draft guidance entitled "Presenting Risk Information in Prescription Drug and Medical Device Promotion" which set forth the factors that FDA reviewers look for in deciding whether a particular promotional piece has adequate risk disclosure. In this document, the agency said: "It is important to emphasize that when FDA evaluates the risk communication in a promotional piece, FDA looks not just at specific risk-related statements, but at the net impression—i.e., the message communicated by all elements of the piece as a whole. The purpose of the evaluation is to determine whether the piece as a whole conveys an accurate and non-misleading impression of the benefits and risks of the promoted product. Manufacturers should therefore focus not just on individual claims or presentations, but on the promotional piece as a whole. A promotional communication that conveys a deceptive net impression of the product could be misleading, even if specific individual claims or presentations are not misleading."

♦ **Companies may make a claim for products in advertising and promotional labeling only when that claim is consistent with the FDA-approved labeling or, in some cases when the labeling is not up to date, based on "substantial evidence," or "substantial clinical experience."** (As a practical enforcement matter, FDA generally does not permit claims to be made solely on the basis of "substantial clinical experience," but this language remains in the FDA regulations.) This requirement has been controversial. Even if information is well accepted in the medical community, it may not, in FDA's view, be used in company promotional material if it is not included in FDA-approved labeling or based on what FDA regards as "substantial evidence."

FDA's rationale in restricting the use of "off-label" information in company promotional materials is that it could mislead healthcare providers and consumers into believing a product is effective for a use when it has not been shown effective to FDA's satisfaction. Further, FDA believes that if companies are permitted to disseminate off-label information, it will remove any incentive they have to conduct needed research on that use. Congress addressed this issue in 1997 legislation, the Food and Drug Administration Modernization Act (FDAMA). This matter also has been addressed in litigation (the Washington Legal Foundation case) and is central to ongoing debates about FDA's policies and its exercise of its enforcement discretion.

In January 2017 FDA issued a draft guidance that explained how companies can use in promotional materials information that is not contained in the product labeling, but that is "consistent" with the labeling. The agency said it considers three factors in making such an assessment and then went on to delineate in some detail how it applies those three factors. The factors deal with specific questions that the company should address, such as whether the information in question is contradicted in the labeling and whether the information would lead to an unsafe or ineffective use of the product.

The draft guidance set forth what is not consistent with the labeling:

♦ Information about the use of a product to treat or diagnose a different disease or condition than the product is approved to treat or diagnose;

♦ Information about the use of a product to treat or diagnose patients who are not included in the product's approved patient population (e.g., a device is cleared for use in individuals with cystic fibrosis (CF) for diagnosing a specific CF gene mutation and a firm's communication provides information about using the device in individuals who do not have CF to determine if they are carriers of the CF gene);

♦ Information about the use of a product to treat a different stage, severity, or manifestation of a disease than the product is approved to treat (e.g., a product is approved/cleared only to treat severe asthma, and a firm's communication provides information about using the product to treat patients with mild asthma).

The draft guidance helps companies feel comfortable when they use, in promotional materials, information not specifically contained in labeling, but which is "consistent with labeling."

♦ **Material facts about the product must be disclosed in company promotional materials.** If an advertisement or promotional piece fails to mention a material fact that would influence the prescribing, use, or purchase of a product, then the piece could be regarded by FDA as being violative.

♦ **The rules governing advertising and "promotional labeling" apply to any product-specific information issued or caused to be issued by a company, *either directly or through any agent*.** FDA has made clear that third parties hired by a company to speak publicly about a product in a promotional context must keep the remarks within approved labeling and otherwise comply with the same rules that apply to company employees.

The rules governing advertising and promotional labeling apply to any product-specific information issued or caused to be issued by a company, either directly or through any agent.

The same principle applies to an advertising or public relations agency hired by a medical products company to promote a product, and it further applies when a company provides money to a third-party organization to issue information on behalf of one of its products. The indictment in the spring of 2006 by the U.S. Attorney in the Eastern District of New York of a physician for allegedly promoting "off-label" uses on behalf of a pharmaceutical company underscores the government's concern with off-label promotion. (The physician pleaded guilty to a misdemeanor).

Specific FDA Policies

As mentioned above, in the view of FDA, promoting a marketed product for an unapproved use could pose a potential threat to the public health or could reduce a manufacturer's incentive to perform the studies and research necessary to obtain FDA approval of such indications.

*Off-label promotion
FDA believes that promoting a marketed product for an unapproved use could pose a significant potential threat to the public health.*

FDA rules and enforcement policy seek to discourage drug and device companies from disseminating information about "off-label" uses. This policy is controversial, as the argument has been made that the standard for dissemination of "off-label" information in a nonpromotional context should be whether the claim itself is medically justified and supported, even if it has not been incorporated into the official FDA labeling. The argument is premised on the fact that FDA labeling lags behind science, and drug and medical device companies should be entitled to provide truthful and non-misleading information.

Some of the specific kinds of "off-label" promotional activities that FDA objects to are saying or implying in an advertisement that a drug is useful for a particular use when it has not been shown to be (for example, FDA objected to a photograph in an advertisement for a drug that depicted a young woman, when the drug was indicated for older women); posting information on the Internet that indicates that a medical device is useful for a broad range of procedures when it was approved under a 510(k) application only for a limited type of procedure; or suggesting that a drug is useful as first-line therapy when it was approved only as second-line therapy.

One particular issue that companies have grappled with is the issuance of articles that appear in the peer-reviewed medical literature and that contain, even in minor references, information that is off-label. In January 2009, FDA issued a guidance that set forth its criteria for when companies could distribute peer-reviewed medical journal articles. Many companies use the provisions in the "reprint guidance" to provide reprints of peer-reviewed medical journal articles to healthcare professionals, with full disclosure that the reprint contains off-label information. FDA updated this guidance in February 2014, clarifying when and how companies can distribute textbooks and third-party clinical practice guidelines that contain off-label information about a company product.

The commercialization of a product before approval is another issue. The agency's view was set forth in 1994 correspondence which expressed its interpretation of section 312.7 ("scientific exchange") of the regulations:

> Prior to approval, promotional materials provided by the sponsor are often inaccurate with respect to the indications and risk information that ultimately appear in the approved product labeling. This inaccuracy occurs because the sponsor does not know what indications and other information the final product labeling will contain. Additionally, the sponsor's assessment of the drug may be overly optimistic, exaggerating efficacy while minimizing risk. Thus, the sponsor's biases may be incorporated into the promotional materials it provides prior to approval of final product labeling. Such promotional materials do not fulfill the needs of healthcare providers or benefits managers to obtain balanced,

accurate information about new drugs, but instead disseminate misinformation and create potential risk and misuse.

FDA has a somewhat different policy for medical devices in the pre-approval stage, recognizing that purchasers need to commit large sums of money to buy certain devices. Medical device companies may notify potential customers about a new product whose 510(k) application is still being reviewed by FDA, but may make no conclusory claims with regard to effectiveness or safety, and may not take orders for the product.

In January 2017 FDA issued a draft guidance on how manufacturers can communicate with payors and others who deal with the price of drugs and devices (this does not apply to healthcare professionals in their prescribing capacity or to consumers/patients). The draft guidance, "Drug and Device Manufacturer Communications With Payors, Formulary Committees, and Similar Entities – Questions and Answers – Guidance for Industry and Review Staff," was in response to requests from many sources for FDA to clarify where the safe harbors are for such communications.

In the draft guidance the agency addressed standards for the communication of healthcare economic information (HCEI). The draft guidance said that HCEI "shall not be considered false or misleading if, among other things, it is 'based on competent and reliable scientific evidence [CARSE].' FDA considers HCEI to be based on CARSE if the HCEI has been developed using generally accepted scientific standards, appropriate for the information being conveyed, that yield accurate and reliable results. In evaluating whether the amount and type of evidence that forms the basis for a particular communication of HCEI meets the generally accepted scientific standards for such information, FDA will consider the merits of existing current good research practices for substantiation developed by authoritative bodies (e.g., International Society for Pharmacoeconomic and Outcomes Research (ISPOR), Patient-Centered Outcomes Research Institute). For example, when evaluating HCEI based on indirect treatment comparisons in the absence of data from head-to-head controlled clinical trials, FDA may refer to guidelines issued by external expert bodies regarding current rigorous methodologies and best practices for such comparisons (e.g., network meta-analyses)."

The draft guidance also set forth, for the first time, FDA's views on what types of information could be communicated to payors about investigational drugs. The FDA said such information could include:

♦ Product information (e.g., drug class, device design)

♦ Information about the indication sought, such as information from the clinical study protocol(s) about endpoint(s) being studied and the patient population under investigation (e.g., number of subjects enrolled, subject enrollment criteria, subject demographics)

♦ Factual presentations of results from clinical or preclinical studies (i.e., no characterizations or conclusions should be made regarding the safety or effectiveness of the product)

♦ Anticipated timeline for possible FDA approval/clearance

♦ Product pricing information

♦ Targeting/marketing strategies (e.g., outreach activities planned to generate prescriber awareness about the product)

♦ Product-related programs or services (e.g., patient support programs)

The draft guidance recommended that companies make clear during the investigational stages that the product has not been found to be safe or effective. "Communications between firms and payors that represent that an investigational product is FDA-approved/cleared or otherwise safe or effective for the purpose(s) for which it is under investigation would not be appropriate," the draft guidance stated.

The draft guidance thus provided direction for companies in an increasingly important area of communications, namely how to communicate with payors about information not in the labeling (i.e., HCEI) and what kind of information can be provided in the investigational stage without fear of enforcement.

Another principal concern of FDA is comparative claims made by companies for their products. In an environment in which competition in the medical products industries is intense, all companies seek to differentiate their products, and all want to claim that their product is superior. Examples of comparative claims are "drug of choice," "unsurpassed," or "more effective."

Comparative claims: FDA requires that any claim of superiority for a prescription drug be supported by "substantial evidence" and not be based solely on a comparison of labeling information.

FDA requires that any claim of superiority for a prescription drug be supported by "substantial evidence," usually two adequate and well-controlled studies or in some cases a single large multicenter trial. The studies must be "head-to-head" (i.e., they must be designed prospectively to directly compare the products). Generally, the agency wants two such studies, but it will permit a limited claim (e.g., our product is better absorbed, or works faster, or is more easily swallowed by patients) to be made on the basis of a single study. FDA prohibits a claim of superiority based solely on a comparison of data in the two products' labeling.

In addition, if a comparative claim is made, it cannot be false or misleading and cannot leave out other measurements by which the company's product is inferior to its competitor.

Two kinds of comparative claims that companies have increasingly been making involve cost-effectiveness (our product is more cost-effective than our competitor's) or quality-of-life claims (our product helps patients obtain a high quality of life, either in absolute terms or in comparison with our competitor's product). FDA generally requires that any such claims be proven by studies. Quality-of-life claims must report not just positive findings but also negative ones found in the study.

COMMUNICATIONS TECHNIQUES

In the modern world, there are many ways for information to be communicated. FDA does not object to the use of any specific mode of communication for medical products information. Medical information can be provided to health-care providers, consumers, managed care purchasers, or anyone else in various formats, and with whatever communication mechanisms exist: electronic or print, television commercials or journal advertising, Internet, or CD/DVD. What FDA is concerned about is the content of these materials and whether it is false and/or misleading in any way.

Requirements that apply to specific formats and methods of communication are as follows:

♦ **Reminder ads:** FDA regulations permit companies to sponsor advertising that does not mention the indications or uses for a product, but that is intended to "remind" readers or viewers of the name. Such advertising may state the name (including the generic name); the ingredients; the dosage form; and the name and address of the manufacturer, packager, or distributor. The advertisement, however, may not mention what the product is used for, and may not make a safety or efficacy claim or any other representation, including a graphic representation, about the use of the product. Such advertising is exempt from the requirement for a "brief summary." "Reminder ads" may not appear for drugs for which there is a "boxed" warning in the FDA-approved labeling, or, in the case of older drugs, whose efficacy has not been reaffirmed by FDA.

Reminder ads are exempt from risk summaries.

♦ **Press releases:** FDA does not have a specific regulation or guidance applying to press releases, but does regard product-specific releases as "promotional labeling." While some attorneys dispute whether FDA has

While some attorneys dispute whether FDA has the authority to regulate press releases, as a practical matter both the drug and devices industry generally accede to FDA's authority.

451

the authority to regulate press releases, as a practical matter both the drug and devices industry generally accede to FDA's authority. Based on FDA expectations (as derived from various enforcement actions and statements by FDA), the agency expects promotional press releases to contain "fair balance" within the release itself. Because they are regarded by FDA as "promotional labeling" rather than advertising, FDA expects that press releases be accompanied by the full package insert, not just a "brief summary" of risks.

Press releases often contain disclaimers that help put the product into regulatory context (e.g., in a research announcement for a product not yet approved, it is best to make clear that the product is not approved or that an application is pending before FDA, if that is the case). Press releases issued before product approval must avoid saying that the product has been shown to be safe and effective, and should avoid any statements that might be construed as promotional, such as words like "promising" or "breakthrough."

♦ **Video news releases:** These 90-second electronic versions of press releases are regarded by FDA as "promotional labeling," and therefore under FDA policy must contain balanced information if they are product-specific.

♦ **Materials for investors:** Investor-directed press releases and other materials, such as annual reports, are technically subject to the same regulatory requirements as promotional materials, according to FDA policy. FDA, however, recognizes that these materials are not usually intended to be used in a product promotion context and that the primary audience is not prescribers. FDA's enforcement priorities are geared accordingly. For example, an annual report handed out at a medical meeting might be regarded as promotional if it contains certain information about approved products, and FDA might consider taking enforcement action if the report were disseminated for promotional purposes. The same report issued only to investors may not raise the same concerns. FDA does not require annual reports issued to investors that mention ongoing research or newly approved products in an investment context to include the labeling as an attachment. FDA has a formal working relationship with the Securities and Exchange Commission in regulating investor materials.

In 2013 FDA issued a Warning Letter to a company whose chief executive officer appeared on an investment show on CNBC, a cable station that caters to investors. The concern was statements by the CEO in two interviews that FDA regarded as off-label. This letter represented one of the few times that FDA had sought corrective measures for statements made in an investment context, even though anyone watching CNBC at that time would have seen the interviews at issue.

♦ **Scientific meetings:** The sponsorship by companies of medical and other meetings has been controversial. The concern by FDA and other government agencies is that companies will use the meetings to promote off-label uses of their products, or that companies will exert control over meetings that are depicted as independent.

Any scientific meeting that is under the content control of a company and that is product-specific must meet all criteria for fair balance and full disclosure. FDA, however, does not regulate the content of legitimate continuing medical education (CME) funded by medical products companies, as long as the CME grant is provided to a third party and the CME is conducted independently of the funding company.

CME is not regulated by FDA if it is independently conducted.

Companies that fund CME generally have standard contracts with providers that set forth a specific relationship that is intended to ensure independence of the program, the presenters, and the derivative material, such as monographs or publications. In evaluating whether a CME program is truly independent, FDA looks at about a dozen factors, most particularly who controls the program agenda and speaker selection. The Accreditation Council for Continuing Medical Education accredits CME programs and has issued rules to assure a high level of independence from commercial interests.

♦ **Internet:** FDA actively regulates information on the Internet sponsored by medical product companies. In January 2014 FDA issued a draft guidance that described what companies must submit to the agency involving Internet promotions. The draft guidance said that "a firm is responsible for product promotional communications on sites that are owned, controlled, created, influenced, or operated by, or on behalf of, the firm … Such product promotional communications may include firm-sponsored microblogs (e.g., Twitter), social networking sites (e.g., Facebook), firm blogs, and other sites that are under the control or influence of the firm." The draft guidance also said that "a firm is responsible for promotion on a third-party site if the firm has any control or influence on the third-party site, even if that influence is limited in scope." In addition, draft guidance said that "a firm is responsible for the content generated by an employee or agent who is acting on behalf of the firm to promote the firm's product."

♦ **Homemade materials:** Company personnel in the field may seek to create their own promotional materials to provide to healthcare professionals. Homemade materials can contain misleading claims and/or lack risk information. FDA discourages this practice, and most companies have specific policies prohibiting the creation of homemade materials. These policies generally state that sales representatives who want to distribute their own materials must go through the company's approval process.

Companies prohibit "homemade" materials as a matter of policy.

♦ **Requests for information:** FDA issued a draft guidance in December 2011 on how companies can respond to unsolicited requests for product information that is outside of labeling. Under the draft guidance, companies are not permitted to encourage or solicit requests for off-label information. The draft guidance said there are two categories of unsolicited requests— those that are received "privately," that is, one-on-one, and those that are received publicly, for example at a public meeting. A "private request," the draft guidance said, should be handled by the company's medical or scientific staff, which should be independent from the sales or marketing department. The response should be accompanied by labeling, references for the information, and a clear statement that the use described in the response is not approved or cleared by FDA. Records should be kept of the request and response.

For "public" requests, the draft guidance said, a company should respond only when one of its products is mentioned. The response should convey that the question pertains to an unapproved or uncleared use. No substantive off-label information should be provided to the group; rather, the individual asking the question should be invited to follow up with the company's medical or scientific affairs department. Further, the draft guidance said, company representatives must clearly disclose their involvement with the company and the response may not be promotional.

♦ **Direct-to-consumer promotion:** Most countries, including those in the European Union, do not permit companies to advertise prescription drug promotional information directly to consumers. The United States is the only country other than New Zealand that permits DTC advertising of prescription products. Companies in the United States also target other promotional materials directly to the consumer, such as materials that may be distributed in a physician's waiting room.

FDA requires that all consumer-directed information must meet the same criteria for accuracy, truthfulness, fair balance, and full disclosure as materials intended for healthcare professionals. Print advertising must fairly present the risks as well as benefits, and also must include the "brief summary" or a consumer version of it.

Advertising of prescription drugs on commercial television is permitted, but it must make "adequate provision" for consumers to obtain further information.

Under a policy announced by FDA in August 1997, and reiterated in August 1999, advertising of prescription drugs on commercial television also is permitted, but it must make "adequate provision" for the consumer to obtain further information via the Internet, a toll-free number, or some other means. FDA encourages disease-oriented or "help-seeking" advertising to consumers that does not mention any product name, but that identifies a disease condition and urges consumers to see their doctors.

Court Cases

A celebrated legal case involving the promotion of medical products was brought by the Washington Legal Foundation (WLF). In 1993, WLF filed a citizen's petition with FDA objecting to the agency's policies restricting the ability of pharmaceutical companies to provide scientific information to healthcare professionals that is truthful and non-misleading but not consistent with FDA-approved labeling for the product. This case evolved into protracted litigation that lasted until 2000.

The case focused on the right of pharmaceutical companies to provide healthcare professionals with truthful and non-misleading scientific information, including reprints of peer-reviewed materials and sponsorship of CME programs. WLF took the view that the criteria for such communication should be whether the information itself was truthful, not whether the information was consistent with the FDA-approved labeling.

On July 30, 1998, the court enjoined FDA from seeking to limit any pharmaceutical manufacturer's ability to disseminate to healthcare professionals any off-label information published in a peer-reviewed journal, to disseminate bona fide textbooks, or suggest content or speakers for an independent CME program, even when off-label uses are to be discussed. This decision was later vacated.

In 2000, during oral argument on appeal, FDA stated that it viewed its CME guidance as establishing a "safe harbor" for pharmaceutical company sponsorship of medical education, and would take enforcement action against companies that provided peer-reviewed articles to healthcare professionals only if the information itself was false and/or misleading or contrary to the public health. In March 2000, FDA published a notice in the *Federal Register* that reiterated its "safe harbor" position.

FDA's articulation of its policy did not resolve the uncertainty. WLF returned to court to seek clarity, but on November 30, 2000, the district court denied the request. The court criticized FDA for failing to resolve the issue: "After six years' worth of briefs, motions, opinions, congressional acts and more opinions, the issue remains 100% unresolved, and the country's drug manufacturers are still without clear guidance as to the permissibility of this conduct." *Washington Legal Foundation v. Henney*, 128 F. Supp. 2d 11, 15 (D.D.C. 2000).

There have been several more recent cases that have related to FDA's regulation of promotional materials, including cases where First Amendment issues have been raised.

For example, one case involved Scott Harkonen, a physician, who was CEO of a drug company, InterMune. He was accused of issuing a deceptive press release in 2002 to boost sales of a drug marketed by InterMune. He was indicted in 2008 for issuing the release, which the government alleged was false and misleading because of the way that it described a clinical trial of the drug Actimmune. A federal jury in San Francisco convicted Harkonen in September 2009 and a judge sentenced him to six months of home confinement and fined him $20,000. He appealed the conviction but did not prevail. In a separate matter, InterMune agreed in 2006 to pay $36.9 million to settle claims under the False Claims Act that it marketed Actimmune for unapproved uses and caused false claims for reimbursement from government health programs. *Harkonen v. Sebelius*, No. C 13-0071 PJH (N.D. Cal. Oct. 22, 2013).

An important case that raised First Amendment issues in terms of the government's authority to regulate was *Sorrell v. IMS Health Inc.* (131 S. Ct. 2653 (2011)). The Supreme Court held unconstitutional a Vermont law restricting pharmaceutical manufacturers' ability to use prescriber information for marketing purposes. The Court applied a "heightened scrutiny" standard and found that "speech in aid of pharmaceutical marketing . . . is protected by the First Amendment."

In a 2-1 decision in December 2012, the Second Circuit Court of Appeals vacated the criminal conviction of a pharmaceutical sales representative, Alfred Caronia, who promoted a narcolepsy drug for "off-label" uses. Caronia maintained that the information he provided was medically truthful. After a jury trial, Caronia was found guilty of conspiracy to introduce a misbranded drug into interstate commerce. Caronia appealed, saying his conviction violated his First Amendment rights. The Second Circuit agreed, finding that the conviction violated his First Amendment right to free speech. The court said that "the government cannot prosecute pharmaceutical manufacturers and their representatives under the FDCA for speech promoting the lawful, off-label use of an FDA-approved drug." This decision, which was widely publicized and discussed, did not noticeably change FDA's enforcement actions. The agency issued a statement saying that the conviction was overturned more on technical procedural grounds than on substantive grounds. *United States v. Caronia*, No. 09-5006, slip op. (2d Cir. Dec. 3, 2012).

In *Amarin Pharma, Inc. v. FDA* (119 F. Supp. 3d 196 (S.D.N.Y. 2015)), the district court applied *Caronia* and held that all truthful and non-misleading speech is protected, including proactive, promotional statements made by a pharmaceutical manufacturer regarding off-label use of its drugs.

In general, cases like *Sorrell*, *Caronia*, and *Amarin* have been viewed as raising questions about the constitutionality of FDA's regulation of manufacturer speech. They prompted FDA to initiate efforts to examine its oversight of promotional materials. For example, on November 9-10, 2017, FDA held a hearing at which members of the public testified about their views of the regulatory oversight. Views ranged from those who stated that FDA needed to be even more aggressive with its policies and enforcement to those who stated that FDA needed to set clear guidelines and permit companies to communicate truthful and non-misleading information not in the approved labeling.

Even while most court cases have raised doubts about the FDA policies for regulating manufacturer communications, there also have been conflicting cases. For example, in *United States ex rel. Polansky v. Pfizer, Inc.* (No. 14-4774, 2016 WL 2865610 (2d Cir. May 17, 2016)), the Second Circuit said in a False Claims Act case that promotional speech regarding off-label use is impermissible if "it evidences that a drug is intended for such off-label use and is therefore 'misbranded.'"

In January 2017, just before the presidential inauguration, FDA issued a 60-page memorandum called "Memorandum: Public Health Interests and First Amendment Considerations Related to Manufacturer Communications Regarding Unapproved Uses of Approved or Cleared Medical Products" (Memorandum). According to FDA, "The Memorandum provides additional background on the issues FDA is considering as part of its comprehensive review, including a discussion of First Amendment considerations."

In the Memorandum, FDA said:

> Firm communications regarding unapproved uses of approved/ cleared medical products implicate several substantial government interests related to health and safety. Among these are motivating the development of robust scientific data on safety and efficacy; maintaining the premarket review process for safety and efficacy of each intended use in order to prevent harm, protect against fraud, misrepresentation, and bias, and to prevent the diversion of health care resources toward ineffective treatments; ensuring required labeling is accurate and informative; protecting the integrity and reliability of promotional information regarding medical product uses; protecting human subjects receiving experimental treatments; ensuring informed consent; maintaining incentives for clinical trial participation; protecting innovation incentives, including statutory grants of exclusivity; promoting the development of products for underserved patients; supporting informed decision-making for patient treatment; and furthering

scientific understanding and research. All of these interests relate to FDA's larger substantial interest in protecting and promoting public health.

The Memorandum generally was regarded as an FDA defense of the legal status quo with regard to manufacturer communication, while the same time taking into account First Amendment issues. These paragraphs summarize the FDA position:

> As shown above, there can be, in certain instances, a tension between the public health interests directly advanced by the premarket review requirements and other aspects of the FDA Authorities and other important interests—particularly with regard to patient treatment decisions. As important and successful as the FDA Authorities have been, and continue to be, in incentivizing the successful development of more and better treatments that are safe and effective for more patients with different diseases, the reality remains at any point in time that for some patients, approved/ cleared therapies are not available or have failed. While the goal of promoting robust research and development of new products to meet these underserved patients remains important to the public health, the latitude for health care providers to prescribe or use approved/cleared medical products for unapproved uses for their patients functions as a critical safety valve. Cognizant of this, FDA, in implementing the FDA Authorities, has sought to strike a careful balance, supporting medical decision-making for patients in the absence of better options, but doing so without undermining the measures designed to incentivize the development and approval/ clearance of medical products that would reduce the need to rely on unapproved use, in light of its risks.
>
> FDA's current implementation approach does not proscribe all firm communications about unapproved uses of approved or cleared medical products. FDA has issued guidance documents to describe some of the circumstances when it would not consider a manufacturer's distribution of reprints, clinical practice guidelines, or reference texts regarding unapproved uses of approved/cleared medical products to be evidence of intended use and/or false or misleading. FDA has also issued a draft guidance on responding to unsolicited requests, which states that 'FDA has long taken the position that firms can respond to unsolicited requests for information about FDA-regulated medical products by providing truthful, balanced, non-misleading, and non-promotional scientific or

medical information that is responsive to the specific request, even if responding to the request requires a firm to provide information on unapproved or uncleared indications or conditions of use.' FDA has also described how industry may support scientific or educational activities (such as Continuing Medical Education programs) without being subject to FDA regulation. In addition, it has long been FDA policy not to consider a firm's presentation of truthful and non-misleading scientific information about unapproved uses at medical or scientific conferences to be evidence of intended use when the presentation is made in non-promotional settings and not accompanied by promotional materials. In a similar vein, HHS recently promulgated a rule that clarifies and expands requirements for the submission of certain objective results information from clinical trials to a publicly available website: ClinicalTrials.gov. Most recently, in January 2017 FDA issued two additional draft guidance documents. One draft guidance addresses firms' communications of data and information not contained in their products' approved or required labeling but that are consistent with the FDA approved or -required labeling and clarifies that such communications alone are not considered evidence of a new intended use. The other draft guidance addresses firms' communications with payors and similar entities and provides recommendations on firms' communications to payors of health care economic information that relates to a drug's approved indication, as well as recommendations regarding firms' communications to payors about investigational drugs and devices not yet approved/cleared for any use.

Enforcement

FDA cannot mandate, but does expect, companies to have written policies and procedures for reviewing promotional materials and programs, including an internal review process. The agency also cannot mandate, but does expect, regular training for staff, including the sales force, on regulatory requirements. Training has become a major focus for many companies that want to be sure that everyone in the company, from top management to the sales force, is aware of the company's philosophy toward FDA's rules, especially with regard to how the sales force conducts its activities on a day-to-day basis. Training also is required under Corporate Integrity Agreements (CIAs) signed by companies that settle cases under the False Claims Act or the anti-kickback statute (see below).

Submission to FDA:
Promotional materials
for drugs and biological
products, but not devices,
must be submitted to FDA at
time of first use.

For pharmaceuticals and biological products, FDA regulations require that all product-specific promotional materials must be submitted to FDA at the time of their first use. Promotional pieces for pharmaceuticals are submitted to the FDA Office of Prescription Drug Promotion (OPDP, formerly known as the Division of Drug Marketing, Advertising and Communications) in the Center for Drug Evaluation and Research, and for biologics to the Advertising and Promotional Labeling Staff in the Center for Biologics Evaluation and Research. Medical device and veterinary medicine manufacturers have no requirements for routine submission of promotional materials at time of first use.

FDA enforcement actions generally are premised on its review of materials submitted at the time of their first use by companies and on its own surveillance of the marketplace. Many actions, however, also are based on competitor complaints (i.e., complaints filed by one company against another, or by healthcare professionals). Such complaints often are submitted formally, in writing, to the FDA division responsible for regulating the advertising and promotion of the product. Many companies encourage their employees to gather intelligence about their competitors' promotional activities to assure that regulation is even-handed. In addition, FDA initiated what became known as its "Bad Ad" campaign in which it proactively encouraged physicians to report what they regarded as illegal or inappropriate promotion.

Typically, when FDA detects a violation, it sends the offending company either an "untitled" letter or a Warning Letter. Both identify FDA's concern and seek remedial action, such as discontinuation of the promotional piece at issue. The letters indicate that the agency has concluded that a legal violation has occurred and remedial action is required, such as withdrawal of the violative materials. FDA also may request that a "Dear Health Professional" letter be disseminated. It also can seek other corrective measures, such as employee training or preclearance of any new promotional materials for a period of time.

Enforcement letters usually provide 10 to 15 days for the company to respond and present a plan of action. Companies often seek a meeting or teleconference with FDA to discuss the appropriateness of the remedial action. Enforcement letters are made public upon issuance by FDA, and thus become a potential source of negative publicity, as well as a potent enforcement tool. FDA posts warning and untitled letters on its Internet site (www.fda.gov), along with the violative materials.

FDA has other enforcement options. FDA has the option to seek a seizure, injunction, or criminal action (misdemeanor or felony) against violative companies or activities. FDA usually includes in its "untitled" letters, and always in its Warning Letters, the possibility of more stringent action but as a practical matter a seizure, injunction, or criminal prosecution is unlikely.

OVER-THE-COUNTER PRODUCTS

The FTC has authority over the advertising and promotion of nonprescription drugs and nonrestricted devices, as well as foods and cosmetics. The FTC's authority, which predates FDA's, stems from section 5 of the Federal Trade Commission Act, which gives the commission authority to prevent companies from "using unfair methods of competition . . . and unfair or deceptive acts or practices in or affecting commerce." (The FTC technically retains some legal jurisdiction over prescription drug advertising, but as a practical matter defers to FDA.)

The FTC regulates the advertising and promotion of nonprescription drugs, nonrestricted devices, foods, and cosmetics.

FDA and the FTC work together in cases involving medical products because the FTC does not have a medical staff and any FTC action must be based on FDA-approved labeling of over-the-counter (OTC) drugs or nonrestricted devices. FDA and the FTC operate under a 1971 Memorandum of Understanding that sets forth how the relationship between the two agencies will work. FTC procedures permit companies to engage in formal discussions with staff before any matter is resolved. The usual resolution of an FTC investigation is the signing of a consent decree in which the company admits no wrongdoing but agrees never to repeat the activity to which the FTC has objected. The FTC also has the authority to seek a temporary restraining order or an injunction.

PRESCRIPTION DRUG MARKETING ACT

The use of drug samples—small quantities of a product that are provided free of charge to a physician so that he or she may provide them free to a patient as a "starter"—is addressed in specific legislation, the Prescription Drug Marketing Act (PDMA), a section of the FDCA. The law addressed concern that control over samples was not sufficient to preclude their diversion into commercial channels or, more important, that samples of drugs subject to potential abuse might be readily diverted.

PDMA prohibits the diversion of prescription drugs or biological products into illegitimate commercial channels. It also prohibits the sale of drug samples. The law provides that companies must obtain the signature of a physician for all drug samples. The law also requires recordkeeping and careful storage of samples. Whenever a manufacturer discovers any diversion, it must report this to FDA.

The Prescription Drug Marketing Act, a section of the FDCA, prohibits sale and diversion of drug samples.

FALSE CLAIMS ACT

The federal False Claims Act was originally passed during the Civil War to prevent vendors from defrauding the government. The law was amended in 1986, and a dozen years later the government started using the law to bring actions against the pharmaceutical and medical device industries.

The basic allegation in the cases was that if a drug or device company promoted a product "off-label," and if, as a consequence, the product cost was reimbursed by the government, then that constitutes fraud against the government. The law provides that whistle-blowers can initiate such cases, and the vast majority of cases brought against the drug and device industries have been brought by whistle-blowers, often current or former company employees, who under the law can collect 15 to 30 percent of the fine. These are known as *"qui tam"* cases.

Several dozen such cases have been brought against pharmaceutical and medical device companies, resulting in fines that often have been in the hundreds of millions or even billions of dollars. The cases also have resulted in companies signing Corporate Integrity Agreements (CIAs) with the government. The cases are brought by the Department of Justice in conjunction with the Office of the Inspector General of the Department of Health and Human Services (OIG DHHS), which usually is intimately involved in negotiating the settlements.

DHHS's interest and authority in this area comes from the fact that it administers the Medicaid and Medicare programs, and the OIG DHHS is responsible for preventing fraud and abuse in these programs. (Medicaid is a joint state/federal healthcare reimbursement program for people who cannot afford treatment, while Medicare is a federal program that reimburses for healthcare for the elderly and disabled.)

Many states have their own false claims statutes and state attorneys general also have brought cases and have shared in the settlements.

In one settlement, three corporate officials pleaded guilty to misdemeanors and paid substantial fines for their roles in promotional activities. This reflected the government's interest in pursuing individual liability.

In 2003, OIG DHHS issued a guidance explaining what it expects from pharmaceutical companies to avoid making false claims under the False Claims Act. The guidelines, published in the *Federal Register* on May 5, 2003, set forth standards for internal compliance programs for pharmaceutical manufacturers. The guidance contained both broad principles for compliance, such as encouraging a

The OIG sets standards for internal compliance programs.

corporate culture of compliance, as well as specific policies that companies are expected to adopt and follow.

The guidance set forth seven elements "that have been widely recognized as fundamental to an effective compliance program." The seven elements constitute the basis for much of the contents of CIAs. The seven elements are:

- **Implementing written policies and procedures:** The written policies should "verbalize" the company's commitment to compliance and address specific areas of fraud and abuse, such as the reporting of pricing and rebate information, and sales and marketing practices.

- **Designating a compliance officer and committee:** The compliance officer and committee are responsible for developing and monitoring the compliance program and should report directly to the board of directors or president/chief executive officer of the company.

- **Conducting effective training and education:** All affected employees should be trained substantively at regular intervals.

- **Developing effective lines of communication:** There should be effective communication between the compliance officer and all employees. Companies should establish a telephone hotline for reporting internal complaints. This safeguards the anonymity of complainants and protects whistle-blowers from retaliation.

- **Conducting internal monitoring and auditing:** There regularly should be audits or other risk evaluation techniques to monitor compliance or identify problem areas.

- **Enforcing standards through well-publicized disciplinary guidelines:** Companies should develop policies and procedures to preclude the employment of individuals or companies excluded from participating in federal healthcare programs and to enforce disciplinary action against employees or contractors who have violated the rules.

- **Responding promptly to detected problems and undertaking corrective action:** Firms should implement policies and procedures for identifying and investigating any instances of noncompliance or misconduct.

ANTI-KICKBACK

Another federal law that applies to marketing medical products is the "anti-kickback" law (42 U.S.C. § 1320a-7b). This law, which dates from 1972, is not part of either the FDCA or the False Claims Act; instead, it relates to the Medicaid and Medicare statutes.

The anti-kickback law relates to the Medicaid and Medicare statutes.

The anti-kickback statutes are intended to prevent overuse of and overcharging for medical products that are subject to government reimbursement under either Medicaid or Medicare (or other government-reimbursed healthcare programs). They prohibit any activity in which a medical products company may try to persuade, other than with sound therapeutic arguments, a physician or another healthcare provider or facility to use a particular product.

Specifically, the law, which is enforced by the OIG DHHS, prohibits a company from offering "any remuneration (including any kickback, bribe or rebate) directly or indirectly, overtly or covertly, in cash or in kind" to anyone to induce them to purchase a product or service for which reimbursement may be sought under Medicaid or Medicare. The regulations do provide certain exceptions, also known as "safe harbors," which do permit some marketing activities.

A number of settlements with pharmaceutical and medical device companies have been signed under the anti-kickback law. The cases have entailed significant fines and the signing of CIAs.

PhRMA and AdvaMed codes

PhRMA's Code on Interactions with Healthcare Professionals redefined the relationship between healthcare professionals and the pharmaceutical industry.

In 2002, the Pharmaceutical Research and Manufacturers of America (PhRMA)— the trade association of research-oriented drug companies—adopted a Code on Interactions with Healthcare Professionals. It attempted to redefine the relationship between healthcare professionals and the pharmaceutical industry. It was adopted by the PhRMA Board of Directors and became effective in 2002, and was later updated effective January 2009. The code is voluntary but has been adopted by most companies and become the standard of conduct for drug companies.

In January 2004, AdvaMed, the trade association representing large medical device companies, issued its own code. It was similar to the PhRMA code except in those areas in which pharmaceutical marketing differs from medical device marketing, such as the ability of device companies to promote their products before approval (but not make any claims or take orders).

Specific provisions of the codes include:

♦ **Informational presentations:** Presentations by industry representatives and others speaking on behalf of a company are encouraged. Occasional meals (but no entertainment or recreational events) may be offered as long as the meals: 1) are modest as judged by local standards; 2) occur in a venue and manner conducive to informational communication; and 3) take place in conjunction with activities that provide scientific or educational value.

♦ **Medical education:** Financial support from companies for scientific and educational conferences or professional meetings is permissible provided no strings are attached. Such financial support should be given to the conference's sponsor through a grant.

♦ **Consultants:** Consultants who provide legitimate services to companies may be offered compensation at fair market value as well as reimbursement for travel, lodging, and meal expenses. Token consulting should not be used. It is not appropriate to pay honoraria, travel, or lodging expenses to nonfaculty and non-consultant attendees at company-sponsored meetings.

♦ **Grants:** No grants, scholarships, subsidies, support, consulting contracts, or educational or practice-related items or other remuneration should be provided or offered to a healthcare professional in exchange for prescribing products. Nothing should be offered or provided in a manner or under conditions that would influence or interfere with the independence of a doctor's prescribing practices.

♦ **Gifts:** Gifts to physicians are not permitted under the PhRMA code unless they are of an educational nature. This provision eliminated pens, pads, and other items provided by drug companies, as well as items for display in medical offices.

In January 2006, another PhRMA code, setting forth principles for DTC advertising, took effect. This is a voluntary code with which most major pharmaceutical companies have agreed to comply. It states that "all DTC information should be accurate and not misleading, should make claims only when supported by substantial evidence, should reflect balance between risks and benefits, and should be consistent with FDA approved labeling."

Further, these principles also state that "DTC television and print advertising for prescription drugs should clearly indicate that the medicine is a prescription drug, to distinguish such advertising from other advertising for non-prescription products." Companies should "spend an appropriate amount of time to educate health professionals about a new medicine or a new therapeutic indication before commencing the first DTC advertising campaign" and "should submit all new DTC television advertisements to the FDA before releasing these advertisements for broadcast. . . . DTC television and print advertising should include information about the availability of other options such as diet and lifestyle changes where appropriate for the advertised condition" and "DTC

There has been a significant increase in the number of DTC advertising campaigns for prescription drugs submitted to the agency for an advisory opinion.

television and print advertisements should be targeted to avoid audiences that are not age appropriate for the messages involved."

The adoption of the PhRMA principles led to a significant increase in the number of DTC advertising campaigns for prescription drugs submitted to the FDA for an advisory opinion.

Conclusion

FDA's regulation of marketing practices by medical products companies—specifically their promotional programs—has become a highly specialized and especially dynamic field within food and drug law. The rules are set forth in a variety of ways—in FDA regulations, in guidances, and in enforcement actions—but are constantly refined in public discussions by regulators. The policies and their nuances continue to evolve as new products are introduced and new means of communications become available.

In essence, however, the key principles underlying FDA regulation have been constant. Programs and materials must be truthful, they must prominently disclose risk information, "scientific exchange" but no commercialization may take place before a product is approved, and there may be no efforts by medical products manufacturers to persuade or induce healthcare providers to use products for uses not approved by FDA.

Chapter 15

Review of FDA Inspections and Related Regulations

Ronald F. Tetzlaff, Ph.D., PAREXEL Consulting, Duluth, GA & David L. Chesney, DL Chesney Consulting, LLC, Exeter, NH

Key Points

- FDA inspections are administrative investigations to determine whether the inspected company is in compliance with the Federal Food, Drug, and Cosmetic Act (FDCA) or other laws enforced by the Food and Drug Administration (FDA).
- Inspectors' actions must comply with general statutory standards of reasonableness (time, limits, manner) and specific procedures as provided by law.
- Inspections may be initiated for routine purposes, for cause, or as a follow-up to prior adverse findings. This chapter explains the more common reasons for inspections, with a focus on Good Manufacturing Practice (GMP) inspections.
- FDA employees who conduct inspections have a wide variety of backgrounds. Inspections are conducted by FDA investigators, chemists, microbiologists, engineers, and various scientists having specialized education and training.
- Effective preparation and management of FDA inspections may significantly influence the outcome.
- FDA has put in place a variety of policies, procedures, and forms with a bearing on inspections. These are public documents and companies are well advised to be familiar with their content and purpose.
- Companies may facilitate FDA inspections by following general guidelines for effective communication and interaction with inspectors and other agency officials.
- A trained person should act as escort for FDA personnel during the course of the inspection.
- A conference room or office should be set aside for FDA's use during the inspection. A separate conference room should serve as the company's command post for the inspection.

INTRODUCTION

One of the principal functions of the Food and Drug Administration (FDA) is to conduct inspections of facilities that manufacture, process, pack, or hold foods, drugs, medical devices, biologicals, cosmetics, tobacco products, and other products that are subject to FDA regulation. The purpose of

FDA inspections is to determine whether regulated products have been pro-cessed, packed, or held under conditions that may result in such products being adulterated or misbranded within the meaning of the Federal Food, Drug, and Cosmetic Act (FDCA), or whether products lacking FDA approval (where approval is required) are being sold and shipped. FDA inspections conducted within the United States and its territories are usually unannounced (most medical device inspections, inspections of sponsors of clinical trials, clinical trial sites, Institutional Review Boards (IRBs), and foreign inspections, with some exceptions, are pre-announced). FDA inspections may include examination of manufacturing sites, contract laboratories, warehouses, and quality control laboratories for evidence of violations, including reviews of production and laboratory control records to determine if conditions and practices are in com-pliance with applicable laws and regulations.

FDA inspections are usually unannounced, and may include examination of manufacturing sites, contract laboratories, warehouses, and quality control laboratories for evidence of violations.

Inspections are also conducted under what FDA terms its "bioresearch monitor-ing" inspections program. These inspections are done at sponsors' clinical trials sites, contract research organizations (CROs), and/or sites where clinical inves-tigations are conducted to determine compliance with applicable regulations, commitments made in relevant submissions (e.g., Investigational New Drug (IND) applications and investigational device exemption (IDE) applications), and to assess data integrity. Under FDA-approved INDs or IDEs, sponsors are permit-ted to use investigational drugs and devices to obtain safety and effectiveness data needed to support New Drug Applications (NDAs) and premarket approval (PMA) applications. In addition, under the bioresearch monitoring program, FDA inspects IRBs for compliance with 21 C.F.R. Parts 50 and 56, nonclinical (animal safety testing) laboratories for compliance with the Good Laboratory Practice (GLP) regulations (21 C.F.R. Part 58), and bioanalytical laboratories that support bioequivalence and bioavailability testing of generic drugs, for compli-ance with 21 C.F.R. Part 320.

Specially trained investigators and laboratory personnel conduct FDA inspec-tions. FDA inspection approaches vary for each of the different types of regulat-ed products. For example, most inspections of food-manufacturing facilities and warehouses are intended to determine if products have been processed, packed, or held under insanitary conditions whereby they may have been contaminated with filth, rendered injurious to health, or are otherwise unfit for consumption. For drugs, medical devices, and biologicals, FDA inspections evaluate the ad-equacy of controls used to ensure the identity, strength, quality, or purity of such products, and to verify that they are in conformance with applicable compendia.

When FDA detects violative conditions or practices during its inspections, evidence is collected to support recommendations for regulatory sanctions against individuals, companies, and/or products, when deemed necessary. Evidence may be in the form of direct observations by investigators, copies of production and control records, and reports to prove violations of laws and regulations, as well as shipping records to prove the connection with interstate commerce necessary to establish federal jurisdiction. Sometimes, samples of products or extraneous material are collected for analysis to support inspection observations.

Inspections that detect significant violations, such as insanitary conditions or noncompliance with current Good Manufacturing Practice (cGMP) regulations, may lead FDA to initiate legal proceedings to effect corrective actions, or to punish responsible persons. Before proceeding to litigation, however, FDA frequently (but not necessarily) will issue a Warning Letter to advise management of the nature of the violations and the applicable sections of the law that the agency is prepared to invoke against the company or individual. When such warnings are ineffective, or if conditions are egregious or pose imminent health hazards, FDA may initiate formal administrative or judicial actions such as seizures, criminal prosecutions, or civil monetary penalties, temporary restraining orders, or permanent injunctions to prevent continued distribution of violative products in interstate commerce. Commonly, civil actions (product seizures and injunctions) are resolved through negotiated settlements in the form of consent decrees, but occasionally these matters proceed to trial.

FDA authority to conduct inspections is derived from section 704 of the FDCA (21 U.S.C. § 374), which defines the conditions under which FDA may conduct its inspections. Generally, inspections may extend to a factory, warehouse, laboratory, or other establishment that manufactures, processes, packs, or holds foods, drugs, devices, and cosmetics. Inspections may encompass facilities, records, finished or unfinished products, files, papers, records, and other documents. Regulations that are relevant to FDA inspections or cGMPs include, but are not limited to, the following:

FDA authority to conduct inspections is derived from the FDCA, which defines the conditions under which FDA may conduct its inspections.

♦ food-related regulations, including infant formulas (21 C.F.R. Part 106);

♦ low-acid canned food (21 C.F.R. Part 113) and food (GMPs) (21 C.F.R. Part 110);

♦ dietary supplements (21 C.F.R. Part 111), bottled water (21 C.F.R. Part 129), fish and fishery products (21 C.F.R. Part 123), animal foods (21 C.F.R. Part 507), and others;

♦ human and veterinary finished pharmaceuticals, including GMP regulations (21 C.F.R. Parts 210 and 211) and medicated animal feeds and premixes (21 C.F.R. Parts 225 and 226);

♦ medical devices, mainly the Quality System Regulation (21 C.F.R. Part 820) and Medical Device Reporting regulation (21 C.F.R. Part 803); and

♦ biologicals, such as biological products (21 C.F.R. Part 600) and blood and blood components (21 C.F.R. Parts 606 and 640).

GMP regulations for drugs, biologics, devices, and some foods are binding (i.e., have the force and effect of law), but food GMPs found at 21 C.F.R. Part 110 are considered to be interpretive and serve as guidance to the food industry. FDA has not promulgated GMPs for the cosmetics industry.

FDA Inspection Authority

Federal Food, Drug, and Cosmetic Act (FDCA)

The FDCA is the principal law that provides FDA authority to conduct factory inspections. It provides FDA with the authority to inspect any factory, warehouse, or establishment in which foods, drugs, devices, or cosmetics are manufactured, processed, packed, or held for introduction into interstate commerce (or after such introduction) or any vehicle being used to transport or hold such food, drugs, devices, or cosmetics in interstate commerce. The FDCA also defines prohibited acts and provides for regulatory and administrative sanctions that enable FDA to bring noncomplying companies or persons into compliance with the law. The Food and Drug Administration Modernization Act of 1997 (FDAMA) amended the provisions of the FDCA and the biological provisions of the Public Health Service Act, including a number of sections that deal with FDA inspection authority (such as new provisions that extended FDA's authority to have access to records for over-the-counter (OTC) drugs). Further changes to inspection provisions were made through passage of the Food and Drug Administration Safety and Innovation Act (FDASIA), signed into law on July 9, 2012.

FDAMA amended the provisions of the FDCA and the biological provisions of the Public Health Service Act, including a number of sections that deal with FDA inspection authority.

The following chapters of the FDCA are relevant to the FDA inspection process:

Chapter	Topic
III	Defines what acts are prohibited and provides for certain administrative and criminal sanctions (penalties)
IV	Provides the basic definition of what constitutes adulteration and misbranding for foods
V	Defines adulteration and misbranding for drugs
VI	Defines adulteration and misbranding for cosmetics
VII	Establishes FDA authority to conduct inspections
VIII	Provides requirements for imports and exports
IX	Tobacco products

FDA's General Inspection Authority

Chapter VII of the FDCA confers general inspection authority on FDA. It authorizes duly accredited FDA personnel to enter and inspect certain types of regulated facilities at "... reasonable times, and within reasonable limits and in a reasonable manner...." The specifics of what constitutes a "reasonable time" are not defined in the statute, but precedents exist that establish that a "reasonable time" is any time regulated activities are being conducted, without regard to time of day, day of the week, or even if the day is a national holiday. It is the conduct of regulated activities that creates a reasonable time for inspection. Other specifics of the "reasonableness standard" have been the subject of debate for many years, such as whether the agency has statutory authority to take photographs during inspections.

In 1952, the Supreme Court ruled that the factory inspection provisions of the 1938 FDCA were too vague to be enforced as criminal law (*United States v. Cardiff*). As a result, Congress passed the Factory Inspection Amendments in 1953 to provide clarification to the 1938 act. These amendments provided for FDA to present manufacturers with a written notice of inspection at the beginning of an inspection, and written reports of observations at the conclusion of the inspection. The amendments also required FDA to provide written receipts for samples, as well as reports of analysis for certain types of samples (FDCA § 704). The provision for a written report of observations at the conclusion of an inspection forms the basis for today's Form FDA-483.

Upon initiating an inspection, FDA personnel must display appropriate credentials and give to "... the owner, operator or agent in charge..." a written notice of inspection. For this purpose, the agency uses the Notice of Inspection, Form FDA-482.

Upon initiating an inspection, FDA personnel must display appropriate credentials and give the owner, operator, or agent in charge a written notice of inspection.

Section 704 of the FDCA confers to FDA specific authority to conduct inspections of any factory, warehouse, or establishment where food, drugs, devices, tobacco products, or cosmetics are manufactured, processed, packed, or held for introduction into interstate commerce (or after such introduction). This section authorizes duly designated FDA personnel to determine whether such products have been manufactured, processed, packed, or held under conditions whereby they may become adulterated or misbranded within the meaning of the law. Examples of the authority provided by Section 704 include, but are not limited to the following:

♦ "(A) to enter, at reasonable times, any factory, warehouse, or establishment in which food, drugs, devices, tobacco products, or cosmetics are manufactured, processed, packed, or held, for introduction into interstate commerce or after such introduction . . . , and "(B) to inspect, at reasonable times and within reasonable limits and in a reasonable manner, such factory, warehouse, establishment, or vehicle and all pertinent equipment, finished and unfinished materials, containers, and labeling therein."

♦ "In the case of any factory, warehouse, establishment, or consulting laboratory in which prescription drugs, nonprescription drugs intended for human use, restricted devices, or tobacco products are manufactured, processed, packed, or held, the inspection shall extend to all things therein (including records, files, papers, processes, controls, and facilities) bearing on whether prescription drugs, nonprescription drugs intended for human use, restricted devices, or tobacco products which are adulterated or misbranded within the meaning of this chapter, or which may not be manufactured, introduced into interstate commerce, or sold, or offered for sale by reason of any provision of this chapter, have been or are being manufactured, processed, packed, transported, or held in any such place, or otherwise bearing on violation of this chapter."

♦ Section 704 also grants FDA authority to request records in lieu of conducting on-site inspections. For example, section 704(4)(A) states: "Any records or other information that the Secretary may inspect under this section from a person that owns or operates an establishment that is engaged in the manufacture, preparation, propagation, compounding, or processing of a drug shall, upon the request of the Secretary, be provided to the Secretary by such person, in advance of or in lieu of an inspection, within a reasonable timeframe, within reasonable limits, and in a reasonable manner, and in either electronic or physical form, at the expense of such person. The Secretary's request shall include a sufficient description of the records requested.

"(B) Upon receipt of the records requested under subparagraph (A), the Secretary shall provide to the person confirmation of receipt.

"(C) Nothing in this paragraph supplants the authority of the Secretary to conduct inspections otherwise permitted under this chapter in order to ensure compliance with this chapter."

While FDA inspection authority for regulated products is relatively broad, the FDCA contains notable provisions where inspection authority is specifically excluded. For example, section 704 states:

No inspection authorized by the preceding sentence or by paragraph (3) shall extend to financial data, sales data other than shipment data, pricing data, personnel data (other than data as to qualification of technical and professional personnel performing functions subject to this chapter), and research data (other than

> data relating to new drugs, antibiotic drugs, devices, and tobacco products and subject to reporting and inspection under regulations lawfully issued pursuant to section 355(i) or (k) of this title, section 360i of this title, section 360j(g) of this title, or subchapter IX and data relating to other drugs, devices, or tobacco products which in the case of a new drug would be subject to reporting or inspection under lawful regulations issued pursuant to section 355(j) of this title).

For new drugs and medical devices and for licensed biological products, FDA must act on requests for regulatory approvals (including but not limited to NDAs, Abbreviated New Drug Applications (ANDAs), PMAs for devices, Biologics License Applications (BLAs), and other similar submissions). FDA decisions are based upon information and data contained in applications submitted by sponsors. To verify the accuracy and completeness (integrity) of such information and data relative to pending or approved applications, FDA has authority to access both facilities (on-site inspections) and records. Failure to allow access to records to which FDA is lawfully entitled is a prohibited act under section 301 of the FDCA. A refusal may cause the agency to seek an administrative inspection warrant to compel such access. An administrative inspection warrant affirms FDA's existing statutory authority and may interpret certain aspects in more specific terms than provided by statute. However, an administrative inspection warrant is not a search warrant and does not broaden FDA's authority beyond existing statutory limits. For example, an administrative inspection warrant may be sought to compel a company to allow FDA to take photographs during an inspection (subsequent to a refusal to permit photography) on the grounds that photographs are sometimes necessary to a "reasonable" inspection. This specific use of administrative inspection warrants is not common. When it does occur, it may be controversial, but serves to illustrate the potential use of such warrants for situations that are less egregious than outright refusal to permit entry. Normally, inspection warrants are obtained *ex parte*, and when served, FDA personnel may be accompanied by Deputy U.S. Marshals, present to ensure compliance with the warrant.

With the FDA pre-approval inspection program, FDA investigators routinely request access to new drug and biologic development records. The same is true for medical device design history files, which are mandated by the Quality System Regulation (QSR). FDA investigators expect access to records that are retained by personnel with "research" functions or responsibilities if the data support product applications. FDA generally will not be deterred from seeking access on the grounds that access is not permitted because testing performed represents "discovery" rather than "developmental" research, after a submission has been filed based on the development data. If the data has been submitted to FDA as part of the basis for approval of an application, verification of its integrity (accuracy, truthfulness, and completeness) is provided for via inspection.

There are other exemptions from inspection that are provided by statute. Section 704(a)(2) of the FDCA states that FDA authority does not include access to records and facilities that manufacture prescription drugs and restricted devices in four specific instances: 1) pharmacies that are in conformance with local laws (provided their activities are limited to dispensing and selling drugs or devices at retail); 2) practitioners who are licensed by law to prescribe or administer drugs (or use devices) if the manufacture or processing is for use in the course of their professional practice; 3) persons who manufacture such products solely for use in teaching, research, or chemical analysis where such products are not for sale; and 4) any other classes of person as designated by FDA by regulation to be exempt upon finding that inspection is not necessary for the protection of public health.

Upon completion of an inspection, FDA personnel must leave a written report with the owner, operator, or agent in charge.

Section 704(b) requires that FDA, upon completion of an inspection, leave with the owner, operator, or agent in charge a written report that identifies any conditions or practices observed by the employee

> . . .which, in his judgment, indicate that any food, drug, device, tobacco product, or cosmetic in such establishment (1) consists in whole or part of any filthy, putrid, or decomposed substance, or (2) has been prepared, packed, or held under insanitary conditions whereby it may have become contaminated with filth or whereby it may have been rendered injurious to health . . . .

FDA generally records its observations on a form known as an FDA-483 (List of Inspectional Observations). While the statute itself only mandates that a report be issued for adulteration-related observations, FDA has for many years included other inspection-related observations on the form as a matter of policy. Certain exceptions are described in Chapter 5 of FDA's *Investigations Operations Manual*, which is available at http://www.fda.gov.

When FDA collects a physical sample during the course of an inspection, a written receipt for samples must be provided to the owner, operator, or agent in charge. Such receipt (FDA Form FDA-484) must be issued upon completion of the inspection. In the case of food samples collected during an inspection, section 704(d) requires the following: "Whenever in the course of any such inspection of a factory or other establishment where food is manufactured, processed, or packed, the officer or employee making the inspection obtains a sample of any such food, and an analysis is made of such sample for the purpose of ascertaining whether such food consists in whole or in part of any filthy, putrid, or decomposed substance, or is otherwise unfit for food, a copy of the results of such analysis shall be furnished promptly to the owner, operator, or agent in charge."

The provisions in section 704(d) apply only to foods and do not extend to samples of drugs, devices, or cosmetics that are collected during FDA inspections, nor does it apply to results of food analysis other than ascertaining if food consists in whole or part of any filthy, putrid, or decomposed substance or is otherwise unfit for food.

FDA employees authorized to conduct inspections, while acting in the course of their official duties, are authorized to possess controlled substances as per 21 C.F.R. § 1301.24(a)(1) and other sections; e.g., 21 C.F.R. § 1309.26(a)(1). This permits FDA investigators to collect samples of controlled substances during inspections and other special assignments. The Form FDA-484 prepared by the FDA investigator, however, must contain FDA's Drug Enforcement Administration (DEA) Registration Number and that of the establishment from which the products are obtained. All other inventory controls required by DEA regulations apply to FDA and to anyone providing samples of controlled substances to an FDA investigator.

For many years, controversies have persisted about the legal requirements for process validation in the GMPs, and their application to research and development activities. While there may be some "gray areas" between "pure research" and new drug development activities, firms should expect FDA to routinely request access to the records supporting process validity. While some firms have been reluctant to provide FDA access to drug development records based on the erroneous assumption that FDA is not entitled to "research" data, the FDCA provides FDA with authority to access and copy records and reports required under the new drug provisions. Drug development involves a continuum from "pure" research activities (i.e., discovery related) through transition phases where the activities clearly have a bearing on GMP or validation issues. Therefore, the statutory exemption from access to research data should be considered applicable only until the point when the data is intended to be used in support of an application for FDA approval to permit use of the new drug or medical device in clinical trials (and beyond). At that stage in the development process, the research data that forms the basis of claims made in the relevant submission may be subject to review during FDA inspections. Correspondingly, research data that is not relevant to any current submission to the agency would be considered exempt from inspection, because it has no bearing on the status of any marketed product or on the validity of any submission to FDA.

While there may be some "gray areas" between "pure research" and new drug development activities, firms should expect FDA to routinely request access to the records supporting process validity.

CHANGES TO INSPECTION AUTHORITY RESULTING FROM FDASIA PROVISIONS RELATING TO SAFETY AND SECURITY OF THE DRUG SUPPLY CHAIN

Title VII of the FDASIA legislation changed several aspects of FDA inspection authority to enhance control over the drug supply chain.

Title VII of the FDASIA legislation changed several aspects of FDA inspection authority to enhance control over the drug supply chain. These changes are summarized as follows:

♦ Under sections 701 (Domestic Establishments) and 702 (Foreign Establishments) of FDASIA Title VII, FDA must create and maintain a data base of all registered drug manufacturing facilities using a Unique Facility Identifier (UFI) to facilitate scheduling of inspections. The electronic system that supports this requirement is mandated by section 704 of FDASIA Title VII.

♦ The previous statutory requirement for biennial inspections (once every two years) of each registered facility has been changed to permit FDA to schedule inspections based on the risk posed by each facility. Many registered facilities present very low risk while others present much higher risk, based on a variety of factors specified in the legislation, such as product type, technology employed, and inspection history. FDA may now take those factors into consideration in deciding how often to inspect a given facility (see section 705 of FDASIA Title VII). FDASIA also authorizes FDA to enter into agreements with foreign governments to recognize those governments' inspections of FDA-registered foreign establishments and to take that information into consideration when implementing a risk-based inspection scheduling scheme.

♦ FDASIA provides specific authority for FDA to demand the production of certain records relating to drug manufacturing remotely, without sending investigators to the facility for an in-person examination of the records (see section 706 of FDASIA Title VII).

♦ Prior to FDASIA, the refusal to permit a lawful inspection, in whole or in part, was (and still is) a prohibited act that exposed the person making the refusal to potential criminal penalties. When refusals occurred, FDA historically resorted to obtaining an administrative inspection warrant for domestic facilities, but had no similar recourse for facilities outside U.S. borders. Under FDASIA, if the refusal takes place in a drug manufacturing facility, the drug products made in that facility are deemed to be adulterated. This enables FDA to proceed against the products themselves, not just the companies and individuals responsible for the refusals. (See FDASIA § 707.) On July 12, 2013, FDA published a Draft "Guidance for Industry: Circumstances that Constitute Delaying, Denying, Limiting, or Refusing a Drug Inspection," which further explains how the agency intends to implement this provision (see section 707 of FDASIA Title VII).

♦ Section 709 of FDASIA Title VII extends the authority for FDA to administratively detain products to drugs. Previously the authority was limited to medical devices.

CURRENT GOOD MANUFACTURING PRACTICE CONCEPTS

The 1962 Drug Amendments granted FDA authority to promulgate regulations and added a provision that required companies to comply with "current good manufacturing practices."

The 1962 Drug Amendments added two important sections that are relevant to FDA inspections. FDA was granted authority to promulgate regulations and a provision was added that required pharmaceutical manufacturers to comply with "current good manufacturing practices" (FDCA § 501(a)(2)(B)). Although the law did not define what constituted "current good manufacturing practices," the FDCA was amended to allow FDA to publish regulations to define its requirements and expectations. FDA published its interpretation of cGMPs in 1963 (currently 21 C.F.R. Parts 210, 211 for human and veterinary drug products, and 21 C.F.R. Parts 225, 226 for medicated premixes and medicated feeds for animals).

Since the passage of the 1962 Drug Amendments the FDA has promulgated a number of regulations for other commodities besides drugs that are required to be manufactured under conditions that comply with "current good manufacturing practices." The following are examples of the key regulations that have been promulgated to define cGMPs for specific commodities. It should be noted, however, that the term "current good manufacturing practice" is limited to drugs and medical devices in the statute. Conceptually, the idea of cGMP has been extended to include regulations governing manufacturing of foods for human and animal consumption, but the statutory basis of cGMP is derived from the drug and device adulteration provision of the FDCA as cited above.

♦ **Foods**—Examples of food commodities for which FDA has promulgated regulations that specifically include requirements for current good manufacturing practice include: Infant Formula (21 C.F.R. 106), Dietary Supplements (21 C.F.R. Part 111); Human Food (21 C.F.R.117), Fish and Fishery Products (21 C.F.R. Part 123), Bottled Water (21 C.F.R. Part 129), and Animal Foods (21 C.F.R. Part 507).

Following is a brief summary of food-related regulations and applicable cGMP requirements from 21 C.F.R., Chapter 1 (Subchapter B, Foods for Human Consumption, and Subchapter E, Animal Drugs, Feeds, and Related Products):

21 C.F.R. Part 106 – Infant Formula Requirements Pertaining to Current Good Manufacturing Practice, Quality Control Procedures, Quality Factors, Records and Reports, and Notifications. This regulation defines "... minimum current good manufacturing practices that are to be used in, and the facilities or controls that are to be used for, the manufacture, processing, packing, or holding of an infant formula." This regulation is considered to be binding [i.e., "The failure to comply with any regulation in this subpart in the manufacture, processing, packing, or holding of an infant formula shall render such infant formula adulterated under section 412(a)(3) of the Federal Food, Drug, and Cosmetic Act (21 U.S.C. 350a(a)(3)); ..." For example, this regulation defines an infant formula to be adulterated if it is manufactured, processed, packed, or held in a facility that does not comply with provisions of several other Parts of 21 C.F.R. such as 1) Part 107, § 107.100 (Infant Formula Nutrient Requirements; 2) Part 113, Thermally Processed Low-Acid Foods Packaged in Hermetically Sealed Containers); and 3) Part 114, § 114.3(b) (Acidified Infant Formula). [Authority: 21 U.S.C. 321, 342, 350a, 371 (see 79 Fed. Reg. 8059 (Feb. 10, 2014)).]

21 C.F.R. Part 111—Current Good Manufacturing Practice in Manufacturing, Packaging, Labeling, or Holding Operations for Dietary Supplements. This regulation defines the requirements for facilities that manufacture package, label, or hold a dietary supplement, including a product that is packaged or labeled by another person and products that are imported or offered for import in any state or territory of the United States, the District of Columbia, or the Commonwealth of Puerto Rico. [Authority: 21 U.S.C. 321, 342, 343, 371, 374, 381, 393; 42 U.S.C. 264 (see 72 Fed. Reg. 34,942 (June 25, 2007)).]

21 C.F.R. Part 113 – Thermally Processed Low-Acid Foods Packaged in Hermetically Sealed Containers. This regulation defines the criteria that are to be applied by FDA " ... in determining whether the facilities, methods, practices, and controls used by the commercial processor in the manufacture, processing, or packing of low-acid foods in hermetically sealed containers are operated or administered in a manner adequate to protect the public health." The criteria are outlined in §§ 113.10, 113.40, 113.60, 113.81, 113.83, 113.87, 113.89, and 113.100. [Authority: 21 U.S.C. 342, 371, 374; and 42 U.S.C. 264 (see 44 Fed. Reg. 16,215 (Mar. 16, 1979)).] The low-acid canned food regulations (21 C.F.R. Part 113) and the companion rules for acidified food (21 C.F.R. Part 114) were issued as a consequence of a number of botulism outbreaks that occurred during the 1960s and 1970s involving food products packaged in hermetically sealed containers. These regulations define the minimum requirements and controls necessary to ensure such products are processed in a manner that ensures they are safe.

21 C.F.R Part 117 – Current Good Manufacturing Practice, Hazard Analysis, and Risk-Based Preventive Controls for Human Food. This regulation defines the current good manufacturing practice requirements for human food including the criteria to be applied " ... in determining whether a food is:

(1) Adulterated within the meaning of: (i) Section 402(a)(3) of the Federal Food, Drug, and Cosmetic Act in that the food has been manufactured under such conditions that it is unfit for food; or (ii) Section 402(a)(4) of the Federal Food, Drug, and Cosmetic Act in that the food has been prepared, packed, or held under insanitary conditions whereby it may have become contaminated with filth, or whereby it may have been rendered injurious to health; and (2) In violation of section 361 of the Public Health Service Act (42 U.S.C. 264)." FDA applies this regulation during inspections of food facilities to determine whether "(b) The operation of a facility that manufactures, processes, packs, or holds food for sale in the United States if the owner, operator, or agent in charge of such facility is required to comply with, and is not in compliance with, section 418 of the Federal Food, Drug, and Cosmetic Act or subpart C, D, E, F, or G of this part is a prohibited act under section 301(uu) of the Federal Food, Drug, and Cosmetic Act. (c) Food covered by specific current good manufacturing practice regulations also is subject to the requirements of those regulations." [See 80 Fed. Reg. 56,145 (Sept. 17, 2015), as amended at 81 Fed. Reg. 3715 (Jan. 22, 2015).]

21 C.F.R. Part 123 – Fish and Fishery Products. This regulation defines the cGMP requirements for ". . . determining whether the facilities, methods, practices, and controls used to process fish and fishery products are safe, and whether these products have been processed under sanitary conditions . . . ." [See 60 Fed. Reg. 65,197 (Dec. 18, 1995), as amended at 80 Fed. Reg. 56,167 (Sept. 17, 2015).]

21 C.F.R. Part 129 – Processing and Bottling of Bottled Water. This regulation defines the criteria that are to be applied by FDA ". . . in determining whether the facilities, methods, practices, and controls used in the processing, bottling, holding, and shipping of bottled drinking water are in conformance with or are operated or administered in conformity with good manufacturing practice to assure that bottled drinking water is safe and that it has been processed, bottled, held, and transported under sanitary conditions." The criteria are outlined in §§ 129.20, 129.35, 129.37, 129.40, and 129.80 [see 80 Fed. Reg. 56,167 (Sept. 17, 2015)].

21 C.F.R. Part 507 – Current Good Manufacturing Practice, Hazard Analysis, and Risk-Based Preventive Controls for Food for Animals. This regulation defines the criteria for determining whether an animal food is adulterated within the meaning of the FDCA, including section 402(a)(3) (i.e., an animal food manufactured under conditions that render it unfit for food) and section 402(a)(4) (i.e., "has been prepared, packed, or held under insanitary conditions whereby it may have become contaminated with filth, or whereby it may have been rendered injurious to health."). An animal food is also deemed to be adulterated if it is "In violation of section 361 of the Public Health Service Act (42 U.S.C. 264)." This regulation stipulates that ". . . The operation of a facility that manufactures, processes, packs, or holds animal food for sale in the United States if the owner, operator, or agent in charge of such facility is required to comply with, and is not in compliance with, section 418 of the Federal Food, Drug, and Cosmetic Act or subparts C, D, E, or F of this part and § 507.7 is a prohibited act under section 301(uu) of the Federal Food, Drug, and Cosmetic Act. (c) Animal food covered by specific current good manufacturing practice regulations also is subject to the requirements of those regulations." This regulation allows facilities to choose with which regulation to comply when a facility has product(s) covered by multiple regulations. For example, § 507.1(d) states "(d) Except as provided by § 507.12, if a facility is required to comply with subpart B of part 507 and is also required to comply with subpart B of part 117 of this chapter because the facility manufactures, processes, packs, or holds human food and animal food, then the facility may choose to comply with the requirements in subpart B of part 117, instead of subpart B of part 507, as to the manufacturing, processing, packing, and holding of animal food at that facility. If a facility is required to comply with subpart C of part 507 and is also required to comply with subpart C of part 117 of this chapter, then the facility may choose to comply with the requirements in subpart C of part 117 as to the manufacturing, processing, packing, and holding of animal food at the facility, instead of subpart C of part 507, provided the food safety plan also addresses hazards for the animal food, if applicable, that require a preventive control. When applying the requirements of part 117 of this chapter to animal food, the term 'food' in part 117 includes animal food." [AUTHORITY: 21 U.S.C. 331, 342, 343, 350d note, 350g, 350g note, 371, 374; 42 U.S.C. 243, 264, 271 (see: 80 Fed. Reg. 56,337 (Sept. 17, 2015).]

♦ **Devices**—In 1996 FDA promulgated the Quality System Regulation (QSR) (21 C.F.R. Part 820) which defines cGMP for medical device facilities. The QSR applies to the methods, facilities, and controls that are used during the design and manufacture (including packaging, labeling, storage, installation, and servicing). These regulations define, among other things "... the methods used in, and the facilities and controls used for, the design, manufacture, packaging, labeling, storage, installation, and servicing of all finished devices intended for human use. The requirements in this part are intended to ensure that finished devices will be safe and effective and otherwise in compliance with the Federal Food, Drug, and Cosmetic Act (the act). This part establishes basic requirements applicable to manufacturers of finished medical devices."

FDA's statutory authority is found in the following sections of the FDCA: 501, 502, 510, 513, 514, 515, 518, 519, 520, 522, 701, 704, 801, 803 of the act (21 U.S.C. 351, 352, 360, 360c, 360d, 360e, 360h, 360i, 360j, 360l, 371, 374, 381, 383, respectively).

FDA considers the requirements for current manufacturing practices that are contained in the QSR Regulations to be binding as per § 820.1, Scope, that states: "The failure to comply with any applicable provision in this part renders a device adulterated under section 501(h) of the act. Such a device, as well as any person responsible for the failure to comply, is subject to regulatory action."

See 61 Fed. Reg. 52,654 (Oct. 7, 1996), as amended at 65 Fed. Reg. 17,136 (Mar. 31, 2000); 65 Fed. Reg. 66,636 (Nov. 7, 2000); 69 Fed. Reg. 29,829 (May 25, 2005); 72 Fed. Reg. 17,399 (Apr. 9, 2007); 75 Fed. Reg. 20,915 (Apr. 22, 2010); 80 Fed. Reg. 29,906 (May 22, 2015).

♦ *cGMPs for Finished Pharmaceuticals*—These were promulgated in 1963 and have been updated a number of times over the years (usually in reaction to incidents or problems) (21 C.F.R. Part 211). The cGMPs describe the minimum FDA requirements for conforming to the cGMP requirements of the FDCA.

Active Pharmaceutical Ingredients (API) are not within the scope of 21 C.F.R. 211. There are no binding FDA cGMP regulations for API. FDA relies on non-binding guidance, Guideline Q7 of the International Conference on Harmonization (ICH), to convey expectations for API cGMP concepts.

FDA published the cGMP regulations for finished pharmaceuticals as being legally binding requirements; i.e., they define the minimum cGMP that must be followed for the production and control of finished pharmaceuticals for administration to humans and animals (43 Fed. Reg. 45,077 (Sept. 29, 1978)). The cGMPs describe the minimum FDA requirements for conforming to the current good manufacturing practices that are cited in the FDCA. Although the cGMPs are substantive, they do not spell out in detail how firms are expected to satisfy the requirements. The cGMPs require that firms have in place standard operating procedures (SOPs) that provide the additional detail needed to apply the regulations to a specific site, and that such SOPs be followed. This is the manner in which the cGMPs are made relevant to specific local circumstances.

The cGMPs included within 21 C.F.R. 211 are considered broad "umbrella" regulations in that they apply to all finished pharmaceuticals for humans and animals. The language of the regulation is broad enough to describe the requirements for all dosage forms (tablets, capsules, oral liquids, topicals, trans-dermals, parenterals, etc.), and the requirements apply to both prescription and OTC drugs. Because they apply across the board to all finished drug products, the regulation contains ample use of subjective terms (such

The cGMPs are considered broad "umbrella" regulations in that they apply to all finished pharmaceuticals for humans and animals.

as adequate, appropriate, sufficient, and others). (Conceptually, the same is true for the cGMP regulations for medicated animal feeds and pre-mixes; see 21 C.F.R. 225 and 226.)

The drug GMPs were originally published by FDA in 1963 under 21 C.F.R. Part 133 (63 Fed. Reg. 6385 (June 20, 1963)). Since then, the GMP regulations were re-codified under 21 C.F.R. Part 211. The most notable revision occurred in 1978 (43 Fed. Reg. 45,077 (Sept. 29, 1978)). The preamble to the 1978 revision provides background about the changes that were made by FDA including the position of the FDA Commissioner related to comments received for the proposed rule and the rationale for the final requirements. The authority for 21 C.F.R. Part 211 is found at U.S.C. 321, 351, 352, 355, 360b, 371, 374, 42 U.S.C. 216, 262, 263a, 264. FDA's website contains a summary the revisions made to 21 C.F.R. Part 211 between 1978 and 2010 (https://www.fda.gov/Drugs/DevelopmentApprovalProcess/Manufacturing/ucm206756.htm).

In 2012 the FDASIA legislation made an important change to the statutory GMP requirement at § 501(a)(2)(B) of the FDCA by adding the following at the end of the section: "For purposes of paragraph (a)(2)(B), the term 'current good manufacturing practice' includes the implementation of oversight and controls over the manufacture of drugs to ensure quality, including managing the risk of and establishing the safety of raw materials, materials used in the manufacturing of drugs, and finished drug products." In effect, this codifies previously existing agency policy regarding management of the drug supply chain by drug companies. FDA has published draft guidance to begin the process of implementing this section, but as of this writing has not modified the regulations to reflect the statutory change. The agency issued draft "Guidance for Industry: Contract Manufacturing Arrangements for Drugs: Quality Agreements" in May 2013 as a first step in clarifying how this requirement will be interpreted for inspection purposes.

♦ **Drug Regulations** (21 C.F.R. Parts 300–499)—FDA has promulgated extensive regulations covering many of the administrative details concerning procedures that must be followed when submitting NDAs and ANDAs to FDA. These sections contain detailed requirements for filing NDAs and ANDAs, as well as the requirements for various drug products. The requirements for submissions for postapproval change have been affected directly by FDAMA, which added section 506A to the FDCA. The major effects of this section on FDA inspections are the statutory requirement to validate postapproval changes, and the subdivision of supplements into four principal types: Pre-approval supplement; Changes Being Effected (30 days); Changes Being Effected (immediate); and Annual Report submissions. This is quite similar to the previous scheme except for the addition of the

Changes Being Effected (30 days) provision. Manufacturers filing this type of submission must wait 30 days before implementing the change to allow FDA an opportunity to review the change and comment (or object).

New drugs that are intended to be administered to humans or animals must be manufactured in accordance with the cGMP regulations, and the NDAs must certify conformance. If production is done in laboratory research facilities or pilot plant production facilities, the procedures may be different from those used in full-scale production facilities. NDAs must include detailed descriptions of manufacturing and control procedures. If changes are made from NDA commitments, it may be necessary to obtain prior approval from FDA or to notify FDA following the change.

◆ Applications for FDA Approval to Market a New Drug or Antibiotic (21 C.F.R. Part 314)—This section describes requirements for NDAs and various administrative actions followed by the agency for reviewing and approving applications.

◆ Other Postmarketing Reports (21 C.F.R. § 314.81)—FDA inspections frequently are triggered as a result of firms filing an NDA Field Alert Report (FAR) as provided for by this section. Applicants are required to submit, within three working days of receipt, information about products that: 1) involve any incident that causes a drug product or its labeling to be mistaken for another (e.g., label mix-up); 2) failure of a distributed product to meet specifications listed in applications; or 3) significant change or deterioration of the drug product (such as physicochemical deterioration or microbiological contamination). NOTE: Licensed biologics that are also drugs are not covered by this regulation, but rather, by the Biological Product Deviation Reporting (BPDR) requirements at 21 C.F.R. 600.14. While similar in many ways to the requirements for FARs, a key difference in the BPDR regulation is that the report must be submitted within 45 working days rather than three days as is the case for FARs.

◆ **Annual Report** *(21 C.F.R. § 314.81)*—Sponsors holding approved NDAs must file annual reports. During postapproval inspections, FDA inspection teams review the content of NDAs and the annual reports to compare actual conditions at the facility against commitments. FDA investigators will verify that annual reports have been filed, and that information contained in them is accurate and complete for significant new information. Such information includes summaries about any matter that may affect the safety, efficacy, or labeling including summaries of actions taken in response to new information or intentions to take actions such as supplements, and new warnings initiating new studies. FDA may verify

During postapproval inspections, FDA inspection teams review the content of NDAs and the annual reports to compare actual conditions at the facility against commitments.

that annual reports contain distribution data showing the quantity of the drug product distributed and summary of labeling changes made, as well as copies of representative package labels, inserts, etc. FDA will be alert for the presence or absence of reports of new information about experiences, investigations, studies, or tests that involve physical, chemical, or micro-biological properties that may affect FDA conclusions about the safety or effectiveness of the drug. Finally, FDA will review documentation about any changes to manufacturing and controls that do not require submissions of supplements under Part 314.70 and the various other summaries that are related to nonclinical and clinical studies.

♦ ***Drug Master Files*** *(21 C.F.R. § 314.420)*—A Drug Master File (DMF) is a submission to FDA that may be used to provide confidential detailed information about facilities, processes, or articles used in the manufactur-ing, processing, packaging, and storing of one or more human drugs. The submission of a DMF is not required by law or FDA regulation, and a DMF is not a substitute for an IND application, NDA, ANDA, or export application. There is no process whereby a DMF is "approved" or disapproved by FDA. During the conduct of pre-approval inspections FDA inspection teams fre-quently review copies of applicable DMFs that relate to containers, closures, and facilities. FDA will carefully compare commitments made in DMFs (such as specifications, test methods, release limits, and the like) against the cor-responding specifications, methods, or release limits that are in place at the user firm. If discrepancies are noted, this may result in an FDA citation.

Five DMFs and the rules for submitting them are listed in 21 C.F.R. § 314.420:

♦ Type I (now rescinded), see below.

♦ Type II covers drug substances, drug substance intermediates, and material used in their preparation.

♦ Type III covers packaging material, including toxicological data on these materials, if such data is not otherwise available.

♦ Type IV covers excipients, colorants, flavors, essences, or materials used in their preparation, including toxicological data.

♦ Type V covers "accepted reference information," which does not fit any of the above categories. FDA actively discourages this type of DMF. If a firm desires to submit one, prior consultation with FDA is required.

In January 2000, FDA announced a revision of the regulation governing DMFs. FDA removed the provision for submitting Type I DMFs (which formerly cov-ered facilities, operating procedures, and personnel) and the agency no longer permits information submitted in a Type I DMF to be incorporated by reference in IND applications, NDAs, ANDAs, or amendments or supplements to any of these. FDA's stated intention is to eliminate submissions of information that is not needed for FDA to conduct its inspections of manufacturing facilities or is not needed for its review of the chemistry, manufacturing, and controls sections of applications (such as INDs, NDAs, and ANDAs). The effective date of this change was July 10, 2000.

♦ ***Bioavailability and Bioequivalence*** *(21 C.F.R. Part 320)*—This section describes FDA expectations and procedures for determining the bioavailability or bioequivalence of drug products. Companies submitting full or abbreviated NDAs are required to submit evidence demonstrating bioavailability of the drug product or to request a waiver from the bioavailability requirement. The regulation describes changes reported in supplements for which bioavailability studies may be required, such as changes in manufacturing process that alter product formulation or strength beyond variations permitted in the approved application, or labeling changes, or the establishment of a new dosage regimen. This section also describes FDA requirements for requesting a waiver from bioavailability or bioequivalence testing requirements.

♦ ***Biological Product Regulations*** *(21 C.F.R. Parts 600–680)*—Used by FDA for the enforcement of section 351 of the Public Health Service Act, these regulations are similar in content to the drug GMP regulations. Licensing provisions and procedures for Establishment License Applications (ELAs) and Product License Applications (PLAs) are described as are the establishment standards for manufacturing whole blood for transfusions, blood components, and blood derivatives. It is important to note that all biological products are by definition also drugs or medical devices as defined in the FDCA, and thus are subject to both statutes. Therapeutic biologicals are most commonly drugs, though some exceptions exist that are devices. Most biological devices are *in vitro* diagnostic products such as monoclonal antibody test kits, and certain reagents used in blood grouping and typing.

Biological product regulations are similar in content to the drug GMP regulations.

Preparing for an Inspection

Inspections are conducted generally by FDA investigators, most of whom are assigned to one of FDA's district offices. As this edition goes to press, FDA is involved in a restructuring of its headquarters and field-organizational units that are responsible for performing inspections and reviewing the findings of FDA inspections. As part of its "Pharmaceuticals FY2016 Program Alignment Action Plan," described below in the section "Recent Inspection Trends," FDA is

Inspections are conducted generally by FDA investigators, most of whom are assigned to one of FDA's district offices.

establishing internal reporting relationships that are based on product specialty (rather than by regional/geographic boundaries). For example, under the proposed reorganiztion, FDA investigators who do pharmaceutical inspections will still live and work in district office areas, but will functionally report to a centralized medical products group in FDA headquarters. Likewise, food investigators will report to a food-oriented headquarters component, and so on. The overall objective is to increase specialization, more closely coordinate inspection activities with FDA headquarters Centers along product lines, and reduce variability in the interpretation and application of enforcement policy around the country and internationally. The details of how this change will be implemented are yet unknown, but it is clear that FDA is changing its organizational structure to allow a more focused approach to its inspections of regulated commodities.

Investigators may be assisted during inspections by laboratory analysts, engineers, microbiologists, FDA headquarters technical experts, and other specialists. FDA also performs inspections abroad for products that are intended to be shipped into the United States. Some investigators are members of the Commissioned Corps of the U.S. Public Health Service, assigned to FDA. These employees are distinguished by the fact that they use military rank titles such as Lieutenant Commander, and often wear military-style uniforms while on duty. For practical purposes, these employees are no different than any other FDA investigator in terms of the operations they conduct.

FDA maintains files of previous inspection reports, communications with industry, and the results of sample testing. Before performing an inspection, the inspection team usually will review these records to determine whether previous inspections have encountered significant discrepancies or violations. If previous inspections have found problems, the follow-up inspection will assess the adequacy of corrective actions. For pharmaceutical, biologic, and medical device inspections, preparation also may include the review of product approval applications to determine compliance with commitments made to the agency. Previously issued FDA-483s are usually reviewed prior to each inspection, as are the associated narrative Establishment Inspection Reports (EIRs). The inspection team will be alert for patterns and trends that reflect evidence of continuing noncompliance, and/or issues that may suggest potential problems in areas not covered previously.

FDA inspection team members also will review appropriate regulatory standards for the facility to be inspected. For example, the team may utilize applicable compendia, such as the U.S. Pharmacopoeia or National Formulary; relevant trade association guidelines; documents that may constitute industry standards; the *Investigations Operations Manual*, which guides the investigators in procedural matters; and the *Compliance Program Guidance Manual*, which contains several hundred documents that describe inspection procedures for particular industries. While FDA investigators may use industry guidelines and standards as references, they are not permitted to impose them as legal requirements.

When preparing for an FDA inspection of a company that has multiple sites, FDA offices often will coordinate their activities to determine whether violations suggest a larger systemic problem. When FDA finds repeated violations at multiple sites for a single company, the agency may consider taking stronger, corporate-wide measures, including the issuance of injunctions.

FDA INSPECTION TECHNIQUES

During a typical FDA inspection, one or more FDA investigators arrive unannounced at a facility. (See the introductory portion of this chapter for exceptions to the unannounced inspection practice.) FDA inspections may be as short as a few hours or last several weeks or months depending on the purpose. A typical inspection of a food-processing facility may last for a few days and a complex inspection of a pharmaceutical manufacturer may require more than two weeks. If FDA detects significant objectionable conditions, the inspection may be extended as necessary.

FDA inspections may be as short as a few hours or last several weeks or months depending on the purpose.

FDA inspection approaches vary considerably depending on the commodities manufactured at the facility. Typically, inspections of food manufacturers concentrate on basic sanitation and employee practices. For example, FDA will examine warehouse areas for evidence of rodents, insects, or other vermin, and will observe manufacturing equipment and employee practices for evidence of inadequate cleaning or insanitary employee practices. FDA also is alert for conditions that may lead to food safety issues, such as conditions that may promote microbiological growth in food products, or unsafe handling of insecticides, cleaning agents, and other hazardous materials.

The scope of an inspection of a pharmaceutical manufacturer will depend upon the purpose of the inspection, the type of product (which determines the applicable regulations), any special concerns such as current complaints, and other factors. For example, FDA inspections of pharmaceutical manufacturers usually include examinations of the facilities and personnel for basic sanitation. In addition, FDA will examine manufacturing and control records to verify conformance with applicable GMPs. Drug products must be manufactured according to manufacturing instructions that have been reviewed and double-checked by

The scope of the inspection will depend upon the purpose of the inspection, the type of product, any special concerns such as current complaints and other factors.

at least two persons. The weighing and addition of ingredients must be verified by at least two persons, and personnel must record each significant step in the manufacturing and control operations. Appropriate "in-process" inspections and tests are required to ensure products meet specifications, and before any batch can be released, it must be tested against predetermined specifications. The GMP regulations specify the types of records that must be maintained and the document retention requirements. FDA investigators will examine laboratory facilities and laboratory control records to ensure that appropriate records are being maintained and that test methods are suitable for the intended use. Before any batch can be released it must be tested according to an approved method, and if a product is covered by an official compendial monograph (such as the U.S. Pharmacopoeia), it must be tested to confirm conformance to this standard.

A major focus of recent FDA drug and device inspections has been the review of product process validation, as well as the activities surrounding the development of drug formulations and the design of medical devices. Recent FDA inspections at drug manufacturers have detected significant data integrity lapses that has led to greater inspection attention to the procedures, processes, and controls used by drug manufacturers to ensure the accuracy and completeness of data and information that is required by applicable laws and regulations. FDA expects firms to provide adequate assurances that drugs have the identity, strength, quality, and purity characteristics that they purport or are represented to possess. When FDA inspections detect non-compliance with GMPs or data integrity lapses, FDA may withhold approval of pending product applications or may invoke regulatory sanctions against marketed products.

During FDA inspections, the team will review records covering the manufacturing and testing of any or all batches made to date, and the documents that establish the firm is capable of consistently producing a product that meets predetermined specifications (i.e., verify that processes are validated). If early development activities are found by FDA to be deficient or not well documented, firms may not be in a position to justify the validity of their conclusions about the safety and effectiveness of their drug product.

Recent Inspection Trends

FDA applies a quality system approach—as opposed to the more traditional facility- or product-oriented approach—to medical device, pharmaceutical, and biologic inspections.

For many years, FDA inspectors have adopted a "quality system" approach, as opposed to the more traditional facility- or product-oriented approach. FDA has an established methodology for use of this approach in medical device inspections, known as the Quality System Inspection Technique (QSIT). The QSIT approach is now standard for medical device inspections that focus on compliance with the Quality System Regulation, 21 C.F.R. Part 820.

Since 2002, FDA has also applied a quality system approach to pharmaceutical and biologic inspections. FDA has adopted a six-system definition for purposes of inspection as follows:

1. The *Quality System* includes a wide variety of areas that involve how the company manages its quality operations. Included here are non-conformance investigations, the responsibilities and authority of the Quality Unit, the requirement for annual review of product quality performance, and other overall quality management functions.
2. The *Facilities and Equipment System*, which, as the name implies, involves evaluation of the adequacy of the environment and equipment used to produce drugs and biologics.
3. The *Materials System*, which includes evaluation of components, containers and closures, packaging and finishing materials, etc.
4. The *Production System*, which includes review of the controls used to keep manufacturing operations running in compliance with GMP.
5. The *Packaging and Labeling System*, which again as the name implies, involves evaluation of controls to assure that products are properly packaged and carry the correct labels and associated labeling.
6. The *Laboratory Controls System*, which involves evaluation of the procedures, controls, and methods used in the laboratory for the analysis of materials, in process and finished products.

Associated training, change control, and records pertinent to each of the systems are reviewed within the context of the systems themselves.

The quality system approach currently used by FDA differs slightly depending on whether the product is a drug (generally regulated by the Center for Drug Evaluation and Research (CDER)) or a biologic (generally regulated by the Center for Biologics Evaluation and Research (CBER)). Both CDER and CBER have issued compliance programs to FDA Field Offices describing how the quality system approach is to be used for the products they regulate. Both compliance programs (7356.002, "Drug Manufacturing Inspections" and 7345.848, "Inspection of Biological Drug Products") provide for either an abbreviated or comprehensive approach, depending on the history of the company, current concerns, and findings of the inspection. The reader is referred to the cited compliance programs, available at http://www.fda.gov, for further details.

It should be noted that FDA, as part of its "Pharmaceuticals FY2016 Program Alignment Action Plan," is currently reexamining its pharmaceutical GMP inspection approach in an effort to make observations more relevant to impact on product quality and patient safety (see http://www.fda.gov/AboutFDA/CentersOffices/ucm477083.htm). One of the FDA initiatives, known as the "New Inspection Protocol Program" (NIPP) is still under development as this chapter goes to press. The NIPP is a new paradigm that is intended to provide a quality-focused approach to inspections using expert investigators and streamlined inspection reporting. If adopted, the proposed NIPP approach will allow FDA investigators to have an inspection format that uses expert-level questions. Such an approach is intended to allow inspection findings to be semi-quantified (i.e., to measure both observations that do not conform to regulatory requirements as well as report conditions that exceed expectations). For those in the pharmaceutical industry, the NIPP initiative bears watching, as significant changes to FDA's drug GMP inspection approach may require modification of company inspection readiness activities and procedures in the future.

Due to the increasing globalization of the pharmaceutical industry and the increased importance of supply chain integrity, FDA has expanded its presence in foreign countries.

Due to the increasing globalization of the pharmaceutical industry and the increased importance of supply chain integrity, FDA has expanded its presence in foreign countries, establishing local offices in China, India, Central America, South Africa, Europe, and other locations. While FDA personnel assigned to these offices conduct inspections, a primary purpose of these offices is to establish working relationships with counterpart agencies in the various nations, and to gain firsthand intelligence about the state of the industry in each locale. Foreign inspections continue to be supported by staff based in the United States, including a dedicated Foreign Inspection Cadre of approximately 15 investigators whose job is limited to foreign inspections. Currently other district office based personnel, national expert-level investigators, and personnel from the Centers continue to support foreign inspections as in the past.

Two Controversial Inspection Issues: Photography and Affidavits

Photography During Inspections

FDA has for many years taken the position that photography is sometimes necessary to a reasonable inspection.

FDA has for many years taken the position that photography is sometimes necessary to a reasonable inspection, and therefore is "just another evidence-gathering tool" authorized under the general "reasonableness" standard of section 704 of the FDCA. However, industry lawyers often take the position that because the law does not specifically authorize photography, FDA has no right to take photographs, and some companies have policies or procedures that state that FDA personnel will not be allowed to take photographs.

FDA's *Investigations Operations Manual* (IOM) provides the following instructions to investigators in the event they need to take photographs:

Do not request permission from management to take photographs during an inspection. Take your camera into the firm and use it as necessary just as you use other inspectional equipment. If management objects to taking photographs, explain that photos are an integral part of an inspection and present an accurate picture of plant conditions. Advise management the U.S. Courts have held that photographs may lawfully be taken as part of an inspection.

The IOM goes on to cite two court cases in support of the agency's position. Nevertheless, the question of whether or not FDA has the right to take photographs during an inspection remains a subject of debate. Opinions in the industry and the legal community vary, and some disagree with the agency's position on the matter. In practice, FDA infrequently takes photographs except during food inspections, most commonly to show gross insanitary conditions. However, it is possible during any inspection (including pharmaceutical and medical device facilities) that the agency may proceed to take photographs. When FDA encounters a refusal to permit photography, FDA has used two enforcement options as follows: 1) go to court (ex parte) to seek an administrative inspection warrant to compel the inspected company to allow photography (FDA has been successful in obtaining such warrants, and has also included provisions mandating photography during inspections in consent decree settlement); and 2) to deem products to be adulterated for limiting photography per provisions of section 707 of FDASIA as described below.

In practice, FDA rarely takes photographs except during food inspections, most commonly to show gross insanitary conditions.

These controversies not withstanding, FDA has long held that it has the right to take photographs during its inspections. FDASIA includes in section 707 a prohibition against delaying, denying, limiting, or refusing inspection. This section amends section 501 of the FDCA by adding the following to the definition of conditions that constitute an "adulterated" drug: "(j) If it is a drug and it has been manufactured, processed, packed, or held in any factory, warehouse, or establishment and the owner, operator, or agent of such factory, warehouse, or establishment delays, denies, or limits an inspection, or refuses to permit entry or inspection.

It is notable that the law itself (section 707 of FDASIA) specifically requires FDA to define the circumstances that constitute delaying, denying, limiting, or refusing a drug inspection. For example, section 707 explicitly states: "Not later than 1 year after the date of enactment of this section, the Secretary of Health and Human Services shall issue guidance that defines the circumstances that would constitute delaying, denying, or limiting inspection, or refusing to permit entry or inspection, for purposes of section 501(j) of the Federal Food, Drug, and Cosmetic Act (as added by subsection(a)). (Deadline 21 USC 351 note.)."

While FDASIA does not explicitly require companies to allow FDA to take photographs, FDA has published a guidance document that provides its interpretation of section 707 of FDASIA ("Guidance for Industry: Circumstances that Constitute Delaying, Denying, Limiting, or Refusing a Drug Inspection," October 2014). The FDA guidance indicates that FDA may deem a drug to be adulterated if it ". . . has been manufactured, processed, packed, or held in any factory, warehouse, or establishment and the owner, operator, or agent of such factory, warehouse, or establishment delays, denies, or limits an inspection, or refuses to permit entry or inspection."

While information contained in this guidance document is not necessarily binding per se, the guidance reflects the agency's current thinking.

It is important to note that the FDA guidance contains the following statement, bearing in mind that the authority provided for in this section of FDASIA pertains to drug products: "Photographs are an integral part of an FDA inspection because they present an accurate picture of facility conditions. Not allowing photography by an FDA investigator may be considered a limitation if such photographs are determined by the investigator(s) to be necessary to effectively conduct that particular inspection. Examples of conditions or practices effectively documented by photographs include, but are not limited to: evidence of rodents or insect infestation; faulty construction or maintenance of equipment or facilities; product storage conditions; product labels and labeling; and visible contamination of raw materials or finished products."

In this section of the guidance, FDA is in effect stating that the refusal to permit photography may be considered by the agency to constitute an unreasonable limitation of a drug facility inspection as that term is used in section 707 of FDASIA Title VII, and therefore may result in the products made at that facility being deemed to be adulterated. It is also important to note that FDA has issued at least one Warning Letter to a drug manufacturer that refused to allow photography during an FDA inspection. For example, a Warning Letter dated September 26, 2016 issued to a company in Japan stated that "The FDA investigator documented that your firm limited and/or refused an FDA inspection. Under the Federal Food, Drug, and Cosmetic Act (the FD&C Act), as amended by the Food and Drug Administration Safety and Innovation Act (FDASIA), section 707, 21 U.S.C. 351(j), your drugs are adulterated in that they have been manufactured, processed, packed, or held in an establishment where the owner or operator has limited inspection and refused inspection." Among the violations cited in the Warning Letter was the issue of limiting photography as follows: "During the inspection, our investigator attempted to take pictures of the (b)(4) apparatus used to manufacture drugs for U.S. distribution. Your quality assurance manager impeded the inspection by preventing our investigator from photographing this piece of equipment."

To avoid potential regulatory consequences resulting from a refusal to allow photographs, prudent companies have developed procedures that do not refuse photography, but define the conditions for which photographs may be permitted and those where photographs are contraindicated (including the rationale for limiting photographs in areas where there may be a safety hazard or risk to the product or process associated with taking photographs (such as risk of explosions in areas with volatile solvents, risk to products being manufactured in controlled environments, disruptions of manufacturing or control operations (such as sensors and detectors) from camera flashes, etc.). Rather than to outright refuse to allow photographs, prudent companies will attempt to work with the FDA investigator to achieve an alternative that is acceptable to both FDA and the company. If a company decides not to allow photographs to be taken during an FDA inspection, the final decision should be based on advice from legal counsel with an awareness of the potential consequences that may arise if FDA deems products to be adulterated based on limiting the inspection in violation of section 707 of FDASIA.

Affidavits

FDA investigators are trained to prepare affidavits to link evidence collected to documents that establish the connection with interstate commerce that is necessary for FDA to establish jurisdiction. Such affidavits may be written and provided to company personnel with a request that personnel sign them. There is no statutory mandate requiring company personnel to sign these affidavits. Here again, the decision whether to sign is one best made by legal counsel after consideration of all the facts. In the experience of the authors, however, many if not most, pharmaceutical companies have policies that require company personnel not to read, agree to, or to sign affidavits that are prepared by FDA personnel during inspections. FDA personnel are familiar with policies and are not likely to be upset by company personnel declining to sign an affidavit.

Many, if not most, pharmaceutical companies have policies that require company personnel not to read, agree to, or to sign affidavits that are prepared by FDA personnel during inspections.

FDA-483s

The stated purpose of the List of Inspectional Observations (Form FDA-483) is to cite observations concerning filth, insanitary conditions, or danger to health. In practice, however, FDA reports a wide variety of inspectional observations on the FDA-483, including deviations from approved protocols in clinical trials, recordkeeping problems, deviations from GMPs, and many other general observations related to inspection findings.

The reverse side of the FDA-483 states a dual purpose: 1) for the purposes required by statute and 2) to assist firms to comply with the provisions of the act. The latter category accounts for the majority of FDA-483 observations. Following each inspection, the FDA team prepares an EIR that describes observations made during the inspection and includes exhibits to support findings (including photographs, production and control documents, records of interstate commerce, etc.). The EIR is reviewed and endorsed by district personnel. Reports that are endorsed as violative are referred to district management for a decision about appropriate compliance action(s). When necessary the case is forwarded to the appropriate FDA headquarters Center for final review and disposition.

HOSTING FDA INSPECTIONS

This section describes some of the important points that companies should consider when hosting inspections conducted by FDA employees. It includes information about the types of FDA employees who usually conduct inspections and the logistical issues associated with hosting an inspection. Also described are some common sense etiquette issues (i.e., "do's and don'ts"), as well as methods to deal with requests that are outside the scope of FDA's inspection authority.

Types of Employees Who Conduct FDA Inspections

Inspections are conducted by FDA investigators, chemists, microbiologists, engineers, and various scientists having specialized education and training.

FDA employees who conduct inspections have a wide variety of backgrounds. Inspections are conducted by FDA investigators, chemists, microbiologists, engineers, and various scientists having specialized education and training. Every employee who participates in an inspection must possess official FDA credentials and must properly display them to an appropriate official of the company at the beginning of each inspection. Each FDA employee is required by law to present a written notice to the owner, operator, or agent in charge before beginning an inspection. FDA uses the "Notice of Inspection" (Form FDA-482) to provide this notice. However, a Form FDA-482 is not normally issued for foreign inspections.

The titles of FDA employees who conduct inspections may vary. Each of the more common titles, with a brief description of the duties, follows:

♦ Consumer Safety Officer (CSO)—This is an official job title for personnel management purposes within FDA, and some employees may identify themselves using the CSO job title. The employees who identify themselves as "investigators" are usually CSOs, although several other specialized positions exist in the CSO job series. For example, also included are the following "functional" titles: Investigator, Compliance Officer, Reviewer, Program Analyst, Small Business Representative, Interstate Travel Sanitation

Specialist, Sanitarian, Shellfish Specialist, Food Service Specialist, and others. Various FDA headquarters-based personnel who sometimes participate in inspections are also included in the CSO job series.

♦ Commissioned Corps Officers—Commissioned officers of the U.S. Public Health Service are on assignment to the agency in a variety of positions, including as investigators. These employees may provide one of the titles given above for CSO positions, or may use their military title as a member of the commissioned corps, such as Commander, Captain, etc. Commissioned corps officers hold the same status and authority as civil service FDA employees.

♦ Consumer Safety Inspector (CSI)—The CSI is a para-professional level position. CSIs carry out such activities as collecting samples and inspecting warehouses. Many CSIs operate exclusively in import-related activities, mainly collecting samples of products offered for importation at the point of entry into U.S. commerce. CSIs usually identify themselves by that title, but may use the title of "Inspector."

♦ Analyst—An analyst normally works in FDA laboratories, but occasionally may participate in on-site inspections. Functional job titles include chemist, microbiologist, biologist, or entomologist. Infrequently, certain para-professional laboratory personnel, such as physical science technicians, may assist on inspections. Laboratory personnel occasionally conduct inspections alone, but normally they are present to assist the investigators with laboratory portions of more complex inspections.

♦ Special Agent, Office of Criminal Investigations (OCI)—Special agents rarely take part in regulatory inspections. If a special agent from OCI is participating in an FDA inspection, his or her presence would provide a signal that the inspection has a special or unusual purpose. Companies that are visited by special agents should consider this to be highly unusual, and should consider seeking the advice and assistance of legal counsel. Special agents have full police powers, including the right to carry firearms and make arrests. A special agent, however, may be assigned to accompany an investigator on an inspection as part of his or her on-the-job training or orientation to agency operations. Companies should ask for and expect to be provided with a full and complete explanation about the purpose of a special agent's presence during a regulatory inspection.

Logistics While an Inspection Is in Progress

A trained person should act as escort for FDA personnel during the course of the inspection. For complex industries, it is advisable to have multiple persons who can fill this role. There may be multiple FDA staff present for the inspection, and an escort should be available for each FDA employee. One or more

There may be multiple FDA staff present for the inspection, and an escort should be available for each FDA employee.

persons should be designated to act as scribe to maintain an accurate transcript of questions, answers, and any significant discussions about issues, concerns, or corrective actions reported to FDA.

The person(s) serving as scribe should not be the designated escort. The escort should not be burdened by trying to take notes while meeting the needs of FDA personnel (such as monitoring FDA activities and responding to requests from the investigators). Written policies or procedures should be prepared in advance, describing how inspections are to be handled by the firm. The policy or procedure should include, but not be limited to, the company's position on such matters as access to areas of the company, photography, affidavits, collection of samples, providing copies of documents, and granting FDA requests for interviews with company employees.

A conference room or office should be set aside for FDA's use during the inspection, as needed. This facilitates review of the large number of documents that may be requested by FDA. The location of the conference room may be near document storage areas, photocopying resources, or production areas depending on the inspection objectives. For lengthy inspections (several weeks or longer) companies may wish to consider dedicated clerical support for the FDA team during the inspection.

A separate conference room should be available to serve as the company's command post for the inspection. This room should be near, but not too near, the room dedicated to FDA's use. It should be located in an area of the company not subject to inspection by FDA, such as administrative office space, to enable frank discussions to take place without risk of them being overheard by the investigators.

Companies are encouraged to have daily debriefings of all company personnel who were involved with FDA during the course of an inspection.

Companies are encouraged to have daily debriefings of all company personnel who were involved with FDA during the course of an inspection. Debriefings should include key issues covered by FDA, topics discussed, information provided, any allegations of violations made by the investigators, corrective actions taken or promised, and any other significant issues.

After the inspection, the company should prepare its own final report, providing a permanent record of the inspection. The record furnishes the company's perspectives and is supported by original notes taken by company personnel during the inspection. Each company should establish a policy as to whether to keep permanent copies of the notes taken during an inspection. If notes are maintained, procedures should define how they are to be identified (signed and dated), how they will be preserved, and by whom. The benefits of having the notes available in the event of litigation must be weighed against any possible adverse consequences of maintaining potentially problematic information. The final decision on retention of original notes should be determined with advice of legal counsel.

Managing the Exit Discussion

At the conclusion of an inspection and prior to leaving the premises, FDA will issue a Form FDA-483, List of Inspectional Observations, if FDA has found conditions or practices in the facility which in the judgment of the inspection team may cause a food, drug, or device to become adulterated under the provisions of the FDCA. As a matter of FDA policy, the inspection team will afford the personnel of the inspected company to have an opportunity to present their views and ask questions during the exit discussion.

While most companies will discuss the List of Observations with the FDA inspection team to better understand the basis for each observation, some companies elect not to comment during the exit discussion, preferring to comment only in writing and after the fact. Each company must decide the best strategy in this regard. Ultimately the decision whether or not to hold an exit discussion may depend on the advice of counsel. Opting not to have the exit discussion precludes an important opportunity to ensure FDA understands the company's position, and to ensure that the company understands the basis for FDA's findings. Even if the company does not agree, understanding FDA's position is critical for preparation of an appropriate response.

Some companies elect not to comment during the exit discussion, preferring to comment only in writing and after the fact.

If a decision is made to participate in an exit discussion, among the objectives of the discussion should be the following, at a minimum:

♦ ensure a correct understanding of FDA's reason for citing items on the 483 (even if the company disagrees, a clear understanding will be essential to a good response);

♦ ensure that the facts stated on the 483 are accurate;

♦ ensure that the wording of the 483 is complete and not misleading (for instance, inadvertent omission of a word like "not" from a sentence may change the entire meaning); and

♦ request that FDA delete items from the 483 if the inspection team agrees they are inaccurate or erroneous. (FDA policy is to delete items that can be shown to be in error or not factually correct.)

Ensure that the right people are present for the discussion. Generally, this means senior management and subject matter experts for topics that were covered during the inspection. It is best to avoid having large numbers of people present who will not be contributing substantively to the discussion and those who have little or no authority to make commitments for the company.

It is important to decide in advance who will control the discussion from the company's perspective, and who will speak for the company regarding actions in response to the 483 and who may offer time lines for corrections. Care should be taken to avoid characterizing FDA's observations as "violations" or "deviations"; instead, simply refer to them as FDA-483 "items" or "citations."

The decision of whether or not to have counsel present for the exit discussion is best determined on a case-by-case basis. In the experience of the authors, most companies elect not to have counsel present unless there appears to be an imminent risk of enforcement action, or a significant dispute has arisen over FDA authority. The ultimate decision is best left to senior management in collaboration with counsel.

Responding in Writing to the FDA-483

While there is no statutory requirement that requires a company to respond either orally or in writing to the FDA-483, such responses are a nearly universal practice in all segments of the FDA-regulated industry. Failing to promptly respond in writing is likely to be perceived negatively by FDA enforcement personnel. In the *Federal Register*, Vol. 74, No. 153, Tuesday, August 11, 2009, FDA published a statement of policy that establishes a 15-business-day time frame to respond to an FDA-483. As a matter of policy, when FDA is considering whether to escalate an enforcement action to a Warning Letter or more serious step following an inspection, FDA will not take into consideration a company's response that has been submitted more than 15 business days after the inspection was completed. Therefore, if a company wants FDA to consider its viewpoint, it is prudent to submit the response to the FDA-483 within the 15 business-day time frame.

Etiquette Points for Dealing with FDA Investigators

The etiquette for dealing with FDA staff is fairly straightforward and is based on an understanding of FDA inspection authority, FDA policy for the conduct of inspections, the company's policy, and an understanding of FDA's ethical restrictions. FDA staff work under a very restrictive standard of ethical conduct, which is repeatedly and strongly reinforced over the course of their employment with the agency. The standard is one of avoidance of even an appearance of a conflict of interest. Therefore, it is inadvisable to offer anything of more than nominal value. Refreshments such as coffee, tea, or soft drinks are generally acceptable and will not be seen as inappropriate. The utmost care should be taken to avoid any offer that could be construed as a bribe or gratuity.

Requests Outside the Scope of FDA Authority

Historically, FDA has taken the position that during an inspection it may ask for any type of information, but will insist upon access only to statutorily mandated areas and information. In practice, FDA investigators will routinely request whatever information they believe they need, and will not, as a rule, take the initiative to explain to the company being inspected just which types of information must be provided versus information requested on a purely consensual basis. Historically, FDA has taken the position that it is the company's responsibility to know the difference.

Historically, FDA has taken the position that during an inspection it may ask for any type of information, but will insist upon access only to statutorily mandated areas and information.

For these reasons, FDA investigators may sometimes request access to areas or information that are outside the scope of the general inspection authority under section 704. The investigators usually will answer questions from the company if asked whether release of the information or access to the area is within the scope of section 704. Since it may be assumed, however, that the investigator's interests are served by obtaining the information on a consensual basis, caution and careful consideration are required before a company accedes to a request that is outside FDA's statutory authority.

There are cases where a company may decide to agree to such a request. For example, if an investigator asks about a company's annual volume of business (a common question), and such information is already a matter of public record, a company may decide that answering will serve to promote goodwill and honest communication while not disclosing information of a proprietary or damaging nature. The factors to be considered in deciding whether to supply information to FDA when the company is not legally required to do so include, among others:

♦ understanding the reason for FDA's request;

♦ an assessment of the potential adverse consequences of disclosure;

♦ an assessment of the benefits of cooperating with the inspector's request versus not cooperating; and

♦ an assessment of the ease with which the agency may be able to obtain the information from alternative sources, and whether the procedure of obtaining the information in that way might expose the company to questions at suppliers, customers, or others.

There is no statutory requirement or precedent that requires FDA to inform a company (or individual persons) of their rights during the context of an FDA inspection.

Note: There is no statutory requirement or precedent that requires FDA to inform a company (or individual persons) of their rights during the context of an FDA inspection. While companies have argued that FDA investigators should provide Miranda warnings or similar warnings to company officials (especially when the agency develops an awareness that the matter under investigation may be referred for criminal prosecution), courts have consistently found that Miranda warnings are not required in the context of an FDA inspection. The FDA *Investigations Operations Manual* instructs investigators to provide Miranda warnings only when the person being interviewed is in custody or under detention, and therefore is not free to leave.

Forms Commonly Used During FDA Inspections

FDA uses several forms for a wide variety of purposes during regulatory inspections. The forms are commonly referred to by either their name or their number. For example, the Notice of Inspection may be referred to as the "Notice of Inspection," the "Notice," the "FDA-482" or simply the "482." FDA employees and industry representatives use the terms interchangeably. The forms FDA-482, FDA-483, and FDA-484 are designed to comply with statutory requirements imposed on FDA by section 704 of the FDCA (see details below). The majority of the current content of section 704 of the FDCA was established through the Factory Inspection Amendments to the FDCA in 1953, with some subsequent modification by the 1997 FDAMA.

FDA-482, Notice of Inspection

Form FDA-482 cites authorities granted by other laws enforced by FDA, and therefore it is used for all inspections, regardless of which law is being enforced.

This form is issued to the "owner, operator, or agent in charge" of a facility at the beginning of an inspection. Its purpose is to comply with the provisions of section 704(a) of the FDCA that require that written notice be given before an inspection is undertaken. The form lists the name and address of the facility being inspected, and bears the signature(s) and typed or printed name(s) of the FDA employee(s) conducting the inspection. The form cites the sections of the law that grant inspection authority. In addition to the FDCA, the form cites authorities granted by other laws enforced by FDA, and therefore it is used for all inspections, regardless of which law is being enforced. This is convenient for the agency, because in many cases the inspection is in fact being conducted under authority granted by more than one statute. For example, an inspection of a licensed blood bank may be conducted under both the FDCA and section 351 of the Public Health Service Act.

FDA-483, Inspectional Observations

This form is issued at the conclusion of the inspection in accordance with section 704(b) of the act. By law, the investigators must list those observations which, in their judgment, may indicate that a food, drug, medical device, or cosmetic processed, packed, or held on the inspected premises consists in whole or in part of a filthy, putrid, or decomposed substance, or has been prepared, packed, or held under insanitary conditions whereby it may have become contaminated. As previously described, the agency uses this form to cite a wide variety of observations, far beyond the scope of what is required by statute. Generally speaking, the form is used to list all potential violations that can be directly observed by the investigators. Certain exceptions exist for issues that generally involve suspected violations that cannot be easily established through inspection observations, such as the adequacy of label claims, status of a drug as a new drug, and other issues. The *Investigations Operations Manual*, Chapter 5, lists these exceptions.

This form is also used to list recordkeeping violations, GMP deviations, discrepancies noted in the review of clinical trial records, and a host of other conditions and practices that range far from its statutorily mandated use. If the FDA employee(s) believe it is necessary to re-initiate any part of the inspection after the FDA-483 has been issued, they will issue a new FDA-482 and another inspection will officially commence.

FDA-484, Receipt for Samples

This form is used to account for any physical evidence removed from the premises being inspected. Product samples (raw materials, in-process goods, and finished products) are listed on the FDA-484, as are samples of extraneous material that may be taken to document conditions observed during the inspection. Extraneous material may include live or dead insects, rodent filth, foreign material, spillage, residues, bacterial swabs, and so forth. Documentary evidence such as labels, copies of production records, invoices, and shipping records are not listed on the FDA-484.

Practices may vary as to the timing of issuance of the FDA-484. Some investigators will issue the form each day when samples are collected. Others will wait until the conclusion of the inspection and issue the form then, to cover all samples collected during the inspection. While firms are undergoing an inspection, it is advisable to request that the form be issued daily when samples are collected, to keep management fully apprised of any materials leaving the premises. The inspected firm also may elect to charge FDA for the materials taken, as they sometimes amount to a considerable value.

Firms undergoing inspection should request that Form FDA-484 be issued daily when samples are collected, to keep management fully apprised of any materials leaving the premises.

Controlled substances present a special case. FDA investigators and special agents are authorized to collect samples of controlled substances under DEA regulations. In these cases immediate completion of all required paperwork, including the FDA-484, is essential.

FDA-463, Affidavit

This form is often prepared by the inspecting FDA employee at the conclusion of an inspection. This form historically has been used primarily to document the connection with interstate commerce necessary to establish jurisdiction, but in recent years its use has expanded to serve as a vehicle to also document individual responsibility. The FDA employee may represent that the statements related to the individual employee job responsibility are intended to qualify the individual to make the statements that follow on the affidavit. Many FDA employees will refer to such statements to bolster other evidence of individual responsibility that has been gathered during the inspection.

Affidavits come in several forms, with individual form numbers. All have basically the same purpose. There are several fill-in-the-blank affidavits that are intended to serve common purposes, such as a "Dealer's Statement," "Warehouseman's Statement," affidavits for use with United Parcel Service shipments, and so forth. The FDA-463 is the most common one, however, and is simply a blank page with the necessary introductory wording preprinted on it with a space for the affiant's name and the name of the FDA employee taking the statement.

In regulatory inspections, FDA uses affidavits principally to establish linkage between evidence that is collected by investigators and the element of interstate commerce.

In regulatory inspections, FDA uses affidavits principally to establish linkage between evidence that is collected by investigators and the element of interstate commerce. Should the inspection lead to legal action and a trial, the agency's lawyers will subpoena the original records and call the affiant to testify, using the affidavit as a record of his or her prior statements.

Because company attorneys often advise their clients not to sign FDA affidavits, investigators are trained to read the affidavit out loud and ask if the statements are true. When a verbal affirmation is received, the investigator will so annotate the affidavit, and will secure a witnesses' signature if possible. The investigator will ask the proposed affiant why he or she is not willing to sign, and also will annotate the reason given. For this reason, many attorneys advise their clients not to read or listen to the content of FDA affidavits. The decision of whether to read, sign, or verbally affirm an affidavit should be made based on advice of legal counsel. Experienced FDA investigators are accustomed to this response and will generally not press the matter further when they encounter refusals to sign or listen to the content of affidavits.

Other Forms

Other forms for special purposes may come into play during a regulatory inspection. Examples include facsimile forms used to make manual "true copies" of invoices or shipping documents; consumer complaint forms used by the agency to record complaints; the FDA-472, a special form of the FDA-484 issued to truck drivers or operators of other interstate conveyances; and various other special purpose forms such as checklists used to record inspectional observations.

FDA Policies and Administrative Procedures

The actions of FDA employees are directed by a variety of internal policies, procedures, guidelines, and guidance documents that are issued by FDA headquarters units.

The *Investigations Operations Manual* contains a wide range of information, from administrative matters to detailed instructions for preparing and routing of inspection reports. Instructions found in its chapters include instructions for filling out FDA forms and expense reports, and policies and guidance for how to effectively interact with company managers. This manual contains basic reference information that is used on a day-to-day basis by investigators.

The manual is of primary importance during litigation involving FDA inspections because it defines the standard of conduct and procedures that FDA personnel are expected to follow during their day-to-day activities. The manual provides the basis of the presumption of official regularity in the performance of duty. Investigators are expected to justify and obtain approval for any deviation from established procedures outlined in the manual.

Most compliance programs are now available from FDA's Internet website and are valuable references for use in preparing for particular types of FDA inspections.

The *Compliance Program Guidance Manual* is a compilation of specific instructions for directed inspections of segments of the industries regulated by FDA. The manual is divided into chapters by industry. It serves as the primary document that guides the conduct of most inspections. Most compliance programs are now available from FDA's Internet website and are valuable references for use in preparing for particular types of FDA inspections.

FDA *Compliance Policy Guides* (CPGs) are internal policy documents. FDA describes issues and responses in simple policy statements, which field personnel use during their inspections to support their findings. Many CPGs establish informal internal action levels for analytical findings on regulatory samples.

Others establish "direct reference" procedures, where the local FDA office can expedite the processing of regulatory actions by eliminating the need for technical or policy reviews by headquarters staff. If "direct reference" criteria are met, the district may initiate legal proceedings without the need for concurrence and prior approval by some of the usual reviewing offices in FDA headquarters. CPGs are not enforceable documents because they have not been subjected to notice-and-comment rulemaking.

The *Regulatory Procedures Manual* is maintained by the Office of Enforcement within the Office of Regulatory Affairs (ORA). It addresses policies and procedures for processing regulatory actions by the field force. It also establishes standard format and provides certain standardized templates with language for pleadings in criminal and civil cases. In addition, the manual provides regulatory guidance in certain other non-litigation matters, such as product recalls.

The *Investigations Training Manual* consists of a series of outlines used during the initial orientation/basic training program for new investigators. This manual provides training in the basic provisions of the FDCA and other laws enforced by FDA, and orientation to the major reference documents, programs, and procedures used by field personnel. The manual is used heavily by new investigators during their initial months on the job, but usually is not often referred to following completion of basic training.

FDA *Field Management Directives* (FMDs) are documents that address administrative and compliance matters dealt with by the field force. Most of the topics in these documents are of limited significance for inspections. Exceptions include FMDs on recall management, consumer complaints, and the classification of EIRs.

FDA *Staff Manual Guides* are issued at the highest level of the agency, and are mainly human resources and financial management documents. They also contain formal delegations of authority, establish position names, describe procedures for the issuance of official credentials, and state policies involving ethical conduct and other matters that have bearing on regulatory inspections.

Inspection Technical Guides and their earlier versions known as Inspection Bulletins are produced and distributed by ORA. These documents are short, focused technical references on topics relevant to inspections.

All of the aforementioned manuals and publications are accessible from FDA's website, http://www.fda.gov.

Chapter 16

FDA Enforcement: How It Works

Vernessa T. Pollard, Partner, & Anisa Mohanty, Associate, McDermott Will & Emery, LLP, Washington, D.C.

Key Points

- The Food and Drug Administration (FDA) has broad discretion to decide which violations of law it will take action against, and what kind of action it will take.

- The primary objective of FDA's enforcement program is to promote compliance with the Federal Food, Drug, and Cosmetic Act (FDCA), and with FDA regulations promulgated under authority of that act. By promoting compliance, FDA also deters regulated companies and individuals from conducting their businesses in ways that create substantial risks of noncompliance.

- Some enforcement actions may be brought directly by FDA against products, individuals, or companies. Other enforcement actions must be brought by the Department of Justice (DOJ) on behalf of FDA. In either setting, the evidence for these actions almost always arises from FDA inspections and/or investigations by FDA.

- The enforcement tool that FDA uses most frequently is a 483 list issued at the conclusion of an FDA inspection. This tool has been effective in promoting compliance through corrective action. Where FDA believes that a company's response to a 483 has been inadequate, it may issue a Warning Letter seeking more robust or comprehensive corrective action.

- The issuance of adverse publicity is a form of FDA enforcement that can have a dramatic and immediate effect on a company or a product or both.

- FDA may bring seizure actions to remove violative products from commerce. Such products may be seized without any notice to the company or prior judicial hearing.

- FDA may recommend, and DOJ may bring, injunction cases to prevent a company from continuing to manufacture and market products in a way that does not comply with FDA regulations.

- DOJ may file criminal charges against individuals and companies for violations of either the FDCA or other federal criminal laws, or both. An individual may be prosecuted for violating the FDCA even if he or she did not know of or participate in the events that led directly to the violation. It is enough if the individual had the power and authority to prevent or correct the violation but failed to do so. The existence of this doctrine of "strict liability" has been an important underpinning of FDA enforcement for more than 60 years, although few of such cases have been brought in the past decade.

INTRODUCTION

The Food and Drug Administration (FDA) is a law enforcement organization. It enforces the law through a variety of administrative actions and, with the approval and assistance of the Department of Justice (DOJ), through judicial actions. The agency can take action against products, companies, and individuals. FDA has broad discretion to decide which violations it will take enforcement action against; what kind of action to take; and which products, companies, or individuals to bring the action against. FDA takes enforcement actions to remove violative products from the market or prevent their distribution in the first place, to obtain compliance with FDA requirements, to punish persons responsible for causing violations, and to deter others from violating FDA requirements in the same or similar ways.

THE SOURCE OF FDA'S ENFORCEMENT POWERS

FDA's enforcement power comes primarily from the Federal Food, Drug, and Cosmetic Act.

FDA's enforcement power comes primarily from the Federal Food, Drug, and Cosmetic Act (FDCA). FDA is empowered to take enforcement action against products that are either "adulterated" or "misbranded" as defined in the FDCA, and against companies and individuals that cause products to become adulterated or misbranded. FDA also can prevent the marketing of products that are required to be approved by the agency but do not have approval.

The FDCA is not static; it has been amended by Congress repeatedly since it was first enacted in 1938. Many of the amendments expand FDA's enforcement powers by defining conduct that constitutes a crime or authorizing FDA to take an ever-enlarging array of enforcement actions. In 2009, Congress amended the FDCA to give FDA new regulatory authority over an entire industry—tobacco products.

In addition to the violations defined in the FDCA, FDA can define and establish requirements that are "binding" and have "the full force and effect of law." FDA does this by promulgating regulations—all of which are codified in Title 21 of the U.S. Code of Federal Regulations (C.F.R.). For this reason, when FDA promulgates a regulation, interpreting some requirement in the FDCA, it is establishing a new, more specific, legal requirement. Then FDA can take enforcement action against noncompliance of the requirement.

FDA also promotes compliance by issuing informal guidance documents that announce its interpretation of the FDCA and FDA regulations. These guidance documents are not legally binding on either FDA or the industries regulated by it. They influence how companies act, however, because FDA usually will not take enforcement action if a company is operating consistent with its advice.

FDA's Enforcement Philosophy

A primary guiding principle in FDA's enforcement policy is to use all appropriate legal means to secure compliance with FDA laws and regulations.

♦ FDA encourages and expects compliance with the laws and regulations it enforces.

♦ FDA conducts inspections and investigations of the industries it regulates to continuously assess compliance and discover noncompliance.

♦ FDA protects the public health by using its enforcement tools, both administrative and judicial, according to the seriousness of the violation and the impact and consequences of that violation.

Historically, FDA has made decisions regarding enforcement action by weighing six factors:

♦ the seriousness of the violation,

♦ the number of people affected by the violative conduct or product,

♦ the extent to which people would be affected,

♦ the strength of the evidence of the violation,

♦ the likelihood of success of the enforcement action, and

♦ the need for FDA to resolve the problem.

How FDA Brings Enforcement Actions

For the most part, enforcement actions are built on evidence of noncompliance with FDA requirements that is gathered by FDA investigators from the district offices during FDA inspections or by agents in FDA's Office of Criminal Investigations (OCI), supplemented by information obtained from other sources. The agency also may rely on information that a company submits to meet FDA requirements (such as adverse reaction reports) or that a company submits voluntarily (such as information about product recalls).

For most administrative and civil judicial actions, compliance officers in the district office evaluate the evidence. The district office makes an initial decision about whether a violation exists, its significance, the need for enforcement action, and the kind of action that seems appropriate. In some situations, the power to initiate an enforcement action rests with the district office. In other situations, the district office must submit a recommendation for enforcement action to the Office of Compliance in the FDA Center that has jurisdiction over the product. That office may either authorize the action or, if required by FDA internal procedures, obtain further review and concurrence of the proposed action from either FDA's Office of Regulatory Affairs or the Office of the Chief Counsel (OCC), or both. For criminal enforcement, the evidence is most often reviewed and assessed by OCI.

Enforcement actions are built on evidence of noncompliance with FDA requirements.

Types of Enforcement

FDA may bring enforcement actions through either administrative or judicial procedures.

FDA may bring enforcement actions through either administrative or judicial procedures. Administrative enforcement may be brought by the agency itself; it does not need either approval from DOJ to initiate the action or an order from a federal court to impose a sanction. As a result, administrative enforcement can be resource-efficient for FDA. Individuals and companies that are the subject of FDA administrative enforcement actions may challenge those actions in court but, in most instances, a court will not intervene in FDA's decision to initiate an administrative action until there is a final agency action. For some administrative actions, FDA regulations or established practice require the agency to provide an opportunity for a hearing, or an informal meeting, before FDA makes its decision.

Judicial enforcement actions involve DOJ and the federal courts. FDA does not have the power to go to court itself to obtain an order against a product, company, or individuals. Rather, the agency may recommend to DOJ that an action be filed on its behalf. The department may either accept FDA's recommendation, modify it (by revising the alleged violations, naming different products or persons as defendants, or changing the type of action to be sought), or decline the recommendation altogether. Enforcement of the FDCA is brought in federal court in the state in which the products are located, the facility in which the products were manufactured is located, or where the company or individuals who may have been responsible for the violation do business.

These two types of enforcement action—administrative and judicial—are not mutually exclusive. First, FDA repeatedly has announced that it is free to use either or both to accomplish its enforcement objectives. Second, FDA's inability to resolve a problem administratively often will be used to justify a subsequent request to DOJ for judicial enforcement. Finally, the mere threat of judicial enforcement, particularly prosecution, provides FDA with significant leverage in discussions with potential defendants to obtain a lesser administrative sanction. Both types of enforcement actions have two predictable consequences. They lead to greater FDA scrutiny of the responsible companies in the future and they decrease FDA's confidence in the companies and individuals against whom enforcement actions have been brought.

ENFORCEMENT TRENDS

Over the past decade, FDA has altered significantly its approach to enforcement actions. The agency has developed compliance policies and procedures that are more varied, more resource-efficient, and swifter than many of the traditional enforcement actions. As a result, FDA's current enforcement approach relies more heavily on administrative (rather than judicial) enforcement actions; greater coordination between district offices and the relevant FDA offices of compliance and of product evaluation; greater coordination with state enforcement authorities, and with professional and trade associations; greater use of adverse publicity; greater reliance on rulemaking to promote compliance; and the use of informal policy guidance documents to encourage companies to meet FDA's compliance expectations even if those expectations are not legally binding. In the area of judicial enforcement, FDA has focused on cases involving fraud, intentional or knowing violations of the FDCA, and on cases involving product defects with significant consequences for users.

Recent enforcement trends reflect FDA's efforts to maintain a robust and credible enforcement program in an era of limited resources. While there have been fewer FDA seizure and injunction cases in the past decade, the number of criminal convictions has increased. In addition, FDA has cooperated with DOJ in its review of evidence and initiation of actions under the False Claims Act. These cases usually involve both criminal and civil dispositions and are based on off-label promotion, including charges of misbranding under the FDCA.

While there have been fewer FDA seizure and injunction cases in the past decade, the number of criminal convictions involving fraud and intentional offenses has increased.

Congressional expansion of FDA's regulatory authority is not always matched by a commensurate increase in the agency's budget. Thus, FDA continuously re-evaluates its enforcement programs to identify ways to maintain deterrence and promote compliance with the resources it has. One agency strategy is to focus on enforcement actions that will have a substantial impact, and to pursue those actions vigorously. It has been persistent in obtaining full compliance in those circumstances where it has taken action. In this regard, FDA enforcement is both opportunistic and unpredictable.

ADMINISTRATIVE ENFORCEMENT

FDA has a wide variety of administrative enforcement powers. Many are informal and can be imposed without significant review within the agency. Others are brought only after extensive review. Many of FDA's administrative enforcement powers apply to all FDA-regulated products; some apply only to certain products.

List of Inspectional Observations

The core of FDA's enforcement programs has been, and remains, the inspections conducted by FDA investigators.

The core of FDA's enforcement programs has been, and remains, the inspections conducted by FDA investigators. These inspections gather the evidence of noncompliance that supports the agency's enforcement actions. During the period from 2011–2016, FDA conducted, on average, about 24,000 inspections per year of manufacturing, retail, and related facilities in the United States.[1] During the years 2008–2011, FDA increased its inspections of facilities outside this country that make products for sale in the United States (from about 950 in 2008[2] to about 1,900 in fiscal year 2016[3]).

At the conclusion of an FDA inspection, the FDA investigators may issue a List of Inspectional Observations (FDA Form 483). This form—provided to a company following a facility inspection—identifies those observations that, in the opinion of the investigator, are deviations from FDA requirements. FDA investigators issue 483 Lists of Observations in about 40 percent of all inspections. Out of about 17,700 inspections in fiscal year 2016,[4] FDA issued a total of about 4,500 Form 483s, in about 25 percent of all inspections.[5] A 483 should be viewed not only as part of an FDA inspection but also as an FDA enforcement action because, almost without exception, it results in corrective action by a company to achieve compliance with FDA requirements. FDA expects that the company's corrective actions not only address the investigator's specific observations but also will address the systems, procedures, or organizational structure that may, unless changed, permit a recurrence of the noncompliances or similar deficiencies to those listed in the 483.

In most circumstances, a company's response to the 483 will resolve the noncompliance and no further enforcement action will be sought. A company can, however, expect a follow-up inspection during which FDA will look to verify that corrective measures described in the 483 response have been effectively implemented.

Warning Letters

An FDA Warning Letter is just that: a written warning from FDA that a company is, in the agency's view, not operating in compliance with FDA requirements.

The primary purpose of the letter is to achieve voluntary compliance by threatening judicial enforcement if the company's noncompliance is not remedied.

In the late 1980s and early 1990s, Warning Letters became the most prominent type of FDA enforcement action. Even after that peak, during the period from 1993 to 2002, FDA issued, on average, about 1,200 Warning Letters per year. However, from 2003 through 2010, that number decreased to, on average, about 550 per year. In fiscal year 2011, FDA issued 1,720 Warning Letters.[6] In fiscal year 2012, that number increased significantly to 4,882. The primary source of this increase was more than 4,000 tobacco retailer Warning Letters issued for alleged violations of tobacco sale and marketing restrictions. In fiscal year 2016, FDA issued 14,590 Warning Letters.[7]

Whether a Warning Letter is initiated by the district or the Center, a Warning Letter represents a formal declaration by the agency that the operations and conditions at a facility do not comply with FDA requirements and that products manufactured in that facility will continue to be either adulterated or misbranded unless the company changes its systems, policies, procedures, or performance.

In most cases, a Warning Letter is based on the results of an FDA inspection that the agency believes has demonstrated reasonably significant deviations from FDA requirements. Therefore, the noncompliant circumstances described in the Warning Letter closely parallel the key items in the 483. In most cases, but not all, if a company has made an adequate and sufficiently comprehensive response to the 483, FDA will not issue a Warning Letter. An adequate response to the 483, however, does not mean that a Warning Letter will not be issued.

In most cases, a Warning Letter is based on the results of an FDA inspection that the agency believes has demonstrated reasonably significant deviations from FDA requirements.

The basic elements of a Warning Letter are fairly straightforward. The letter summarizes the facts or circumstances found during an FDA inspection, labeling review, adverse reaction report, recall, or some other underlying event. The letter asserts that those facts or circumstances cause the recipient's products to be adulterated or misbranded, and describes the facts giving rise to a finding of noncompliance. The letter provides the recipient with 15 working days to notify the agency of the corrective actions that the company has taken or intends to take. Finally, the letter notifies the recipient that a failure to make an adequate response may lead to a product seizure, an injunction, or some other enforcement action.

A Warning Letter may, in some circumstances, be more than a warning. In many settings, the issuance of a Warning Letter results in the facility that is the subject of the letter being put on "compliance hold." As a result, FDA may not approve a pending product application or re-issue an export certificate for a product manufactured at that facility until the issues raised in the letter are resolved to FDA's satisfaction.

Typically, Warning Letters will advise the recipient that the instance(s) of non-compliance described in the letter should not be read as a comprehensive list, and that the recipient has an obligation to consider the issues raised by the Warning Letter as they may apply to other of the company's products or activities. This standard language reflects FDA's effort to maximize the degree of corrective action obtained from issuing the Warning Letter. It also underscores the need for companies to review the significance of the letter beyond the particular instances of noncompliance described in it.

The legal authority for a Warning Letter is found in the section of the FDCA that allows FDA to issue "a suitable written notice or warning" when it believes that a violation exists but has chosen not to pursue a judicial sanction, at least initially. While the issuance of a warning is authorized, it is not required. In addition, FDA is under no obligation to issue a Warning Letter before recommending a judicial enforcement action. FDA has found Warning Letters to be effective in obtaining compliance and has chosen to use them in numerous situations where, in earlier years, it may have recommended a seizure action or an injunction. Recently, FDA has started using Warning Letters to obtain specific and targeted corrective actions. For example, certain Warning Letters issued in 2012 requested that companies hire a third-party consultant and submit to the relevant FDA compliance office a certification and reports demonstrating that the consultant has conducted a Good Manufacturing Practice (GMP) audit to verify the companies' corrective actions. In 2016, FDA continued to focus on GMP Warning Letters to active pharmaceutical ingredient (API) suppliers, specifically related to data integrity.

Warning Letters are public information.

Like 483s, Warning Letters are public information. Many Warning Letters are automatically made available by FDA to the public and press, without the need for a formal Freedom of Information request. Therefore, once issued, they stand as a public accusation by FDA that a company's operation does not meet FDA standards and that the company's product(s) violate the law. Moreover, FDA routinely sends a copy of Warning Letters to federal procurement agencies, such as the Department of Defense and the Veterans Administration. These referrals can lead to a decision to terminate federal government contracts to purchase products implicated in the Warning Letter. These are a few of the many reasons why, as a practical matter, a company almost always will provide a comprehensive written response to a Warning Letter.

The primary objective when responding to a Warning Letter is to demonstrate a serious and significant effort by the company to address the allegations of noncompliance. FDA expects, and most companies provide, a response that goes beyond any particular examples or circumstances of non-compliance referenced in the letter to include a comprehensive, "systemic" solution designed to preclude a recurrence of the problems. While some deficiencies may be amenable to specific corrections, many can be addressed only through new or revised company policies and procedures, organizational restructuring, employee training, and/or other broad-based activities. Nevertheless, companies generally do not promise more than they can or are willing to deliver. Therefore, most companies try to describe their corrective actions as precisely as possible, often including particular targeted completion dates or implementation schedules.

If FDA discovers that commitments made in a response to a Warning Letter have not been met and there is no compelling explanation, the recipient can anticipate a significant escalation of FDA enforcement action. Accordingly, commitments that are made in response to a Warning Letter should not be made lightly; well-counseled companies assess realistically what changes they are prepared to make, in what amount of time, and how broadly the changes will be applied throughout the company. In considering the extent of its commitments for corrective action, companies generally keep in mind that FDA views a Warning Letter as a "second bite at the apple" (because the company's response to the underlying 483 is seen as inadequate). Thus, in most circumstances, companies will significantly "up the ante" in undertaking corrective actions beyond those described in their 483 response.

If a company disagrees with the alleged instances of noncompliance discussed in the Warning Letter, it may decide to explain why a change is unnecessary or would create even greater problems. In some circumstances, a company that disagrees with the agency may choose to make a change anyway because the company believes that it is unlikely that it will be able to convince FDA that its present processes and procedures are adequate. Often, a company will express its disagreement with FDA and explain its position, but implement changes anyway.

As is apparent, a Warning Letter can result in a significant amount of corrective actions by a company. While these corrections are the principal objective in FDA issuing the letter, it serves another important FDA enforcement purpose: a Warning Letter documents that the company, and the particular person to whom it is addressed, has received formal notice that the company's operations are not satisfactory. If the same or similar noncompliances continue, the existence of this "prior notice" or "prior warning" may be a significant element in FDA persuading DOJ to bring either an injunction action or a criminal prosecution.

A Warning Letter documents that the company, and the particular person to whom it is addressed, has received formal notice that the company's operations are not satisfactory.

Because a Warning Letter can result in nearly as much corrective action as can be obtained through a judicial injunction action, and because injunctions are resource-intensive for FDA and require approval by DOJ, FDA is much more likely to issue a Warning Letter than it is to seek an injunction where it believes that a company's policies, processes, and procedures need to be changed in order to prevent continued noncompliance.

Untitled Letters and "It Has Come to Our Attention" Letters

In recent years, FDA has also notified companies of violations that do not meet its threshold for regulatory significance for a Warning Letter through Untitled Letters. These letters are intended to serve as formal, documented notification of a violation of law and give companies an opportunity to come into compliance without threat of further FDA action. Following significant First Amendment litigation, such as *United States v. Caronia*, 703 F.3d 149 (2d Cir. 2012) (holding that the government may not prohibit or criminalize truthful off-label promotional speech); *Amarin Pharma, Inc. v. FDA*, 119 F. Supp. 3d 196 (S.D.N.Y. 2015) (holding that the government may not pursue misbranding provisions under the FDCA for statements that were truthful and non-misleading); and *United States v. Vascular Solutions, Inc.*, Cr. No. 14-926 (W.D. Tex. 2016) (jury finding that speech that is "solely truthful and not misleading" cannot be basis for misbranding charge), FDA has increasingly issued Untitled Letters rather than Warning Letters to manufacturers for off-label promotions. This represents a shift in enforcement philosophy over the agency's approach to issue Warning Letters.

FDA has also issued "It Has Come to Our Attention" Letters. The agency appears to issue these when it needs to clarify information before it issues an Untitled Letter, Warning Letter, or schedule an inspection.

Adverse Publicity

The FDCA authorizes FDA to issue publicity to warn the public about possible adverse consequences associated with the use of the products it regulates. This statutory authority provides FDA with a broad platform to not only issue public advisories but also to publicize significant enforcement actions.

FDA routinely issues press announcements of its enforcement actions.

As a matter of general practice, FDA routinely issues press announcements of its enforcement actions, such as the issuance of a Warning Letter, the institution of a seizure, the signing of a consent decree of injunction, or even a criminal conviction. Thus, there can be no assurance that FDA will refrain from seeking publicity about any of these events. Because the effects of FDA-initiated adverse publicity can be devastating to a product or company, the agency's ability to issue such publicity cannot be taken lightly. Indeed, an FDA press release about a public health problem with a product can be the most immediate and effective form of enforcement action—it can end the product's marketability. FDA has significant media and public credibility, particularly when it comes to product-specific safety concerns.

While FDA may be willing to provide notice to a company that publicity about it or one of its products is about to issue, it generally does not negotiate with the company about the text of the FDA announcement. In most cases, FDA will not share the text of a press communication with a company in advance. Thus, a company can try to contain the potential adverse effects of FDA publicity by issuing its own, preemptive statement. Ultimately, however, there is relatively little a company can do in most circumstances to significantly diminish the effect of an agency adverse press release.

Although FDA routinely issues press releases for enforcement actions, it is most likely to issue a press release to announce a criminal prosecution, an enforcement action against a large corporation, or an enforcement action that involves a well-recognized product or brand. Where FDA has initiated judicial enforcement, a press release may be issued by the U.S. Attorney's Office that is responsible for handling the case. Many U.S. Attorneys' Offices routinely issue press releases about criminal cases.

Adverse publicity issued by either FDA or DOJ may be reported in the local media and, in many circumstances, may become a national story. Any adverse publicity issued by FDA will be reported by the food, drug, and device trade press, and often by the investment community press. The "news" or other story may also be spread by various blogs or other forms of social media.

FDA may publicize the results of its enforcement action by means other than a standard "press release." These include interviews with the press; appearances on television and radio talk shows; speeches at consumer programs, medical and professional association meetings, and professional conferences; descriptions of the enforcement action in congressional testimony; or providing information to be released during a congressional hearing.

While FDA seeks publicity only when it deems necessary, it routinely publishes lists of violative products that have been recalled or have been the subject of other enforcement action in its enforcement report. Some of these reports are repeated or summarized in the trade press, including trade publications that report on specific types of FDA enforcement actions, such as Warning Letters and inspectional observations.

Of course, adverse publicity based on an FDA enforcement action can result merely because the action is public. Indictments in criminal cases, complaints in injunction and seizure cases, Warning Letters, 483s, and other FDA enforcement initiatives are all public documents. Copies of these documents can be obtained from a court, from FDA, and, in many cases, through the Internet. Copies of these documents also can be obtained from FDA under the Freedom of Information Act, either in the name of the requestor or anonymously by obtaining copies through a requesting service.

Recalls

With very few exceptions, product recalls by companies are voluntary.

With very few exceptions, product recalls by companies are voluntary. As a result, FDA is often unaware of the recall until it has begun. When a company recalls a product because it is adulterated or misbranded, FDA counts that as an enforcement action even though it is undertaken voluntarily.

Although companies are not required by law to report most recalls to FDA, recalls of FDA-regulated products are reported to the agency regularly by companies in deference to FDA's request that it be advised. Because a recall involves the removal from the market of a product that is adulterated or misbranded within the meaning of the FDCA, companies report their recalls so that FDA knows that the products are already being removed from commerce and, therefore, an enforcement action is unnecessary. Companies also report their recalls to FDA to maintain a good relationship with the agency, and to demonstrate that they have the capacity to identify their own noncompliance and the willingness to take action without being forced to do so.

From 1998 to 2007, companies increased the number of recalls from approximately 3,500 per year to more than 5,500 in 2007. During fiscal year 2009, FDA recorded approximately 2,700 "recall events" involving about 8,000 products. In fiscal year 2010, FDA recorded approximately 3,800 recall events involving about 9,300 products. In 2012, these numbers peaked with approximately 4,000 events involving about 9,500 products. However, in fiscal year 2016, FDA recorded approximately 2,800 recall events involving about 8,300 products.[8] Each recall may affect one particular manufactured lot of a product or all of a product made during a substantial period of time. Some recalls involve many products.

There are, of course, many reasons for a company to recall a product quite apart from FDA; these include a desire that customers not receive an inferior product, a desire to limit exposure to liability litigation if a user were injured as a result of use of a product (a use that could have been avoided by a recall), a desire to avoid adverse publicity associated with the distribution of a defective or inferior product, and a desire to maintain the reputation of the company or of the product/brand.

Most companies that decide to recall a product adhere to FDA's recall guidelines. These guidelines advise companies to follow a recall strategy that addresses the depth of the recall (to the wholesale or retail level); the need for a public warning; a communication plan to notify wholesalers, retailers, hospitals, and others being asked to return the product; and a process for checking the effectiveness of the recall.

A recall strategy addresses:
- *the depth of a recall,*
- *the need for a public warning,*
- *a communication plan, and*
- *a process for checking the effectiveness of the recall.*

The agency can and often does request that a company conduct a recall. When FDA learns about the distribution of a product that it believes presents a significant public health risk or a gross fraud, and where a company has not taken action to remove the product from the market, FDA may contact the company directly and request that the company conduct a recall.

If a company does not respond to such a request, FDA in effect can initiate the recall on its own by contacting the company's accounts—distributors, warehousers, hospitals, or individuals—and advising them directly of FDA's conclusion that the product is adulterated or misbranded and should not be used.

During these FDA-initiated recalls, the agency may request that the product be returned to the manufacturer. FDA has initiated a recall in this way very rarely, and there is no direct statutory authority for such a recall. The basis for an FDA-initiated recall would appear to be FDA's authority to notify the public of any dangers associated with the use of FDA-regulated products together with its authority to seek adverse publicity. While companies may complain about FDA initiating a recall, the agency will do so when it concludes that a significant public health problem exists, that other enforcement actions may be inefficient or burdensome, and that the company has not itself taken adequate action.

Although FDA lacks general authority to order a product recall, Congress specifically has provided FDA with that authority in five product areas:

◆ Medical Devices: FDA may order a company to conduct a recall if it finds "a reasonable probability that a device intended for human use could cause serious adverse health consequences or death." Before ordering a recall of a dangerous medical device, FDA must provide the company with an opportunity for an informal hearing to discuss whether a recall is necessary. FDA can exercise this authority even if the company already has voluntarily recalled some of the product.

◆ Biologics: FDA can order the recall of a licensed biological product if it presents "an imminent or substantial hazard to the public health."

◆ Tobacco Products: FDA may order the immediate cessation of distribution, and subsequently a recall of a tobacco product where FDA has found that there is a "reasonable probability that the tobacco product contains a manufacturing or other defect not ordinarily contained in tobacco products on the market that would cause serious adverse health consequences or death." The responsible person has an opportunity for an informal hearing within 10 days of FDA's order.

◆ Infant Formula Products: FDA can order the recall of infant formula products that lack the required nutrients or are otherwise adulterated or misbranded.

◆ Foods: Where FDA determines that there is a reasonable probability of adulteration or misbranding of a food and that "the use of or exposure to [the food] will cause serious adverse health consequences or death" to humans or animals. FDA may, initially, order the cessation of distribution of the food. Before ordering a recall, FDA must give the responsible company an opportunity to take a recall voluntarily.

Enforcement Concerning Product Approvals

The FDCA provides that FDA may withdraw its product approval.

Many FDA-regulated products can be sold only if FDA approves an application for marketing. By the same token, the FDCA provides that FDA may withdraw its approval in a number of circumstances, including noncompliance with good manufacturing practice (GMP) requirements, false or misleading labeling, new evidence that the product is no longer safe or effective, or the submission of false statements to FDA.

To withdraw a product approval, FDA must publish a notice in the *Federal Register* of its intention to withdraw and invite comments from the company holding the approval as well as others. Next, the agency must publish a notice of an administrative hearing to decide whether the approval should be withdrawn. In most circumstances, however, no hearing is held. Rather, FDA and the company marketing the product settle the dispute, usually by agreeing to an orderly withdrawal of the product from the market or by agreeing on a labeling change.

When a public health hazard exists, FDA may temporarily suspend its approval of certain product applications without any prior notice or opportunity for an administrative hearing. FDA approvals of new drug and new animal drug applications may be suspended summarily if FDA finds that the product creates an "imminent hazard" to the public health. An approved biologics license can be summarily suspended if continued distribution would create a danger to health. FDA may revoke a permit to make thermally processed foods in hermetically sealed containers if the manufacturer is not in compliance with FDA's low-acid canned foods regulations.

FDA may temporarily suspend the approval for a drug, but only after providing an opportunity for an informal hearing. If there is reasonable probability that the continued distribution of the drug would cause serious adverse health consequences or death, the agency may order the temporary suspension of the distribution of drugs covered by an approved New Drug Application (NDA) or Abbreviated New Drug Application (ANDA) but only after it has provided an opportunity for a hearing on any disputed facts. The suspension of distribution of an NDA or ANDA drug is authorized if FDA finds that the applicant has engaged in bribery or submitted false statements, or has engaged in flagrant and repeated material violations of the drug GMP requirements so that such violations undermine the safety of the drugs and have not been corrected within a reasonable period of time.

FDA may refuse to review a product application if the agency concludes that the data in the pending application is unreliable and possibly fraudulent.

In addition to withdrawing or temporarily suspending product approvals, FDA may refuse to review one or more of a company's product applications, even if they contain the required evidence of safety and effectiveness, if FDA concludes that data in the pending application is unreliable and possibly fraudulent. This deferral of review is one element of FDA's "Application Integrity Policy." When FDA questions the reliability of data in a pending product application and invokes this policy, the company that submitted the application must do four things for FDA to proceed with its review:

♦ cooperate with FDA in looking for the cause of any wrongdoing that has resulted in the submission of false or unreliable data;

♦ identify to FDA those individuals who were or may have been associated with any wrongdoing, and remove them from positions of authority on FDA matters;

♦ conduct a comprehensive internal review to assess the integrity of its product development and application processes; and

♦ provide a written commitment to FDA to develop a corrective action plan.

In addition, FDA may conduct its own "validity assessment" to ensure that any potential causes of unreliable or false data have been identified and remedied. These activities can take a long time, depending on the apparent source and scope of the data integrity problem. Some companies have had FDA review of their product applications deferred for one to three years while they undertook the prescribed corrective program.

Enforcement Against Imported Products

FDA, working with U.S. Customs and Border Protection (Customs), has authority to prevent products from entering U.S. commerce if those products appear to be adulterated or misbranded, or otherwise violate the FDCA.

When a product is identified by an importer as an FDA-regulated product, that declaration is communicated to FDA by an electronic link between Customs and the agency. If FDA requests, Customs will hold the product for FDA examination or sampling. In fact, FDA examines only a very small portion of the FDA-regulated products that are offered for importation each year—around 2 percent. This reflects the enormous volume of import entries of FDA-regulated products each year and the lack of FDA resources available. If FDA decides to take an enforcement action against an import, however, its powers are significant.

FDA examines only a small portion of FDA-regulated products that are offered for importation each year.

First, the standard for taking enforcement action is relatively low. FDA may refuse entry into U.S. commerce if the product merely "appears" to be violative. Second, FDA's interference with an import can have a significant economic impact, particularly for perishable products or products with short shelf lives. Thus, even the temporary detention of an import for examination pending a final decision on entry often leads to "voluntary" corrective action by the importer without the issuance of a formal refusal of entry. Finally, FDA may block importations of products by placing an automatic detention on all products that meet the detention criteria. For example, if FDA has evidence demonstrating that a certain product made in a particular country has regularly been shown to be contaminated, FDA can issue, on the basis of that historical data, an automatic detention to preclude the importation of all entries of that product from that country.

Because products can be refused entry on the basis of examination, sampling, or "otherwise," and because importation of products from outside the United States traditionally has been considered a privilege, not a right, FDA's significant authority to control the importation of violative products has been generally sustained. A few courts, however, have questioned whether such FDA detention criteria are individual enforcement actions that the agency may pursue at its discretion, or whether they are "rules" that FDA can impose only after rulemaking. Notwithstanding this unresolved legal issue, FDA has established an effective, even if very selective, enforcement process for those imports that the agency has resources to assess.

The issue of FDA's ability to effectively "guard the border" against noncompliant products has been seriously assessed in the past few years. FDA has observed that the nation increasingly relies on other countries to produce the food, drugs, devices, and cosmetics that are consumed here. Fifteen to 20 percent of all foods, nearly two-thirds of fruits and vegetables,[9] half the medical devices, about 40 percent of finished drug products, and about 80 percent of active pharmaceutical ingredients (APIs) used to make finished drug products for sale in the United States are manufactured abroad.[10] In fiscal year 2015, it was estimated that 34 million shipments of FDA-regulated products were imported into the country.[11] To address this situation, FDA has, among other strategies, established foreign offices in China, India, Europe, Latin America, and the Middle East. It also has increased its inspection of foreign establishments. In addition to its import entry authority, FDA has begun to issue Warning Letters to foreign manufacturing facilities. In 2016, FDA issued a number of Warning Letters to foreign manufacturing facilities for data integrity and API quality.

The issue of FDA's ability to effectively "guard the border" against noncompliant products has been seriously assessed in the past few years.

As a result of congressional action to prevent acts of bioterrorism by the use of poisonous food, FDA is authorized to detain any food offered for import into the United States if the agency has "credible evidence" that the food presents a threat of "serious adverse health consequences or death" to humans or animals. The importer or owner of the food may appeal FDA's decision. In addition, food establishments must register with FDA, and FDA is authorized to hold any imported food if the foreign manufacturing facility is not registered. To allow FDA to exercise its regulatory powers over imported food, companies must give FDA notice of their intent to import foods into the United States prior to its arrival at an American port. Moreover, under the FDA Food Safety Modernization Act (FSMA), signed into law in January 2011, FDA is authorized to require importers to perform supplier verification activities and to obtain certifications that imported foods comply with safety requirements.

FDA is authorized to detain any food offered for import into the United States if the agency has "credible evidence" that the food presents a threat of "serious adverse health consequences or death" to humans or animals.

Congress further expanded FDA's authority to protect the safety of the U.S. drug supply under the Food and Drug Administration Safety and Innovation Act (FDASIA), which was signed into law in July 2012. Although primarily focused on drugs and devices, the statute gives FDA expanded enforcement authority for other products. For example, FDASIA specifies that violations that occur outside of the United States are subject to enforcement in the United States if the individual or entity intended to import the violative FDA-regulated product into the United States or committed acts in furtherance of the violation in the United States. FDASIA also expanded FDA's authority with respect to current Good Manufacturing Practices (cGMP) and authority to enforce requirements related to supply chain management.

Civil Money Penalties

For certain products, Congress has authorized the agency to obtain a civil money penalty. A civil money penalty is a fine that is assessed against a company, an individual, or both. FDA has civil money penalty authority in 10 program areas. In most of them, FDA has been authorized to impose the penalty itself, administratively. In a few areas, only federal courts have the authority to impose the penalty.

FDA has the authority to impose a civil money penalty for most violations of FDA requirements applicable to medical devices. FDA can impose these fines administratively; it does not need the approval of DOJ or an order from a court. For many violations, FDA can assess a penalty only if the violation is "significant" or "knowing," or a company can avoid a fine by showing that, notwithstanding the violation, it has operated in "substantial compliance" or that there have been no product defects or significant adverse consequences as a result of the violation. FDA may impose a civil money penalty of up to $15,000 for each violation or up to $1,000,000 for all violations involved in a single civil money penalty proceeding. A company or an individual that has been fined by FDA may appeal the fine to a federal court of appeals.

FDA also may seek a civil money penalty against companies or individuals for violating provisions of the FDCA covering radiation-emitting products. Violations that could lead to a fine include the manufacture or distribution of an electronic product that does not meet applicable federal standards, issuing false certificates of compliance with standards, or the failure to permit an FDA inspection or make an FDA-required report. For radiation-emitting products, FDA cannot impose a civil money penalty administratively. Therefore, FDA must request that DOJ file a complaint for a penalty in a federal court.

Under the Prescription Drug Marketing Act (PDMA), FDA is authorized to seek civil money penalties but only against companies, not individuals. A company can be assessed a fine if a representative of the company has been convicted of selling drug samples or if the company fails to report to FDA the fact that any of its representatives have been convicted of such violation. Under certain circumstances, a company can avoid a civil money penalty by demonstrating that it could not reasonably have been expected to have detected the violation, notwithstanding its having an internal audit system to detect possible wrongdoing by its employees. The fines that may be imposed range from $50,000 to $1,000,000, depending on the number of violations, the similarity of violations if more than one company representative is involved, and the number of violations that have occurred within a certain time period. FDA has asserted its authority to impose penalties in this area administratively, although the PDMA refers only to the assessment of a civil money penalty by a federal court.

FDA also may impose a civil money penalty against a company that has failed to comply with an FDA order to recall a defective biological product. The penalty is not imposed for the distribution of the product but for failing to comply with FDA's recall order. Thus, this penalty resembles a fine for contempt and, accordingly, is based on each day of continued noncompliance with the FDA recall order, up to $100,000 per day.

The Generic Drug Enforcement Act of 1992 gave FDA authority to impose civil money penalties administratively for a number of prescribed violations involving ANDAs. Civil penalties may be assessed against companies or individuals for making false statements, failing to disclose a material fact, destroying evidence, obstructing an FDA investigation, or bribing or attempting to bribe an FDA employee. In addition, a company may be assessed a civil money penalty if it uses the services of an individual who has been debarred by FDA from work on drug products. The maximum fine is $250,000 for an individual and $1,000,000 for a company, for each violation.

FDA also may impose a penalty under the National Childhood Vaccine Injury Act of 1986 (for destroying, altering, or falsifying documents submitted by a vaccine manufacturer under the childhood compensation program) and under the Mammography Quality Standards Act of 1992 (for a testing facility's failure to obtain the required certificate for operation or for failing to comply with applicable standards). In addition, the Food Quality Protection Act of 1996 authorized civil money penalties for introducing into interstate commerce a food that contains an unsafe pesticide.

The Food and Drug Administration Amendments Act (FDAAA), enacted in 2007, authorized FDA to impose a civil money penalty if a company fails to comply with FDA requirements to register clinical trials and their results in the National Institutes of Health registry or submits registration or study data information that is false or misleading. A penalty of $10,000 may be imposed; violations that are not corrected within 30 days are subject to a civil penalty of up to $10,000 per day until the violation is corrected. The FDAAA also requires drug companies to develop risk evaluation and mitigation strategies and established new postapproval safety labeling requirements. The amendments also authorized civil money penalties against companies that issue false or misleading direct-to-consumer advertisements, up to $500,000 if violations recur.

In the Family Smoking Prevention and Tobacco Control Act (FSPTCA), signed into law in June 2009, Congress authorized FDA to impose administratively civil money penalties against any person or company that "violates a requirement of this Act." The law authorizes penalties in the range of $250,000 per violation to $1,000,000 for all violations adjudicated together, as well as up to $10,000,000 for violations that continue after FDA notice. Separately, the act authorizes civil money penalties in the range of $250 to $10,000 against retailers who sell tobacco products in violation of the act or the restrictions on sales in FDA regulations. Between 2009 and 2016, FDA initiated more than 8,290 civil money penalty actions against tobacco retailers.[12]

Except where explicitly required by the statute, FDA can impose a civil money penalty without a showing of knowing, willful, or intentional conduct by the person who is fined.

FDA has established procedures for imposing civil money penalties. Under these procedures, the penalty process is initiated by filing a "complaint" alleging the violations on which the proposed penalty is based. If a defendant does not want to challenge the allegations in a complaint, a penalty can be assessed without any further proceedings. If the company or an individual challenges the complaint, FDA and the defendant may settle the case and agree upon a fine, or, if they are unable to reach agreement, the case will go forward. Either there will be a hearing or the hearing officer may decide that there are no genuine issues of material fact justifying a hearing, and he or she may issue a decision on the basis of stipulated facts and other documentation presented by both sides.

In a civil money penalty proceeding, subpoenas can be issued by FDA and by the defendant. There is no right to issue subpoenas, however; the hearing officer may accept or reject a request for the issuance of a subpoena by either party.

FDA has used its civil money penalty authorities infrequently.

FDA has used its civil money penalty authorities infrequently. Part of the reason is that some of these authorities are relatively new. Another reason is that developing a penalty case is resource intensive and may not be as attractive as other enforcement actions because the penalty itself does not correct the problem and FDA does not gain control over the operation of the company as it does by an injunction.

Referral to State Authorities

Given the common definitions of adulteration and misbranding between federal and state laws, and a significant degree of similarity in enforcement authorities, FDA has the option of asking the state authorities to take an enforcement action.

Nearly all states have adopted food, drug, and device laws nearly identical to the FDCA. Most of those states amend their laws to incorporate significant new amendments to the FDCA. More than 20 states have provisions in their laws by which amendments to the FDCA are automatically adopted into and become part of the state law. Given the common definitions of adulteration and misbranding between federal and state laws, and a significant degree of similarity in enforcement authorities, FDA has the option of asking the state authorities to take an enforcement action. The state authorities may take enforcement action against any product manufactured or distributed within their state that violates state law.

To foster cooperation and coordination between FDA and the states, the agency works cooperatively with the National Association of Attorneys General (NAAG). In recent years, the states' Attorneys General have had a particular interest in bringing enforcement actions involving consumer fraud. Once one state has initiated an action, the Attorneys General in other states often will file or threaten to initiate enforcement actions in their states. This strategy has often resulted in an "agreement" between the company and the Attorneys General for many states in which a company undertakes corrective action, such as stopping certain promotional claims and issuing "corrective advertising."

The states' Attorneys General have often worked with both the DOJ and FDA's OCI in the development of cases for alleged healthcare fraud involving state Medicaid programs, and the states often receive a portion of the disposition of the False Claims Act case when the federal settlement is reached.

In addition to enforcement tools similar to those of FDA, state health officials have two additional tools. First, state officials usually can suspend the license of a manufacturer, distributor, or retailer to practice within the state. (Almost all businesses must obtain a state license to operate.) Second, in all states but one, health officials have the authority to embargo violative products on the spot.

In addition to referring certain noncompliant conduct for state enforcement action, FDA may commission state health officials to gather evidence for the agency to use in its federal enforcement action under the FDCA.

Debarment

In limited settings, FDA has the power to debar either a company or an individual. FDA's debarment authority applies to ANDAs, may implicate other drugs and, under the bioterrorism laws, applies to food importation.

In limited settings, FDA has the power to debar either a company or an individual.

An individual who has been debarred may not provide any services to a company that has any FDA approved or pending drug product applications. Thus, when a company submits a drug product application, it must certify to FDA that it has not used the services of any debarred individual in developing or submitting the application.

An individual may be debarred if he or she has been convicted of a felony under federal law for illegal conduct relating to the development or approval of any drug product. An individual also may be debarred if that individual has been convicted of a felony relating to the regulation of any drug, not just activity concerning approval. Debarment may be based on the fact that the individual has been convicted of any one of a number of other federal or state crimes, or "materially participated" in any conduct that was the basis of a conviction, even though that individual was not convicted. Finally, FDA may debar an officer or director of a company or some other "high managerial agent" if that person knew that others at the company were engaging in criminal conduct but did not report that conduct to FDA or the appropriate compliance official within the company.

When a drug company has been debarred, FDA will not accept or review any ANDA submitted by that company. In other words, during the period a company is debarred, FDA will not approve any new ANDAs for that company, although the company may continue to submit and FDA may continue to approve other product applications, and the company may continue to manufacture and distribute any drugs for which it already obtained FDA marketing approval. A company may be debarred if it has been convicted of a felony relating to the development or approval of any ANDA or if that company has been convicted of certain specified federal crimes or state law. FDA may not debar either an individual or a company until it has provided an opportunity for a hearing on any disputed issues of material fact.

Because companies can be debarred only if they have been convicted of a crime, FDA is somewhat limited in its ability to exercise this power because it must await action by DOJ or by a state Attorney General to file criminal charges against a company and obtain a conviction.

The names of individuals and companies that have been debarred are published in the *Federal Register*. Because companies can be debarred only if they have been convicted of a crime, FDA is somewhat limited in its ability to exercise this power because it must await action by DOJ or by a state Attorney General to file criminal charges against a company and obtain a conviction.

From the beginning of the debarment program in 1993 to present, FDA has permanently debarred about 102 individuals and approximately 41 other individuals have been debarred for designated periods of time, most often three to five years.[13] FDA has not yet debarred any company.

Congress has authorized FDA to debar persons who are convicted of a felony relating to food importation or who have engaged in a pattern of offering for import adulterated food that presents a threat of serious adverse health consequences or death to humans or animals.

ADDITIONAL ENFORCEMENT POWERS

Congress has amended the FDCA numerous times since its initial passage in 1938. Many of the amendments have established new or elevated requirements for market entry, addressed specific operational functions of FDA, enhanced the agency's inspection powers, or provided new enforcement authority. Four amendments enacted over the past 20 years have and are likely to have a significant impact on FDA's enforcement powers and their role in protecting the public health—the Safe Medical Devices Act (SMDA), FSPTCA, FSMA, and, most recently, FDASIA.

Medical Devices

In addition to its standard enforcement tools for regulated products, the agency has additional specific enforcement powers regarding medical devices. These authorities were provided by Congress primarily in the SMDA.

The Safe Medical Devices Act provides for additional enforcement authorities against noncompliant medical devices.

For medical devices, an FDA investigator has the power, during an inspection, to order that a device be detained if the investigator has reason to believe that it is adulterated or misbranded. The detention may last only 20 days and is designed to provide FDA with an opportunity to decide whether to bring a seizure action against the product or to obtain an injunction against the company. If FDA decides that it needs more time to consider its next step, however, the period of detention may be extended an additional 10 days.

FDA also may order that a device manufacturer issue a notification to distributors, retailers, doctors, or users of a device if the agency has concluded that the device presents an unreasonable risk of substantial harm to the public and that notification is necessary to eliminate that risk. The only prerequisite to FDA invoking this authority is to "consult with the persons who are to give the notice." In effect, this provision authorizes FDA to mandate that a manufacturer distribute adverse information about its product, which is likely to result in modification of the conditions under which the device is used, cessation of the use of the device due to anxiety associated with the notification, or the return of the device by those who believe that it is no longer safe.

FDA may order a device manufacturer to "immediately cease distribution" of a device and to "immediately notify health professionals and device user facilities. . . to cease use" of it. FDA may invoke this authority if it finds that there is a reasonable probability that the device would cause serious adverse health consequences or death. FDA may make that finding on its own and issue a cease distribution order without giving the company an opportunity for any hearing. FDA must provide an opportunity for such a hearing, however, within 10 days after issuing its order. At that time, the agency may withdraw or modify the order, or it may amend the order to require the company to recall the device. In other words, this statutory provision gives FDA the authority to issue both an injunction and a mandatory recall administratively.

Drugs

Under FDASIA, FDA extended its detention authority to include drugs if the agency has reason to believe that a drug is adulterated or misbranded.

Tobacco Products

The FSPTCA was, to a substantial degree, modeled after the FDA regulatory regime for medical devices.

The FSPTCA was, to a substantial degree, modeled after the FDA regulatory regime for medical devices. As a result, as with devices, FDA has its standard administrative and judicial enforcement tools as well as product detention, manufacturer notification, and the ability of FDA to order the immediate cessation of distribution, followed by mandatory recall. In addition, as with devices, there are various restrictions on the sale and advertising of tobacco products. Indeed, because FDCA amendments reflect Congress's resolution of product-specific issues, the FSPTCA contains a number of prohibitions and limitations that, if not complied with, result in a tobacco product being adulterated, misbranded, or otherwise violative. For example, under the FSPTCA and the regulations that it created, tobacco products may not be sold with descriptors such as "light" or "low" and cigarettes may not be flavored. FDA may also issue regulations that establish standards for, and limitations on, the ingredients and characteristics of tobacco products, including reducing the levels of addictive nicotine. In 2016, FDA expanded its initial authority over cigarettes, smokeless tobacco, and cigarette tobacco and/or roll-your-own tobacco to all tobacco products through the deeming rule.

Food

Under FSMA, the agency may now order the cessation of distribution of food and its recall from the market, if the requisite criteria are met. Importers are required to perform supplier verification and obtain certification that food imports meet safety standards. FSMA also authorizes enhanced FDA inspectional access to food facility records and establishes new recordkeeping requirements for foods designated as high risk.

JUDICIAL ENFORCEMENT

Three types of judicial enforcement:
- *seizure*
- *injunction*
- *prosecution*

The FDCA authorizes three types of judicial enforcement: product seizure, injunction, and prosecution. The first two are civil sanctions; the last is criminal.

Seizure

Under section 304 of the FDCA, a product that is adulterated or misbranded is subject to seizure. Products may be seized in a manufacturing facility, a warehouse, or distribution facility; from a truck or other carrier of the product; from a retail store; from a hospital or doctor's office; or from a consumer. In most cases, seizures are made at the facility where the products were made, or from the warehouse or distribution center where they are held.

At one time, FDA pursued more than 200 seizures each year. During the past several years, FDA has used seizure actions very infrequently—only four in fiscal year 2016.

FDA can recommend a seizure to the U.S. Attorney in the state where the products are located. If the U.S. Attorney agrees to initiate the seizure action, he or she will file a "complaint" in the federal court. The complaint identifies the products and describes the ways in which they are adulterated or misbranded, or both. After the complaint is filed, the clerk of the court issues a warrant for the "arrest" (the seizure) of the products. Usually, a Deputy U.S. Marshal will make the seizure. In nearly all situations, products are seized where they are found ("in place"), and cannot be moved or handled without the court's permission.

There is no judicial hearing before the products are seized, so once the seizure is accomplished, FDA has—temporarily—won the case. After that, the court will condemn the products or it can find that the allegations in the complaint have not been proven and release the products from seizure.

Recently, FDA has used seizures in three settings: seizures designed to remove from the market products that FDA believes present a serious public health risk, seizures of products that violate the law in a way that FDA wants to publicly highlight, and "mass seizures." FDA may recommend a "mass seizure" of all products that have been manufactured or are being warehoused under violative conditions. Typically, a mass seizure will be brought where the products are alleged to be adulterated because they have not been manufactured in compliance with GMP regulations, or they have been manufactured or held under insanitary conditions. Where such manufacturing or storage conditions exist, all of the products are adulterated. A mass seizure can significantly disrupt normal business operations. As a result, there is often a prompt resolution.

In the vast majority of seizure cases, the products are condemned either by default or consent. One reason for this success rate is that FDA usually does not recommend a seizure action unless it has reasonably strong evidence that the

In the vast majority of seizure cases, the products are condemned either by default or consent.

products are adulterated or misbranded. Another is the absence of a judicial hearing before the seizure is accomplished—the owner of the seized products is at a substantial disadvantage because the products remain under seizure during the lengthy judicial process. Thus, it is often in the owner's best business interest to resolve the seizure promptly.

In many seizures, the owner or manufacturer allows the products to be condemned by "default." When this occurs, the court usually will order that they be destroyed. In other situations, the manufacturer will file a claim to the seized products and enter a consent decree agreeing that the court may condemn them. Where products are condemned as part of a consent decree, the decree usually gives the owner or manufacturer an opportunity to recondition them—by relabeling, sorting, cleaning, or similar procedures—in order to salvage as many of them as possible for distribution. Under typical FDA consent decrees, FDA decides whether the products have been reconditioned successfully. Once they have been reconditioned and FDA has released them, the products may be distributed just like any other product because they are no longer in violation of the FDCA. Condemned products that cannot be reconditioned to FDA's satisfaction will be destroyed.

In recent years, FDA has been able to settle a seizure action through a consent decree that not only resolves the seizure but also includes injunctive language designed to address the underlying causes of the violations. In this way, FDA uses the seizure as leverage to obtain manufacturer agreement to an even broader decree—one that is frequently more rigorous than FDA would have otherwise secured.

On a few occasions, the owner or manufacturer not only believes that the seized products are not adulterated or misbranded but also that FDA supervised reconditioning is not acceptable. In those cases, the owner or manufacturer will contest the seizure with the hope of demonstrating to the court that the products are not violative and should be released for distribution as is. At trial, the government has the burden of showing, by a preponderance of evidence, that the seized products are violative.

Injunction

An injunction is a court order that the company cease manufacture and distribution of products unless and until the company complies with FDA requirements.

Through an injunction FDA hopes to force a company to make significant changes in its operations. An injunction is a court order that the company cease manufacture and distribution of products unless and until the company complies with FDA requirements. A court will issue an injunction if it believes that, without an injunction, violations are likely to recur. The injunction is designed to prevent such recurrence. Usually FDA will seek injunctive relief only after other enforcement actions have been unsuccessful in bringing about corrective action. Most often, FDA will seek injunctive relief for persistent violations of its

GMP regulations, or for repeated noncompliance with FDA requirements for labeling and promotion.

FDA recommends injunction actions to the Office of Consumer Protection Litigation, the part of DOJ assigned to review FDA cases. Typically, the complaint for injunction proposed by FDA will identify, in substantial detail, those practices that FDA believes do not comply with its regulations. It is FDA's hope that after reading the lengthy complaint a judge would be inclined to enter an order of injunction against the defendants.

It is FDA's policy that an injunction case should be brought not only against the company but also against company officials who have the most direct responsibility for the alleged violations. Thus, for example, an injunction might include as defendants the company president, the vice president for operations, the director of quality assurance, and possibly, the plant manager. It has been FDA's experience that by naming corporate individuals as defendants it obtains the maximum amount of cooperation in achieving compliance, as well as the maximum amount of deterrence against other corporate officials who have similar responsibilities in their companies.

There are three types or phases of an injunction. If the alleged violations create a significant and immediate public health risk, FDA will request that DOJ seek a temporary restraining order (TRO). If a court enters a TRO, it will prevent the company from shipping violative products for up to 20 days until there can be a further judicial hearing. A TRO can be entered without a formal hearing before the court. In most cases, however, a court will not enter a TRO without some informal opportunity for a company to appear and offer either an explanation or some assurance about the operations of the company. A court can enter a TRO, however, without any representative from the company being present.

Whether or not a TRO is sought, most FDA injunctions include a request for "preliminary" relief. A preliminary injunction usually prevents the defendants from making or distributing products until the noncompliant procedures and practices are corrected, and until there can be a full judicial hearing on a permanent injunction. In many cases, however, a preliminary injunction may be in effect for several weeks. During that time, a company may negotiate with DOJ to settle the case. A preliminary injunction may be entered only after a judicial hearing.

Most FDA injunctions include a request for "preliminary" relief.

If neither a TRO nor a preliminary injunction has been entered, the company may continue to operate until a full hearing on a permanent injunction is held and the court has ruled. Usually, FDA seeks both a preliminary and a permanent injunction. In some cases, however, where violations have persisted over a long time but the consequences are not particularly significant, FDA may seek only a permanent injunction.

FDA has pursued injunctive relief somewhat selectively in recent years.

FDA has pursued injunctive relief somewhat selectively in recent years. In the years 2011 to 2016, FDA recommended approximately 100 actions to DOJ—on average, about 17 per year.[14] Most of these injunction cases are based on alleged violations of FDA's GMP regulations for drugs and devices. As a result, resolution of most GMP injunctions is very burdensome on the defendant company.

Most injunction actions filed on behalf of FDA are resolved through the entry of a consent decree of permanent injunction that has been negotiated between DOJ and the defendants. This often occurs because the defendants decide that FDA has sufficient evidence to win an injunction after judicial hearing or they want to resolve the dispute with FDA as quickly as possible. A consent decree may be agreed to even before the complaint for injunction is filed. This occurs when the DOJ attorney provides the potential defendants (through their lawyers) with a copy of the complaint that DOJ intends to file in court and a copy of a proposed consent decree of permanent injunction. Most consent decrees of injunction contain four standard provisions:

- First, the defendants must cease manufacture and distribution "unless and until" they make a number of corrections in their policies and procedures, which are specified in the consent decree itself. In some cases, a consent decree may allow the company to continue to manufacture and ship its products—or most of them—while it is implementing corrective action and undergoing verification of such action by external audit. Such "going forward" decrees are less disruptive for companies although the required remedial programs are usually comprehensive, very burdensome, and can take years to be fully implemented. Consent decrees may permit the enjoined company to continue to make and distribute medically necessary products.

- Second, the defendants must submit a written report to FDA describing the corrections they have implemented or intend to implement to achieve compliance. The corrective actions are often developed with the assistance of outside GMP experts.

- Third, the defendants must retain an independent expert consultant to review their operation and to report to the defendants, and certify to FDA, that the company is in compliance. Based on the consultant's report, the defendants also must certify to FDA that they are in compliance.

- Finally, FDA will make an inspection, at the defendants' expense, to verify that the company is operating in compliance with the FDCA, and that the corrections are adequate and have been fully implemented.

In addition, the defendants usually must agree to hold all the products in their possession or under their control on the date the consent decree is entered until FDA determines that the products are suitable for release or until the products are reconditioned to FDA's satisfaction. In this way, nearly every injunction action contains within it a mass seizure. As is apparent, meeting the terms of a consent decree of injunction is resource intensive for the defendant company. It is time consuming and expensive and may involve significant changes in the way the company operates.

The terms of the consent decree will generally reflect the specific underlying nature of noncompliance with FDA requirements alleged in the complaint, as well as the significance of the noncompliance, the type of product, the consequences for users if the product is not in compliance, and the regulatory history of the company and the individual defendants. It will also reflect DOJ's assessment of the defendants' ability to demonstrate that effective corrective actions have already been implemented, and that the likelihood that the violations will recur is significantly reduced. Finally, the terms of the consent decree will reflect the "give and take" of the negotiation processes.

As a result, a consent decree may impose requirements or give FDA additional powers not conferred by the FDCA itself. For example, companies often are required to have their operations audited routinely by an independent expert and to submit the audit reports to FDA even after they are allowed to resume operations under the consent decree. Some consent decrees require the defendants to conduct ongoing employee training programs. Under some decrees, FDA is authorized to order recalls of the defendants' products. In a consent decree based on allegations of unsubstantiated advertising, the defendants may be required to recall and destroy all material that promotes a product for an unapproved use, submit new promotional material to FDA for advance approval, and conduct a corrective advertising program including issuance of "Dear Doctor" letters and corrective advertisements to appear in journals named by FDA. In some recent consent decrees, the defendants have agreed to pay FDA's costs in investigating and bringing the injunction action, or they have been required to set aside an amount of money to ensure adequate funds for process improvements even after the resumption of operations under the consent decree.

A consent decree may impose requirements or give FDA additional powers not conferred by the FDCA itself.

Two recent appellate courts have upheld FDA's position that the government can obtain equitable monetary relief—restitution or disgorgement—as part of an injunction under the FDCA. The theory of this relief is that companies should not be allowed to retain the profits they have made from the sale of violative products before the injunction was entered. So far, FDA has sought this additional relief selectively and important legal issues about its imposition remain.

Complaints for injunction and consent decrees are public documents. Injunction actions are widely reported by FDA trade press and, depending upon the nature of the problem and the size of the defendants, often are reported in the lay press.

Even though a consent decree is agreed to by both FDA and the defendants, it is a court order just as if it had been entered by the court after the defendants had challenged the injunction and lost. Because a consent decree is a court order, any knowing violation of it constitutes a contempt of court. The power of the court to hold individuals in contempt undoubtedly is designed to encourage compliance with the decree.

Because a consent decree is a court order, any knowing violation of it constitutes a contempt of court.

Developing injunction cases is time consuming for FDA. In addition, there is no guarantee that DOJ will agree to file an injunction that FDA recommends, although in most cases the department accepts FDA's recommendation. While the primary burdens of a consent decree fall upon the defendants, FDA has certain obligations to monitor and supervise the defendants' compliance activities. Thus, an injunction is not completely a one-way street. For these reasons, FDA does not recommend injunction cases lightly. It usually reserves this type of enforcement for companies that have failed repeatedly, after notice from the agency, to adequately correct significant noncompliance with FDA requirements.

Criminal Prosecution

While the FDCA identifies numerous "prohibited acts," most criminal cases are based on either the shipment of adulterated or misbranded products in interstate commerce or the manufacture of a product under conditions that cause it to be adulterated or misbranded. Any individual or company that engages in those prohibited acts or causes any such violation may be punished, criminally. FDA's policy is to recommend criminal charges against individuals as well as companies. FDA believes that criminal charges against the company alone, without individual defendants, do not provide adequate deterrent or adequate punishment.

Under FDA criminal law an individual can be prosecuted even without knowing about the violative conduct or without intent to violate the law.

The most fundamental feature of FDA criminal law is that an individual can be prosecuted even without knowing about the violative conduct or without intent to violate the law. Rather, the prosecution is based on the individual's responsibility for the conduct that results in the violation, as reflected in the individual's power and authority in the company. This "strict liability" basis for criminal prosecution is based upon two Supreme Court decisions. The first, *United States v. Dotterweich*, was decided in 1943. In that case, the Supreme Court said that a violation of the FDCA is committed by all company officials who are "responsible" for the violative conduct.

More than 30 years later, the Supreme Court reaffirmed and amplified the standard of criminal strict liability under the FDCA in its decision in *United States v. Park*. The Court described the standard for criminal liability under the FDCA this way:

> The Act imposes not only a positive duty to seek out and remedy violations when they occur but also, and primarily, a duty to implement measures that will ensure that violations will not occur. The requirements of foresight and vigilance imposed on responsible corporate agents are beyond question demanding and even onerous but they are no more stringent than the public has the right to expect of those who voluntarily assume positions of authority in business enterprises whose services and products affect the health and well being of the public that supports them.

> ... [It is enough if the] defendant had, by reason of his position in the corporation, responsibility and authority either to prevent in the first instance or promptly to correct the violation complained of, and that he failed to do so. ... We are satisfied that the Act imposes the highest standard of care and permits conviction of responsible corporate officials, who in light of this standard of care, have the power to prevent or correct violations.

The Court also observed that:

> ... those corporate agents vested with the responsibility, and power commensurate with that responsibility, to devise whatever measures are necessary to ensure compliance with the Act bear a "responsible relationship" to, or have a "responsible share" in, violations.

The "strict liability" basis for criminal prosecution is based upon two Supreme Court decisions.

Under the strict liability standard of the "Park doctrine," a person who has a responsible relationship to the violations may be prosecuted for a failure to detect, prevent, or correct the violations. The only legal defense under the Park doctrine is a showing that the violation occurred notwithstanding "extraordinary" efforts to prevent it. In such a circumstance, the courts have held that compliance is, in effect, impossible. Of course, any individual defendant may show that he or she did not stand in a responsible relationship to the violative conduct because the defendant lacked the necessary power or authority. For that reason, the individual would try to demonstrate that he or she was powerless to prevent the violation and cannot be convicted for what was impossible.

The ability to recommend a criminal prosecution based on the Park doctrine provides FDA with a substantial amount of discretion in choosing targets for criminal action. FDA's recommendations for prosecution under the Park doctrine were few and far between. Since 2000, FDA referred only a handful of Park, strict liability criminal cases to DOJ. In addition, DOJ hesitated to file criminal charges against individuals based only on the Park doctrine. Rather, DOJ preferred to bring criminal charges against individuals who have intentionally or fraudulently violated the law or who have been grossly negligent or have recklessly disregarded the FDCA.

In 2010, however, FDA began to take steps to revive the Park doctrine. It revised its criteria—nonbinding considerations—for recommending strict liability criminal cases and in 2011 published them in its *Regulatory Procedures Manual*. The criteria are not novel; they reflect the potential defendants' authority to prevent or correct a violation, as well as actual knowledge of the circumstances resulting in a violation. In addition, FDA will consider whether the violation involves harm to the public, is serious, or widespread; whether the issue or product defect was obvious; or whether it reflects a failure to respond to prior notice or warnings. In recent years, FDA has referred and DOJ has accepted a number of prosecution cases against individuals under the Park doctrine.

Most recently, the U.S. Supreme Court denied the defendants' Petition for Writ of Certiorari in *United States v. DeCoster*. In *DeCoster*, the lower court held the defendants criminally liable without actual knowledge of the wrongful conduct but, rather, vicarious liability, where supervisory parties were held liable for the actionable conduct of a subordinate based on the relationship between the two parties.

Whatever the outcome of FDA's renewed focus on criminal cases, the recent focus of criminal enforcement has been on knowing or intentional violations of the FDCA or other cases involving fraud. These cases are usually investigated by FDA's Office of Criminal Investigations. Between fiscal year 2011 and fiscal year 2016, OCI accounted for approximately 4,093 criminal convictions.[15]

OCI investigates cases concerning willful misconduct involving FDA-regulated products, obstruction of justice, submitting false information to FDA, mail fraud, wire fraud, racketeering, criminal conspiracy, and product tampering.

Most of these violations are defined by the federal criminal laws, not the FDCA. In some of these cases, while the investigation has focused on federal, non-FDCA felonies, the defendants may resolve the investigation by agreeing to plead guilty to FDCA Park violation. Even where a plea bargain may involve a conviction for an FDCA violation, the penalties associated with these cases often include fines of several million dollars and periods of incarceration for some defendants.

With the assistance of the DOJ, OCI investigators often use evidence-gathering tools that are not available to FDA. These include grand jury subpoenas for evidence, grants of immunity to individuals in exchange for their cooperation against targets of the investigation, and electronic surveillance (wiretapping). OCI investigators often work with agents from the Federal Bureau of Investigation (FBI) and other federal law enforcement investigative agencies to develop these cases.

In recent years, a new area of law enforcement has become the primary context in which most FDA criminal charges are included. These are cases brought to enforce the False Claims Act (FCA), which establishes penalties against companies that "cause" doctors and hospitals to submit claims for Medicare and Medicaid reimbursement, claims that are considered false because the medication for which payment is sought is for an unapproved, off-label use. These "healthcare fraud" cases are usually based on whistleblower reports and are investigated and developed by the Department of Health and Human Services Inspector General's office, FDA's OCI, and the FBI. Because nearly all of these cases involve off-label promotion of drugs, allegations of criminal misbranding under the FDCA are usually brought and the settlement of the majority of these cases includes companies or individuals pleading guilty to FDCA criminal misbranding charges, including felony violations. While the largest portion of the fines accessed in these settlements are civil penalties under the FCA and payments to states, some of the fines are based on the criminal FDCA violations, as well as criminal violations of other, related laws, such as the anti-kickback laws and various fraud statutes. Penalties for violations of the FDCA and other criminal statutes in these cases have often included companies being required to enter into corporate integrity agreements—aggressive remediation programs much like those imposed under an FDA injunction—and have resulted in terms of imprisonment for some individuals. Conviction for healthcare fraud can also result in corporate and individual exclusion from federal healthcare programs. These FCA/misbranding cases have been most noteworthy for their very substantial fines, in excess of $2 billion in one recent settlement. It has been reported that in the past decade, fines and penalties from settlement of cases alleging off-label promotion have totaled more than $10 billion.

Conviction for healthcare fraud can result in corporate and individual exclusion from federal healthcare programs.

The vast majority of criminal cases involving FDA are resolved by conviction of the defendants as part of a plea bargain. For a corporate defendant, the plea bargain may involve not only the payment of a fine but also an agreement to establish a corporate compliance program or corporate integrity agreement that contains many elements of an FDA injunction. For individuals, a plea bargain may involve not only a recommendation regarding a fine or against imprisonment but also may involve an agreement by the defendant not to participate in certain FDA-regulated activities.

Violations of the FDCA under the Park doctrine are misdemeanors.

Violations of the FDCA under the Park doctrine are misdemeanors. Violations of the FDCA with intent to defraud or mislead and most violations of the federal criminal laws are felonies. The distinction between misdemeanors and felonies, however, has been significantly affected as a result of federal fines and sentencing laws and the U.S. Sentencing Guidelines under which fines against corporations and periods of incarcerations of individuals may be calculated under a complex scheme that considers various factors outside of the misdemeanor/felony distinction. In addition, a company can be placed on corporate probation, a sentence that has some of the characteristics of an FDA injunction. Under the Guidelines, a company can reduce the level of its fine if it can demonstrate that, notwithstanding the violations, it had an effective corporate compliance program designed to detect and prevent violations of law.

Conclusion

FDA enforcement has been an effective deterrent in promoting compliance among FDA-regulated companies. FDA has a variety of effective enforcement tools available to it and broad discretion in deciding which tools to use to remedy violations of the FDCA. FDA has the greatest flexibility and control in taking administrative enforcement actions. These are often as effective as judicial enforcement and do not require the concurrence of DOJ. However, recent enforcement actions based on collaborative FDA/DOJ investigations have resulted in penalties that have significantly enhanced the deterrent effect of enforcement.

Endnotes

1. *See* U.S. Food and Drug Admin., Inspection Classification Database Search, *available at* https://www.accessdata.fda.gov/scripts/inspsearch.
2. Susan Laska, Deputy Director, Division of Foreign Field Investigations, U.S. Food and Drug Admin., "Division of Foreign Field Investigations," https://www.fda.gov/downloads/AboutFDA/Transparency/Basics/UCM255116.pdf.
3. *Supra* note 1.
4. *Id.*
5. U.S. Food and Drug Admin., Inspection Observations, https://www.fda.gov/iceci/inspections/ucm250720.htm.

6. *See* U.S. Food and Drug Admin., Enforcement Activity, https://www.fda.gov/iceci/enforcementactions/ucm247813.htm.

7. *Id.*

8. *Id.*

9. *See* U.S. Dep't of Health and Human Services, Food and Drug Admin., Justification of Estimates for Appropriations Committees Fiscal Year 2015, https://www.fda.gov/downloads/aboutfda/reportsmanualsforms/reports/budget-reports/ucm388309.pdf.

10. Deborah M. Autor, Deputy Comm'r for Global Regulatory Operations and Policy, U.S. Food and Drug Admin., Statement before U.S. Senate Committee on Health, Education, Labor and Pensions, "Securing the Pharmaceutical Supply Chain" (Sept. 14, 2011), available at https://www.fda.gov/newsevents/testimony/ucm271073.htm.

11. Howard Sklamberg, Deputy Comm'r for Global Regulatory Operations and Policy, Remarks to the Food and Drug Law Institute's 2016 Annual Conference (May 6, 2016), https://www.fda.gov/NewsEvents/Speeches/ucm500314.htm.

12. See U.S. Food and Drug Admin., "FDA protects kids from illegal sales of e-cigarettes, e-liquids and cigars," Sept. 15, 2016, https://www.fda.gov/NewsEvents/Newsroom/PressAnnouncements/ucm520865.htm.

13. See U.S. Food and Drug Admin., FDA Debarment List (Drug Product Applications), *available at* https://www.fda.gov/ICECI/EnforcementActions/FDADebarmentList/default.htm.

14. *Supra* note 6.

15. U.S. Food and Drug Admin., "Cumulative number of convictions at the end of the quarter," https://www.accessdata.fda.gov/scripts/fdatrack/view/track.cfm?program=ora&id=ORA-OCI-Criminal-Convictions-and-Monies-Recovered.

Chapter 17

Managing an FDA Regulatory Crisis

William Vodra, Retired Partner, Arnold & Porter Kaye Scholer LLP, Washington, D.C. &
Wayne L. Pines, APCO Worldwide Inc., Washington, D.C.

Key Points

- A crisis for a company regulated by the Food and Drug Administration (FDA) may take many forms, but usually it involves public allegations of legal violations that endanger consumers, resulting in legal proceedings and negative publicity that can threaten the company's reputation and even its survival.
- The crisis often will be based on either an apparent or real risk to the public health or a plausible charge of fraud.
- Although every crisis has acute phases that must be properly managed, the company facing the crisis will have to make a prolonged and steady commitment of resources. Endurance and patience are essential.
- Five principles of crisis management are:
  - o Recognize a possible crisis early and act accordingly.
  - o Get ahead of the potential crisis by anticipating its possible scope.
  - o Staff the crisis adequately.
  - o Ensure truth and consistency in public statements.
  - o Deal effectively with FDA and other constituencies.
- Not all crises can be prevented, but good crisis management programs contribute to limiting and resolving the unavoidable crisis.

Characteristics of a Crisis for an FDA-Regulated Firm

Anyone working in the food and drug field will meet the greatest challenges during a "regulatory crisis." Every business tries hard to prevent a disaster, but despite the best of these efforts, one still may be encountered. For firms that are regulated by the Food and Drug Administration (FDA), the nature of the products subject to regulation means that crises inevitably will occur.

Crises pose unusual and unique demands on a company. Important steps should be taken early during a crisis to manage it as well as possible. Crisis prevention activities may assist in containing the unavoidable crisis.

The characteristics of a regulatory crisis include:

- allegations of violations of FDA law that endanger consumers;
- public awareness of these allegations;
- legal or regulatory proceedings initiated by FDA or other parties; and
- significant threats to the company's reputation or products, and perhaps to the company and key employees as well.

A "regulatory crisis" is not a normal confrontation with FDA. Any business regulated by FDA has numerous and diverse opportunities to run afoul of regulations. Indeed, during an intensive audit by the agency, any regulated company making any regulated product on any particular day could likely be found in violation of some legal requirement. These "routine" violations generally do not trigger any formal FDA action. The agency looks at whether a business is substantially in compliance with legal requirements, determined in part by whether the firm has control of its operating processes and systems. If FDA believes the systems generally are under control, the agency usually will bring the "routine" violations to the company's attention and recommend voluntary remedial action.

In a regulatory crisis, the alleged violations plausibly create an immediate and significant danger to consumers.

In a regulatory crisis, the alleged violations plausibly create an immediate and significant danger to consumers. The injury would result from one or more of three common elements:

- a product is unsafe as made, labeled, used, or promoted;
- consumers are being defrauded; or
- the government is failing to protect the public because it was misled by the company.

If no risk of serious harm to users of the product is perceived, a confrontation between FDA and a company over the alleged violations will rarely develop into a "crisis."

A regulatory crisis inevitably involves public awareness. Normally, "routine" violations result in a relatively private dialogue between the regulatory agency and the regulated firm. When news media make the public aware of the alleged misconduct, however, a regulatory crisis can explode. Perceptions about the business and its products are always at the core of the situation. Firms supplying foods, drugs, medical devices, cosmetics, and other FDA-regulated items must maintain a high degree of consumer and healthcare professional confidence. For example, when new information about a prescription drug becomes public, raising safety concerns, negative publicity suggesting a new hazard or concealed information inevitably will cause prescriptions for these drugs to fall.

In a regulatory crisis, therefore, a firm is challenged to maintain the trust of the consuming public in its products and in its corporate image.

During a regulatory crisis, parties other than the company and FDA inevitably become active players. Furthermore, important events and pressures emerge in many arenas at the same time. For example, a company may be faced simultaneously with different lawsuits asserting claims for product liability, securities law violations, wrongful discharge of employees, unfair trade practices, or denial of insurance coverage. Inquiries can be initiated by congressional committees, corporate directors, and federal agencies in addition to FDA. Investigative news reporters can start a search for scandal. Similar regulatory activities, litigation, and investigations may erupt in other countries where the product is marketed or the firm does business.

A regulatory crisis is marked also by enormous stresses within a company. Sales of the products under scrutiny may plummet and certainly will if there are readily available alternatives. The sales force, if operating on a commission basis, immediately loses personal income. Workers in production and distribution areas may be laid off if sales soon do not recover. Even employees not directly responsible for the involved products may worry about the company's ability to respond to the emergency. In short, morale is put in jeopardy throughout the organization.

If the company's securities are publicly traded, values of shares of stock may fall. Pharmaceutical and medical device stocks are particularly sensitive to FDA actions. In May 2007, after the *New England Journal of Medicine* published a study purporting to show that Avandia (rosiglitazone) increased the risk of heart attacks in diabetic patients, the manufacturer's stock price dropped more than 10 percent within days, wiping out $15 billion in market value. Such precipitous declines expose firms to litigation for alleged failure to disclose risks (thus overvaluing the stock), as well as hostile takeover bids. Even without these dire consequences, management remains answerable to existing shareholders for loss in market value. In the short term, a crisis will require senior executives to devote significant energy to responding to Wall Street analysts. In 2016, after FDA's medical evaluation of a promising new drug found the risks to be too high, the price of the company's stock plummeted by almost 90 percent.

Further, the potential exposure of the company to cumulative sanctions—criminal prosecution, civil fines and penalties, disgorgement of profits or restitution to consumers, debarment from government procurement programs, and punitive damages in private litigation—can be staggering. Bankruptcy is not unheard of; it was the fate of Able Laboratories following a crisis involving the

A regulatory crisis could result in:
- *plummeting sales,*
- *share values falling,*
- *cumulative sanctions, or*
- *civil and criminal liability.*

reliability of generic drug products. Managing these risks can demand resources for years after the immediate crisis has passed.

Finally, individuals within the company may be exposed to civil and criminal liability, as well as debarment from further employment in the industry. The ability of law-respecting "white collar" employees faced with allegations of criminal wrongdoing to bear up under investigations, hearings, depositions, and media coverage is highly variable. This personal element frequently is overlooked in the heat of activities, but can be critical to the firm's ability to survive the crisis intact.

These stresses give a regulatory crisis dimensions that often are not appreciated until it is experienced. Within the company during a crisis, profound interpersonal tensions can emerge. Resources previously committed to future projects are diverted to addressing the problems at hand. Root cause assessments may turn individuals and operating units against each other.

Employees begin to consider new career opportunities. The more serious and prolonged the crisis, the more intense becomes the pressure on the company to find a quick and decisive resolution. Management's ability to keep the organization functioning can be severely challenged.

Although a regulatory confrontation may originate between a company and FDA at any time, it becomes a regulatory crisis when it spreads into the public domain and invites other parties to become involved.

Evolution of a Crisis

Major crises tend to fall into two patterns: the public health crisis and the fraud crisis.

Major crises tend to fall into two patterns: the "public health" crisis and the "fraud" crisis.

The preponderance of the most serious FDA regulatory crises have begun with a real or perceived danger to the public health associated with a marketed product. In some circumstances, the questions relate to product quality and alleged contamination of a product, whether for example by diethylene glycol in toothpaste, melamine in pet food, oversulfated chrondroitin sulfate in heparin, or *E. coli* on spinach. Other situations emerge from new discoveries questioning the safety of an established product. Newspapers routinely break stories about possible links between products and terrifying hazards, even when the underlying studies are preliminary and inconclusive. In recent years, American society has been buffeted by scares such as whether antidepressants and anti-acne drugs cause patients to commit suicide, whether preservatives in childhood vaccines cause autism, whether a widely used class of anti-arthritis drugs triggers heart attacks, and whether drug-coated coronary stents are more dangerous than earlier "bare-metal" stents. In response to intense criticism for failing to disclose data on potential product safety issues, FDA often publicizes early notices about unconfirmed reports of possible risks. These situations seem to explode with little prior warning. FDA on occasion will take the risk of being wrong about certain potential hazard product situations, rather than wait for all the information to be available.

When a food, drug, device, or cosmetic in active use is discovered—or merely alleged—to present a significant risk of illness, injury, or death, both the company and FDA must deal with urgent health questions:

♦ Should the product be temporarily or permanently removed from the market?

♦ Should new warnings or risk minimization controls restrict use of the product?

♦ Should consumers be advised to get medical care?

These issues must be addressed promptly and with a public conclusion— even if that conclusion is no more than a conscious choice to defer any action until more information is available.

A public health crisis need not present any actual dangers to the public. Consumer advocacy groups, scientific researchers, investigative journalists, members of Congress, and even organizations with political agendas unrelated to FDA regulation can make widely publicized accusations that specific products or classes of products are endangering the public health. In every case, Congress and the public expect FDA to review the data dispassionately and to reach a reasoned conclusion about the merits of the allegations. Even when the allegations ultimately prove baseless, the mere fact that they were made can have long-term adverse consequences for the product. For example, public attacks linking Bendectin, a drug for morning sickness during pregnancy, with birth defects were unequivocally rejected by FDA as unsupported by any scientific evidence; nevertheless, continued product liability litigation and hostile publicity led the manufacturer to remove the product from the market.

A public health crisis need not present any actual dangers to the public.

After any immediate remedial actions are taken to address a public health crisis, FDA almost always will investigate whether the firm either could have prevented the problem or actively concealed it. The search is always looking to answer the critical pair of questions: what did the company know and when did the company know it?

Allegations that company officials knew a product was dangerous but hid that information from the public and regulators make great headlines and can profoundly influence future events. To illustrate, each of the most prominent criminal prosecutions of pharmaceutical manufacturers in the 1980s (Eli Lilly & Co. for Oraflex, Smith Kline & French for Selacryn, and Hoescht AG for Merital) followed public claims that the drug firm had evidence that its product could cause a fatal side effect prior to marketing, failed to disclose that evidence adequately to FDA during premarket review, and, as a result, was able to sell the product with insufficient warnings.

A fraud crisis also may emerge independent of any prior public health crisis. In this situation, it is alleged that the firm committed fraud on someone—FDA, other government bodies, or the public—in connection with obtaining approval of or marketing a product. The assertions may relate to misrepresentations in or omissions from applications submitted to FDA, to misleading promotional claims, or to inconsistent statements made to other bodies or to investors. The public accountability of FDA and the agency's concern for the integrity of its processes require these allegations to be pursued diligently. For example, FDA brought a successful prosecution against a company and its chief executive officer, based on charges that it knowingly and deceptively marketed an approved product for sterilizing reusable surgical devices.

Many of the examples just discussed first appeared to be "public health" crises, with widespread stories of illness or deaths linked to the products. But in each case, as well as the other examples, the crisis evolved into a "fraud" crisis where the company was under a lengthy investigation for misconduct.

Duration of a Crisis

To most outsiders, a crisis seems like a bomb explosion: noisy and brief. The public perceives crisis activities as short-lived or episodic. The situations flare, attract considerable attention, and soon become forgotten. The public health problem, for example, is addressed promptly: the product is removed, re-labeled, or given a "clean bill of health." A fraud crisis attracts attention episodically: when the allegations are first exposed; whenever there are important subsequent revelations; and, if litigation results, when cases are brought or tried.

A fraud crisis attracts episodic attention:
- *when allegations are first exposed*
- *whenever there are important subsequent revelations*
- *if litigation results, when cases are tried*

This image is deceptive for those actually involved in an FDA regulatory crisis. For a business, management of the problems can require continuing resources for many months or years. The company still must respond to the potential litigations and investigations that are spun off by the initial controversy. Probably it will engage in its own internal investigation and analysis of "what went wrong" and "how could we do better." And it may need to implement changes in personnel and procedures as a result of the crisis.

Understanding how long a crisis might last is important for a company. The problems will divert resources for extended periods and require recurring management attention. As patience wears thin, the desire for a "quick fix" will intensify.

HANDLING A CRISIS IN TODAY'S BUSINESS WORLD

The common recommendation for crisis management involves having designated teams available, written procedures, training exercises, and mock rehearsals. There is great merit in this approach, but in the corporation of today, other strategies are needed. Many firms no longer have the capacity for training and rehearsing. Moreover, given regular personnel turnover, the potential benefits from developing and maintaining a state of readiness may not appear to managers and directors to be worth the investment.

In the corporation of today, different crisis management strategies are needed.

Thus, additional ways must be found to prepare for managing the future regulatory crisis.

Contemporary crisis management requires at least five elements:	
1	Recognize a possible crisis early and act accordingly.
2	Get ahead of the potential crisis by anticipating its possible scope.
3	Staff the crisis adequately.
4	Ensure truth and consistency in public statements.
5	Deal effectively with FDA and other constituencies.

The first challenge is to recognize a potential crisis early so that appropriate steps can be taken. This step is perhaps the most difficult to take. Most firms and individuals in a potential—or actual—crisis situation cannot accept easily the possibility that something terrible might happen. Not only does the potential for a crisis suggest that the lives of many people will be disrupted; it implies some failure or error on the part of someone in the organization. By the same token, being the bearer of bad news is neither welcomed nor honored. Consequently, the natural human incentives always work against thinking the unthinkable. This tendency toward complacency frequently can lead a company into giving insufficient attention to an emerging issue while valuable time is lost.

Firms must attempt to get ahead of any potential crisis. To anticipate the possible scope of problems that may have to be addressed, the company must assume a "worst case" scenario.

Firms must attempt to get ahead of any potential crisis. To anticipate the possible scope of problems that may have to be addressed, the company must assume a "worst case" scenario. As with warnings about possible crises, this unpleasant exercise is not welcomed and may be greeted with criticisms of "doom-saying." While it might be hoped that such prognostications at least would soften the shocks when things go from bad to worse, it should not be a surprise that—when predicted scenarios come to pass—people will complain they were not really warned about this or that possibility.

Legal advisers need to assess the company's potential vulnerabilities so that immediate actions can take them into account. These vulnerabilities include potential exposure to enforcement action by FDA or other governmental agencies; claims for damages from consumers, customers and vendors, third-party insurers, employees, and stockholders; and investigations from legislative bodies. Non-lawyers must be involved also, for many of the most pressing demands for rapid response from the company will arise from media and business considerations, not simply legal obligations. Interested and indirectly affected constituencies may include shareholders (particularly major investors and securities analysts); suppliers and distributors; employees and their unions; insurance carriers; and federal, local, and foreign government agencies. These constituencies cannot be overlooked when focusing on the ultimate consumers of the product, lay media, or regulators such as FDA. Once the potential or emerging crisis is identified and its dimensions are sketched out, the company must promptly allocate adequate and qualified resources. Two groups of inside employees are essential to handling the situation: those who will be responsible for corporate management of the crisis and those who uniquely possess the factual background essential to support the crisis management effort. These indispensable people must be made available, even if it means that other assignments do not get accomplished. To help them focus on the crisis, these individuals should have job priorities adjusted promptly.

Beyond these essential persons, the company should ensure that adequate numbers of people with knowledge, skills, or experience appropriate to the demands of the crisis are located and assigned. Transferring people will not be easy, as it necessitates a painful process of choosing priorities among competing needs of the business. Here lies the importance of understanding the potential extended duration of a crisis: projects potentially could be postponed not merely for a few weeks, but indefinitely unless other resources are found.

A further staffing consideration is the ability of each individual to function under prolonged stress. Most scientists, regulatory affairs, marketing, and business management people are not trained to—nor do they wish to—work in the adversarial circumstances of, for example, a criminal investigation by FDA or extended civil litigation. Thus, the composition of a crisis management team should take into account the long-term demands on its members. For a variety of reasons, bringing in outside resources is almost always prudent and necessary. They probably have more experience in crises, particularly if the company and its current management have been fortunate enough to have avoided any FDA crisis in recent memory. They also are not being pulled from other corporate commitments. Finally, they usually are more accustomed to a stressful and adversarial environment. Companies should avoid a natural tendency to attempt to manage the situation using only internal resources; a delay in bringing in the appropriate resources can be costly.

For a variety of reasons, bringing in outside resources is almost always prudent and necessary. They probably have more experience in crises, particularly if the company and its current management have been fortunate enough to have avoided any FDA crisis in recent memory.

During a crisis, it is imperative to ensure the truth and consistency of public statements. A regulatory crisis generally involves allegations that a product appears to endanger the public health. These allegations will become public through news reports. And with communications being 24/7, there is often little time to communicate or respond. With social media, crises can readily get out of hand.

Consequently, the business is pressured to respond to public inquiries and attacks—very often, instantaneously. Carefully managing the media is critical, particularly in the early stages of a crisis and if the crisis starts going viral. In addition, if there are parallel proceedings—such as lawsuits, congressional hearings, or inquiries from other government agencies and/or governments—the company will be making statements in those arenas.

These pressures can be the most difficult for lawyers or regulatory affairs officials. These individuals often prefer to have matters resolved quietly, out of the spotlight, as much as possible. In a regulatory crisis, and in today's media/Internet environment, however, this approach does not serve the company's interests well. The business must maintain consumer and public trust. It may be compelled to undertake remedial actions and self-correction activities to reassure the public. If company officials are so worried about future liabilities that these immediate priorities are ignored, the business will hurt itself for both the short- and long-term.

All public statements must be accurate and truthful, and be capable of being proven so, for they likely will be closely scrutinized in the future in many different circumstances. The company must avoid injuring itself through its public statements. In an era of "spin doctors," the tendency to rebut an allegation with a plausible tale or statement of principle may make the company briefly look good. But if the assertion cannot be substantiated—or worse, later can be proven wrong—the statement will haunt the company for a long time. Moreover, the value of an unsubstantiated assertion is limited, while the risks are not.

All public statements must be accurate and truthful, and be capable of being proven so, for they likely will be closely scrutinized in the future in many different circumstances.

In dealing with press/Internet communications, despite the best public relations effort, no company is going to be able to control media coverage. At most, the story can be influenced toward accuracy and balance.

Companies should avoid the following when making public statements:
- *unsubstantiated assertions*
- *sweeping promises of corrective or remedial actions*
- *inconsistent statements*

Another common tendency of companies is to make sweeping promises of corrective or remedial actions, in an effort to forestall FDA regulatory activity. It is critical to ensure that any promises to government regulators both can be kept and will be kept. FDA has seen firms pledge to undertake changes in manufacturing processes, for example, that were technologically impossible. Such promises undermine credibility and certainly do not deter an FDA enforcement action. Similarly, failure to fulfill a commitment made in the urgency of the hour must be explained later. The explanation that the cost of the commitment proved unacceptable to corporate management will not be favorably received by FDA. The company also should be careful to avoid any inference that the failure to have previously implemented a particular step or activity represents an admission of past legal violations. FDA has been known to interpret an unqualified pledge to take corrective steps as an admission of prior noncompliance.

A third dimension of public statements involves assuring consistency among statements. Given the potential breadth and duration of a regulatory crisis, the company must ensure adequate coordination and communication among those who are making statements on behalf of the firm. Many years ago, one firm was embarrassed (and worse) when a spokesperson in a European country defended the safety of its product on the basis of a particular study; it turned out that the company had previously advised FDA that the integrity of that study could not be established. The challenge of assuring consistency is especially important with respect to assertions made under oath or under legal rules proscribing false statements. Once a firm makes a sworn statement of fact to one government body, it cannot readily deny the truth of the statement before another agency or in court. To be sure, as information changes, prior statements no longer may be fully accurate, but the burden will be on the firm to demonstrate that its information evolved.

The last principle in contemporary management of an FDA crisis is to deal with FDA effectively. As with attempts to control the media during a crisis, efforts to control the actions and responses of FDA generally are doomed to failure. The agency has been mandated by Congress to protect the public and to ensure the integrity of its own processes, by independent investigation and evaluation of the underlying facts. FDA automatically fails in this duty if it accepts a company's story uncritically and without scrutiny. The more serious the alleged threat to the public, the more egregious the alleged fraud on the agency or the consumer, or the more public the allegations become, the greater will be the likelihood that FDA will conduct its own investigation, notwithstanding the statements and promises from the regulated firm.

Complicating the situation is the fact that FDA has two distinct roles, one seeking to protect the public health, the other charged with enforcing the law. In the first capacity, there is no inherent conflict between the agency and the company, which has no interest in injuring its customers. In a metaphorical sense, the marketer sits side-by-side with FDA confronting the public health issue with the best science and medicine both can bring to bear. Cooperation and candor assist both in resolving the safety issues.

But when the question is "What did the company know and when did it know it?", FDA and the firm are in an adversarial mode. In this situation, cooperation and candor may result in facilitating a criminal prosecution. Because the Federal Food, Drug, and Cosmetic Act contains strict criminal liability penalties, the intent or good faith of the firm and its officers is irrelevant to conviction. This fact infuses interactions between the company and FDA with inherent tensions and problems for lawyers, regulatory affairs personnel, and business managers.

To complicate the situation further, FDA has no voluntary disclosure program analogous to those of the Department of Defense or Environmental Protection Agency. These programs provide incentives to companies to reveal instances of violations in exchange for a commitment by the government not to impose the most severe sanctions legally available. Because of the strict liability provisions of the FDCA, voluntary disclosure of any violation is tantamount to an admission of criminal wrongdoing.

Because of the strict liability provisions of the Federal Food, Drug, and Cosmetic Act, voluntary disclosure of any violation is tantamount to an admission of criminal wrongdoing.

Despite these special burdens, the regulated business must communicate with FDA throughout a regulatory crisis. In doing so, it should avoid unnecessary confrontations, recognizing the high levels of stress already present. These interactions are not occasions for company employees to vent their past frustrations with regulatory processes at FDA. Nor should irrelevant agendas be incorporated into the situation.

The most sensitive and difficult communication between a company and FDA during a crisis involves "bad news." For the reasons just outlined, the natural tendency is to say nothing. If FDA is likely to learn the bad news eventually, however, the firm should be the first to tell the agency. This process permits the company to put the information into context and offer appropriate explanations. Disclosure also may enhance the credibility of the company with the agency.

Dealing with FDA during a crisis involves complex and difficult choices. Handling the interactions effectively will never guarantee an outcome that the company might consider optimal. Unnecessary confrontations and a loss of credibility, however, will increase the probability of an undesirable outcome from the firm's perspective.

CRISIS MINIMIZATION THROUGH COMPLIANCE

Even with good preparations, a crisis can still occur. To minimize the impact of a crisis, it is important to have a good understanding of how to deal with the inevitable consequences. Well-documented compliance programs can limit the scope and duration of any public health crisis and reduce the potential for a subsequent fraud crisis. Two components are a closed-loop self-correcting compliance system and good documentation of compliance decisions.

FDA is interested in knowing whether a firm has control of its operating systems and processes. FDA looks at two key factors: the "closed-loop" design of each system and the documentation of the critical decisions.

From the perspective of FDA, every regulated activity is or should be governed by a system. Each system should contain five fundamental elements:	
1	Written specifications or performance goals that the activity is to attain,
2	Written operating procedures by which the activity is to be conducted in order to meet the specifications or goals,
3	Training employees in the procedures,
4	Monitoring activity to detect failures to meet the specifications or goals, and
5	A self-correcting mechanism to identify the cause of each failure and institute appropriate remedial action.

The fifth element, shown above, gives the system its "closed-loop" nature. Once the system has identified a failure, in theory it can identify what corrective action is needed. In somewhat oversimplified terms, the problem arose because:

♦ the specifications did not include all of the necessary targets for the system to attain; or

♦ the specifications were adequate but the operating procedures were deficient in assuring the correct conduct of the activity; or

♦ the specifications and procedures were both adequate, but employees were insufficiently trained to follow the procedures; or

♦ the specifications, procedures, and training were adequate, but adherence to the training and procedures was insufficiently ensured.

The effort to identify the source of the failure, sometimes termed a "root cause analysis," not only permits the system to restore itself to compliance; it is also an essential prerequisite to meaningful corrective action.

FDA believes that these five elements should exist for all aspects of FDA-regulated activities, from the manufacture of individual products, to the development of labeling and promotional material, to the research and development process for new products, to the identification and reporting of adverse events. Good crisis prevention programs will ensure that each regulated operating system or activity has all five elements in place and functioning.

The primary contribution of these crisis prevention programs to crisis management lies in providing the company an opportunity to identify the situation early and to initiate steps to limit the scope and duration of any public health crisis. Secondarily, the existence of strong internal closed-loop systems may lead FDA to conclude that enforcement actions are not needed to bring about compliance from the company. Many of the elaborate and intrusive consent decrees obtained by the agency against individual firms reflect a sense that FDA had lost confidence in each firm's ability to get its own house in order and under control.

Documentation of internal decisions represents the second major crisis prevention activity of importance to FDA. The agency recognizes that its investigations have 20/20 hindsight accuracy. What is ultimately pivotal to initiating enforcement action against the firm is the agency's assessment of how the company performed when making the decisions that are now under FDA review. Successful prosecutions are less likely if the firm's actions were reasonable; the fact that a decision proved wrong does not make it unreasonable, even in hindsight.

Nevertheless, an action that looks reasonable in *post hoc* argument may not prevent enforcement actions. What the agency is looking for is a conscious decision, not inadvertent actions. Hence, FDA will look for documentation that shows the company made a decision that was:

♦ reasonable,

♦ reasoned,

♦ timely, in that it occurred within the applicable time limits (e.g., by FDA reporting regulations or prior to product release in accordance with good manufacturing practices), and

♦ documented contemporaneously.

Documentation leading to a company's reasoned decision can defuse and resolve questions about the company's conduct.

The last three items avoid *post hoc* arguments to defend actions that might have been reasonable.

The benefit of such documentation to crisis management is that it can defuse and resolve questions about the company's conduct. If a firm can demonstrate through memoranda or other papers generated at the time decisions were being made that it promptly reached a reasoned decision, taking into account what was known and what the law required, all that FDA—or any private litigant—can argue in a court is that a different decision would have been more reasonable. Because the law generally recognizes that reasonable persons can disagree, these documents provide an important defense.

Conclusion

An FDA regulatory crisis may not be avoidable. If and when it strikes, a firm that is prepared to respond early and effectively will have an enormous advantage. The company that is not faces serious threats to its reputation, financial health, and potentially, its very survival.

Chapter 18

Research and the FDA

Gary L. Yingling, J.D., B.S.Pharm., M.S., & Ann M. Begley, J.D., B.S.N., Morgan Lewis, Washington, D.C.

Key Points

- Each of the Food and Drug Administration's (FDA's) six substantive Centers has its own requirements for research.
- Experimental animal research is regulated closely by both the U.S. Public Health Service and the U.S. Department of Agriculture to ensure the humane treatment of laboratory animals.
- In clinical research, the essential purpose of an Institutional Review Board is to review research to assure it meets the ethical obligations of a clinical study, whereas the principal investigator controls the integrity of the research and manages the other professionals conducting the research. The sponsor must monitor the study and the principal investigator's research to assure compliance.
- To assure that persons involved as subjects in a clinical study are properly informed, FDA requires that investigators obtain written informed consent from study subjects.
- When submitting clinical research information to FDA for review, a major consideration will be the integrity of the data.

INTRODUCTION

Research is central to the mission of the Food and Drug Administration (FDA)—not just research that FDA does itself, but more particularly the research that companies must submit to gain approval to market their products in the United States. This chapter provides an overview of the regulatory framework for research required by the Centers for the various products regulated by FDA.

Each of FDA's six substantive Centers has its own requirements for research. The Centers require research studies to gain approval or marketing authorization for at least some of the products subject to their jurisdiction. The Center for Drug Evaluation and Research (CDER), the Center for Biologics Evaluation and Research (CBER), and the Center for Devices and Radiological Health (CDRH) each have statutory, regulatory, and guidance documents creating standards and expectations of how the research is to be conducted. The Center for Veterinary Medicine (CVM) has similar expectations, but they are not as detailed, and the Center for Food Safety and Applied Nutrition (CFSAN) and the Center for Tobacco Products (CTP) are evolving and continuing to develop their expectations.

FDA's research requirements and expectations have significant impact on how research is conducted in the United States and, to some degree, in other countries. These regulatory standards continue to develop as new methodologies and technologies emerge.

Animal Research

A number of years ago, animal research was not the subject of government regulation and there was little dialogue relative to the ethical treatment of animals. Not so today. While not the subject of significant regulation by FDA, experimental animal research is regulated closely by both the U.S. Public Health Service (PHS) and the U.S. Department of Agriculture (USDA). Both PHS and USDA have established rules and standards governing the humane treatment of laboratory animals. Of particular relevance to those conducting preclinical research are USDA's Animal Welfare Regulations, which include provisions covering the licensing and registration of research facilities, as well as attending veterinarians; standards for adequate veterinary care; record-keeping requirements; compliance quality standards; and various other research practices (see 9 C.F.R. Chapter 1, Subchapter A, Parts 1-3). These regulations require all animal research laboratory facilities to register and submit to federal inspection. Also, researchers are required to adhere to Good Laboratory Practices (GLPs) when conducting animal experiments (21 C.F.R. Part 58) if the collected research data is going to be submitted to FDA in support of a product application.

Each facility is required to establish and maintain an Institutional Animal Care and Use Committee to review and approve study protocols for proposed research involving the use of animals and to monitor ongoing animal studies.

Additionally, each facility is required to establish and maintain an Institutional Animal Care and Use Committee (IACUC) to review and approve study protocols for proposed research involving the use of animals and to monitor ongoing animal studies. Under this system, there are instances when an IACUC will not allow an experiment because it is considered torture to the animal. For example, 20 years ago one could remove both of a rat's kidneys making the animal uremic as part of an experimental design (bilateral nephrectomy). Today, it would be unethical to approve such a study design and an IACUC would most likely approve no greater than a 5/6 removal of the kidneys. While such limitations on experimental design do create challenges, most can be overcome without compromising the objectives of the proposed study.

While most of the animal research is performed in order to submit data to CDER, CBER, and CDRH, some is performed to address CFSAN safety concerns, and much of the more sophisticated animal studies are conducted for CVM to prove the effectiveness of animal drugs in treating food-producing animals.

Clinical Research

FDA expects that all clinical trials will be conducted in accordance with Good Clinical Practice (GCP) standards, which are intended to represent current best practices in the conduct of human subject research in terms of design, conduct, performance, monitoring, auditing, recording, analyses, and reporting of clinical trials or studies. The purpose of GCP is to provide a level of public confidence that the rights, safety, and well-being of subjects are protected and the data collected meets expected standards of quality, reliability, and integrity.

Institutional Review Board

Regulatory controls on clinical research start with the Institutional Review Board (IRB). Research involving human subjects that raises any questions of safety cannot be undertaken without having the proposed experiment, protocol, and informed consent reviewed by an IRB. An IRB is responsible for ensuring that the health and rights of human test subjects are adequately protected in a clinical research setting.

The origin of the IRB dates back to 1964, when the Declaration of Helsinki was adopted by the World Medical Assembly and one of the recommendations was that research be reviewed by an independent committee. The Department of Health, Education and Welfare issued a policy in 1971 governing federally funded studies that required research to be reviewed by "an appropriate institutional committee" charged with determining whether the rights and welfare of subjects are protected. The Belmont Report, a 1979 document issued by the National Commission for the Protection of Human Subjects of Biomedical and Behavioral Research, stated that an ethical review of research was necessary to protect human subjects. The federal policy resulted in two different sets of regulations governing human subject protection. Fifteen agencies have codified by separate regulation the "Common Rule," which covers most federally funded research. An example of the Common Rule is set forth in the Department of Health and Human Services (DHHS) regulation. 45 C.F.R. Part 46. FDA's human subject protection regulation is similar to the Common Rule but takes into account FDA's unique authority as it relates to investigational products.

21 C.F.R. Part 56. New requirements under the 21st Century Cures Act, however, will require FDA to work toward harmonization with the Common Rule to the extent possible consistent with law, and so further alignment and less differences between the two regulations may occur in the near future.

FDA and the Office for Human Research Protections (OHRP) (within the DHHS) have specific regulations governing the various types of IRBs that may be established, their responsibilities and membership, and the need for minutes reflecting their decision making. The essential purpose of an IRB is to review research to assure it meets the ethical obligations of a clinical study. The IRB can be an academic IRB, organized within an academic institution such as a university; an IRB organized by a clinical site that is conducting studies; or an independent IRB that acts as an IRB for clinical investigators or others who do not wish to undertake the obligation of creating an IRB organization. Today, many institutions with their own IRBs will nonetheless contract out certain studies to independent IRBs for review, particularly where multi-site studies are concerned. Additional information regarding FDA's regulation of the IRB and the board's composition and responsibilities can be found in Chapter 5 of this book.

The essential purpose of an IRB is to review research to assure it meets the ethical obligations of a clinical study.

In the drug and device area, both FDA and OHRP exercise inspectional jurisdiction. FDA's inspection is normally done as part of an on-site inspection by an FDA bioresearch monitoring professional, while most of OHRP's are done by correspondence and conference calls. While the styles may be different, the objectives are the same. Each agency wants to assure that the IRB is fulfilling its ethical obligations to protect the human subject in clinical research.

Informed Consent

To assure that persons involved as subjects in a clinical study are properly informed, FDA requires that investigators obtain written informed consent from study subjects for "all clinical investigations regulated by FDA" that support product applications (21 C.F.R. Part 50). The informed consent statement/ form, simply stated, must explain to the person who is considering whether to become a clinical subject the following: the purpose of the study; its potential benefits, if any; and the risks that are potentially associated with participation in the study. The objective is to provide sufficient information so the person can make an informed decision on whether to participate in the study.

FDA and OHRP have created regulations that specifically address the information that must be included in the informed consent document.

FDA and OHRP have created regulations that specifically address the information that must be included in the informed consent document. Some of the required elements of informed consent include descriptions of reasonably foreseeable risks, benefits that may be reasonably expected, the duration of the research activity, and who to contact with questions about the research or a subject's rights during the study. The informed consent must be written using language understandable to the subject (e.g., fifth-grade level; translated); it must be reviewed and approved by the IRB; it must provide the subject with sufficient opportunity to consider whether or not to participate in the study; and the informed consent must be signed by the subject or the subject's legal representative to confirm the patient was informed (see 21 C.F.R. § 50.25; 45 C.F.R. § 46.116(a)).

It really does not matter whether the study concerns a food ingredient, a drug, cosmetic, or device; the expectation is that a person being asked to participate in a research study should be provided with complete and understandable disclosure of the benefits and risks of study participation and provide his or her informed consent on a form examined and approved by an IRB. During an inspection of a clinical study, one of the main focal points of an FDA bioresearch monitoring inspection or an OHRP audit will be whether the written informed consent that was signed by the study subject or representative fulfills the FDA or DHHS regulation of fully and properly informing the subject. Failure to inform has often been the basis for FDA to disallow data or OHRP to question a research institution's compliance.

The Sponsor/Sponsor-Investigator

The sponsor is the person or organization who takes responsibility for, funds, and initiates a clinical investigation. Among other things, the sponsor is responsible for monitoring the conduct of the study being conducted by the principal investigator (PI) to assure compliance, ensuring that FDA and all participating investigators are notified about new adverse effects or risks associated with the investigative drug, and overseeing collection and analysis of the study data. The sponsor may be a pharmaceutical company, a private or academic organization, or an individual. The sponsor-investigator, however, is an individual who both initiates and conducts a clinical investigation and under whose immediate direction the investigational drug or device is being administered and dispensed. It is the sponsor or sponsor-investigator who generally seeks FDA approval before beginning a clinical study.

Among other things, clinical study sponsors must list most studies on the National Institutes of Health's (NIH's) website (www.clinicaltrials.gov) before the enrollment of the first subject. The sponsor must submit to FDA a certification of compliance with the NIH listing requirement when it submits its investigational product application. Study results information must be posted by the sponsor sometime after the conclusion of the study.

Principal Investigator

The principal investigator has primary responsibility for the FDA clinical research process.

When one considers clinical research performed for the purpose of making a scientific data submission to FDA, careful attention should be paid to the PI because that person has primary responsibility for the FDA clinical research process. It is the PI who controls the integrity of the research and manages the other professionals conducting the research. FDA, by requiring the drug/biologic investigator to sign a Form 1572, places the ultimate responsibility for the clinical investigation on the PI. A Form 1572 is a "Statement of Investigator" Form. No investigator may participate in an investigation until he/she provides the sponsor with a completed and signed Form 1572 (21 C.F.R. § 312.53(c)). By signing the form, the investigator agrees, among other things, to conduct the investigation according to the approved protocol, to personally conduct or supervise the described investigation, to inform patients that drugs are being used for investigational purposes, to ensure that requirements related to informed consent and IRBs are met, to report any adverse events that occur in the course of the investigation to the sponsor, to report to the IRB unanticipated problems involving risks to the subjects and others, and to ensure compliance with all other applicable FDA regulations. The PI must also submit certain financial disclosure information to the sponsor before commencing a study. The purpose of this information is to allow the sponsor to assure that necessary protocol measures are in place to prevent potential bias.

In the device process, the PI must sign an agreement with the sponsor which will include language that commits the PI to following the FDA regulations governing device studies.

Whether the investigational product is a drug or a device, the PI is responsible to several different parties in the research process. For example, when the study protocol is not followed, FDA holds the PI responsible. The IRB looks to the PI to advise it of unanticipated problems and to properly perform the informed consent process. When a contract research organization (CRO) is employed, the CRO will expect the PI to follow the procedures for coordinating the research and enrolling patients. Finally, the sponsor will expect the PI to enroll patients, provide accurate and complete case report forms, submit adverse event reports, and follow the protocol. The data collected by the PI are a critical part of the drug/device application process. As can be seen from these expectations, the PI is the foundation on which all studies are based.

Clinical research is first and foremost data collection, and the clinical site is only as good as its data collection process.

The most significant challenge for sponsors and FDA is that few physicians doing their first clinical study as a PI understand that clinical research is not clinical medical practice. Clinical research is first and foremost data collection, and the clinical site is only as good as its data collection process. The average medical professional who agrees to perform a clinical study and signs a 1572 or device letter agreement may have little understanding of the time and effort that will be required of the staff or the investigator personally. The PIs remain ultimately responsible if there are problems at the study site. The obligation is significant because the investigator can face criminal and civil sanctions should the staff fail to fill out the case report forms correctly. Unfortunately, many PIs do not fully appreciate the level of responsibility they have assumed and fail to properly educate themselves or their staff. (See "FDA Guidance for Industry—Protecting the Rights, Safety, and Welfare of Study Subjects—Supervisory Responsibilities of Investigators," available at www.fda.gov/cder/guidance/index.htm.)

CENTER FOR FOOD SAFETY AND APPLIED NUTRITION

Food additives, color additives, and Food Contact Notifications require the submission of scientific studies and data to support marketing.

Almost all of the studies to support food-related substances are focused on safety and involve the use of various animal models and some tissue testing. Parties are expected to submit both supportive and other data when making submissions to FDA (i.e., provide FDA with information supporting approval of their submission, as well as information of which they are aware that does not necessarily support approval of their submission).

When submitting data to FDA for review, a major consideration will be whether the collected data is statistically significant. For example, were enough animals placed in the study to provide a statistically significant result? Most submissions also require a statement certifying that the study was conducted in accordance with GLPs. GLPs for nonclinical laboratory studies are discussed at 21 C.F.R. Part 58. These regulations include requirements pertaining to organization and personnel, facilities, testing, test and control articles, study protocols, and recordkeeping among other things. While one might think that all laboratories practice GLPs, this is not the case; many laboratories have not adopted the procedures necessary to satisfy GLP standards. Data from a laboratory that does not practice GLPs will, in all likelihood, be rejected by FDA. As to studies in humans being submitted to CFSAN, they are very rare so the Center has no formal policy or procedure for submitting a pretesting application. One area in foods that often does include human testing is taste panels, but normally a taste test falls outside the definition of "research." Moreover, such testing is rarely submitted to FDA.

CENTER FOR VETERINARY MEDICINE

The CVM is concerned with both pharmaceutical and food testing in that the Center is charged with approval of animal feeds, animal drugs, and the level of drug that may be present in the animal tissue to be eaten by humans. This creates a unique situation not found in any of the other Centers. CVM has oversight responsibility relative not only to animal feeds, but also with respect to the pharmaceuticals given to animals and the level of the pharmaceutical present in the animal tissue at the time of slaughter.

CVM has oversight responsibility relative not only to animal feeds, but also with respect to the pharmaceuticals given to animals and the level of the pharmaceutical present in the animal tissue at the time of slaughter.

For the most part, testing in animals is similar to safety testing for human foods in that it requires no pretesting submission to FDA. CVM, however, is increasingly focused upon the potential implications associated with the presence of residual levels of drugs that remain in animal tissue of food products ingested by humans. Where the drug is being tested in a food-producing animal and the intent is to use the tissue from that animal for human food, CVM will require research testing that evaluates not only the effect of the drug on the animal, but also the level of residue of the drug in the animal tissue to be eaten by human consumers.

Where questions of animal and consumer safety are involved, an Investigational New Animal Drug (INAD) application (referred to in the regulations as a "Notice of Claimed Investigational Exemption for a New Animal Drug") must be filed with FDA before shipping the test article in interstate commerce. Studies evaluating the impact of such drug residues on human health will likely be required (21 U.S.C. § 360b(j)). The legal requirements for conducting studies, tests, and investigations under an INAD exemption are located at 21 C.F.R. Part 511. Among other things, these include labeling the product as investigational, ensuring that the test product is used for tests only in animals and not humans, maintaining adequate shipment records, and actually filing the INAD application. Usually this responsibility lies with the sponsor. Trials using the investigational drug may commence at any time following the submission of the INAD to FDA so long as the regulatory requirements mentioned above are satisfied. Additionally, animals treated with the investigational product may not be used for food until expressly authorized by FDA. Before conducting a study, drug sponsors are encouraged to consult with the agency on study design.

New animal drugs used for tests *in vitro* and in laboratory research animals are less strictly regulated and covered by the provisions of 21 C.F.R. § 511.1(a). Generally, if the animal tissue is not going to be used as a human food, then submission of an application prior to testing is not required.

Center for Drug Evaluation and Research and Center for Biologics Evaluation and Research

Unlike preclinical research, clinical drug research with human subjects requires FDA notification and involves more active FDA oversight. This is meant to protect the safety and general well-being of the human test subjects participating in the study and to ensure the integrity of the collected test data.

Before a clinical trial can begin, FDA must be notified to be sure the proposed test/experiment/research will be useful and not result in a study that would expose subjects to the risk of research without providing data that would be useful in a drug approval. To be sure the research will be of value, a well-designed and IRB-approved protocol should be used that includes appropriate controls such as informed consent and study monitoring. FDA requires that an Investigational New Drug (IND) application be submitted to the agency at least 30 days before the drug or biologic is shipped and administered to a test subject. Among other things, the IND should be accompanied by a copy of the IRB-approved protocol and any preclinical laboratory data supporting the proposed investigation. An FDA Form 1571 should be submitted, which identifies the phase of the study and specifies the sponsor's commitment to follow regulatory requirements.

Before a clinical trial can begin, FDA must be notified to ensure that the research will be useful and not result in a study that would expose subjects to the risk of research without providing data that would be useful in a drug approval.

An FDA Form 1572 signed by the PI should also be filed with the IND. By signing the FDA Form 1572, the PI commits to conducting the study in accordance with FDA regulations, including properly obtaining informed consent from each study participant, following the protocol, accurately recording all collected data, and ensuring that all of the investigational product is accounted for. In addition, the PI may work with sub-investigators who also must be listed in the filing with FDA so that the agency knows who is involved in conducting the study. During the 30-day period before the study is allowed to start, FDA will review the IND to assure that research is appropriate and the subjects will not be subjected to unreasonable risk. If the agency does not place a clinical hold on the IND within 30 days, then the IND becomes effective and the sponsor can begin the clinical trial. As a practical matter, the sponsor will generally seek some type of assurance from FDA that the sponsor can proceed with the study before actually starting; there have been times when FDA has delayed beyond 30 days in providing its view and the study has been placed on clinical hold.

Once the IND has been at the agency for 30 days and assuming that a clinical hold has not been placed on the IND, the sponsor/CRO can notify the PI that subjects can be enrolled into the study provided they meet the inclusion/

exclusion criteria of the protocol and are properly consented into the study. During the study, the PI or the staff collect data from the subject and record it in the patient's clinical records and the case report forms (CRFs) for forwarding to the CRO or sponsor for review and analysis.

During the clinical study, it is likely that the PI will be monitored by the sponsor/ CRO to assure that the PI is following the protocol and fully understands the study. If problems are identified at the clinical site, the monitor may try to educate the PI or the site may be closed because the quality of the research is such that it cannot be relied on to support any study conclusions. If the monitoring visit goes well, the PI will continue to enroll patients until the enrollment criteria have been met or the study is stopped. At that point, the PI will submit any data (CRFs) not already submitted and either destroy or return any unused drug. The PI's assignment is then concluded. Now the sponsor takes over the leadership role, analyzing the data from various PIs and conducting a statistical evaluation to see if the data supports a conclusion that the drug is better than a placebo.

CENTER FOR DEVICES AND RADIOLOGICAL HEALTH

Many devices can be proven to be effective based on nonclinical data.

Clinical research in the medical device area is only a little different from that performed in the area of drugs. As noted earlier, the PI does not sign a 1572, but instead agrees in a letter to the sponsor to follow FDA's medical device regulations. The Center also does not require as much clinical research; many devices can be proven to be effective based on nonclinical data, including various physical measurements or animal data.

CDRH also does not require a pre-submission for almost all clinical studies. The Center has concluded that there are two types of clinical studies with medical devices. The first type involves a study in which the clinical risk associated with the device is considered not serious, and is called a "Non-Significant Risk" study. In those cases, FDA has concluded that there is no real need in having an investigational device exemption (IDE) application formally submitted to FDA for review. Instead, the agency relies on the IRB to make the risk determination. If the IRB says there is no significant risk and approves the study, the sponsor/ CRO does not need to file an IDE and the study may begin immediately (see 21 C.F.R. § 812.150). If, however, the IRB says the device does present a significant risk, then the sponsor/CRO must submit an IDE 30 days before the first patient is enrolled.

The IDE submission for the significant risk device is similar to the IND and is governed by 21 C.F.R. Part 812. In the case of an IDE submission, FDA has 30 days to make a decision on the application, and the sponsor must have FDA approval prior to sending the device to the PI. The PI can then seek to enroll patients who meet the study criteria and complete the informed consent process. Once the study is complete, any devices not used are to be returned to the sponsor.

CENTER FOR TOBACCO PRODUCTS

As the newest Center at FDA, the CTP's regulation of tobacco-related research is evolving. Under the Family Smoking Prevention and Tobacco Control Act of 2009 (Tobacco Control Act), a company must submit a Premarket Tobacco Product Application (PMTA) to FDA to seek marketing authorization for "new tobacco products," i.e., a product that is not "grandfathered" (one that was on the market prior to February 15, 2007, the so-called grandfather date). In 2016, CTP released the much anticipated final deeming rule, extending its tobacco authority to all "newly deemed" tobacco products including, but not limited to, e-cigarettes and other electronic nicotine delivery systems (ENDS), cigars (including premium cigars), and components or parts of tobacco products. Because many of these products were not on the market prior to the grandfather date, many of them will need to submit a PMTA. In late 2011, FDA issued draft guidance describing its expectations as to the PMTA content, including content reporting human and nonclinical testing. Under the act, the PMTA must include information that establishes that the new tobacco product is "appropriate for the protection of the public health," which FDA understands to require an analysis of whether there is an increased or decreased likelihood that existing users will stop using such products, or that non-users will start using such products.

The Tobacco Control Act also requires submission of an application for modified risk tobacco products (MRTPs), which are products that claim to reduce the harm or the risk of tobacco-related diseases (e.g., "low," "light," and "mild" claims). In early 2012, FDA issued a draft guidance describing its expectations as to these applications, which will also be expected to include reporting of human and nonclinical testing. The FDA guidances additionally describe expectations as to nonclinical studies; specifically, they should evaluate the tobacco product for toxicity, abuse liability, impacts on users and non-users, and other health risks.

The CTP funds and completes research to bring science-based regulation to the manufacturing, marketing, and distribution of tobacco products, and has identified seven areas for further research: product diversity; addiction; toxicity and carcinogenicity; health consequences; communication; marketing; and economics and policy. CTP works with the National Institutes of Health (NIH) to complete the Population Assessment of Tobacco and Health (PATH) Study. The PATH Study is a large, national longitudinal study of how the use of tobacco products affects the health of the American public that provides information about the marketing, manufacture, and distribution of tobacco products. About 46,000 people are participating in the PATH Study.

FDA has stated that it plans to issue regulations providing conditions under which new tobacco products can be investigated in humans, but until that time, it is exercising discretion in enforcing the PMTA and MRTP review requirements. In the meantime, however, it states that clinical studies must be designed to evaluate health risks of the new tobacco product, and that compliance with 21 C.F.R. Parts 50 and 56 is recommended. FDA recommends that parties planning to conduct clinical research contact the agency to discuss such plans. While no research-related regulations have been issued to date, in July 2017, FDA issued a draft guidance to assist the tobacco industry and investigators on how to effectively meet with the CTP to discuss research and development plans for tobacco products.

Conclusion

As noted, FDA's Centers for drugs, biologics, and medical devices have specific statutory and regulatory requirements governing the practice of preclinical and clinical research. Several of these requirements, such as the approval of the study by an IRB, and obtaining the informed consent of study participants, are required for all studies submitted to FDA. It is important for PIs and sub-investigators to fully appreciate their responsibility to ensure that the patient is properly informed, the recordkeeping is accurate, and there is adherence to GCPs.

CVM focuses primarily on pharmaceutical research in food-producing animals while CFSAN focuses on nonclinical research, and CTP rules on research conduct are evolving. Each of the Centers is concerned with the quality of the research.

Chapter 19

International Regulation

Sam Halabi, *The University of Missouri School of Law, Columbia, MO* & *Richard Kingham,*
Covington & Burling LLP, Washington, D.C.

Key Points

- Nearly every industrialized nation maintains regulatory systems comparable to the Food and Drug Administration's (FDA's), although those systems are not always based on the U.S. model.
- Food and drug law is not a recognized specialty outside of North America because most developed countries have not established agencies like FDA.
- Most advanced regulatory systems are in the European Union (EU), Canada, Australia, and Japan.
- EU regulation governing foods, drugs, and similar products is adopted through the European Commission.
- The first European medicines directive required member states to establish premarket approval systems. Today, requirements for marketing authorization applications are harmonized.
- Medical device legislation in Europe relies on a standards-based approach to harmonization.
- Cosmetics legislation in Europe provides for ingredient declarations using common European nomenclature, and requires manufacturers to maintain product dossiers.
- The EU has issued numerous directives, regulations, and decisions affecting food regulation.
- Health Canada is the primary federal regulator in Canada.
- In Australia, drugs, devices, and similar products are regulated by the Therapeutics Goods Administration; foods are regulated by several agencies.
- The Ministry of Health, Labor, and Welfare conducts food and drug regulation in Japan.
- The China Food and Drug Administration is the responsible national agency in China.
- The United States is unusual in the high degree to which it seeks to regulate exports.
- Efforts to coordinate international food and drug regulation and reduce obstacles to trade take three forms: international cooperation, harmonization of regulations and standards, and mutual recognition. Only the last of these actually eliminates duplicative approval requirements, but it has proved the most difficult to achieve.
- Rarely, coordination may also occur through disputes under international trade law.

Introduction

Nearly every industrialized nation maintains regulatory systems comparable to the Food and Drug Administration's (FDA's), although those systems are not generally organized along the lines of the U.S. system. In recent years, the United States has borrowed ideas from other countries, and there is a growing trend toward international harmonization of food and drug regulation.

It is thus essential to have at least a general understanding of international food and drug regulation. This chapter focuses on three topics: regulatory systems outside the United States, FDA regulation of exports and other matters affecting international trade, and international harmonization initiatives.

Foreign Regulatory Systems

"Food and Drug Law" is not a recognized specialty outside North America for the simple reason that most developed countries in Europe and elsewhere have not established agencies like FDA. Instead, regulation of products under FDA's jurisdiction is commonly entrusted to several agencies, often in different ministries or departments. Within product categories, enforcement is sometimes divorced from policymaking and product-approval functions.

Many countries are now looking to the EU as an alternative to the FDA model.

The most advanced regulatory systems are in the European Union (EU), Canada, Australia, and Japan. The regulatory system in China is less well developed, but is increasingly relevant because of the importance of the Chinese market to U.S. manufacturers. Perhaps the most important jurisdiction is the EU, which is now the biggest unified market in the industrialized world. As of 2014, the EU comprised 28 member states with a total population of 507 million, compared to 317 million in the United States. On March 29, 2017, the United Kingdom initiated the legal process to withdraw from the EU, which will require practitioners to follow negotiations to understand which EU directives will continue to bind the UK along with other aspects of British access to the EU market and vice versa. Generally, the EU's efforts to harmonize national regulation of consumer products provide a lesson in what can reasonably be expected from such initiatives. Many countries are now looking to the EU as an alternative to the FDA model.

European Union

The Legal Framework

◆ Sources of EU Food and Drug Law

There are two main sources of food and drug regulation in the EU: harmonizing regulations issued by the EU and judicial decisions under provisions of the EU Treaty that correspond roughly to the Interstate Commerce Clause of the U.S. Constitution.

◆ Free Movement of Goods

The EU Treaty guarantees free movement of goods among the member states, and regulations that create obstacles to free movement may be struck down by the courts if they are not justified on specific grounds identified in the treaty (e.g., protecting the health and safety of consumers), or are not "proportional" to the public interests that justify them. The European courts have developed a substantial body of case law relating to national rules on foods, drugs, cosmetics, and other consumer products. Decisions have rendered unenforceable, for example, a French law defining "cassis de Dijon" and a 16th-century German beer-purity law that prohibited use of additives.

◆ Harmonization Measures

Beginning in the 1960s, the EU (then the European Economic Community) issued a series of measures aimed at harmonizing national regulations of consumer goods so that products are assured free movement and requirements for duplicative national approvals are minimized. The pace was accelerated greatly in 1985, when the EU set the deadline of December 31, 1992, for the issuance of more than 300 measures required to complete the "internal market." Amendments in 1986 to the EU Treaty furthered this "EC-92" initiative by eliminating provisions that allowed individual member states to veto harmonization measures.

Beginning in the 1960s, the EU issued a series of measures aimed at harmonizing national regulations of consumer goods.

Today, the EU maintains comprehensive systems of measures governing foods, drugs, and similar products. The extent of actual harmonization, however, varies greatly among product categories. The following is a brief summary of the major measures.

Medicines

The first medicines directive, issued in 1965, required member states to establish premarket approval systems based on proof of efficacy, safety, and quality. Today, requirements for marketing authorization applications are harmonized, as are provisions for labeling, advertising, regulation of wholesalers, good clinical practice, good laboratory practice (GLP), good manufacturing practice (GMP), and other matters.

Until 1995, marketing authorizations for medicines were granted country-by-country, and divergent decisions were common. Efforts to establish a coordinated "multistate procedure" (an early version of mutual recognition) were largely ineffective, because there was no mechanism to enforce harmonized decisions.

◆ The European Medicines Agency

Since 1995, a London-based independent agency, the European Medicines Agency, has been responsible for coordinating EU drug approval procedures.

Since 1995, a London-based independent agency, the European Medicines Agency (EMA), has been responsible for coordinating EU drug-approval procedures. Marketing authorization applications for new biotechnology products and many new chemical entities must be submitted to the EMA, and applications for certain other innovative products may be submitted on an optional basis. An expert body (the Committee for Medicinal Products for Human Use) reviews applications and renders opinions to the European Commission (the executive branch of the EU), which issues approvals that are effective throughout the EU.

For other products, national approvals also are available. Products that are intended to be marketed in more than one member state, however, must be submitted through mandatory mutual recognition or "decentralized" procedures that are backed up by a binding arbitration process administered by the EMA. Almost all new innovative medicines today are, however, authorized through the EU-wide centralized procedure.

◆ Current Issues

EU law provides periods of data exclusivity after new drugs are approved, during which "generic" marketing authorization applications (the EU equivalent of Abbreviated New Drug Applications) cannot be submitted. Under legislation that took effect in 2005 (which applies to innovative products for which marketing authorization applications were submitted after the effective date), the EU recognizes a uniform protection period that is often referred to as "8 + 2 + 1." Generic applications cannot be filed until eight years after the reference product is approved, and generic products cannot enter the market until the end of the tenth year, but this period can be extended to 11 years if a medically significant new use is authorized within the first eight years after the reference product is approved. A special system has been established for approval of follow-on biological products (referred to as similar biological medicinal products, or biosimilars).

An orphan drug regulation provides a 10-year period of marketing exclusivity, and there are incentives for investment in research on medicines for pediatric use, including the potential for a six-month extension of supplemental protection certificates (the equivalent of patent term restoration in the U.S.). As of May 2016, clinical trials used to support approval applications are governed by Clinical Trials Regulation (CTR) EU No 536/2014, which significantly revised procedures for clinical trials. Applications are submitted to an EU "portal," and when studies are done in multiple member states, there are procedures to coordinate the review and approval process. The directive also increases the amount of data concerning clinical trials that is available to the general public.

Medical Devices

Separate directives establish uniform regulatory requirements for marketing active implantable medical devices (e.g., pacemakers), medical devices, and *in vitro* diagnostics. All of these directives rely on a "new approach" to harmonization developed by the EU to facilitate the EC-92 initiative. The directives establish relatively general "essential requirements." Products that comply with those requirements are labeled with a mark of conformity (the CE mark) and are entitled to move freely throughout the EU, subject to a "safeguard clause" allowing national enforcement actions in extraordinary circumstances. Essential requirements are supplemented by standards issued by the European standard-setting bodies. Conformity to standards is not mandatory, but constitutes presumptive evidence of compliance with essential requirements.

Manufacturers are legally responsible for determining whether their products conform to essential requirements and thus may bear the CE mark. Conformity assessment procedures depend on the risk classification of a device, which is determined by principles in the medical device directives. For the lowest risk devices, conformity assessments may be performed by manufacturers without any intervention by third parties. Manufacturers must notify member state governments when such products are introduced to the EU market.

Manufacturers are legally responsible for determining whether their products conform to essential requirements.

Conformity assessments for higher-risk devices require interaction with "notified bodies" (quasi-governmental entities designated by member state governments). This may consist of product-specific design reviews or certification of quality systems, or both. Quality systems certifications are based on a European version of the International Organization for Standardization (ISO) 9000 series of standards, with modifications specific to medical devices. A new Medical Device Regulation (MDR) was officially published on May 5, 2017 and entered into force on May 26, 2017. Manufacturers of currently approved medical devices will have a transition time of three years until May 26, 2020 to meet the requirements of the MDR.

Cosmetics

A directive first issued in 1976 established a general safety requirement for cosmetics; set harmonized labeling requirements; prohibited or restricted certain ingredients; and required affirmative listing of specified categories of ingredients (ultraviolet filters, preservatives, and color additives). The European Commission, working with a scientific committee and the member state governments, periodically revises the ingredient lists.

The directive provided for ingredient declarations, using a common European nomenclature, and required manufacturers to maintain product dossiers. The dossiers must include reports of safety evaluations, which are subject to inspection by member state governments. Manufacturers must submit notifications when products are introduced in the EU. The directive also includes a ban on testing of cosmetic products and new cosmetic ingredients in animals.

The EU has adopted a cosmetics regulation that supersedes the directive and applies directly in the member states. There are requirements for premarket notification (but not premarket approval) through a centralized system for finished products containing nanomaterials, reporting of serious, undesirable effects to government authorities, and other enhanced regulatory responsibilities. The basic framework, however, remains the same, and enforcement will continue to be the responsibility of the member states.

Foods

♦ Harmonizing Measures

The EU has issued numerous directives, regulations, and decisions affecting food regulation

The EU has issued numerous directives, regulations, and decisions affecting food regulation. These include "horizontal" measures on labeling, additives, contaminants, hygiene, and food-contact materials, and "vertical" measures establishing standards for particular foods (e.g., chocolate, fruit juices, mineral waters, and sugars). The European Food Safety Authority advises the European Commission on all matters with a direct or indirect impact on food safety, and other technical issues relating to food legislation. Not all aspects of food regulation are harmonized, however, and there is still scope for national variations.

♦ **Free-Movement Principle**

A 1989 EU "communication" seeks to prevent member states from enforcing national requirements that create obstacles to free movement unless there is a clear public health or consumer protection benefit, and requires member states to establish expedited procedures for approving imports from other EU countries that comply with food regulations in the country of origin.

OTHER JURISDICTIONS

Canada

♦ **Laws and Agencies**

The principal federal statute is the Food and Drugs Act (passed in 1953, but with predecessor legislation dating back to 1860), supplemented by the Food and Drug Regulations and numerous guidance documents. Health Canada (the Department of Health) is the primary federal regulator, although certain aspects of food regulation are entrusted to Agriculture and Agri-Food Canada, other federal departments, and a Canadian Food Inspection Agency established in 1997.

The principal federal statute in Canada is the Food and Drugs Act (passed in 1953, but with predecessor legislation dating back to 1860), supplemented by the Food and Drug Regulations and numerous guidance documents.

Health Canada maintains a system of premarket approval for new drugs, for which applicants submit new drug submissions and obtain notices of compliance. A procedure for abbreviated new drug submissions provides for an eight-year data exclusivity period to protect innovators, with provision for linkage to patent expiry. A separate system governs medicines containing old active ingredients, for which submissions are required to obtain drug information numbers or GP numbers.

For many years, Canada maintained a relatively simple notification system for most medical devices, with more elaborate requirements for safety substantiation of specified products. Health Canada now maintains a premarket screening procedure in which the level of scrutiny depends on relative risk based on classification principles similar to those used in the EU. The ISO 9000 series of standards for quality systems also plays a role.

The Food and Drug Regulations contain requirements for labeling of cosmetics and for notifications of new products, and Health Canada has issued guidelines on permissible claims. Drug/cosmetic products are permitted, but must be registered as proprietary medicines and meet other requirements for drugs (e.g., GMP).

Food additives require prior approval, and the Food and Drug Regulations establish requirements for labeling. Health Canada has issued numerous informal guidelines, including detailed guidance on health-related claims for foods.

Australia

Drugs, devices, and similar products are regulated by the Therapeutic Goods Administration (TGA) in the Commonwealth Department of Health and Ageing. Foods are regulated by several federal and state agencies, with many requirements established by Food Standards Australia New Zealand. Cosmetics that are not classified as drugs are subject only to general regulations for consumer products. The TGA has entered into a mutual recognition agreement with the EU concerning medical device regulation.

Japan

Drugs, devices, foods, and cosmetics are regulated at the national level by the Ministry of Health, Labor, and Welfare.

Drugs, devices, foods, and cosmetics are regulated at the national level by the Ministry of Health, Labor, and Welfare (MHLW). The Pharmaceutical Affairs Law governs drugs, devices, and cosmetics, while the Food Sanitation Law governs foods.

Drugs ordinarily require a manufacturing or import license (*kyoka*) and a product license (*shonin*). Data requirements for marketing authorization applications are set out in guidelines issued by the MHLW. New chemical entities are subject to a period of postmarket "re-examination," during which abridged applications for generic copies are not accepted. There are simplified procedures for approval of products containing established active ingredients.

Medical device regulation was recently revised, and the current system assigns devices to several classes based on relative risk. Product approvals are no longer required for the lowest risk devices, but quality standards apply.

Cosmetic products require premarket approval. Applications for products containing novel active ingredients require safety data, as do those for "quasi-drugs," a category that includes many products regulated as ordinary cosmetics in Europe and the United States.

Food imports require prior notification. Detailed labeling requirements apply, and there is a system of premarket approval of food additives, with different requirements for "chemical compound additives" and substances of natural origin.

China

Drugs, devices, foods, and cosmetics are regulated at the national level by the China Food and Drug Administration, with significant responsibilities also entrusted to authorities in the provinces, autonomous regions, and municipalities. For drug registration/approval purposes, drugs are classified into three categories: chemical drugs, biological drugs, and traditional Chinese medicines. Drug manufacturing and distribution are subject to license requirements, including patent information, formula, manufacturing processes, and uses, as are clinical trials. Separate systems have been established for licensing imported drug products, with provision for a six-year period of data exclusivity for new chemical entities. There are special licensing systems for traditional Chinese medicines and ethnomedicines, vaccines, blood products, and diagnostic reagents. In addition, licensing requirements apply to medical devices, cosmetics, and many food products.

FDA Regulation of Foreign Trade

General Controls on Exports

Every developed country regulates imports of foods, drugs, and similar products, but the United States is unusual in the degree to which it seeks to regulate exports. Section 801 of the Federal Food, Drug, and Cosmetic Act (FDCA) permits exports of foods, drugs, and other articles that are adulterated or misbranded under U.S. law if they conform to the specifications of foreign purchasers, do not conflict with foreign law, and meet certain other requirements. FDA has narrowly interpreted the exemption provisions of the section to restrict exports of banned color additives, aflatoxin-contaminated feedstuffs, and similar products. The agency has asserted that exporters bear the burden of proving compliance with foreign law and has demanded proof of compliance, including letters from foreign government officials.

The United States is unusual in the degree to which it seeks to regulate exports.

Exports of Unapproved Drugs and Devices

◆ Historical Background

Unapproved drugs (and, since 1976, unapproved devices) have presented the most difficult problem. By a quirk of legislative drafting in 1938, the New Drug Application requirement was not linked to the adulteration and misbranding provisions of the FDCA. As a result, the export exemption in section 801 was ineffective for unapproved new drugs. It is unclear whether Congress intended this result, because it chose seven years later (without discussion) to regulate penicillin, and later other antibiotics, under the adulteration provisions and thus make them eligible for the export exemption.

♦ FDA Enforcement Policy

In the decades following 1938, FDA consistently took the position that exports of unapproved new drugs were prohibited. The agency extended the ban not only to finished products but also to bulk pharmaceuticals, applied the export restriction to foreign trade zones, and prohibited import of unapproved products intended solely for re-export.

The agency permitted exports of "chemical intermediates" used to manufacture drug substances, on the theory that they were not new drugs, but refused to apply a similar policy to precursors of biological products.

♦ The 1968 and 1976 Amendments

By the 1960s, the U.S. ban on exports of unapproved drugs, whatever its historical origins, had become a matter of political significance. Consumer groups drew attention to the "dumping" of unsafe and ineffective medicines in developing countries and urged the United States to provide moral leadership to the industrialized world. When it enacted the Animal Drug Amendments of 1968 and the Medical Device Amendments of 1976, Congress specifically incorporated special procedures for FDA approval of exports of banned or unapproved devices in a conscious effort to drastically deter such exports.

♦ The 1986 Export Amendments

By the 1980s, the political climate had changed. There was increased concern about the competitiveness of U.S. businesses in world markets, and manufacturers argued that U.S. export controls served mainly to encourage companies to locate research and manufacturing facilities abroad.

In 1984, FDA issued regulations permitting exports of unapproved drugs for clinical trials, subject to permits. In 1986, Congress enacted amendments that allowed exports of unapproved drugs to any of 21 listed countries, subject to specified conditions, including FDA permits. The legislation included special provisions for unfinished biologics and drugs for tropical diseases.

♦ Current Law

The FDA Export Reform and Enhancement Act of 1996 lifted the import/re-export ban, allowed exports of unapproved drugs and premarket approval devices to any country if they were approved in one of several designated jurisdictions, permitted exports for clinical trials in the listed jurisdictions, and eliminated the requirement for prior approval of most exports (although a simple notification was still required). The legislation also authorized FDA to expand the list of designated countries and to permit, on a case-by-case basis, exports of products not approved in listed countries.

The FDA Export Reform and Enhancement Act of 1996, among other things, lifted the import-re-export ban.

INTERNATIONAL INITIATIVES

Efforts to coordinate international food and drug regulation and reduce obstacles to trade take three forms: international cooperation, harmonization of regulations and standards, and mutual recognition. Only the last of these actually eliminates duplicative approval requirements, but it has proved the most difficult to achieve.

Efforts to coordinate international regulation and reduce obstacles take three forms:
- *international cooperation,*
- *harmonization of regulations and standards, and*
- *mutual recognition.*

Cooperative Agreements

♦ General

Information exchanges and other cooperative efforts among government agencies have existed for many years. FDA, for example, began "tri-partite" meetings with drug regulators in the United Kingdom and Canada more than 25 years ago, and the World Health Organization (WHO) has long maintained an international clearinghouse for information on adverse drug reactions. FDA officials now meet periodically with their counterparts in the European Commission.

More recently, FDA has entered into formal information-sharing agreements with the EU and Japanese authorities relating to drug approvals, inspections, and safety reporting. In 2003, FDA and the EMA agreed to procedures for providing joint scientific advice to pharmaceutical companies on development of new drug products, an agreement that was extended indefinitely in 2010. The agencies may share staff and observe the work of the other's scientific committees as well as share information about ongoing evaluations and safety concerns for medicines.

Responding to public concern about imports of contaminated drugs, cosmetics, and other products, FDA has established inspection posts in countries that export significant quantities of products to the United States.

♦ Memoranda of Understanding

FDA's more formal cooperative agreements with foreign regulatory agencies are commonly set out in memoranda of understanding (MOUs), exchanges of letters, and similar documents. Typically, these are signed by FDA and its counterparts in foreign countries, but approval by the U.S. Secretary of State may also be required. Agreements cover a wide range of topics, from information exchanges to mutual acceptance of inspections and product standards.

The precise legal status of these agreements has never been entirely clear. They are not treaties within the meaning of the U.S. Constitution, and they cannot supersede FDA's obligations under U.S. statutes or regulations. Some FDA officials have expressed concern that such agreements might impermissibly delegate FDA enforcement functions to foreign governments. Nevertheless, MOUs and similar agreements have great practical importance for the industrial sectors affected.

Harmonization

International efforts to harmonize food and drug regulatory standards have proliferated.

In recent years, international efforts to harmonize food and drug regulatory standards have proliferated. WHO, the Organization for Economic Cooperation and Development (OECD), international standard-setting bodies (especially the ISO), and numerous sectoral and regional organizations have played a role in the process. The Uruguay Round amendments to the General Agreement on Tariffs and Trade (GATT) (now part of the World Trade Organization), including the Agreement on Sanitary and Phytosanitary Measures and the Agreement on Technical Barriers to Trade, signed in 1994, enhanced the significance of these initiatives, because signatory countries now may be required to justify failure to implement agreed-upon international standards.

♦ Major Initiatives

Codex Alimentarius

Among the oldest efforts is the Codex Alimentarius Commission, established by the United Nations Food and Agriculture Organization and the WHO in 1962 to develop international standards for foods. The Codex Commission, whose members include representatives of more than 150 countries, aims to protect the health of consumers and ensure fair international trade in food. Major areas of activity include food labeling, food additives and contaminants, food hygiene, pesticide residues, veterinary drug residues, analytical methods, and food inspection. The Codex Commission is advised by expert committees, such as the Joint Expert Committee on Food Additives and the Joint Meeting on Pesticide Residues.

Although the United States has long participated in Codex activities, it has given a relatively low priority to implementing Codex standards.

International Conference on Harmonization

The International Conference on Harmonization of Technical Requirements for Registration of Pharmaceuticals for Human Use (ICH), established in 1990, has been an extraordinarily productive initiative. Sponsors include FDA; the Japanese MHLW; the European Commission; and the national trade associations of the pharmaceutical industries in the United States, the EU, and Japan, with coordination from the International Federation of Pharmaceutical Manufacturers & Associations. Other governments and international entities participate as observers.

From its inception, the ICH decided not to seek mutual recognition, but to focus instead on harmonization of technical requirements for product registration. Activities have been undertaken in the areas of safety (e.g., toxicology testing), efficacy (clinical testing), and quality (manufacturing and chemistry). The result has been a series of consensus documents that participants transpose into guidelines or regulations. The volume of documents has been considerable. In some cases, however, full implementation requires issuance of new regulations or other legislation; this has proved difficult to accomplish, especially in the United States. The ICH has also developed a "common technical document" (CTD) to help harmonize marketing authorization applications.

Medical Devices

The International Device Regulators Forum, with participants from the United States, Canada, the EU, Japan, and other countries, is seeking to duplicate the accomplishments of the ICH for medical devices. One of the greatest forces for international harmonization of medical device regulation has been the ISO 9000 series of quality systems standards, which can be used as the basis for external certification of companies' systems for controlling the design, testing, production, and distribution of any product or service. The EU's decision to use modified versions of ISO 9001 and 9002, coupled with notified-body certifications, as one means of compliance with its medical device directives greatly enhanced the significance of the standards, as did FDA's decision to incorporate major elements of the standards in its regulations governing GMPs for devices.

The International Device Regulators Forum, with participants from the United States, Canada, the EU, Japan, and other countries, is seeking to duplicate the accomplishments of the ICH for medical devices.

♦ Effect of GATT and Other World Trade Organization Agreements

International agreements aimed at eliminating nontariff barriers to trade lend increased importance to harmonization initiatives. Much attention has been devoted to the North American Free Trade Agreement (NAFTA), but the World Trade Organization (WTO) is potentially more significant, because it includes an effective enforcement mechanism.

Under WTO agreements, measures that might affect international trade must not be stricter than necessary for protection of human, animal, or plant health; must not be maintained without sufficient scientific evidence; and must be based on scientific principles. The WTO's Dispute Settlement Understanding provides a forum, which may adjudicate one member's dispute with another member over its food, drug, device, and cosmetics measures.

Mutual Recognition

FDA maintains agreements with many countries on shellfish sanitation inspections.

FDA traditionally has been reluctant to enter into broad mutual recognition agreements with foreign countries, and such agreements have often been confined to narrow sectors or areas of regulation. For example, the existence of OECD guidelines for GLP, based in large measure on the U.S. GLP regulations, made it possible for FDA to enter into MOUs with several countries for mutual acceptance of GLP inspections. FDA maintains agreements with many countries on shellfish sanitation inspections. Mutual recognition, however, has proved much more difficult to accomplish for product sectors that are subject to premarket approvals and similar controls. A 1997 U.S./EU Mutual Recognition Agreement, which covered six product sectors (including drugs and medical devices), proved much less useful than was hoped. In particular, an arrangement for mutual recognition of GMP inspections for pharmaceuticals was never put in operation, largely due to FDA's reluctance to accept the results of inspections by certain national authorities in the EU.

In 2012, FDA entered into its only systems recognition agreement with New Zealand's Ministry for Primary Industries (MPI). The agreement acknowledges that FDA and MPI have comparable food safety regulatory systems that lead to equivalent levels of food safety assurance. The agreement resulted only after a long, resource-intensive period of negotiations and verification investigations including onsite visits. As of 2016, pursuing further mutual recognition agreements was not an FDA priority.

Index

CPSIA information can be obtained
at www.ICGtesting.com
Printed in the USA
FSHW021035141219
64807FS

9 781935 065845